Computer Networks

Computer Networks

Editor:

Ivan Stanimirović, Ph.D.

ArclerPress

www.arclerpress.com

Computer Networks

Editor: Ivan Stanimirović, Ph.D.

708 3rd Avenue, 6th Floor
New York
NY 10017
United States of America
www.arclerpress.com

ISBN: 978-1-68094-443-3

Library of Congress Control Number: 2016951133

About the Editor

Ivan Stanimirović, Ph.D.

Ivan Stanimirović gained his PhD from University of Niš, Serbia in 2013. His work spans from multi-objective optimization methods to applications of generalized matrix inverses in areas such as image processing and computer graphics and visualisations. He is currently working as an Assistant professor at Faculty of Sciences and Mathematics at University of Niš on computing generalized matrix inverses and its applications.

Contents

List of Contributors

Khalid Kh. Sharaf
Computer Science, Alaqsa University, Gaza, Palestain

AbuBaker Elhussein
Computer Engineering, Africa University, Khartom, Sudan

Changwang Zhang
School of Computer Science, National University of Defense Technology, Changsha, China
Department of Computer Science, University College London, Gower Street, London WC1E 6BT, United Kingdom

Zhiping Cai
School of Computer Science, National University of Defense Technology, Changsha, China

Weifeng Chen
Department of Math & Computer Science, California University of Pennsylvania, USA

Xiapu Luo
Computing Department, Hong Kong Polytechnic University, China

Jianping Yin
School of Computer Science, National University of Defense Technology, Changsha, China

Chao Zhou
Institute of Computer Science & Technology, Peking University, Beijing 100871, PR China

Xinggong Zhang
Institute of Computer Science & Technology, Peking University, Beijing 100871, PR China

Zongming Guo
Institute of Computer Science & Technology, Peking University, Beijing 100871, PR China

Keerti Tiwari
Department of Electronics and Communication Engineering, Jaypee University of Information Technology, Waknaghat, Solan 173234, India

Davinder S. Saini
Department of Electronics and Communication Engineering, Chandigarh College of Engineering and Technology, Chandigarh 160019, India

Sunil V. Bhooshan
Department of Electronics and Communication Engineering, Jaypee University of Information Technology, Waknaghat, Solan 173234, India

Eduardo da Silva
Department of Informatics, Federal University of Parana (UFPR), 81531970 Curitiba, Brazil
Department of Informatics, Catarinense Federal Institute (IFC), 89245000 Araquari, Brazil

Luiz Carlos Pessoa Albini
Department of Informatics, Federal University of Parana (UFPR), 81531970 Curitiba, Brazil

Niranjan Kumar Ray
Department of Computer Science & Engineering, Silicon Institute of Technology, Bhubaneswar 751024, India

Ashok Kumar Turuk
Department of Computer Science & Engineering, National Institute of Technology, Rourkela 769008, India
Shahrukh Khalid
Telecommunication Engineering, Hamdard University, Sharae Madinat Al-Hikmah, Muhammad Bin Qasim Avenue, Karachi 74600, Pakistan

Athar Mahboob
Khawaja Fareed University of Engineering & Information Technology, Rahim Yar Khan 64200, Pakistan

Choudhry Fahad Azim
Faculty of Engineering Sciences and Technology, Hamdard University, Sharae Madinat Al-Hikmah, Muhammad Bin Qasim Avenue, Karachi 74600, Pakistan

Aqeel Ur Rehman
Department Computer Science, Hamdard University, Sharae Madinat Al-Hikmah, Muhammad Bin Qasim Avenue, Karachi 74600, Pakistan

Shin-ichi Kuribayashi
Department of Computer and Information Science, Seikei University, Japan

Christopher Köhnen
[1]City University London, Department of Electrical and Electronic Engineering, London EC1V 0HB, UK

Christian Überall
City University London, Department of Electrical and Electronic Engineering, London EC1V 0HB, UK

Muttukrishnan Rajarajan
City University London, Department of Electrical and Electronic Engineering, London EC1V 0HB, UK

Rudolf Jäger
Department for Information Technology, Electrical Engineering & Mechatronics, Technische Hochschule Mittelhessen-University of Applied Sciences, Wilhelm-Leuschner-Straße 13, 61169 Friedberg, Germany

Veselin Rakočević
City University London, Department of Electrical and Electronic Engineering, London EC1V 0HB, UK

Christian Köbel
Departamento de Telecomunicaciones y Telemática, Instituto Superior Politécnico José Antonio Echeverría ISPJAE, Calle 114, No. 11901, e/Ciclovía y Rotonda, Marianao 19390, La Habana, Cuba

Walter Baluja García
Departamento de Telecomunicaciones y Telemática, Instituto Superior Politécnico José Antonio Echeverría ISPJAE, Calle 114, No. 11901, e/Ciclovía y Rotonda, Marianao 19390, La Habana, Cuba

Joachim Habermann
Department for ICT, Electrical Engineering & Mechatronics, THM University of Applied Sciences, Wilhelm-Leuschner Straße 13, 61169 Friedberg, Germany

Rakesh Matam
Indian Institute of Information Technology, Guwahati, Assam 781001, India

Somanath Tripathy
Indian Institute of Technology Patna, Patna, Bihar 800013, India

Martin Ellis
School of Computing Science, University of Glasgow, Glasgow G12 8QQ, UK

Dimitrios P. Pezaros
School of Computing Science, University of Glasgow, Glasgow G12 8QQ, UK

Theodore Kypraios
School of Mathematical Sciences, University of Nottingham, Nottingham NG7 2RD, UK

Colin Perkins
School of Computing Science, University of Glasgow, Glasgow G12 8QQ, UK

Fan Wang
School of Computer Science and Technology, Dalian University of Technology, Dalian, China

Yan Yang
School of Computer and Information Technology, Liaoning Normal University, Dalian, China

Kunpeng Wang
School of Computer Science and Technology, Dalian University of Technology, Dalian, China

Xiaopeng Hu
School of Computer Science and Technology, Dalian University of Technology, Dalian, China

Ning Zhang
School of Computer Science and Technology, Dalian University of Technology, Dalian, China

Adewale Adeyinka A
Covenant University, Canaanland, Ota, Nigeria

Adagunodo Emmanuel R
Obafemi Awolowo University, Ile-Ife, Nigeria

John Samuel N
Covenant University, Canaanland, Ota, Nigeria

Ndujiuba Charles
Covenant University, Canaanland, Ota, Nigeria

Yu Nakata
Graduate School of Information, Science and Technology, Osaka University, 1-5, Yamadaoka, Suita, Osaka 565-0871, Japan

Shin'ichi Arakawa
Graduate School of Information, Science and Technology, Osaka University, 1-5, Yamadaoka, Suita, Osaka 565-0871, Japan

Masayuki Murata
Graduate School of Information, Science and Technology, Osaka University, 1-5, Yamadaoka, Suita, Osaka 565-0871, Japan

Omar Said
IT/ College of Computers and Information Technology Taif University Taif, Saudi Arabia.

Mehedi Masud
CS/ College of Computers and Information Technology Taif University Taif, Saudi Arabia.

Preface

Computer networks represent a main component of the economy of information. Their appliance spans from WiFi to cellular networks, enabling the foundations of the Web. Some fundamental problems of computer networking, from performing distributed applications to multiple-access and bandwidth allocation, are being investigated. For each problem, various design strategies are developed to assess its performance in practical applications. Many interconnections are considered in computer networking, and various aspects of computer system analysis using queueing network models are illustrated by particular case studies. A number of important modelling techniques are summarized in the algorithmic form, for all main widely-used networking technologies. Network Management is the process of controlling a complex data network so as to maximize its efficiency and productivity. An architecture for dynamic network reconfiguration is presented in the first section of the book, giving the auto reconfiguration using the directory server, which is used to store and maintain configuration information.

The following seven chapters of the book present various techniques to improve Ad hoc networks and appliance of technologies such as Low-rate Distributed Denial-of-Service (LDDoS) and multiple-input and multiple-output (MIMO) technology. The remaining content of this book focuses on the advances of specific methods and algorithms in the field of QoS framework and Internet. The specific advances discussed in this book include the use of ordered successive interference cancellation, new QoS frameworks, as well as the advances in Internet of things.

The recently proposed TCP-targeted LDDoS attacks send fewer packets to attack legitimate flows by exploiting the vulnerability in TCP's congestion control mechanism. Congestion Participation Rate (CPR) metric is presented as well as a CPR-based approach to detect and filter LDDoS attacks by their intention to congest the network. The major innovation of the CPR-base approach is its ability to identify LDDoS flows. The effectiveness of CPR is analysed theoretically by quantifying the average CPR difference between normal TCP flows and LDDoS flows and showing that CPR can differentiate them.

In computer networks systems, multiple-input and multiple-output, (MIMO) technology can be employed because of the enormous benefits it offers. It is the technique of using multiple antennas at the transmitter to propagate signal through multiple propagation paths to multiple antennas at the receiver. This can be used to significantly increase communication performance, measured by data throughput, and link reliability without additional bandwidth or increased transmit power. It achieves this goal by spreading the same total transmit power over the antennas to achieve an array gain that improves the spectral efficiency, channel capacity and link reliability. These benefits are not without setbacks due to mutual coupling of the antennas, correlation of the signals and the degree of matching between the receiver and the load. Some general expressions are formulated showing the impact, on the capacity of the MIMO channel, by both antenna coupling and spatial correlation due to the propagation environment. Due to heterogeneous channel conditions in MIMO wireless networks, it is challenging for video broadcasting to map scalable video layers to proper MIMO transmit antennas to minimize the average overall video transmission distortion. Channel scheduling problem for broadcasting scalable video content over MIMO wireless networks is investigated. An adaptive channel scheduling based unequal error protection (UEP) video broadcasting scheme is proposed. In the scheme, video layers are protected unequally by being mapped to appropriate antennas, and the average overall distortion of all receivers is minimized. This scheme is formulated into a non-linear combinatorial optimization problem.

Ordered successive interference cancellation (OSIC) is adopted with minimum mean square error (MMSE) detection to enhance the multiple-input multiple-output (MIMO) system performance. The optimum detection technique improves the error rate performance but increases system complexity. Therefore, MMSE-OSIC detection is used which reduces error rate compared to traditional MMSE with low complexity. The system performance is analyzed in composite fading environment that includes multipath and shadowing effects known as Weibull-Gamma (WG) fading. Along with the composite fading, a generalized noise that is additive white generalized Gaussian noise (AWGGN) is considered to show the impact of wireless scenario. This noise model includes various forms of noise as special cases such as impulsive, Gamma, Laplacian, Gaussian, and uniform. Consequently, generalized function is used to model noise. The average symbol error probability (ASEP) of MIMO system is computed for 16-quadrature amplitude modulation (16-QAM) using MMSE-OSIC detection in WG fading perturbed by AWGGN.

Multicast is an indispensable communication technique in wireless mesh network (WMN). Many applications in WMN including multicast TV, audio and video conferencing, and multiplayer social gaming use multicast transmission. An algorithm called SEMRAW (SEcure Multicast Routing Algorithm for Wireless mesh network) is developed to be resistant against all known active threats including wormhole attack. SEMRAW employs digital signatures to prevent a malicious node from gaining illegitimate access to the message contents.

802.11-based wireless mesh networks (WMNs) as last mile solutions frequently become bottlenecks in the overall Internet communication structure. The lack of end-to-end capacity on routes also affects vertical traffic coming from or flowing towards external networks, such as the Internet. The presented approach aims to increase the overall network performance by exploiting channel diversity and to additionally favor vertical traffic. To achieve this, first a general system that modifies an existing mesh node architecture is proposed, in order to prepare a more efficient resource management and to enhance the restricted transmission capacity in standard WMNs. Quality-of-Service parameters were improved, and more efficient use of multiple radios could be reached.

The high increase of bandwidth-intensive applications like high definition video streaming in home and small office environments leads to QoS challenges in hybrid wired/wireless local area networks. These networks are often not QoS aware and may contain bottlenecks in their topology. A novel autonomous system for hybrid QoS in local area networks is investigated, called QoSiLAN, which does not rely on network infrastructure support but on host cooperation and works independently of the access technology. Also, a new QoS Signalling Protocol, policing and admission control algorithms are presented, as well as a new lightweight statistical bandwidth prediction algorithm for autonomous resource management in LANs. This new QoS framework enables link based, access-medium independent bandwidth management without network support.

Ad hoc networks lack support of infrastructure and operate in a shared bandwidth wireless environment. Presently, such networks have been realized by various adaptations in Internet Protocol (IP) architecture which was developed for infrastructure oriented hierarchical networks. Ad hoc networks suffer from additional problems like IP address autoconfiguration, service provisioning, efficient bandwidth utilization, and node identification. IDHOCNET is a novel implementation of service provisioning and application development framework in the ad hoc context. Moreover how identifiers can completely replace the IP addresses to run the IP based applications is shown.

Secure Middleware for Ad Hoc Networks (SEMAN), which provides a set of basic and secure services to MANETs is presented, aiming to facilitate the development of distributed, complex, and flexible applications. SEMAN considers the context of applications and organizes nodes into groups, also based on these contexts. The middleware includes three modules: service, processing, and security.

An energy conservation technique, called Location Based Topology Control with Sleep Scheduling for ad hoc networks is developed. It uses the feature of both topology control approach and power management approach. Like the topology control approach, it attempts to reduce the transmission power of a node, which is determined from its neighborhood location information. A node goes to sleep state based on the traffic condition as that of power management approach.

In the Internet, Autonomous Systems exchange traffic through interconnected links. As traffic demand increases, more traffic becomes concentrated on such links. A method to identify the hierarchical nature of traffic aggregation on the Internet topology is developed and used to discuss the long-term changes in traffic flow. A new evolution process that attempts to reduce this traffic concentration is investigated. It increases the number of links in the deeper level in the hierarchy, thus relaxing the traffic concentration.

Internet of things is a promising research due to its importance in many commerce, industry, and education applications. Recently, new applications and research challenges in numerous areas of Internet of things are fired. Different proposed architectures of Internet of things, research challenges and open problems are discussed. The concept of Internet of things database is introduced and it is discussed about the future vision of Internet of things.

Editor
Ivan Stanimirović, Ph.D.

CHAPTER 1

SIMPLE ARCHITECTURE FOR AUTOMATIC CONFIGURATION IN DYNAMIC NETWORK

Khalid Kh. Sharaf[1] and AbuBaker Elhussein[2]

[1]Computer Science, Alaqsa University, Gaza, Palestain

[2]Computer Engineering, Africa University, Khartom, Sudan

ABSTRACT

Network Management assures that the network operates efficiently at all times. Network Management is the process of controlling a complex data network so as to maximize its efficiency and productivity. Since communication networks have reached a high level of complexity, their management is more difficult to be performed. The international standardization have simplified the study by adopting five principal functional cooperating areas: Configuration Management, Fault Management, Security, Management, Performance Management, Accounting Management. The configuration management deals with the setting, changing and restoring network device like bridges, routers, switches, and links etc. In this paper we will present an architecture for dynamic network reconfiguration, this architecture provide the auto reconfiguration using the directory server, which is used to store and maintain configuration information. The configuration information is organized using the standard Directory Enabled Networks specification thereby allowing effective exchange of network.

INTRODUCTION

Network management means different things to different people. In some cases, it involves a solitary network consultant monitoring network activity with an outdated protocol analyzer. In other cases, network management involves a distributed database, auto polling of network devices, and high-end workstations generating real-time graphical views of network topology changes and traffic. In general, network management is a service that employs a variety of tools, applications, and devices to assist human network managers in monitoring and maintaining networks. We describe the main tasks of the network management in the following points:

- Protecting the network (e.g. intrusion detection)
- Detecting failed components (interfaces, links, hosts, routers)
- Monitoring traffic patterns (recommend needed upgrades, cap certain types of traffic)
- Detect abnormal traffic (rapid changes in routing tables, huge spikes in BW usage)

The ISO has contributed a great deal to network standardization. Its network management model is the primary means for understanding the major functions of network management systems [3]. This model consists of five conceptual areas first, performance management, second configuration management, third fault Management, forth security management and the fifth is accounting management, we will discuss the ISO model in the next section.

Citation: Khalid Kh. Sharaf, AbuBaker Elhussein, Simple Architecture for Automatic Configuration in Dynamic Network, International Journal of Networks and Communications, Vol. 4 No. 1, 2014, pp. 12-19. doi: 10.5923/j.ijnc.20140401.02.

In other hand we need to network management system (NMS) to do the maintenance and configuration of network devices, servers and services, as well as continual monitoring of the operation of all the devices within the network, so the NMS is very important elements of a successfully functioning computer network. In order to ensure the reliable and secure management of devices and services, it is necessary to design a network in such a manner that it provides configuration management. Another aspect of the successful management of computer networks concerns the network protocols used for this purpose like SNMP, CMIP, and WBEM.

Finally, this paper is organized as follows. Section 2 contains, Network management functionalities. Section 3 contains, Issues and Trends Configuration Management. Section 4 contains, Network Management Architecture. Section 5 contains, Suggested architecture. Section 6 contains, Dissection. Section 7 contains, Related work. Section 8, contains, Concludes the paper.

NETWORK MANAGEMENT FUNCTIONAL-ITY'S

Based on the recommendations of ISO (international standard organizations), five important network management subsystems have been identified

1. ***Configuration management*** *supports activities for* controlling physical, electrical, and logical inventories, managing changes distributed software, and so on. The configuration management deals with the setting, changing and restoring network devices like computers, bridges, routers, switches and links etc. [1]. Improper change of configuration of any device can have huge destructive effect on the network an may also obstruct services for the users. We will present the overview of configuration management in the next section.
2. ***Fault management*** is very important part of network management which refers to a collection of activities assuring dynamic maintenance of network services. Real-time performance degradation is detected by initiating controlling functions (diagnosis, repair, test, recovery, backup, etc.). A fault management requires quick finding and appropriate correction of any fault or problem. In more systematic manner the whole process can be divided in following phases [2]: Identification and characterization of faults, Correlation among issues of faulty behavior, Diagnosis and finding of cause, Repair and restoration to take network back to normal State and Effectiveness evaluation for future reference as well as accounting. Network devices and links need to be managed and monitored to detect any faults. Immediate recognition and identification of faults can play a vital role in efficient fault management and to minimize the effect of faults as well. Correlation and diagnosis can provide information about the cause, effect and possible solution. Repair and restoration is required to eliminate the fault as well as its effect and take the network back to its previous working and faultless state.

The effectiveness of the repairs and fault management process needs to be evaluated and possibly documented to monitor damage caused by faults and the costs of repairs [3].

A single failure of a network device or link in large networks can build up an overall failure effect like congestion and denial of service etc. It means that the effect of a single failure in network can cause a lot of trouble by generating cascading alarms for the management system which makes it impossible to manage dynamically and in real time. Recent research efforts are looking at simplifying this procedure by correlating the alarms generated by the same fault [4].

3. ***Performance management*** evaluates if service levels are maintained, identifies actual and potential bottlenecks, and establishes trends for management decision making and planning. An operational data base with performances is included. Performance management includes the observation and monitoring of the performance of not only the network devices but also of the overall network, in terms of user perceived performance [3]. Among a wide range of activities that come under performance management some are: analyzing network to identify bottleneck devices and links, monitoring link availability and performance, measuring network bandwidth and traffic utilization, analyzing traffic usage patterns to know applications' and users' network behavior and monitoring Quality of Service (QoS) to get information about user experience on the network.

Traffic classification is one of the areas that has attained a lot of attention from research community in the recent past. Classifying network traffic on the basis of application, transport layer protocol, users etc. is an effective tool for trend analysis required for appropriate designing, dynamic monitoring and resource provisioning of networks. Such traffic analysis is also used for management of network in terms of security, fault repairs and accounting etc.

4. ***Security management*** ensures the network protection by analyzing the risks, implementing a network security plan, and monitoring success strategies. Special functions include the surveillance of security indicators, partitioning, password administration, and warning or alarm messages on violations. Network security management includes all actions required to protect network, its components and services to keep it in most usable state with maximum integrity and continuity of operation [5]. In simple words, network security deals with effectively detecting network security threats and optimally choosing methods and tools to get rid of their effects and damage. In general, the network security threats can be in shape of Virus, Trojan horse, Worms, Vandals, IP spoofing, Sniffing, man in the middle attack, DoS attacks etc. [3, 5]. Network security primarily concerns with the attacks that use computer network to launch and need to be analyzed as well as eliminated in the network. Two different types of approaches can be used to keep network secure: one that find security threats in real time on active network data and second, that analyze recorded data to find intruders and unauthorized users. Appropriate type of method is used depending on a number of factors like; severity of threat, importance of keeping network secure, type and scope of network, loss of revenue and reputation in case of successful security attack etc. Discovering security problems by detecting anomalous behavior in

otherwise normal state of network has been an active area of research in recent past. The network traffic that does not obey already defined normal behavior pattern is distinguished and usually analyzed for possible security threat. A huge number of techniques have been adopted for effective anomaly detection in network traffic based on statistical data, payload and header analysis, user behavior, AI and ML concepts.

5- ***Accounting management*** is the process of collecting, interpreting, processing, and reporting information referring to costs of processing and resource allocation, as well as bill notifications. Network accounting management deals with measuring network utilization to regulate and apportion network resources to its users. Accounting plays a vital role in minimizing network problems due to unfair use of resources. Appropriate and reasonable means and measures are to be taken to provide required services to the users and billing and other related tasks are to be carried out accordingly, as well [6]. Business strategies and acquisition of revenues greatly depend on proper implementation and supervision of accounting policies. One of the factors to consider while designing accounting management strategies is the speed with which data can be handled. Network processors are proposed for stable, reliable and high performing accounting management systems [7]. Due to the complexity in handling user based accounting, single flat accounting methods have been used for charging all users, no matter how differently they are accessing network services. Such simple methods may not be applicable for multi service level networks. A number of approaches have been proposed for differential charging based on the service levels [4]. Because of its importance in network configuration, we consider a stand-alone sixth subsystem, Network Planning.

6. ***Network planning*** determines the optimal network (based on data for network performance), traffic flow, resource utilization, network requirements, technological trade-off, and estimated growth of present and future applications. Interfaces to modeling devices are part of the planning process.

ISSUES AND TRENDS CONFIGURATION MANAGEMENT

In this section we discuss tow terms, first term, configuration management issues and the second term, trends in configuration management.

1. Configuration Management Issues

The present configuration management approaches involve complex labor-intensive processes. They are also error prone and costly. There are several reasons for these issues faced by traditional configuration management practices.

- Configuration management typically involves configuration of vendor-specific network elements spread across several management domains. The network elements may have their respective vendor-specific proprietary configuration methods to effect configuration changes. Configuration management also has to deal with multi-service networks.
- An example of a multi-service network may be an ATM/SONET backbone integrated with IP services. Configuration management in such a scenario requires labor-intensive processes involving detailed knowledge of the network, and the respective configuration tools associated with the network.
- The traditional configuration management methods are based on the centralized manager/agent model. This approach involves centralization of configuration intelligence in a central management station like the SNMP Manager. However, an increase in the number and complexity of network elements can increase the complexity and overload the central management station. Besides, the central management station may have limited access to multiple heterogeneous management domains.
- The traditional configuration management approaches involve distribution of configuration data across heterogeneous databases present in several management domains. The lack of a common, unifying information repository hinders effective information exchange across the network. The traditional configuration management approaches also lack elaborate schema standardization required to effectively model the configuration of network elements and services.

2. Trends in Configuration Management

The current configuration management practices such as the Simple Network Management Protocol (SNMP) approach or the Command Line Interface (CLI) approach perform the configuration of network elements on an individual basis, which is a major drawback in the configuration and management of large scale networks and emerging network services. Configuration management in such cases is also prone to configuration inconsistencies that may result in failures or performance degradation. In general, traditional configuration practices cannot effectively provide configuration management services to large-scale networks spread across several management domains. The automation of configuration management aims to address this issue by providing effective and consistent configuration of large-scale networks. The Directory-enabled network management and Policy-based network management are emerging technologies that are being used to implement automation of configuration management. Directory-enabled network management involves maintaining configuration information in a special repository known as directory. The network resources (devices, operating systems, management tools, and applications) use the directory to perform the following functions–provide information about themselves, discover other resources, and obtain configuration information from other resources. The DEN environment allows heterogeneous network elements and services to function as interoperating components of the network. Fig. 1 depicts Directory-enabled network management

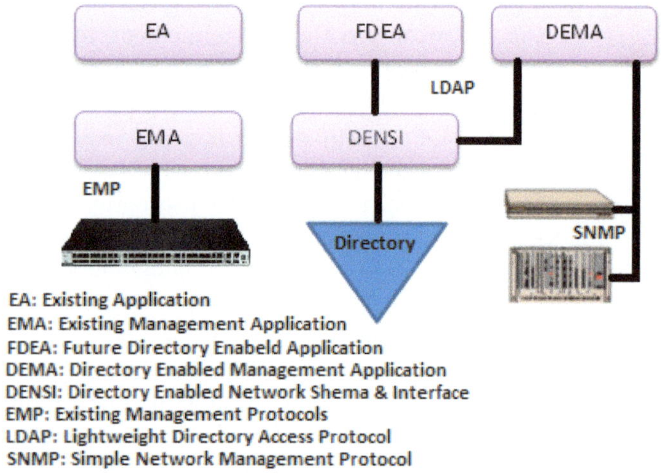

Figure 1: Directory-enabled network management.

The standard DEN specification is used to model the configuration information maintained in the directory. The standard network management protocols (such as SNMP) are used as the means of communication with the network elements. The Lightweight Directory Access Protocol [8, 9] is used to access the directory. Policy-based network management [10, 11] uses policies to describe network behavior with a high level of abstraction. A policy is a representation of an objective to be implemented in the management domain and is applied using a set of policy rules. A policy rule is comprised of a set of conditions and a corresponding set of actions. Policy-based network management defines two key elements Policy decision points (PDP) and Policy enforcement points (PEP). PDP is a process that makes decisions based on the policy rules. The PEP is an agent running on or within a resource that enforces the policy decision. Policy-based network management employs the Common Open Policy Service (COPS) protocol [12] to standardize the communication between the PDP and the PEP. The policies are stored in a policy repository. The policy repository may be a directory or any other storage device such as a relational database. Fig. 2 depicts Policy-based network management.

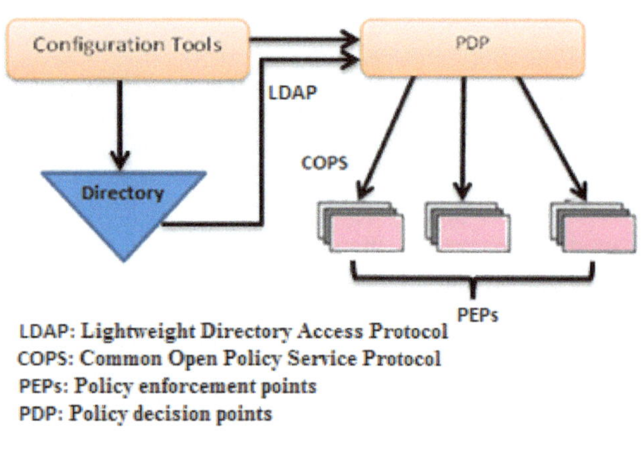

Figure 2: Policy-based Networking.

The PDP monitors the network state by evaluating configuration data obtained from various sources such as the SNMP management station or directly from the SNMP management agents. In the latter case, SNMP communication is required between the PDP and the management agent. The proponents of the widely deployed SNMP standard have proposed the idea of improving the SNMP protocol to effectively perform dynamic network configuration.

The IETF Configuration Management with SNMP (SNMP CONF) working group has been involved in promoting SNMP as an effective protocol for dynamic network configuration. The SNMPCONF working group has been involved in developing MIB modules necessary to facilitate configuration management, specifically MIB modules which describe network characteristics that can be used by management entities making policy decisions at a network level or a device level. However, the SNMP protocol needs to address a number of issues in order to be effective for dynamic network configuration. SNMP needs to support more functionally rich operations, rather than the simple GET and SET operations. SNMP also needs to support a flexible management information model rather than the relatively rigid Structure of Management Information (SMI) model. Therefore, the IETF Next Generation Structure of Management Information (SMing) working group is involved in developing a standards-track specification for the next generation data definition language for specifying network management data. The working group has used the SMIng language developed in the IETF Network Management Research Group as a starting point. SMIng represents a superset of the SMIv2 (Structure of Management Information v2) and the SPPI (Structure of Policy Provisioning Information). The SNMP and Policy-based network management methods involve centralization of configuration management. The configuration decisions are made by the management station in case of SNMP and by the PDP in case of Policy-based network management. The centralization of network management leads to scalability problems, particularly in case of large-scale heterogeneous networks. Although it is possible to implement Policy based Networking (PBN) in a distributed manner, PBN aims at implementing an effective decision making architecture. The DEN specification on the other hand aims at effective modeling of the network and providing a centralized repository that can be directly accessed by the network resources in order to perform configuration management tasks.

NETWORK MANAGEMENT ARCHITECTURE

Most network management architectures use the same basic structure and set of relationships (Fig. 3 illustrate the network management architecture). End stations (managed devices), such as computer systems and other network devices, run software that enables them to send alerts when they recognize problems (for example, when one or more user-determined thresholds are exceeded). Upon receiving these alerts, management entities are programmed to react by executing one, several, or a group of actions, including operator notification, event logging, system shutdown, and automatic attempts at system repair. Management entities also can poll end stations to check the values of certain variables. Polling can be automatic or user-initiated, but agents in the managed devices respond to all polls. Agents are software modules that first compile information about the managed devices in which they reside, then store this information in a management database, and finally provide it (proactively or reactively) to management entities within network management systems (NMSs) via a network management protocol. Well-known network management protocols include the Simple Network Management Protocol (SNMP) and Common Management Information Protocol (CMIP).

Management proxies are entities that provide management information on behalf of other entities. The following figure depicts a typical network management architecture.

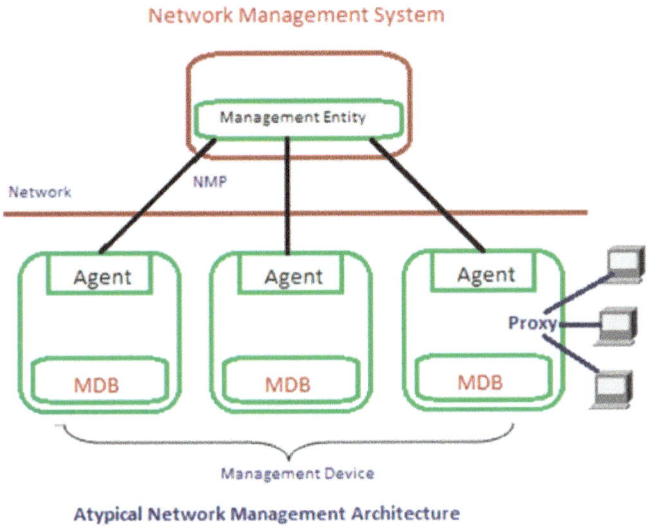

Figure 3: Atypical Network Management Architecture.

SUGGESTED ARCHITECTURE

In this section we present the proposed architecture which is used Directory service to provide dynamic automatic configuration networks. The specification of Directory-enabled network is used to model the heterogeneous network elements and services. Automatic interaction in response to changes in policy configuration is necessary for automatic configuration, so the use of Directory-based automatic configuration allows this important interaction. There are two categories of configuration data to satisfy auto configuration. first category such as routing algorithms or IP addresses, where configuration data is associated with relatively static configuration parameters. Second such as quality of service policies or security policies, where configuration data is associated with providing information service. The directory-enabled network specification is used to model both the categories of configuration data.

Fig. 4 illustrate the general architecture of Directory based Automatic configuration of networks, where the human manager uses to some tools specify configuration policies and download the configuration policies to the directory server. This tools named configuration tools, which is connected with the directory server by Lightweight Directory Access Protocol.

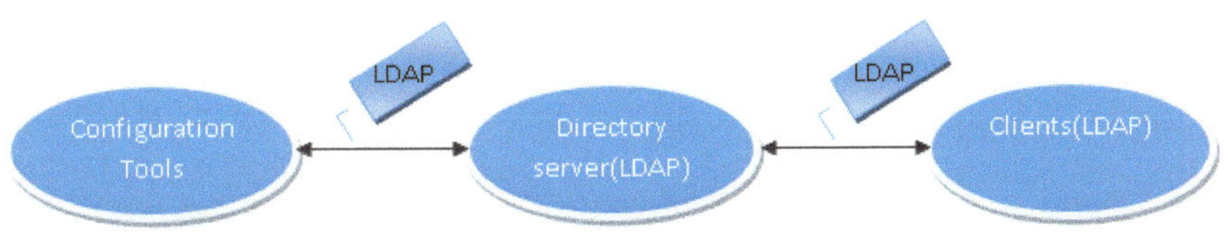

Figure 4: Directory-based automatic configuration of networks

And the clients connected with the directory server by Lightweight Directory Access Protocol, subsequently The network element doing the reconfiguration automatically After inform about any related change in the configuration policies to the server (any change occur in the configuration policies will dynamically recorded in the directory server) by implementing one of the following two techniques:

- periodic polling of the directory, the network element periodically connects to the directory and refreshes it's configuration data.
- invoking a persistent search operation on the directory, The persistent search operation[13] alters the standard Lightweight Directory Access Protocol search operation so that it does not end after the initial set of entries matching the search criteria are returned. Instead, the Lightweight Directory Access Protocol server keeps the search operation active.

The periodic polling of the directory is facing the problem of overload on the network elements, directory server and network resources, on the other hand, invoking a persistent search operation on the directory provides Lightweight Directory Access Protocol clients and servers participating in persistent search an active channel through which entries that change (and additional information about the changes that occur) can be communicated [14]. The persistent search operation suffers from the drawback that it requires an active TCP connection, which otherwise may not have been kept active. The maintenance of an active TCP connection between the Lightweight Directory Access Protocol clients and the server constitutes undesirable overhead at the server level and also results in increased utilization of network resources, particularly in cases where persistent search is invoked by a large number of Lightweight Directory Access Protocol clients.

Fig. 5 illustrate the suggested architecture of Automatic Configuration.

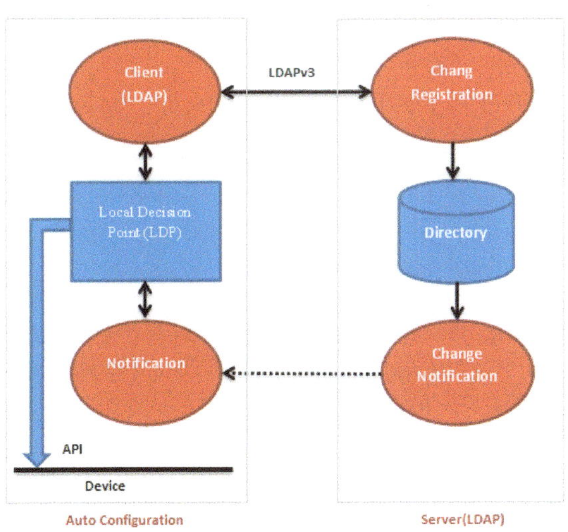

Figure 5: Suggested Architecture

The directory server includes the functionality to implement the change registration and change notification mechanisms. The auto-configurable network element consists of three important functional units :

- Lightweight Directory Access Protocol client,
- Local Decision Point
- Notification unit.

The Lightweight Directory Access Protocol client allows the network element to receive initial configuration information from the directory at the time of startup. The Lightweight Directory Access Protocol client also enables the network element to register change registration requests at the directory server. If the changes made to the directory match the criteria specified by a change registration request, then the directory server performs change notification. The directory server notifies the notification unit of the concerned network element (s) about the changes in the configuration information. In case of the pull model of change notification, the notification unit informs the Lightweight Directory Access Protocol client, which in turn establishes an Lightweight Directory Access Protocol session with the directory server and retrieves the changed configuration information. The Lightweight Directory Access Protocol client transfers the changed configuration information to the Local Decision Point. In case of the push model of change notification, the directory server provides the notification unit with the changed configuration information, which in turn passes the information to the Local Decision Point.

The DEN specification involves a set of classes that are applicable to all management domains, such as physical or logical aspects of managed entities or other aspects that are part of a managed environment. The DEN specification also involves classes related to specific management domains such as System, Device, Network, Database, User, and Service Level Agreement, etc. The network element may subscribe to changes in properties that represent the element or to properties related to the domain or network in accordance with its configuration goals. The Local Decision Point configures the network element in accordance with the changed configuration policies. The Local Decision Point uses the appropriate application programming interface (API) to implement the self-configuration of the network element. The Local Decision Point may use SNMP API to configure the management information base (MIB) of the device or may use COPS API to implement changes in the policy information base (PIB) of the network element. The Lightweight Directory Access Protocol v3 protocol provides means to implement secure transfer of information between the Lightweight Directory Access Protocol server and the Lightweight Directory Access Protocol client [16]. The notification messages may be transmitted using any suitable data communications protocol. The Local Decision Point uses network programming [17] to implement the self-configuration of the network elements by downloading and installing appropriate software. The standard network programming interfaces such as IEEE P1520 APIs can be used for this purpose [18, 19].

DISSECTION

Suggested Architecture provides dynamic notification of changes in the directory to the network elements without requiring an active Lightweight Directory Access Protocol session. Lightweight Directory Access Protocol has the important services offered by Lightweight Directory Access Protocol.

We present the following points:

- Lightweight Directory Access Protocol control is a mechanism that allows additional parameters to be added to previously defined Lightweight Directory Access Protocol operations.
- Lightweight Directory Access Protocol extended operation is a mechanism that allows for new Lightweight Directory Access Protocol operations to be defined to enhance the base set of Lightweight Directory Access Protocol operations. For example, Lightweight Directory Access Protocol extensions have been developed to provide dynamic directory services.
- The dynamic directory services store information that only persists in its accuracy and value when it is being periodically refreshed.
- The Lightweight Directory Access Protocol extended operations provide change registration and change notification services to the network elements.
- The network elements use the change registration extended operation to register at the directory server for change notification.
- The registration is followed by the termination of the Lightweight Directory Access Protocol session.
- The network elements specify the directory entries that are to be monitored as part of the change registration extended operation.
- The directory server maintains a list of all valid registration requests and associates the requests with the related network elements.
- The directory server monitors the directory information tree (DIT) for any changes. The changes to the DIT are compared to the change registration requests registered at the server.
- If the changes made to the DIT match the criteria specified by a change registration request, then the directory server performs the change notification extended operation.
- The change notification extended operation notifies the related network element (s) regarding the associated changes made to the DIT, which may represent changes in the configuration policies.
- The change notification extended operation may be implemented using two different models, push model or pull model.
- The pull model involves notifying the network element about the changes to the DIT.
- The network element is required to reconnect to the directory server in order to access the changed configuration information.
- The push model of change notification involves automatic transfer of the changed information from the directory server to the network element.
- The push model has the advantage of reducing the response time to changes in configuration information,

as it does not involve the Lightweight Directory Access Protocol connection setup and data request associated with the pull model of change notification.

- The change registration extended operation allows the network element to specify the change notification method-pull model or push model. This allows the network element to implement the change notification approach most suited with regards to the frequency of change of configuration information and importance of the changed configuration information.

RELATED WORK

The directory-enabled network (DEN) specification is an extension of the Common Information Model (CIM) of Distributed Management Task Force (DMTF). CIM is an object-oriented approach to the management of information and systems, and the automatic configuration (suggested architecture) uses the standard DEN specification to model network elements and services. There are many object-oriented approaches to model networks. The OSI CMIP proposal was based on object-oriented models to organize instrumentation of managed resources at agent's [20]. NETMATE [20], Dolphin [21], and NESTOR [22] have also used object-based approaches to model networks. The NESTOR system [23] provides an architecture for network self-management and organization. NESTOR automates configuration management by using policy scripts that access and manipulate respective network elements via a resource directory server (RDS). The MANDATE (MAnaging Networks using Database TEchnology) system [23] is a database system designed for effective management of large enterprise networks. In [24], the directory has been used to provide a framework for Directory-enabled SNMPv3 management. The network elements, that are typically SNMP agents access the configuration data maintained in the directory and translate the data into SNMP MIB attributes. This architecture suffers from the drawback that, the network elements perform only initial configuration tasks and do not support dynamic automatic configuration.

CONCLUSIONS

The suggested architecture uses the standard DEN specification to model network elements and services. The DEN specification is an extension of the Common Information Model (CIM) of DMTF. CIM is an object-oriented approach to the management of information rectory services, and network programming to provide auto configuration of networks. The fundamental purpose of DEN is to provide a common, unifying repository that is used to store data and information about the data (metadata) for multiple applications to share and use. The directory information is replicated among multiple directory servers using directory replication. The use of a logically centralized, physically distributed repository enables DEN to define an approach to manage the network as opposed to an element in the network. This approach makes configuration management using DEN fundamentally different from and advantageous compared to other traditional approaches. The other major advantage of using DEN to perform configuration management is the rich information model provided by the DEN specification to describe a multi-service network. The DEN specification allows many disparate services and technologies to be conceptually, logically, and physically modeled as a single cooperating platform. This feature of the DEN specification allows configuration management to be performed easily and effectively across several heterogeneous management domains. In the suggested architecture, the configuration information is maintained in a standard directory. The network elements register for change notification at the directory server using a directory service. The directory server notifies the network elements about any related changes in the configuration information. The network elements upon receiving the changed configuration data are able to perform automatic configuration. Automatic configuration allows increased scalability, as the network elements are able to automatically adapt themselves to the new configuration policies so I think the automatic configuration is able to eliminate configuration inconsistencies, reduce configuration management tasks, and is able to provide a unifying framework for effective enterprise management.

ACKNOWLEDGMENTS

We would like to thank Dr. Abu Baker El Hussain for their useful comments and help.

REFERENCES

1. Network Configuration Management, http://networkdictiona ry.com/ networking/ncm.php, Oct 2010.
2. J. Kurose and K. Ross, "Computer Networking", fifth edition, Pearson education, 2010.
3. Network Change and Configuration Management: Optimize Reliability, Minimize Risk and Reduce Costs, An Enterprise Management Associates White Paper, 2008.
4. B.Stiller, P. Reichl, J. Gerke, H. Hasan and P. Flury," Charging and Accounting in High-speed Networks", Journal on Future Generation Computing Systems 19 (2003) 101-109, Elsevier 2003 What is Network Security, http://www.cc.boun .edu.tr/ networksecurity. Html, Oct 2010.
5. Network Management Basics, http://www.cisco.com/en/US/ docs/internetworking/technology/handbook/ NM Basics.html, Nov 2010.
6. J. Liu, T. He and X. Li, "An Accounting Management System for High-speed Network Building on Network Processor", In proceedings of APAN Network Research Workshop, 2004.
7. M. Wahl, T. Howes, and S. Kille, "Lightweight directory access protocol (v3),"IETF, RFC2251, Dec.1997.
8. Mark Wilcox, Implementing LDAP, Wrox Press, 1999.
9. Wang Changkun, "Policy-based network management," in Proc. Int. Conf.Commun. Technol., vol. 1, 2000.
10. Y. Nomura et al., "A policy based networking architecture for enterprise networks," in Proc. IEEE Int. Conf. Commun., 1999.
11. D. Durham et al., "The COPS (common open policy service) protocol," IETF, RFC 2748, Jan. 2000.
12. Smith et al., "Persistent search: A simple LDAP change notification.

13. Dfg Y. Yaacovi, M.Wahl, and T. Genovese, "Lightweight directory access protocol (v3): Extensions for dynamic directory services," IETF, RFC 2589, May 1999.

14. M. Wahl et al., "Authentication methods for LDAP," IETF RFC, 2829, May 2000.

15. D. Tennenhouse et al., "A survey of active network research," IEEE Commun.Mag., vol.35, no. 1, 1997.

16. Programming interfaces for IP networks, White Paper IEEE P1520/TS/IP001. Available at http://www.ieee-pin.org/doc/ draft docs/IP/ p1520tsip001-rev0.4.pdf.

17. Programming interfaces for IP routers and switches, an architectural framework document, " IEEE P1520/TS/IP003. Available at.

18. http://www.ieee-pin.org/doc/draft ocs/IP/p1520tsip003-04dec98.pdf.

19. ITU-T, "Information technology, open systems interconnection, structure of management information: Guidelines for the definitions of managedobjects," Recommendation X.772, ISO/IEC 10165-4, 1992.

20. A. Dupuy et al., "NetMate: A network management environment," IEEE Network Mag., 1991.

21. A. Pell et al., "Managing in a distributed world," in Proc. 4th IFIP/IEEE Int. Symp. Integrated Network Management, 1995.

22. Y. Yemini, A. Konstantinou, and D. Florissi, "NESTOR: An architecture for network self-management and organization," IEEE J. Select. Areas Commun., vol. 18, no.5, May 2000.

23. J. Haritsa et al., "MANDATE: Managing networks using database technology,"IEEE J. Select. Areas Commun., vol. 11, 1993.

24. S. Omari and R. Boutaba, "Directory supported management with SNMPv3,"in Proc. 10th IFIP/IEEE International Workshop on Distributed Systems Operation and Management (DSOM'99), Zurich, Switzerland, Oct. 1999.

CHAPTER 2 FLOW LEVEL DETECTION AND FILTERING OF LOW-RATE DDOS

Changwang Zhang [a,b], Zhiping Cai [a], Weifeng Chen [c], Xiapu Luo [d], and Jianping Yin [a]

[a] School of Computer Science, National University of Defense Technology, Changsha, China

[b] Department of Computer Science, University College London, Gower Street, London WC1E 6BT, United Kingdom

[c] Department of Math & Computer Science, California University of Pennsylvania, USA

[d] Computing Department, Hong Kong Polytechnic University, China

ABSTRACT

The recently proposed TCP-targeted Low-rate Distributed Denial-of-Service (LDDoS) attacks send fewer packets to attack legitimate flows by exploiting the vulnerability in TCP's congestion control mechanism. They are difficult to detect while causing severe damage to TCP-based applications. Existing approaches can only detect the presence of an LDDoS attack, but fail to identify LDDoS flows. In this paper, we propose a novel metric – Congestion Participation Rate (CPR) – and a CPR-based approach to detect and filter LDDoS attacks by their intention to congest the network. The major innovation of the CPR-base approach is its ability to identify LDDoS flows. A flow with a CPR higher than a predefined threshold is classified as an LDDoS flow, and consequently all of its packets will be dropped. We analyze the effectiveness of CPR theoretically by quantifying the average CPR difference between normal TCP flows and LDDoS flows and showing that CPR can differentiate them. We conduct ns-2 simulations, test-bed experiments, and Internet traffic trace analysis to validate our analytical results and evaluate the performance of the proposed approach. Experimental results demonstrate that the proposed CPR-based approach is substantially more effective compared to an existing Discrete Fourier Transform (DFT)-based approach – one of the most efficient approaches in detecting LDDoS attacks. We also provide experimental guidance to choose the CPR threshold in practice.

INTRODUCTION

Distributed Denial-of-Service (DDoS) attacks [1] have been identified as a major threat to today's Internet services. Being a new kind of DDoS attacks, TCP-targeted Low-rate Distributed Denial-of-Service (LDDoS) [2] attacks are more efficient in terms of causing damage to legitimate flows and more difficult to detect when compared to traditional flooding-based DDoS attacks.

Traditional flooding-based DDoS attacks employ a "sledge-hammer" approach of high-rate transmission of packets, which obviously distinguishes themselves from normal data flows in statistical characteristics. Many of the proposed approaches for detecting DDoS attacks have been based on these statistical characteristics [3], [4], [5], [6] and [7].

LDDoS attacks are quite different from the traditional flooding-based DDoS attacks as they exploit the vulnerabilities in TCP's congestion control mechanism. Instead of sending

Citation: Changwang Zhang, Zhiping Cai, Weifeng Chen, Xiapu Luo, Jianping Yin, Flow level detection and filtering of low-rate DDoS, Computer Networks, Volume 56, Issue 15, 15 October 2012, Pages 3417-3431, ISSN 1389-1286, http://dx.doi.org/10.1016/j.comnet.2012.07.003.

continuous network traffic, an LDDoS attacker sends periodically pulsing data flows, which may dramatically reduce the average rate of attack flows. LDDoS attacks have already been observed in the Internet2 Abilene backbone [8], thus presenting a new challenge to the security of the Internet.

When facing large scale LDDoS attacks, existing defense approaches can only detect the presence of the LDDoS attack, but cannot determine whether a particular flow is an attack flow or not. In this paper we propose a novel metric "Congestion Participation Rate" (CPR) to identify LDDoS flows. The CPR-based approach exploits the fact that LDDoS flows actively induce network congestion whereas normal TCP flows actively avoid network congestion. That is, normal TCP flows will tend to send fewer packets during network congestion whereas LDDoS flows would not. The Congestion Participation Rate (CPR) can accurately capture this fundamental difference, and hence allow us to identify LDDoS flows. Our contributions are summarized as follows:

- We propose a novel metric – Congestion Participation Rate (CPR) to identify LDDoS flows by measuring the intention of network flows to congest the network. To the best of our knowledge, it is the first metric that could recognize LDDoS flows by quantifying each flow's intention of congesting the network.
- We propose and implement a CPR-based approach to detect and filter LDDoS attacks. The CPR-based approach is an originality innovation that can effectively identify LDDoS in a per-flow basis in large-scale LDDoS attacks as far as we are concerned.
- We conduct intensive experiments, including both ns-2 simulations and test-bed experiments, to validate our analytical results and evaluate the performance of the CPR-based approach. The experimental results demonstrate that the CPR-based approach is effective for all of the LDDoS attacks considered while the existing Discrete Fourier Transform (DFT)-based approach is only effective for a small set of LDDoS attacks.
- We obtain the trade-off between the detection rate and the false positive rate for the CPR-based approach through a comprehensive set of experiments. This trade-off provides experimental guidance for choosing a CPR threshold in practice.

It is worth noting that the CPR-based approach is designed to distinguish between normal TCP flows and LDDoS flows. Differentiating normal UDP flows and LDDoS flows will be investigated in future work. The LDDoS attacks in this paper, if not declared otherwise, precisely refer to TCP-targeted LDDoS attacks including Shrew attacks [2]and Pulsing DoS (PDoS) attacks [9]. The CPR-base approach is also designed to counter TCP-targeted LDDoS attacks [2] and [9].

The rest of the paper is organized as follows. Section 2 presents the modeling of LDoS attacks and LDDoS attacks. Section 3 defines the metric of CPR, describes the CPR-based approach and analyzes the boundaries of average CPR for normal and attack flows. Intensive experiments based on ns-2 simulations and real network configurations are presented in Sections 4 and 5 respectively. Section 6 discusses several important issues related to the deployment of the CPR-based approach. Section 7 reviews existing work that is directly related to the proposed approach. Finally we conclude the paper in Section 8.

MODELING LDDOS ATTACKS

In this section we model the LDDoS attacks. Our target is to detect and filter LDDoS attack flows. A flow is uniquely determined by a 5-tuple (*Source IP, Source Port, Destination IP, Destination Port, Protocol*). We use four parameters (T_a,T_b,R_b,s) to describe an LDoS attack flow, where T_a is the LDoS attack period, T_b is the LDoS attack burst width (or pulsing width), R_b is the LDoS attack burst rate (or pulsing rate), and *s*is the starting time of the attack flow (see Fig. 1).

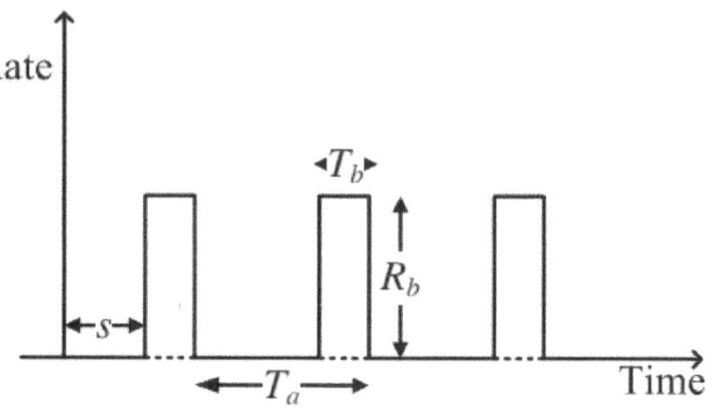

Figure 1: LDoS attack flow.

An LDDoS attack consists of multiple LDoS attack flows, F_1,F_2 … F_n, that may originate from different machines distributed on the Internet. Assuming that T_a,T_b and R_b are identical for every LDoS flow F_i, we define an LDDoS flow group as a set of attack flows that have the same starting time *s*. The starting time of an LDDoS flow group is just the starting time of each flow in the group. We assume that the starting gap between consecutive LDDoS flow groups remains constant in an LDDoS attack. For example, in Fig. 2, sg_1 represents the starting gap between LDDoS flow groups 1 and 2, and sg_2 represents the starting gap between LDDoS flow groups 2 and 3. Our assumption corresponds to that both sg_1 and sg_2 are equal to a constant in an LDDoS attack. This starting gap is denoted as σ. We further assume that each group has an identical number, *m* , of flows.

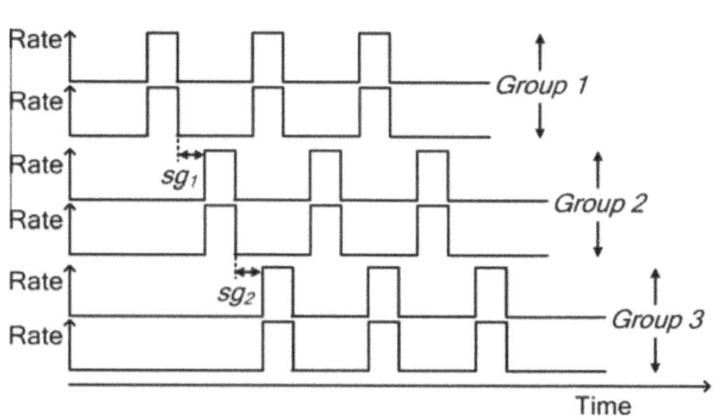

Figure 2: An LDDoS attack. There are 3 LDDoS flow groups in this LDDoS attack. sg_1 is the starting gap between LDDoS flow groups 1 and 2. sg_2 is the starting gap between LDDoS flow groups 2 and 3. In modeling LDDoS attacks, we assume that both sg_1 and sg_2 are equal to a constant in an LDDoS attack.

Based on the definition and assumption above, we describe an LDDoS attack using four parameters (n,g,m,σ), where *n* is the total number of flows in the attack, *g* is the number of attack flow groups, and *m* is the number of members in an LDDoS flow group. It is clear that $n = mg$ based on the above assumptions.

It is worth noting that the aforementioned assumption only eases the classification of LDDoS attacks and is not required by our detection system.

Based on these assumptions and definitions, we classify LDDoS attacks into four categories (Fig. 3), according to how the three characteristics $T_a T_b$, and R_b are being distributed among multiple flows in an LDDoS attack. Although our classification is by no means complete, it is enough for us to analyze the characteristics of the LDDoS attacks and to conduct experiments to evaluate our approach.

- Attack Frequency Intensification (AFI) 51¼e<WW LDDoS attack($n > 0$, $g = n$, $m = 1$, $= Ta/g$)
- The first category represents the LDDoS attacks whose aggregate attack period is equally distributed among *n* flows. The attack frequency of the aggregate flow is intensified by *n* times, compared to the frequency of each attack flow.
- Attack burst Width Intensification (AWI) LDDoS attack($n > 0$, $g = n$, $m = 1$, $\sigma = T_b$)
- The second category corresponds to the case when the aggregate burst width of an LDDoS attack is equally distributed among *n* flows. An attack burst of a flow is immediately followed by a burst from another flow. In this case, the attack burst width of the aggregate attack flow is intensified by *n*times.
- Attack burst Rate Intensification (ARI) LDDoS attack($n > 0$, $g = 1$, $m = n$, $\sigma = 0$)
- The third category describes the LDDoS attacks in which *n* flows start at the same time, and the burst rate of the aggregate attack flow is intensified *n* times.
- Mixed Intensification (MI) LDDoS attack

  ($n > 0$, $g > 1$, $m > 1$, $\sigma > 0$)

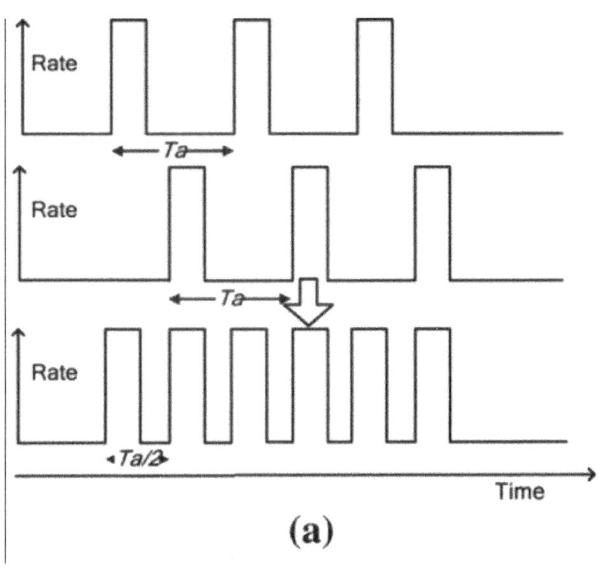

(a)

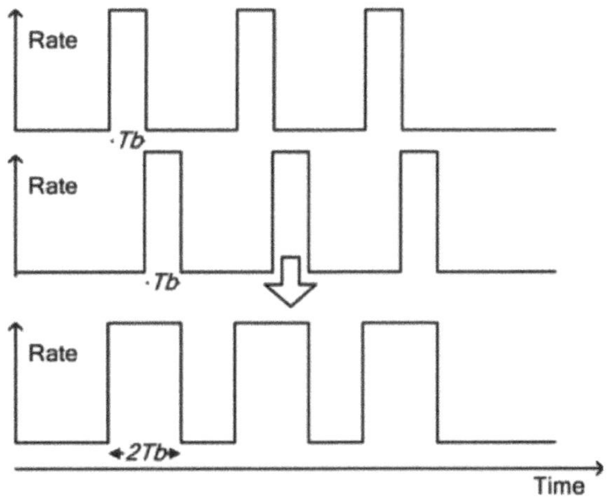

(b)

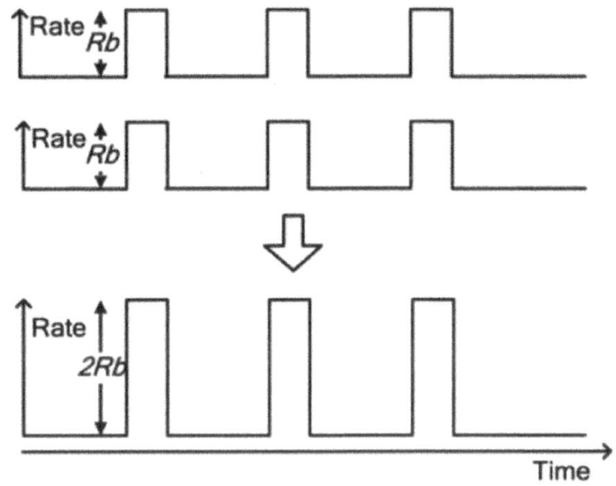

(c)

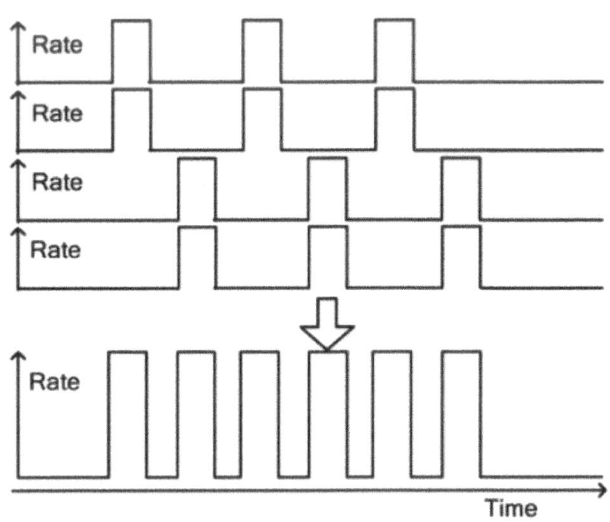

(d)

Figure 3: LDDoS attack categories (a) Attack Frequency Intensification (AFI), (b) Attack burst Width Intensification, (c) Attack burst Rate Intensification, and (d) Mixed Intensification. The unit for Rate is Bytes/s and the unit for time is second.

The last category can be considered as the combination of the previous three.

Let T_a, T_b and R_b be the parameters for a single attack flow, and T_a^+, T_b^+, and R_b^+ be the parameters for the aggregate flow of an LDDoS attack. Table 1 demonstrates the relationship between T_a^+, T_b^+, R_b^+, and T_a, T_b, R_b.

Table 1: Aggregate flow of LDDoS attacks

LDDoS categories	Aggregate flow		
	T_a^+	T_b^+	R_b^+
AFI	T_a/n	T_b	R_b
AWI	T_a	$T_b \times n$	R_b
ARI	T_a	T_b	$R_b \times n$
MI	$(T_a/n, T_a)$	$(T_b, T_b \times n)$	$(R_b, R_b \times n)$

THE CPR-BASED APPROACH

In this section, we first propose the metric of CPR and then describe our CPR-based approach to detect and filter LDDoS attack flows.

Congestion participation rate

A major difference between normal TCP flows and LDDoS flows is that normal TCP flows actively avoid network congestion due to TCP's congestion control mechanism, whereas LDDoS flows actively induce network congestion to degrade network performance.

Motivated by this difference, we propose Congestion Participation Rate (CPR) to distinguish between an LDDoS flow and a normal TCP flow. Consider a router through which different flows (normal TCP flows and LDDoS attack flows) pass (see Fig. 4), at time *t*, we sample the incoming link of the router for a duration *d* and count the number of packets from every flow F_i, denoted as $S_{i,t}$. At the same time, we monitor the packet queue in the router. If there is at least a packet dropped at the packet queue (because the queue is full) during *d*, we consider that the outgoing link of the router is congested at time *t*. After a series of sampling *T* , we define the CPR of flow F_i as

$$\theta_i = \sum_{t \in T*} S_{i,t} \Big/ \sum_{t \in T} S_{i,t} \qquad (1)$$

where T^* is the set of sampling epochs when the outgoing link is congested. In other words, the θ_i is the ratio of the incoming packets in congestion to the total incoming packets from flow F_i. It is worth noting that the packets are sampled at the incoming link before they enter the packet queue or be dropped when the packet queue is full (due to the congestion of the outgoing link). Thus the packet number measured here is for the packets sent by a flow to the router. It is normally larger than the number of the packets from the flow that are forwarded by the router, as some of the packets may be dropped due to congestion.

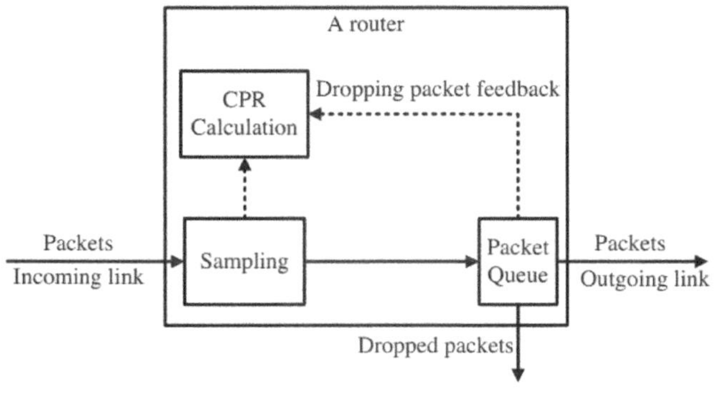

Figure 4: Calculation Congestion Participation Rate (CPR) on a router.

Since LDDoS flows actively induce network congestion while normal TCP flows actively avoid network congestion, the CPR of an LDDoS flow is expected to be considerably bigger than that of a normal TCP flow.

The detecting and filtering approach

Fig. 5 shows the block diagram of our CPR-based approach for detecting and filtering LDDoS. This approach is expected to be deployed on a router where we want to detect and filter LDDoS attack flows. In the diagram, the flow size estimation module is a functional module that is already included in most Internet routers (for example Cisco NetFlow [10]). The CPR metric mainly works in the LDDoS Attack Detection module.

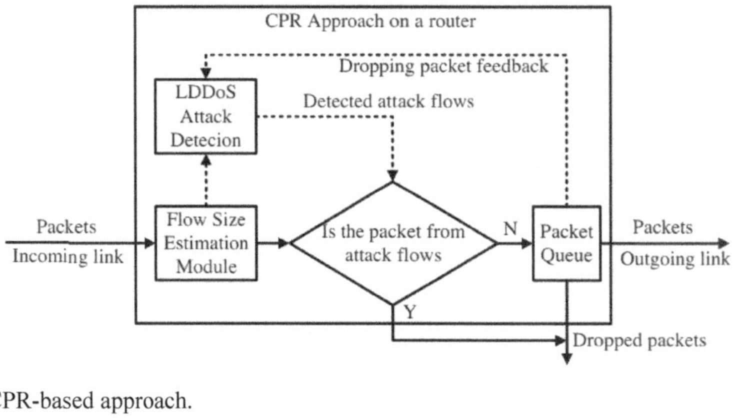

Figure 5: Block diagram of the CPR-based approach.

The router keeps CPR for every flow. A flow is considered as an LDDoS attack flow if its CPR is higher than a threshold τ. We investigate this threshold analytically in Section 3.3and use experiments to demonstrate how to determine the threshold in practice in Section 4.4.

When an LDDoS flow is detected, we drop all packets from the detected flow until its CPR becomes smaller than the threshold τ. A normal TCP flow may be mistakenly interpreted as an attack flow if it is initiated and starts to send data while the network is congested. To mitigate it, after a flow is regarded as an LDDoS flow, we keep on measuring its CPR. If its CPR becomes smaller than the threshold, the flow will once again be considered as a normal flow and its packets will pass the router successfully. A normal TCP flow that was misclassified as an attack flow will reduce its CPR by sending data when the network is not congested.

In the extreme scenario, the LDDoS attack can throttle all normal TCP flows and the aggregate rate of the LDDoS flows is also very close to the bottleneck bandwidth of network. There is almost no packet will be dropped in the scenario and consequently no network congestion can be observed. When no network congestion can be observed from a scenario, the CPRs of both LDDoS flows and normal TCP flows all tend to be 0 according to the definition in (1). This is problematic for the CPR-based approach to distinguish LDDoS flows. To solve this problem, we turn on the Random Early Detection (RED) [11] queue management mechanism on the router where we install the CPR-based module. In the extreme scenario mentioned above, the RED mechanism actively drops packets from the pulsing LDDoS flows. Normally, RED drops packets in order to send congestion signals back to the sources. As will be covered in Section 4, the CPR-based approach with RED effectively detects LDDoS attacks in this scenario. We configure the RED mechanism to be based on packet count as opposed to packet bytes because the packet-count RED is more sensitive to the small packets sent in an LDDoS attack flow.

Bounds of the congestion participation rates

In this subsection, we theoretically analyze the average CPR difference between normal TCP flows and LDDoS flows, which is critical for our approach to identify attack flows. More precisely, we conduct a worst-case analysis by computing the minimum average CPR difference between normal TCP flows and LDDoS flows. It is worth noting that, this section does not aim to establish a complete analytical model for CPR bounds, but to analyze the relationship between CPR bounds and several network parameters that are directly measureable. As stated in Section 3.3.3, to get the exact value of those CPR bounds, one sill needs to experimentally measure several network parameters.

Since LDDoS flows tend to have a higher CPR than normal TCP flows, the minimum average CPR difference is obtained by subtracting the upper bound of normal TCP flows' average CPR from the lower bound of the average CPR of LDDoS flows. We obtain the theoretical equations for these two bounds in this subsection and verify the results through experiments in a real network in Section 5. Table 2 lists the notation used in our analysis.

Table 2: Notations and abbreviations for network traffic.

Notations	Definition
r_{TCP}	The average ratio of packets dropped to all incoming packets from normal TCP flows
r_{LDDoS}	The average ratio of packets dropped to all incoming packets from LDDoS flows
B	The maximum bandwidth of the outgoing link of a router (Mbps)
ρ_{TCP}	The average aggregate peak incoming rate (Mbps) of normal TCP flows
ρ_{LDDoS}	The average aggregate peak incoming rate (Mbps) of LDDoS flows
δ_{TCP}	The average aggregate packet-dropping rate (Mbps) of normal TCP flows
δ_{LDDoS}	The average aggregate packet-dropping rate (Mbps) of LDDoS flows
z	The average packet size
T^*	The packet-dropping period of time
T	The total time period

When a network's bandwidth is sufficiently high, packets are unlikely to be dropped in the network, and an LDDoS attack cannot throttle normal TCP traffic either. Therefore we focus on the scenario that a network's bandwidth is lower than users' demands, i.e., the network is relatively high loaded. This can be represented as $\rho_{TCP}+\rho_{LDDoS}>B$.

Consider the following scenarios. In a time period T, a set of normal TCP flows and LDDoS attack flows with average aggregate peak incoming rates ρ_{TCP} and ρ_{LDDoS} go through a router with outgoing bandwidth B. Since $\rho_{TCP}+\rho_{LDDoS}>B$, network congestion and packet dropping will happen. Let $T^*\subseteq T$ be the time when the outgoing link is in congestion and packets are dropped. We investigate the CPR through the ratio r of dropped packets to all incoming packets in this time period

T. More specifically, we want to establish the relationship between CPR and r. Note that r is the packet drop ratio that can be measured directly from network traffic.

Upper bound of the CPR for normal TCP flows

Although many sophisticated TCP models have been proposed [12], [13], [14] and [15], we found that the simple model proposed in this subsection is sufficient for determining the upper bound of normal TCP flows' CPR.

We first consider the situation when there is no LDDoS attack flow, i.e., all flows are normal TCP flows. The situation when attack flows are present will be described next.

When there are only normal TCP flows, the traffic in time period T can be depicted in Fig. 6, which is obtained from our testbed experiment results. We assume that the packet dropping is all due to network congestion. When the outgoing link is congested, the buffers of routers are fully filled, and ρ_{TCP} is higher than B. That is the reason for packet dropping. Thus, we have (2).

$$\delta_{TCP} = \rho_{TCP} - B \qquad (2)$$

From Fig. 6, one can see that the number of packets dropped in time period T is $(T^* \times \delta_{TCP})/z$, whereas the total number of incoming packets in T is $(T^* \times \rho_{TCP})/z + ((T-T^*) \times B)/z$, which gives us r_{TCP} in (3).

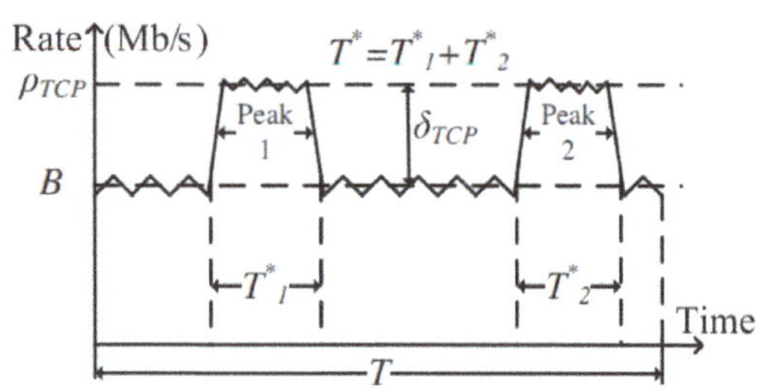

Figure 6: Normal TCP traffic (when there is no attack).

Intuitionally, r_{TCP} is the ratio of the shaded area to the area enclosed by the Rate curve and the Time axis (from 0 to T) in Fig. 7, i.e., the area enclosed by the bold curves.

$$r_{TCP} = \frac{T^* \times \delta_{TCP}/z}{T^* \times \rho_{TCP}/z + (T - T^*) \times B/z} = \frac{T^* \times \delta_{TCP}}{T^* \times \rho_{TCP} + (T - T^*) \times B} \qquad (3)$$

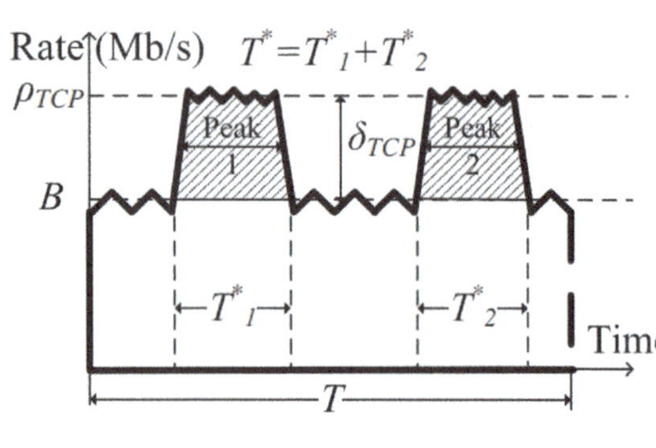

Figure 7: Illustration of r*TCP*.

According to the definition of CPR in (1), we have the CPR of the aggregate TCP flows, θ_{TCP}, as

$$\theta_{TCP} = \frac{T^* \times \rho_{TCP}/z}{T^* \times \rho_{TCP}/z + (T - T^*) \times B/z} = \frac{T^* \times \rho_{TCP}}{T^* \times \rho_{TCP} + (T - T^*) \times B} \qquad (4)$$

Fig. 8 graphically illustrates the calculation of θ_{TCP} in (4). θ_{TCP} is the proportion of the shaded area to the area enclosed by the bold curves.

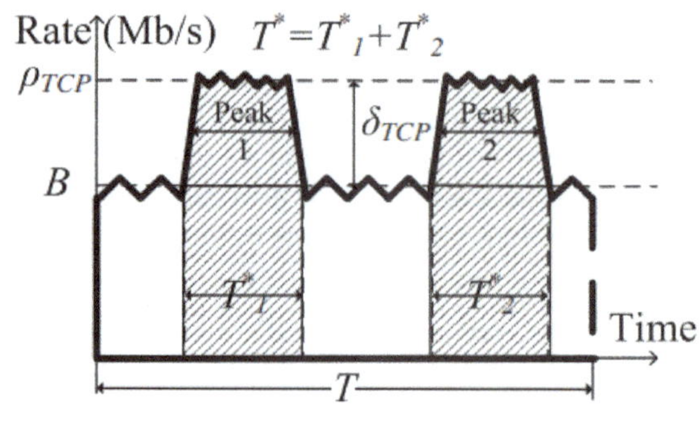

Figure 8: Illustration of θ_{TCP}.

Eqs. (3) and (4) yield the relationship between the CPR of the aggregate TCP flows, θ_{TCP}, and r_{TCP} in (5):

$$\theta_{TCP} = \begin{cases} \frac{\rho_{TCP}}{\delta_{TCP}} \times r_{TCP} & (\delta_{TCP} > 0) \\ 0 & (\delta_{TCP} = 0) \end{cases} \qquad (5)$$

In (5), when $\delta_{TCP}=0$, no packet dropping is observed. Consequently, $T^*=0$ and $\theta_{TCP}=0$.

From (2) and (5), we get (6):

$$\theta_{TCP} = \frac{\rho_{TCP}}{\rho_{TCP} - B} \times r_{TCP} = \frac{1}{1 - B/\rho_{TCP}} \times r_{TCP}(\rho_{TCP} > B) \ \ldots \qquad (6)$$

From (6), we can see that the average CPR of normal TCP flows without attacks is determined by B/ρ_{TCP} and r_{TCP}, which in practice can be obtained from network traffic. In other words, once we obtain B, ρ_{TCP} and r_{TCP}, we can use (6) to get θ_{TCP}. In Section 5, the accuracy of (6) is validated by real network traffic.

When LDDoS attack flows are present with normal TCP flows in the network, normal TCP flows would be forced by the LDDoS flows to send packets only in the off-period of the attack (when the network is not congested) or may even stop sending. Thus the CPR of normal TCP flows in this case is smaller than the one in the first case as shown in (6). Therefore θ_{TCP} in (6) represents the upper bound of the CPR of normal TCP flows.

Lower bound of the CPR for LDDoS flows

The lower bound of the average CPR for the aggregate LDDoS flows should be achieved in the extreme scenarios described in Section 3.2, i.e., when the aggregate rate of attack flows is very close to the bottleneck bandwidth. Fig. 9 illustrates the scenarios where two aggregate bursts with rate ρ_{LDDoS} very close to bandwidth B were sent one after the other with an interval between them. The network is congested during two bursts T_1 and T_2. However, since ρ_{LDDoS} is close to B, the number of dropped packets may be very small if no Active Queue Management (e.g., RED) is being deployed. As previously described, our CPR-based approach employs RED to actively drop packets from the pulsing LDDoS flows. In Fig. 9, T_1^* and T_2^* represent the packet-dropping period (mainly due to the RED) in the two bursts. Note that in the figure, both T_1^* and T_2^* are represented as a single period for illustrative purposes. In fact, there may be multiple short periods distributed within each burst. However, this simplification does not affect our analysis below.

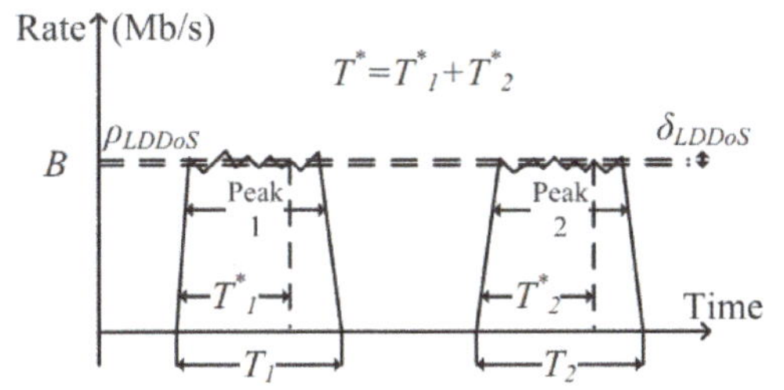

Figure 9: The meticulously planned LDDoS attack traffic.

In this situation, we can get (7) and (8).

$$r_{LDDoS} = \frac{(T_1^* + T_2^*) \times \delta_{LDDoS}/z}{(T_1 + T_2) \times \rho_{LDDoS}/z} = \frac{(T_1^* + T_2^*) \times \delta_{LDDoS}}{(T_1 + T_2) \times \rho_{LDDoS}} \quad (7)$$

$$\theta_{LDDoS} = \frac{(T_1^* + T_2^*) \times \rho_{LDDoS}/z}{(T_1 + T_2) \times \rho_{LDDoS}/z} = \frac{(T_1^* + T_2^*)}{(T_1 + T_2)} \quad (8)$$

From (7) and (8), we can get (9).

$$\theta_{LDDoS} = \begin{cases} \frac{\rho_{LDDoS}}{\delta_{LDDoS}} \times r_{LDDoS}(\delta_{LDDoS} > 0) \\ 0(\delta_{LDDoS} = 0) \end{cases} \quad (9)$$

In (9), when $\delta_{LDDoS}=0$, no packet dropping is observed. Consequently, $T^*=0$ and $\theta_{LDDoS}=0$. If no RED is deployed, r_{LDDoS} and δ_{LDDoS} could drop to 0, resulting in the CPR for the LDDoS flow to be 0 as well. Under these conditions no attack flows will be detected. However, when we turn on RED on the router, packets will be dropped and attack flows will be detected. r_{LDDoS} and δ_{LDDoS} in (9) are mainly determined by the RED mechanism in practice, as will be described in the next section.

Minimum average CPR difference between TCP and LDDoS flows

The minimum average CPR difference is obtained by subtracting the upper bound of normal TCP flows' average CPR (θTCP) from the lower bound of the average CPR of LDDoS flows (θ_{LDDoS}). In order to calculate θ_{TCP} and θ_{LDDoS} based on (6) and (9), several parameters need to be measured from network traffic, including B ,ρ_{TCP},r_{TCP},ρ_{LDDoS},δ_{LDDoS}, and r_{LDDoS}.

Note that $\rho_{TC}P$ and ρ_{LDDoS}, which respectively represents the average aggregate peak incoming rate of normal TCP flows and LDDoS flows, are normally higher than B – the bandwidth of the outgoing link of a router. They could be measured at a router by sampling packets from its incoming link before those packets enter the packet queue or be dropped when the packet queue is full (packets that manage to enter the packet queue will be finally sent to the outgoing link of the router).

We measure these parameters in three test-bed experiments in Section 5 and show the calculation results – θ^e_{TCP} and θ^e_{LDDoS} – in Table 6. According to Table 6, the minimum-average-CPR differences between normal TCP and LDDoS flows (θ^e_{DIF}, which equals to $\theta^e_{LDDoS} - \theta^e_{TCP}$) are 62.05%, 69.49%, and 73.46% for those three test-bed experiments, resulting in an overall minimum-average-CPR difference of 68.3%.

SIMULATION EXPERIMENTS

In this section we present our experiment results obtained from ns-2 [16]. Section 4.1tests the influence of the RED mechanism on the approach. Section 4.2 evaluates the performance of the CPR-based approach in the presence of different LDDoS attacks. Section 4.3 evaluates the performance of the approach in a challenging scenario – distinguishing LDDoS flows from short-lived HTTP flows. Section 4.4 evaluates the trade-off between the detection rate and the false positive rate of our CPR-based approach that provides a quantitative guideline to determine the CPR threshold τ in practice.

Dumbbell network topologies are commonly used in congestion control studies [17]. Fig. 10 shows the experimental topology, which consists of two routers (R_0, R_1), 30 users ($User_1 \cdots User_{30}$), 20 attackers ($Attacker_1 \cdots Attacker_{20}$), 30 servers ($Server_1 \cdots Server_{30}$), and a victim server (Victim Server). The link between two routers is the bottleneck link with a bandwidth of 5 Mbps and one-way propagation delay of 6 ms. All the other links have a bandwidth of 10Mbps and a one-way propagation delay of 2 ms. In this topology, $User_i$ communicates with $Server_i$ ($i = 1 \cdots 30$) using FTP (generated by *Application/FTP* using Newreno TCP in ns-2), and 20 attackers send UDP packets (generated by *Application/Traffic/CBR* in ns-2) to attack the Victim Server. The queue size of the bottleneck link is 50. A RED based on packet count is deployed at router R_0 on the queues of the bottleneck link. Other links use DropTail queues. A CPR-based detection module is installed at router R_0 where most normal TCP packets are dropped when an LDDoS attack is present. For comparison, we also install a module based on Cumulative Amplitude Spectrum (CAS) [18] at R_0, CAS uses Discrete Fourier Transform (DFT) to locate anomalies caused by LDDoS flows.

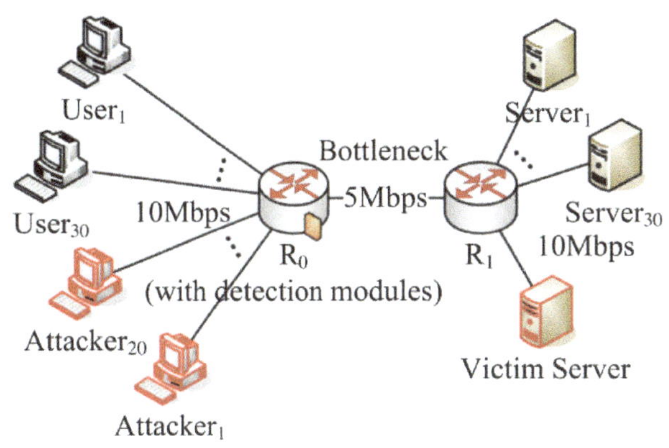

Figure 10: Topology of the simulation network.

A set of simulations are conducted and outlined in each of the following subsections. Each simulation lasts for 240 s. LDDoS attack traffic begins at 120 s and continues until 220 s. In Sections 4.1, 4.2 and 4.3, normal TCP traffic (the FTP flows from User to Server) begins at 20 s and ends at 240 s. While in Section 4.4, it begins at a random time between

20 s and 240 s, and ends at 240 s. In this section, we use a 7-tuple$(n,g,m,\sigma,T_a,T_b,R_b)$ to describe the parameters of an LDDoS attack.

RED on our approach

We first explore the influence of the RED mechanism on normal TCP flows, LDDoS flows and their CPRs. We consider an AFI LDDoS attack with parameters $(n = 20,\ g = 20,\ m = 1,\ \sigma = 1\text{ s},\ T_a = 20\text{ s},\ Tb = 200\text{ ms},\ R_b = 5\text{ Mbps})$. Here R_b is chosen to be close to the bandwidth of the bottleneck to represent the extreme situation to our CPR-based approach as described in Section 3.2.

Then using the same parameters we repeat the experiment two times. The first time we employ DropTail on the bottleneck queue at router R_0 and the second time we employ RED. The sampling frequency is $f = 1000$ Hz in both experiments and the results are shown in Table 3.

Table 3: RED vs DropTail

AQM	ρ_{na}	r_{na}	ρ_a	r_a	θ_{TCP}	θ_{LDDoS}
DropTail	4.9 Mbps	10.6%	1.0 Mbps	7.6%	13.5%	14.4%
RED	4.9 Mbps	10.6%	3.1 Mbps	25.0%	12.5%	85.9%

In Table 3, ρ_a and ρna represent the average rates of normal TCP flows when there is an attack and when there is no attack, respectively. rna represents the ratio of dropped packets to all packets at router R_0 when there is no attack and r_a is the one when there is an attack. θ_{TCP} represents the average *CPR* of the normal TCP flows and θ_{LDDoS} is for the LDDoS flows.

The results in Table 3 indicate that when there is no attack RED has no obvious influence on the normal TCP flows (ρ_{na} and r_{na} are almost the same for DropTail and RED). However, when LDDoS attacks are present, RED significantly improves the throughput of normal TCP. Note that in this case, RED drops 25% packets, much more than the 7.6% from DropTail. In other words, when the aggregate rate of the LDDoS flows is very close to the bottleneck bandwidth of network, deploying RED is able to drop more attack packets while increasing the throughput of the normal TCP flows. Admittedly RED might also drop more legitimate packets than DropTail here, however it achieves a higher normal-TCP-flow throughput ρ_a than DropTail. The throughput ρ_a of normal TCP flows is considered to be more important than its drop ratio r_a when a network is under an LDDoS attack.

Table 3 shows that under DropTail, the CPR-based approach may not be able to distinguish an LDDoS attack flow from a normal TCP flow since the two CPRs are close to one another. However, it is also clear that the CPR-based approach under RED is able to detect an attack flow since the two CPRs are significantly different under RED.

LDDoS attacks

In this subsection, we conduct experiments to compare the effectiveness of our proposed CPR-based approach and the CAS approach [18] on detecting LDDoS attack flows under different categories of LDDoS attacks. Parameters of the experiments are listed inTable 4, where for each of the three categories (AFI, AWI and ARI), we select a range of values for one variable and fix all the others. For example, for the AFI LDDoS attack, we vary the attack period T_a for each single attack flow from 20 s to 40 s. The italic values in the table list the parameters corresponding to the aggregate attack flow. They are calculated according to Table 1, which demonstrates the relationship between the parameters of each LDDoS flow (T_a,T_b, and R_b) and their aggregate flow $(T_a^+, T_b^+, \text{and } R_b^+)$. The results for the MI LDDoS attack are not presented here and can be provided upon request, but this category is just the combination of other three and the results are quantitatively comparable.

Table 4: Parameters of LDDoS attacks experiments

Categories	LDDoS attack				Single flow			Aggregate flow		
	n	g	m	σ	T_a (s)	T_b (ms)	R_b (Mbps)	T_a^+ (s)	T_b^+ (ms)	R_b^+ (Mbps)
AFI	20	20	1	$T_a/20$	[20,40]	200	5	*[1,2]*	*200*	*5*
AWI	20	20	1	T_b	1	[0.1,10]	5	*1*	*[2]*	*5*
ARI	20	1	20	0	1	200	[0.01,0.25]	*1*	*200*	*[0.2,5]*

Fig. 11 shows the results for the AFI LDDoS attack. Both the CPR-based approach and the CAS-based approach are quite effective for this category of the LDDoS attack. It is worth noting that the difference between normal TCP flows and LDDoS flows in CPR (around 0.6) is larger than that in CAS (around 0.4). We also observe that the average CPRs do not change too much as T_a increases. This is because the CPR is calculated based on a ratio (Eq. (1)). When the attack period T_a increases, the attackers tend to send fewer packets. However, the ratio of the incoming packets in congestion to the total incoming packets measured by a router may remain unchanged. This explains the similar observations in Fig. 12 and Fig. 13.

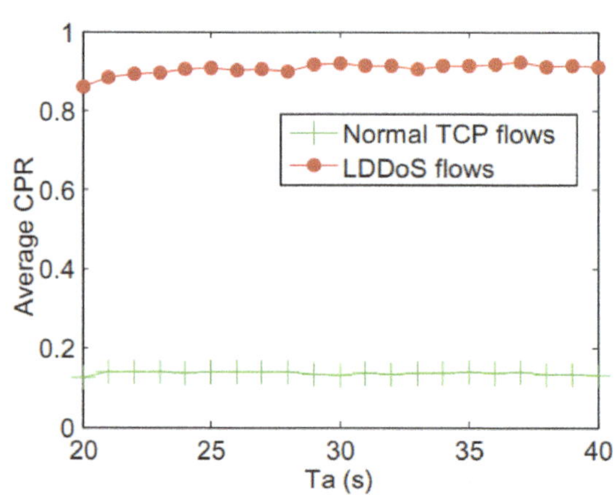

(a)

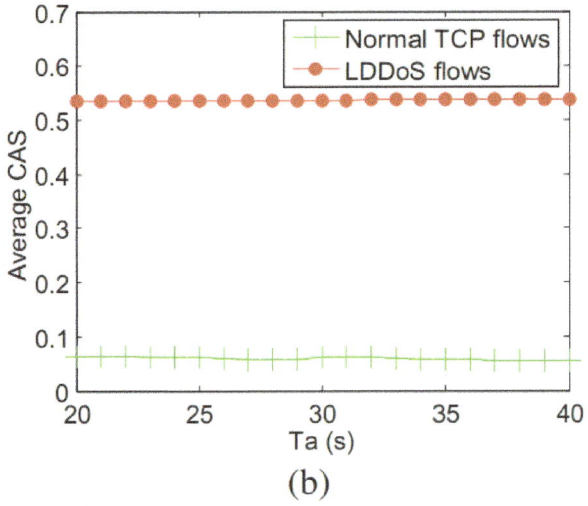

Figure 11: AFI LDDoS attack experiment.

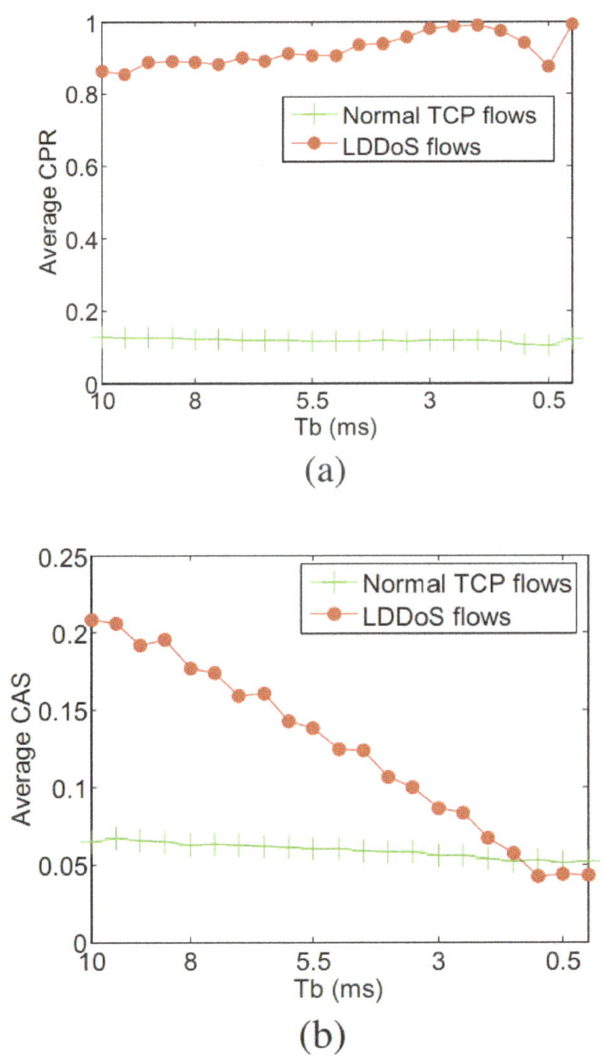

Figure 12: AWI LDDoS attack experiment.

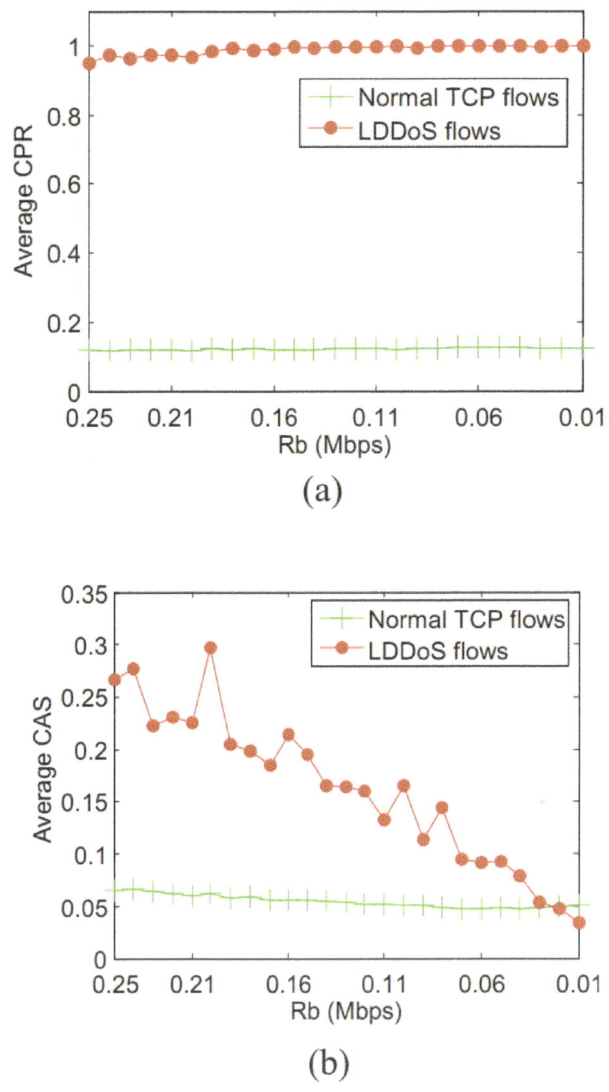

Figure 13: ARI LDDoS attack experiment.

Fig. 12 shows the results for the AWI LDDoS attack. Our CPR-based approach is still effective – the difference in the average CPR for normal TCP flows and LDDoS flows is evident. However, as T_b decreases (from 10 ms to 0.1 ms), the average CAS of the attack flows under the CAS-based approach also decreases. When T_b is around 0.5 ms, the average CAS of the normal TCP flows and the LDDoS flows is about the same.

Fig. 13 shows the results for the ARI LDDoS attack. Similar to previous results, our CPR-based approach is still effective whereas the effectiveness of the CAS-based approach decreases as R_b decreases (from 0.25 Mbps to 0.01 Mbps).

These experimental results clearly demonstrate that our CPR-based approach works well for all three categories (AFI, AWI, and ARI) of LDDoS attacks whereas the CAS-based approach only works for AFI LDDoS. CAS distinguishes LDoS flows from normal TCP flows using their spectrum difference in low frequency band. It works well for small-scale LDoS attacks. However, an attacker can dramatically reduce the burst width $T_b$and burst rate R_b of each LDDoS flow by launching large-scale LDDoS attacks, including LDoS attacks with spoofing IP addresses. The spectrum difference in low frequency band between an LDoS flow and a normal TCP flow decreases when T_b andR_b of each LDDoS flow are reduced.

For this reason DFT-based approaches, such as CAS, are not effective in detecting large-scale LDDoS attacks.

HTTP traffic

LDDoS flows can be short lived so that their traffic pattern is similar to that of normal short-lived flows like HTTP flows. Therefore, it is challenging to distinguish LDDoS flows from HTTP flows. In this subsection, we evaluate the performance of the CPR-based approach for distinguishing LDDoS flows from HTTP flows.

HTTP traffic in our experiment is generated by PackMime generator [19], that uses real Internet traces. The network topology is similar to that in Fig. 10, but with only 10 users (this is due to the limit of PackMime), 10 servers, and 10 attackers. Let R_c represent the average number of new connections started per second in PackMime. We investigate the relationship between R_c and the average *CPRs* of normal HTTP flows and LDDoS flows. The experimental results are shown in Fig. 14. One can see from the figure that the difference between the average CPR of normal HTTP flows and that of LDDoS flows increases as R_c increases. Thus it is not harder but easier for our CPR-based approach to distinguish LDDoS flows from normal HTTP flows when there are more normal HTTP flows.

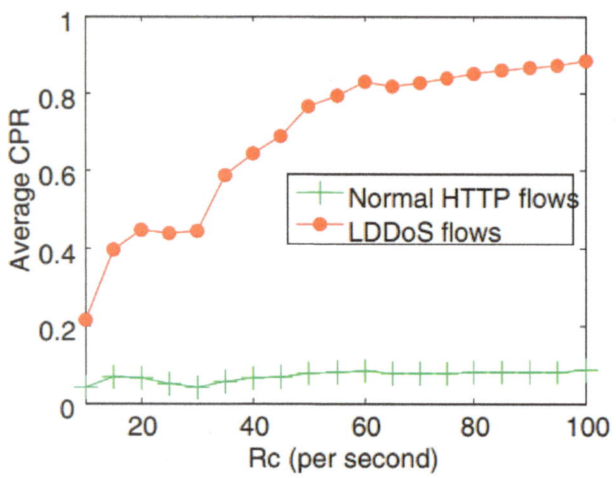

Figure 14: LDDoS attacks with HTTP traffic.

Trade-off of detection rate and false positive rate

In this subsection, we conduct experiments based on MI LDDoS attacks to systematically understand the principle of our CPR-based approach. The parameters of the LDDoS attack are (n=20,g=5,m=4,T_g,T_a,T_b,R_b), where $T_a \in [0.5, 5]$ s, $T_b \in [25]$ ms, and $R_b \in [0.75, 1.5]$ Mbps. It took over 36 h to conduct hundreds of experiments that still use the dumbbell network shown in Fig. 10. In these experiments, each user starts to send normal TCP traffic at a random time between 20 s and 240 s, and stops sending at 240 s. This simulates users' random behavior on the Internet.

Fig. 15a depicts the probability distribution of CPR of normal TCP flows and LDDoS flows. Clearly, the CPRs of these two different flows are distributed on the two ends between 0 and 1, with a small overlap in the middle.

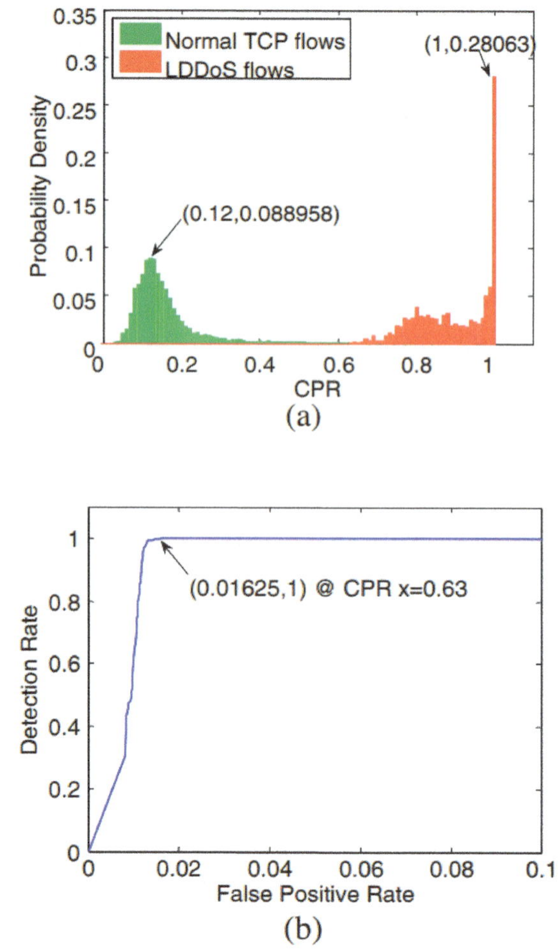

Figure 15: Receiver Operating Characteristic (ROC) experiment.

Fig. 15a also provides experimental guidance for choosing the CPR threshold in practice. From the figure, for any given CPR $x \in (0,1)$, one can obtain the experimental likelihood (Hx) that the average CPR of LDDoS flows is higher than x, which is the ratio of the red area on the right side of x to the whole red area. Similarly, one can obtain the likelihood (Lx) that the average CPR of normal TCP flows is smaller than x . Based on this, one can choose the CPR threshold τ to be x to achieve detection rate Hx with a false positive rate ($1 - Lx$). Obviously, a higher x corresponds to a lower Hx and a higher Lx. This trade-off is indicated in the Receiver Operating Characteristic (ROC) curve in Fig. 15b, where each point on the ROC curve corresponds to a CPR $x \in (0,1)$ in Fig. 15a. For example, when x=0.63, we can achieve a 100% detection rate with a 1.625% false positive rate.

REAL NETWORK AND INTERNET TRACE EXPERIMENTS

In addition to the simulation conducted using ns-2, we set up a test-bed shown in Fig. 16to further evaluate the performance of the CPR-based approach. Entities in the test-bed are all PCs, whose function, OS and installed software are listed in Table 5. In the test-bed experiments, normal TCP flows include short-lived TCP (e.g., SSH) and long-lived TCP (e.g., FTP). We use these two kinds of TCP flows to represent the mixed TCP traffic on the real network. We modify the TFN2K [20], a well-known DDoS attack tool, to label its attack flows by the

ID field in the IP header. We also add LDDoS attack function to the TFN2K and correct its header-checksum algorithm. We name the refined program as TFN2K4R (Tribe Flood Network 2000 For Research). TF2K4R is used to generate labeled LDDoS traffic. The labels are used to verify the detection rate of our CPR-based approach.

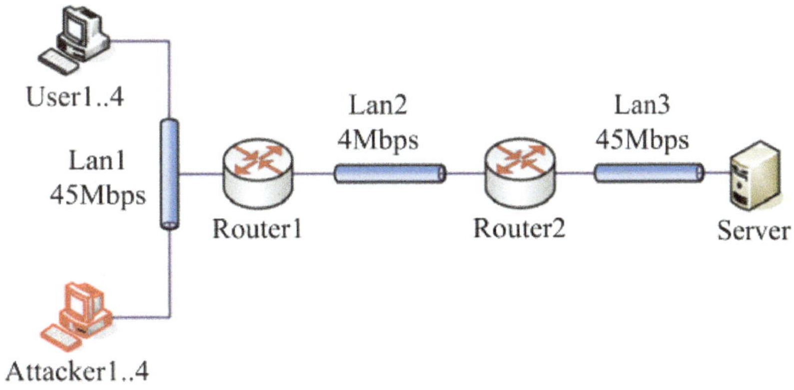

Figure 16: Topology of the test-bed.

Table 5: Setup of test-bed machines

Entities	Function	OS	Software
User1···4	Client	Debian 4	FTP, SCP
Attacker1··· 4	Attack	Debian 4	TFN2K4R
Router1 & 2	Packet forwarding Packet dumping	Debian 4	Tcpdump
Server	Server	Debian 4	vsftpd, ssh

In the experiments User1 and User2 use FTP (long-live TCP flows) to upload a 32 MB file to Server while User3 and User4 use SCP (short-lived TCP flows) to transfer 50 copies of a 0.5 MB file to Server. For the attack, we fix the first six parameters in the 7-tuple$(n,g,m,\sigma,T_a,T_b,R_b)$ and vary the last parameter R_b. The first six parameters are fixed as $n = 4$, $g = 1$, $m = 4$, $\sigma = 0$, $T_a = 1$ s, and $T_b = 200$ ms. The setting of these fixed parameters means that four attackers each simultaneously start an LDoS attack $(T_a = 1$ s, $T_b = 200$ ms, R_b, $s = 5$ s$)$. A total of three experiments are conducted, each with a different R_b. Table 6 presents the average CPR for different flows, where θ_{FTP} is the average CPR for long-lived FTP flows (User1 and User2), θ_{SCP} is the average CPR for short-lived SCP flows (User3 and User4), and θ_{LDDoS} is the average *CPR* for LDDoS flows. θ^e_{TCP} is the estimated average CPR of normal TCP flows calculated using(6) and θ^e_{LDDoS} is the estimated average CPR of LDDoS flows calculated using (9). θ^e_{DIF} is the estimated average CPR difference between normal TCP flows and LDDoS flows, which equals to $\theta^e_{LDDoS} - \theta^e_{TCP}$.

Table 6: Analysis of real network experiments.

R_b (Mbps)	θ_{FTP} (%)	θ_{SCP} (%)	θ_{LDDoS} (%)	θ^e_{TCP} (%)	θ^e_{LDDoS} (%)	θ^e_{DIF} (%)
0.25	3.27	4.19	67.1	4.15	66.2	62.05
0.5	5.95	5.43	78.7	6.51	76.0	69.49
1	8.02	8.37	84.9	7.84	81.3	73.46

Table 6 shows a clear difference between the average CPR of LDDoS flows (θ_{LDDoS}) and normal TCP flows (θ_{FTP} and θ_{SCP}). It is also noticeable that the calculated θ^e_{TCP} and θ^e_{LDDoS} are quite close to the measured CPR (θ_{FTP}, θ_{SCP} and $\theta LDDoS$), which indicates that our analysis in Section 3.3 is reasonable.

We further use real Internet traffic to validate our CPR-based approach. The LBNL/ICSI Enterprise Trace [21] is collected at a medium-sized enterprise site – one of the most possible places to install our approach. We use (6) to estimate the average CPR of the TCP flows contained in the traces. The collected trace did not record dropped packets, thus we cannot calculate the drop-packet-ratio r_{TCP} needed in (6). Instead, we use the out-of-sequence packets [22] to approximate r_{TCP}. The average CPR of the normal TCP flows for the three traces selected from [21] are 0.93%, 0.77%, and 0.70%, respectively. This is because the traces were collected when the network was not congested (the ratio of out-of-sequence packet is very small) and their CPR values tend to be zero. Since currently there is no LDDoS attack trace publically available, using real attack traffic to validate our CPR-based approach remains one of our future work.

DISCUSSION

Our CPR-based approach is an online algorithm that can be easily implemented in a router because its basic mechanism is simply counting packets, and then calculating the CPR based on Eq. (1), whose accuracy has been verified in the previous section. In this section we discuss practical issues related to the implementation of the CPR-based approach.

Flow table sizes

Compared to existing approaches on detecting LDDoS attacks [9], [18], [23], [24], [25],[26] and [27], our CPR-based approach is capable of detecting whether a flow is an attack flow or a normal TCP flow. A flow table is required to maintain the CPR of all the flows passing through the router where the CPR-based approach is installed. Our CPR-based approach requires 19.44 MB memory to maintain 11,341,289 flows in an ISP trace with OC48 speed (conducted in.[28], [29] and [30]) using a bloom filter calculator [31] with the probability of false positive of 0.001. However, the CPR-based module should be installed on routers to which the bottleneck link, to the potential victim, is connected. Such routers are unlikely to be ISP routers since they are unlikely to be bottleneck [32]. Consequently the number of flows our CPR-based approach needs to maintain will be considerably less than the one in the ISP trace leading to smaller size memory requirements. Additionally, as will be discussed in the next subsection, Multilevel Bloom Filter techniques have been proposed, which can be used to further reduce the flow table size.

Besides the flow table, our CPR-based approach also needs a flow size estimation, which can be achieved through existing solutions implemented at current routers such as Cisco NetFlow [10].

IP address spoofing

According to the way it generates spoofed source addresses, IP address spoofing can be classified into two types: fixed spoofing and random spoofing. Fixed spoofing generally does not cause a large-space overhead for our approach, as its source addresses are chosen from a predefined list [33]. While random spoofing would drastically increase the flow table size needed in our approach because a flow is defined based on IP addresses. There are already a number of solutions to tackle IP spoofing [34], such as Network Ingress Filtering [35]. However, since none of the solutions are widely deployed, we describe an alternative technique "Multilevel Bloom Filters" that can be integrated into our approach to mitigate the large-space-overhead problem caused by random spoofing.

Multilevel Bloom Filters (MBF) have been shown to be an effective approach for mitigating the large-space-overhead problem by providing a trade-off between the space requirement and the false positive rate [36]. The MBF technique is inspired by the success of the Stochastic Fair Blue (SFB) [36] algorithm, which is a scalable approach to record and update the state information of flows through Multilevel Bloom Filters. According to [36], the MBF effectively gives the algorithm N^L unique "buckets" using $L \times N$ number of bins (L levels with N bins in each level). That is, we can save $(1-L\times N/N^L)\times 100\%$ of required buffer or memory space by using Multilevel Bloom Filters. For example, we can save up to $(1-2\times 23/23^2) = 91.3\%$ of the required memory by using a MBF with $L = 2$ and $N = 23$. In our recent work.[37], we have employed MBF techniques and observe an efficient memory save using the approach with an affordable false positive rate.

UDP traffic

Our CPR-based approach has been demonstrated to work effectively in distinguishing normal TCP flows from LDDoS flows. Since UDP flows normally do not reduce their transmission rate when the network is congested, we believe that the current CPR-based approach will treat a UDP flow as an attack flow if the UDP flow behaves non-responsively. Further investigation on differentiating UDP flows and attack flows, and the fairness issue will be investigated in future work.

Integration of RED

The motivation of employing the RED [11] queue management mechanism together with our approach is to improve the performance of our approach in the extreme scenario described in Section 3.2. The the RED [11] mechanism enable our CPR-based approach to still be effective in detecting LDDoS attack flows in that very extreme scenario. Although the RED mechanism is found to be notably vulnerable to LDoS attacks[37] and [38], it does not introduce vulnerabilities, because our approach detects and filters attack flows while simultaneously protecting RED from being exploited.

Adversarial analysis

Finally we briefly discuss how difficult it would be for an attacker to evade our CPR-based approach.

The various types of LDDoS attacks shown in Fig. 3 may adopt different detection evasion strategies while causing the same damage to normal flows. For example, AFI LDDoS attacks could enlarge the attack period T_a for each attack flow; AWI LDDoS attacks could narrow the attack burst width T_b of each attack flow; ARI LDDoS attacks could reduce the attack burst rate R_b for every attack flow and MI LDDoS attacks could employ one or several of the aforementioned strategies. We have evaluated the performance of the proposed approach under AFI, AWI, and ARI LDDoS attacks in Section 4.2 and against MI LDDoS attacks in Section 4.4. Experimental results show that the Congestion Participation Rate (CPR) is a reliable and robust metric for identifying LDDoS attack flows for all LDDoS attack categories listed in Fig. 3.

Generally, an attacker might want to lower the CPR value by sending fake pulses that do not cause network congestion. Although fake pulses may lower the CPR value of an LDDoS flow, as long as the flow still sends packets during congestion periods, it will be detected since it still has a higher CPR than a normal TCP flow.

The only way to completely evade our CPR-based detection is to send all the attack packets using the TCP congestion control mechanism, in other words, to make an LDDoS flow behave like a normal TCP flow. In this case, the LDDoS flow hardly achieves any obvious attack effects. To summarize, to the attacker, there is a trade-off between mounting an effective attack but being detected or evading our approach but loosing attack effectiveness.

RELATED WORK

LDoS attacks were proposed by Kuzmanovic [2] in 2003, which were also called shrew[2] attacks and Pulsing DoS (PDoS) attacks [9]. LDDoS attacks are LDoS attacks that are launched from hosts distributed on the Internet. Since LDoS was initially proposed in [2], a series of variants of LDoS attacks have been discussed, including:

- Reduction of Quality (RoQ) attacks [39] that exploit the performance vulnerability during a system's adaptation process. RoQ attacks could dramatically reduce the service quality of a network element, or deprive it of a large amount of its capacity, by only occupying a small fraction of its capacity [39].
- LDoS attacks targeting application servers (LoRDAS attacks) [40]. LoRDAS attacks can reduce the availability of an application server in a controlled manner by generating pulsing service request, using only low-rate traffic.

These LDoS variants are not directly addressable by the CPR-based approach proposed in this paper. Adopting the CPR-based approach to address these new variants is part of our future work.

Presently approaches to detect and filter LDoS attacks mainly consider two characteristics of LDoS attacks. One is the pulsing high rate characteristic and the other is the periodical characteristic.

Kuzmanovic [2] and Sarat [23] proposed approaches that explore the pulsing high rate characteristic of LDoS attacks. Active Queue Management (AQM) mechanisms (such as SRED [41]) were used to mitigate LDoS attacks. Their approaches were easy to deploy and effective at improving the performance of normal TCP flows in the presence of LDoS attacks. However, the adaptive mechanisms in AQM algorithms are also targets of LDoS attacks. RED-like algorithms [11], [36] and [42], as typical representatives of AQM algorithms, have already been found to be considerably vulnerable to LDoS attacks [37] and [38].

Shevtekar [24] proposed an approach based on the traffic anomaly of all the expired flows to detect LDoS attacks, considering the pulsing (short-lived) characteristic of the LDoS attacks. This approach has the capability to detect LDoS attacks even when the source and destination IP addresses are spoofed. Unfortunately it only identifies the presence of attacks, and not the identity of the attack flows.

Sun's approach [25] based on Dynamic Time Warping (DTW) examined the periodical characteristic of LDoS attacks. This approach can detect LDoS attacks that employ variable attack pulsing periods. However, since this DTW-based approach used the similarity between real-time LDoS flows and the sampled LDoS flows, it is only effective for the *aggregate* flow of LDDoS attacks. In other words, it can only detect the presence of an LDDoS attack, but fails to identify whether a given flow is an LDDoS flow or not.

Discrete Fourier Transform (DFT)-based approaches proposed by Chen [18] and Wei[26] consider both the periodical characteristic and the pulsing high rate characteristic of LDoS attacks. They explore the difference between the traffic spectrum of attack flows and that of normal flows. DFT-based approaches are considered to be one of the most efficient approaches in detecting LDoS attacks. However, they have difficulties in identifying single flows in large-scale LDDoS attacks.

Luo [9] proposed an approach based on wavelet transform after considering the influence of LDoS attacks on the input TCP data traffic and output TCP ACK traffic. This approach considers both the attack flows' characteristics and their influence on network traffic. An extension to this approach is their Vanguard detection system that employs more metrics to detect various LDoS attacks [43]. These approaches are both limited by their ability to only detect the aggregate flow of an LDDoS attack.

The Shrew Attack Protection (SAP) mechanism.[44] mitigates the LDoS attack by giving priority to flows with high packet loss rate. While SAP can maintain high throughput for TCP flows under certain LDoS attacks and always prevent TCP sessions from closing, it has obvious performance degradation when the attack uses the ports protected by SAP.

The generalized entropy metric and the information distance metric were proposed in[45] to detect LDDoS attacks. This approach has advantages in terms of detection speed and false positive rate. The impracticality of this approach is rather unfortunate with successful implementation relying on gaining full control of all the routers in the network.

A mathematical model [46] and a defense technique [47] were proposed for LDoS attacks targeting application servers [40]. The model and defense technique are stimulating, but more experiments and analyses are needed to test their effectiveness for LDDoS attacks targeting TCP traffic [2] that are studied in this paper.

In a large-scale LDDoS attack, the attack period of each single attack flow could be very long. Its peak rate could be very small, and the pulsing period could be very short. Thus the average rate of every single attack flow could be very low, even lower than a normal flow in a large-scale LDDoS attack. This is the main reason that existing approaches can only detect the aggregate flow of an LDDoS attack, rather than a single attack flow. The Congestion Participation Rate (CPR)-based approach proposed in this paper can detect single LDDoS attack flows.

In addition to existing LDoS detection approaches, flow-level Active Queue Management (AQM) mechanisms are also relevant to our approach as they detect and limit unresponsive [48] flows, including FRED [49], RED-PD [50], SFB [51], CHOKe[52], etc. However, most existing flow-level AQMs aim to maintain fairness among traffic flows instead of detecting LDDoS flows. Moreover, some of them (RED-

PD[50] and SFB[51]) have already been identified as being vulnerable to LDoS attacks [37] and [38].

CONCLUSIONS

In this paper, we have proposed an effective and efficient approach to detect and filter TCP-targeted LDDoS attacks [2] and [9] based on a novel metric – Congestion Participation Rate (CPR). The CPR-based approach can achieve per-flow-level detection of LDDoS attacks. We have analytically expressed the upper bound of the average CPR for normal TCP flows and the lower bound of the average CPR for LDDoS flows, using several network parameters that are directly measureable. We have implemented the CPR-based approach and conducted comprehensive experiments in both ns-2 and test-bed. The experiment results have demonstrated that, compared to the existing Discrete Fourier Transform (DFT)-based approach, the CPR-based approach is effective for all LDDoS attacks considered, while the DFT-based approach is effective for a limited set of LDDoS attack types.

We should note here that the CPR-based approach requires the router where it is deployed to turn on the Random Early Detection (RED) [11] queue management mechanism, to work properly on an extreme scenario described in Section 3.2. The RED mechanism is already supported by most existing routers (such as the WRED in Cisco routers).

In the future work, we will reduce the required memory size by implementing MBF techniques in the CPR-based approach. Another promising direction we hope to achieve is the deep integration of our CPR-based approach with the RED mechanism. Lastly, the CPR metric proposed in this paper could be applied to detect a number of variants of LDDoS attacks, such as LDDoS attacks against application servers [40] and LDDoS attacks against 3G/WiMax wireless networks [53].

ACKNOWLEDGMENT

This work is supported in part by the National Natural Science Foundation of China (Nos.61070198, 60970034, 61170287, and 60903040) and the Engineering and Physical Sciences Research Council of UK (No. EP/G037264/1).

REFERENCES

1. C. Douligeris, A. Mitrokotsa, DDoS attacks and defense mechanisms: classification and state-of-the-art, Computer Networks 44 (2004) 643–666.
2. A. Kuzmanovic, E.W. Knightly, Low-rate TCP-targeted denial of service attacks – (the shrew vs. the mice and elephants), in: ACM SIGCOMM, Karlsruhe, Germany, 2003, pp. 75–86.
3. G. Loukas, G. Oke, Protection against denial of service attacks: a survey, Computer Journal 53 (2010) 1020–1037.
4. M. Li, An approach to reliably identifying signs of DDOS flood attacks based on LRD traffic pattern recognition, Computers & Security 23 (2004) 549–558.
5. R.K.C. Chang, Defending against flooding-based distributed denialof-service attacks: a tutorial, IEEE Communications Magazine 40 (2002) 42–51.
6. T. Peng, C. Leckie, K. Ramamohanarao, Survey of network-based defense mechanisms countering the DoS and DDoS problems, ACM Computing Surveys 39 (2007).
7. P. Owezarski, On the impact of DoS attacks on internet traffic characteristics and QoS, in: Proceedings of the International Conference on Computer Communications and Networks (ICCCN), 2005, pp. 269–274.
8. M. Delio, New Breed of Attack Zombies Lurk, 2011.
9. X. Luo, R.K.C. Chang, On a new class of pulsing denial-of-service attacks and the defense, in: Network and Distributed System Security Symposium (NDSS), San Diego, CA, 2005, pp. 2–5.
10. CiscoSystems, NetFlow Services Solutions Guide, 2007. .
11. S. Floyd, V. Jacobson, Random early detection gateways for congestion avoidance, IEEE/ACM Transactions on Networking 1 (1993) 397–413.
12. J. Padhye, V. Firoiu, D.F. Towsley, J.F. Kurose, Modeling TCP Reno performance: a simple model and its empirical validation, IEEE/ACM Transactions on Networking 8 (2000) 133–145.
13. I. Yeom, A.L.N. Reddy, Modeling TCP behavior in a differentiated services network, IEEE/ACM Transactions on Networking 9 (2001) 31–46.
14. N. Cardwell, S. Savage, T. Anderson, Modeling TCP latency, in: IEEE INFOCOM 2000.
15. M. Allman, W.M. Eddy, S. Ostermann, Estimating loss rates with TCP, SIGMETRICS Perform, Evaluation Review 31 (2003) 12–24.
16. S. McCanne, S. Floyd, The Network Simulator – ns-2, 2008. .
17. A. Shevtekar, N. Ansari, Do low rate DoS attacks affect QoS sensitive VoIP traffic? in: IEEE International Conference on Communications (ICC), 2006, pp. 2153–2158.
18. Y. Chen, K. Hwang, Collaborative detection and filtering of shrew DDoS attacks using spectral analysis, Journal of Parallel and Distributed Computing 66 (2006) 1137–1151.
19. J. Cao, W.S. Cleveland, Y. Gao, K. Jeffay, F.D. Smith, M. Weigle, Stochastic models for generating synthetic HTTP source traffic, in: IEEE INFOCOM, 2004, pp. 1546–1557.
20. CERT, Advisory CA-1999-17 Denial-of-Service Tools, 2000. .
21. V. Paxson, R. Pang, M. Allman, M. Bennett, J. Lee, B. Tierney, LBNL/ ICSI Enterprise Tracing Project (collection), 2007. .
22. C. Fraleigh, S. Moon, B. Lyles, C. Cotton, M. Khan, D. Moll, R. Rockell, T. Seely, C. Diot, Pocket-level traffic measurements from the sprint IP backbone, IEEE Network Magazine 17 (2003) 6–16.
23. S. Sarat, A. Terzis, On the effect of router buffer sizes on low-rate denial of service attacks, in: International Conference on Computer Communications and Networks (ICCCN), San Diego, CA, 2005, pp. 281–286.

24. A. Shevtekar, N. Ansari, A router-based technique to mitigate reduction of quality (RoQ) attacks, Computer Networks 52 (2008) 957–970.
25. H.B. Sun, J.C.S. Lui, D.K.Y. Yau, Defending against low-rate TCP attacks: Dynamic detection and protection, in: IEEE International Conference on Network Protocols (ICNP), Berlin, GERMANY, 2004, pp. 196–205.
26. W. Wei, Y.B. Dong, D.M. Lu, G. Jin, H.L. Lao, A Novel mechanism to defend against low-rate denial-of-service attacks, in: S.Z.D.D.C.H.T.B.W.F.Y. Mehrotra (Ed.), IEEE International Conference on Intelligence and Security Informatics (ISI), San Diego, CA, 2006, pp. 261–271.
27. A. Kuzmanovic, E.W. Knightly, Low-rate TCP-targeted denial of service attacks and counter strategies, IEEE/ACM Transactions on Networking 14 (2006) 683–696.
28. A. Kumar, M. Sung, J. Xu, J. Wang, Data streaming algorithms for efficient and accurate estimation of flow size distribution, in: ACM SIGMETRICS, 2004, pp. 177–188.
29. C. Cranor, T. Johnson, O. Spataschek, V. Shkapenyuk, Gigascope: a stream database for network applications, in: SIGMOD, 2003, pp. 627–651.
30. B. Grot, W. Mangione-Smith, Good memories: enhancing memory performance for precise flow tracking, in: ANCHOR, 2005.
31. Thomas, Bloomfilter Calculator, 2009. .
32. A. Akella, S. Seshan, A. Shaikh, An empirical evaluation of wide-area Internet bottlenecks, in: ACM SIGCOMM Conference on Internet Measurement (IMC), Miami Beach, FL, USA, 2003, pp. 101–114.
33. C. Wei, Y. Dit-Yan, Defending against TCP SYN flooding attacks under different types of IP spoofing, in: Proceedings of the International Conference on Networking, International Conference on Systems and International Conference on Mobile Communications and Learning Technologies (ICNICONSMCL), 2006, pp. 38–38.
34. T. Ehrenkranz, J. Li, On the state of IP spoofing defense, ACM Transactions on Internet Technology 9 (2009).
35. P. Ferguson, D. Senie, RFC2827: Network Ingress Filtering: Defeating Denial of Service Attacks which employ IP Source Address Spoofing, 2000.
36. F. Wu-Chang, D.D. Kandlur, D. Saha, K.G. Shin, Stochastic fair blue: a queue management algorithm for enforcing fairness, in: IEEE INFOCOM, 2001, pp. 1520–1529.
37. C. Zhang, J. Yin, Z. Cai, W. Chen, RRED: robust RED algorithm to counter low-rate denial-of-service attacks, IEEE Communications Letters 14 (2010) 489–491.
38. X.P. Luo, R.K.C. Chang, E.W.W. Chan, Performance analysis of TCP/ AQM under denial-of-service attacks, in: IEEE International Symposium on Modeling, Analysis and Simulation of Computer and Telecommunication Systems (MASCOTS), Atlanta, GA, 2005, pp. 97–104.
39. M. Guirguis, A. Bestavros, I. Matta, Exploiting the transients of adaptation for RoQ attacks on Internet resources, in: IEEE International Conference on Network Protocols (ICNP), Berlin, Germany, 2004, pp. 184–195.
40. G. Macia-Fernandez, J.E. Diaz-Verdejo, P. Garcia-Teodoro, Evaluation of a low-rate DoS attack against iterative servers, Computer Networks 51 (2007) 1013–1030.
41. T.J. Ott, T.V. Lakshman, L. Wong, SRED: stabilized RED, in: IEEE INFOCOM, 1999.
42. S.S. Kunniyur, R. Srikant, An adaptive virtual queue (AVQ) algorithm for active queue management, IEEE/ACM Transactions on Networking 12 (2004) 286–299.
43. X. Luo, E.W.W. Chan, R.K.C. Chang, Detecting pulsing denial-ofservice attacks with nondeterministic attack intervals, Eurasip Journal on Advances in Signal Processing (2009).
44. C.-W. Chang, S. Lee, B. Lin, J. Wang, The taming of the shrew: mitigating low-rate TCP-targeted attack, IEEE Transactions On Network Service Management 7 (2010).
45. Y. Xiang, K. Li, W. Zhou, Low-rate DDoS attacks detection and traceback by using new information metrics, IEEE Transactions on Information Forensics and Security 6 (2011) 426–437.
46. G. Macia-Fernandez, J. Diaz-Verdejo, P. Garcia-Teodoro, Mathematical model for low-rate DoS attacks against application servers, IEEE Transactions on Information Forensics and Security 4 (2009) 519–529.
47. G. Macia-Fernandez, R.A. Rodriguez-Gomez, J.E. Diaz-Verdejo, Defense techniques for low-rate DoS attacks against application servers, Computer Networks 54 (2010) 2711–2727.
48. S. Floyd, K. Fall, Promoting the use of end-to-end congestion control in the Internet, IEEE/ACM Transactions on Networking 7 (1999) 458– 472.
49. D. Lin, R. Morris, Dynamics of random early detection, SIGCOMM Computer Communication Review 27 (1997) 127–137.
50. R. Mahajan, S. Floyd, D. Wetherall, Controlling high-bandwidth flows at the congested router, in: Proceedings of IEEE International Conference on Network Protocols (ICNP), 2001, pp. 192–201.
51. W.-c. Feng, K.G. Shin, D.D. Kandlur, D. Saha, The blue active queue management algorithms, IEEE/ACM Transactions on Networking 10 (2002) 513–528.
52. R. Pan, B. Prabhakar, K. Psounis, CHOKe – a stateless active queue management scheme for approximating fair bandwidth allocation, in: Proceedings of Annual IEEE International Conference on Computer Communications (INFOCOM), 2000, pp. 942–951.
53. P.P.C. Lee, T. Bu, T. Woo, On the detection of signaling DoS attacks on 3G/WiMax wireless networks, Computer Networks 53 (2009) 2601– 2616.

CHAPTER 3

OPTIMAL ADAPTIVE CHANNEL SCHEDULING FOR SCALABLE VIDEO BROADCASTING OVER MIMO WIRELESS NETWORKS

Chao Zhou, Xinggong Zhang, and Zongming Guo

Institute of Computer Science & Technology, Peking University, Beijing 100871, PR China

ABSTRACT

Video broadcasting is an efficient way to deliver video content to multiple receivers. However, due to heterogeneous channel conditions in MIMO wireless networks, it is challenging for video broadcasting to map scalable video layers to proper MIMO transmit antennas to minimize the average overall video transmission distortion. In this paper, we investigate the channel scheduling problem for broadcasting scalable video content over MIMO wireless networks. An adaptive channel scheduling based unequal error protection (UEP) video broadcasting scheme is proposed. In the scheme, video layers are protected unequally by being mapped to appropriate antennas, and the average overall distortion of all receivers is minimized. We formulate this scheme into a non-linear combinatorial optimization problem. It is not practical to solve the problem by an exhaustive search method with heavy computational complexity. Instead, an efficient branch-and-bound based channel scheduling algorithm, named TBCS, is developed. TBCS finds the global optimal solution with much lower complexity. The complexity is further reduced by relaxing the termination condition of TBCS, which produces a $(1-\varepsilon)$-optimal solution. Experimental results demonstrate both the effectiveness and efficiency of our proposed scheme and algorithm. As compared with some existing channel scheduling methods, TBCS improves the quality of video broadcasting across all receivers significantly.

INTRODUCTION

The broadcast nature of wireless medium allows a single source to simultaneously communicate information with multiple receivers. However, one major challenge for wireless broadcasting arises from heterogeneous network conditions of different receivers. Moreover, the potentially low bandwidth and high bit error rate also become significant obstacles for wireless communication providers to offer high quality multimedia services. To overcome such obstacles, multi-input multi-output (MIMO) systems, which have been investigated to simultaneously transmit multiple bit streams to achieve high data rate wireless multimedia communication [1], have emerged as one of the most prominent techniques. MIMO channel can be decomposed into a series of independent SISO subchannels [2], and it is suitable for transmitting multiple video substreams simultaneously. Meanwhile, the technology of scalable video coding (SVC)[3] and [4] enables media providers to generate a single embedded bitstream, from which appropriate subsets can be extracted to meet various requirements of a broad range of users. These conditions

Citation: Chao Zhou, Xinggong Zhang, Zongming Guo, Optimal adaptive channel scheduling for scalable video broadcasting over MIMO wireless networks, Computer Networks, Volume 57, Issue 15, 29 October 2013, Pages 3039-3050, ISSN 1389-1286, http://dx.doi.org/10.1016/j.comnet.2013.07.010.

inspire us to combine the advanced MIMO and SVC techniques to improve the video broadcasting performance. SVC video consists of layers with different contribution to video quality, which makes it possible be transmitted with unequal error protection (UEP) [5], [6] and [7]. In MIMO unicast, UEP can be easily achieved by mapping video layers to antennas in the order of antenna's signal to noise ratio (SNR) strength [6]. However, it is not trivial for video broadcasting over MIMO wireless networks, and this has not drawn enough research attention.

Adaptive channel scheduling, which denotes mapping video layers to proper antennas to improve video transmission performance, faces great challenges for scalable video broadcasting over MIMO wireless networks. It mainly arises from that each transmit antenna corresponds to multiple receivers with different and independent SNR strength, and the corresponding SNR strength for each transmit antenna among multiple receivers forms a vector. For example, in Fig. 1, antenna At_1 is corresponding to three receivers (At_1 − User1, At_1 − User2, At_1 − User3), whose SNR strength form the vector $\gamma_1 = [\gamma_{11}, \gamma_{12}, \gamma_{13}]$. It is the same for antenna At_2. since sets of vectors cannot be sorted, UEP cannot be achieved by mapping video layers to antennas in the order of antenna's SNR strength as done in MIMO unicast. Besides, the inter-layer dependencies among SVC video layers further make the problem challenging.

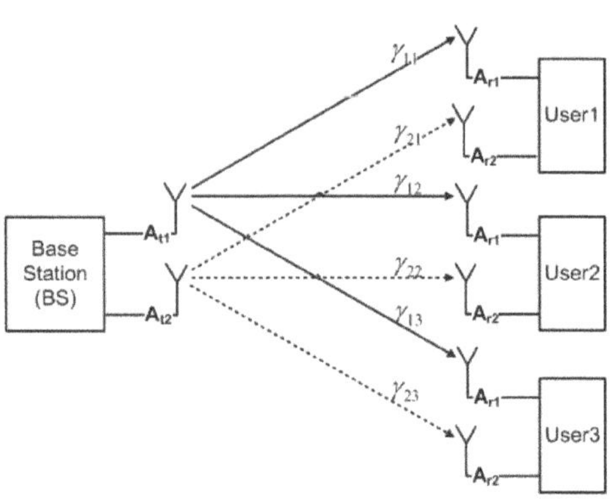

Figure 1: Example of video broadcasting in MIMO wireless networks.

In this paper, we have studied this problem and proposed a novel adaptive channel scheduling based scalable video broadcasting scheme, which greatly improve the received video quality. By mapping each video layer to certain transmit antenna, the video layers are protected unequally and the overall average video quality is improved. Since each antenna faces multiple users with various network conditions as Fig. 1shows, and there exists inter-layer dependencies among SVC video layers, the channel scheduling problem is a non-linear combinatorial problem. It can be solved using an exhaustive search method, which has the highest accuracy level and computational complexity. In order to reduce the complexity and make it suitable for practical implementation, a branch-and-bound framework is adopted to find an adaptive channel scheduling algorithm. Specifically, by partitioning the original problem into some simple sub-problems, we are able to derive the upper and lower bounds of the average overall video distortion. Then an efficient branch-and-bound based channel scheduling algorithm (TBCS) is presented by incorporating these bounds into the branch-and-bound framework. With bounding and pruning techniques, TBCS finds the global optimal solution with much lower complexity than the exhaustive search method. Moreover, by relaxing termination conditions of TBCS, the complexity is further reduced and a (1 − ε)-optimal solution is produced. Through simulations, TBCS is shown to be effective and efficient. As compared with existing channel scheduling schemes, the simulation results reveal significant performance improvements in TBCS.

The main contributions of our work are summarized as:

- We are among the first to investigate the channel scheduling problem for salable video broadcasting over MIMO wireless networks where video layers are broadcasted to all users simultaneously over multiple antennas. Different from traditional multiuser problem over MIMO broadcast channel where different information is conveyed to different users by multiple transmit antennas, the antennas are shared by all users who receive all streams broadcasted over the antennas in our proposed scheme.
- We formulate it into a non-linear combinatorial optimization problem, and an efficient channel scheduling algorithm is proposed by employing the branch-and-bound framework. Specifically, by mapping the video layers to antennas according to the order of antennas' average PER, we derive the upper bound of the average overall video transmission distortion. On the other hand, we transform the channel scheduling problem to an assignment problem by relaxing some constraints, and then the lower bound of the average overall video transmission distortion is derived.
- By relaxing the termination condition of TBCS, a (1 − ε)-optimal solution is produced to balance the needs for the complexity and accuracy of the proposed algorithm.

This paper is organized as follows. We review related work in Section 2. In Section 3, we describe our proposed system and formulate the proposed scheme into a non-linear combinatorial optimization problem. In Section 4, we propose a branch-and-bound framework to solve the channel scheduling problem. First, we derive the upper bound (Section 4.2) and and lower bound (Section 4.3) of the average overall distortion respectively, then an efficient branch-and-bound based channel scheduling algorithm is proposed, which produces the global optimal solution (Section 4.4). Also, an acceleration mechanism is presented to further reduce the computational complexity (Section 4.5). We show simulation results in Section 5, and conclude the paper in Section 6.

RELATED WORK

In recent years, MIMO systems have emerged as one of the most prominent techniques [1], [8], [9] and [10] to provide high data rate wireless communications. Spatial multiplexing techniques [1] and [10] have been investigated to simultaneously transmit independent data in order to achieve high data rate wireless multimedia communications. For MIMO broadcast, the capacity region is still an open issue since broadcast channels are non-degraded generally. But the optimal sum rate, and the suggestive pre-coding scheme are now completely known. Caire and Shamai [11] are the first to give the optimal sum capacity of MIMO broadcast channel by explicitly maximizing the Dirty Paper [12] lower bound and minimizing the Sato's upper bound [13] in the case which, as it turns out, is equal. But its computational complexity is high and it is hard to be extended to more general cases [14]. Yang [15] extends the channel scheduling scheme from unicast MIMO network to multicast MIMO network. In [16], dynamic resource allocation is studied to maximize system's capacity, and a low complexity suboptimal algorithm is proposed for practical implementation. Literature [17] investigates multi-resolution broadcast systems for WCDMA cellular mobile networks, including MIMO technology. However, all of these previous works focus on maximizing system's capacity and belong to parallel transmission (PT) [18] MIMO. In PT MIMO, all the content is treated equally and it is not suitable for video communication, since video content generally contains bits with different importance, and needs to be protected unequally when transmitted over error-prone wireless networks. In unicast, UEP in MIMO can be easily achieved by mapping video layers to multiple transmit antennas in the order of antenna's signal to noise ratio (SNR) strength [6]. While in MIMO broadcast networks, it becomes challenging. This is mainly because that each transmit antenna corresponds to multiple end users, and the SNR strength of each transmit antenna forms a vector asFig. 1 shows.

The idea of scalable video for multiuser communications is well-known. Without loss of generality, multiuser MIMO is used to convey different information to different users by multiple transmit antennas. In [19], the authors propose a video broadcasting scheme via pre-coding and SNR-Scalable video coding. By packet extraction and pre-coding, users will receive different quality of videos. There are some other research works on multiuser MIMO [20], [21] and [22]. However, we differ from them in several major ways. For the purpose of clarity, we take [19] as example to compare our proposed scheme with these works. First, by the pre-coding matrix which is consist of some orthogonal sub-matrices, the antennas are divided into some independent groups and each user will only receive the stream transmitted by a certain group of antennas in [19]. In our proposed scheme, each user will receive the streams transmitted over all antennas. Therefore, this kind of multiuser video transmission schemes have great limitation in the number of users that the number of transmit antennas is no smaller than the sum of all users receive antennas as assumed in [19]. We have no such limitation on both the number of users and number of antennas since all users multiplex the same transmit antennas. At last, in [19], some streams are transmitted multiple times at the transmitter side which wastes bandwidth and power resource, for example, the base layer must transmitted in each group of antennas for each user. While in our proposed scheme, each video layer is only mapped to a certain antenna and broadcasted to all users.

Very few UEP schemes have been proposed for broadcasting scalable video over MIMO wireless networks where multiple antennas have been sufficiently multiplexed for broadcasting multiple streams to all users concurrently. In [23], UEP is achieved by using diversity embedded space time codes (DESTC), which provides UEP to different video layers, thereby delivering high quality video to users with good network conditions while still providing acceptable quality to users with poor network conditions. But the authors assume that all receivers employ single receive antenna, which greatly simplifies the problem. Moreover, DESTC is not flexible enough to adapt to the complex network environment because it add different amount of redundancy to different streams without considering the instantaneous channel conditions. A novel JSCC framework for scalable video transmission has been proposed in [24], in which power allocation, channel coding and modulation are jointly optimized to achieve UEP and improve the system performance. The computational complexity is very high and it is not suitable for practical implementation. In [25], UEP is achieved for scalable video broadcasting over cooperative wireless networks through power allocation. However, all of these previous works treat transmit antennas equally and neglect their various qualities. In fact, the qualities of transmit antennas are time-varying, and video transmission performance can be greatly improved by mapping video layers to antennas properly.

To the best of our knowledge, none of previous research work considers achieving UEP for scalable MIMO video broadcasting through channel scheduling. In this paper, we investigate this problem, and an adaptive channel scheduling based video broadcasting scheme is proposed. We formulate this scheme into a non-linear combinatorial problem. By adopting the branch-and-bound framework, an effective and efficient low-complexity channel scheduling algorithm is proposed.

PROBLEM FORMULATION

In this section, the proposed system architecture is described at first. Then we formulate the adaptive channel scheduling based scalable video broadcasting scheme into a non-linear combinatorial optimization problem.

System description

Fig. 2 shows the block diagram of our proposed system, where all transmitter and receivers are equipped with multiple antennas. Here we only show one receiver for the purpose of clarity, and all receivers have the same signal processing diagrams. At the transmitter side, the input video sequence is encoded to generate multiple video layers by H.264/SVC [3] and [4]. Combining with the feedback SNR strength and video layers' unequal importance, the video layers are periodically switched among multiple transmit antennas using our proposed TBCS algorithm. Then the video layers are broadcasted to all receivers simultaneously. At the receiver side, each receiver needs to estimate the post-processing SNR strength of each transmit antenna and send it back to the transmitter by employing pilot symbols [26]. The transmitted video sequences are reconstructed after demodulation and channel decoding.

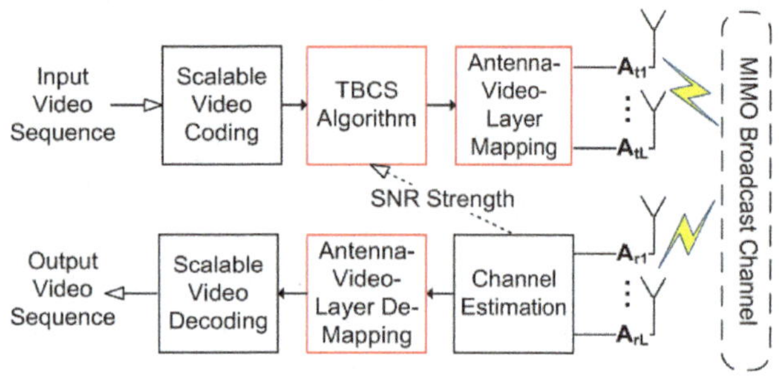

Figure 2: Proposed system diagram.

Without loss of generality, it is commonly assumed that the channel is block fading [27], i.e., the channel remains constant over some consecutive symbol periods (determined by the coherence time) and then changes in an independent fashion to a new realization. The above video broadcasting system can be treated as K virtual MIMO unicast systems except that all receivers have the same transmitter, and K is the total number of receivers[28]. Then, for each virtual MIMO system with Mt transmit antennas and Mr receive antennas over flat-fading channel, the system equation between the transmitter and kth receiver is

$$\mathbf{y}_k = \sqrt{\frac{E_s}{M_t}}\mathbf{H}_k\mathbf{x} + \zeta_k \tag{1}$$

where $\mathbf{H}_k$ is the complex channel matrix between the transmitter and kth receiver with size Mr × M_t, $\mathbf{x}$ is the M_t × 1 transmitted signal vector, $\mathbf{y}_k$ is the M_r × 1 received signal vector at kth receiver, ζ_k is the M_r × 1 noise vector with elements distributed according to $CN(0,N_0)$, and E_s is the total average energy available at the transmitter over a symbol period having removed losses due to propagation and shadowing.

The channel matrix $\mathbf{H}_k$ is estimated by existing estimation methods such as maximum-likelihood (ML) and minimum mean-squared error (MMSE) techniques discussed in [26]at kth (1 ⍰ k ⍰ K) receiver. More details of channel estimation can also refer to literature [6]. The transmitted signals are detected by linear ZF (zero-forcing) receivers, which are much more practically attractive than non-linear receivers due to their low complexity. Then, the post-processing SNR strength of ith transmit antenna for kth receiver, γ_{ik}, is obtained as

$$\gamma_{ik} = \frac{E_s}{M_t N_0 \left[\mathbf{H}_k^H \mathbf{H}_k\right]_{ii}^{-1}} \tag{2}$$

where $[\cdot]_{ii}$ denotes ith diagonal entry of the matrix inside the square bracket, and $\mathbf{H}^H$ denotes the Hermitian of $\mathbf{H}$.

In this work, we focus on exploiting the potential UEP ability of channel scheduling for scalable video broadcasting over MIMO system. To eliminate the effect of channel coding and modulation, which can also achieve UEP, we fix the modulation level and channel coding rate for all video layers. In fact, our proposed channel scheduling method can be incorporated with these methods to further improve the system performance, one of the incorporation examples is our previous JSCC work [29]. Specifically, M-QAM and RS (N, m) are used for modulation and channel coding, where N is block size, and m is the number of source bits in each block. Then, combining with the feedback SNR strength in Eq. (2), we can easily derive the block error rate b_{ik}(i ⩽ Mt, k ⩽ K) between transmit antenna i and receiver k as follows:

$$b_{ik} = 1 - \sum_{j=0}^{N-m} \binom{N}{j} \rho_{ik}^{j} (1-\rho_{ik})^{(N-j)} \tag{3}$$

where $\rho_{ik} \approx \frac{\sqrt{M-1}}{\sqrt{M}\log_2\sqrt{M}} \operatorname{erfc}\left(\sqrt{\frac{3\gamma_{ik}}{2(M-1)}}\right)$ is the bit error rate (BER) between ith transmit antenna and kth receiver, and erfc (·) is the complementary error function.

Problem formulation

Suppose the transmitter is equipped with M_t antennas, user k is equipped with M_r^k antennas, and the video sequence is encoded into L layers. Generally, each video layer is broadcasted over one transmit antenna or dropped at the transmitter side due to the data-rate constraints. We define $\mathbf{A}_{L\times Mt}$={aij} as channel scheduling matrix to denote the mapping relationship between video layers and transmit antennas, and its entries $a_{ij} \in \{0, 1\}$. Let $a_{ij} = 1$ if ith video layer is transmitted over jth transmit antenna, or $a_{ij} = 0$ otherwise. Then, we have

$$\sum_{j=1}^{M_t} a_{ij} \leqslant 1 \tag{4}$$

when $\sum_{j=1}^{M_t} a_{ij} = 1$, it denotes video layer i is mapped to one of the antennas, and $\sum_{j=1}^{M_t} a_{ij} = 0$ denotes video layer i is mapped to no antenna and dropped at the transmitter side. Then, we derive the video layer's PER matrix $\mathbf{P}$L×K = {Pjk} as a function of matrix $\mathbf{A}_{L\times Mt}$ as follows:

$$P_{ik} = \begin{cases} \sum_{j=1}^{M_t}(a_{ij}b_{jk}) & \text{if } \sum_{j=1}^{M_t} a_{ij} = 1 \\ 1 & \text{if } \sum_{j=1}^{M_t} a_{ij} = 0 \end{cases} \tag{5}$$

where P_{ik} denotes the ith video layer's PER for user k, b_{ik} is the block error rate between ith transmit antenna and receiver k and it is given in Eq. (3).

We employed the quality model proposed in [30] to estimate the end-to-end video transmission distortion in our work. According to [30], the video quality (PSNR) after decoding all the first n layers is given as

$$\tilde{d}_n(q_n) = d_n(\tilde{m}, q_n) = b_1 \log_{10}((\tilde{m}_n)^s + 1) \cdot q_n + b_2 \tag{6}$$

where b_1 and b_2 are model parameters, the value of s depends on the frame type, and q_n is the value of quantization parameter (QP) for layer n. More details about this can refer to literature [30] and the references therein. Then, the weight of each video layer is written as:

$$w_i = \begin{cases} \tilde{d}_1(q_1) & \text{if } i = 1 \\ \tilde{d}_i(q_i) - \tilde{d}_{i-1}(q_{i-1}) & \text{if } i \geqslant 2 \end{cases} \tag{7}$$

For the purpose of clarity, we omit the subscript of matrixes $\mathbf{A}$ and $\mathbf{P}$ in the following of the paper. Now, we get the end-to-end video transmission distortion $D_k(\mathbf{P}(\mathbf{A}))$ for user k:

$$\mathcal{D}_k(\mathbf{P}(\mathbf{A})) = \sum_{i=1}^{L} w_i \left(1 - \prod_{j=1}^{i}(1 - P_{jk})\right) \tag{8}$$

and the overall average distortion for all users is:

$$D(\mathbf{P}(\mathbf{A})) = \frac{1}{K}\sum_{k=1}^{K} \mathcal{D}_k(\mathbf{P}(\mathbf{A})) \tag{9}$$

Moreover, we can also get the video bit-rate for each video layer according to literature [30] and we denote r_i as the video bit-rate of layer i. Under the assumption that RS (N, m) is used for channel coding, video layer i would consume the data-rate of r'_i for transmission with

$$r'_i = r_i \frac{N}{m} \tag{10}$$

We assume the data-rate capacity of antennas i is R_i. Since a fixed modulation order on all antennas is used, we have $R_1=R_2=\cdots=R_{Mt}=R$. Then, the proposed adaptive channel scheduling based video broadcasting scheme is formulated as:

$$\begin{aligned}\{\mathbf{A}^*\} &= \arg\min_{\{\mathbf{A}\}} \quad D(\mathbf{P}(\mathbf{A}))\\ \text{subject to} &\quad \sum_{i=1}^{L} r'_i a_{ij} \leqslant R, \quad \forall j \leqslant M_t\\ &\quad \sum_{j=1}^{M_t} a_{ij} \leqslant 1, \quad \forall i \leqslant L\\ &\quad a_{ij} = \{0,1\}, \quad \forall i \leqslant L,\ j \leqslant M_t\end{aligned} \tag{11}$$

The above optimization problem aims to minimize the average overall video transmission distortion through adaptive channel scheduling, i.e., selecting the optimal matrix $\mathbf{A}^*$. However, due to the heterogeneous network conditions of different receivers and inter-layer dependencies among SVC video layers, solving this problem is challenging. Exhaustive search method finds the optimal solution by searching the whole solution space, whose size is M_t^L. Its computational complexity increases heavily with the number of transmit antennas and video layers, and it is not suitable for practical implementation.

BRANCH-AND-BOUND BASED ADAPTIVE CHANNEL SCHEDULING

In this section, we adopt the branch-and-bound framework to solve above channel scheduling problem, and an efficient branch-and-bound based channel scheduling algorithm is proposed. We first briefly describe how to adopt the branch-and-bound framework into channel scheduling. Then, the upper and lower bounds of the average overall distortion for each subproblem are derived in detail. At last, we present TBCS to solve the optimization problem in Eq. (11).

Branch-and-bound based channel scheduling

Branch-and-boundisaniterativemethodforsolvingoptimization problems, especially for discrete and combinatorial problems. A branch-and-bound procedure has two components. The first one, which is called branching, is to partition a problem into subproblems. The procedure is repeated recursively to each of the subproblems and all produced subproblems naturally form a tree structure, i.e., the branch-and-bound tree. Its nodes are the constructed subproblems. The leaves of the tree are also call theProblem List. The other component is bounding, which is a fast way of finding upper and lower bounds for the optimal solution for each subproblem.

The core of this approach is an observation that, for a minimization problem, if the lower bound for a subproblem s_2 is higher than the upper bound for any other subproblem s_1, $s_2$and the branch rooted at s_2 can be safely discarded from the tree, thus the computational complexity can be reduced. This procedure is called pruning. Besides, for each iterative, the subproblem with the smallest lower bound is selected and further partitioned. The algorithm terminates when the lower bound is equal to the upper bound.

In our proposed adaptive channel scheduling based video broadcasting scheme, we partition the problem into subproblems by selecting available transmit antennas for the video layers orderly, i.e., we first select a transmit antenna for the base layer, then for the first enhancement layer, and so on. When computing the upper and lower bounds of the average distortion for the nodes in the dth layer of the branch-and-bound tree, we only need to compute the bounds for the remaining L − d video layers. This is because all the first d video layers have been mapped to certain antennas, and their corresponding distortion is determined.

In order to reduce the iterations, pruning procedure is used to discard nodes from the tree. The key of pruning is to obtain the bounds for each node. For our proposed minimization problem, any feasible solution can be treated as the upper bound. On the other hand, an lower bound is found by solving a relaxed problem. The details of deriving these bounds are presented in Section 4.2 and Section 4.3 respectively.

Before presenting how to derive the upper and lower bounds, we present Proposition 1as follows, which servers as an intuition to develop the distortion bounds.

Proposition 1.

In unicast, when the scalable video layers are mapped to multiple transmit antennas according to the order of PER (the base layer is transmitted over the antenna with the smallest PER, the first enhancement layer is transmitted over the antenna with the second smallest PER, and so on), the minimum video transmission distortion is obtained.

Proof.

In unicast, assuming that there are L video layers and L transmit antennas, we then denote Pi as the PER of ith transmit antenna, and assume that the PERs satisfy$P_1 < P_2 \cdots < P_L$. We also define G=[G[1],G[2],…,G[L]] as the video-layer-antenna mapping order, which denotes that i th video layer is mapped to G[i] th antenna. According to Proposition 1, when G[i]=i(∀1⍰i⍰L), the minimum video transmission distortion can be obtained:

$$\mathcal{D}^* = \sum_{i=1}^{L} w_i * \left(1 - \prod_{s=1}^{i}(1 - P_s)\right)$$

We prove Proposition 1 through proof by contradiction. Assume that there exists another mapping order G′=[G′[1],G′[2],…,G′[L]], whose corresponding distortion, D′, is smaller than D*, i.e., $\mathcal{G}'[i] \neq i \ \&\ \mathcal{D}' < \mathcal{D}^*,\ \exists 1 \leqslant i \leqslant L$. Then the distortion D′ is written as:

$$\mathcal{D}' = \sum_{i=1}^{L} w_i * \left(1 - \prod_{s=1}^{i}(1 - P_{\mathcal{G}'[s]})\right)$$

Then

$$\Delta\mathcal{D} = \mathcal{D}^* - \mathcal{D}' = \prod_{s=1}^{i}(1 - P_{\mathcal{G}'[s]}) - \prod_{s=1}^{i}(1 - P_s) \leqslant 0$$

Above inequality comes from that in $\prod_{s=1}^{i}(1 - P_s)$, $P_s(\forall 1 \leqslant s \leqslant i)$ is s th smallest PER of all transmit antennas, so

$\prod_{s=1}^{i}(1-P_s)$ is always no smaller than $\prod_{s=1}^{i}(1-P_{\mathcal{G}'[s]})$. Then we derive that ΔD≤0, i.e., D*≤D'.

Moreover, if and only if

$$\prod_{s=1}^{i}(1-P_{\mathcal{G}'[s]})=\prod_{s=1}^{i}(1-P_s),\quad \forall 1\leqslant i\leqslant L$$

the inequality takes the equal sign, i.e., D'=D*, and $\mathcal{G}'[i]=i,\ \forall 1\leqslant i\leqslant L$. This is contradictory with the assumption that $\mathcal{G}'[i]\neq i\ \&\ \mathcal{D}'<\mathcal{D}^*,\ \exists 1\leqslant i\leqslant L$. Therefore, we conclude Proposition 1 is correct.

Upper bound

The objective of above optimization problem is to minimize the average overall video transmission distortion by selecting the optimal channel scheduling matrix **A***. For this proposed minimization problem, any matrix that satisfies the constraints described in Eq.(11) is a feasible solution, and its corresponding average overall distortion is an upper bound. Though it is very easy to find such matrixes, it is not trivial to find an appropriate matrix which obtains a tight upper bound. This is very crucial for reducing the number of iterations.

In Proposition 1, we show that the optimal matrix **A*** can be easily obtained according to the order of antenna's PER in MIMO unicast. The proposition also denotes that the principle of channel scheduling is to map important video layers to antennas with better channel quality (low PER). MIMO broadcast channel is a vector channel, i.e., each transmit antenna corresponds to multiple receivers, and the corresponding PER forms a vector. Since sets of vectors cannot be sorted, it is hard to determine which antenna has the best or worst channel quality. In order to find a feasible solution providing a tight upper bound, average PER of each transmit antenna is adopted to denote its channel quality in TBCS. Then, the channel scheduling problem is similar to that in unicast. It is worth to noticing that more than one video layers may be mapped to the same antenna when the data-rate constraints are satisfied, thus we cannot simply map the video layers to transmit antennas in the order of their average PER according to Proposition 1. However, the intuition of mapping video layers to antennas behind Proposition 1 is that from the lowest layer to the highest layer, we map video layer i to antenna j when it has lowest average PER and its remaining available data-rate is no smaller than the required rate r'_i. Then, the remaining available data-rate of antenna j is updated by subtracting r'_i. This process is iterated until all video layers have been mapped to appropriate antennas or there is no antennas whose remaining available data-rate satisfies the data-rate constraints. Though the solution is not optimal, its performance is much better than random channel scheduling, and a much tighter upper bound is obtained.

We denotes P_i^{avg} as the average PER of ith antenna, then we have

$$P_i^{avg}=\frac{1}{K}\sum_{k=1}^{K}b_{ik} \tag{12}$$

For nodes in dth layer of the branch-and-bound tree, each of the first d(1 ≤ d ≤ L) video layers has been mapped to a certain transmit antenna respectively. This denotes that the values $a_{ij}(1\leqslant i\leqslant d,\ 1\leqslant j\leqslant Mt)$ have been determined as described in Section 4.1. Then for ∀d < i ≤ L, 1 ≤ j ≤ M_t, the value of aij is derived as follows:

$$a_{ij}=\begin{cases}1, & \text{if } P_j^{avg}=\min(\Psi_i)\\ 0, & \text{otherwise}\end{cases} \tag{13}$$

where Ψi is the set of antenna's average PER, excluding the antennas whose remaining available data – rate is no smaller than r'_i. Until now, we have obtained the values for all entries in matrix **A**. According to formula Eqs. (2), (3), (4), (5), (6), (7),(8) and (9), the upper bound D^{upper} of the average overall distortion can be easily derived.

Lower bound

In order to obtain the lower bound of average overall distortion, we first define an efficiency matrix **V** = $\{v_{ij}\}$ to denote video layers' distortion, and its entry v_{ij} denotes ith video layer's average distortion among all users when it is mapped to jth transmit antenna. The entries are dependent due to the inter-dependence among video layers. We derive approximate expression of lower bounds for the entries in **V**, which have eliminated the dependence among them. Then, the primal problem is transformed into a standard assignment problem (AP), and the optimal solution (minimal total average distortion) of this AP is the primal problem's lower bound.

Now, we give details of deriving the lower bound of average overall distortion. For the nodes in dth layer of the branch-and-bound tree, the values $a_ij(1\leqslant i\leqslant d,\ 1\leqslant j\leqslant M_t)$ have been determined as described in the above section. Then we can easily derive $P_{ik}(1\leqslant i\leqslant d,\ 1\leqslant k\leqslant K)$ according to Eq. (5). Now the average overall distortion of the first d video layers is

$$\mathcal{D}^d=\frac{1}{K}\sum_{k=1}^{K}\sum_{i=1}^{d}w_i\left(1-\prod_{j=1}^{i}(1-P_{jk})\right) \tag{14}$$

Therefore, in order to obtain the lower bound of the average overall distortion, we only need to derive the lower bound of average distortion for the remaining L − d video layers. According to the inter-dependence among video layers, v_{ij} is written as

$$v_{ij}=\frac{1}{K}\sum_{k=1}^{K}w_i\left(1-\prod_{s=1}^{i}(1-P_{sk})\right),\quad \forall d+1\leqslant i\leqslant L \tag{15}$$

where for user k (1 ≤ k ≤ K), $P_{ik}=b_{jk}$ since ith video layer is mapped to jth antenna, and Psk(1 ≤ s ≤ d) are constant as explained in the second paragraph of this sub-section. Therefore, v_{ij} is only depending on $P_{sk}(d+1\leqslant s\leqslant i-1)$. Now we can write Eq. (15) as

$$\begin{aligned}v_{ij}&=\frac{1}{K}\sum_{k=1}^{K}w_i\left(1-\prod_{s=1}^{d}(1-P_{sk})\prod_{s=d+1}^{i-1}(1-P_{sk})(1-P_{ik})\right)\\&\leqslant\frac{1}{K}\sum_{k=1}^{K}w_i\left(1-\prod_{s=1}^{d}(1-P_{sk})\prod_{s=d+1}^{i-1}(1-\min(\Psi_{s,j}^{k}))(1-b_{jk})\right)\\&=v'_{ij}\end{aligned} \tag{16}$$

where $\Psi_{s,j}^{k}$ is the set of antenna's PER for user k, excluding those whose remaining available data-rate is no smaller than r'_i. When a layer is mapped to a certain antenna, its remaining available data-rate is updated by the video layer's bit-rate including redundancy bit-rate. The intuition of this inequality comes from Proposition 1, and it is derived by selecting the feasible antenna with smallest PER for sth ($d + 1 \leqslant s \leqslant i - 1$) video layer iteratively. Moreover, for any video layer i, when there is no antenna whose remaining available data-rate is no smaller than r'_i, or $\Psi^k_{s,j}$ is a null set, it denotes video layer i must be dropped at the transmitter side. In this case, we simply set $v'_{ij} = w_i$.

Since v'_{ij} is a lower bound of v_{ij} and it is independent from each other, the efficiency matrix **V′** for the assignment problem is written as:

$$\mathbf{V}' = \begin{pmatrix} v'_{(d+1)1} & \cdots & v'_{(d+1)(L-d)} \\ \vdots & \ddots & \vdots \\ v'_{L1} & \cdots & v'_{L(L-d)} \end{pmatrix} \quad (17)$$

This assignment problem can be solved by any existing algorithms, such as dynamic programming or recursive iteration algorithms. Its optimal solution, denoted as $D^{(L-d)}$, is the lower bound of the remaining L − d video layers' total distortion for the primal problem. Then, we derive the lower bound of the average overall distortion of all video layers as

$$\mathcal{D}^{lower} = \mathcal{D}^{d} + \mathcal{D}^{(L-d)} \quad (18)$$

Adaptive channel scheduling algorithm

We incorporate these bounds into the branch-and-bound framework, and an efficient branch-and-bound based channel scheduling algorithm is proposed. Compared with exhaustive search method, TBCS finds the global optimal solution with much lower complexity.

Fig. 3 illustrates the convergence of TBCS as d increase. For a certain selected node in the branch-and-bound tree, d denotes both its layer-index in the tree and the number of video layers that have been assigned antennas for this node. The figure shows that when d = L, i.e., the selected node is a leaf in the branch-and-bound tree, the upper bound is equal to the lower bound and the algorithm terminates. The pseudo code for the branch-and-bound based channel scheduling algorithm is given in Algorithm 1. The algorithm consists of three major components: (i) Partition component partitions the primal problem into subproblems, (ii) Bounding component derives the upper and lower bounds of each subproblem, (iii) Iteration and Pruning component compares the bounds and delete some subproblems to reduce the complexity.

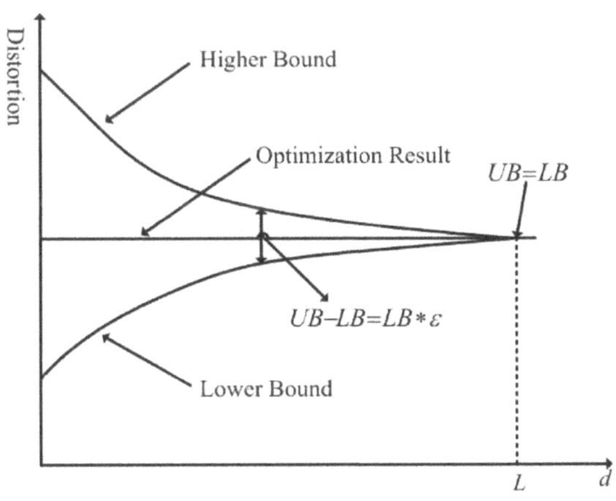

Figure 3: Convergence of TBCS as d increases, and d denotes the number of video layers that have been mapped to certain antennas.

Moreover, we accelerate the convergence of TBCS and further reduce the complexity by relaxing its termination condition. The algorithm terminates when the upper bound reaches 1 + ε of the lower bound, i.e., UB − LB = LB * ε, and a (1 − ε)-optimal solution is produced. The details of this acceleration mechanism are presented in Section 4.5.

Enhancement

Instead of terminating the algorithm when the bounds are equal, we introduce a (1 − ε)-optimal solution method to accelerate the convergence of TBCS, i.e., TBCS terminates when the upper bound reaches 1 + ε of the lower bound. Let the global optimal objective value be G ⩽ UB , we have $LB \geqslant \frac{1}{1+\varepsilon}UB \geqslant \frac{1}{1+\varepsilon}G = (1 - \varepsilon + \varepsilon^2 - \varepsilon^3 + \cdots) \approx (1 - \varepsilon)G$, for $0 \leqslant \varepsilon \ll 1$. By relaxing the termination condition, we greatly speed up the convergence of the branch-and-bound algorithm.

Algorithm 1.

Branch-and-bound based channel scheduling algorithm

Initialization:

obtain the original problem as Prob 1;
optimal solution $sol \leftarrow \varnothing$;
problem list $\mathcal{S} \leftarrow \{\text{Prob } 1\}$;
upper bound $UB \leftarrow \infty$;
lower bound $LB \leftarrow 0$;
feasible antenna set $\mathcal{A} \leftarrow \{1, 2, \ldots, M_t\}$;
layer-index for the selected *node* in the *branch-and-bound tree* $d_1 \leftarrow 0$;
get the upper bound UB_1 and solution $\mathbf{A}_1$ as described in Section 4.2;
get the lower bound LB_1 as described in Section 4.3;
$UB \leftarrow UB_1$;
$LB \leftarrow LB_1$;

Iteration and Pruning:

select Prob l with the smallest LB_l in $\mathcal{S}$;
$LB \leftarrow LB_l$;
if $UB_l < UB$ **then**
  $sol \leftarrow \mathbf{A}_l$;
  $UB \leftarrow UB_l$;
end if
if $UB \leqslant (1 + \varepsilon)LB$ **then**
  stop with solution *sol*;
else
  remove all Prob k in $\mathcal{S}$ with $LB_k \geqslant \frac{UB}{1+\varepsilon}$;
end if

Partition:

for the selected Prob l;
while $\mathcal{A} \neq \varnothing$ **do**
  select antenna m in $\mathcal{A}$, and map the $(d_l + 1)$th video layer to antenna m;
  update $\mathcal{A}$
  $d_{l_m} \leftarrow d_l + 1$
  obtain a new problem Prob l_m;
end while

Bounding:

```
solve all the partition Probs l_m to get solution A_{l_m}
and bounds UB_{l_m} and LB_{l_m};
remove Prob l from problem list S;
for each m do
   if LB_{lm} ≤ UB/(1+ε) then
      add Prob l_m into problem list S;
   end if
end for
if S == ∅ then
   stop;
else
   goto the Iteration & Pruning procedure;
end if
```

ILLUSTRATIVE SIMULATION RESULTS

In this section, we present illustrative simulation results to show how the proposed channel scheduling scheme is able to achieve UEP, and how TBCS finds the global solution with much lower complexity than exhaustive search method. In order to evaluate both the effectiveness and efficiency of our proposed scheme and algorithm, we have compared them with exhaustive search method, which always achieves the optimum with the highest computation complexity. Besides, we have also compared them with Min–Max channel scheduling scheme (which selects antennas in the ascending order of the maximal PER of each row in matrix $BL_{x}K$, and the inspiration comes from [31]) and random channel scheduling method (RCS, which randomly assigns a transmit antenna for each video layer and it is similar to PT MIMO [18]). The video sequences, mobile,foreman and crew, are tested. These sequences are selected because of their different characteristic motion and spatial details. All test sequences are 300 frames with a frame rate of 30 fps and encoded by the JSVM reference encoder [4] to generate an embedded scalable video stream with eight layers.

We assume that the channel conditions of the users are independent. For user $k(1 \leqslant k \leqslant K)$, the MIMO channel is under independent Rayleigh fading, and elements in channel matrix $\mathbf{H}_k$ are obtained from Clarke and Jakes' model [32]. Noise vector ζk is from i.i.d. Gaussian collection with zero mean, independent real and imaginary parts, with variance σ^2. Equal power is allocated to each transmit antenna and 16-QAM is used for modulation. Also, RS codes [33] are adopted to protect the transmitted bit streams since it maintains maximum erasure protection while produces a minimum of redundancy. We allocate the same channel codes for all video layers. Although unequal power allocation and channel coding can also achieve UEP, these methods are beyond the scope of this paper. In this paper, we focus on achieving UEP only through channel scheduling and it can be easily incorporated into these existing UEP schemes. For the detection of transmitted video signals, linear ZF receivers [34] are adopted.

Complexity analysis

We conduct experiments to show the computational complexity of TBCS versusexhaustive search method. The number of iterations is adopted as the comparison criterion. Fig. 4 illustrates the iterations of both exhaustive search method and TBCS under different number of video layers with the number of transmit antennas Mt = 4. The figure shows that exhaustive search method always has higher iterations than TBCS. In order to find the global optimal solution, exhaustive search method has to search the whole solution space, whose space size is M_t^L. While the computational complexity of TBCS is mainly depending on the tightness of both the upper and lower bounds, branching and pruning techniques, and parameter ε. Their effectiveness is demonstrated through simulation results in the next subsections. In the case that ε = 0, TBCS finds the optimal solution, but it has much lower complexity than exhaustive search method, this also demonstrates the efficiency of TBCS.

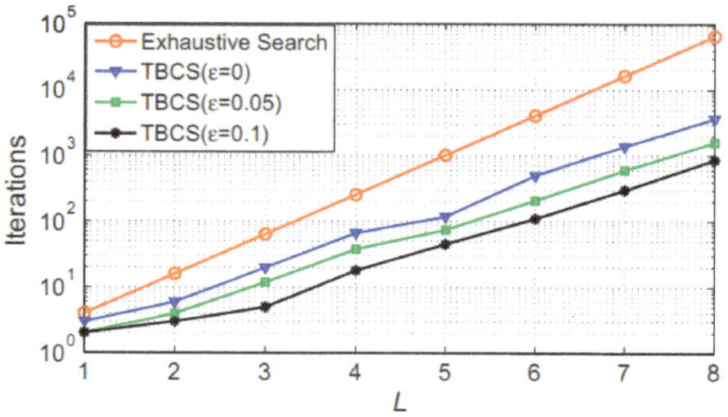

Figure 4: Complexity performance. The iterations of exhaustive search method and TBCS with different ε versusthe number of video layers L. The number of antennas Mt = 4, the number of users K = 50, average SNR = 20 dB.

From this figure, we also find that the iterations gap between exhaustive search method and TBCS is becoming bigger as L increases. This is mainly because that in exhaustive search method, the number of iterations is only depending on the number of video layers when Mt is constant, and it is increasing exponentially. While in TBCS, the video layers have been mapped to antennas orderly. Thus, when some important video layers (base layer and some relative low enhancement layers) are mapped to antennas with very poor channel quality, many nodes would be pruned from the branch and bound tree through the pruning procedure. This greatly reduces the searching space and computational complexity.

BER performance

We then compare both the short-term and long-term average BER of different schemes. The number of transmit antennas is four and the number of video layers is eight in the simulations. Elements in channel matrix $\mathbf{H}_k$ are obtained from Clarke and Jakes' model[32]. For purpose of clarity, the parameter ε is set to zero in TBCS, and we only plot the average BER of four layers (the lowest two layers and the highest two layers, i.e., the base layer, enhance-1, enhance-6 and enhance-7) of different schemes in this subsection.

The short-term average BER of video layers with average SNR = 20 dB is illustrated inFig. 5. The figures clearly demonstrate that the short-term average BER is timely fluctuated from 10^{-6} to 10^0. Thus, video layers should be mapped to different transmit antennas according to their importance. Specially, in order to protect base-layer bit stream during bad status, mapping it to the best antenna is indispensable. In RCS scheme, all video layers are treated equally and mapped to transmit antennas randomly. The average BER of all video layers are fluctuated from 10^{-6} to 10^{0} as Fig. 5(a) shows, and UEP is not achieved. The Min–Max scheme assigns the antennas to video layers in the ascending order of the maximal PER of each row in matrix $\mathbf{B}_{L\times K}$[31], and the average BER of video layers is illustrated in Fig. 5(b). The figure shows that the average BER still does not strictly have the same order with that of video layers' priorities. However, when compared with RCS, important video layers are given more protection in some degree. For example, the average BER of the lowest two layers is generally lower than the highest two layers. Our proposed branch-and-bound algorithm finds the optimal video-layer-antenna mapping order and Fig. 5(c) shows its average BER results of different video layers. This figure obviously manifests that an unequal average BER according to the importance of bit stream is accomplished. However, at some points, such as when t = 0.2 and t = 0.9, the average BER of lower video layers is not always lower than that of higher layers. This is because channel scheduling is a non-linear mapping problem due to the inter-dependence among video layers, and simply mapping video layers to multiple antennas according to the order of average BER is only a feasible solution. Though it cannot guarantee the solution's optimality, it generally achieves much better performance than RCS. This is why we adopt the average PER as the criterion to denote antenna's channel quality and find an upper bound of the average overall distortion in TBCS, the details have been explained in Section 4.2.

We also compare the long-term average BER of each video layer under different SNR strength and the results are illustrated in Fig. 6. In RCS scheme, the long-term average BER will be converged since all the video layers are treated equally and mapped to multiple transmit antennas randomly. Fig. 6(a) demonstrates this. The figure shows that all video layers nearly have the same average BER, and no UEP is achieved. On the other hand, the long-term average BER performance illustrated in Fig. 6(b) shows that low video layers have lower average BER than the high layers in Min–Max scheme. However, the gap of the average BER among video layers is small.

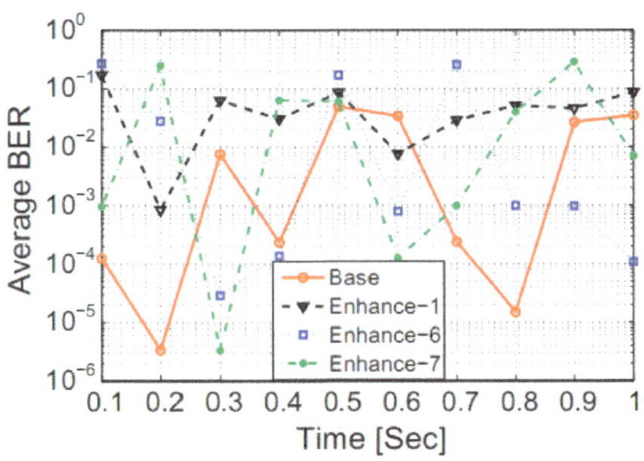

(a) RCS.

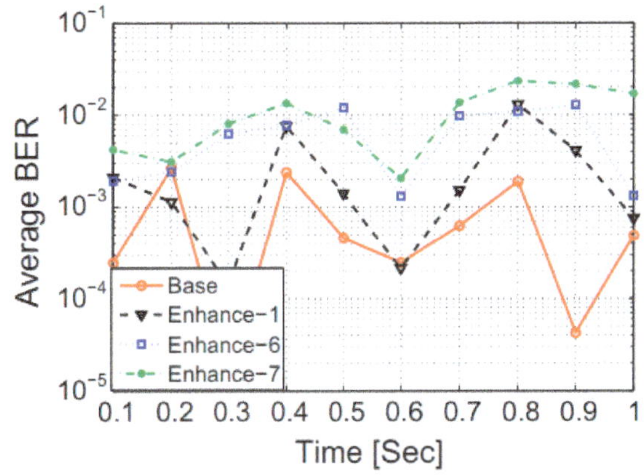

(b) Min-Max.

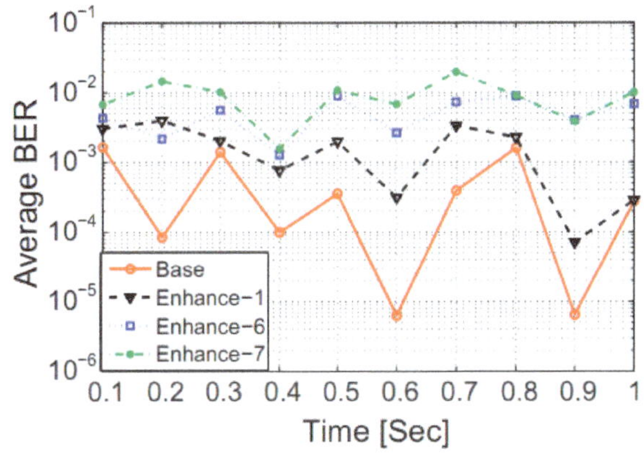

(c) TBCS.

Figure 5: Short-term average BER of different schemes. The number of users K = 50, average SNR = 20 dB, and$\varepsilon = 0$.

It is mainly because that Min–Max only gives more protection to important video layers in some degree, and it cannot guarantee that optimal UEP is achieved. In Fig. 6(c), we plot the long-term average BER of TBCS. The figure clearly shows that UEP is achieved, and the gap of the average BER among video layers is bigger than that in Min–Max scheme. When comparing all the three sub-figures in Fig. 6, we can find that the low average BER of the important video layers (e.g. base layer, the first enhancement layer) is achieved by sacrificing the BER performance of high video layers. This is reasonable in video communication since video signal contains bits of different importance. And it is indispensable to protect the bits discriminatively and give more protection to the important bits.

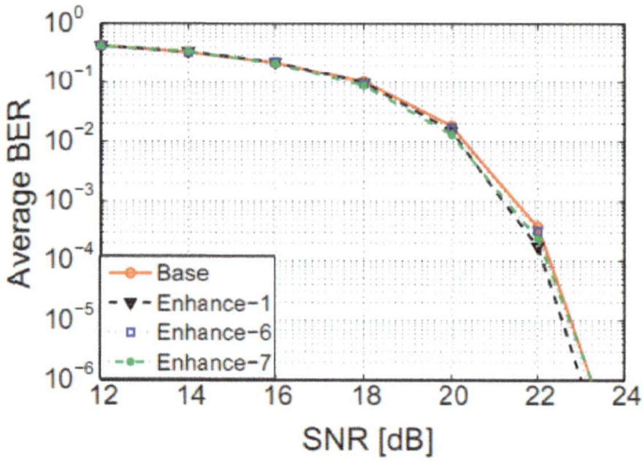

(a) RCS.

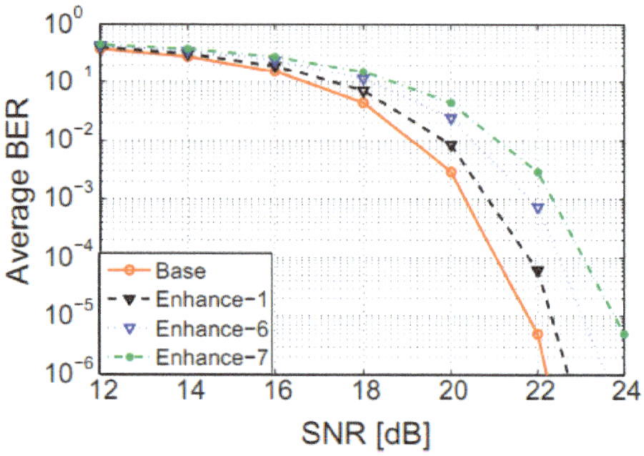

(b) Min-Max.

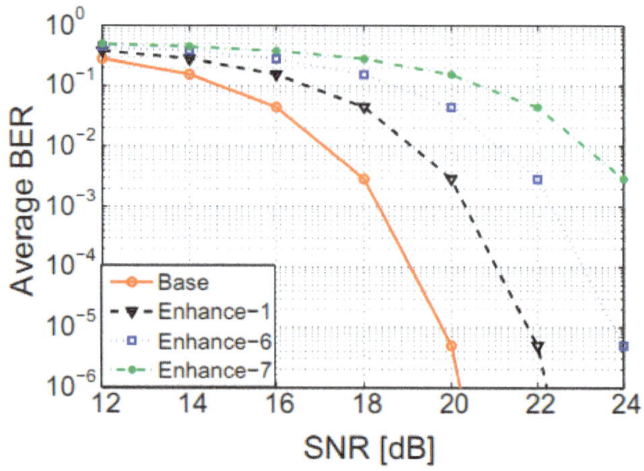

(c) TBCS.

Figure 6: Long-term average BER of different schemes. The number of users K = 50, and ε = 0.

Reconstructed video PSNR performance

We conduct experiments to show the reconstructed average overall PSNR of the decoded video sequences over various average SNR strength and number of receivers. Three video sequences, mobile, foreman and crew, are tested and encoded into eight layers.

First, we evaluate the reconstructed average PSNR performance over various SNR strength and the results are illustrated in Fig. 7. The number of receivers K = 50 and parameter ε = 0. All the three figures, Fig. 7(a–c), undoubtedly show that the PSNR improvement is achieved by TBCS against both RCS and Min–Max schemes. The performance improvement is from the obtained UEP, which is achieved by adaptive channel scheduling. Particularly, the gap of PSNR among the schemes in the low SNR region is outstanding since the high BER makes it indispensable to give more protection to the important video layers. As the average SNR strength increases, the superiority of channel scheduling becomes inconspicuous. Suppose that SNR strength of any antenna is high enough to broadcast video layer reliably, channel scheduling is becoming unnecessary. Therefore, the gap of PSNR among the schemes is very small in the high SNR region.

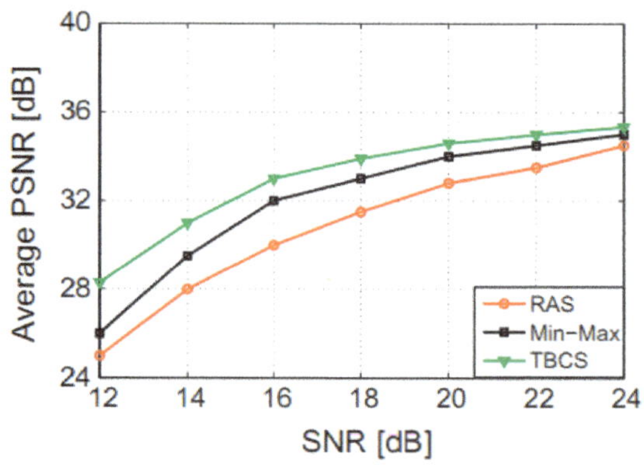

(a) Reconstructed average PSNR of *mobile*.

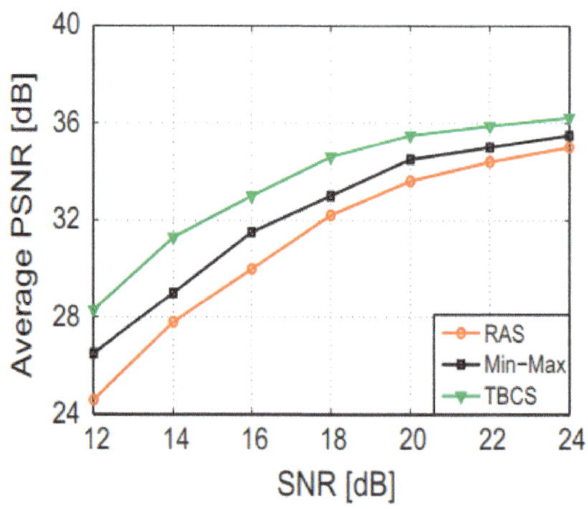

(b) Reconstructed average PSNR of *foreman*.

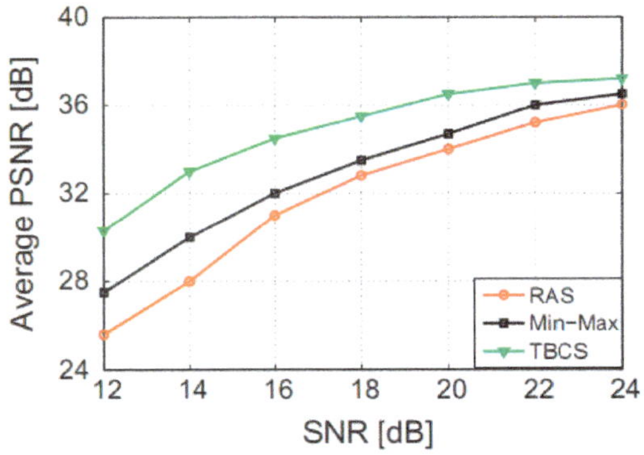

(c) Reconstructed average PSNR of *crew*.

Figure 7: The reconstructed average PSNR performance of different schemes under various SNR strength. The number of users K = 50, and ε = 0.

We also compare the schemes under different numbers of receiver, and the results are illustrated in Fig. 8. The average SNR strength is 20 dB and parameter ε = 0. From the figures we find that PSNR is decreasing as the number of users K increases. The reason is that the heterogeneity of channel condition is becoming considerable as the number of users increases, and the performances of all schemes are deteriorated. When the number of users K is large enough, the quality differentiation among antennas is becoming inconspicuous since each antenna is corresponding to K subchannels, and the gap of PSNR among the schemes becomes small. Meanwhile, the figures also clearly show that TBCS always performs the best, this demonstrates the effectiveness of TBCS under various channel conditions.

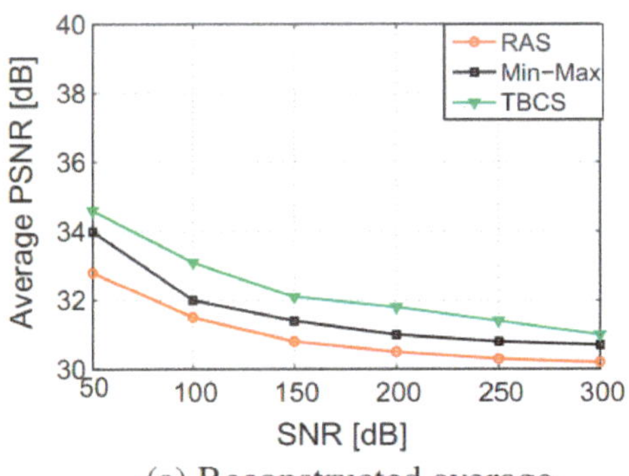

(a) Reconstructed average PSNR of *mobile*.

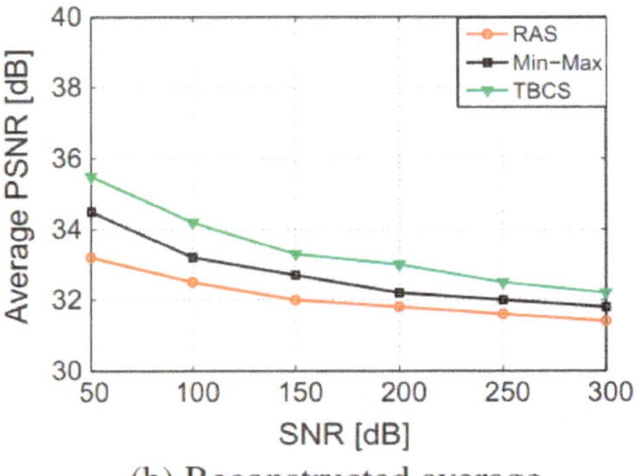

(b) Reconstructed average PSNR of *foreman*.

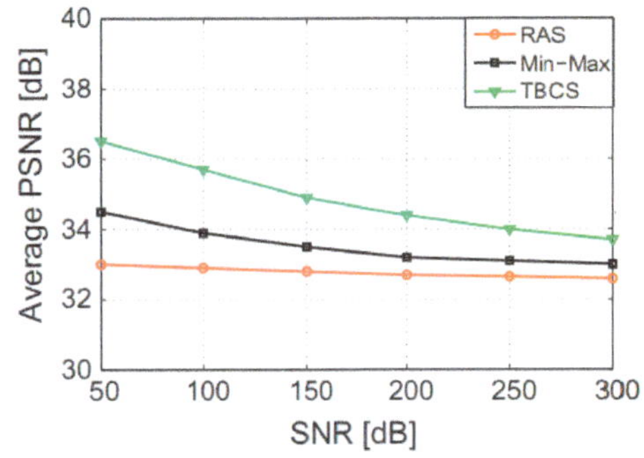

(c) Reconstructed average PSNR of *crew*.

Figure 8: The reconstructed average PSNR performance of different schemes under various number of users. Average SNR = 20 dB, and ε = 0.

We then examine the influence of parameter ε on received video quality. The video sequence, crew, is tested, and the number of users K = 50. Fig. 10 plots the average PSNR of the reconstructed video given different ε. The figure shows that average PSNR decreases as ε increases. The reason is as follows. When ε = 0, TBCS finds the optimal solution and has the same PSNR performance with exhaustive search method. Whenε > 0, TBCS terminates when $LB \geqslant \frac{1}{1+\varepsilon}$ UB as described in Section 4.5, and a (1 − ε)-optimal solution is produced, which is equal to the upper bound of the distortion. As ε increases, the algorithm converges more quickly with higher distortion. From Fig. 4 andFig. 10, we can also conclude that TBCS is flexible to various applications. For example, if the applications require high video quality, the parameter ε should be set small. On the other hand, if the applications require low delay, ε can be set big relatively.

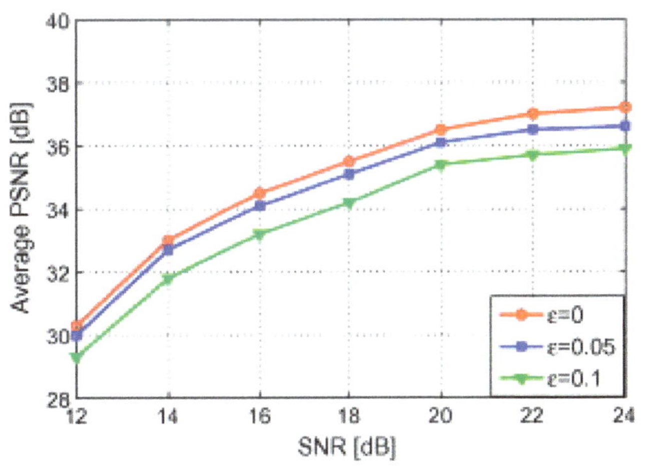

Figure 10: The influence of parameter ε on average PSNR performance. The number of users K = 50.

At last, we investigate the reconstructed video PSNR performance of TBCS against the channel estimation error. In Fig. 9, we show the results with perfect channel matrix $\mathbf{H}_k$ versus channel estimation error where Hk is estimated by ML. Moreover, to investigate the robustness of TBCS under heavy estimation error, we also plot results when we add 15% disturbances to the feedback SNR strength. Specifically, from the channel matrix, we get the SNR strength of each antenna according to Eq. (2). Then, each of the SNR strength γik is disturbed by randomly adding a noise, and the noise is a variable randomly selected from the range of $[-0.15 * \gamma_{ik}, 0.15 * \gamma_{ik}]$. At last, the performance of RCS is illustrated as the benchmark. The figures show that when channel matrix is estimated by ML, the PSNR performance is very close to the case when channel matrix is known perfectly. This demonstrates the effectiveness of our proposed scheme and algorithm in practical applications. When the estimation error is heavy which is simulated by adding 15% disturbances to the feedback SNR strength in our experiments, the PSNR is close to RCS, but it is never worse than RCS. This is because when the estimation error is too big, it provides little useful information for optimizing channel scheduling and the channel scheduling result is similar to RCS. This demonstrates the robustness against channel estimation error.

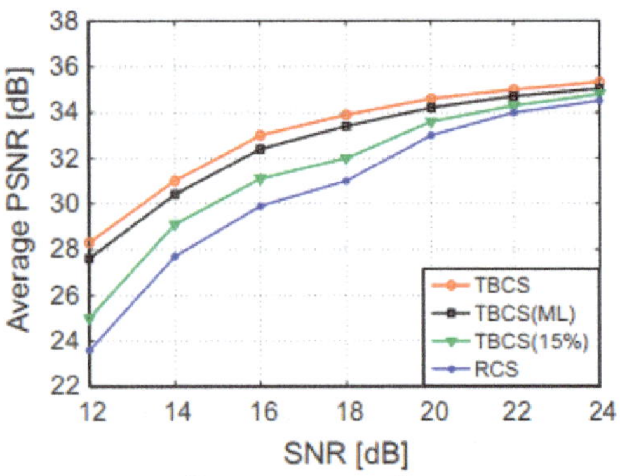

(a) Reconstructed average PSNR of *mobile*.

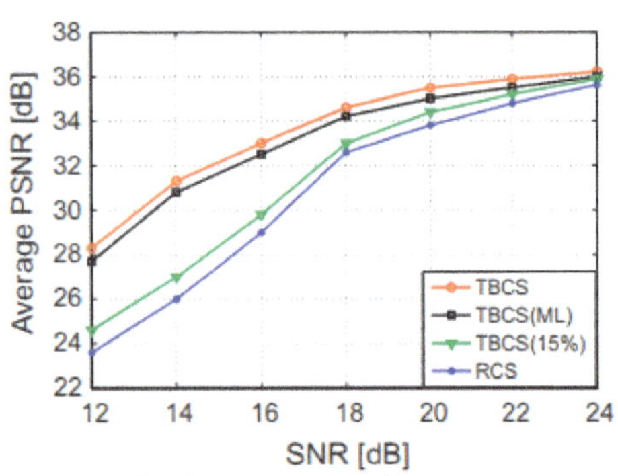

(b) Reconstructed average PSNR of *foreman*.

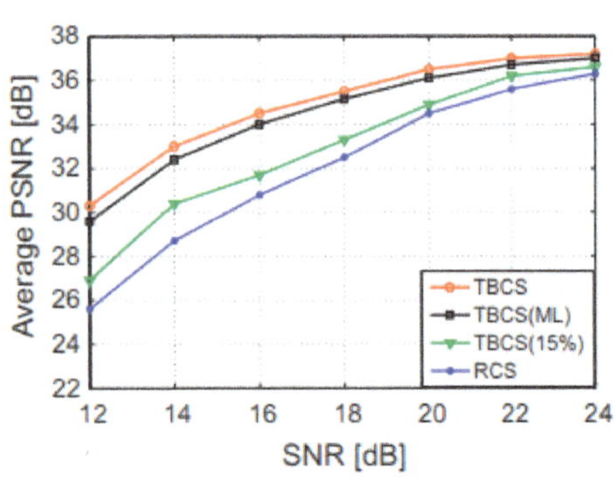

(c) Reconstructed average PSNR of *crew*.

Figure 9: The reconstructed average PSNR performance against channel estimation error. The number of usersK = 50.

CONCLUSION

In this paper, we have investigated the channel scheduling problem for scalable video broadcasting over MIMO wireless networks. According to the feedback SNR strength, the scalable video layers are periodically scheduled among multiple antennas. We formulate it into a non-linear combinatorial optimization problem. The computational complexity is very high by using exhaustive search method. Instead, by adopting the branch-and-bound framework, an efficient low-complexity channel scheduling algorithm is proposed. Moreover, at the expense of performance loss, the complexity is further reduced by relaxing termination condition of TBCS, and a $(1 - \varepsilon)$-optimal solution is produced. Our proposed scheme is very flexible that UEP is achieved only by switching the video layers among multiple antennas. It can be easily incorporated into most of the existing UEP video transmission schemes. At last, simulation results demonstrate both the effectiveness and efficiency of our proposed scheme and algorithm.

ACKNOWLEDGMENTS

This work was supported by National High-tech Technology R&D Program (863 Program) of China under Grant 2013AA013504, National Natural Science Foundation of China under contract No. 61071082 and National Key Technology R&D Program of China under Grant 2012BAH18B03.

REFERENCES

1. P.W. Wolniansky, G.J. Foschini, G.D. Golden, R.A. Valenzuela, VBLAST: an architecture for realizing very high data rates over the rich-scattering wireless channel, in: IEEE Int. Symp. on Signals, Syst. Electron., 1998, pp. 295–300.
2. D. Gesbert, M. Shafi, D. shan Shiu, P. Smith, A. Naguib, From theory to practice: an overview of MIMO space-time coded wireless systems, IEEE J. Sel. Areas Commun. 21 (3) (2003) 281–302.
3. T. Wiegand, G. Sullivan, J. Reichel, H. Schwarz, M. Wien, Joint Draft of SVC Amendment, Joint Video Team (JVT), Doc. JVT-W201.
4. H. Schwarz, D. Marpe, T. Wiegand, Overview of the scalable video coding extension of the H.264/AVC standard, IEEE Trans. Circ. Syst. Video Technol. 17 (9) (2007) 1103–1120.
5. M.K. Jubran, M. Bansal, L.P. Kondi, Low-delay low-complexity bandwidth-constrained wireless video transmission using SVC over MIMO systems, IEEE Trans. Multimedia 10 (8) (2008) 1698–1707.
6. D. Song, C.W. Chen, Scalable H.264/AVC video transmission over MIMO wireless systems with adaptive channel selection based on partial channel information, IEEE Trans. Circ. Syst. Video Technol. 17 (9) (2007) 1218–1226.
7. Y.P. Fallah, H. Mansour, S. Khan, P. Nasiopoulos, H.M. Alnuweiri, A link adaptation scheme for efficient transmission of H.264 scalable video over multirate WLANs, IEEE Trans. Circ. Syst. Video Technol. 18 (7) (2008) 875–887.

8. S.M. Alamouti, A simple transmit diversity technique for wireless communications, IEEE J. Sel. Areas Commun. 16 (8) (1998) 1451– 1458.
9. V. Tarokh, H. Jafarkhani, A.R. Calderbank, Space-time block coding for wireless communications: performance results, IEEE J. Sel. Areas Commun. 17 (3) (1999) 451–460.
10. G.J. Foschini, Layered space-time architecture for wireless communication in a fading environment when using multielement antennas, Bell Labs Tech. J. (1996) 41–59.
11. G. Caire, S. Shamai, On the achievable throughput of a multiantenna Gaussian broadcast channel, IEEE Trans. Inf. Theory 49 (7) (2003) 1691–1706.
12. M. Costa, Writing on dirty paper, IEEE Trans. Inform. Theory 29 (1983) 439–441.
13. H. Sato, An outer bound on the capacity region of broadcast channel, IEEE Trans. Inform. Theory 24 (1978) 374–377.
14. S. Vishwanath, N. Jindal, A. Goldsmith, On the capacity of multiple input multiple output broadcast channels, IEEE Int. Conf. Commun. 3 (2002) 1444–1450.
15. Y. Yang, On the capacity of maximum selection in MIMO multicast network, IEEE Conf. on Comput. Commun. (2008) 1–5.
16. J. Xu, S.-J. Lee, W.-S. Kang, J.-S. Seo, Adaptive resource allocation for MIMO-OFDM based wireless multicast systems, IEEE Trans. Broadcast. 56 (1) (2010) 98–102.
17. A.M.C. Correia, J.C.M. Silva, Nuno M. B Souto, et al., Multi-resolution broadcast/multicast systems for MBMS, IEEE Trans. Broadcast. 53 (1) (2007) 224–234.
18. H. Zheng, K.J.R. Liu, Space-time diversity for multimedia delivery over wireless channels, IEEE Int. Symp. Circ. Syst. 4 (2000) 285–288.
19. J. Xu, R. Hormis, X. Wang, MIMO video broadcast via transmitprecoding and SNR-scalable video coding, IEEE J. Sel. Areas Commun. 28 (6) (2010) 456–466.
20. G. Caire, S. Shamai, On the achievable throughput of a multi-antenna Gaussian broadcast channel, IEEE Trans. Inf. Theory 49 (7) (2003) 1691–1706.
21. J. Xu, R. Hormis, X. Wang, Scalable video multicast on broadcast channels, IEEE Global Telecommun. Conf. (2009) 1–8.
22. Y. Yang, On the capacity of maximum selection in MIMO multicast network, IEEE Conf. Comput. Commun. (2008) 1–5.
23. C. Bilen, E. Erkip, Y. Wang, Layered video multicast using diversity embedded space time codes, IEEE Int. Symp. Sarnoff (2009) 1–5.
24. H. Xiao, Q. Dai, X. Ji, W. Zhu, A novel JSCC framework with diversitymultiplexing-coding gain tradeoff for scalable video transmission over cooperative MIMO, IEEE Trans. Circ. Syst. Video Technol. 20 (7) (2010) 994–1006.
25. C.-H. Kuo, C.-M. Wang, J.-L. Lin, Cooperative wireless broadcast for scalable video coding, IEEE Trans. Circ. Syst. Video Technol. 21 (6) (2011) 816–824.
26. B. Hassibi, B. Hochwald, How much training is needed in multipleantenna wireless links?, IEEE Trans Inf. Theory 49 (4) (2003) 951– 963.
27. E. Biglieri, J. Proakis, S. Shamai, Fading channels: informationtheoretic and communications aspects, IEEE Trans. Inform. Theory 44 (6) (1998) 2619–2692.
28. E. Biglieri, R. Calderbank, A. Constantinides, A. Goldsmith, A. Paulraj, H.V. Poor, MIMO Wireless Communications, Cambridge Univ. Press, Cambridge, UK, 2007.
29. C. Zhou, X. Zhang, Z. Guo, A novel JSCC scheme for scalable video transmission over MIMO systems, IEEE Int. Image Process. (2012) 2277–2280.
30. H. Mansour, Y. Fallah, P. Nasiopoulos, V. Krishnamurthy, Dynamic resource allocation for MGS H.264/AVC video transmission over link-adaptive networks, IEEE Trans. Multimedia 11 (8) (2009) 1478– 1491.
31. D. Lu, D.K.C. So, Performance based receive antenna selection for VBLAST systems, IEEE Trans. Wireless Commun. 8 (1) (2009) 214–225.
32. R.H. Clarke, A statistical theory of mobile-radio reception, Bell Syst. Tech. J. 47 (1968) 957–1000.
33. S. Lin, D.J. Costello, Error Control Coding-Fundamentals and Applications, Prentice-Hall, Englewood Cliffs, NJ, 1983.
34. A. Paulraj, R. Nabar, D. Gore, Introduction to Space-Timewireless Communications, Cambridge Univ. Press, Cambridge, UK, 2003.

CHAPTER 4

ASEP OF MIMO SYSTEM WITH MMSE-OSIC DETECTION OVER WEIBULL-GAMMA FADING CHANNEL SUBJECT TO AWGGN

Keerti Tiwari[1], Davinder S. Saini[2], and Sunil V. Bhooshan[1]

[1]Department of Electronics and Communication Engineering, Jaypee University of Information Technology, Waknaghat, Solan 173234, India

[2]Department of Electronics and Communication Engineering, Chandigarh College of Engineering and Technology, Chandigarh 160019, India

ABSTRACT

Ordered successive interference cancellation (OSIC) is adopted with minimum mean square error (MMSE) detection to enhance the multiple-input multiple-output (MIMO) system performance. The optimum detection technique improves the error rate performance but increases system complexity. Therefore, MMSE-OSIC detection is used which reduces error rate compared to traditional MMSE with low complexity. The system performance is analyzed in composite fading environment that includes multipath and shadowing effects known as Weibull-Gamma (WG) fading. Along with the composite fading, a generalized noise that is additive white generalized Gaussian noise (AWGGN) is considered to show the impact of wireless scenario. This noise model includes various forms of noise as special cases such as impulsive, Gamma, Laplacian, Gaussian, and uniform. Consequently, generalized Q-function is used to model noise. The average symbol error probability (ASEP) of MIMO system is computed for 16-quadrature amplitude modulation (16-QAM) using MMSE-OSIC detection in WG fading perturbed by AWGGN. Analytical expressions are given in terms of Fox-H function (FHF). These expressions demonstrate the best fit to simulation results.

INTRODUCTION

In multiple-input multiple-output (MIMO) systems, the role of spatial multiplexing (SM) and spatial diversity is to provide high data rate and reliable communication, respectively. However, a tradeoff occurs between diversity and multiplexing for multiple access channels [1]. The demand to achieve high data rate is increasing for next generation communication systems. Using diversity, a simple detection can be formed at the cost of capacity reduction. Thus, spatial multiplexing is recommended for achieving significant capacity gain with improved transmission rate. However, demultiplexing at the receiver is still an issue for efficient system design.

A variety of detection techniques exist in literature to improve the system performance [2–7]. Zero forcing (ZF) and minimum mean square error (MMSE) are simple detection techniques although they lead to the reduced error performance [3, 4]. Maximum likelihood (ML) detection provides an optimal error rate performance. However, the hardware complexity increases with the increase in transmitter antennas and modulation order. Therefore, ordered successive

Citation: Keerti Tiwari, Davinder S. Saini, and Sunil V. Bhooshan, "ASEP of MIMO System with MMSE-OSIC Detection over Weibull-Gamma Fading Channel Subject to AWGGN," Journal of Computer Networks and Communications, vol. 2016, Article ID 7918456, 7 pages, 2016. doi:10.1155/2016/7918456

interference cancellation (OSIC) is recommended with MMSE for improving the error rate performance [5]. In [5–8], efficient approaches have been investigated to develop OSIC and to reduce the complexity of receiver for Vertical-Bell Laboratories Layered Space-Time (V-BLAST) system. In [9], antenna selection has been used for OSIC detection to enhance the error rate performance. Also, a near-optimal selection technique has been proposed to decrease the complexity without substantial performance reduction. Different detection ordering such as signal-to-noise ratio (SNR) based, column norm based and, signal-to-interference plus noise ratio (SINR) based ordering has been investigated. It is examined that postdetection SINR based ordering achieves the best performance among all three ordering techniques [10]. Hence, MMSC-OSIC detection is used in this paper to achieve the improved error rate performance with adaptable complexity level in composite fading scenario. Identifying an efficient detection technique is still under investigation in MIMO systems.

Various small scale multipath channel models including Rayleigh, Rician, Nakagami-m, and Weibull have been recommended to analyze the wireless system performance. Large scale fading can be modeled using log-normal (LN) or Gamma distribution. Both the small scale and large scale fading effects can be observed simultaneously due to rapidly changing wireless environment. Therefore, channel modeling of composite fading which comprises multipath as well as shadowing effects is imperative to figure out. Also, it is important to resolve a number of practical problems with interference effects in MIMO wireless communications. The composite channel models such as RayleighLN, shadowed-Rician, Gamma-Gamma, K, generalized-K, correlated shadowed-κ-$-\mu$ [11–17], and comparatively newfangled Weibull-Gamma (WG) [18, 19] are widely used to incorporate both small scale fading and shadowing. Gamma models are simpler and more accurate than LN models and hence preferred in recent approaches. The WG composite distribution is appropriate for MIMO system design in the present wireless scenario due to its extensive flexibility, experimental efficiency, and analytical conformity. Weibull fading model is adaptive for modeling severe and nonsevere multipath fading conditions, Gamma model is used for shadowing, and collectively WG composite fading model is formed to quantify both the effects. WG fading model is a generic model and it includes Rayleigh-Gamma or K and exponential-Gamma distributions as its special cases. Consequently, this model approximates several other fading models [11, 18].

Both higher and lower modulation orders have been considered in multipath fading with the existence of AWGN [20–22]. However, the deviation of actual noise is possible; therefore, generic noise model is required. In power line communication (PLC), the system performance is extensively affected by additive and multiplicative power line noises. Further, the additive noise is categorized into background noise and impulsive noise. The background noise and impulsive noise models follow Nakagami-m and Middleton class A distribution, respectively, although the multiplicative PLC noise induces fading in the received signal power. Also, the system error rate performance has been evaluated in the presence of such noise scenarios [23–25]. The generalized Gaussian distribution (GGD) is the emerging research interest for modeling different noise effects. This generic noise model considers various forms of noise such as impulsive, Gamma, Gaussian, Laplacian [26]. Rectangular quadrature amplitude modulation (QAM) is defined by a combination of in-phase and quadrature phase pulse amplitude modulation (PAM) signals. This modulation technique has been used to compute average symbol error probability (ASEP) using Gaussian $\mathcal{Q}$ -function in composite fading scenario perturbed by additive white generalized Gaussian noise (AWGGN) [27].

To the best of our knowledge, the MIMO system performance has not been evaluated for composite WG fading channel with the consideration of generalized noise. To improve the MIMO system performance spatial multiplexing (SM) is used with efficient detection technique, that is, MMSE-OSIC. The expressions derived for ASEP in [27] are analyzed again which were previously limited to single-input single-output (SISO) system. To achieve the high data rate of the wireless link, higher order modulation techniques are preferred, although they are less flexible to noise and interference. Exact analytical expressions are computed in terms of Fox-H function (FHF) for 16-QAM in SM-MIMO WG fading subject to AWGGN. Two special cases of AWGGN, namely, AWGN and Laplacian noise, are considered. AWGN is popularly known and Laplacian noise has also achieved attention in the signal processing and wireless systems to model impulsive noise. In addition, the variations of fading and shadowing parameters are also illustrated.

The rest of the paper is organized as follows. In Section 2, system model and proposed detection technique are described. Section 3 provides the simulation results and analysis for ASEP of SM-MIMO in WG fading subject to generic noise along with specified detection technique. Finally, the paper is concluded in Section 4.

SYSTEM AND CHANNEL MODEL

Consider a MIMO system having $Nr \times Nt$ antennas, where N_t and N_r denote the number of transmit and receive antennas, respectively. X is the transmit signal modulated by 16-QAM and multiplied by a composite flat fading channel envelope $\mathcal{H}$. Previously, the noise is generally considered as AWGN. However, the AWGGN noise $\mathcal{N}$ is assumed here with zero mean and variance σ^2 . MIMO system model is represented as

$$Y = \mathcal{H}X + \mathcal{N}. \tag{1}$$

The probability density function (PDF) of the AWGGN noise is described in [28, Equation (6.2)] over $n \in \Re$ as

$$\mathcal{P}_{\mathcal{N}}(n \mid m_n, \sigma, \eta) = \frac{\eta\psi}{2\Gamma(1/\eta)} \exp\left(-\psi^{\eta} |n - m_n|^{\eta}\right), \tag{2}$$

where η and m_n denote shaping parameter of N and mean, respectively $(\eta \in \Re^+, m_n \in \Re^+)$. Furthermore, the coefficient ψ can be defined by normalizing the noise power using normalizing coefficient ψ_0 with respect to η as

$$\psi = \frac{\psi_0}{\sigma} = \sqrt{\frac{2\Gamma(3/\eta)}{N_0\Gamma(1/\eta)}}, \tag{3}$$

where $\Gamma(\cdot)$ denotes Gamma function, $\psi_0 = \sqrt{\Gamma(3/\eta)/\Gamma(1/\eta)}$, $\sigma^2 = E[\mathcal{N}^2] - m_n^2 = N_0/2$, N_0 is the power per positive frequency of AWGGN, and $E[\cdot]$ is expectation operator.

The random variable of AWGGN distribution rigorously depends on its shaping parameter η. This distribution reveals a superior fit to the quantified noise statistics with the changing physical channel conditions and forms various noise categories as special cases of AWGGN. For η=2, η=1, η = 0.5, and η=0, it characterizes the prominent Gaussian, Laplacian, Gamma, and impulsive noise, respectively. Consequently, for $\eta = 1/2$ and $\eta = 1/3$, the statistical properties and accurate simulation technique have been developed in the presence of AWGGN [29].

The PDF of the received signal envelope χ given in [30] is simplified to form WG distribution defined over $x \in (0,\infty)$ and represented as

$$\mathscr{P}_{\chi}(x) = \frac{2}{\Gamma m}\left[\frac{(m+1)\Gamma(1+1/k)}{\Omega}\right]^{m} \cdot x^{2m-1}\Gamma\left[\left(1-\frac{m}{k}\right),0,\left(\frac{(m+1)\Gamma(1+1/k)}{\Omega}\right)^{m}x^{2},\frac{1}{k}\right], \quad (4)$$

where $\Gamma(\cdot,\cdot,\cdot,\cdot)$ is extended incomplete Gamma function, which is given as $\Gamma(\xi,s,a,\mu) = \int_{s}^{\infty} x^{\xi-1}\exp(-x-ax^{-\mu})dx$, $(s \in \Re^{+}), (\xi,a,\mu) \in \mathbb{C}$ [28, Equation (6.2)]. k and m denote fading figure and shadowing shaping parameter, respectively, where $0.5 \leq k < \infty$, $0 \leq m < \infty$, and $\Omega = E[\chi^2]$ $(0 \leq \Omega < \infty)$ is the average power of the received signal envelope.

The SNR γ for received symbols in the presence of AWGGN follows WG PDF, which is defined over $\gamma \in (0,\infty)$. The average SNR per symbol is $\overline{\gamma} = E[\gamma] = E[\chi^2]E_x/N_0$, where E_x is the energy of transmitted symbols. By exchanging variables, PDF is represented in the form of SNR as

$$\mathscr{P}_{\gamma}(\gamma) = \frac{1}{\Gamma m}\left[\frac{(m+1)\Gamma(1+1/k)}{\overline{\gamma}}\right]^{m} \cdot \gamma^{m-1}\Gamma\left[\left(1-\frac{m}{k}\right),0,\left(\frac{(m+1)\Gamma(1+1/k)}{\overline{\gamma}}\right)^{m}\gamma,\frac{1}{k}\right]. \quad (5)$$

Equation (5) can be expressed in terms of the FHF using [28, Equation (6.22)], [31, Equations (2.1.4), (2.1.5) and (2.1.11)] and simplifying [32, Equation (8)] as

$$\mathscr{P}_{\gamma}(\gamma) = \frac{1}{\Gamma m\gamma}H_{0,2}^{2,0}\left[\frac{(m+1)\Gamma(1+1/k)\gamma}{\overline{\gamma}}\Bigg|_{(1,1/k),(m,1)}^{-}\right], \quad (6)$$

where

$$H_{p,q}^{m,n}\left[z\Big|_{(b_k,B_k)_{1,q}}^{(a_j,A_j)_{1,p}}\right] = \frac{1}{2\pi i} \cdot \int_{c}^{-} \frac{\prod_{k=1}^{m}\Gamma(b_k,B_k s)\prod_{j=1}^{n}\Gamma(1-a_j,A_j s)}{\prod_{k=n+1}^{p}\Gamma(a_j,A_j s)\prod_{k=m+1}^{q}\Gamma(1-b_k,B_k s)} z^{-s}ds, \quad (7)$$

where $H_{p,q}^{m,n}(\cdot)$ is FHF defined in [31, Equation (1.1.1)], [33] and c represents Mellin-Barnes contour.

MMSE-OSIC DETECTION

MMSE detection technique maximizes the postdetection SINR by minimizing mean-square error (MSE). In OSIC, SINR based ordering improves the performance of linear detection technique by maximizing SINR. This technique maintains the low complexity for designing hardware. It holds number of linear receivers in which each receiver classifies one of the parallel data streams with detected signal components. These signal components are successively canceled from the received signal at each stage [34].

The MMSE detection technique explained in [10] offers the 1st estimated stream with the 1st row vector of the MMSE weight matrix W_{MMSE} which is given by

$$W_{\text{MMSE}} = \left(\mathscr{H}^{\dagger}\mathscr{H} + N_0 I\right)^{-1}\mathscr{H}^{\dagger}, \quad (8)$$

where $(\cdot)\dagger$ denotes the Hermitian operator. In MMSE detection, to determine the required statistical information of N_0, the ith row vector $w_{i,\text{MMSE}}$ of W_{MMSE} is obtained by

$$w_{i,\text{MMSE}} = \underset{w=(w_1,w_2,\ldots,w_{N_t})}{\arg\max} \frac{|wh_i|^2 E_x}{\sum_{j=1,j\neq i}^{N_t} E_x |wh_i|^2 + N_0\|w\|^2}, \quad (9)$$

where hi is the ith column vector of the channel matrix and $\|\cdot\|$ is the Frobenius norm of matrix. $_{(i)}$ denotes the ith order detected symbol which depends on the order of detection; hence, this symbol may be different from the transmit signal at the ith antenna. The sliced value of $_{(i)}$ is given by $\widehat{x}_{(i)}$. The remaining signal is represented by

$$\widetilde{Y} = Y - \sum_{j=1}^{i-1}\widehat{x}_j h_j. \quad (10)$$

Assume that $\widehat{x}_j$, $j = 1,2,\ldots,i-1$, is accurately generated. When $x_{(1)} = \widehat{x}_{(1)}$ it means the interference is canceled and $_{(2)}$ can be estimated. When $x_{(1)} \neq \widehat{x}_{(1)}$ then error propagation takes place. The entire performance of OSIC technique is affected by the order of detection. The erroneous outcomes in the previous stages cause the error propagation.

Primarily, signals containing a higher postdetection SINR are detected in SINR based ordering. The linear MMSE detection with the postdetection SINR is represented by

$$\text{SINR}_i = \frac{E_x |w_{i,\text{MMSE}}h_i|^2}{\sum_{r\neq i} E_x |w_{i,\text{MMSE}}h_r| + N_0\|w_{i,\text{MMSE}}\|^2}, \quad i = 1,2,\ldots,N_t. \quad (11)$$

Once the selection of the N_t SINR values using W_{MMSE} is completed, the corresponding layer with the highest SINR is chosen. The second detected symbol is selected by canceling the interference due to first detected symbol from the received signals. If rth symbol is canceled first, then $\mathscr{H}$ of (8) is transformed into (12) by deleting the channel gain vector as per rth symbol:

$$\mathscr{H}^{(r)} = [h_1 \; h_2 \; \cdots \; h_{r-1} \; h_{r+1} \; \cdots \; h_{N_t}]. \quad (12)$$

Again, W_{MMSE} is calculated after substituting $\mathscr{H}$ of (8) by (12). Then, $N_t - 1$ SINR values (i.e., $(\text{SINR}_i)_{i=1,i\neq r}^{N_t}$) are computed by selecting the symbol containing highest SINR. After canceling the next symbol with the highest SINR, the same process is continued with the remaining signal. The total number of calculated SINR values is generated by $\sum_{j=1}^{N_t} j = N_t(N_t+1)/2$.

The OSIC technique can offer diversity order greater than $N_r - N_t + 1$ for all symbols. Following the ordering approach, the diversity order of the first detected symbol is also greater than $N_r - N_t + 1$. Nevertheless, the diversity order of remaining symbols depends on whether the previously detected symbols are exact or not. Suppose all the symbols are exact; then, the diversity order of the ith detected symbol is $N_r - N_t + i$. The ith detected symbol is different from the one transmitted from the ith transmit antenna. Since the ordering is based on SINR for MMSE detection, therefore, (11) is used to improve the ASEP performance.

AVERAGE SYMBOL ERROR PROBABILITY FOR M-QAM

The symbol error probability (SEP) has been given in [35, Equation (10)] for QAM in the presence of AWGN. The formation of M-QAM signal constellation is given by two independent in-phase and quadrature M-ary PAM signals, where M_I-ary PAM and $M_{\mathcal{Q}}$-ary PAM are in-phase and quadrature signals, respectively, and $M = M_I M_{\mathcal{Q}}$. Given that, GGD and Gaussian distribution demonstrate the identical symmetry properties. According to [27], the identical symmetry properties can be used to define SEP of M-QAM, given as

$$\begin{aligned}\mathscr{P}(\text{SEP}) &= 2\left(1-\frac{1}{M_I}\right)\mathcal{Q}_\eta(\mathscr{A}_I) + 2\left(1-\frac{1}{M_{\mathcal{Q}}}\right)\mathcal{Q}_\eta(\mathscr{A}_{\mathcal{Q}}) \\ &\quad - 4\left(1-\frac{1}{M_I}\right)\left(1-\frac{1}{M_{\mathcal{Q}}}\right)\mathcal{Q}_\eta(\mathscr{A}_I)\,\mathcal{Q}_\eta(\mathscr{A}_{\mathcal{Q}}),\end{aligned} \tag{13}$$

where $\mathscr{A}_I = \mathscr{D}_I/\sigma$, $\mathscr{A}_{\mathcal{Q}} = \mathscr{D}_{\mathcal{Q}}/\sigma$, and $\mathscr{D}_I$ and $\mathscr{D}_{\mathcal{Q}}$ denote the decision distances for in-phase and quadrature phase components, respectively. $\mathcal{Q}(\cdot)$ is generalized-$\mathcal{Q}$ function for $x \geq 0$ defined in [32] as

$$\mathcal{Q}_\eta(x) = \frac{\eta\psi_0}{2\Gamma(1/\eta)}\int_x^\infty e^{-\psi_0{}^\eta t^\eta}\,dt. \tag{14}$$

In [32, A.5], the representation of (14) in the form of FHF using [33, Equation (8.3.2/21), (A.4)] is given as

$$\mathcal{Q}_\eta(x) = \frac{1}{2\Gamma(1/\eta)} H_{1,2}^{2,0}\left[\psi_0{}^\eta |x|^\eta \Big|_{(1/\eta,1),(0,1)}^{(1,1)}\right]. \tag{15}$$

The ASEP is obtained by averaging the conditional SEPs in (13) under slow fading conditions over the PDF of γ. Then, $\mathscr{P}(\gamma)$ is represented by

$$\begin{aligned}\mathscr{P}r(S_e) &= 2\left(1-\frac{1}{M_I}\right)\mathfrak{T}(\mathscr{A}_I) \\ &\quad + 2\left(1-\frac{1}{M_{\mathcal{Q}}}\right)\mathfrak{T}(\mathscr{A}_{\mathcal{Q}}) \\ &\quad - 4\left(1-\frac{1}{M_I}\right)\left(1-\frac{1}{M_{\mathcal{Q}}}\right)\mathfrak{I},\end{aligned} \tag{16}$$

where

$$\mathfrak{T}(x) = \int_0^\infty \mathcal{Q}_\eta(\sqrt{\gamma}x)\,\mathscr{P}_\gamma(\gamma)\,d\gamma, \tag{17}$$

$$\mathfrak{I} = \int_0^\infty \mathcal{Q}_\eta(\sqrt{\gamma}\mathscr{A}_I)\,\mathcal{Q}_\eta(\sqrt{\gamma}\mathscr{A}_{\mathcal{Q}})\,\mathscr{P}_\gamma(\gamma)\,d\gamma. \tag{18}$$

It is difficult to formulate $\mathfrak{T}(\cdot)$ and $\mathfrak{I}$ using the conventional expressions of WG distribution and GGD. Therefore, alternative expressions (6) and (15) are used to compute simplified analytical expressions for $\mathfrak{T}(\cdot)$ and $\mathfrak{I}$ and then resulting expression for the ASEP. In (17), $\mathfrak{T}(x)$ consists of an integral including the product of two FHFs which is comparable to that of [32] considering the normalized value of fading shaping factor and severity of shadowing. Unlike [32], we prefer an efficient SINR based ordering for MMSE detection to improve the error rate performance of MIMO system. Using [27] and [31, Equation (1.1.1)], $\mathfrak{T}(x)$ can be represented in the form of FHF by a closed form expression given as

$$\mathfrak{T}(x) = \frac{1}{\eta\Gamma(1/\eta)\Gamma m} \cdot H_{2,3}^{2,2}\left[\frac{(m+1)\Gamma(1+1/k)}{x^2\psi_0{}^2\bar{\gamma}}\Big|_{(1,1/k),(m,1),(0,2/\eta)}^{(1-1/\eta,2/\eta),(1,2/\eta)}\right], \tag{19}$$

$$\mathfrak{I} = \frac{1}{2\eta\Gamma(1/\eta^2)\Gamma m} H_{2,1;0,2;1,2}^{0,2;2,0;2,0}\left[\frac{(m+1)\Gamma(1+1/k)}{\mathscr{A}_I{}^2\psi_0{}^2\bar{\gamma}}, \left(\frac{\mathscr{A}_{\mathcal{Q}}}{\mathscr{A}_I}\right)^\eta \Big|_{(1,1/k),(m,1),(1,1),(1/\eta,1),(0,1)}^{(1-1/\eta;2/\eta,1),(1;2/\eta,1),(0;2/\eta,1)}\right]. \tag{20}$$

Substituting (6) and (15) in (18), an integral which includes the product of three FHFs is used to describe (20). Then, using [36, Equation (2.3)], $\mathfrak{I}$ is expressed in terms of the FHF of two variables known as the bivariate Fox-H function (BFHF).

Substituting (19) and (20) in (16), the ASEP of M-QAM is computed. This ASEP expression is given for rectangular $(M_I \neq M_{\mathcal{Q}})$, square $(M_I = M_{\mathcal{Q}})$ QAM in arbitrary WG fading with AWGGN. Consequently, it maintains substantial range of noise and fading parameters. The commonly considered noise cases of AWGGN in composite fading scenario are as follows.

Case 1 (WG fading with Laplacian noise). The first special case of AWGGN emerges when $\eta=1$, and the noise is considered Laplacian. Taking $\eta=1$, $\mathfrak{T}(x)$ is represented as

$$\mathfrak{T}(x) = \frac{1}{\Gamma m} H_{2,3}^{2,2}\left[\frac{(m+1)\Gamma(1+1/k)}{2x^2\bar{\gamma}}\Big|_{(1,1/k),(m,1),(0,2)}^{(0,2),(1,2)}\right]. \tag{21}$$

Using [31, 36], FHF and BFHF functions are well explored and utilized to make a simplified form of (21) by reducing number of terms in $H_{\cdot,\cdot}^{\cdot,\cdot}(\cdot)$ as

$$\mathfrak{T}(x) = \frac{1}{\Gamma m} H_{1,2}^{2,1}\left[\frac{(m+1)\Gamma(1+1/k)}{2x^2\bar{\gamma}}\Big|_{(1,1/k),(m,1)}^{(1,2)}\right]. \tag{22}$$

Similarly, $\mathfrak{I}$ can be written as

$$\mathfrak{I} = \frac{1}{2\Gamma m} H_{2,1;0,2;1,2}^{0,2;2,0;2,0}\left[\frac{(m+1)\Gamma(1+1/k)}{2\mathscr{A}_I{}^2\bar{\gamma}}, \left(\frac{\mathscr{A}_{\mathcal{Q}}}{\mathscr{A}_I}\right)\Big|_{(1,1/k),(m,1),(1,1),(1,1),(0,1)}^{(0;2,1),(1;2,1),(0;2,1)}\right]. \tag{23}$$

Using [36, Equation (1.1)], for the description of BHFH and [28, Equations (6.29) and (6.42)], $\mathfrak{I}$ is represented as

$$\mathfrak{I} = \frac{1}{2\Gamma m} H_{1,2}^{2,1}\left[\frac{(m+1)\Gamma(1+1/k)}{2\left(\mathscr{A}_I{}^2 + \mathscr{A}_{\mathcal{Q}}{}^2\right)\bar{\gamma}}\Big|_{(1,1/k),(m,1)}^{(1,2)}\right]. \tag{24}$$

Equations (22) and (24) are used to calculate ASEP when Laplacian noise is present.

Case 2 (WG fading with AWGN). For $\eta=2$, (19) and (20) can be rearranged to find the ASEP in AWGN environment. Again, the expressions for $\mathfrak{T}(x)$ and $\mathfrak{I}$ are reduced as

$$\mathfrak{T}(x) = \frac{1}{2\sqrt{\pi}\Gamma m} \cdot H_{2,3}^{2,2}\left[\frac{(m+1)\Gamma(1+1/k)}{2x^2\bar{\gamma}}\Big|_{(1,1/k),(m,1),(0,1)}^{(1/2,1)(1,1)}\right],$$

$$\mathfrak{I} = \frac{1}{14.5\Gamma m} H_{2,1;0,2;1,2}^{0,2;2,0;2,0}\left[\frac{(m+1)\Gamma(1+1/k)}{2\mathscr{A}_I{}^2\bar{\gamma}}, \left(\frac{\mathscr{A}_{\mathcal{Q}}}{\mathscr{A}_I}\right)^2 \Big|_{(1,1/k),(m,1),(1,1),(1/2,1),(0,1)}^{(1/2;1,1),(1;1,1),(0;1,1)}\right]. \tag{25}$$

Here, $m\rightarrow\infty$ eliminates the effect of shadowing. When $m\rightarrow\infty$, WG distribution follows Weibull distribution and $m\rightarrow\infty$, $k=1$ converted WG distribution into Rayleigh distribution [30, Table 1]. Thus, the fading scenario can be changed by setting the parameters m and k.

SIMULATION RESULTS AND ANALYSIS

To evaluate the MIMO system performance, 16-QAM modulation is used as a function of SNR for the generalized case of noise. Therefore, distinct values of η and arbitrary values of m and k are taken into consideration. The in-phaseto-quadrature phase decision distance ratio is represented as $R_{\mathrm{ddr}} = \mathscr{D}_I/\mathscr{D}_Q = \mathscr{A}_Q/\mathscr{A}_I$. For this case, the average total energy per symbol ET is given as $E_T = 10.5\bar{\gamma}\mathscr{D}_I^2 + 2.5\bar{\gamma}\mathscr{D}_Q^2 = 0.5(21 + 5R_{\mathrm{ddr}}^2)\bar{\gamma}\mathscr{D}_I^2$ and hence $E_T/\sigma^2 = 0.5(21 + 5R_{\mathrm{ddr}}^2)\bar{\gamma}\mathscr{A}_I^2$ [27]. Taking a fixed $R_{\mathrm{ddr}} = (10.5)^{1/2}$, the identical average energies of the in-phase and quadrature signals are obtained.

The impact of the parameter R_{ddr} is emerged to observe the system performance. When $R_{\mathrm{ddr}} = 1$, the most favorable case occurs; this implies that the in-phase and quadrature distance are identical for both the Laplacian and Gaussian noise. For $R_{\mathrm{ddr}} = (10.5)^{1/2}$, same energy is obtained between the in-phase and quadrature signal; thus the system performance is reduced with a small amount, that is, approximately 1 dB SNR reduction for large SNRs. When the quadrature signal contains 10.5 times the average energy of the inphase signal, for this instant loss is more essential as it gets approximately 4 dB SNR loss for large SNRs, comparative to the aforementioned case, where $R_{\mathrm{ddr}} = 1$.

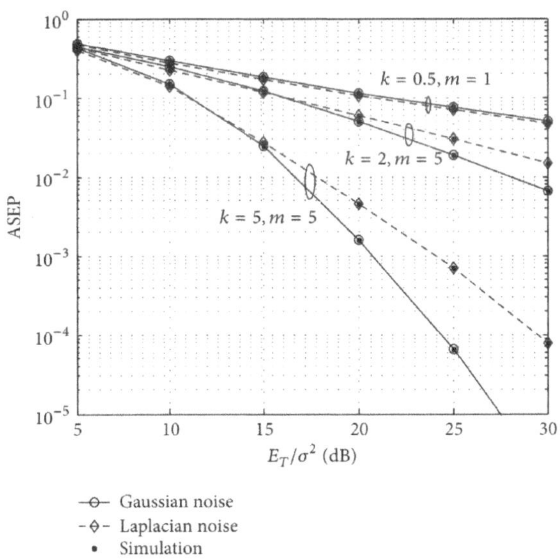

Figure 1: ASEP of 2 × 2 MIMO system using MMSE-OSIC over WG fading channel subject to Laplacian and Gaussian noise.

Firstly, composite WG fading is considered in Laplacian noise environment. To obtain Weibull and Rayleigh fading, the parameters are settled to $m\rightarrow\infty$ and $m\rightarrow\infty$, $k=1$, respectively. Figure 1 depicts the ASEP as a function of average SNR per symbol ET/σ^2 for both Gaussian and Laplacian cases of noise. In addition, distinct values of m and k are chosen to determine the severity of fading. Analytical results presented in this paper by (19) and (20) demonstrate the perfect match of the simulation results. The performance of the system is improved by increasing both the parameters m and k. Results shown in Figure 1 illustrate that the ASEP performance in Laplacian noise is superior to that of Gaussian noise for lower SNR or less than 15 dB SNR. However, for high SNR, less fading ($k\geq2$), the situation is upturned and ASEP performance improves in the Gaussian noise compared with Laplacian noise. For severe fading ($m = 0.5$), Laplacian noise offers better results than Gaussian noise.

Afterward, Weibull and Rayleigh fading which are the special cases of WG fading are considered. In Figure 2, Rayleigh fading case is taken into account. In this case, system gives superior performance by diminishing η, which validates the previous result in which the Laplacian noise gives better performance than the Gaussian noise in severe fading. It is previously mentioned that large fading parameter refers to less fading. In Figure 3, the ASEP is demonstrated as a function of the SNR per QAM symbol in Weibull fading environment ($k=5$) with AWGGN for which $\eta = 8, 2, 0.5, 0.25$. In this case, when the less fading condition occurs, the different two regions are investigated. At low SNR, the ASEP decreases with increasing η and at high SNR it improves by increasing η.

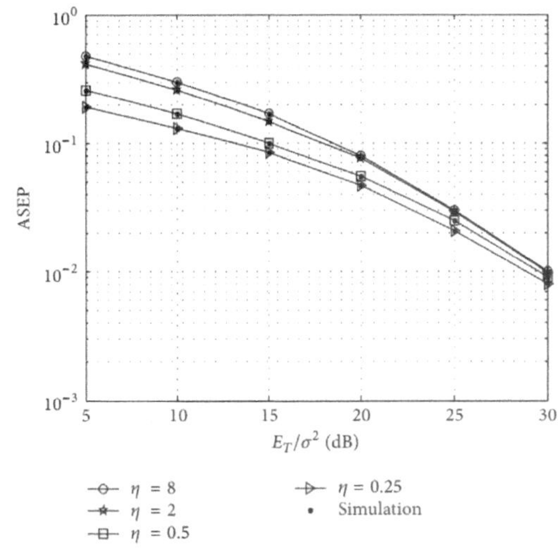

Figure 2: ASEP of 2 × 2 MIMO system for 16-QAM using MMSE-OSIC over Rayleigh fading channel with arbitrary values of η.

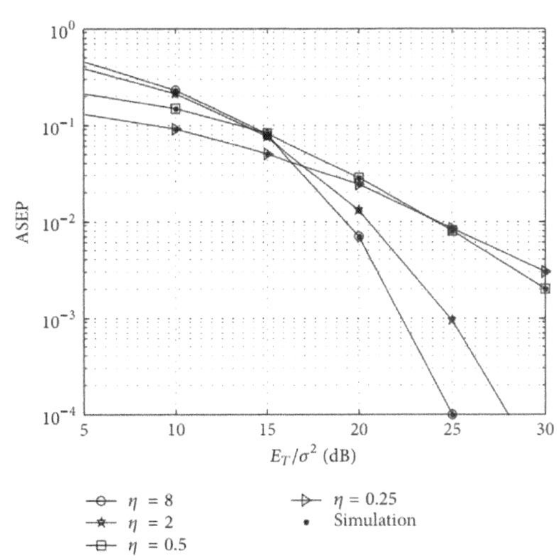

Figure 3: ASEP of 2 × 2 MIMO system for 16-QAM using MMSE-OSIC detection over Weibull fading channel () with arbitrary values of η.

CONCLUSION

This paper evaluates the ASEP performance of MIMO system in composite WG fading environment subject to AWGGN.

Analytical expressions for ASEP are derived using 16-QAM consisting of two independent in-phase and quadrature signals of PAM. The MMSE-OSIC detection is used to improve the error rate performance of MIMO system. It is concluded from the results that the ASEP performance in Laplacian noise is better than that of Gaussian noise for low SNR. However, in less fading, performance is degraded for high SNR and improved error performance is obtained in Gaussian noise compared with Laplacian noise. In severe fading, improved error rate performance can be achieved in the presence Laplacian noise compared with Gaussian noise. In Rayleigh fading case, the system gives superior performance for low noise shaping parameter η. This result again proves that the Laplacian noise gives better performance than the Gaussian noise in severe fading. In Weibull fading, the different two regions are inspected for lower amount of fading or large fading parameter. Moreover, the ASEP reduces with η at low SNR and it increases by η at high SNR. Simulation results validate the analytical results.

COMPETING INTERESTS

The authors declare that there are no competing interests regarding the publication of this paper.

REFERENCES

1. E. Biglieri, R. Calderbank, A. Constantinides, A. Goldsmith, A. Paulraj, and H. V. Poor, MIMO Wireless Communications, Cambridge University Press, Cambridge, UK, 2007.
2. Y. Lee, H.-C. Shih, C.-S. Huang, and J.-Y. Li, "Low-complexity MIMO detection: a mixture of ZF, ML and SIC," in Proceedings of the 19th International Conference on Digital Signal Processing (DSP ‹14), pp. 263–268, Hong Kong, August 2014.
3. C. Siriteanu, S. D. Blostein, A. Takemura, H. Shin, S. Yousefi, and S. Kuriki, "Exact MIMO zero-forcing detection analysis for transmit-correlated rician fading," IEEE Transactions on Wireless Communications, vol. 13, no. 3, pp. 1514–1527, 2014.
4. Y. Jiang, M. K. Varanasi, and J. Li, "Performance analysis of ZF and MMSE equalizers for MIMO systems: an in-depth study of the high SNR regime," IEEE Transactions on Information Theory, vol. 57, no. 4, pp. 2008–2026, 2011.
5. H. Zhang, H. Dai, and B. L. Hughes, "Analysis on the diversity-multiplexing tradeoff for ordered MIMO SIC receivers," IEEE Transactions on Communications, vol. 57, no. 1, pp. 125–133, 2009.
6. T.-H. Liu, "Some results for the fast MMSE-SIC detection in spatially multiplexed MIMO systems," IEEE Transactions on Wireless Communications, vol. 8, no. 11, pp. 5443–5448, 2009.
7. Y. Song, C. Liu, and F. Lu, "Lattice reduction-ordered successive interference cancellation detection algorithm for multiple-input–multiple-output system," IET Signal Processing, vol. 9, no. 7, pp. 553–561, 2015.
8. Y. Song, C. Liu, and F. Lu, "The optimal MMSE-based OSIC detector for MIMO system," IEICE Transactions on Communications, vol. E99-B, no. 1, pp. 232–239, 2016.
9. Y. Bae and J. Lee, "Low complexity antenna selection for V-BLAST systems with OSIC detection,"EURASIP Journal on Wireless Communications and Networking, vol. 2011, article 6, 7 pages, 2011.
10. Y. S. Cho, J. Kim, W. Y. Yang, and C. G. Kang, MIMO-OFDM Wireless Communications with MATLAB, John Wiley & Sons, 2010.
11. P. M. Shankar, Fading and Shadowing in Wireless Systems, Springer, New York, NY, USA, 2012.
12. T. Hashem and M. I. Islam, "Performance analysis of MIMO link under fading channels," in Proceedings of the 17th International Conference on Computer and Information Technology (ICCIT ‹14), pp. 498–503, Dhaka, Bangladesh, December 2014.
13. A. Abdi and M. Kaveh, "K distribution: an appropriate substitute for Rayleigh-lognormal distribution in fading-shadowing wireless channels," Electronics Letters, vol. 34, no. 9, pp. 851–852, 1998.
14. M. Matthaiou, N. D. Chatzidiamantis, G. K. Karagiannidis, and J. A. Nossek, "On the capacity of generalized-K fading MIMO channels," IEEE Transactions on Signal Processing, vol. 58, no. 11, pp. 5939–5944, 2010.
15. M. R. Bhatnagar and M. K. Arti, "On the closed-form performance analysis of maximal ratio combining in shadowed-rician fading LMS channels," IEEE Communications Letters, vol. 18, no. 1, pp. 54–57, 2014.
16. M. R. Bhatnagar, "On the sum of correlated squared κ-μ shadowed random variables and its application to performance analysis of MRC," IEEE Transactions on Vehicular Technology, vol. 64, no. 6, pp. 2678–2684, 2015.
17. M. R. Bhatnagar and M. K. Arti, "Performance analysis of AF based hybrid satellite-terrestrial cooperative network over generalized fading channels," IEEE Communications Letters, vol. 17, no. 10, pp. 1912–1915, 2013.
18. P. S. Bithas, "Weibull-gamma composite distribution: alternative multipath/shadowing fading model,"Electronics Letters, vol. 45, no. 14, pp. 749–751, 2009.
19. K. Tiwari and D. S. Saini, "SER improvisation of MIMO-MRC system over Weibull-Gamma fading channel," in Proceedings of the International Conference on Signal Processing and Communication (ICSC ‹15), pp. 70–73, IEEE, Noida, India, March 2015.
20. N. C. Beaulieu, "A useful integral for wireless communication theory and its application to rectangular signaling constellation error rates," IEEE Transactions on Communications, vol. 54, no. 5, pp. 802–805, 2006.
21. G. K. Karagiannidis, "On the symbol error probability of general order rectangular QAM in nakagami-m Fading,"

IEEE Communications Letters, vol. 10, no. 11, pp. 745–747, 2006.

22. H. A. Suraweera and J. Armstrong, "A simple and accurate approximation to the SEP of rectangular QAM in arbitrary Nakagami-m fading channels," IEEE Communications Letters, vol. 11, no. 5, pp. 426–428, 2007.

23. A. Mathur and M. R. Bhatnagar, "PLC performance analysis assuming bpsk modulation over nakagami-m additive noise," IEEE Communications Letters, vol. 18, no. 6, pp. 909–912, 2014. ·

24. A. Mathur, M. R. Bhatnagar, and B. K. Panigrahi, "PLC Performance analysis over Rayleigh fading channel under Nakagami-m additive noise," IEEE Communications Letters, vol. 18, no. 12, pp. 2101–2104, 2014.

25. A. Mathur, M. R. Bhatnagar, and B. K. Panigrahi, "Performance evaluation of PLC under the combined effect of background and impulsive noises," IEEE Communications Letters, vol. 19, no. 7, pp. 1117–1120, 2015.

26. R. Viswanathan and A. Ansari, "Distributed detection of a signal in generalized Gaussian noise," IEEE Transactions on Acoustics, Speech, and Signal Processing, vol. 37, no. 5, pp. 775–778, 1989.

27. H. Soury, F. Yilmaz, and M.-S. Alouini, "Error rates of M-PAM and M-QAM in generalized fading and generalized gaussian noise environments," IEEE Communications Letters, vol. 17, no. 10, pp. 1932–1935, 2013.

28. M. A. Chaudhry and S. M. Zubair, On a Class of Incomplete Gamma Functions with Applications, Chapman & Hall/CRC, Boca Raton, Fla, USA, 1st edition, 2002.

29. M. Nardon and P. Pianca, "Simulation techniques for generalized Gaussian densities," Working Papers145, Departement of Applied Mathematics, Università Ca› Foscari Venezia, 2006.

30. F. Yilmaz and M.-S. Alouini, "A new simple model for composite fading channels: second order statistics and channel capacity," in Proceedings of the 7th International Symposium on Wireless Communication Systems (ISWCS ‹10), pp. 676–680, IEEE, York, UK, September 2010.

31. A. A. Kilbas and M. Saigo, H-Transforms: Theory and Applications (Analytical Methods and Special Functions), CRC Press, New York, NY, USA, 1st edition, 2004. ·

32. H. Soury, F. Yilmaz, and M.-S. Alouini, "Average bit error probability of binary coherent signaling over generalized fading channels subject to additive generalized Gaussian noise," IEEE Communications Letters, vol. 16, no. 6, pp. 785–788, 2012.

33. A. P. Prudnikov, Y. A. Brychkov, and O. I. Marichev, Integrals and Series: More Special Functions, vol. 3, Gordon and Breach Science Publishers, New York, NY, USA, 1990.

34. G. D. Golden, C. J. Foschini, R. A. Valenzuela, and P. W. Wolniansky, "Detection algorithm and initial laboratory results using V-BLAST space-time communication architecture," Electronics Letters, vol. 35, no. 1, pp. 14–15, 1999.

35. N. C. Beaulieu, "A useful integral for wireless communication theory and its application to rectangular signaling constellation error rates," IEEE Transactions on Communications, vol. 54, no. 5, pp. 802–805, 2006.

36. P. K. Mittal and K. C. Gupta, "An integral involving generalized function of two variables," Indian Academic Science, vol. 75, pp. 117–123, 1972.

CHAPTER 5

SEMAN: A NOVEL SECURE MIDDLEWARE FOR MOBILE AD HOC NETWORKS

Eduardo da Silva[1,2] and Luiz Carlos Pessoa Albini[1]

[1]Department of Informatics, Federal University of Parana (UFPR), 81531970 Curitiba, Brazil

[2]Department of Informatics, Catarinense Federal Institute (IFC), 89245000 Araquari, Brazil

ABSTRACT

As a consequence of the particularities of Mobile Ad Hoc Networks (MANETs), such as dynamic topology and self-organization, the implementation of complex and flexible applications is a challenge. To enable the deployment of these applications, several middleware solutions were proposed. However, these solutions do not completely consider the security requirements of these networks. Based on the limitations of the existing solutions, this paper presents a new secure middleware, called Secure Middleware for Ad Hoc Networks (SEMAN), which provides a set of basic and secure services to MANETs aiming to facilitate the development of distributed, complex, and flexible applications. SEMAN considers the context of applications and organizes nodes into groups, also based on these contexts. The middleware includes three modules: service, processing, and security. Security module is the main part of the middleware. It has the following components: key management, trust management, and group management. All these components were developed and are described in this paper. They are supported by a cryptographic core and behave according to security rules and policies. The integration of these components provides security guarantees against attacks to the applications that usethe middleware services.

INTRODUCTION

Mobile Ad Hoc Networks (MANETs) are very attractive in several scenarios, as [1] soldiers carrying out information on a battlefield; people sharing information during a meeting; attendees using notebooks in an interactive conference; rescuers working after disasters. MANETs are dynamically established without any fixed infrastructure or centralized administration, and their operation is held by the nodes themselves [2].

Citation: Eduardo da Silva and Luiz Carlos Pessoa Albini, "SEMAN: A Novel Secure Middleware for Mobile Ad Hoc Networks," Journal of Computer Networks and Communications, vol. 2016, Article ID 3136853, 18 pages, 2016. doi:10.1155/2016/3136853

On the other hand, these characteristics also impose several challenges, and the major ones are related to security. In addition to conventional wireless communication problems, the dynamic topology facilitates action of adversaries, making MANETs susceptible to both passive and active attacks [2]. In a passive attack, an unauthorized adversary tries to discover or to use system information without interaction with the network, while in an active one, the adversary tries to break into the system aiming to affect its operation [3]. Due to these particularities, the development of applications for MANET is not an easy task [4].

In general networks, to support the resolution of heterogeneity, scalability, and resource sharing problems and to allow the implementation of more complex and flexible applications, middleware solutions have been successfully used [5]. These solutions aim to provide interoperability and other services, as distribution of functionality, scalability, load balancing, and fault tolerance [6].

Several middleware solutions have also been proposed to support applications and services on MANETs. These solutions are message-oriented [7] and were classified, in a previous work [4], on tuple space-based, P2P-based, context-based, cross-layer, and application-oriented solutions. A complete analysis and comparison of these middleware solutions can be found in [4].

To support MANETs characteristics, a middleware must be lightweight in terms of the amount of processing, memory, and bandwidth consumption, to maintain its overhead as small as possible. Further, it must self-adapt to the dynamic environment and handle unpredictable message loss. Considering the security requirements of MANETs and since the middleware handles all the communication between a client and an application, it must also considers the security requirements [6]. However, middleware solutions do not consider, or consider only partially, the security requirements of the MANETs. As a consequence, security can be considered the main drawback of the solutions reported on [4]. Thus, the need for developing a middleware arises which considers the security challenges of MANETs and contains a set of components to provide secure services to applications.

This paper proposes a new Secure Middleware for Mobile Ad Hoc Networks, called SEMAN (Secure Middleware for Mobile Ad Hoc Networks). The middleware is based on groups, which are formed considering the context information. Group members exchange information which can be used on decision making and services provisioning. SEMAN has a security module which aims to ensure the system confidentiality and the resistance to following malicious attacks: selfish, byzantine, impersonation, and Sybil. The contributions of this paper are the new architecture of a secure middleware for MANETs; the design of a context-based group management and definition of strategies to the secure group communication; the integration of trust management and evaluation services; and an identity-based key management scheme integrated with the SEMAN cryptographic core.

The remaining of the paper is composed of six sections. Section 2 presents the network and the attack model. Section 3 introduces SEMAN: Secure Middleware for Mobile Ad Hoc Networks. Section 4 details the security model of SEMAN and how it can ensure security for middleware clients. Section 5 presents a scheme for secure group communication based on key agreements. Section 6 presents the integration of the security components to provide security to applications on different scenarios. Finally, Section 7 presents the conclusions and some research directions.

NETWORK AND ATTACK MODEL

The proposed middleware considers an asynchronous network composed of n mobile nodes, denoted by $N_1,\ldots,_n$. The description of SEMAN considers the notation presented as follows:

G_1: cyclic additive group with order p,

G_2: cyclic multiplicative group with order p,

e: bilinear pairing in which : $G_1 \times G_1 \rightarrow G_2$,

$H_1(x)$: hash function in which $H_1(x) = \{0,1\}^* \rightarrow \mathbb{G}_1^*$,

$H_2(x)$: hash function in which $H_2(x) = \mathbb{G}_2 \rightarrow \mathbb{Z}_p^*$,

N_F: founder nodes,

N_i: identification of node i,

SK_i: private key of node i,

PK_i: private key of node i,

MSK: master private key of system,

MPK: master public key of system,

MSK_i: share of master private key hold by node i.

It is assumed that only trust nodes participate in group initialization phases.

SEMAN aims to protect the network against some malicious attacks as selfish, byzantine, impersonation, and Sybil. Even though SEMAN may be effective against other attacks, they were not considered in this paper.

i.*Selfish Attacks.* A node presents a selfish behavior either as a consequence of a malicious and intentional act or to save its own resources. But regardless the reason, the selfish behavior may compromise the network activities and any decisionmaking scheme which needs the cooperation of nodes. To guarantee the security against a selfish behavior, SEMAN group operations are structured considering the secret sharing (t over n) technique, in which $n - (t + 1)$ nodes may be unavailable, or present a selfish behavior, and the system is able to attend the requests. Further, trust management component provides information about the behavior of nodes in a context. Thus, if a node is selfish and does not participate on group activities, the other nodes will be aware of this behavior through the trust management component.

2. *Byzantine Attacks.* A malicious node may perform a byzantine attack against the system, issuing false information or making decisions on behalf of a group. Thus, a byzantine attack may compromise the reliability of the middleware operations. The strategy to organize nodes into groups using secret sharing technique t-over-n increases the system protection against these attacks. Then, a malicious node must compromise, at least, other t nodes to perform any malicious activity on behalf of a group, making its actions more difficult and limited. Also, similar to selfish attack, the trust management provides ways for nodes to inform other ones if they detect some byzantine behavior. Thus, based on trust information, byzantine nodes can be isolated.

3. *Impersonation Attacks.* An attacker may steal the identity of a node and compromise the system reliability issuing false information on behalf of this node. A key management service is implemented to prevent this kind of attack against the system. All secure services provided by the middleware use cryptography. By using the key management, the middleware ensures that an identity belongs to the node that is using it.

Thus, an attacker needs to compromised the entire key management component to be success on this kind of malicious action. Also, a secure communication service provided by the group management is implemented which increases the reliability of SEMAN against impersonation attacks, ensuring that only members of a closed group are able to decrypt a message sent to this group.

4. *Sybil Attack.* In a Sybil attack, a malicious node creates a false identity and gets the authorization of other nodes to have this false identity accepted in the system. Then, system reliability is affected, since a unique node may perform several activities on behalf of a group. Similar to impersonation attack, key management helps to prevent the action of a Sybil attacker. As the identity of a node is certified by the key management, it is necessary that an attacker compromises the key management scheme to be able to create a false identity and issue a valid public/private key pair to this new identity. Also, the secure communication of the group management component increases the reliability of SEMAN against this attack. As the secure communication service ensures that only the members of a closed group are able to decrypt a message sent to a group, it prevents a node from creating a false identity and from using this identity to receive messages sent to a group that it is not a member of.

This section presented the network characteristics addressed in this work and the attack model considered. Four kinds of attacks and how they may compromise the network behavior, performance, and operations were described.

SECURE MIDDLEWARE FOR MOBILE AD HOC NETWORKS

This section describes the SEMAN, the new context-based middleware that utilizes a group approach to support decision making related to security. Based on [4], context-based solutions are more suitable for MANETs. Further, the group approach facilitates the nodes organization on the contexts and security-related decision making. Figure 1 illustrates how applications may use the middleware to perform a reliable communication over an unreliable physical channel.

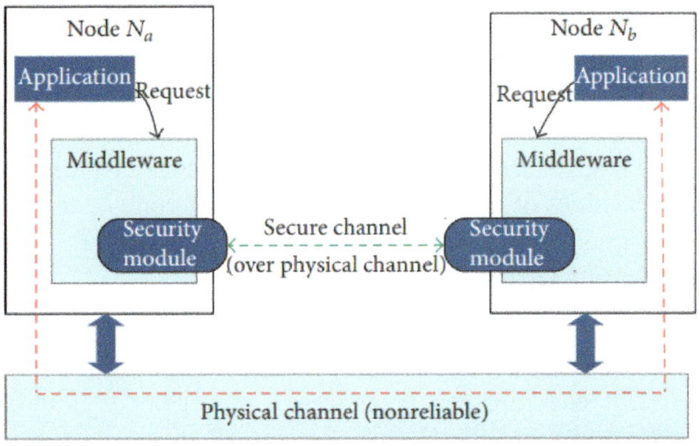

Figure 1: Reliable communication using a secure middleware.

SEMAN provides support to secure and reliable communications between multiple nodes in scenarios susceptible to malicious attacks. It is composed of distributed modules and a set of group-based cryptographic operations. To support middleware operations, nodes with similar requirements form groups. These groups, called context groups, are self-organized and dynamically formed with no user interaction, considering only applications profiles and requirements. Services are provided and utilized by the applications in a context and, consequently, they are made available to nodes that belong to groups of this context.

SEMAN is composed of a communication interface, a catalog, and three modules: services, processing, and security, as illustrated in Figure 2. Applications requests may be sent either to the middleware or to lower layers. Without loss of generality, only the former scenario is considered in this paper. All message exchanges between the middleware and the applications are performed by using the communication interface, which classifies messages and deliveries them to the correct module or application.

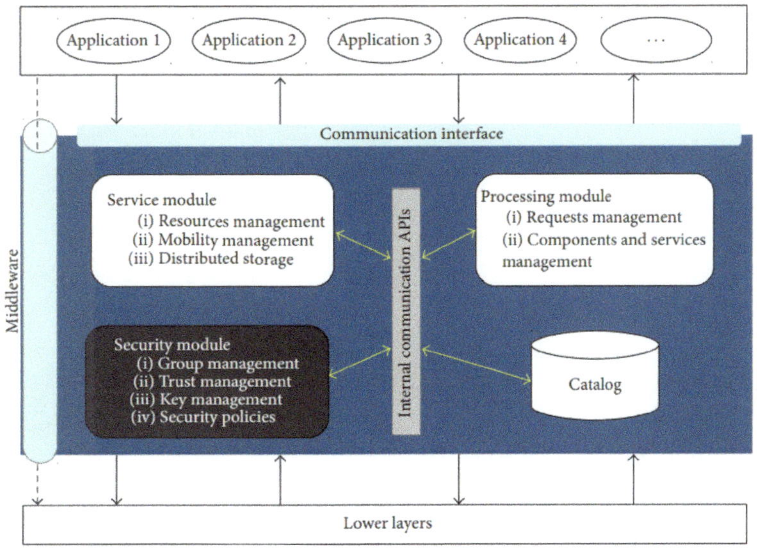

Figure 2: Architecture of the secure middleware.

The catalog is composed of a nonvolatile memory and is responsible for keeping all pending requests and security information about applications and nodes, like cryptographic keys, trust information, credential, and so forth. It is important to ensure the resistance in, at least, three scenarios: (i) node crash; (ii) network disconnection; and (iii) long delays in service provisioning. These situations may result either from a malicious action or from the dynamic behavior of MANETs.

The next subsections present the main characteristics and functionalities of the three modules and their components.

Services Module

The services module is responsible for keeping a list and details of all services and applications hosted by the node to other nodes. It encompasses the resource management, mobility management, and distributed storage. All these components are accessed by internal and external applications.

Resource Management

A service that provides information about location and availability of resources, as nodes, remote services, and contents, is very important for MANETs [8]. This service must consider the following restrictions: (i) mitigate the communication overhead, avoiding unneeded updates about available resources; (ii) be independent of nodes geographical position; and (iii) be independent of routing protocol. This component must consider the resources discovery and allocation, as well as their location management.

Resource management must offer, at least, four subcomponents, as depicted in Figure 3: allocation, registration, discovery, and location of resources. Each subcomponent requests and provides information to processing and security modules. For example, the security module provides information about nodes and applications authorization, while the resource allocation subcomponent provides information about the use of resources to the processing module.

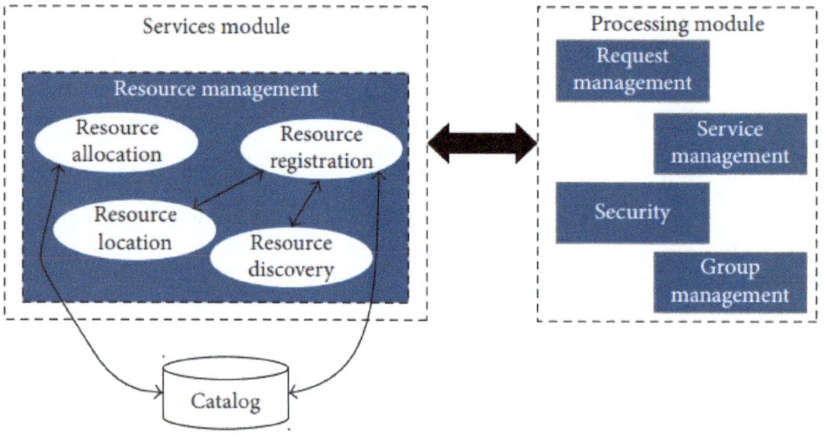

Figure 3: Components of resource management module.

Information about resources is locally stored and available to all local applications that use the middleware services. Also, this information can be available to other nodes, considering their context and permissions. The control access is maintained by security module and is based on context group formation.

Mobility Management

This component is particularly important, since mobile nodes can move and change their geographical positions unpredictably, affecting the performance of distributed applications. Besides nodes mobility, this service must consider the applications mobility, which can migrate from a node to another. To provide an effective service to applications, it contains three subcomponents, as depicted in Figure 4: location management, transfer management, and disconnection management.

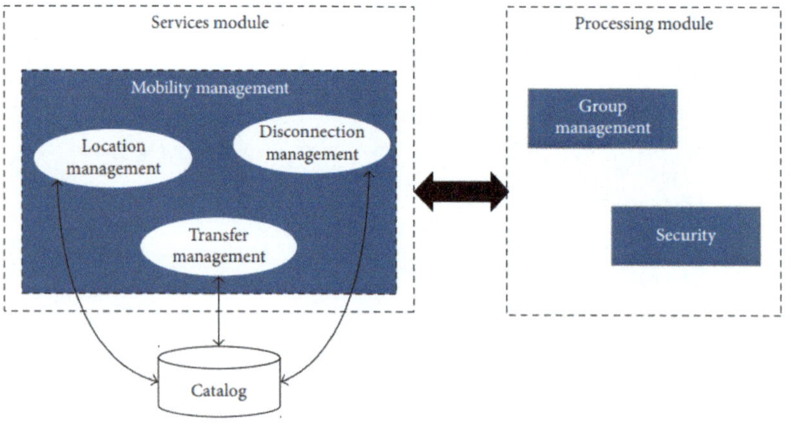

Figure 4: Components of mobility management module.

Location management must provide information about nodes physical location to applications. Thus, it is assumed that members of a group keep their location up-to-date in this group. Transfer management must allow mobile applications to keep the connection during a migration. It aims to mitigate the delay of applications transfers and to eliminate applications losses resulting from the migration. Finally, disconnection management must provide information about the reachability or disconnections of nodes that provide services through SEMAN.

Distributed Storage

This component allows nodes to store their information in a distributed, secure, dynamic, and self-organized way. It does not depend on any specific node availability and must be highly resistant to malicious attacks. Its main objective is to distribute context information to nodes of a group related to this context. This context information is fragmented into the network, and the absence of some nodes should not affect the stored data retrieval.

It is composed of four subcomponents, illustrated in Figure 5: data distribution, data retrieve, replica management, and data exclusion. All these components have a relationship with security and group management modules.

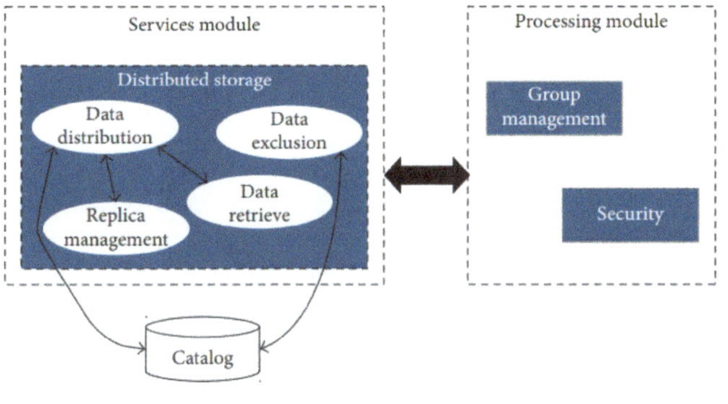

Figure 5: Components of distributed storage component.

Data distribution is responsible for disseminating information to remote nodes. Data retrieve handles the access requests and locates remote data. Replica management is responsible for keeping enough active replicas to ensure the information availability and the data consistency. Exclusion data guarantees that when requested, data will be excluded from all remote nodes in which it is stored.

Processing Module

Processing module is responsible for keeping the central operation of SEMAN. It is composed of requests management and services and components management.

Requests Management

This component is responsible for keeping a registration of all services requests made to the middleware. It keeps the registration of both pending and attended requests.

An application is able to use, simultaneously, one or more services provided by the middleware. Due to the dynamic characteristics of MANETs, applications may not be aware of which services are being provided in a given time or which nodes are hosting these services. Figure 6 depicts how a service request is operated by SEMAN. Upon receiving a request, the request management component gets the security parameters with the security module. Then, it must check the availability of the requested service with the resource management component. If the service is provided by the middleware, it stores the information about the request into the catalog, performs the required communications with other components, and sends the request to the corresponding nodes.

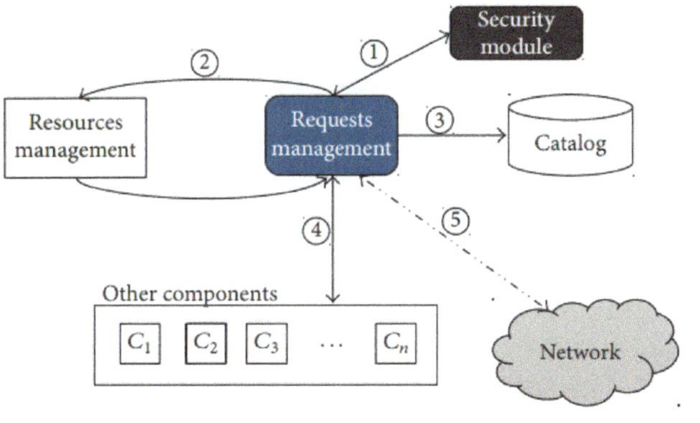

Figure 6: Services requests.

As services may be provided by more than one node, SEMAN might(1)request the service to all nodes that provide it, increasing the service availability and reducing the reply time;(2)distribute the requests among nodes that provide it, making a load balance; or(3)choose the more reliable node based on previous experiences.

During the service provisioning, the middleware may provide mechanisms to prevent malicious attacks. It must authenticate and authorize applications. Also, all messages exchanged with the middleware must be ciphered, to prevent eavesdropping.

Services and Components Management

This component has a simple but essential function to the middleware operation. It is responsible for keeping a registration of all services and components provided by SEMAN. When a user wants to make a service available, through the middleware, this services must be previously registered. All relevant information of the new service, as security policies and context, must be stored into catalog. Then, other nodes can be informed about the availability of the new service.

This component must provide primitives to the registration of new services, as well the query of provided services. Similarly, for each registered component, it is necessary to store information about access strategies and services requirements.

Conclusion

This section presented an overview of SEMAN, its modules, and main characteristics. All next section will detail the security operations and module and how they will provide security to the middleware applications.

SECURITY MODULE

This module is the central point of SEMAN. Its components, as depicted in Figure 7, include key management, trust management, and group management. These components operate with cryptographic operations and security policies components, which provide basic security primitives to the module.

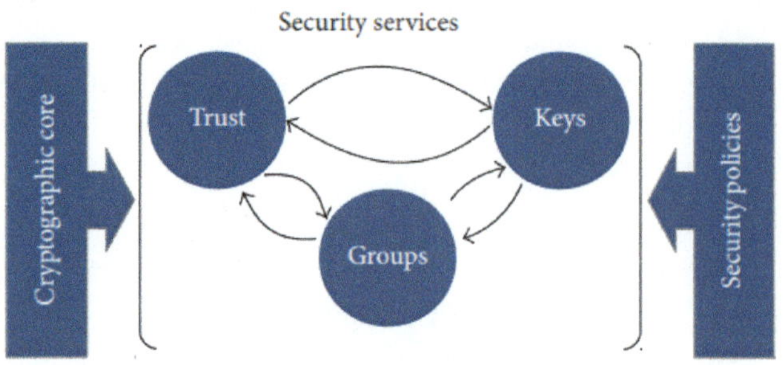

Figure 7: Security module diagram.

Security services use a context-based group approach. All management operations and decision making are based on information provided by other members of the context group. Thus, nodes cooperate among themselves to increase the reliability of available services. However, the use of all components is not mandatory.

Cryptographic Core

To ensure that messages are not prone to eavesdropping, all messages must be ciphered. Though any cryptographic mechanism can be used, identity-based ones seem to be more suitable for MANETs [9]. Symmetric schemes impose a high cost to manage pairwise secret keys, and when compared with traditional certificate-based asymmetric schemes, identity-based cryptography (IBC) presents at least three advantages [10]:(1)does not require certificates, mitigating certificates storage, distribution, and verification cost;(2)makes easy noninteractive key agreement, reducing communication and processing overhead;(3)removes the requirement of destination public keys authentications before message sending.

Another advantage to use IBC on MANETs is that they have a simple key management and a reduced storage cost, if compared with other methods. On IBCs, the identity of a user, as e-mail or IP, is used to derive the node public key. Thus, all nodes are able to disclose the public key of other nodes without data exchange. However, IBCs present a drawback. Private key is generated and available by an entity known as Private Key Generator (PKG). This characteristic imposes an implementation challenge, since PKG can be a single point of failure. To mitigate the impact of a central PKG, in this work the PKG is distributed over the network.

Cryptographic Operations

SEMAN considers the use of identity-based cryptography. Any IBC can be used, depending on middleware requirements. Without loss of generality, the Boneh and Franklin scheme is employed [11].

The main algorithms to perform cryptographic operations and to support the secure communication between nodes are composed of configuration and extraction and encryption and decryption. The former two are detailed on Section 4.4, which discusses the key management, since they are related to system initialization and key issuing.

The encryption and decryption algorithms are presented as follows. Let $k \in Z+$ be a security parameter from security module and G a generator of BDH parameter

(1) Encryption: to encrypt M using a public key of node i, follow the next steps:

A. CALCULATE $PK_i = H_1(N_i)$;

B. CHOOSE A RANDOM $r \in \mathbb{Z}_q^*$;

C. GENERATE THE ENCRYPTED TEXT $C = \langle rP, M \oplus H_2(g_i^r) \rangle$ IN WHICH $g_i = \hat{e}(N_i, PK_i) \in G_2^*$.

(2) Decryption: let $C = \langle U, V \rangle$ be the encrypted text using the public key of node i. To decrypt the message the private key SK_i is necessary. The following formula shows as text may be decrypted:

$$V \oplus H_2(\hat{e}(SK_i, U)) = M. \quad (1)$$

The proof of these algorithms can be found in [11].

Trust Management

Though cryptography may be used to ensure communication security, it does not provide information about the reliability of the nodes [12]. Further, many cryptographic mechanisms, such as key management [13, 14], rely on some degree of preestablished trust between nodes. However, trust in any kind of open network is very difficult to be valued and has received a lot of attention from the security community [15].

In a previous work [16, 17], TRUE was presented to evaluate the trust between pairwise communicating nodes. TRUE uses the concept of trust chains formed between nodes by direct monitoring and recommendations of physical neighbors. It supports applications in an autonomous and dynamic way, while keeping the ability to resist malicious attacks. In this approach, each node creates in a self-organized strategy a trust network based on context, to provide trust information represented by a direct graph $G_{tr} = (V_{tr}, E_{tr})$, in which vertexes V_{tr} are the nodes and edges E_{tr} are the trust relationships between them. The trust network, or trust graph, contains all trust information which a node has about other nodes in a context. This information, or evidences, is gathered via direct interaction or by recommendations, considering the system security policies. The trustworthiness of a node is always locally computed, with no kind of message exchange, based on the trust network. In the next subsection are briefly presented the operation of the TRUE and its procedures and an evaluation of the proposed service.

Building Context-Based Trust Networks

When joining the system, each node N_i creates its own trust network $G_{tr}^i = (V_{tr}^i, E_{tr}^i)$ in a self-organized way. Initially, nodes have knowledge only about nodes with which they have direct trust relations, and only such data is stored in the trust network. Then, in predetermined time intervals (ΔT_{ex}), nodes exchange trust evidences with their physical neighbors, propagating trust values through the network in an epidemic behavior [18, 19].

During trust information exchange, each node evaluates the

relevance of the received evidences by calculating the trustworthiness of the sender. Then, it decides whether it accepts or not such evidences, based on local policy rules. If it accepts the trust evidences, then it incorporates the received information on its context-based trust network. Otherwise, trust evidences are discarded.

Trust Evaluation

To evaluate the trust on node N_u, node N_x must either have a direct connection with node n_u in G^x_{tr} or it finds at least one trust chain (TC) from N_x to N_u in G^x_{tr}. Trust chains represent a transitive trust from N_x to N_u. The trust network graph G^x_{tr} is depicted in Figure 8. As node Nx can find several different trust chains between itself and Nu in G^x_{tr}, each chain is denoted as $TC^i_{(N_x,N_u)}$.

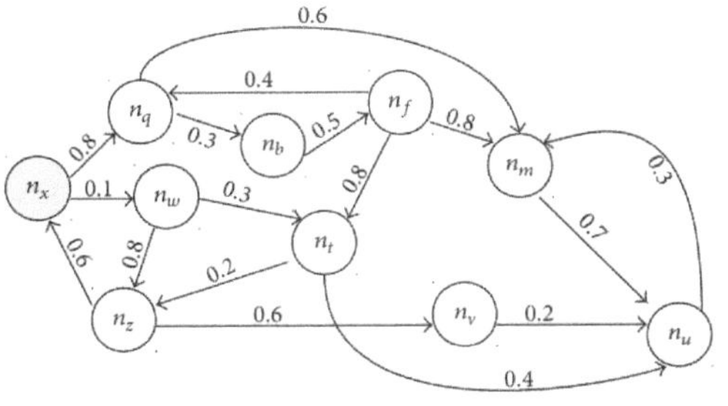

Figure 8: Example of trust chain G^x_{tr} from node n_x.

If N_x has a direct trust with N_u, only this value is considered on trust evaluation. Otherwise, it tries to find a trust path in G^x_{tr}. Upon finding a chain, node N_x must compute its trust. Consider N_1 to N_m as the m intermediary nodes in the ith trust chain, denoted as $TC^i_{(N_x,N_u)}$; (2) estimates the trustworthiness of $TC^i_{(N_x,N_u)}$.

$$TC^i_{(N_x,N_u)} = TV_{(N_x,N_1)} \times \prod_{i=1}^{m-1} TV_{(N_j,N_{j+1})} \times TV_{(N_m,N_u)}. \quad (2)$$

Returning to Figure 8, there are several chains between n_x and n_u, for example,

(1) chain $(N_x \to N_q \to N_m \to N_u)$, trust chain value $TC^1_{(N_x,N_u)} = 0.8 \times 0.6 \times 0.7 = 0.336$;

(2) chain $(N_x \to N_q \to N_b \to N_f \to N_m \to N_u)$, trust chain value $TC^2_{(N_x,N_u)} = 0.8 \times 0.3 \times 0.5 \times 0.8 \times 0.7 =$ 0.067.

Furthermore, nodes can use a threshold value for each edge of the trust chain (β value). If at least one edge of the trust chain has a trust value below this threshold, the chain is discarded. After calculating the trust value for all chains, the trust value $TV_{(N_x,N_u)}$ can be calculated applying a weighted mean as follows:

$$TV_{(N_x,N_u)} = \frac{\sum_{i=1}^{k} \left(TC^i_{(N_x,N_u)} \times \left(1/\left|TC^i_{(N_x,N_u)}\right|\right)\right)}{\sum_{i=1}^{k} \left(1/\left|TC^i_{(N_x,N_u)}\right|\right)}. \quad (3)$$

The weighted mean reduces the impact of transitivity in trust chains. In fact, the greater the chain, the less reliable it is. Thus, this method aims to privilege small chains, following a social perspective.

Key Management

SEMAN employs identity-based cryptography (IBC) [20] to perform its cryptographic operations, which requires an entity acting as a Private Key Generator (PKG). As the PKG knows the master private key, it is able to decrypt or sign messages on behalf of any client, without any active attack and without being detected. This problem is known as key escrow. These issues have been considered the main drawback that leads to the low adoption of IBC outside closed environments [21]. Boneh and Franklin suggested distributing the PKG to handle these problems using secret sharing schemes (n, t), in which n nodes form a distributed PKG (D-PKG) and only a subset of t+1 nodes is able to compute the master private key [11].

Several identity-based key management schemes have been designed for MANETs and most of them consider the distribution of the PKG [9]. However, proposed schemes do not consider all characteristics of these networks.

In a previous work [22], the Identity-based Fully Self Organized (*i*FUSO) key management service was presented, which can be integrated with SEMAN. The *i*FUSO considers an asynchronous network composed of n nodes, represented by N_1, N_2,...,N_n, in which malicious nodes can compromise at most t nodes and t<n. It considers that only trusted nodes participate in the system initialization. Nodes which initialize the system are called founding nodes, denoted by N_F.

These nodes form the distributed PKG (D-PKG) in a fully distributed way. No node knows the master private key, since it is distributed in t-over-n threshold scheme. Also, to adapt to the dynamism of the network, *i*FUSO allows nodes to join or leave the D-PKG.

To prevent the system from cryptanalysis attacks, the iFUSO provides a way to update public and private keys of nodes, similar to [23, 24]. The key update may occur either periodically according to a predetermined interval, or reactively when the number of revoked nodes reaches a threshold value. Nodes are able to update their public keys autonomously and their private key by requesting to the D-PKG. Further, the FUSO supports both implicit and explicit revocations.

Initialization

The *i*FUSO must be initialized by a set of m founding nodes (NF), which must be able to securely exchange information to initialize the system. As the first step of the initialization, nodes must determine.

(1) the system size n and the security threshold t;

(2) p, q: two large prime numbers, in which q divides (p–1);

(3) G_1: a cyclic additive group with order p;

(4) a generator $g \in G_1$;

(5) G_2: a cyclic multiplicative group with order p;

(6) the pairing type making sure that there exists a bilinear paring $e : G_1 \times G_1 \to G_2$ of the chosen type;

(7) $G = \langle e, G_1, G_2 \rangle$.

This step can be performed jointly by nodes which are initializing the group, or proposed by one node to the others.

To initialize the system, founding nodes set up the DPKG, generating the master public key and its corresponding master private key.The D-PKG is built in a distribute t-over-n way among the n founding nodes.

New Members Joining the D-PKG

G. In a MANET it is very important for a D-PKG to be highly dynamic and decentralized, and new nodes must be able to join the distributed PKG at any time. Thus, these nodes must receive a share of MSK, computed by at least t members of the D-PKG.

If a new node N_k wants to join the D-PKG, it must contact at least t members of the D-PKG to get the corresponding information from these nodes. The join of new nodes to the D-PKG must follow the following:

(1) node N_k selects t members of D-PKG, denoted by Ω;

(2) node N_k requests each node of Ω to be accepted as a member of the D-PKG;

(3) each node $Nj \in \Omega$ sends a piece of information $f(j,k) = S_j^k$ back to N_k;

(4) after receiving t replies, N_k can compute its polynomial share MSK_k using a Lagrange interpolation.

Issuing Node Private Key

The iFUSO is composed of a number of continuous, nonoverlapping key update phases, denoted by p_Δ, in which Δ represents the phase index. As in [23], each p_Δ is associated with a unique binary phase string denoted as str_Δ. For each N_i, its public key is represented by $PK_i = H_1(N_i)$ while the corresponding private key is represented by $SK_i = (PK_i)^{MSK}$. Recalling that in the iFUSO no node knows MSK, which is generated and stored in a fully distributed way. To retrieve its private key SK_i, node N_i must request the D-PKG for it and to wait for at leasttreplies. Thus, the following steps must be executed:

(1) N_i must select at least t nodes from the D-PKG. This set of nodes is denoted by Ψ. To minimize the requesting time, the Ψ has all nodes of the D-PKG;

(2) N_i requests its share of SKi to each node in Ψ;

(3) each node $N_j \in \Psi$ sends back to N_i a share of the private key $\sigma_i^j = (PK_i)^{MSK_j}$;

(4) upon receiving at least t replies, N_i computes its private key SK_i as

$$SK_i = \prod_{k \in \Psi} (\sigma_i^k)^{\lambda_k}, \tag{4}$$

in which $\lambda_k = \prod_{k \in \Psi}(k/(k-i))$ are appropriate Lagrange coefficients.

Key Renewing

To prevent attacks against the distributed PKG and potential threats resulting from compromised keys, a technique similar to the one proposed in [23], known as key update or key renewing, is employed. Security solutions based on key update are common practices on MANETs [25–27]. In the iFUSO, a new key update phase p_{i+1} starts after a predetermined time threshold. As all nodes must update their keys, if the members of the distributed PKG do not update the key of a given node N_a, it is (implicitly) considered revoked.

Each node Na can autonomously update its public key $PK_{a,p_i} = (H_1(N_a), H_1(str_i))$, in which $str_i = str_{i-1} + 1$. On the other hand, generating the phase private key involves at least t members of the D-PKG. A given node N_z, member of the D-PKG, sends a request to at least $t-1$ other members of the D-PKG.

Key Revocation

The iFUSO also provides techniques to verify if the public key of a node is revoked. Key revocations must be handled within the system, as nodes must be able to immediately verify the status of a public key [28]. Almost all key management schemes for MANETs consider the key revocation based on expiration time [29]. However, this is not sufficient since nodes must be able to revoke keys before expiration, as consequence of a compromise key or malicious behavior.

Thus, iFUSO supports both implicit and explicit revocations. If any node is not allowed to recover the common private key during a given phase p_i, then it is neither able to encrypt nor able to decrypt any information during this phase and is considered implicitly revoked.

On the other hand, the explicit revocation of the iFUSO is based on a list of revoked nodes stored by nodes themselves. Upon detecting the misbehavior of node N_a, node N_b generates a signed accusation message against N_a, which must be sent to the D-PKG. To avoid the interception of the accusation message, it is sent via broadcast encryption. This technique, besides decreasing the communication cost of revocation, increases the security since the malicious nodes are not able to read the accusation message.

Upon receiving an accusation message against N_a from N_b, a member of the D-PKG, will drop it if N_b has been previously revoked. Otherwise, it saves the accusation message. To prevent false accusations against legitimate nodes, a node N_a is diagnosed as compromised just when the accusations against it reach a revocation threshold γ in a predetermined time window. The value of γ defines the trade-off between the false accusations tolerance and the compromise detectability. Once the revocation threshold is reached, a key revocation against node N_a is generated and published.

Group Management

This section presents how the group management must be carried out to support the activities of SEMAN. It this paper, a group is a set of nodes sharing common interests and willing to cooperate on activities related to this interest. This "common interest" is also called context. Context information must be frequently updated and made available to other nodes, to allow the efficient organization of groups [30].

Due to several varieties of services provided by a middleware, many kind of distinct groups may be formed, with different mobility pattern, lifetime, organization strategies, internal politics, and joining rules characteristics. However, independent of group characteristics, system must provide resources management to allow the creation and update of existing groups and their profiles.

To support several kinds of applications, with strong and light security restrictions, two group management techniques are used: yellow pages and closed groups. Yellow pages groups, or open groups, provide primitives allowing nodes to freely form groups and to avail services related to its context. As these groups are open, they do not consider the trustworthiness of their members. Thus, these groups are indicated to services that require a lower trust level or when applications themselves are responsible for this task.

Closed groups use trust management information at their formation. Thus, all services provided by members of a closed context group obey the preestablished security requirements. Also, both internal and external group secure communication are allowed.

Storage Information about Existing Groups

In SEMAN, context groups are considered services available in the network. Information about the existence of groups and their main features must be available to nodes that want to participate in these groups or to enjoy services provided by them. To this end, it is important that the middleware provides ways to manage this information and make it available during its operations. Many architectures were proposed to organize the service provisioning on MANETs. An initial study about these architectures can be found in [31]. Solutions can be classified into with directories and without directories.

In the first approach, information about groups is stored in a directory which can be centralized or distributed. Nodes which store information about directories are called server nodes. Every time a node wants to provide a data, it finds out some server node and requests the storage of this data. On the other hand, a node that wants to use this data needs only to contact a server node and gets a list of nodes which are providing it.

In the second approach, information about groups is not stored in a directory and must be propagated or requested when needed. Thus, when a node wants to provide a service in the network, it diffuses this information, in order to reach the higher number of nodes. It can be employed by global or controlled flooding techniques. When a node wants to use a service and it does not have local information about this service, it requests such an information in the network, via global or controlled flooding.

There is not a consensus about which strategy is more suitable for MANETs. Group discovery is considered good when presenting a high availability, keeping a low communication cost and small delays. Thus, if the network has just few service requirements, a strategy without directories with on demand queries would be more suitable. On the other hand, a network with many services but with few queries would generate unnecessary communications to keep information about these services.

Any one of these architectures may be used on SEMAN. In this work, the use of a fully distributed directories architecture is considered. When a new group is created, its information is disseminated in the network. All nodes locally store information about groups. Thus, every time a node needs information about a group, it may get it locally, without delays or additional costs.

Yellow Pages

The first group formation strategy in the SEMAN is called yellow pages. This technique, based in the traditional yellow pages, works as a directory of services, fully open and dynamic. Group formation is directly related to some kind of provided service. When a node wants to provide a service, it informs the middleware, which propagates this information to all other nodes, to make them aware of the new service.

When another node wants to use a service, it requests to the middleware a list of nodes which are providing the service. Based on this list, the node may request or not the service considering information from the trust management module.

This kind of approach is important in providing services without a high level of security. Any node can freely participate in a group and provide a given service. Client applications can, therefore, determinate the trust level they want in a service. Thus, the middleware, based on information provided by the trust management module can select the more trustworthy nodes which are providing the service.

Formation of an Open Group. Before initiating a group, a node needs to certify that there is no other group with the same characteristics of the new one. To this, it queries its local directory. If the group already exists, the node joins this group (Section 4.5.2). Otherwise, it creates the new group.

When a node wants to form a new context group, it defines all main features of this group, as identifier, mobility pattern, context information, service provided, and initial nodes. Other information may be included to make the group management easier. Then, it disseminates this information through the network, as discussed in Section 4.5.1.

Joining and Leaving an Open Group. When a node wants to participate in an open group G_α, it needs to create a message informing that it is providing the same services as described in the group G_α profile. Then, it must disseminate this information through the network, in order that all nodes be aware that it is providing such services. Note that there is no strategy to block the participation of nodes on open groups. Any node may send a message informing that it is participating in this group.

Similarly, when a node wants to leave a group, it just creates a message informing that it is leaving the group and disseminates this information through the network. However, as this message is not mandatory, or nodes may leave unpredictably and involuntary the network, is necessary some technique are necessary to ensure the consistency of nodes participating in a group. Thus, the node which has created the group, or the older one, periodically performs queries to members, checking their availability. So, at the end of a cycle, a list of available nodes is disseminated into network. It is important that checking interval be not so small in order to prevent a high communication overhead.

Using Secure Services of Open Groups. Open groups do not provide native secure communication methods between members or to service requests. As nodes are able to freely join groups, the group key establishment is difficult. But this does not block that services provided by open groups require ciphered and signed message requests.

When a node wants to request any service to members of an open group, it makes a request directly to these nodes, by using either unicast or multicast messages. If it wants to use ciphered messages, it may use the security primitives provided by the middleware for communication between nodes, supported by cryptographic operations and key management components.

Closed Groups

While some services may be supported by an open group management scheme, other services require a more controlled management. In this case, the middleware provides a dynamic closed group management service to applications. These groups are formed based on applications context, interest, and security requirements.

An example of closed groups is the key management described in Section 4.4 and in [22], which requires a high trustworthy and restrict service. This section describes the closed group management operations, as group formation, new members joining, and leaving.

Closed Group Formation. As previously assumed, groups are formed based on applications context. Each node is able to autonomously promote the formation of a group without a central entity or a group manager. During the group formation, the creator node must only specify the group profile and security requirements.

A group may be composed of a set of nodes, with a unique assumption: these nodes must be able to securely exchange information to initialize the group. Then, to start a group nodes must determinate

(1) group size n and the security threshold t;

(2) p and q: two large prime numbers, in which q divides $(p - 1)$;

(3) G_1: a cyclic additive group of order p;

(4) generator $g \in G_1$;

(5) G_2: a cyclic multiplicative group of order p;

(6) the paring type to ensure that exists a bilinear paring $e : G_1 \times G_1 \rightarrow G_2$ to the choose paring;

(7) $G = \langle e, G_1, G_2 \rangle$.

These values must be defined by all nodes through an agreement approach or may be proposed by a founder node to the other ones. After that, each founder node must have the following public elements:

(1) prime numbers p and q;

(2) generator g and cyclic additive group G_1;

(3) cyclic multiplicative group G_2;

(4) $\mathbb{Z}_q^*$: an elliptic field with order q;

(5) $H_1(x)$: a hash function in which $H_1(x) = \{0,1\}^* \rightarrow \mathbb{G}_1^*$;

(6) $H_2(x)$: a hash function in which $H_2(x) = \mathbb{G}_2 \rightarrow \mathbb{Z}_p^*$.

To initialize the group, nodes must generate a public identification of this group and a signature. This signature is distributed between group members by using a threshold cryptographic scheme (m, t) among the m founder nodes, as follows:

(1) Each node N_i chooses a bivariate symmetric polynomial function $f(x, y)$ over $\mathbb{Z}_q^*$ in which the two variables x and y must be at most order t. The polynomial function is described as

$$f_i(x, y) = \sum_{k=0}^{t} \sum_{j=0}^{t} a_{k,j}^i x^k y^j, \tag{5}$$

in which $a_{k,j}^i \in \mathbb{Z}_q^*, a_{k,j}^i = a_{j,k}^i$, and $a_{0,0}^i = z_i$.

(2) Each N_i computes $f_l^i(x)$ for all N_l founder nodes as

$$f_l^i(x) = f_i(x, l) = \sum_{k=0}^{t} \sum_{j=0}^{t} a_{k,j}^i x^k l^j. \tag{6}$$

Then, N_i securely sends $f_l^i(x)$ to N_l.

(3) Each node N_i computes its share of the signature Sign_i:

$$\text{Sign}_i = f_i(x) = \sum_{j=1}^{n} f_i^j(x) = \sum_{j=1}^{n} f_j(x, i) = f(x, i). \tag{7}$$

(4) Signature Sign is not known by any node but is defined as

$$\text{Sign} = \sum_{N_i \in m} \text{Sign}_i \bmod q. \tag{8}$$

Each node N_i, after computing its share Sign , publishes g^{Sign_i}. When nodes receive t shares, they are able to compute the group identity as $\text{ID} = \sum_{i=1}^{t} g^{\text{Sign}_i}$. Then, the group identity ID can be published to all other nodes.

After group formation, nodes which want to collaborate in a specific context or interest must search a group and request its participation in this group. As each group is set with its profile and security requirements, nodes themselves may decide whether available groups attend their own interests.

Joining. As describe in Section 4.5.3, each closed group has its profile and requirements. Thus, nodes themselves may decide on participating or not of a group. If a node N_x wants to join a group G_α it must request to G_α members the participation authorization. To be able to join G_α, N_x needs the approval of at least t members. The following steps must be performed:

(1) node N_x chooses t nodes of group G_α, denoted by Ω;

(2) node N_x requests each node of Ω to be accepted as member of group G_α;

(3) each node $N_j \in \Omega$ sends an information share $f(j, k)$ back to node N_k;

(4) upon receiving t replies, N_x may compute its polynomial share Sign_x by using Lagrange interpolation:

$$\text{Sign}_k = S_k(x) = \sum_{j=1}^{t} \lambda_j S_j^k = \sum_{j=1}^{t} \lambda_j f(j, k) = f(x, k). \tag{9}$$

After computing Sign_x, N_x is able to participate in all group operations.

Members Exclusion. When a node does not attend anymore the security or trust requirement of a group, it must have its participation revoked. To this, signed accusation messages are employed with a list of revoked associations. When a given node N_x has a number of accusations higher than a threshold γ, it has its association revoked. The value of γ is a group parameter, defined on its creation profile.

When a node N_α, based on information provided by trust management, believes that N_x does not satisfy anymore the group requirements, it issues a signed accusation message and sends it to all other group members. To thwart excluded nodes from receiving this message, the signed accusation message must be unknown by them. Thus, a variant of the identity-based broadcast encryption proposed on [32] is used.

Let E be the set of excluded nodes; then node N_a generates the parameters for the broadcast encryption:

(1) $\forall i \in \mathrm{N} \setminus \mathrm{E}$ computes $\mathrm{PK}_i = H_1(N_i)$;

(2) it randomly selects $r \in \mathbb{Z}_P^*$ and $\forall i \in \mathrm{N} \setminus \mathrm{E}$ computes $s_i = H_2(\hat{e}(\mathrm{PK}_i^r, \mathrm{MPK}))$;

(3) it randomly selects $k \in \mathbb{Z}_P^*$ and computes a message encrypting key $K = \hat{e}(g, g)^k$;

(4) it randomly selects $\alpha \in \mathbb{Z}_P^*$;

(5) it computes $\mathrm{Hdr} = (C_1, C_2, C_3)$ in which

$$C_1 = g^r;$$
$$C_2 = (g^\alpha)^k;$$
$$C_3 = \left\{c_i = \left(g^{1-1/\alpha}\right)^{1/s_i}\right\}_{N_i \in \mathcal{N} \setminus \mathcal{E}}. \tag{10}$$

After that, N_a has the key K and Hdr and uses K to encrypt the accusation message K, generating C_K. Finally, N_z broadcasts the ciphered message (Hdr, C_K).

When a nonrevoked node N_b receives this message, it is able to retrieve the accusation message K encapsulated in the header Hdr, using its private key SK_b, as follows:

(1) computes $s_i = H_2(\hat{e}(\mathrm{SK}_b, C_1))$;

(2) retrieves c_i from C_3 and computes

$$\hat{e}\left(C_2^{-1}, c_i^{s_i}\right) \times \hat{e}\left(g, C_2\right)$$
$$= \hat{e}\left(\left((g^\alpha)^k\right)^{-1}, \left(\left(g^{1-1/\alpha}\right)^{1/s_i}\right)^{s_i}\right) \times \hat{e}g, (g^\alpha)^k$$
$$= \hat{e}\left(g, g\right)^{-k(\alpha-1)} \times \hat{e}\left(g, g\right)^{k\alpha} = K. \tag{11}$$

With K, node N_b is able to decrypt the encrypted message C_K, extracting the accusation message K. Upon receiving γ accusations, each node creates an association revocation register and stores it locally in a revoked associations list. This list may be made publicly available to all nodes, in order that external member be aware that N_x is no longer authorized to provide service in name of the group.

Conclusion

This section presented the security module and its components. Cryptographic operations, trust management, group management, and key management components were detailed. Also, how these components will ensure security to the middleware was explained.

SECURE GROUP COMMUNICATION

To allow secure group communication, the use of a group key agreement protocol is proposed. This kind of protocol allows that a group of users exchange information over an insecure and public communication channel and agree on a secret key to be used to derive a session key. Then, the session key can be used to ensure requirements as authentication, confidentiality, and integrity.

The group key agreement approach is attractive to dynamic networks since it does not require the presence of a central controller or a leader. In this case, all users generate the key session. Thus, no node is able to control or to predict the session key. This kind of approach has been widely employed in distributed and collaborative applications, as file sharing, distributed computing, and audio and video conferences, among others.

Several proposals to session group key establishment can be found in the literature [33–35]. Any scheme that makes use of identity-based approach may be easily employed in the SEMAN. Without the loss of generality, the scheme proposed by Zhang et al. in [35] is assumed. An advantage of this scheme is that it allows outside group nodes to send ciphered messages to group members. This makes the secure service request to closed groups easier.

In the key agreement, members of a group G_α issue signed messages. The union of all signed messages issued by them form a group encryption key, called GEK_α, which may be public. However, only members of the group are able to derive the group decryption key GDK_α. The next subsections present the key agreement operations and the group encryption and decryption key generation.

Agreement

A given node N_i, with the private key SK_i and member of group G_α, must perform the following steps to carry out the key agreement:

(1) to choose a random number $\eta_i \in \mathbb{Z}_q^*$;

(2) to compute $r_i = g^{\eta_i}$;

(3) to choose a random number $k \in \mathbb{Z}_q^*$;

(4) to compute $g_1 = g^k$;

(5) for all $1 \le j \le n$, to compute $f_j = H_2(N_j)$, in which $H_2(x)$ is a hash function;

(6) for all $1 \le j \le n$, to compute $z_{i,j} = \mathrm{SK}_i f_j^{\eta_i}$;

(7) to publish $\sigma_i = (r_i, \varrho_i, \{z_{i,j}\}_{j \in \{1,\ldots,n\}, j \ne i})$

In this case, ϱ_i is the identity-based signature on value r_i. Element $z_{i,j} = \mathrm{SK}_i f_j^{\eta_i}$ is not published, but kept secret by node n_i.

Encryption Key Generation and Use

To get a group encryption key, a node firstly checks the n tuple of signature message $(r_1, \varrho_1), \ldots, (r_n, \varrho_n)$. If all signatures are valid, then it computes

$$w = \prod_{i=1}^{n} r_i,$$
$$Q = \hat{e}\left(\prod_{i=1}^{n} H_1(N_i), g_1\right). \tag{12}$$

Then, it sets the group encryption key as $\mathrm{GEK} = (w, Q)$. To encrypt a message M, any node, member or not of the group, generates a ciphered text as follows:

(1) selects $\rho \in \mathbb{Z}_q^*$;

(2) computes $c_1 = g^\rho$, $c_2 = w^\rho$, and $c_3 = M \oplus H_3(Q^\rho)$;

(3) generates the ciphered text $c = (c_1, c_2, c_3)$.

After the ciphered text c generation, it can be sent through the network and only members of destination group are able to decrypt the transmitted message.

Decryption Key Generation and Use

Each node N_i checks the n tuples of signed messages $(r_1, \varrho_1), \ldots, (r_n, \varrho_n)$. If all signatures are valid, node N_i computes $\mathrm{GDK} = \prod_{j=1}^{n} z_{j,i}$ and makes the following verification:

$$\hat{e}(\mathrm{GDK}_i, g) \stackrel{?}{=} \hat{e}(f_i, w) \cdot Q. \tag{13}$$

If the equation is correct, node N_i accepts the key GDK as decryption group key. Otherwise, it aborts the procedure.

When a node Ni, member of group, receives a ciphered message $c = (c_1, c_2, c_3)$, it uses the decryption key GDK as

$$M = c_3 \oplus H_3\left(\hat{e}(\mathrm{GDK}, c_1)\hat{e}\left(f_i^{-1}, c_2\right)\right) \tag{14}$$

Conclusion

This section presented how to provide a secure group communication through SEMAN. How nodes may use cryptographic services to make an agreement and provide secure group communication to applications was discussed.

COMPONENTS INTEGRATION IN DIFFERENT SCENARIOS

Policy management component is responsible for supporting the security module integrating the trust, key, and group management components. Thus, the development of strategies is fundamental to provide security in several scenarios in which applications may be provided by SEMAN.

This section discusses some cases, which show how the middleware may be used in different scenarios. Security parameters described to each scenario are configured on the security policy component, part of the security module. It is important to point out that several scenarios can be found in a unique network. Some applications may be better suitable to open scenarios, while other ones require a more rigorous security control. SEMAN allows the configuration of these different scenarios, since applications and nodes are organized into context, with profiles and security parameter set according to provided services.

Three scenarios are presented:

(i) open: indicated to applications which do not require a high security control;

(ii) partially restrict: indicated to applications which require an intermediary security support but do not require a rigid control on their operations;

(iii) restrict: indicated to applications which require a high security level on their operations.

To each presented scenario, distinct security policies are indicated. Table 1 illustrates how security components may be set to proposed scenarios. However, these scenarios parameters and politics are not static, and new environments and configurations may be proposed and configured by middleware users.

Table 1: Security policies for distinct scenarios

	Trust	Key	Groups
Restrict	Block evidence exchanges with nonreliable nodes	Allow the service to be provided to each distinct group t value greater than $n/2$	Prioritize closed group creation Trust restriction to group joining
Partially restrict	Trust values of α and β between 0.4 and 0.6	A unique system to all the middleware t value greater than $n/2$	Prioritize closed group creation Allow the service providing in closed groups
Open	Trust values of α and β less than 0.4	A unique system to all the middleware Small t value Great interval between updates	Most part of provided services in open groups

Next subsections detail these scenarios and how security components may be integrated in the service provisioning to applications. Each scenario discusses how SEMAN can ensure the desired security and the communication overhead imposed by it. However, the measurement of this kind of overhead is a complex task, since these values depend on several factors: group size, update interval, threshold values, and others. Then, a more realist approximation of the overhead is a future work.

Open Scenarios

A first scenario that SEMAN may be employed is an open environment, which requires a less rigorous security control. Several applications may provide services in an open scenario. An example is the data and file distributed storage service. In this case, users may share, for a while, data or files that do not require a high level of confidentiality and availability, as video or audio files.

(1) Trust management: adopting TRUE, values of α and β may be small, less than 0.4. Then, middleware will consider more nodes reliable on evaluated context. As a consequence, more nodes will be considered reliable to provide services in this context.

(2) Key management: using *i*FUSO, values of t may also be small, less than $m/2$, in which m is the members of D-PKG. Also, update interval may be high. Then, system overhead is reduced while the service is offered to users considering the defined parameters.

(3) Group management: in open scenarios, services may be provided in open groups, and users themselves can query the trust management component to decide by the use or not of the offered services.

Note that, in this scenario, a unique great group may be used to the key management of the entire middleware. Then, all applications which need cryptographic services use the same service.

To all other services provided in the network, the trust management may provide trust information on the context of these services. For example, a resource localization service have a different context than a distributed storage. Nodes which provide these services may be organized into open groups, but their users may use trust values to choose the best servers to their requirements.

Figure 9 illustrates a possible configuration of the security module to satisfy applications in an open scenario. In this case, the "data sharing" application requests services to the middleware. Services and processing modules reply application requests and, if necessary, make queries to the security module. In this scenario, trust management provide two contexts: "sharing" and "KeyManagement" Both have α and β values lower than 0.4.

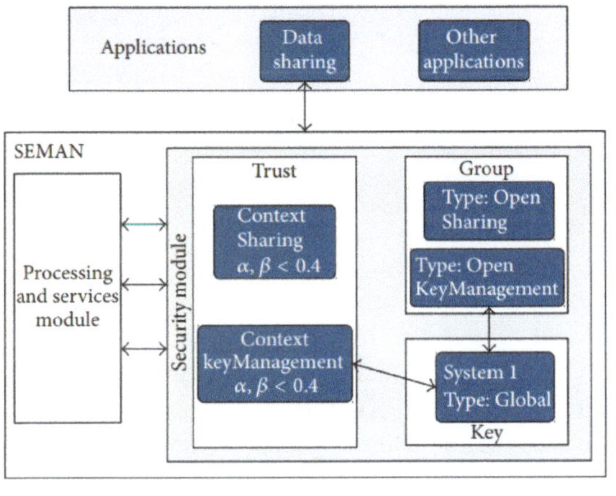

Figure 9: Open scenario.

The context KeyManagement is queried by the key management system for key issuing, revocation, and update. Though trust management values will be considered in the key issuing, threshold values to the acceptance are small. Thus, any node may request participation as a D-PKG member, making the group open, but the private master key is issued only if this node satisfies a minimal trust requirements.

The other context is called Sharing and may be queried by applications on the acceptance or not of services provided by members of an open group named "Sharing." Note that any node is able to participate in this group. If necessary, group members or client applications may query the global key management system to check the identity authenticity of any group member.

With these configurations, middleware provides just some security guarantees to applications. Applications which perform queries to trust management may receive unreliable information, since system is susceptible to false accusation attacks. The key management is vulnerable to impersonation attacks, since an attacker needs to compromise a small number of D-PKG members to be accepted and to receive its own private key or even to be a D-PKG member.

Partially Restrict Scenarios

A second scenario is a partially restrict scenario, in which an intermediary security control is necessary. A service example which can be classified as partially restrict is the resource localization. In this case, it is important to provide guarantees of nodes authenticity, but at same time it does not need to block any node to provide a service to applications.

In this case, security parameters and threshold values may be set with more restrictions than previous scenario. Hereafter, some suggestions are presented:

(1) trust management: using TRUE, α and β values may be between 0.5 and 0.7. Then, middleware will exchange information with nodes that have an intermediary trust evaluation in the context. As a consequence, the communication overhead will be smaller than previous scenario, while it keeps a higher control of transmitted information;

(2) key management: with *i*FUSO, t value for the master key sharing should be higher than $m/2$, to prevent network partitioning attacks. Further, key update intervals may not be large, to block unreliable nodes to be on the system for a long time;

(3) group management: in this scenario, some applications may be provided in closed groups, but the majority may be organized into open groups. Thus, even all nodes being able to join a group and to provide services in this context, client applications may use trust management information to select the best node to request a service.

Note that in this scenario, a unique group may be used to the middleware-wide key management. Thus, all applications which need cryptography use the same service. As on open scenarios, the trust management must have information of a context which will be queried by key management, for example key-management. For all other provided services, the trust management may provide trust information on their own context.

Figure 10 illustrates how SEMAN components may be integrated to satisfy security requirements on partially restrict scenarios. "Resource location" application requests services to the middleware, which are received by the services and processing modules. When necessary, some queries are made to the security module. Two contexts are envisaged: KeyManagement and Location. On both contexts, trust management α and β values are between 0.5 and 0.7.

As in open scenarios, KeyManagement context is queried by the key management for key issuing, revocation, and update. However, only nodes of the closed group named "KeyManagement" are accepted to be members of the DPKG. Thus, the participation of nodes as D-PKG members is more restrictive, making the system more reliable. Also, α and β parameters of the KeyManagement context may be increased, to ensure more security to key management and to client applications.

The other context is called Location and may be queried by application itself in the acceptance or not of services provided by members of group named "Location." As in the open groups, any node may be member of this group and, if necessary, client applications may query the global key management to check the identity authenticity of a node.

With these configurations the system should be protected against impersonation attacks. Also, higher α and β values make the propagation of false accusations against a node reputation more difficult. Thus, the middleware ensures, to users, the authenticity of nodes which are participating in these groups.

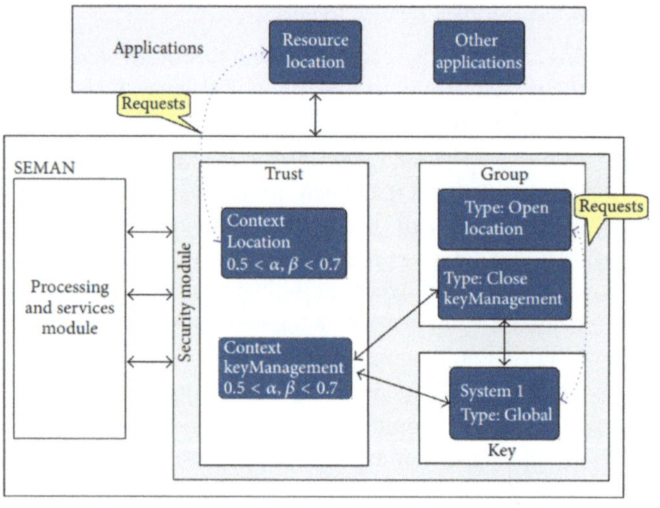

Figure 10: Partially restrict scenarios.

Restrict Scenarios

The third scenario is a restrict environment, in which a more rigorous security control is necessary. This context considers the applications which cannot be compromised in face of attacks. These applications perform, in general, essential tasks to users and, if affected by malicious attacks, may compromise the integrity of provided services. Examples are the e-commerce or financial transactions.These services may receive the guarantee from the middleware that they are protected against malicious attacks.

In this case, security parameters and threshold values must be set with many restrictions. The following are some suggestions:

(1) trust management: if TRUE is adopted, α and β values must be higher than 0.7. Then, middleware will exchange information only with reliable nodes in related context. As a consequence, less nodes will be able to join groups of this context;

(2) key management: with *i*FUSO, t values for master key sharing must be higher than $m/2$. Further, update phase interval cannot be high. Then, the system overhead is increased, but services provided will ensure security against malicious attacks;

(3) group management: in restrict scenarios, applications must be provided in closed groups, with a more restrictive control on group joining.

Note that for this kind of scenario, different key management group may be used, for each application. Thus, more restrictive applications may have their own contextrelated key management. This blocks malicious nodes, even the ones not participating in the group that is providing a service, to be a D-PKG member. On the other hand, a global key management scheme may be implemented to provide service to groups with less restrictive applications. For all other services, the trust management may provided trust information on the services context.

Figure 11 illustrates the integration of SEMAN components on restrict scenarios. E-commerce application requests services to middleware. Requests are received by the services and processing modules that if necessary query the security module. Two contexts are envisaged: DPKG-Transaction and Transaction. On both contexts, trust management has α and β values higher than 0.7

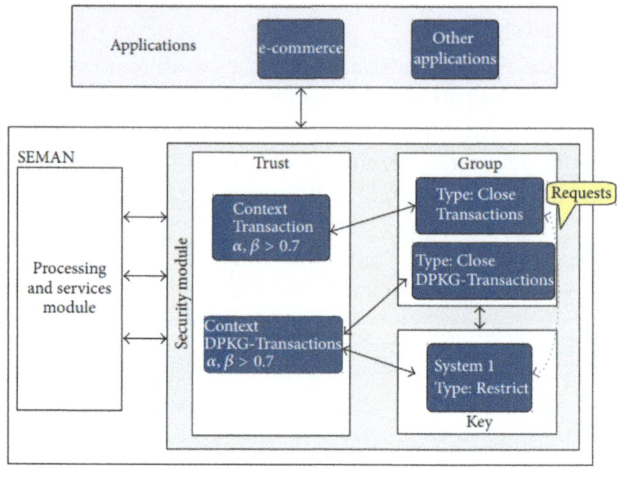

Figure 11: Restrict scenarios.

The DPKG-Transaction is queried by the key management of closed group "Transaction." To this, group management allows the formation of a closed group called "DPKGTransaction," which has only the nodes that satisfy the requirements to be a D-PKG member. These D-PKG members make queries to the closed group "Transactions" to check nodes reliability and issue private keys to them.

The other context is called Transactions and it is queried by members of closed group with same name, which are responsible for the acceptance or not of a new member, or by the exclusion of a current member. Unlike previous scenarios, to participate in a group, nodes need to satisfy the trust requirements defined by group policies, increasing the system security and protection against malicious attacks.

Hybrid Scenarios

Three distinct scenarios of security module configuration were presented. However, in practice, each application which is using the middleware services may present a different scenario. For example, at the same time, middleware may provide services to applications that require a high level of security and also to an open one. Thus, SEMAN security policies must be directed to applications and services contexts which use the security module.

A recommendation to the use of SEMAN in these scenarios is the setting of a global key management, which satisfies all services. Thus, the entire network is supported by a unique D-PKG and all users have a unique public/private key pair to use on all applications. Trust management must offer information about users in two contexts: key-management and key-management-dpkg.

Trust information about first context (key-management) is used by key management when D-PKG members perform users private key issuing, update, or revocation. In this case, users with trust value in this context less than a threshold (that must be high) will not have their keys issued or update by D-PKG members.

Trust information of the second context (key-management-dpkg) is used by D-PKG members on decisions about the acceptance or not of new D-PKG member. These restrictions must be higher than the key issuing restrictions. For example, a node can be authentic and has the right to have its private key issued by a D-PKG. However, it cannot be reliable enough to be member of D-PKG.

With a secure key management, middleware ensures the protection of cryptographic operations against malicious attacks and the authenticity of members. Thus, each application may be provided inside a context of closed or open groups, which requires a high level of reliability or allows that services to be provided by any node. Thus, each application will be protected against malicious actions depending of its own policies.

Conclusion

This section presented a study of some scenarios which SEMAN may be employed to satisfy applications requirements.

CONCLUSIONS AND FUTURE DIRECTIONS

This paper proposed secure context-based middleware, called SEMAN, which employs a group approach to support security making decisions. The middleware architecture and an overview of its operations were discussed. Also, how SEMAN services must be provided and how group approach may be applied to ensure the security were presented.

SEMAN has three modules: services, processing, and security. The first two are responsible for providing services and for requests management. Security module is responsible for ensuring the security to applications that use the services provided by SEMAN. This module is composed of trust, key, and group management components. All these components were detailed, focusing on how they can be used to ensure the security to applications.

Security module components are integrated through policies management which is responsible for security parameters of each provided service. Further, all activities are supported by identity-based cryptographic operations. The integration of these components was discussed in distinct scenarios, in which some configuration suggestions were presented to satisfy applications requirements.

SEMAN provides security against selfish, impersonation, Sybil, and byzantine attacks. But other attacks can be found on MANET and may affect the middleware efficacy. At the end, some scenarios in which SEMAN may be employed were presented. These scenarios are classified into open, partially restrict, and restrict. Table 2illustrates the expected overhead in each presented scenario. SEMAN does not impose a high communication overhead. Key management, for example, needs more messages exchanges during a group creation and update. However, key updates do not occur frequently.

Table 2: Expected communication overhead.

	Trust	Key	Groups
Restrict	Low	Low	High
Partially restrict	Medium	Low	Medium
Open	High	Very low	Low

Group management presents an overhead that depends on the way groups are organized. Closed groups have higher overhead than open ones. However, even closed groups have a higher communication cost only during group formation. Further, secure group communication allows multicast messages, decreasing the quantity of individual messages.

Trust management imposes a higher communication overhead when groups are open and, then, α and β values are smaller. However, even this higher quantity of messages is performed just among neighbor nodes, not affecting the entire network.Then, security module of SEMAN can be used to ensure the security requirements of application while not imposing a high communication overhead to network.

To increase the system reliability, new services can be integrated to SEMAN and may be performed in future work, as integrating with analysis tools of external environment, to help automatic and dynamic configuration of security policies; proposing the integration of SEMAN with other certificateless public key cryptography; implementing and evaluating the middleware in real scenarios; and designing an accounting scheme integrated with trust management to impede that denial of service attacks overhead the system with false control messages. Further, a study should be performed in order to reduce de requirements of exponential and pairing computations. Authors suggest the use of certificateless public key cryptography, or other alternative models, comparing their computational cost.

ACKNOWLEDGMENTS

This study is partially funded by CNPq, Grants 448004/2013-6.

REFERENCES

1. B. Wu, J. Chen, J. Wu, and M. Cardei, “A survey of attacks and countermeasures in mobile ad hoc networks,” in Wireless Network Security, Y. Xiao, X. S. Shen, and D.-Z. Du, Eds., Signals and Communication Technology, chapter 12, pp. 103–135, Springer, New York, NY, USA, 2007.
2. P. Papadimitratos and Z. J. Haas, “Securing mobile ad hoc networks,” in The Handbook of Ad Hoc Wireless Networks, chapter 21, pp. 457–481, CRC Press, Boca Raton, Fla, USA, 2005.
3. R. Shirey, RFC 2828: Internet Security Glossary, EUA, Marina del Rey, Calif, USA, 2000, http://www.ietf.org/rfc/rfc2828.txt.
4. E. da Silva and L. C. P. Albini, “Middleware proposals for mobile ad hoc networks,” Journal of Network and Computer Applications, vol. 43, pp. 103–120, 2014.
5. P. A. Bernstein, “Middleware: a model for distributed system services,” Communications of the ACM, vol. 39, no. 2, pp. 86–98, 1996.

6. J. Al-Jaroodi, I. Jawhar, A. Al-Dhaheri, F. Al-Abdouli, and N. Mohamed, "Security middleware approaches and issues for ubiquitous applications," Computers and Mathematics with Applications, vol. 60, no. 2, pp. 187–197, 2010.
7. S. Hadim, J. Al-Jaroodi, and N. Mohamed, "Trends in middleware for mobile ad hoc networks," Journal of Communications, vol. 1, no. 4, pp. 11–21, 2006.
8. I. Chlamtac, M. Conti, and J. J.-N. Liu, "Mobile ad hoc networking: imperatives and challenges," Ad Hoc Networks, vol. 1, no. 1, pp. 13–64, 2003.
9. E. da Silva, A. L. dos Santos, L. C. P. Albini, and M. N. Lima, "Identity-based key management in mobile ad hoc networks: techniques and applications," IEEE Wireless Communications, vol. 15, no. 5, pp. 46–52, 2008.
10. H.-Y. Chien and R.-Y. Lin, "Improved ID-based security framework for ad hoc network," Ad Hoc Networks, vol. 6, no. 1, pp. 47–60, 2008.
11. D. Boneh and M. Franklin, "Identity-based encryption from the weil pairing," in Advances in Cryptology—CRYPTO 2001, J. Kilian, Ed., vol. 2139 of Lecture Notes in Computer Science, pp. 213–229, Springer, London, UK, 2001.
12. X. Li, J. Slay, and S. Yu, "Evaluating trust in mobile ad hoc networks," in Proceedings of the Workshop of International Conference on Computational Intelligence and Security (CIS ‹05), Springer, Xi›an, China, 2005.
13. J. van der Merwe, D. Dawoud, and S. McDonald, "A survey on peer-to-peer key management for mobile ad hoc networks," ACM Computing Surveys, vol. 39, no. 1, article 1, Article ID 1216371, 2007.
14. M. Nogueira, G. Pujolle, E. Silva, A. Santos, and L. Albini, "Survivable keying for wireless ad hoc networks," in Proceedings of the IFIP/IEEE International Symposium on Integrated Network Management (IM ‹09), pp. 606–613, IEEE Communications Society, Long Island, NY, USA, June 2009.
15. M. Blaze, J. Feigenbaum, and J. Lacy, "Decentralized trust management," in Proceedings of the 17th IEEE Symposium on Security and Privacy (SP ‹96), pp. 164–173, Oakland, Calif, USA, May 1996.
16. M. Misaghi, E. da Silva, and L. C. P. Albini, "Distributed self-organized trust management for mobile ad hoc networks," in Networked Digital Technologies, R. Benlamri, Ed., vol. 293 of Communications in Computer and Information Science, pp. 506–518, Springer, 2012.
17. E. da Silva, M. Misaghi, and C. P. Luiz, "True: a trust evaluation service for mobile ad hoc networks resistant to malicious attacks," Journal of Digital Information Management, vol. 10, no. 4, pp. 262–271, 2012.
18. J. W. Mickens and B. D. Noble, "Modeling epidemic spreading in mobile environments," in Proceedings of the 4th ACM Workshop on Wireless Security (WiSe ‹05), pp. 77–86, ACM, Cologne, Germany, September 2005.
19. X. Zhang, G. Neglia, J. Kurose, and D. Towsley, "Performance modeling of epidemic routing," Computer Networks, vol. 51, no. 10, pp. 2867–2891, 2007.
20. A. Shamir, "Identity-based cryptosystems and signature schemes," in Advances in Cryptology, G. R. Blakley and D. Chaum, Eds., vol. 196 of Lecture Notes in Computer Science, pp. 47–53, Springer, New York, NY, USA, 1985.
21. A. Kate and I. Goldberg, "Distributed private-key generators for identity-based cryptography," in Security and Cryptography for Networks, J. A. Garay and R. De Prisco, Eds., vol. 6280 of Lecture Notes in Computer Science, pp. 436–453, Springer, Berlin, Germany, 2010.
22. E. da Silva and L. C. P. Albini, "Towards a fully self-organized identity-based key management system for MANETs," in Proceedings of the 9th International Conference on Wireless and Mobile Computing, Networking and Communications (WiMob ‹13), pp. 717–723, Lyon, France, October 2013.
23. Y. Zhang, W. Liu, W. Lou, and Y. Fang, "Securing mobile ad hoc networks with certificateless public keys," IEEE Transactions on Dependable and Secure Computing, vol. 3, no. 4, pp. 386–399, 2006.
24. H. Luo, J. Kong, P. Zerfos, S. Lu, and L. Zhang, "URSA: ubiquitous and robust access control for mobile ad hoc networks," IEEE/ACM Transactions on Networking, vol. 12, no. 6, pp. 1049–1063, 2004.
25. L. Zhou and Z. J. Haas, "Securing ad hoc networks," IEEE Network, vol. 13, no. 6, pp. 24–30, 1999.
26. J. Kong, P. Zerfos, H. Luo, S. Lu, and L. Zhang, "Providing robust and ubiquitous security support for mobile ad-hoc networks," in Proceedings of the International Conference on Network Protocols (ICNP ‹01), pp. 251–260, Washington, DC, USA, November 2001.
27. S. Yi and R. Kravets, "MOCA: mobile certificate authority for wireless ad hoc networks," in Proceedings of the 2nd Annual PKI Research Workshop (PKI ‹03), National Institute of Standards and Technology (NIST), Gaithersburg, Md, USA, 2003.
28. K. Hoeper and G. Gong, "Key revocation for identity-based schemes in mobile ad hoc networks," in Ad-Hoc, Mobile, and Wireless Networks, T. Kunz and S. S. Ravi, Eds., vol. 4104 of Lecture Notes in Computer Science, pp. 224–237, Springer, 2006.
29. V. Daza, P. Morillo, and C. Ràfols, "On dynamic distribution of private keys over MANETs," Electronic Notes in Theoretical Computer Science, vol. 171, no. 1, pp. 33–41, 2007.
30. O. Courand, O. Droegehorn, K. David et al., "Context aware group management in mobile environments," in Proceedings of the 14th IST Mobile and Wireless Communications Summit, Nokia Research Center, Dresden, Germany, 2005.
31. C. N. Ververidis and G. C. Polyzos, "Service discovery for mobile ad hoc networks: a survey of issues and techniques," IEEE Communications Surveys & Tutorials, vol. 10, no. 3, pp. 30–45, 2008. View at Publisher·
32. J. Hur, C. Park, and S. O. Hwang, "Privacy-preserving identity-based broadcast encryption," Information Fusion, vol. 13, no. 4, pp. 296–303, 2012.

33. D. Augot, R. Bhaskar, V. Issarny, and D. Sacchetti, "An efficient group key agreement protocol for ad hoc networks," in Proceedings of the 6th IEEE International Symposium on a World of Wireless Mobile and Multimedia Networks (WoWMoM ‹05), pp. 576–580, Washington, DC, USA, June 2005.

34. B. E. Jung, "An efficient group key agreement protocol," IEEE Communications Letters, vol. 10, no. 2, pp. 106–107, 2006.

35. L. Zhang, Q. Wu, B. Qin, and J. Domingo-Ferrer, "Provably secure one-round identity-based authenticated asymmetric group key agreement protocol," Information Sciences, vol. 181, no. 19, pp. 4318–4329, 2011.

CHAPTER 6

A HYBRID ENERGY EFFICIENT PROTOCOL FOR MOBILE AD HOC NETWORKS

Niranjan Kumar Ray[1] and Ashok Kumar Turuk[2]

[1]Department of Computer Science & Engineering, Silicon Institute of Technology, Bhubaneswar 751024, India

[2]Department of Computer Science & Engineering, National Institute of Technology, Rourkela 769008, India

ABSTRACT

We proposed an energy conservation technique called Location Based Topology Control with Sleep Scheduling for ad hoc networks. It uses the feature of both topology control approach and power management approach. Like the topology control approach, it attempts to reduce the transmission power of a node, which is determined from its neighborhood location information. A node goes to sleep state based on the traffic condition as that of power management approach. In the proposed scheme, a node goes to sleep state only when its absence does not create local partition in its neighborhood. We preformed extensive simulation to compare the proposed scheme with existing ones. Simulation results show that the energy consumption is lower with increase in the network lifetime and higher throughput in the proposed scheme.

INTRODUCTION

Wireless ad hoc networks do not require any preestablished network infrastructure. They are more suitable for deployment in areas where a fixed backbone network infrastructure is inflexible and/or economically nonviable. Mobile ad hoc networks (MANETs) have variety of applications such as emergency communication services, military communication, and environmental monitoring. However, they suffer from many challenges such as unpredictable mobility, restricted battery power, limited bandwidth, multihop routing, and security. Efforts are being made to address the above issues.

As nodes in MANETs are battery operated, energy efficiency is important design criteria for the longevity of the network. If a node runs out of battery, its ability to route the network traffic gets affected which in turn adversely affects the network lifetime. Network lifetime of MANETs can be enhanced by either maximizing the battery power of nodes or minimizing the total power consumption in the network. Though a considerable progress has been made in the battery technologies in recent years, it is incomparable with the progress made in semiconductor technology yet. This difference has created a gap between the amount of energy needed to operate in a wireless environment and the battery capacity that powered the nodes. Hence, it necessitates the requirement of power conservation techniques to enhance the network lifetime. Such techniques can be applied at different layers of protocol stack.

Citation: Niranjan Kumar Ray and Ashok Kumar Turuk, "A Hybrid Energy Efficient Protocol for Mobile Ad Hoc Networks," Journal of Computer Networks and Communications, vol. 2016, Article ID 2861904, 11 pages, 2016. doi:10.1155/2016/2861904

Nodes in MANET usually transmit packets with maximum power. A packet transmitted with maximum power may reach the destination with lesser number of hops but can decrease the channel utilization and the remaining energy of the node to a greater extent. Energy saving can be done at the node level by adjusting the transmission power to a lower level [1–4]. In recent years, many techniques have been proposed to conserve energy in MANETs. Topology control approach is one among them. The primary objective of topology control algorithms is to adjust the network topology by reducing the transmission power at node level and at the same time maintaining the network connectivity. In other words the objective of topology control approach is to remove the energy inefficient links at the node level by reducing the transmission power. The major design goal in most of the topology control protocols is to minimize the maximum power used by a node. Other design goals are to improve the network performance such as throughput, network lifetime by alleviating contention, and interference in the network. In this paper we have proposed an energy efficient technique, where nodes are put into sleep state depending on their connectivity information, and transmission power is determined from the location of next-hop node. The proposed scheme inherits the merit of both topology control approach and power management approach. A node in this scheme goes to sleep state only when its absence does not create local partition in its neighborhood.

The rest of the paper is organized as follows. In Section 2, few of the power control techniques are briefly discussed. Proposed technique is described in Section 3. In Section 4 simulation results are presented and conclusion is drawn in Section 5.

RELATED WORK

Energy conservation strategies for MANET can be broadly classified into two types: (i) power management approach and (ii) topology control approach. In power management approach a node remains in one of the three possible states: (a) active: participating in the network traffic by sending and/or receiving packets, (b) idle: waiting for the traffic, and (c) sleep: switching off its radio transceiver for a particular period and wakeing up at the end of the period. Among the above three states, sleep state consumes lesser amount of energy. Therefore, power management based protocols put as many nodes as possible into sleep state to save energy. However, they are more prone to network disruption. This is because, as the nodes goes to sleep state, the connectivity may be lost. Few representatives of power management approach are discussed in [5–9].

Topology control approach conserves energy by adaptively adjusting the transmission power while maintaining the network connectivity. Most of the topology control protocols require information like location, direction, neighbor, and so forth, to construct the topology. Location information can be obtained by means of global positioning systems (GPS) or other positioning methods. The directional information can be obtained by using angle-of-arrival (AOA) technique. Location based techniques produce more accurate topology but are associated with higher hardware cost. In order to reduce the hardware cost some of the techniques assume that a subset of nodes are equipped with GPS while other nodes get their location information by exchanging message with GPS enabled nodes. Few topology control protocols are discussed below.

Topology optimization for different topologies and communication pattern is addressed by Santi [10]. Protocols like Geographical Adaptive Fidelity (GAF) [11] and SPAN [12] save energy by maintaining a connected dominating set (CDS). GAF identifies the routing prospective nodes and redundant nodes. Redundant nodes are switched off to save energy. In SPAN, few nodes are selected as coordinator, which stay/awake continuously and perform multihop packet routing. Nodes not selected as coordinator remain in power save mode to conserve energy. SPAN saves energy by putting few nodes into sleep state, while communication takes place through coordinator. Bao and Garcia-Luna-Aceves [13] proposed a topology management scheme called Topology Management by Priority Ordering (TMPO) [13], which is based on CDS and minimum determining set (MDS). TMPO uses two-hop neighborhood information to determine CDS and MDS.

Sahoo et al. [14] proposed a distributed power control protocol that constructs a power saving tree without taking the nodes local information into account. In their proposed approach, network topology is maintained by controlling the transmission power. Topology based on neighborhood information is constructed in Adaptive Neighbor-based Topology Control (ANTC) proposed by Mir and Ko [15], where the transmission range is determined adaptively in order to maintain connectivity. Based on the local connectivity, each node selects a backbone that guarantees a hierarchical topology structure. In the scheme proposed by Sheu et al. [16] transmission power is calculated considering sender maximum power, receiver minimum power, and the signal strength of the received packet. Both LFTC and ANTC do not put the node into sleep state to save energy. Gui and Liu [17] proposed a technique to optimize the delay and energy. They modeled link delays as a function of signal to interference noise ratio of the receiving node and its packet forwarding time in the link. The sum of delay and energy consumption is considered as the weight of an edge, and their objective was to find the minimum weight sum of any edge.

A prediction based data reduction strategy for sensor network is proposed in [18]. In this approach a hierarchical least mean square (HLMS) adaptive filter mechanism is used to maximize the lifetime of sensor nodes. Energy saving is achieved by reducing the actual data transmission between a source-sink pair. Both source and sink predict the value of sensed data; if the error is acceptable then sink can use predicted value. Otherwise the source will transmit the sensed data to sink. HLMC acheives better energy saving. However, in dynamic environment when link failure occurs due to node mobility its energy saving is a major concern. A tree based broadcast algorithm for wireless ad hoc network is proposed in [19]. The protocol uses two-hop neighborhood information through the exchange of *Hello* message to construct broadcast tree. The node in the broadcast tree assigned channels in a time-oriented way such that the message forwarded in the broadcast tree is collision free. Simulation results suggest that the protocol achieves lower broadcast redundancy and higher reachability.

A distributed energy efficient multicast routing algorithm is proposed in [20]. The protocol maximizes the lifetime of a source based multicast tree by considering both hop count and energy efficient metric. A weight is assigned to the cost metrics to assign the priority. This helps the protocol to use the cost metrics more efficiently.

A topology control technique *CoopSink* for ad hoc network is proposed in [21]. *CoopSink* considers cooperative communication (CC) employing decode-and-forward approach. CC is used to reduce energy consumption in the network and also provides efficient route to the destination node. The authors claim that *CoopSink* improves the network connectivity and has lower energy consumptions compared to other protocols. X-LMST, an extension of local minimum spanning tree (LMST), is proposed in [22]. Objective of X-MST is to build an energy efficient spanning tree to improve network lifetime. A cost function is proposed to measure the energy efficiency of a node. Network lifetime is enhanced by avoiding the transmission through energy critical nodes.

Two topology control techniques, node-to-cluster topology control (NCTC) and cluster-to-cluster topology control (CCTC), are proposed in [23]. NCTC and CCTC define two different types of links. In both schemes, cooperative links are employed to connect the clusters obtained by the initial topology. Higher energy saving and connectivity are maintained by NCTC and CCTC considering transmitter and receiver cooperation. However, both are based on centralized approach.

The protocols discussed in this section do not put the node to sleep state to save energy.

PROPOSED WORK

In this section, we proposed a power conservation technique for ad hoc network, called Location Based Topology Control with Sleep Scheduling (LBTC). The proposed technique takes into the account the merits of both topology control and power management approach. It uses variable transmission power, like the topology control approach. A sleep scheduling mechanism is introduced where nodes are put to sleep state like the power management approach. However, a node in the proposed scheme goes to sleep state only when it is satisfied that its absence will not create a local partition in its neighborhood [24]. Section 3.1 describes the network model and notation used. The proposed scheme is presented in Section 3.2 and analyzed in Section3.3.

Network Model and Notation

Wireless ad hoc network is modeled as a graph $G = (V, E)$, where V represents the set of nodes and E represents the set of edges. Network consists of n number of heterogeneous nodes randomly deployed in the network. Each node has a unique identity (ID) and is equipped with omnidirectional antenna. It is assumed that nodes are location aware and can calculate their relative distance to their neighboring nodes. Let $P_{max}(u)$ be the maximum transmission power, let $P_{min}(u)$ be the minimum transmission power, and let P_u be the transmission power of a node $u \in V$. Initially nodes transmit with maximum power P_{max}. We assumed that transmission power $P(u)$ can be adjusted between the maximum and minimum value; that is, $P_{min}(u) \leq P(u) \leq P_{max}(u)$. Let P_{uV} be the minimum transmission power required to communicate between nodes u and V, which can be computed as $P_{uv} = D^{\beta} + C$, where D is the Euclidean distance between u and V, β is the path loss exponent, where $2 \leq \beta \leq 4$, and$C$is a constant. Let$G = (V, E)$ be the initial topology of the network and let $G' = (V, E')$ be the topology, obtained when the transmission power control mechanism is applied at nodes. We have further assumed that links are symmetric and the power control technique is applied within the neighborhood of a node.

Neighbor Set

One-hop neighbor set of node u denoted as N_u^1 is defined as the set of nodes that have a direct link to u, when it transmits with power $P(u)$, $P_{min}(u) \leq P(u) \leq P_{max}(u)$.

Two-hop neighbor set of node u denoted as N_u^2 is defined as the set of nodes that have a direct link to the nodes in the set N_u^1. This is represented as

$$N_u^2 = \bigcup_{x \in N_u^1} N_x^1. \qquad (1)$$

The common node between u and V is denoted as$ComNode_{uV}$. A node is said to be a common node between u and V when it lies in the intersection area of nodes u and V. This is represented as

$$ComNode_{uv} = \{i \mid i \in \{N_u^1 \cap N_v^1\}\}, \qquad (2)$$

where N_u^1 and N_v^1 are the one-hop neighbor set of nodes u and V, respectively

Location Based Topology Control with Sleep Scheduling (LBTC)

The proposed scheme operates in two phase. First phase is the link selection phase, while the second is the sleep scheduling phase. In the link selection phase a node determines its transmission power. In sleep scheduling phase a node decides whether to go to sleep state or not depending on the present traffic condition and neighborhood connectivity. A node goes to sleep state only when it satisfies that its neighbors are reachable from each other without its active participation.

Link Selection Phase

In this phase a node u determines its transmission power that is enough to reach any of the nodes in the set N_u^1. Nodes periodically broadcast a *Hello* message with Pmax, which contains sender ID and location information of the sender. On receiving *Hello* message a node computes the transmission power required to transmit to the sender of the *Hello* message and updates its vicinity table which is maintained at each node. The structure of the vicinity table is as follows:

SenID

LocInfo

MinCost

ComNode

DirCost

LinkType.

The meaning of each field in the vicinity table is explained as follows.

SenID. It is identity of the node (Node ID), from which *Hello* message is received.

LocInfo. It is location information of the sender of *Hello* message.

DirCost. It is link cost from the node to the sender of the *Hello* message.

MinCost. It is minimum link cost between the current node and the sender. Current node is the node that is updating its vicinity table. Initially the value in this field is set to that of DirCost. This value is updated when there exists common node i between the current node and SenID such that transmission cost from the current node to SenID node through node i has lower total transmission cost than the DirCost.

ComNode. This field records the common node i through which there exists an energy efficient path between the current node and SenID. It is updated when there exists a common node i between u and V such that $P_{ui} + P_{iV} < P_{uV}$

LinkType. It indicates whether the link between the current node and SenID is direct (one-hop) or indirect (more than one-hop). For direct the entry is zero, else it is one.

Initially, the vicinity table is empty and is updated when a node receives a *Hello* message from its neighbors. To illustrate the updation of vicinity table we consider Figure 1. Let node X with its current location (91, 61) receive a *Hello* message (Z, (101, 61)) from node Z, where coordinate (101, 61) is the current location of node Z. Then, the vicinity table of node X is updated as shown in Table 1. Node X computes the DirCost between itself and Z, which is computed to be 101, assuming β=2 and C=1. DirCost and MinCost field is set to 101 and the LinkType to zero. ComNode is set to null as no common node between X and Z exists at this stage.

Table 1: Vicinity table (node) after receiving message from

SenID	*LocInfo*	*MinCost*	*ComNode*	*DirCost*	*LinkType*
Z	(101, 61)	101	—	101	0

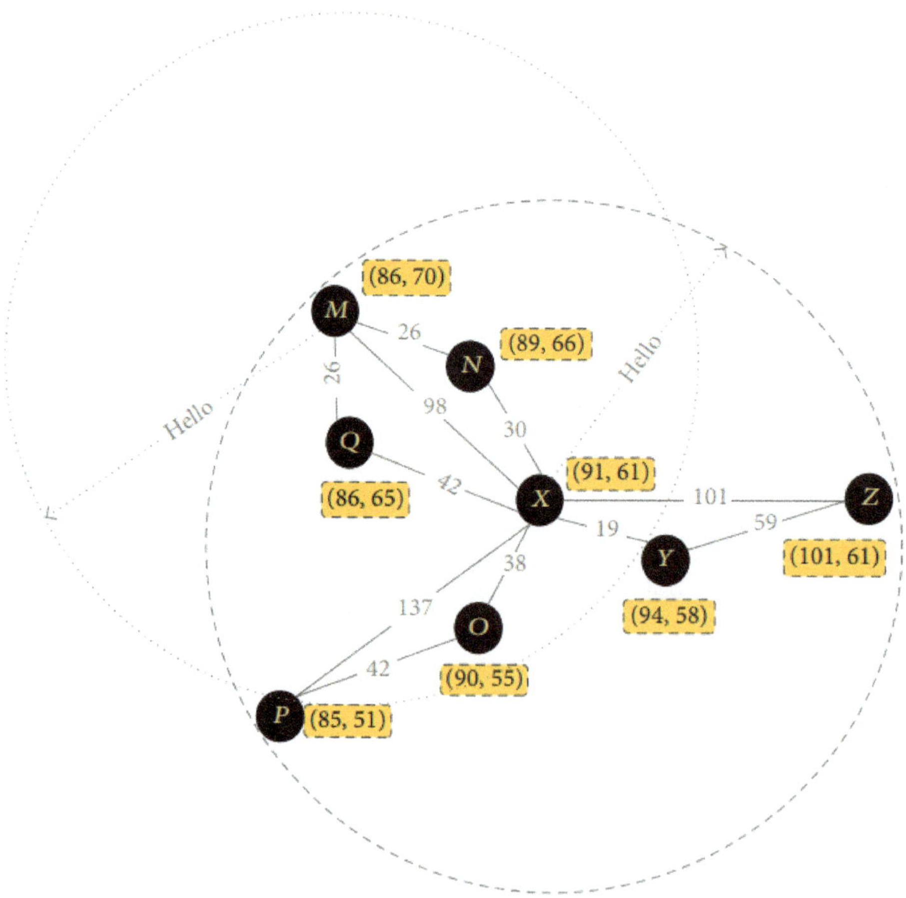

Figure 1: Nodes with location information.

Vicinity table of node X after receiving *Hello* message from all its neighbor is shown in Table 2. After gathering information about its neighbor, node X determines whether there exists any *ComNode* between itself and its neighbor. Nodes Y, N, and O are the *ComNode* between X and Z, X and M, and X and P, respectively. There can be more than one node within the transmission range of a pair of nodes. Only that node is selected as the *ComNode* through which the cost between the pair of nodes is minimum. For example, nodes N, O, P, and Q are within the transmission range of nodes X

and M. But node O is selected as the *ComNode* between X and M. After obtaining the *ComNode*, node X updates the LinkType, *ComNode*, and MinCost field in its vicinity table. The updated vicinity table is shown in Table 3. From the table it is observed that the cost of transmitting from X to Z through node Y is 78, whereas the direct cost is 101. Similarly, the cost of transmitting from X to P through O is 80, whereas the direct cost is 137.

Table 2: Vicinity table (node) after receiving message from neighbors

SenID	*LocInfo*	*MinCost*	*ComNode*	*DirCost*	*LinkType*
Z	(101, 61)	101	—	101	0
Y	(94, 58)	19	—	19	0
M	(86, 70)	98	—	98	0
N	(89, 66)	30	—	30	0
P	(85, 51)	137	—	137	0
O	(90, 55)	38	—	38	0
Q	(86, 65)	42	—	42	0

Table 3: Vicinity table (node) after determining the ComNode between itself and its neighbor.

SenID	*LocInfo*	*MinCost*	*ComNode*	*DirCost*	*LinkType*
Z	(101, 61)	78	*Y*	101	1
Y	(94, 58)	19	—	19	0
M	(86, 70)	56	*N*	98	1
N	(89, 66)	30	—	30	0
P	(85, 51)	80	*O*	137	1
O	(90, 55)	38	—	38	0
Q	(86, 65)	42	—	42	0

From the updated vicinity table, node X computes its transmission power for which it considers only those nodes where the LinkType field is set to zero. Node X considers nodes Y, N, O, and Q as the LinkType field to these nodes which is set to zero. The transmission power of a node is the maximum value in the DirCost field of those nodes considered for computing transmission power. Node X determines its transmission power, which is the maximum value in the DirCost field of nodes Y, N, O, and Q; that is, max (19, 30, 38, 42) = 42. The resulting topology as seen by node X after the link selection phase is shown in Figure 2. It is observed that node X has lesser number of one-hop neighbors than previous as seen in Figure 1.

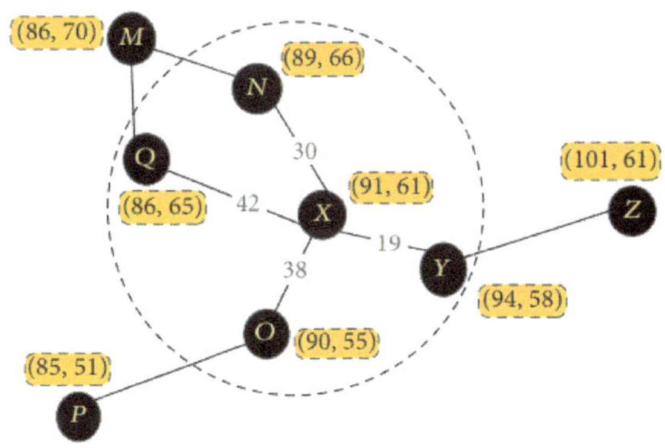

Figure 2: Resulting topology of node after link selection phase.

Sleep Scheduling Phase

In this phase a node decides whether to enter into sleep state or not, depending on the traffic pattern and neighborhood connectivity information. A node remains in one of the following three states: (i) active, (ii) watch, and (iii) sleep. In active state nodes participate in data communication and periodically broadcast a *Hello* message. After the expiry of Hello message period, TH, nodes enter into awatch state. Inwatch state, a node decides whether to go to active state or to sleep state. In active and watch state the radio transceiver of a node is turned on, whereas it is turned off in sleep state. A node in sleep state wakes up at the end of sleep time, TS, and enters into watch state. The state transition diagram between states is shown in Figure 3. In the watch state, a node decides whether to go to active state or sleep state. If the node has some pending traffic, it returns to active state; otherwise it executes a sleep eligibility algorithm, to check whether it can enter into the sleep state.

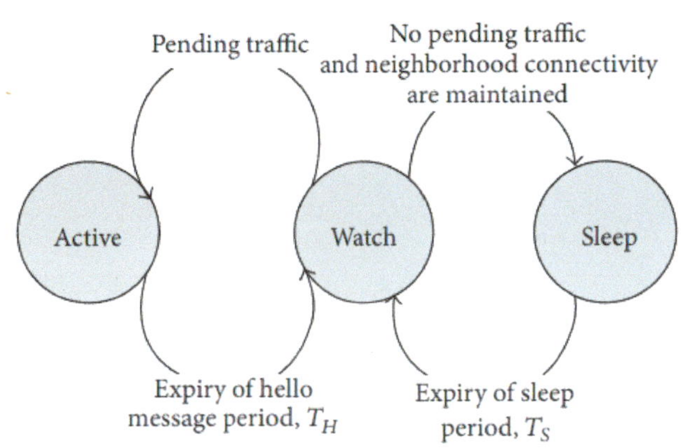

Figure 3: State transition in LBTC.

When a node goes to sleep state it may create a local partition, within its neighborhood. For example, a critical node on a path, when goes to sleep state, creates a local partition. This is because when a critical node goes to sleep state, all paths through that node are broken, and any ongoing traffic through that node gets disturbed. Therefore, before going to sleep state, a node checks whether its absence will create any local partition. In the watch state a node checks for the local partition. If the node has no traffic to participate and its absence does not create a local partition, then the node goes to sleep sate. A node in watch state, having no traffic to transmit, executes the sleep eligibility algorithm given as Algorithm 1.

Assuming that Δ is the maximum degree of a node, the running time of steps (7)–(16) is $O(\Delta^3)$. In steps (17)–(22), node u does the following for each of its N_u^2. If the length of $X(n) \geq 2$, for each pair of $(a, b) \in X(n)$, it initializes CM[a][b] = CM[b][a]. Maximum length of $X(n)$ will be Δ.

So the running time of steps (17)–(22) is $O(\Delta^2)$. Running time of steps (24)–(26) and (27)–(31) are constant. So total running time of Algorithm 1 is $O(\Delta^3)$.

```
Q: No. of neighbor of u, where u executes the algorithm
X(n): Is a set maintained for node n, where n ∈ N_u^2
CM: Connectivity matrix of order Q × Q
/* Initialize */
∀x, y CM[x][y] = FALSE
X(n) ← ∅
procedure Local connectivity
  for i ∈ N_u^1 do
    for each j ∈ N_i^1 do
      if j ∈ N_u^1 then
        Set CM[j][i] = CM[i][j] = TRUE
      else
        X(n) = X(n) ∪ {i}
      end if
    end for
  end for
  for n ∈ N_u^2 do
    if |X(n)| ≥ 2 then
      ∀(a, b) ∈ X(n)
      Set CM[a][b] = CM[b][a] = TRUE
    end if
  end for
  /* Adjust CM */
    if CM[x][y] = CM[y][z] = TRUE then
      Set CM[x][z] = TRUE
    end if
    if ∃(a, b) ∈ N_u^1 and CM[a][b] = FALSE then
      goto active state
    else
      goto sleep state
    end if
end procedure
```

Algorithm 1: Sleep eligibility algorithm.

Analysis

In this subsection, we analyze the network connectivity in the proposed scheme.

Theorem 1 If two nodes are connected before the *link selection* phase, then they are also connected after the *link selection* phase.

Proof. Let $G = (V, E)$ be the network topology before the *link selection* phase and let $G' = (V, E')$ be the network topology after the *link selection* phase. We have to show that, for any u, V $\in V$, if there exists a path in G, then there also exists a path from u to V in G'.

Since G is connected, for any u, V $\in V$, there exists a path from u to V in G. Let the path be $u \xrightarrow{k} v$, where k is the number of links in the path from u to V. We show by means of induction that there also exists a path from u to V; that is, $u \xrightarrow{k'} v$, with k' being number of links in G', where $k' \geq k$.

Let k=1, which means that node V is within the transmission range of node u in G. In G', V will be in either one-hop or two-hop neighbor of u. Therefore, a path from u to V exists in G'.

Let us assume that it is true for k=n; that is, there exists a path in G from u to V with n number of links. Therefore, there also exists a path from u to V in G', and the number of links in the path is greater than or equal to n.

Let $k = n$+1; then the path from u to V with n+1 number of links in G is shown in Figure 4.

The path in Figure 4 can be interpreted as two subpaths one from u to v' with n number of links and the other from v' to V with single link in G. From the induction hypothesis, we know that if there exists a path from u to v' in G with n links then there exists a path from u to v' in G'. From the basis, we know that if there exists a path from v' to V with single link in G then there exists a path from v' to V in G'. Hence there exists a path from u to V in G'. Therefore if G is connected then G' is also connected.

Figure 4: Exemplary network.

In the sleep scheduling phase each node checks the local connectivity within its neighborhood. Partition in a network means global partition, which is not the same as that of local partition. In the process of maintaining local connectivity there always exists a node redundancy due to false alarm of network partition. Therefore, connectivity is always maintained in the proposed scheme.

SIMULATION AND COMPARISON

We simulated the proposed technique using QualNet 4.5 [25] simulator to evaluate its performance. The parameters considered for simulation are shown in Table 4.

Table 4: Simulation parameters

Simulator	QualNet 4.5
Terrain-dimension (meters)	1500 * 1500
Number of nodes	50–100
Node speed	Max = 10 m/s, min = 0 m/s
Traffic type	CBR
Channel frequency	2.4 GHz
Mobility model	Random waypoint
Propagation limit	−111 dbm
Transmit current	220 mA
Receive current	180 mA
MAC protocol	802.11b
Size of packets	512 bytes
Initial battery capacity	300 mAH

For the comparison, we consider two topology control protocols, LFTC [16] and ANTC [15]. Lifetime of *Hello* message is set to *two* sec and *Hello* message interval to *one* sec. The following metrics were considered for performance evaluation.

Throughput

We plot the throughput versus pause time, number of nodes, CBR connection, and packet size in Figures 5(a),5(b), 5(c), and 5(d), respectively. From Figure 5, it is observed that a higher throughput is attainable in the proposed scheme. Higher throughput is attributed to the increase in longevity of the network due to proper adjustment of transmission power in the link selection phase and energy saving in the sleep scheduling phase.

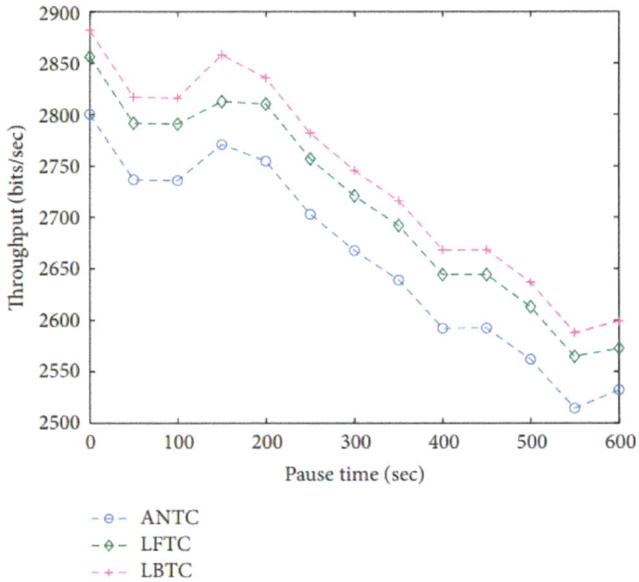

(a) Throughput versus pause time

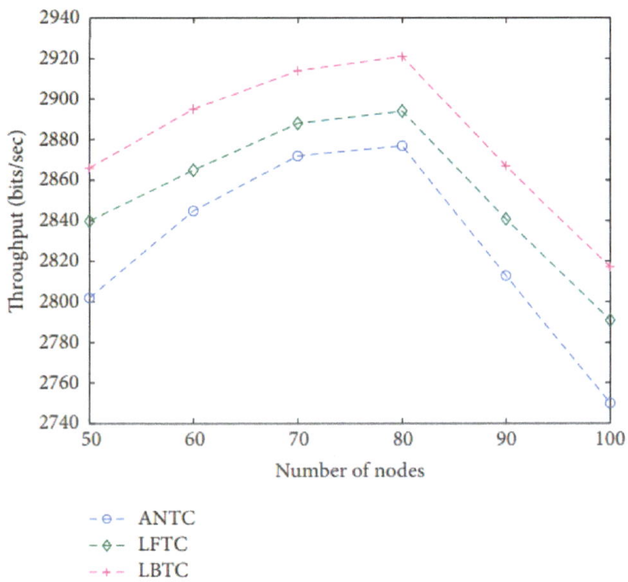

(b) Throughput versus number of nodes

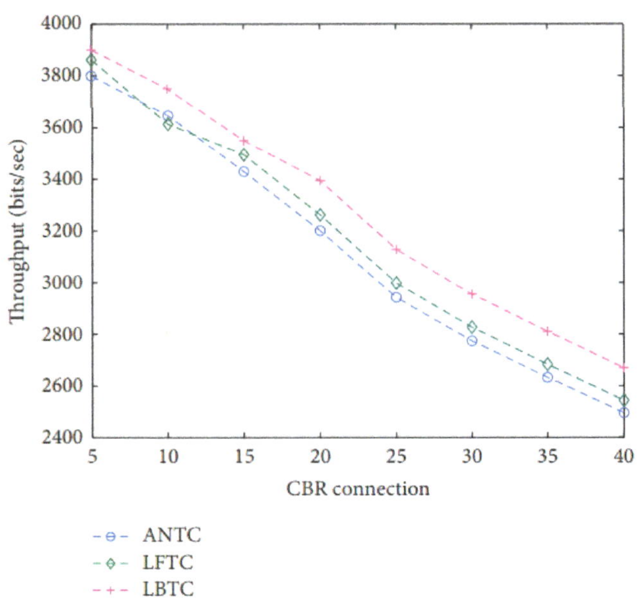

(c) Throughput versus CBR connection

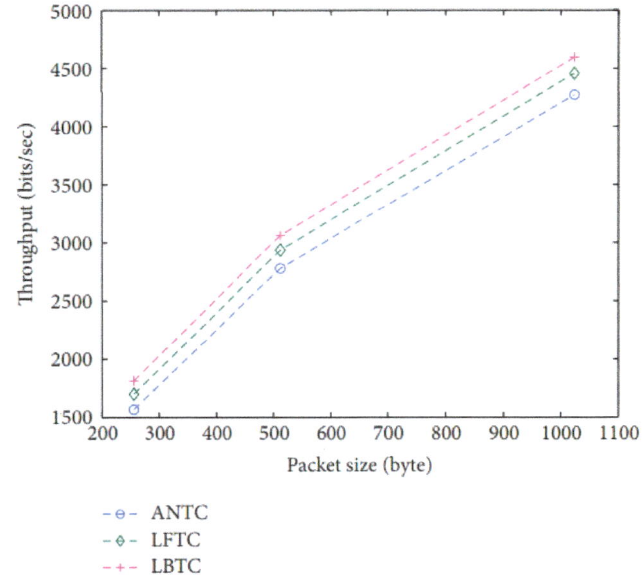

(d) Throughput versus packet size

Figure 5: Network throughput.

Energy Consumption

Energy consumption determines the effectiveness of energy saving scheme. We consider the energy model in [26] for measuring the energy consumption. The plot for energy consumption versus pause time, number of nodes, CBR connection, and packet size is shown in Figures 6(a), 6(b), 6(c), and 6(d), respectively. It is observed from Figure 6 that the proposed LBTC scheme has lower energy consumption. This is because LBTC selects energy efficient links and nodes are put to sleep state, if they do not actively participate in ongoing transmission.

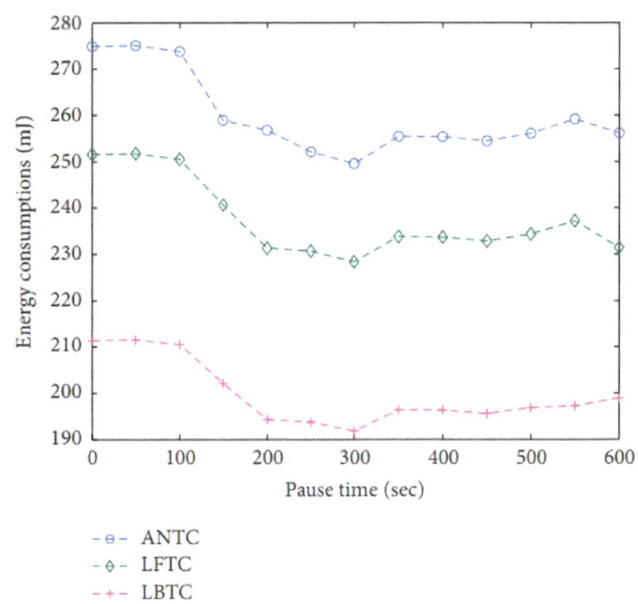

(a) Energy consumption versus pause time

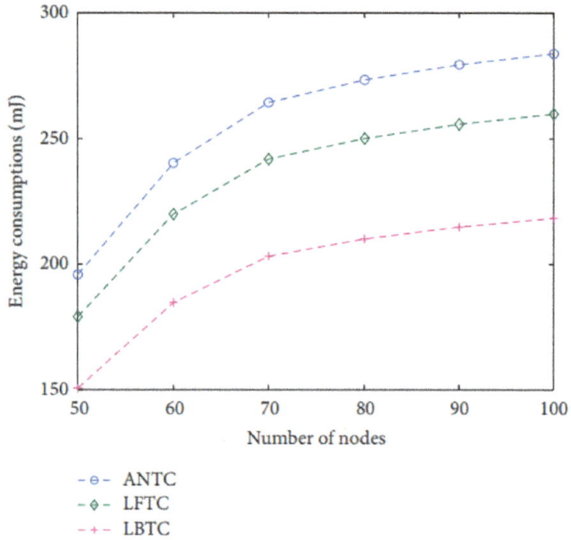

(b) Energy consumption versus number of nodes

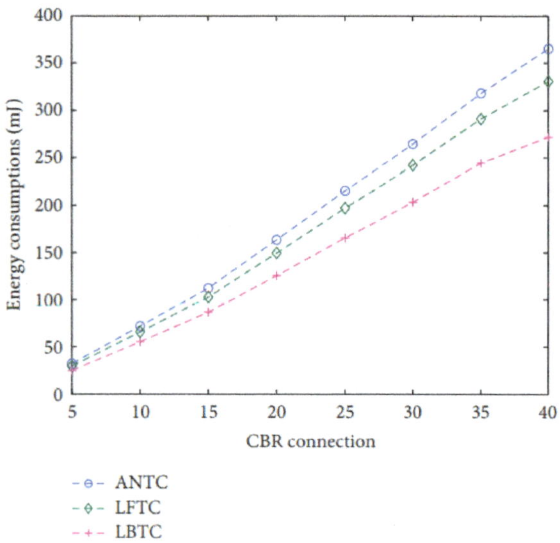

(c) Energy consumption versus CBR connection

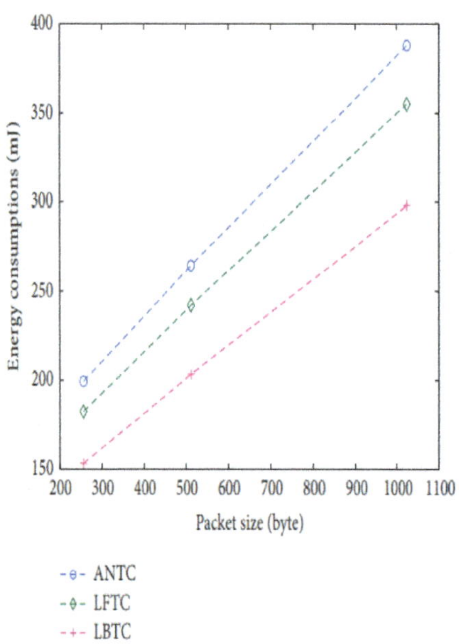

(d) Energy consumption versus packet size

Figure 6: Energy consumption.

Network Lifetime

The plot for network lifetime versus pause time, number of nodes, CBR connection, and packet size is shown in Figures 7(a), 7(b), 7(c), and 7(d), respectively. It is observed that LBTC gives a superior network lifetime because it is energy efficient.

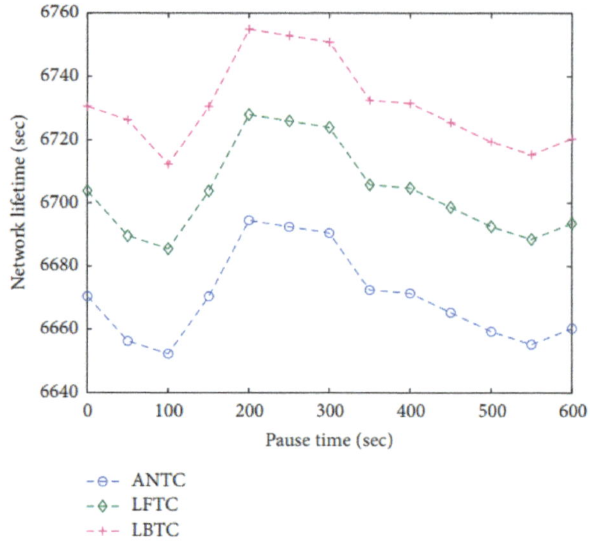

(a) Network lifetime versus pause time

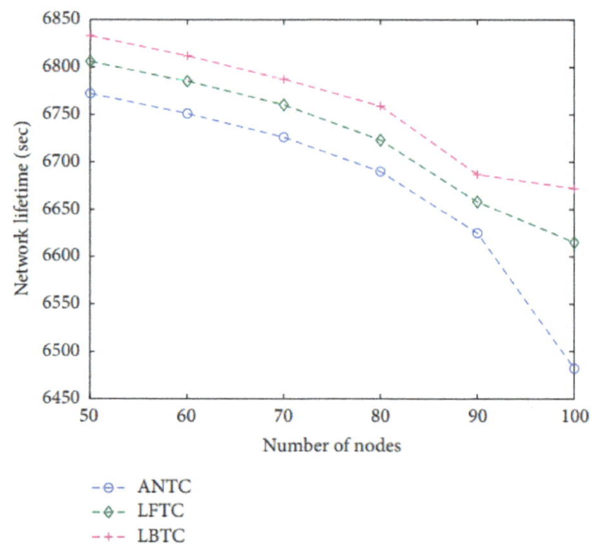

(b) Energy consumption versus number of nodes

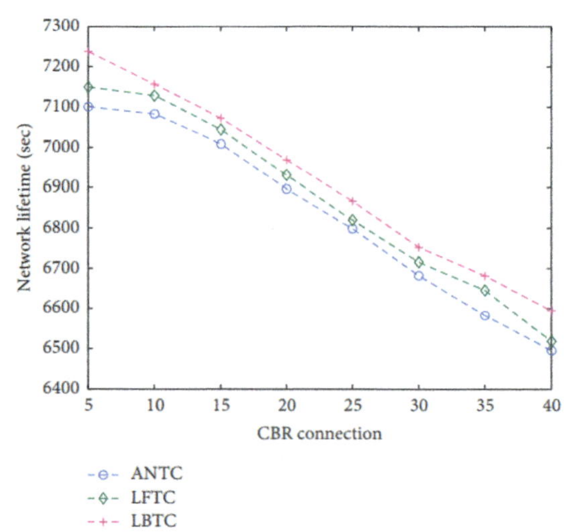

(c) Energy consumption versus CBR connection

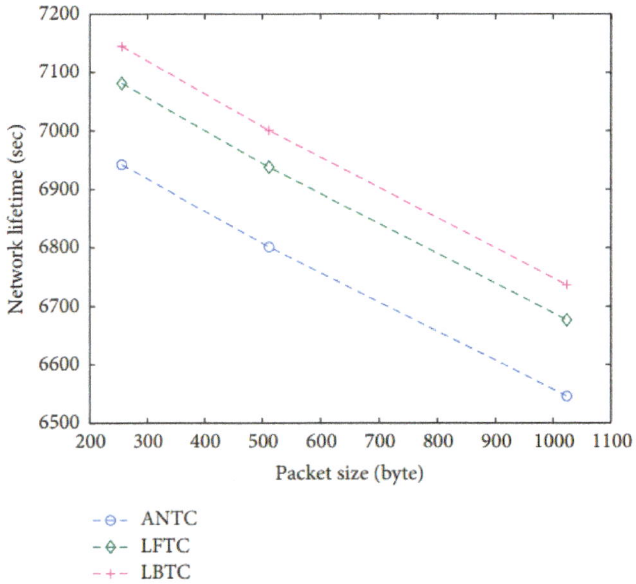

(d) Energy consumption versus packet size

Figure 7: Network lifetime.

Delay

The plot for delay versus pause time, number of nodes, CBR connection, and packet size is shown in Figures8(a), 8(b), 8(c), and 8(d), respectively. From Figure 8, it is observed that LBTC has higher end-to-end delay as compared to LFTC and ANTC. This is due to increase in hop count as nodes transmit with lower power. This observation is consistent with the published report that the average end-to-end delay increases when the transmission power control mechanism is applied [27].

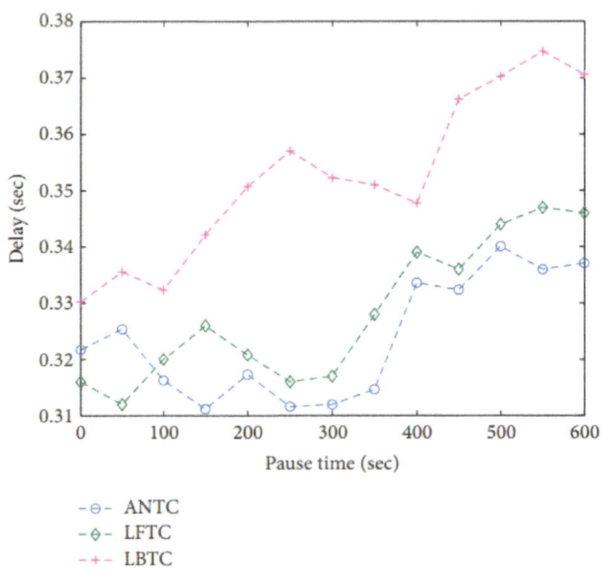

(a) End-to-end delay versus pause time

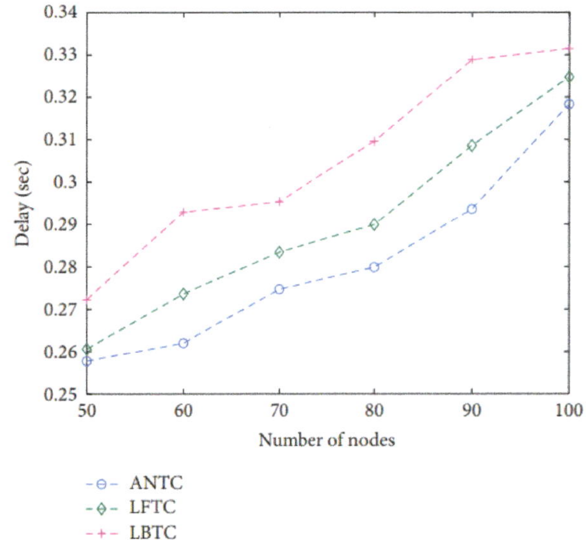

(b) End-to-end delay versus number of nodes

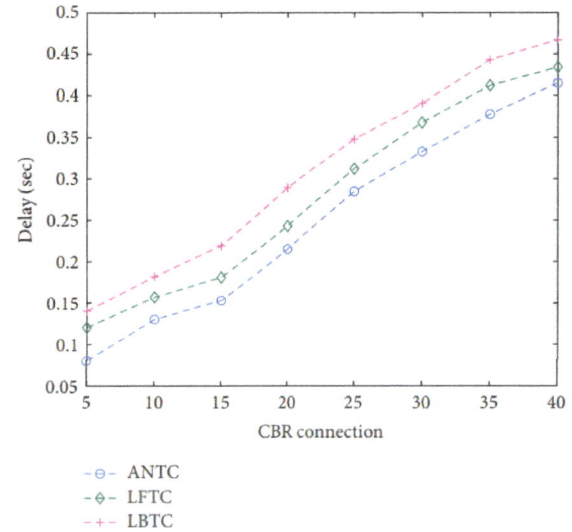

(c) End-to-end delay versus CBR connection

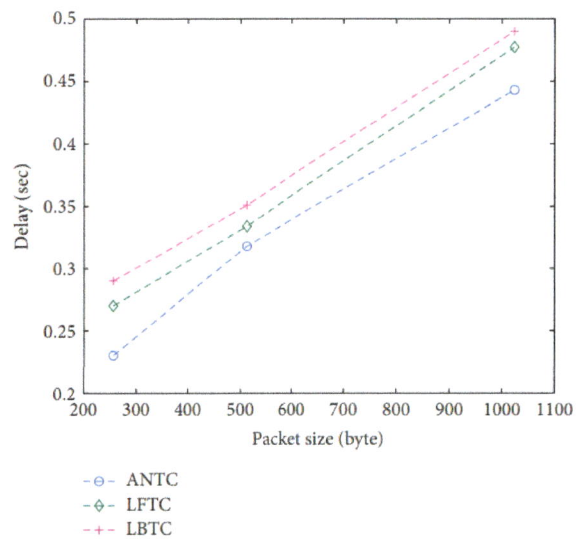

(d) End-to-end delay versus packet size

Figure 8: End-to-end delay.

CONCLUSION

In this paper, we proposed a hybrid energy efficient protocol called LBTC for ad hoc network. The proposed protocol considers the merits of both topology control scheme and power management scheme. It selects energy efficient links, and nodes which do not actively participate in communication are put to sleep state. LBTC is compared with two existing schemes and observed that it is more energy efficient and delivers higher throughput. However, the end-to-end delay is higher. This is because as the transmission power is controlled, packets take more number of hops to travel the destination. In future, we intend to reduce end-to-end delay with enhancing the network lifetime.

REFERENCES

1. M. Krunz, A. Muqattash, and S. J. Lee, "Transmission power control in wireless ad hoc networks: challenges, solutions, and open issues," IEEE Network Magazine, vol. 18, no. 5, pp. 8–14, 2004.
2. M. Chiang, "Balancing transport and physical layers in wireless multihop networks: jointly optimal congestion control and power control," IEEE Journal on Selected Areas in Communications, vol. 23, no. 1, pp. 104–116, 2005.
3. J. Gomez and A. T. Campbell, "Variable-range transmission power control in wireless ad hoc networks,"IEEE Transactions on Mobile Computing, vol. 6, no. 1, pp. 87–99, 2007.
4. X. Zhang, A. Anpalagan, L. Guo, and A. S. Khwaja, "Energy-efficient cooperative MAC protocol based on power control in MANETs," in Proceedings of the IEEE 29th International Conference on Advanced Information Networking and Applications (AINA ‹15), pp. 48–53, IEEE, Gwangju, Republic of Korea, March 2015.
5. IEEE 802.11 Working Group, Wireless LAN Medium Access Control (MAC) and Physical Layer (PHY) Specification, IEEE, 1999.
6. G. De-yun, Z. Lin-juan, and W. Hwang-cheng, "Energy saving with node sleep and power control mechanisms forwireless sensor networks," The Journal of China Universities of Posts and Telecommunications, vol. 18, no. 1, pp. 49–59, 2011.
7. S. Wu, P. Tseng, and Z. Chou, "Distributed power management protocols for multi-hop mobile Ad Hoc networks," Computer Networks, vol. 47, no. 1, pp. 63–68, 2005.
8. R. Zheng and R. Kravets, "On-demand power management for ad hoc networks," Ad Hoc Networks, vol. 3, no. 1, pp. 51–68, 2005.
9. N. K. Ray and A. K. Turuk, "A review on energy efficient MAC protocols for wireless LANs," inProceedings of the 4th International Conference on Industrial and Information Systems (ICIIS ‹09), pp. 137–141, Peradeniya, Sri Lanka, December 2009.
10. P. Santi, "Topology control in wireless ad hoc and sensor networks," ACM Computing Surveys, vol. 37, no. 2, pp. 164–194, 2005.
11. Y. Xu, J. Heidemann, and D. Estrin, "Geography-informed energy conservation for Ad hoc routing," inProceedings of the 7th Annual ACM/IEEE International Conference on Mobile Computing and Networking (MobiCom ‹01), pp. 70–84, Rome, Italy, July 2001.
12. B. Chen, K. Jamieson, H. Balakrishnan, and R. Morris, "SPAN: an energy efficient co-ordination algorithm for topology maintenance in Ad Hoc wireless networks," ACM, Wireless Networks Journal, vol. 8, no. 5, pp. 481–494, 2002.
13. L. Bao and J. J. Garcia-Luna-Aceves, "Stable energy-aware topology management in ad hoc networks," Ad Hoc Networks, vol. 8, no. 3, pp. 313–327, 2010.
14. P. K. Sahoo, J.-P. Sheu, and K.-Y. Hsieh, "Power control based topology construction for the distributed wireless sensor networks," Computer Communications, vol. 30, no. 14-15, pp. 2774–2785, 2007.
15. Z. H. Mir and Y. Ko, "Adaptive neighbor-based topology control protocol for wireless multi-hop networks," EURASIP Journal on Wireless Communications and Networking, vol. 2012, article 97, 2012. ·
16. J. Sheu, S. Tu, and C. Hsu, "Location free topology control protocol in wireless ad hoc networks,"Computer Communications, vol. 31, no. 14, pp. 3410–3419, 2008.
17. J. Gui and A. Liu, "A new distributed topology control algorithm based on optimization of delay and energy in wireless networks," Journal of Parallel and Distributed Computing, vol. 72, no. 8, pp. 1032–1044, 2012.
18. L. Tan and M. Wu, "Data reduction in wireless sensor networks: a hierarchical LMS prediction approach," IEEE Sensors Journal, vol. 16, no. 6, pp. 1708–1715, 2016.
19. L. Tan, X. Zhan, J. Li, and F. Zhao, "A novel tree-based broadcast algorithm for wireless ad hoc networks,"International Journal of Wireless and Mobile Computing, vol. 1, no. 2, pp. 156–162, 2006.
20. S. Zhao, L. Tan, and J. Li, "A distributed energy efficient multicast routing algorithm for WANETs,"International Journal of Sensor Networks, vol. 2, no. 1-2, pp. 62–67, 2007.
21. T. F. Neves and J. L. Bordim, "Topology control in cooperative ad hoc wireless networks," Electronic Notes in Theoretical Computer Science, vol. 302, pp. 29–51, 2014.
22. D. Shang, B. Zhang, Z. Yao, and C. Li, "An energy efficient localized topology control algorithm for wireless multihop networks," Journal of Communications and Networks, vol. 16, no. 4, pp. 371–377, 2014.
23. K. Moon, D.-S. Yoo, W. Lee, and S.-J. Oh, "Receiver cooperation in topology control for wireless ad-hoc networks," IEEE Transactions on Wireless Communications, vol. 14, no. 4, pp. 1858–1870, 2015.
24. N. K. Ray, Techniques to enhance the lifetime of mobile ad hoc networks [Ph.D. thesis], National Institute of Technology, Rourkela, India, 2013.
25. Qualnet 4.5, 2008, http://www.scalable-networks.com/.

26. L. M. Feeney, "An energy consumption model for performance analysis of routing protocols for mobile ad hoc networks," Mobile Networks and Applications, vol. 6, no. 3, pp. 239–249, 2001.

27. P. Siripongwutikorn and B. Thipakorn, "Mobility-aware topology control in mobile ad hoc networks,"Computer Communications, vol. 31, no. 14, pp. 3521–3532, 2008.

CHAPTER 7

IDHOCNET: A NOVEL ID CENTRIC ARCHITECTURE FOR AD HOC NETWORKS

Shahrukh Khalid[1], Athar Mahboob[2], Choudhry Fahad Azim[3], and Aqeel Ur Rehman[4]

[1]Telecommunication Engineering, Hamdard University, Sharae Madinat Al-Hikmah, Muhammad Bin Qasim Avenue, Karachi 74600, Pakistan

[2]Khawaja Fareed University of Engineering & Information Technology, Rahim Yar Khan 64200, Pakistan

[3]Faculty of Engineering Sciences and Technology, Hamdard University, Sharae Madinat Al-Hikmah, Muhammad Bin Qasim Avenue, Karachi 74600, Pakistan

[4]Department Computer Science, Hamdard University, Sharae Madinat Al-Hikmah, Muhammad Bin Qasim Avenue, Karachi 74600, Pakistan

ABSTRACT

Ad hoc networks lack support of infrastructure and operate in a shared bandwidth wireless environment. Presently, such networks have been realized by various adaptations in Internet Protocol (IP) architecture which was developed for infrastructure oriented hierarchical networks. The IP architecture has its known problem and issues even in infrastructure settings, like IP address overloading, mobility, multihoming, and so forth. Therefore, when such architecture is implemented in ad hoc scenario the problems get multiplied. Due to this fact, ad hoc networks suffer from additional problems like IP address autoconfiguration, service provisioning, efficient bandwidth utilization, and node identification. In this paper we present IDHOCNET which is a novel implementation of service provisioning and application development framework in the ad hoc context. We illustrate a number of implemented features of the architecture which include IP address autoconfiguration, identification of nodes by using real world identifiers, IP based services support in ad hoc networks, and a new class of application known as ID based application. Moreover how identifiers can completely replace the IP addresses to run the IP based applications is shown. It is expected that this work will open new research horizons and paradigms for ad hoc networks.

INTRODUCTION

The current Internet is built upon Internet Protocol (IP) architecture [1]. It provides numerous services like Voice over Internet Protocol (VoIP), email, gaming, social networking, e-banking, and so forth. However, the classical IP architecture suffers a number of known issues highlighted in [2, 3] in next generation networks. Such problems include IP address overloaded semantics, multihoming, and mobility. In order to meet the demanding needs from the Internet, a number of proposals in the direction of new architectures have emerged. The most popular trend among the new architectures is the ID/Locator based Split Architecture (ILSA). ILSA based systems are derived from the seminal paper at [4]. A comprehensive taxonomy and a review of such architectures are given in [5].

Continuing with the same premise of problems associated with infrastructure based networks, when IP based architecture is applied in the scenario of ad hoc networks the problems tend to increase manifoldly due to the fact that such networks lack infrastructure support. Additionally, IP addresses have topological meaning but ad hoc networks have flat topology

Citation: Shahrukh Khalid, Athar Mahboob, Choudhry Fahad Azim, and Aqeel Ur Rehman, "IDHOCNET: A Novel ID Centric Architecture for Ad Hoc Networks," Journal of Computer Networks and Communications, vol. 2016, Article ID 6438584, 18 pages, 2016. doi:10.1155/2016/6438584

and may lack hierarchy. There are no centralized servers in ad hoc networks for resolving issues like IP address conflicts using DHCP (Dynamic Host Configuration Protocol) [6] or DHCPv6 [7]. Moreover, there can be no central approach for name resolution like the Domain Name System (DNS) [8]. As a result, there are numerous of proposals in the direction of distributed naming and name resolution [9] for ad hoc networks.

IP address holds a pivotal presence in IP based architecture. For the functioning of a network it is essential that each communicating entity is configured with a unique IP address. Such a requirement is fulfilled with the help of centralized DHCP servers in infrastructure based networks. However ensuring unique IP address in ad hoc networks is a nontrivial issue. IP address conflict problem is studied under the field of IP address configuration services or IP address configuration protocols. In this pursuit various approaches have been proposed to resolve the problem of IP address autoconfiguration in ad hoc networks [10–12]. There are numerous papers suggesting such techniques but practical implementation of IP address conflict resolution schemes is hard to find. In an IP based ad hoc network a fully active IP address conflict scheme should be present to cater for the IP address conflict issues.

Bandwidth preservation is another important consideration in ad hoc networking scenario in which nodes have scarce resources and shared medium. Any measure which could save the number of bytes while transmitting the data is very valuable. A popular bandwidth preservation technique is adoption of an IP header compression scheme. In IP header compression a context or relationship is established within one hop peer. On the basis of the established relationship or context there is a possibility of compressing the IP header at the sender end and decompressing or recovering the complete packet at the receiver end. Thus a large amount of bytes can be saved and IP protocol overhead can be reduced. In ad hoc networking scenario the arrangement of nodes is in multihop fashion; therefore the IP header compression scheme is required to be modified for bandwidth preservation. In IP based networking, realization of a multihop header compression service is an open issue.

From the above discussion it can be analysed that IP based architecture has problems in infrastructure based network realization and such problems become more dominant in ad hoc networking scenarios. Moreover, it is observed that ID/Locator split architectures cannot be directly applied in ad hoc networks due to nonpresence of required infrastructure support. A depiction of ad hoc network node in IP based network, facing multitude problems, is shown in Figure 1.

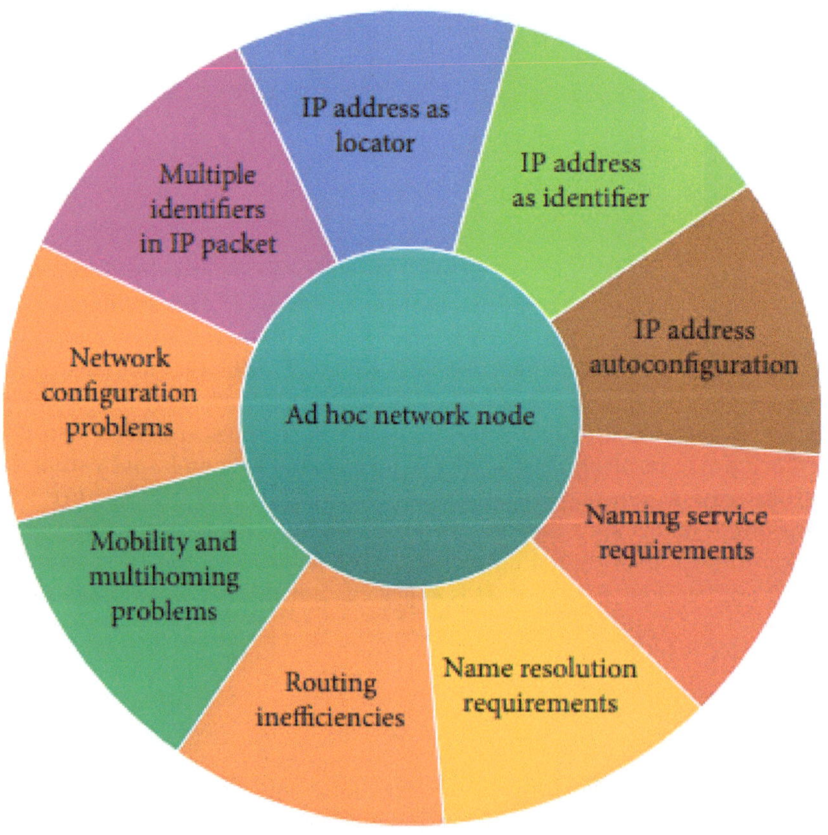

Figure 1: Problem circle of IP architecture based ad hoc networking.

As a step for resolving such problems for ad hoc networks we implemented a preliminary design for IP address autoconfiguration using identifiers [13]. In this paper, we considerably extend our earlier work and propose a novel ID centric networking architecture for ad hoc networks with the following design goals:

(i) Introduction of identifier based paradigm for communication entities.

(ii) An ID based application design.

(iii) Backward compatibility for IP based services and Internet provisioning.

(iv) Use of identifiers like MAC addresses, telephone numbers, and so forth for directly running IP based services.

(v) Multihop header compression when streaming services like VoIP are used.

In order to achieve the above-mentioned goals we implemented a functional prototype network which we call as identifier based ad hoc network (IDHOCNET). The proposed network system has been implemented on Linux based platform and a testbed has been built for conducting test and measurements. The remainder of our paper is organized as follows: Section 2 highlights the practical design considerations and problems, associated with IP based realization of ad hoc networks. Presence of such problems and issues has motivated us for design and development of our proposed ID centric architecture. Section 3 describes various components of our proposed architecture. Section 4 gives process flows of the architecture. Section 5 describes the implementation details of the prototype. Section 6 provides the experimental results. Section 7 compares the framework with respect to existing ad hoc schemes. Finally, Section 8 concludes the paper and presents future work.

REQUIREMENTS, ISSUES, AND CHALLENGES

IP Address Autoconfiguration Service

When IP centric communication is used, it is mandatory for nodes to have unique IP addresses assigned in their interface software. For a large ad hoc network it is very difficult to assign IP addresses manually and ensure the uniqueness of IP addresses. IP address autoconfiguration is an open research field and the large number of proposed schemes exists. Although there are hundreds of proposals, practical implementation of any of such schemes is scarcely available. Most of the autoconfiguration schemes exist for mobile ad hoc network (MANET) due to dominant problems of network merging and partitioning. We give examples of few latest autoconfiguration protocols.

The protocol proposed in [14] uses proxy nodes for assigning IP addresses to the joining nodes. Each proxy node has disjoint set of IP address blocks. Each node has predistributed hash functions for assuring secure communication. The SAAMAN [15] is an IP address autoconfiguration mechanism in which routing is based on geoforwarding mechanism. In order to ensure uniqueness of IP addresses the protocol implements distributed servers known as Distributed Detection Servers (DDS). Extended Prime Number Allocation (EPNA) [16] uses proxy nodes for assigning unique IP addresses. The rule for assignment is based on disjoint IP address generation by prime factor multiple. The protocol in [17] detects duplicate IP address through OLSR routing messages. The same authors have extended their work for merging support in [18]. An IPV6 autoconfiguration scheme is proposed in [19] for Wireless Sensor Networks (WSN) which is based on location information of the sensor nodes. Dynamic WMN (Wireless Mesh Network) Configuration Protocol (DWCP) [20] is an autoconfiguration scheme for Wireless Mesh Networks. The algorithm exploits the hierarchal structure of the WMN. A tree based scheme is proposed in [21] in which root node performs diverse set of functions which includes maintenance of record in its database of all group leaders in the network, maintaining free address information held by group leaders, index of leader of leaders for assignment of new root in case of its own departure from the network, and also performing network merging and partitioning tasks. The group leaders contain disjoint block of IP addresses. Another tree based architecture is proposed in [22] in which IP addresses are assigned by proxy nodes. Control packet overhead is restricted to one-hop peers. The protocol proposed in [22] also supports address reclamation.

Considering the above discussion it is straightforward to see that there is a certain overhead and complexity added when autoconfiguration is used in ad hoc networks for ensuring unique IP addresses.

ID/Locator Based Protocols

A number of proposals for ID/Locator split architecture are in evolutionary stage. Such proposals use identifiers for establishing communication between the entities. ILSA based architectures however require infrastructure components for location indirection. Therefore such proposals cannot be directly used in ad hoc networks. IDHOCNET design is inspired from ILSA in using identifiers for establishing communication between the entities. The basic model of ILSA is shown in Figure 2.

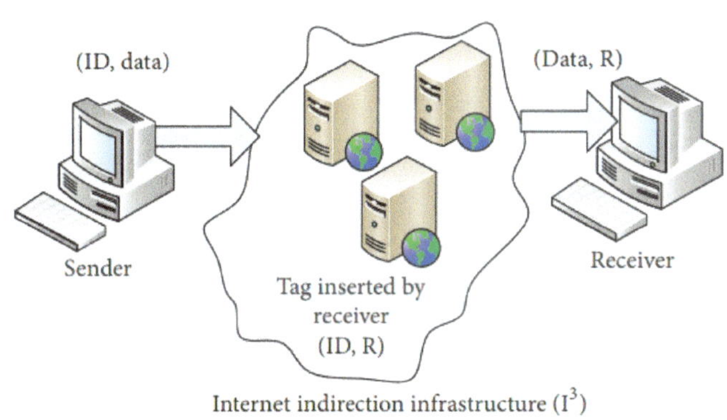

Figure 2: An abstract view of ID/Locator split based architecture.

A receiver can insert its location in Internet indirection infrastructure (I^3) and the sender can send the data intended for the receiver without knowing its location. The sender only sends the data and knows the identifier of the receiver. Each entity is identified by its unique identifier whereas location is maintained by an indirection infrastructure which performs indirection based upon the identifiers of the communication entities. The difference among the various competing proposals is in the way identifiers are represented, indirection infrastructure is implemented, and the means by which ID and locator mapping is carried out. Such architectures are in evolutionary stages and only small scale testing/prototype implementations are done in this regard.

For elucidation purpose we provide brief details of such proposals and kind of mechanisms used by them for various purposes.

Mobile Oriented Future Internet (MOFI) [23] proposed a distributed mapping control of ID and locators. MILSA (Mobility and Multihoming Identifier Locator Split Architecture) [24] proposes the use of composite form of identifiers. An identifier as per MILSA is composed of flat part which uniquely defines an object within a particular domain whereas the hierarchical part defines the unique domain for which a user is a part. Realm Zone Bridging Servers (RZBS) are used for mapping between identifiers and locators. Enhanced MILSA architecture proposes the use of a composite ID as a combination of human readable and cryptographic ID as a single node identifier. A virtualization architecture based on ID/Locator split concept was proposed in [3]. The proposal introduces the usage of virtual machines to build the indirection infrastructure. HIMALIS (Heterogeneity Inclusion and Mobility Adaption through Locator ID Separation in New Generation Network) [25, 26] approaches the ID/Locator split concept by introducing an extra layer between network and transport layer. This layer is the identity sublayer. The function of this layer is to support the session identification for the upper layers. Security features for the proposed infrastructure are based on asymmetric keys. An identifier overlay network (ION) [27] over IP based networks was proposed for supporting mobility. A clean slate approach was proposed in [28] which is based on ID based architecture design. An idea of domain trusted entity is used in which security and authentication features are based on identities of users. Due to a new architecture current IP based services are required to be modified to run on the proposed architecture. Another ID based clean slate approach has also been proposed in [29]. Use of IMSI number as identifiers was proposed in [30] for identity overlay networks.

IP Address as Identifier

In IP centric architecture the IP address is used as the core identifier, as shown in Figure 3, where IP based MANET is formed using OLSR. The IP addresses are used in the protocol header for establishing sessions, running services, and routing the IP packets in the network. In IP based ad hoc networks, especially in mobile ad hoc network (MANET), nodes cannot have dedicated or same IP address throughout their life cycle. Nodes will be required to change their addresses in an automated manner as dictated by the autoconfiguration service. Such events of address changes will cause the communication disruption between the nodes and this certainly is not a desired network attribute. After the change of IP address network wide broadcast and changes are required for ensuring future communication.

```
      *** olsr.org -  0.6.1-git_-hash_d553b5317eeede0bb5f5bb99b93dfa39
-10-18 03:09:44 on rothera) ***

--- 15:01:24.944788 ----------------------------------------------------

IP address        hyst         LQ        ETX
20.0.0.1          0.000  1.000/1.000     1.000
20.0.0.3          0.000  1.000/1.000     1.000

--- 15:01:24.944969 ---------------------- TWO-HOP NEIGHBORS

IP addr (2-hop)  IP addr (1-hop)  Total cost
20.0.0.4         20.0.0.3         2.000
```

Figure 3: Route establishment by OLSR.

As a practical example consider a scenario shown in Figure 3 in which OLSR is running as a routing protocol.

A user has the view of the current topology and sees that it can communicate with another user, if a priori information about destination IP address is known. But we know that IP address may be changed by the user itself. Moreover, due to the presence of an IP address autoconfiguration scheme, there is likely a chance that IP address of the user will be different from the intended one. Therefore, IP address in such scenario cannot be reliably used for establishing communication.

IP Address as Locator

Internet is a hierarchal network. The enforcement of this hierarchy is accomplished by Internet Assigned Numbers Authority (IANA) which delegates series of IP addresses to its suborganization known as Regional Internet Registries (RIRs) shown in Figure 4. Each RIR is responsible for its respective region assign IP addresses to various Internet Service Providers. Therefore a host on Internet bears the topological binding in the form of IP address received through its respective ISP. Therefore IP address structure signifies a hierarchical topology and it has been designed specifically for infrastructure based networks. However, in ad hoc networks and especially in MANET the topology is highly dynamic and changes quickly overtime. Moreover the IP addresses are likely to change frequently. Thus due to variation in the assigned IP address to the interface IP address cannot be reliably used for routing packets to the peers. Moreover in case of changes in the IP address of the peer due to address conflicts the routing table entries will also become stale. The change in such cases will be a complex process to handle. Another proposal for mobile hosts to retain their IP addresses while they roam from one network to another is in the form of Mobile IP (MIP) [31]. However MIP also requires infrastructure components of home agent (HA) and foreign agent (FA) for its functionality. Therefore MIP is also not directly applicable in ad hoc networking context.

Figure 4: Global view of IP address assignment authorities.

Using Identifier for Path Establishment

IEEE 802.11s [32] is an extension or amendment to the IEEE 802.11 standard. It has been designed keeping in view the requirements of ad hoc networks like MANET. As shown in Figure 5, the path is established using MAC addresses of the communication entities. The MAC address in the above case is used for path establishment between the peers and it is responsible for forwarding the data packets. However in the above case the peers still need to use IP addresses for running the applications and in case there is a change of IP address of a particular peer the communication will be disrupted.

```
shahrukh@shahrukh:~$ sudo iw dev mesh0 mpath dump
DEST ADDR         NEXT HOP          IFACE     SN      METRIC  QLEN    EXPTIMED
TIM      DRET     FLAGS
10:fe:ed:19:ea:03 10:fe:ed:19:ea:02 mesh0     65535   0       0       32428529 -
92       0        0        0x19
10:fe:ed:19:ea:04 10:fe:ed:19:ea:02 mesh0     65535   0       0       32428529
92       0        0        0x19
10:fe:ed:19:ea:05 10:fe:ed:19:ea:02 mesh0     65535   0       0       32428529
92       0        0        0x19
10:fe:ed:19:ea:02 10:fe:ed:19:ea:02 mesh0     2       8193    0       32428529
92       0        0      _ 0x14
```

Figure 5: Path establishment using MAC addresses.

Naming and Name Resolution

IP address is not a suitable choice for identification of nodes. As shown in Figure 6, both IPv4 and IPv6 addresses are difficult to remember. Moreover due to dynamicity of ad hoc networks IP address changes; therefore, the node identification is not persistent. Hence, it is necessary to identify nodes using other types of identifiers. In the present literature of ad hoc networks, it is observed that assignment and resolution of names are carried out by various mechanisms [9]. For realization of naming and name resolution in ad hoc networking scenario nodes are required to exchange control packets which cause overhead for their functioning. Moreover, the role of such services is to map an IP to a name. It is apparent that IP address assigned to the node is variable. Moreover the name assigned to the node is also variable. Therefore, to uniquely identify a node in such paradigm will require double efforts, that is, one to ascertain unique IP address and the other to ascertain unique name.

(a)

(b)

(c)

(d)

(d)

Figure 6: Real world ad hoc networking establishment scenarios.

Support of IP Based Applications for Backward Compatibility

A completely clean slate design without the backward compatibility of IP based applications will offer less flexibility and lower chances of adoption by the community. Therefore, any new architecture should support the standard IP architecture until the maturity of the new architecture. However, provisioning of IP oriented services should be done in such a way that known issues of the IP architecture could be minimized.

ARCHITECTURAL ELEMENTS OF IDHOCNET

Domain or Realm Perspectives

In the proposed architecture a network is established in a domain. A domain or realm is a group of communication entities which share common context and same identifier class. In a particular domain a host uses a unique identifier to establish communication with its peers. The choice of identifier class rests with the domain in question. The scale of the domain or realm can be small or large and depends upon the total number of identifiers. Various realms are shown in Figure 6. There can be home scenarios where names can be used for identifying respective users. In domains like school, universities, or organizations identifiers like roll number or office identification numbers can be used. In larger domains like public area or countrywide scenarios identifiers like national identification numbers can be adopted. In much larger scenarios identifiers like global telephone numbers, MAC addresses, IMEI, or IMSI numbers can be used.

As discussed above, IDHOCNET function in a particular domain and users can adopt a particular identifier class to communicate with each other. In a particular location there is a possibility of forming IDHOCNET networks pertaining to different domains as shown in Figure 7. There exists a possibility of allowing interdomain communication. However, in this work we will discuss the communication in a single domain. Each domain uses a unique domain identifier. Security policies can be enforced as per requirement of a domain. However, discussion on security provision and implementation is not the scope of the present work.

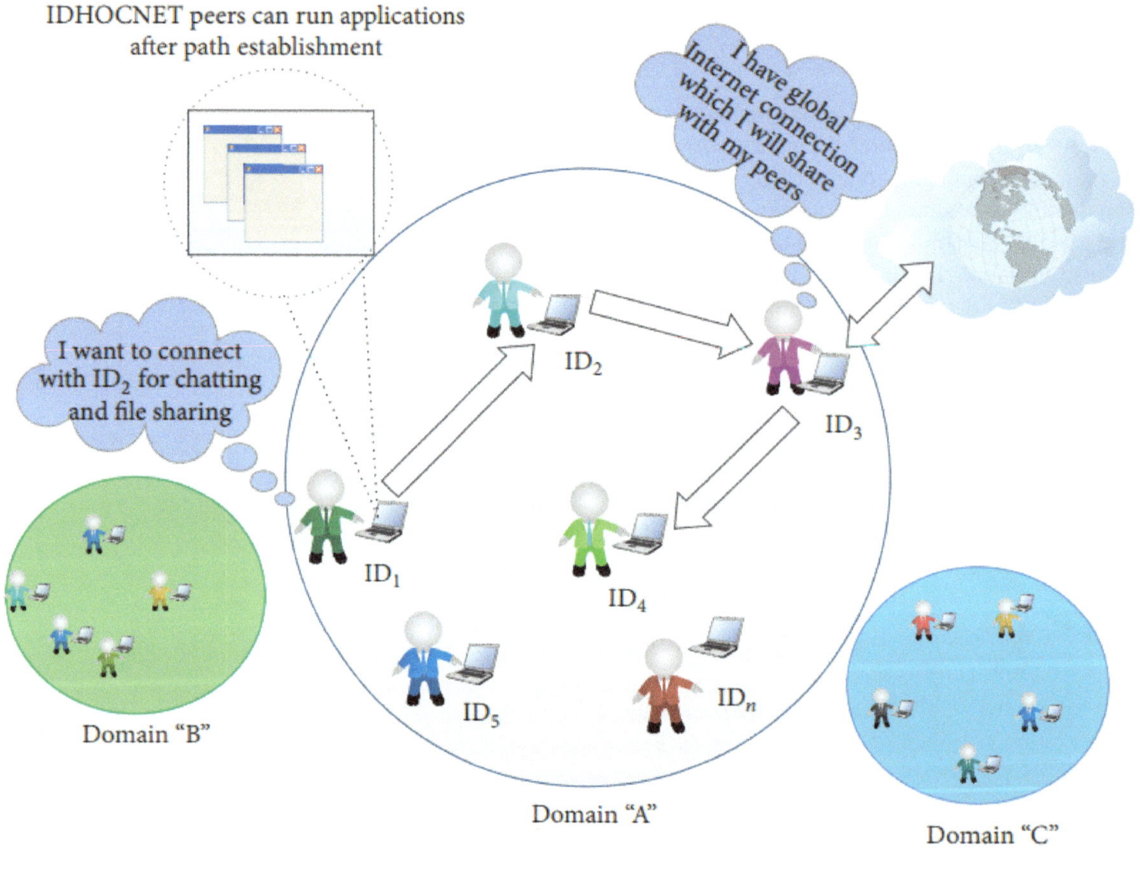

Figure 7: Abstract view of IDHOCNET formation in different domains.

Identifiers Based Communication Model

An identifier is a unique entity in the context of particular ad hoc network. In the strict sense an ideal identifier for use in the architecture is a hardware ID or a burned-in address (BIA) which can be translated in packet headers for establishing the communication. As an example, the architecture can use MAC address as an identifier as it is easily translatable to an ID. As an example an arbitrary MAC address, say, 11:22:33:44:55:66, is a hexadecimal number and its decimal equivalent is 18838586676582. It can be observed that the identifier looks similar to a telephone number which can be remembered or written down in the directory for communicating with the desired party. There are other hardware based identifiers like SIM number, IMSI, IMEI, and so forth. Moreover, there is a proliferation of RFID technology which also holds an identifier. The technology can be used for embedding the identifiers like national identity card number, telephone number, employee number, and so forth.

The identifiers are used for identification of the entities and used for forwarding the data to other entities. As shown in Figure 8, after path establishment process, an entity can forward the data to the destined entity on the basis of next hop identifier.

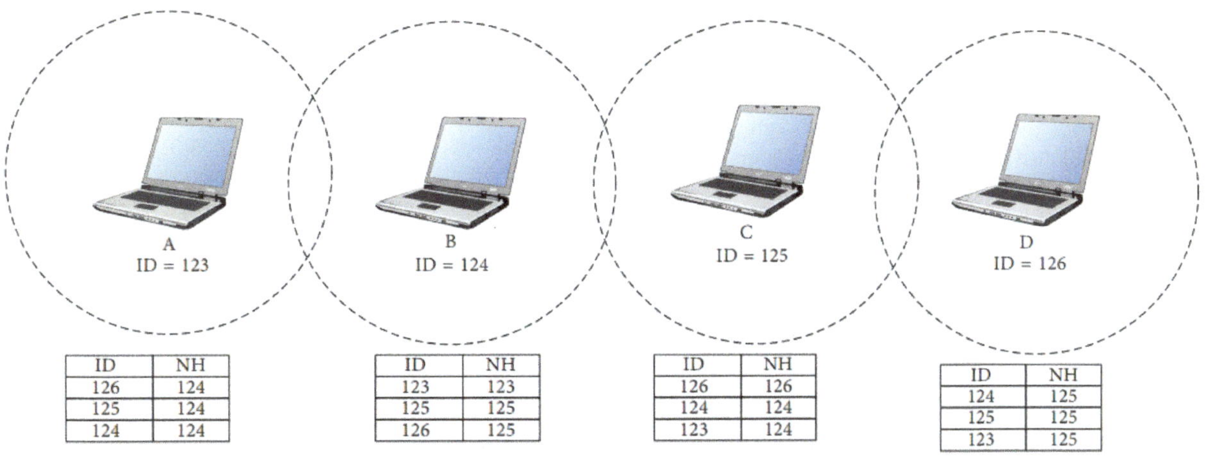

Figure 8: Identifier based path establishment in IDHOCNET.

Protocol Stack of the Architecture

ID centric architecture in comparison with IP based architecture is shown in Figure 9. The proposed ID centric architecture uses minimal pseudo 802.11 header which is added after the radiotap header [33]; thereafter identity layer is added. The minimal 802.11 header is added to device driver requirement [34]. The identity layer is used for end-to-end communication and packet forwarding. Moreover, this layer is also used for identification of the communication entities. The last layer is the application or data layer which contains either IP or ID based application data. The communication interface of the system is based on the Wifi device which is commonly available in all smart phones and laptops. The device is required to be in monitor mode for use by the ID based architecture. Each wireless frame is transmitted by inserting radiotap header which is the standard for transmitting and receiving Wifi frames [34].

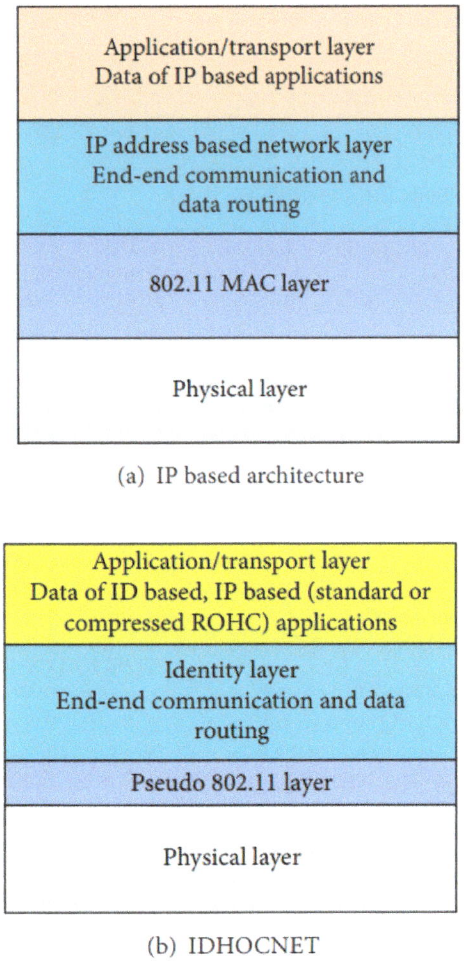

Figure 9: IP Vs IDHOCNET protocol stack comparison.

Frame Structures of Architecture

The system uses various frames, shown in Figure 10. The basic message M is composed of using radiotap header of 9 bytes and minimal pseudo 802.11 header of 4 bytes. A realm identifier is included for realm identification. After these headers, ID based frame is constructed. An ID based frame includes 2 bytes for protocol type. Presently available protocol types shown in Table 1 include Route Request (RREQ), Route Reply (RREP), IP applications, and ID based chat application frames. More frame types can be added to the system as per requirement, after the protocol type field identifiers are added to the frame. The size of the identifiers can vary as per the requirement of the domain or realm. A domain or realm is a collection of ad hoc nodes sharing a common context. For a smaller domain or realm which has limited users smaller size identifiers can be used. In order to suffice the requirement of large scale domain like Internet, 16-byte identifiers can be used. Source and destination identifiers are mandatory identifiers and remain same throughout the life cycle of the frame. For all IP/ID based data frames, intermediate source and intermediate destination identifier are added by each node which forwards the frame to the next node. However, it is possible to exclude the intermediate source identifier to conserve the bandwidth. Type A data packets include intermediate source identifier whereas Type B packets do not have intermediate source identifier.

Table 1: Protocol types of IDHOCNET.

Protocol type	Description
0x00	IP based applications
0x01	Route Request (RREQ)
0x02	Route Reply (RREP)
0x03	ID based applications

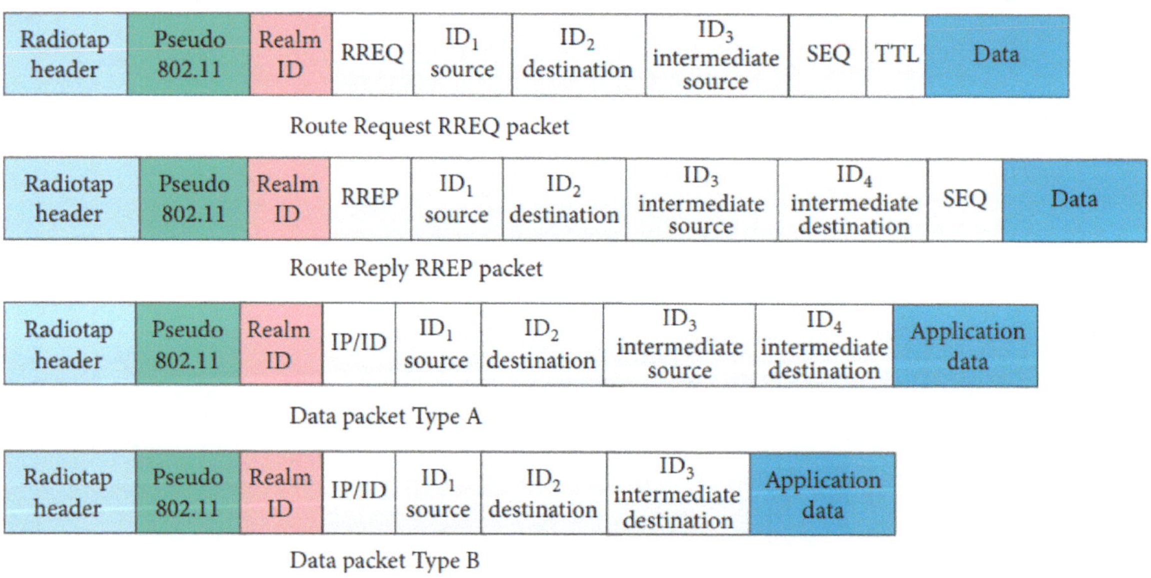

Figure 10: IDHOCNET frames structure.

Processing Steps at Node

Processing steps after reception of a packet at node x are shown in Figure 11. There can be a Route Request (RREQ) or a Route Reply (RREP) packet. Respective actions of RREQ and RREP are elaborated in the path establishment process. If a data packet is received and the next hop destination is known to node x then the packet is relayed to the next hop node. In case the packet is destined for the consumption of node x itself, it is processed as per the application in context.

```
If (M is of type RREQ or RREP) then{
    Process M;
    }

If (M is of type data packet and next hop is known) then {
    Relay M to the next hop;
    }

If (M is of type data packet and the destination is x) then {
    Consume the packet M as per the application in context;
    }
else drop M;
```

Figure 11: Processing steps of received packet M in IDHOCNET.

Placement of IDHOCNET in Host OS

An IDHOCNET node requires support of operating system to perform its core functionalities. IDHOCNET exploits the varieties of socket interfaces to achieve its operations. Figure 12 shows the placement of IDHOCNET in a host operating system. The system supports ID as well as IP based applications. Elaboration of socket interfaces is provided in Section 5.2.

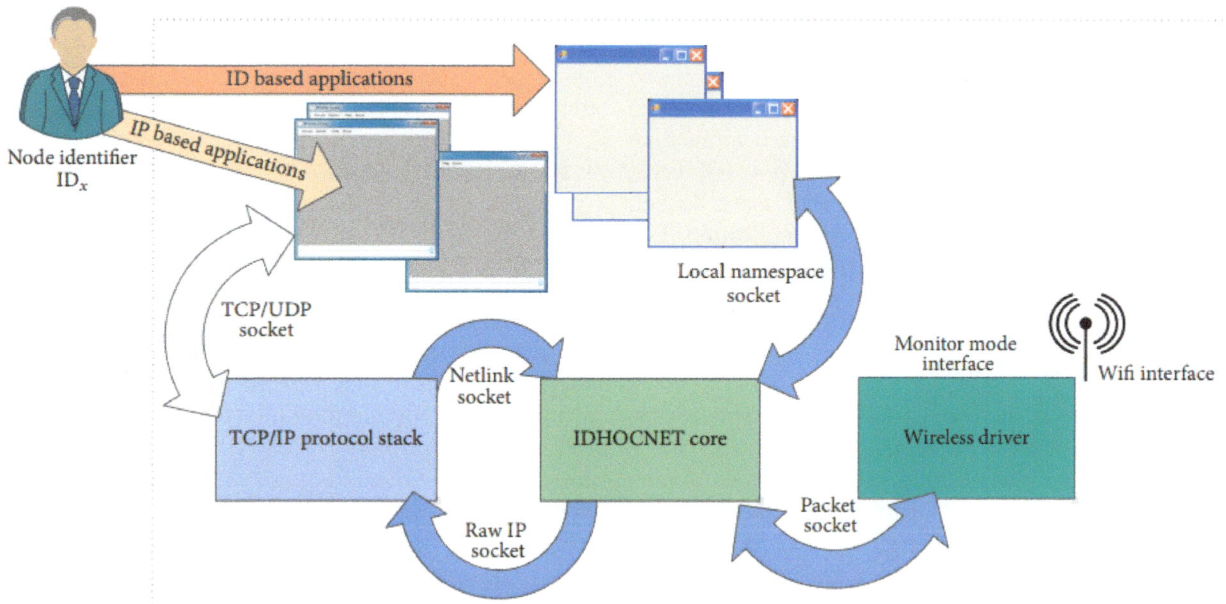

Figure 12: Placement of IDHOCNET in operating system.

Services and Capabilities Announcement

Each host has its own capability and services to offer. The peers may share the information of their capabilities and services through RREQ and RREP messages. Data portion of RREQ and RREP messages contains the capability information. The data of the capability string is defined to let the peers know the types of services being offered. All the intermediate nodes, which process the RREQ and RREP messages, also acquire the services and capabilities information.

Identifiers Based Application Design

The architecture supports a novel application class known as identifier based applications. This class of applications does not require the use of TCP/IP protocol stack for functioning. An ID based application interacts with the ID server through an Interprocess Communication (IPC) method known as local namespace or Unix domain sockets. Novel ID based applications can be designed which can achieve various tasks like chat, voice, ping, and so forth. The ID server application uses a local namespace socket name, say, /tmp/idcore. Each category of ID based application holds a unique protocol number as discussed in the frame types section. At startup, the application uses its unique local namespace socket name, say, /tmp/idapplication, for communication initially with the ID based server application. ID based server application maintains counter of numbers known as dock numbers. These dock numbers are analogous to the port numbers which are used by IP based applications. The flow of ID based application registration with ID based server application is shown in Figure 13.

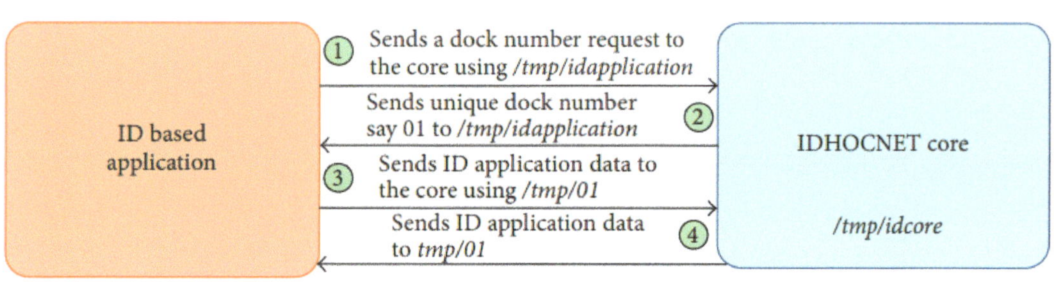

Figure 13: Identifier based application interaction.

At step 1, ID based application requests a dock number from ID based server application. ID server application assigns a unique dock number and registers an entry of application protocol number versus dock number in the ID applications table. At step 2, the server ID based application sends a unique dock number to the ID based application instance. After receiving the dock number ID based application deletes its native namespace socket so that other similar applications can initiate additional instances if required. The ID based application uses the dock number as its local namespace socket throughout its life cycle. At step 3, ID based application sends data to the ID server application. At step 4, ID server application sends data to the respective name space socket. Further illustration of the ID based network application flow is available in Section 4.4 under ID Based Application Process Flow.

Localized IP Networking

In order to support contemporary IP based applications, each node initializes a software defined tap interface. The IP address of the main tap interface (e.g., vnic) acts as the source IP address for all the outgoing IP packets. Whenever a node establishes a contact with a peer, the ID server initializes an alias networking interface and assigns it an IP address. Each pair of main tap interface and the alias network interface acts as a point-to-point network link. Thus a logical Ethernet network as shown in Figure 14 is available at each node for IP application provisioning. Such an implementation of private addresses is also beneficial for ensuring IP address uniqueness and therefore address autoconfiguration service is not required.

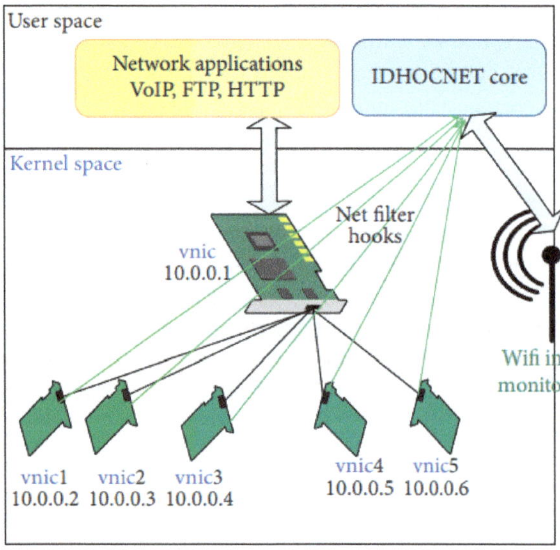

Figure 14: Localized IP address mapping with identifiers.

As shown in Figure 14, ID based networking architecture has Netfilter hook mechanism which captures the outgoing traffic of each private IP address whenever the user uses an IP application. For all the outgoing traffic source IP address remains the same which is the IP address of the vnic peer, whereas the destination IP address varies as per the target user. The outgoing IP based data is captured by the ID based architecture due to the presence of Netfilter hooks. Afterwards an ID based header is added to the IP packet and it is further transmitted by the IDHOCNET node.

ID versus IP Address Binding

A binding with ID and the private IP address is available in the routing table. Furthermore, ID server application also registers an entry in the host configuration file of the operating system. After this entry, IP application can also be run by using the identifier of the remote host. This is possible because IP applications can resolve host IP address through their names available in the host configuration file through gethostbyname() call. Details of the bindings and process flow of IP application are explained in Section 5under IP based application process flow.

User View of the Network

Each user of the ID based network has the view of the connected nodes. This view is populated on the basis of routing table and other peer related information. This view is acquired by the user by sending the command to the ID based server application. A user can see all those nodes which are in direct communication and also those nodes for which the user acts as data forwarding node. This view also gives the information about the private IP addresses of the peers which has been assigned locally by the ID based server application running at the user node. A sample view of a user with ID, say, 1230, is shown in Table 2.

Table 2: User accessible information of network peers.

ID	Name	Next hop	Private IP	Capabilities
1234	Athar	1235	10.0.0.2	ID chat
1236	Aqeel	1235	10.0.0.3	Internet Gateway, @ port 3120, ID chat
1237	Fahad	1235	10.0.0.4	VoIP, ID chat
1238	N/A	1238		N/A
1235	Shahrukh	1235	10.0.0.5	ID chat

OPERATIONAL FLOWS OF THE ARCHITECTURE

Path Establishment Process Flow

In general, the proposed architecture can adapt any reactive or proactive approach (like OLSR or AODV) for path establishment from TCP/IP model by replacing IP address with real identifier. Initially, for the proof of concept an ID based path establishment procedure similar to AODV is used with a number of simplifications for establishing the path between peers. A path or Route Request is initiated whenever a node requires sharing application data with its peer. RREQ initiating node knows the identifier of node to which connection is required. When node A wants to communicate with node D it initiates a Route Request toward node D as shown in Figure 15. When node A transmits the RREQ it is received by node B at reference point 1; at this point node B initiates a reverse path in its routing table so that path to node A gets registered. Similarly node B forwards the Route Request and it is received by node C at point 2 which registers the reverse path for node A. Now node C transmits the Route Request packet and it finally reaches the destination node D at point 3 and registers the path to reach node A. At this instant node D additionally performs 03 in number functions which include instantiating a private IP address, adding an iptables rule for this private IP address and IP versus ID binding is added to host configuration file.

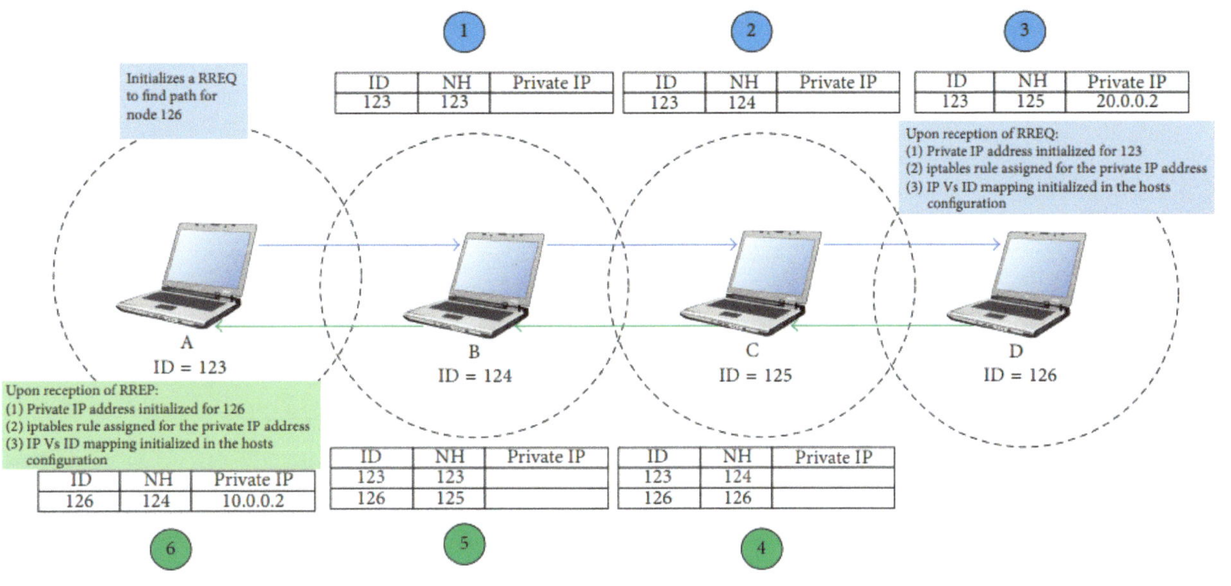

Figure 15: Path establishment process between nodes.

Now node D transmits the Route Reply (RREP) towards node A. In the Route Reply path the packets are forwarded in the unicast manner because path till node A is known. The RREP transmitted by node D first reaches node C at point 4. At point 4 node C also registers path to reach node D. Node C transmits the RREP which reaches node B at point 5. At point 5, node B registers path to reach node D. Finally the RREP transmitted by node B reaches the final destination node A which performs following functions register of the path to reach node D. Similar to the 03 functions performed at node D, node A also instantiates a private IP address for node D, adds iptables rules, and adds an IP versus ID binding in its hosts configuration file. After the path establishment process nodes A and D can run IP or ID based applications.

IP Application Process Flow

Let us consider a scenario wherein after the path establishment process between node A and node D node A starts an IP based application. The application runs between the IP address of the main tap interface with IP address, say, 10.0.0.1, and the synonym interface IP address configuring node A, say, 10.0.0.2. As depicted in Figure 16, at reference point 1 the IP based application generates the IP based data. The data is captured by the associated TCP/UDP socket. The socket passes the data to the protocol stack at reference point 2. At reference point 3, the IP packet is captured by the packet interception system of the ID based server application. At reference point 4, the routing table is referred and identifiers are added. At reference point 5, the packet moves to the packet socket system after composition of wireless headers. At reference point 6, the network driver writes the packet to the Wifi air interface. At reference point 7 the packet leaves the air interface where the intermediate nodes forward the data to the destination node. When the packet reaches the destination node at reference point 8 it is received by the air interface. At reference point 9, the packet socket captures the data and wireless header is stripped off. At reference point 10, whether the packet is destined for the node is checked. At reference point 11 IP addresses compatible to the node are associated with the packet; that is, destination address is changed to main tap interface address, that is, 20.0.0.1, and source address is changed to 20.0.0.2. At reference point 12 raw socket injects the packet back into the protocol stack. At point 13, the TCP/UDP socket captures the packet. At point 14 the active IP application consumes the packet.

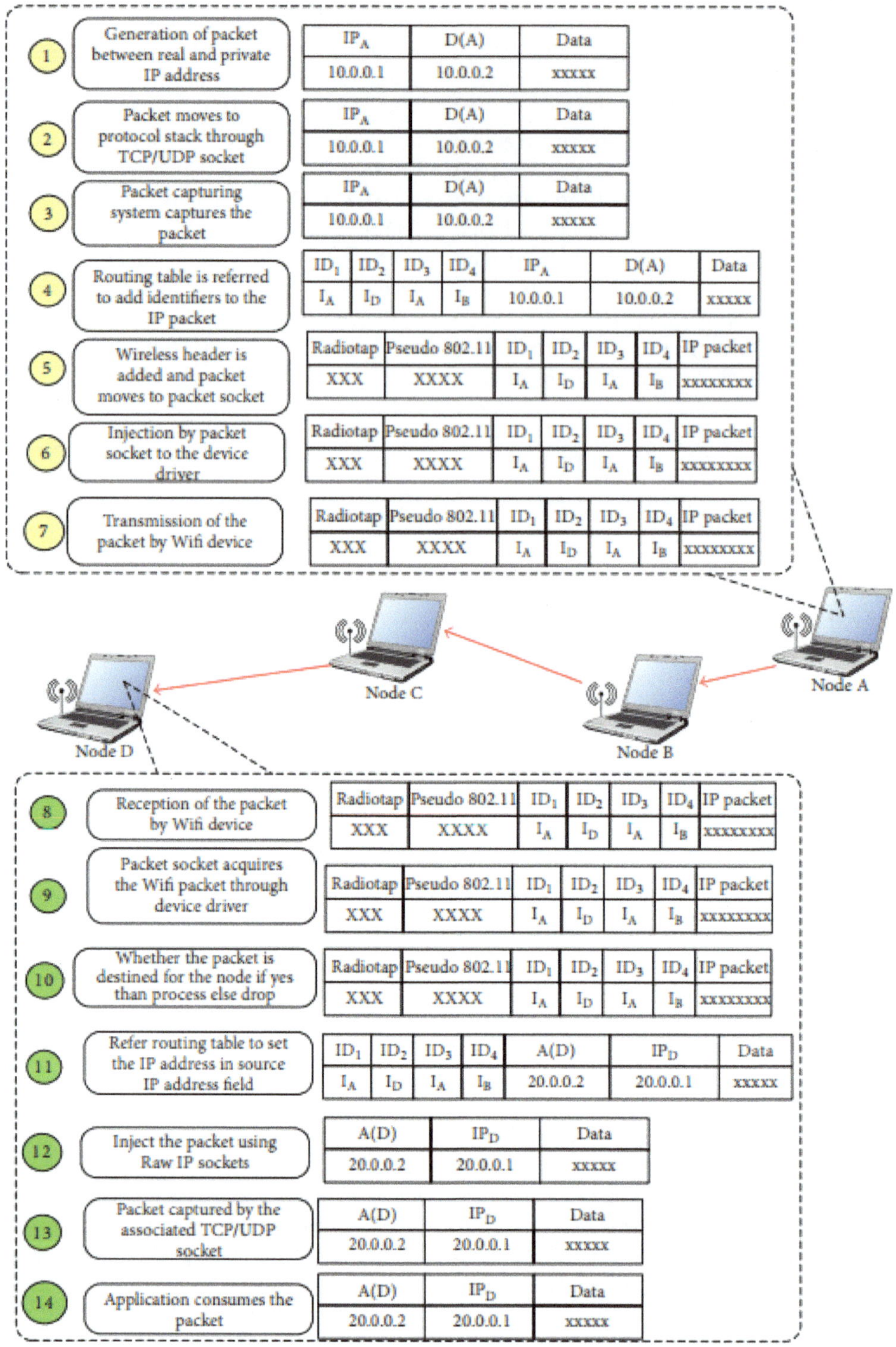

Figure 16: IP application packetwise flow.

Internet Accessibility Process Flow

Users of the ID based network may also have access to the Internet. A gateway node as shown in Figure 17, with an additional wired or wireless interface is used for Internet provision. This node runs a light weight proxy server and listens to the main tap interface IP address at a specific port address, say, 3120. This proxy server forwards the HTTP requests for all the ID based peers to the Internet bearing interface. These requests are captured by the monitor interface and injected to the protocol stack by the ID server application. After the injection of HTTP request packet, an HTTP response is received. The HTTP response is captured by the ID server application due to the configured net filter rule for outgoing IP packets. Each response is encapsulated in ID based packet and transmitted back to the requesting nodes. The users configure their browser's proxy setting with their locally assigned IP or with the identifier of the proxy node. They know the availability of the proxy nodes through the RREQ or RREP processing. When the packet is received at the requesting node then the ID based server application injects the packet and the user can see the response in its Internet browser.

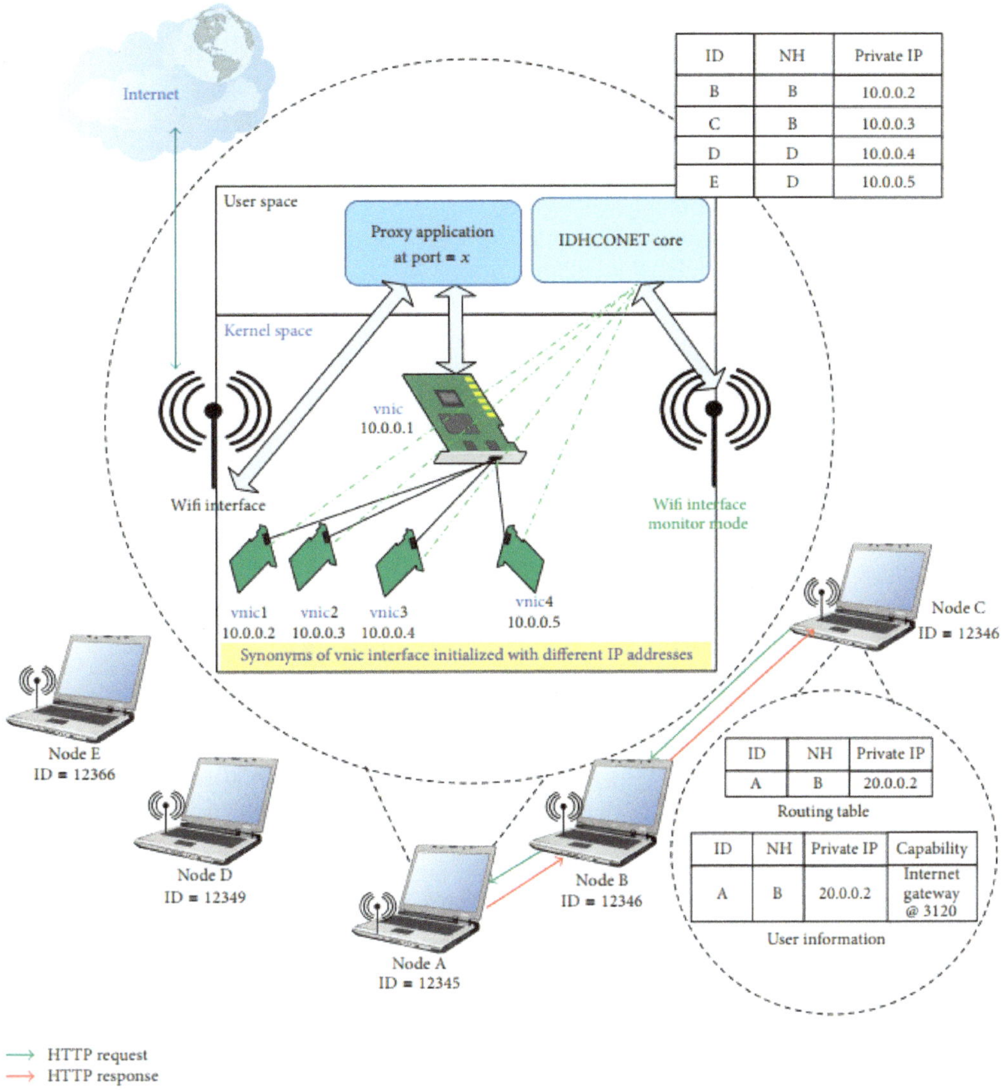

Figure 17: Internet provision through gateway node.

ID Based Application Process Flow

After the path establishment process users can run ID based applications like ID based chat, ID based ping, and so forth. Figure 18 shows the process flow of the ID based application run. Initially both end points start their ID based chat application. The application at both ends registers in the respective ID based server application with application type versus dock number entry. Initially, node A does not know the destination dock number of chat application running at node D. At step 1, node A sends the message to node D with the source dock number 03 and destination dock number as −1. When node D receives the message the ID based application sees in the ID based application table the type of frame and the respective dock number. The server application forwards the data to application available at dock 1. Now node D knows the node A dock number of chat application. At step 2 node D sends message using source dock number 01 and destination dock number 3. When A receives the message it now also knows the dock number of node D chat application. Now both node A and node D can exchange messages.

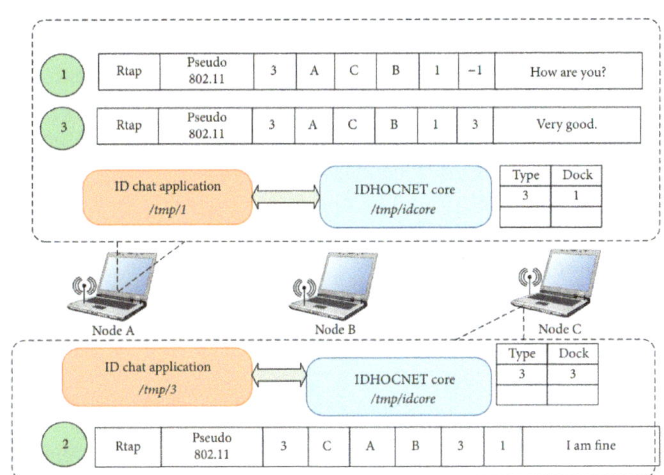

Figure 18: ID application process flow.

IMPLEMENTATION DETAILS

Host Configurations

Laptops with Ubuntu 12.04 LTS operating system were used to

build a host. C++ has been used as the development language. In order to ensure that each host has same software configuration, RemasterSys tool [15] was used. The image supports features like 80211.s mesh networking and OLSR. TL-WN721N device of TPLink was used as Wifi USB interface due to its 802.11s driver support on Linux. However, the proposed system has no restriction and it was tested to work on a number of Wifi devices. The size of the identifiers is 8 bytes which is sufficient to accommodate the IMEI, MAC addresses, global telephone or mobile numbers, and so forth.

Sockets Application Programming Interfaces

The implementation uses different types of sockets API for performing various functionalities and communication provision. Table 3 gives the type and functionality of the socket APIs.

Table 3: User accessible information of network peers.

Socket type	Functionalities
Packet socket	Capturing and transmitting Wifi Packets
Raw socket	Injection of IP packets to local IP addresses
Netfilter socket	Capturing of IP packets against iptables rule
Namespace or Unix domain socket	Intercommunication of ID based application

Packet Capturing System

For supporting the IP based application a Linux Netfilter system [16] is implemented using LibnetFilterQueue and LibnfNetLink [17]. An ID based application automates the process of adding an iptables rule against every private IP address added for the peer by issuing a Linux system command. When a particular packet is received in the callback function of the Netfilter system NF_DROP verdict is issued to further stop the flow of the packet. Identifiers based header is added to the captured packet so that it can be forwarded to the destination node. There are two possibilities that we can either send the uncompressed packet to the destination nodes or an optional ROHC based IP header compression can be applied to the received packet flow. The option is set in the configuration parameters of the software whether ROHC compression is required or not.

Interfaces and Private IP Addresses

The main tap interface (e.g., vnic) and monitor mode interface (e.g., monIf) are initialized at the start of the system through Unix system commands. When a node has active communication with other nodes then virtual interfaces are added to it (e.g., vnic : 1, vnic : 2, . . . , vnic : n). A snap shot of interfaces of IDHOCNET is shown in Figure 19.

```
shahrukh@shahrukh:~$ ifconfig
monIf     Link encap:UNSPEC  HWaddr 10-FE-ED-19-EA-C1-00-00-00-00-00-00-00-00-00-00
          UP BROADCAST RUNNING MULTICAST  MTU:1500  Metric:1
          RX packets:1580 errors:0 dropped:0 overruns:0 frame:0
          TX packets:0 errors:0 dropped:0 overruns:0 carrier:0
          collisions:0 txqueuelen:1000
          RX bytes:510374 (510.3 KB)  TX bytes:0 (0.0 B)

vnic      Link encap:Ethernet  HWaddr b2:07:5d:9c:69:3c
          inet addr:10.0.0.1  Bcast:10.255.255.255  Mask:255.0.0.0
          UP BROADCAST MULTICAST  MTU:1500  Metric:1
          RX packets:0 errors:0 dropped:0 overruns:0 frame:0
          TX packets:0 errors:0 dropped:0 overruns:0 carrier:0
          collisions:0 txqueuelen:500
          RX bytes:0 (0.0 B)  TX bytes:0 (0.0 B)

vnic:1    Link encap:Ethernet  HWaddr b2:07:5d:9c:69:3c
          inet addr:10.0.0.2  Bcast:10.255.255.255  Mask:255.0.0.0
          UP BROADCAST MULTICAST  MTU:1500  Metric:1

vnic:2    Link encap:Ethernet  HWaddr b2:07:5d:9c:69:3c
          inet addr:10.0.0.3  Bcast:10.255.255.255  Mask:255.0.0.0
          UP BROADCAST MULTICAST  MTU:1500  Metric:1

vnic:3    Link encap:Ethernet  HWaddr b2:07:5d:9c:69:3c
          inet addr:10.0.0.4  Bcast:10.255.255.255  Mask:255.0.0.0
          UP BROADCAST MULTICAST  MTU:1500  Metric:1
```

Figure 19: Private address map view.

EXPERIMENTATION, EXPERIENCES, AND RESULTS

Testbed Configuration

Multichip configuration between end points was established for test IP and ID based applications. All IP and ID based applications were tested up to 5 hop configuration settings. All the hosts were configured with identical hardware and software configuration as mentioned in Section 5.1. Channel 10 of Wifi was selected for all testing and applications run. The data was collected by using Wireshark tool.

P2P IP Based Applications Execution

Various IP based applications were tested. After path establishment between the end points, a user issued a ping command for private IP address 10.0.0.2. Moreover, the user was also able to identify the destination directly. In case the identifier is used its IP is resolved by gethostbyname() call available in the IP based applications. A regular VoIP application [18] was tested successfully. The application [18] was based on ALSA library and OPUS codec. A multihop scenario of 04 hops was established for verifying the voice reception between the end points. After the ID based path establishment process between the peers, the voice between the end points was transmitted and received successfully and the two parties were able to clearly hear each other.

Client Server Based IP Application Execution

The framework supports Client Server paradigm of IP based architecture. Apache web server is configured at a node and an application is hosted which tells the current temperature of the surrounding by reading the sensor value. The application was accessed successfully from a client browser by typing the identifier of the server as shown in Figure 20.

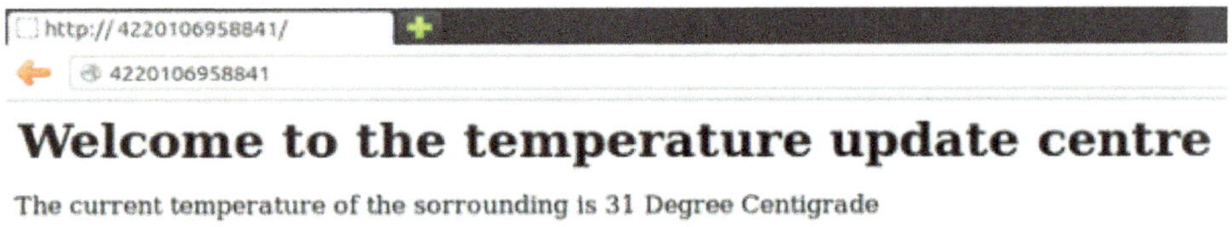

Figure 20: Receiving server response through a web browser.

Moreover, a gateway node with Internet connectivity was added and Internet was accessed in multihop configurations.

P2P ID Based Application Execution

A simple ID based application is designed using the principle and techniques outlined in the architecture details. In Figure 21(a) user with ID 18687085636098 is connected with ID 18687085636099. The multipath is established using the ID based path establishment procedure outlined above. The user sends a message to the destination. After traversing the intermediate nodes the message is received successfully at the destination node as shown in Figure 21(b).

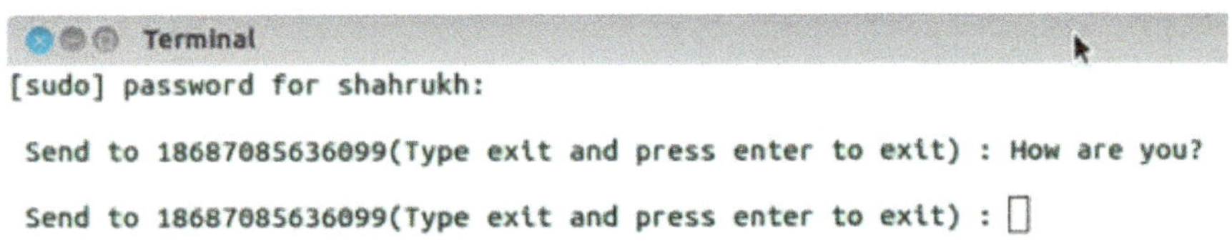

(a) Sending data to the user

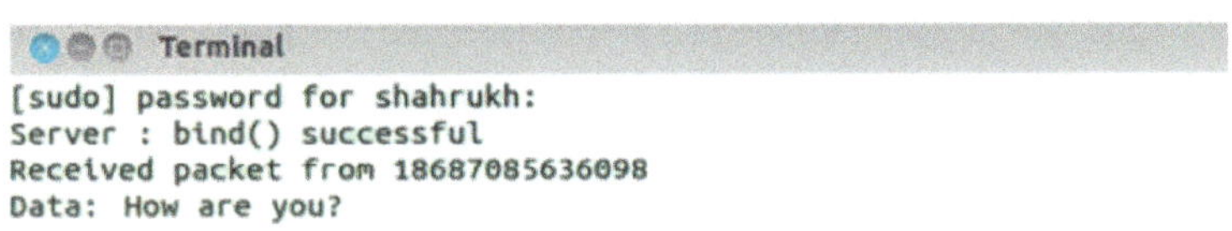

(b) Receiving data at the remote end

Figure 21: P2P ID based application sending and receiving data.

Data Packet Forwarding Overhead Comparison

Transmission size of a frame encapsulating an IPv4 packet of 20 bytes with 30-byte payload under different forwarding mechanism is shown in Table 4. The size of 802.11s link layer based forwarding is highest due to the use of IP addresses and additional MAC addresses. The size of IP layer based forwarding is the same as that of Type A of the IDHOCNET. In order to efficiently conserve the bandwidth Type B header can save an additional 08 bytes. As forwarding is based on identifiers and IP addresses are set at reception and as per the scheme at the node there is a possibility for not sending the source and destination IP addresses in Type A and Type B headers thus saving an additional 08 bytes in case of IPv4 addresses.

Table 4: Data packet comparison using different protocols

Forwarding type	MAC	IP	Payload	Total
Link layer	64	20	30	114
IP layer	52	20	30	102
Type A	52	20	30	102
Type B	44	20	30	94
Type A (No src, des IP)	52	12	30	94
Type B (No src, des IP)	44	12	30	86

RTP/UDP/IP Stream Analysis

In order to estimate the VoIP statistical performance we established a multihop testbed setup, complying with the host configuration discussed in Section 5.1. In each configuration RTPSEND [19] application was used with constant bit rate traffic at 20 msec and constant payload size of 168 bytes. For each configuration, 5000 RTP/UDP/IP packets were collected using OLSR, 80211.s, and finally our ID based protocol with Wireshark tool. ROHC library was used for compression of the RTP/UDP/IP packet when ID based protocol was used. The size of the complete frame also including the radiotap header is shown in Figure 22.

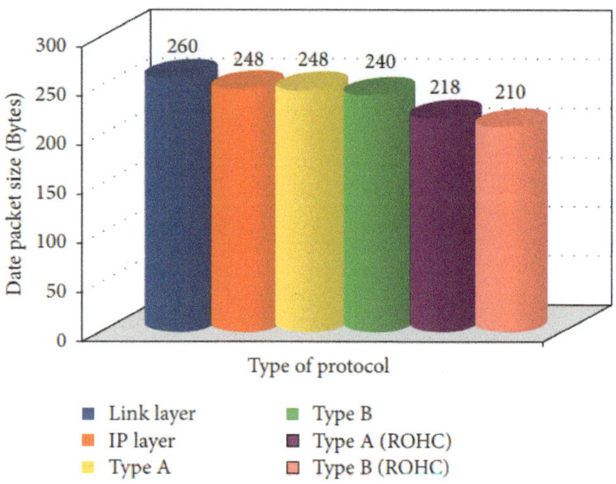

Figure 22: Frame size of RTP/UDP/IP packet under different protocols.

The packet loss ratio was measured during each scenario which is shown in Figure 23. It was observed that 802.11s suffers when more hops were added. The performance of IP layer forwarding and our proposed system using Type A or Type B headers is almost similar.

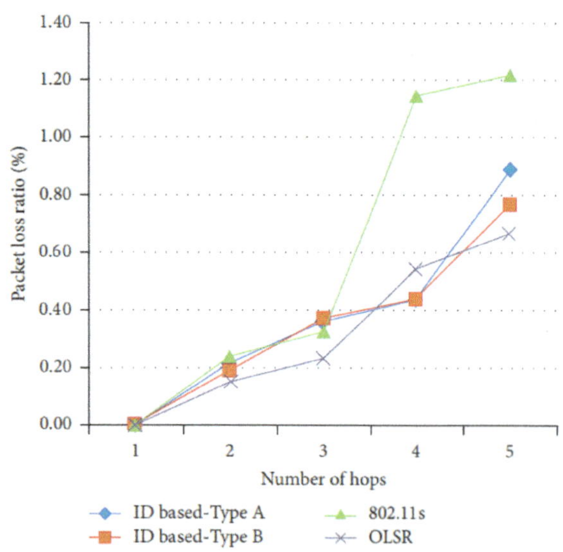

Figure 23: Packet loss ratio under different scenarios.

The jitter performance is shown in Figure 24. The jitter values calculated in different hops reveal that 802.11s performance is worst among the different protocols. The performance of Type A and Type B is better than the IP layer forwarding.

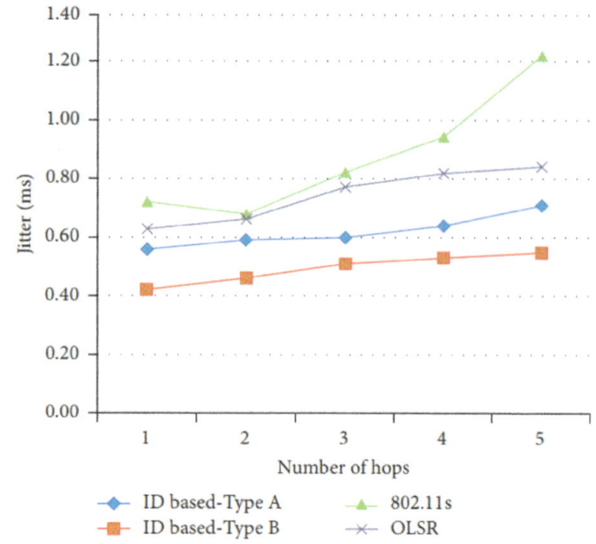

Figure 24: Jitter under different scenarios.

In order to appreciate the amount of bytes saving by the proposed ID based system in comparison to Layer 3 and Layer 2 forwarding by IP based architecture transmitted bytes were collected over the period of three minutes. Figure 25 shows the total transmitted bytes during the total span of 01, 02, and 03 minutes.

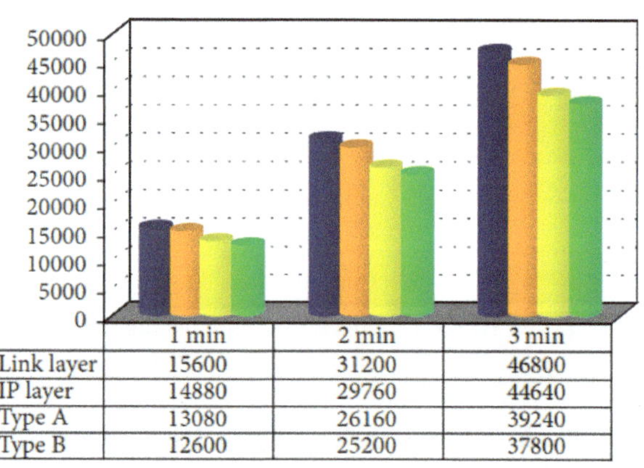

	1 min	2 min	3 min
Link layer	15600	31200	46800
IP layer	14880	29760	44640
Type A	13080	26160	39240
Type B	12600	25200	37800

Figure 25: Total transmitted bytes under different scenarios.

After the lapse of three-minute interval the scheme successfully saves considerable amount of bytes. In comparison with Layer 2 forwarding, Type A saves 7560 bytes, whereas Type B saves 9000 bytes. In comparison with Layer 3 forwarding Type A saves 5400 bytes whereas Type B saves 6840 bytes. It is evident that the ID based protocol is an ideal candidate for usage in real time streaming services like VoIP.

COMPARISON OF FRAMEWORK WITH EXISTING AD HOC NETWORK REALIZATION

The proposed framework provides number of benefits over the existing realization of ad hoc networks based on IP based networking architecture. A comparison is presented in Table 5. In IP based architecture the nodes use IP addresses as end point identification. The usage of the IP addresses is temporary in nature and required to be changed due to address conflicts. Moreover in terms of user point of view, the structure of the IP address is difficult to remember, whereas the proposed ID based framework can use real world identifiers like telephone number, mobile number, MAC address converted into its numeric equivalent, and so forth. As the users are already familiar with such types of identifiers, therefore transition for using identifiers instead of IP addresses will be straightforward and advantageous in terms of ease of use.

The existing ad hoc networking requires additional distributed name assignment and name resolution services [9] for naming support. Addition of such schemes adds complexity and communication overhead. The proposed framework does not require naming and naming resolution thus saves the additional overhead required by the existing ad hoc networking schemes. IP address autoconfiguration service is an essential requirement for existing ad hoc networking scheme for ensuring unique IP addresses throughout the network. The service adds complexity and communication overhead, whereas the proposed scheme implements private addresses at each node; therefore IP address autoconfiguration scheme is not required. Nonusage of IP address autoconfiguration will save bandwidth.

Table 5: Comparison between IDHOCNET and IP based ad hoc networks.

Requirement	Existing ad hoc schemes	Proposed scheme	Merit over IP based networks
End point identification	Uses IP addresses as identifiers.	Supports identifiers like global telephone numbers and MAC addresses.	Identifiers like telephone numbers, mobile numbers can be used.
Name resolution	For naming support it requires the naming and name resolution services [9] for identification support.	Uses identifiers (IDs) for end point identification, no need for resolution requirement throughout network.	No overhead for name resolution thus saving network bandwidth.
IP address autoconfiguration	These schemes require an IP address autoconfiguration service [10–12] to run in the ad hoc network.	It uses private address map for resolving IP address autoconfiguration. The proposed scheme does not suffer from IP address conflicts.	No requirement to run an IP address autoconfiguration scheme thus saving network bandwidth.
Heterogeneous subnets	Special gateway nodes are required for communication between nodes belonging to different subnets.	IP address support is implemented using private address map managed by the node. Therefore each node can have its own subnet.	No requirements for special gateway nodes.
Uniformity	Different schemes for IP address autoconfiguration assume different roles by different nodes like root node, group leader [21], and proxy node [22].	All nodes have similar role in the architecture.	Provides design simplification due to similar role.
Multihop header compression	Simulation studies [35, 36] have been conducted for multihop ROHC in ad hoc contexts. However a practical multihop ROHC implementation does not exist.	Implements a multihop Robust Header Compression scheme.	Supports a practical multihop Robust Header Compression (ROHC) scheme which saves considerable amount of network bandwidth.

In existing ad hoc networking all nodes come under similar subnetwork for communicating with each other. In case of provision of communication between different subnets special gateway nodes are required. This constraint will become dominant in case of mobile ad hoc network if two networks are initialized with different subnetworks. In case of mergers all nodes must come under same subnetwork or the provision of special gateway nodes must be available. In comparison to IP based networks, the proposed scheme can have disjoint subnets due to the private IP address usage at each node.

A number of naming, name resolution, and IP address autoconfiguration schemes demand special roles from ad hoc network nodes. In case of failure of special purpose node the functionality is difficult to maintain, whereas in the proposed ID based scheme all nodes have similar role.

To the best of our knowledge there is no practically implemented multihop IP header compression scheme for IP based ad hoc networks. However, simulation studies for MANET IP header compression (MIPHC) and MIPHC/ROHC schemes [20] have been conducted. These schemes offer less bandwidth conservation as compared to point-to-point ROHC scheme, whereas the proposed framework implements a multihop IP header compression using ROHC library, with similar compression gain offered by ROHC for point-to-point links.

CONCLUSION AND FUTURE WORK

An ID based architecture has been designed and realized for ad hoc networks which is likely to open future research directions. Problems of IP address autoconfiguration along with dual role of IP address as an identifier and locator can be solved by using our proposed methodology. We have provided support for operation of contemporary IP based applications. A novel class of network application known as ID based application has been designed and tested in multihop scenario. The VoIP scenario has been tested using multihop testbed using OLSR, 80211.s, and ID based protocol. The overall overhead of ID based protocol is found to be lower than IP based protocols.

Moreover, the protocol supports ROHC in multihop scenario which will be highly desirable in ad hoc contexts. An overall comparison of our architecture with existing ad hoc networking shows visible benefits. In future, we aim to extend our work by implementing a kernel module for the proposed architecture. The present work does not encompass the security features which is an essential requirement for ad hoc networks; our future work will focus on security provisioning of our ID centric architecture.

REFERENCES

1. J. Postel, "Internet protocol," RFC 791, 1981, https://tools.ietf.org/html/rfc791.
2. R. Jain, "Internet 3.0: ten problems with current internet architecture and solutions for the next generation," in Proceedings of the IEEE Military Communications Conference (MILCOM '06), pp. 1–9, IEEE, Washington, DC, USA, October 2006.
3. C. So-In, R. Jain, S. Paul, and J. Pan, "Virtualization architecture using the ID/Locator split concept for Future Wireless Networks (FWNs)," Computer Networks, vol. 55, no. 2, pp. 415–430, 2011.
4. I. Stoica, D. Adkins, S. Zhuang, S. Shenker, and S. Surana, "Internet indirection infrastructure,"IEEE/ACM Transactions on Networking, vol. 12, no. 2, pp. 205–218, 2004.
5. W. Ramirez, X. Masip-Bruin, M. Yannuzzi, R. Serral-Gracia, A. Martinez, and M. S. Siddiqui, "A survey and taxonomy of ID/Locator Split Architectures," Computer Networks, vol. 60, pp. 13–33, 2014.
6. R. Droms, "Dynamic host configuration protocol," Internet RFCs RFC 1541, 1997.
7. R. Droms, J. Bound, B. Volz, T. Lemon, C. Perkins, and M. Carney, "Dynamic host configuration protocol for IPv6 (DHCPv6)," RFC 3315, 2003.
8. P. Mockapetris and K. J. Dunlap, "Development of the domain name system," ACM SIGCOMM Computer Communication Review, vol. 18, no. 4, pp. 123–133, 1988.
9. M. Masdari, M. Maleknasab, and M. Bidaki, "A survey and taxonomy of name systems in mobile ad hoc networks," Journal of Network and Computer Applications, vol. 35, no. 5, pp. 1493–1507, 2012.
10. L. J. García Villalba, J. García Matesanz, A. L. Sandoval Orozco, and J. D. Márquez Díaz, "Auto-configuration protocols in mobile ad hoc networks," Sensors, vol. 11, no. 4, pp. 3652–3666, 2011.
11. S. Khalid and A. Mahboob, "A survey on Auto-configuration mechanisms for Mobile Adhoc Networks (MANETS)," Journal of Engineering and Applied Sciences, vol. 31, no. 2, 2013.
12. H. Zhou and M. W. Mutka, "Review of autoconfiguration for MANETs," in Wireless Ad-Hoc Networks, H. Zhou, Ed., chapter 6, pp. 123–144, InTech, Rijeka, Croatia, 2012.
13. S. Khalid and A. Mahboob, "Design and implementation of ID based MANET auto-configuration protocol," International Journal of Communication Networks and Information Security, vol. 5, no. 3, pp. 141–151, 2013.
14. U. Ghosh and R. Datta, "A secure dynamic IP configuration scheme for mobile ad hoc networks," Ad Hoc Networks, vol. 9, no. 7, pp. 1327–1342, 2011.
15. S. Rafiul and H. Subrata, "SAAMAN: scalable address autoconfiguration in mobile ad hoc networks,"Journal of Network and Systems Management, vol. 19, no. 3, pp. 394–426, 2011.
16. H. Kumar and R. K. Singla, "Architecture for address auto-configuration in MANET based on extended prime number address allocation (EPNA)," WSEAS Transactions on Computers, vol. 8, no. 3, pp. 549–558, 2009.
17. L. J. G. Villalba, J. G. Matesanz, A. L. S. Orozco, and J. D. M. Díaz, "Distributed dynamic host configuration protocol (D2HCP)," Sensors, vol. 11, no. 4, pp. 4438–4461, 2011.
18. L. Javier, G. Villalba, J. García, A. Lucila, and S. Orozco, "An extension proposal of D2HCP for network merging," Journal of Ubiquitous Systems and Pervasive Networks, vol. 3, no. 1, pp. 35–40, 2011.
19. W. Xiaonan and Z. Shan, "An IPv6 address configuration scheme for wireless sensor networks based on location information," Telecommunication Systems, vol. 52, no. 1, pp. 151–160, 2013.
20. A. Zimmermann, A. Hannemann, and B. Schleinzer, "IP address assignment in wireless mesh networks,"Wireless Communications and Mobile Computing, vol. 11, no. 3, pp. 321–337, 2011.
21. M. F. Al-Mistarihi, M. Al-Shurman, and A. Qudaimat, "Tree based dynamic address autoconfiguration in mobile ad hoc networks," Computer Networks, vol. 55, no. 8, pp. 1894–1908, 2011.
22. X. Wang and H. Qian, "A tree-based address configuration for a MANET," Pervasive and Mobile Computing, vol. 12, pp. 123–137, 2014.
23. J.-I. Kim, H. Jung, and S.-J. Koh, "Mobile oriented future internet (MOFI): architectural design and implementations," ETRI Journal, vol. 35, no. 4, pp. 666–676, 2013.
24. J. Pan, S. Paul, R. Jain, and M. Bowman, "MILSA: a mobility and multihoming supporting identifier locator split architecture for naming in the next generation internet," in Proceedings of the IEEE Global Telecommunications Conference (GLOBECOM '08), pp. 1–6, IEEE, New Orleans, La, USA, November-December 2008.
25. V. P. Kafle and M. Inoue, "Himalis: heterogeneity inclusion and mobility adaptation through locator ID separation in new generation network," IEICE Transactions on Communications, vol. 93, no. 3, pp. 478–489, 2010.
26. V. P. Kafle and M. Inoue, "Locator ID separation for mobility management in the new generation network," Journal of Wireless Mobile Networks, Ubiquitous Computing, and Dependable Applications, vol. 1, no. 2-3, pp. 3–15, 2010.

27. Y. Wang, J. Bi, and X. Jiang, "Mobility support in the internet using identifiers," in Proceedings of the 7th International Conference on Future Internet Technologies (CFI '12), pp. 37–42, Seoul, Republic of Korea, September 2012.
28. P. Martinez-Julia and A. F. Gómez-Skarmeta, "A novel identity-based network architecture for next generation internet," Journal of Universal Computer Science, vol. 18, no. 12, pp. 1643–1661, 2012.
29. B.-O. Kwak, T.-H. Lee, and W. Chun, "ID based communication in domain-insulated autonomous network architecture (DIANA)," in Proceedings of the International Conference on ICT Convergence (ICTC '12), pp. 264–269, IEEE, Jeju Island, South Korean, October 2012.
30. Y. Wang, "UNA: a new internet architecture for user-level multi-homing and mobility," in Proceedings of the 6th International Conference on Future Internet Technologies (CFI '11), pp. 13–18, Seoul, Republic of Korea, 2011.
31. C. E. Perkins, "Mobile IP," IEEE Communications Magazine, vol. 35, no. 5, pp. 84–99, 1997.
32. R. C. Carrano, L. C. S. Magalhães, D. C. M. Saade, and C. V. N. Albuquerque, "IEEE 802.11s multihop MAC: a tutorial," IEEE Communications Surveys & Tutorials, vol. 13, no. 1, pp. 52–67, 2011.
33. G. H. Berg and L. R. Johannes, "Radiotap," http://www.radiotap.org/.
34. M. Vipin and S. Srikanth, "Analysis of open source drivers for IEEE 802.11 WLANs," in Proceedings of the International Conference on Wireless Communication and Sensor Computing (ICWCSC '10), pp. 1–5, Chennai, India, January 2010.
35. B.-N. Cheng, J. Wheeler, B. Hung, S. Moore, and P. Sukumar, "A comparison of IP header compression schemes in MANETs," in Proceedings of the IEEE 32nd International Performance Computing and Communications Conference (IPCCC '13), pp. 1–9, San Diego, Calif, USA, December 2013.
36. B.-N. Cheng, J. Zuena, J. Wheeler, S. Moore, and B. Hung, "MANET IP header compression," inProceedings of the IEEE Military Communications Conference (MILCOM '13), pp. 494–503, IEEE, San Diego, Calif, USA, November 2013.

CHAPTER 8

IMPROVING QUALITY OF SERVICE AND REDUCING POWER CONSUMPTION WITH WAN ACCELERATOR IN CLOUD COMPUTING ENVIRONMENTS

Shin-ichi Kuribayashi[1]

[1]Department of Computer and Information Science, Seikei University, Japan

ABSTRACT

The widespread use of cloud computing services is expected to deteriorate a Quality of Service and toincrease the power consumption of ICT devices, since the distance to a server becomes longer than before. Migration of virtual machines over a wide area can solve many problems such as load balancing and power saving in cloud computing environments.

This paper proposes to dynamically apply WAN accelerator within the network when a virtual machine is moved to a distant center, in order to prevent the degradation in performance after live migration of virtual machines over a wide area. mSCTP-based data transfer using different TCP connections before and after migration is proposed in order to use a currently available WAN accelerator. This paper does not consider the performance degradation of live migration itself. Then, this paper proposes to reduce the power consumption of ICT devices, which consists of installing WAN accelerators as part of cloud resources actively and increasing the packet transfer rate of communication link temporarily. It is demonstrated that the power consumption with WAN accelerator could be reduced to one-tenth of that without WAN accelerator.

INTRODUCTION

Cloud computing services are rapidly gaining in popularity [1]-[3], which enable users to access huge computing resources (processing ability, storage, etc.) distributed over the network from any terminals for a required length of time without any need to worry about where resources are located or how resources are structured internally. The background to this rapid penetration includes the availability of high-speed networks, and the development of virtual computing, grid computing and other advanced computing technologies. In recent years, enterprises are shifting from building their own information systems to using cloud computing services increasingly, because cloud computing services are easy to use and enable them to reduce both their business cost and environmental impacts.

As a lot of servers and storages will be centralized in cloud computing environments, it is necessary to deal with failures and to balance the processing load. It is also required to decrease the power consumption of ICT devices.

In cloud computing environments, migration of virtual machines (VMs) over a wide area can solve many problems such as load balancing and power saving. Migration technology

Citation: Shin-ichi Kuribayashi, Improving Quality of Service and Reducing Power Consumption with WAN accelerator in Cloud Computing Environments, DOI : 10.5121/ijcnc.2013.5103.

is used to move the memory spaces of VMs from one physical server to a different physical server while ensuring service continuity. In particular, live migration is intended to move VMs with virtually no disruption to the services being provided. There are studies that assume that VMs are moved over a wide area rather than keeping them confined in the same site[4]-[13]. Such wide-area migration will improve robustness against wide-area disasters and the effectiveness of load balancing. When a VM is moved to a distant center, the performance may deteriorate (e.g, slow response and decreased throughput) due to an increase in network delay or a reduction in bandwidths. It is required to prevent degradation in performance after live migration of VMs over a wide area. We propose to automatically apply WAN accelerator[14]-[18] (also known as WAN optimization)to prevent degradation in performance when the network delay between the terminal and the center exceeds a certain threshold as a result of moving a VM.

Although ICT makes it possible to reduce power consumption in the country by optimizing physical distribution, optimizing production, and reducing human movements (commuting and business trips) [19],[20], it is required to make efforts to prevent an increase in power consumption of ICT devices as much as possible. Cloud computing, which uses huge computing and network resources, are naturally subject to such efforts. To reduce the power consumed by the entire ICT devices, it is necessary to take coordinated measures to implement power saving in data centers, communication networks and power networks, instead of seeking to save power in each of these independently. The authors have proposed a guideline and a procedure to exchange information needed for this coordination [21]-[23]. With a view to further reducing the power consumed by the entire ICT devices, we present a new power saving measure with WAN accelerators in this paper. Although WAN accelerators have been introduced to prevent degradation in performance caused by a long network delay in WANs originally, they can also dramatically shorten communication time of applications such a file transfer that transfer a huge volume of data continuously but do not require real-time transfer. The reduction in communication time can also reduce the power used by data centers and network devices. Therefore, the introduction of WAN accelerators as part of cloud resources is useful not only for reducing communication time but also for reducing the power consumption by ICT devices.

The rest of this paper is organized as follows. Section 2 proposes to dynamically apply WAN accelerator within the network to prevent the degradation in performance after live migration of VMs over a wide area. This paper does not consider the performance degradation of live migration itself. Section 3 presents a method of reducing the power consumption of the entire ICT devices in a cloud computing environment, which consists of installing WAN accelerators as part of cloud resources actively and increasing the packet transfer rate of communication link temporarily. Section 4 explains the related work. Finally, Section 5gives the conclusions. This paper is an extension of the study in Reference [18].

METHOD OF PREVENTING THE DEGRADATION IN PERFORMANCE AFTER VM LIVE MIGRATION OVER A WIDE AREA

Overview

A lot of servers and storages will be centralized in cloud computing environments. While this approach may bring economic benefits, it may sacrifice communication performance and usability for users because it will increase network delay time and traffic congestion. WAN accelerators, which aim to accelerate a broad range of applications and protocols over a WAN, are widely introduced to cope with this type of problem. For example, in the case where TCP is used, the introduction of a WAN accelerator allows the use of ACK proxy responses, the expansion of the TCP window size, and slow-start control[14]. These features can improve response time and enhance throughput. The use of data compression and caching is also useful because they can reduce both the volume of traffic and the bandwidths used in the network.

When a VM is moved to a distant center, the performance may deteriorate (e.g, slow response and decreased throughput) due to an increase in network delay or a reduction in bandwidths. As a measure to prevent this degradation, this paper proposes to apply WAN accelerator in the network automatically whenever network delay has increased or the bandwidths available have decreased beyond certain specified levels. The proposed method could allow more flexible application of VM migration without requiring any change in the terminal environment. The image of the proposed method is illustrated in Figure 1.

Method of dynamically inserting WAN accelerator after migration of virtual machines

Even when the IP addresses of VMs are changed as a result of wide-area live migration, it could be possible to maintain communication using the methods proposed in References [24]-[28]. Those methods do not support the establishment of a new TCP connection in conjunction with VM migration, even though most of existing WAN accelerators initiate WAN optimization function by establishing a new TCP connection. Therefore, we have chosen to use mSCTP[29]-[31], which supports multi-homing and multiple IP addresses simultaneously.

In mSCTP-based migration, VMs will transfer data using different TCP connections before and after migration, thereby maintaining the sessions between the terminals and servers. Issues form SCTP-based live migration and solutions to them are described and proposed below. It is assumed here that VirtualBox [32] is used as the server virtualization system. The ‘teleportion’ function of VirtualBox supports live migration.

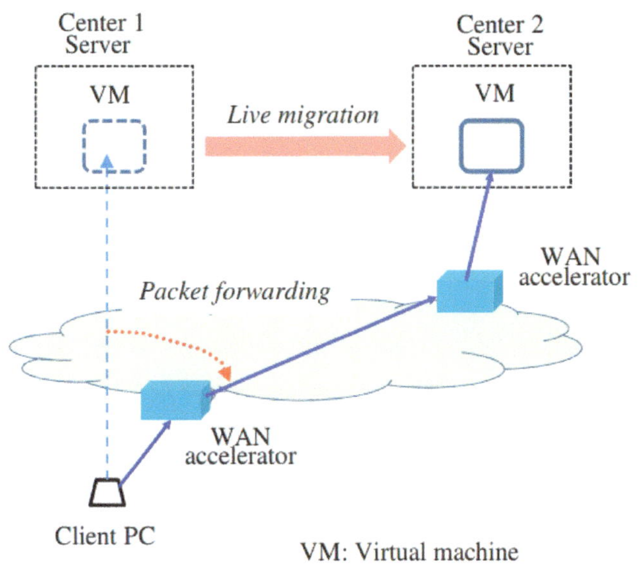

Figure 1: Image of wide-area live migration of VM with WAN optimization function

(1) How client PC finds out the new IP address of the destination VM

It is impossible to know in advance when VM migration will occur. It is proposed that the source server notifies the client terminal of the new IP address of the destination VM using SCTP messages in advance.

(2) When and how to determine migration of VMs

It is generally difficult for an external party to know immediately the timing when VM migration has completed. It is proposed to solve this problem as follows: After VM migration has been completed, VirtualBox's window of the destination server changes from the migration standby & display window to a VM's OS activation window. Completion of VM migration can be recognized by watching for this change. The client PC is notified of this change separately from the mSCTP functions. The reception of this notification prompts the client PC to request the migrated VM on the destination server to establish a new TCP connection.

Figure 2 shows the communication sequence of the entire mSCTP-based live migration that incorporates the solutions described in (1) and (2). The image of connection management in client PCs and servers is illustrated in Figure 3. Each client PC and VM has two different IP addresses. It uses different IP addresses and uses different TCP connections before and after VM migration. The transferred data is first stored in SCTP packets, and is then encapsulated in TCP packets and transmitted.

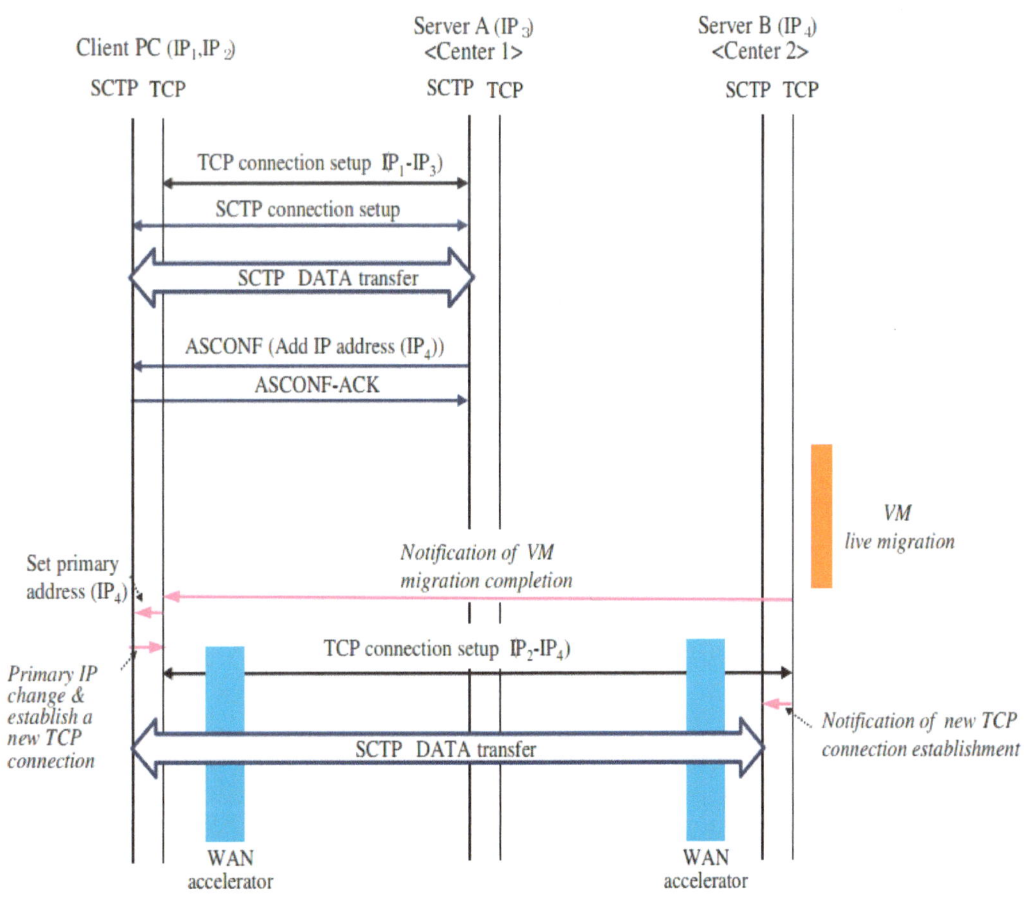

Figure 2: Overview of VM migration sequence with mSCTP

Evaluation of mSCTP-based live migration

Evaluation system configuration

A system shown in Figure 4 was built to verify the operation of the proposed method. The specification of individual devices in the system is as follows:

<Servers>
CPU: Intel Core™ i5, Virtualization system: VirtualBox 4.0.16, Host OS: Windows 7, Guest OS: Windows XP, LAN interface: 100Mbps
<Clients>
CPU: Intel Core™ i5, OS: Windows 7,LAN interface: 100Mbps
<NAS>
1 TB×2, LAN interface: 100Mbps
<Network Emulator>
Maximum speed: 100Mbps, constant delay
<WAN accelerator>

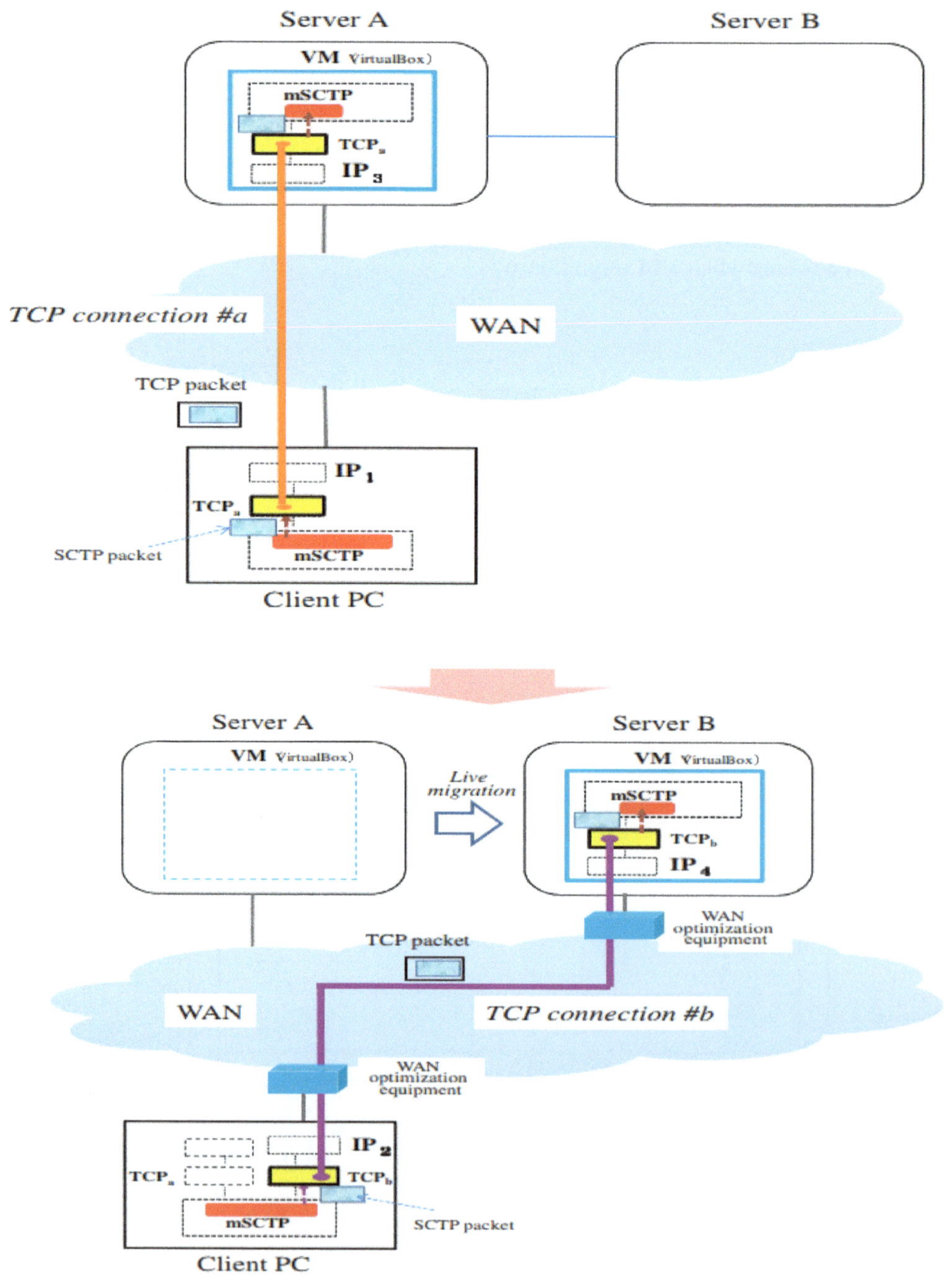

Figure 3: Image of TCP connection exchange in servers and client PC

Verification of the operation

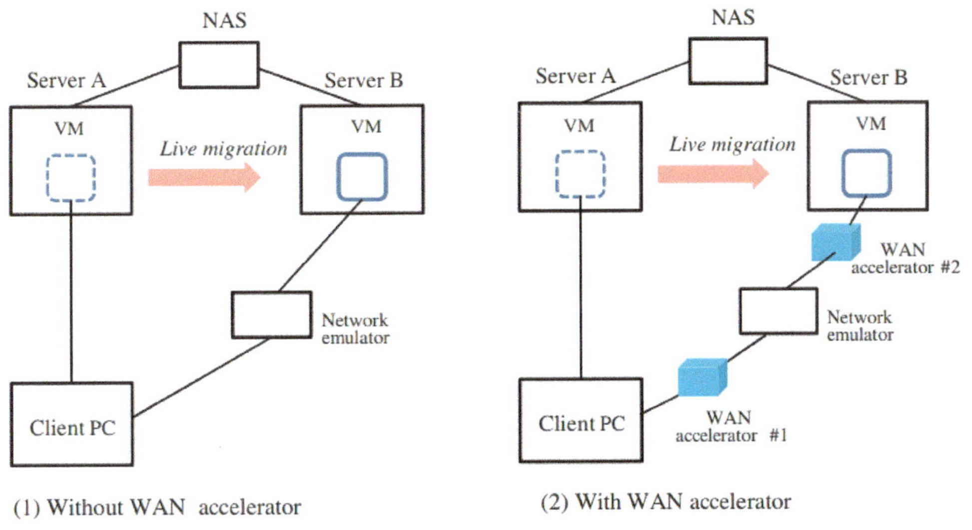

Figure 4: Evaluation system configuration

We have checked the live migration (teleportation) of a VM on Server A to Server B in Figure 4 while the VM is gradually displaying an image, up to the point where the entire image has been displayed. It was assumed that no other communication is in progress. We have found that the image displaying speed is reduced to one-fifth of the speed before the VM migration unless a WAN accelerator is inserted, when the network delay between Server B and the client PC is 300 ms. The insertion of a WAN accelerator after the migration returns the image displaying speed to almost the same speed as in the pre-migration state. It has been also found that the insertion of a WAN accelerator has little impact on VM migration time.

Table 1 shows the time it takes to transfer file data with FTP. d is the network delay between Server B and the client PC and is assumed to be constant. T shows the time which is taken to complete the transfer of all data(50MB) after live migration with WAN accelerator and does not include the time required for live-migration. The value of T is normalized relative to the time required to complete the transfer of all data without live migration. It is clear from Table 1 that WAN accelerator makes it possible to maintain the communication performance similar to that before the migration.

Table 1: Required time to complete the transfer of all data with WAN accelerator

d [ms]	T
250	0.25
500	0.1
750	0.08
1000	0.07

d: Network delay between client and server B after live migration
T: Required time to complete the transfer of all data (50MB) after live migration which is normalized relative to the time without WAN accelerator

METHOD OF REDUCING POWER CONSUMPTION OF ICT DEVICES

Reducing power consumption by applying WAN accelerator

In recent years, enterprises are consolidating servers and storage units in different sites into a single center, in order to utilize those resources efficiently and reduce their business cost. However, the benefit of efficient operation may derive at the expense of reduced performance and inconvenience for users since the distance to those resources becomes longer than before. To prevent these negative effects, WAN accelerators[14]-[17] are increasingly introduced. In TCP, ACK proxy responses at the WAN accelerator side, widening of the TCP window size, etc. can shorten response time and increase throughput. In addition, data compression and caching can reduce traffic in the WAN, thereby preventing congestion and reducing the required bandwidth.

In addition, WAN accelerators can reduce the power consumption of ICT devices. That is, WAN accelerators can dramatically shorten communication time in a file transfer application and some ICT devices can be put in sleep mode for a long time by the shortened time. It can reduce the power consumption of them. This idea could not apply to all applications but is effective for huge data transfer.

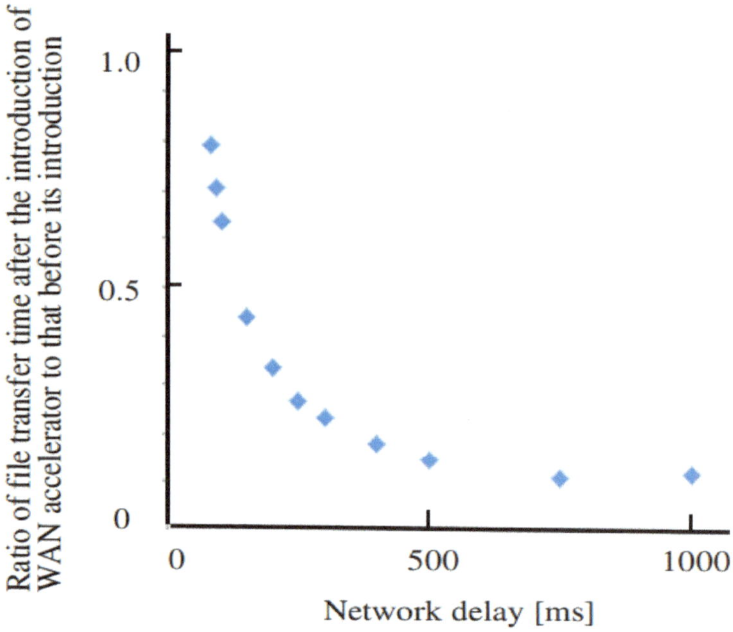

Figure 5: Effect of introducing WAN accelerator

Figure 5 illustrates an example of measurement of time it takes to transfer a fixed-size data file with FTP. The same WAN accelerator (Steelhead) in Section 2.3.1 is also used here. Network delay is assumed to be constant. It shows how the introduction of a WAN accelerator shortens communication time. The vertical axis indicates the ratio of the file transfer time after the introduction of a WAN accelerator to that before its introduction. For example, where the network delay is 500ms, the introduction of WAN accelerator can shorten file transfer time to about 1/10 and thereby the power consumed by the ICT devices connected to the WAN would be reduced by 1/10 at the maximum.

While the individual user can introduce a WAN accelerator on their own, it is effective to install WAN accelerators as part of cloud resources and lease them to users on an hourly basis, as proposed in Reference [17], or for a network provider to apply WAN accelerator transparently. If WAN accelerators are combined with other WAN optimization technologies, such as data compression and caching, it is possible to reduce not only power consumption but also network bandwidth that the network provider needs to install.

Reducing power consumption by increasing the packet transfer rate

As a measure to reduce the power consumption of the network, it has been proposed to reduce the packet transfer rates of communication links when traffic on these links is small [33]-[35]. This idea assumes that the higher the link transfer rate, the more power is consumed. However, in applications, such as file transfer, that transfer a huge volume of data continuously but do not require real-time transfer, the total power consumption can be reduced by increasing the packet transfer rate conversely, thereby shortening the communication time.

Let Th be the communication time in the case where fast transfer is used, Ph be the electric power of the communication link in the same case, Tl be the communication time in the case where slow transfer is used, and Pl be the electric power of the communication link in the same case. As the inequality, $Th/Tl > Ph/Pl$, generally holds, the comparison of the two cases in the total power consumption becomes $Th*Ph < Tl*Pl$. That is, the total power consumption will be smaller when data transfer is faster. In addition, the faster transfer makes it possible not only to reduce the total power consumption of the communications link but also to put the link in sleep mode for a longer time than when slower transfer is used. This can further reduce the power consumption of the link. Furthermore, the higher the probability at which all links connected to a node are put to sleep mode, the higher the probability at which the node itself can be put to sleep mode.

Figure 6 illustrates one example of total power consumption of communication switch which compares the case where a file data is transferred at a constant low speed with the case where a file data is transferred at a high speed. The fixed part in the figure is the total power consumption except NICs. The values of electric power are assumed to be the same as those of our evaluation system. It is also supposed here that the devices are put to sleep after the completion of the transfer. In this example, the power consumption with high speed is only about one-tenth of that with low speed.

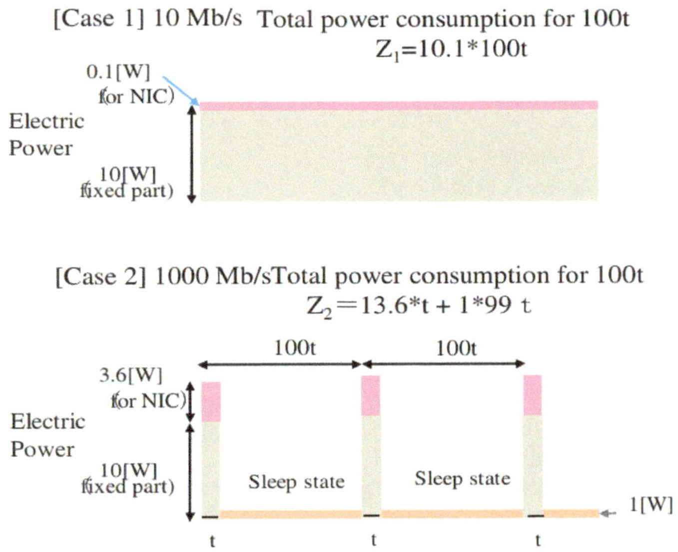

Figure 6: Comparison of total power consumption by link speed

RELATED WORK

A variety of solutions such as Mobile IP [24], SIP mobility [25], TCP migration [26], LISPmob [27], mSCTP [29]-[31]could be applied to mobility management on VM live migration over a wide area. As it is required to establish a new TCP connection to initiate WAN optimization function supported by the existing WAN accelerators, we proposed to adopt mSCTP which supports multiple IP addresses simultaneously in Section 2. Moreover, multiple methods have been proposed to improve or to prevent the degradation of the performance of wide-area live migration itself [4]-[13]. However, most of them do not consider to prevent the degradation in performance after live migration of VM over a wide area.

WAN accelerators have been introduced to prevent degradation in performance caused by a long network delay in WANs originally. They can also dramatically shorten communication time of applications such a file transfer and thereby reduce the power used by data centers and network devices, as proposed in Section 3.1.

As for a measure to reduce the power consumed by the network, Adaptive Link Rate (ALR) technology has been proposed [33]-[35]. This idea assumes that the higher the link transfer rate, the more power is consumed. However, in applications, such as file transfer, that transfer a huge volume of data continuously but do not require real-time transfer, the total power consumption can be reduced by increasing the packet transfer rate conversely, thereby reducing the packet transfer rates of communication links when traffic on these links is small, as proposed in Section 3.2

CONCLUSIONS

This paper has proposed to dynamically apply WAN accelerator within the network when a virtual machine is moved to a distant center, in order to prevent the degradation in performance after live migration of virtual machines over a wide area. mSCTP-based data transfer using different TCP connections before and after migration have been proposed in order to use a currently available WAN accelerator. Assuming VirtualBox for a virtualization system, we have verified the operation of the proposed method, and confirmed that it is possible to prevent degradation in communication performance after migration of virtual machines. This paper has not considered the performance degradation of live migration itself.

Then, this paper has proposed the method to reduce the power consumption of ICT devices in a cloud computing environment, which consists of installing WAN accelerators as part of cloud resources actively and increasing the packet transfer rate of communication link temporarily. It has been indicated that the power consumption with WAN accelerator could be reduced to one-tenth of that without WAN accelerator.

It is necessary to study more specific schemes for the installation of WAN accelerators in a network, conditions that the introduction of WAN accelerator is effective, and details of the operation of WAN accelerators on VM live migration. It is also necessary to study the detailed schemes and required protocols for the installation of WAN accelerator to reduce the power consumption of ICT devices in cloud computing environments.

ACKNOWLEDGEMENT

This work was partly supported by MEXT (Japan) grant-in-aid for building strategic research infrastructures.

REFERENCES

1. Amazon Elastic Compute Cloud (Amazon EC2) http://aws.amazon.com/ec2/
2. Google App for Business http://www.google.com/enterprise/apps/business/
3. J.W.Rittinghouse and J.F.Ransone, "Cloud computing: Implementation, management, and security", CRC Press LLC, Aug. 2009.

4. C. Clark, K. Fraser, S. Hand, J. G. Hansen, E. Jul, C. Limpach, I. Pratt and A. Warfield: "Live Migration of Virtual Machines", Proceedings of the 2nd USENIX Symposium on Networked Systems Design and Implementation, 2005.

5. F. Travostino, P. Daspit, L. Gommans, C. Jog, J. Mambretti, I. Monga, B. Oudenaarde, S. Raghunath and P. Wang: "Seamless Live Migration of Virtual Machines over the MAN/WAN", Elsevier Future Generation Computer Systems, Vol.22, 2006.

6. R. Bradford, E. Kotsovinos, A. Feldmann and H. Schioberg: "LiveWide-Area Migration of Virtual Machines Including Local Persistent State", VEE'07, June 2007.

7. R. Bradford, E. Kotsovinos, A. Feldmann, and H. Schioberg: "Live wide-area migration of virtual machines including local persistent state", Proc. 3rd international conference on Virtual Execution Environments, 2007

8. M. R. Hines and K. Gopalan: "Post-copy based live virtual machine migration using adaptive pre-paging and dynamic self-ballooning", in Proceedings of the ACM/Usenix international conference on Virtual execution environments (VEE'09), 2009.

9. H. Liu, H. Jin, X. Liao, L. Hu and C. Yu: "Live Migration of Virtual Machine Based on Full System Trace and Replay", Proceedings of the 18th International Symposium on High Performance Distributed Computing (HPDC'09), June 2009.

10. W. Voorsluys, J. Broberg, S. Venugopal, and R. Buyya: "Cost of Virtual Machine Live Migration in Clouds: A Performance Evaluation", Proceedings of the 1st International Conference on Cloud Computing, Dec. 2009.

11. T. Hirofuchi, H. Nakada, S. Itoh and S. Sekiguchi: "Enabling Instantaneous Relocation of Virtual Machines with a Lightweight VMM Extension", 10th IEEE/ACM International Conference on Cluster, Cloud and Grid Computing (CCGrid), 2010

12. S. Akoush, R. Sohan, A. Rice, A. W. Moore and A. Hopper: "Predicting the Performance of Virtual Machine Migration", The 18th Annual IEEE/ACM International Symposium on Modeling, Analysis and Simulation of Computer and Telecommunication Systems (MASCOTS'10), August 2010.

13. H. Liu, C.Z. Xu, H. Jin, J. Gong and X. Liao: "Performance and Energy Modeling for Live Migration of Virtual Machines", HPDC'11, June 2011.

14. Y. Zhang, N. Ansari, M. Wu and H. Yu: "On Wide Area Network Optimization", IEEE Communications Surveys & Tutorials, Vol.14, No.4, Fourth Quarter 2012.

15. T. Wolf, S. You, and R. Ramaswamy, "Transparent TCP Acceleration Through Network Processing," in Proc. IEEE Global Telecommunications Conference (GLOBECOM), Dec. 2005, pp. 750–754.

16. J. Lee, P. Sharma, J. Tourrilhes, R. McGeer, J. Brassil and A. Bavier: "Network Integrated Transparent TCP Accelerator", AINA2010.

17. Riverbed, "Optimization for the Public Cloud" http://www.riverbed.com/us/products/cloud_products/cloud_steelhead.php

18. Y. Awano and S. Kuribayashi: "Reducing Power Consumption and Improving Quality of Service in Cloud Computing Environments", Proceeding of the 15-th International Conference on Network-Based Information Systems (NBiS-2012), Sep. 2012.

19. ITU Symposium on "ICTs and Climate Change" Summary Report, London, June 17&18,2008 http://www.itu.int/dms_pub/itu-t/oth/06/0F/T060F0060090001PDFE.pdf

20. "Green IT Initiative in Japan", METI, Japan Oct. 2008 http://www.meti.go.jp/english/policy/GreenITInitiativeInJapan.pdf

21. S.Kuribayashi, "Reducing Total Power Consumption Method in Cloud Computing Environments", International Journal of Computer Networks & Communications (IJCNC) Vol.4, No.2, March 2012.

22. S.Kuribayashi, "Reducing Total ICT Power Consumption with Collaboration Among End systems, Communication Network and Power Network", Proceeding of the 25th IEEE International Conference on Advanced Information Networking and Applications (AINA-2011), Mar. 2011

23. K.Hatakeyama and S.Kuribayashi, "Reducing total energy consumption with collaboration between network and end systems", In Proc. of the 12-th International Conference on Network-Based Information Systems (NBiS2009), Aug. 2009.

24. RFC3775 "IP Mobility Support in IPv6"

25. E. Wedlund and H. Schulzrinne: "Mobility support using sip," Proc. Second ACM International Workshop on Wireless Mobile Multimedia, Sep. 1999.

26. A.C. Snoeren and H. Balakrishnan: "An End-to-End Approach to Host Mobility", 6th ACM/IEEE International Conference on Mobile Computing and Networking (MobiCom '00), 2000.

27. A. Cabellos, etc: "LISPmob: Mobile Networking through LISP", LISPmob white paper.

28. E. Silvera, G. Sharaby, D. Lorenz, and I. Shapira: "IP Mobility to Support Live Migration of Virtual Machines Across Subnets", The Israeli Experimental Systems Conference (SYSTOR 2009), Article 13, 2009.

29. RFC4960 "Stream Control Transmission Protocol" RFC5061 "Stream Control Transmission Protocol (SCTP)Dynamic Address Reconfiguration"

30. M. Riegel and M. Tuxen: "Mobile SCTP Transport Layer Mobility Management for the Internet", Softcom2003.

31. L. Budzisz, R. Ferrús, A. Brunstrom, K. Grinnemo, R. Fracchia,G. Galante and F. Casadevall: "Towards transport-layer mobility: Evolution of SCTP multihoming", Comput. Commun. 31, 5, Mar. 2008.

32. VirtualBox https://www.virtualbox.org/

33. C.Gunaratne, K.Christensen, B.Nordman and S.Suen, "Reducing the Energy Consumption of Ethernet with Adaptive Link Rate (ALR)," IEEE Trans. On computers, Vol.57, No.4, Apr. 2008.

34. IEEE802.3az http://standards.ieee.org/getieee802/download/802.3az-2010.pdf

35. P. Reviriego, K. Christensen, J. Rabanillo and J. A. Maestro, "An Initial Evaluation of Energy Efficient Ethernet," IEEE Communi- cations Letters, Vol. 15, No. 5, pp. 578-580, May 2011.

CHAPTER 9

AUTONOMOUS QOS MANAGEMENT AND POLICING IN UNMANAGED LOCAL AREA NETWORKS

Christopher Köhnen[1], Christian Überall[1], Muttukrishnan Rajarajan[1], Rudolf Jäger[2], and Veselin Rakočević[1]

[1]City University London, Department of Electrical and Electronic Engineering, London EC1V 0HB, UK

[2]Department for Information Technology, Electrical Engineering & Mechatronics, Technische Hochschule Mittelhessen-University of Applied Sciences, Wilhelm-Leuschner-Straße 13, 61169 Friedberg, Germany

ABSTRACT

The high increase of bandwidth-intensive applications like high definition video streaming in home and small office environments leads to QoS challenges in hybrid wired/wireless local area networks. These networks are often not QoS aware and may contain bottlenecks in their topology. In addition, they often have a hybrid nature due to the used access technology consisting of, for example, Ethernet, wireless, and PowerLAN links. In this paper, we present the research work on a novel autonomous system for hybrid QoS in local area networks, called QoSiLAN, which does not rely on network infrastructure support but on host cooperation and works independently of the access technology. We present a new QoS Signalling Protocol, policing and admission control algorithms, and a new lightweight statistical bandwidth prediction algorithm for autonomous resource management in LANs. This new QoS framework enables link based, access-medium independent bandwidth management without network support. We provide evaluation results for the novel bandwidth prediction algorithm as well as for the QoSiLAN framework and its protocol, which highlight the features, robustness, and the effectiveness of the proposed system.

INTRODUCTION

Quality of Service (QoS) becomes more and more relevant to consumer networks, due to the increased usage of High Definition (HD) video streaming, IPTV applications, and Voice over Internet Protocol (VoIP) communication. Nowadays, video streaming is already topping the list of consumer traffic [1] with more than 35% of mobile devices using WiFi connections and even Ultra HD Internet video streaming is evolving. Regarding the consumer Internet video traffic, video streaming is expected to grow further massively from 19% as of 2014 to 53% in 2017, as forecasted by Cisco's Visual Network Index [2]. Currently, most consumer routers and switches support QoS management in local area networks (LANs) on the basis of the Differentiated Services (DiffServ). Additionally, there are already consumer systems in the market, which perform self-organised traffic flow identification and classification for prioritised packet scheduling [3]. This means that, at best QoS is only available for traffic passing the gateway and no QoS guarantees are possible as compared to the QoS model the Resource Reservation Protocol (RSVP) is based on [4]. Therefore, LAN internal traffic remains completely unmanaged, which affects mainly intra-LAN communication like video and audio streaming from Media Network Attached Storage (Media-NAS) devices, which is

Citation: Christopher Köhnen, Christian Überall, Muttukrishnan Rajarajan, Rudolf Jäger, and Veselin Rakočević, "Autonomous QoS Management and Policing in Unmanaged Local Area Networks," Journal of Computer Networks and Communications, vol. 2015, Article ID 790375, 24 pages, 2015. doi:10.1155/2015/790375

a common operation in networked consumer households. Additionally, IntServ protocols, like the RSVP, usually cannot no be found in consumer network hardware. Even Microsoft has dropped support for RSVP in Windows operating systems with the release of WindowsXP [5] in 2001. State-of-the-art LAN management protocol frameworks like H.622 [6] or UPnP-QoS [7] and QoS NSLP [8] emphasise the need for QoS management in LANs. They propose strategies, which rely on network support for session-based QoS to enable bandwidth reservation.

Since the broadband connection and wireless links in a LAN are still bottlenecks for services with high bandwidth requirements, a QoS scheme is required to protect real-time service flows from congestion. Internet providers solve the problem on the last mile by using separate multicast and QoS enabled Internet links for their IPTV delivery. This provider control ends at the router. Problems in a LAN arise mainly when multiple user traffic flows utilize a bottleneck link in the network and one of the flows has real-time media QoS requirements. This problem in unmanaged network scenarios is still a research challenge in state-of-the-art research and technology. The current trend on application side to use rate-adaptive streaming does not solve the problem either. Rate-adaptive streaming aims at reacting on congestion and bandwidth degradation by stepping down the resolution and bandwidth [9], instead of preventing the congestion from not real-time dependent sources.

To overcome these issues we propose a QoS in local area networks (QoSiLAN) framework, which enables QoS service guarantees in the forms of end-to-end bandwidth reservation between the hosts within the LAN, as well as for traffic flows, passing the Internet gateway. The proposed QoSiLAN framework addresses the problem of QoS management in unmanaged LANs, without the essential dependence on network infrastructure support. Its goal is to manage the real-time traffic autonomously with a host-based, cooperative approach. The QoSiLAN framework is designed to work autonomously, taking into account the assumption not to rely on network cooperation, but to support it. Since the QoSiLAN framework completely relies on host cooperation, multiple key technology modules are needed on the hosts in the LAN to support this architecture as depicted in Figure1. For the first time, this paper describes all modules and their interaction algorithms in detail.

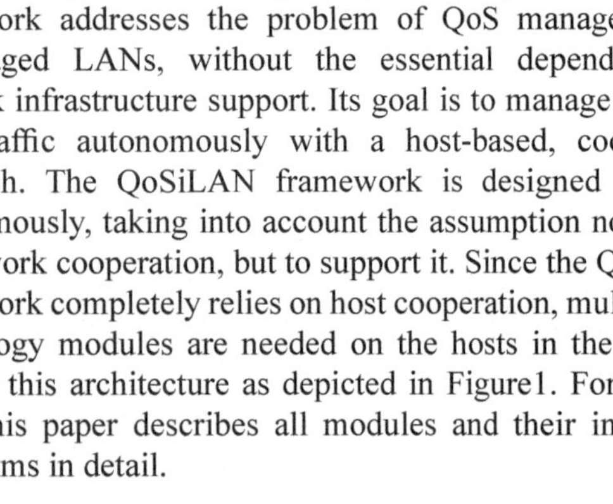

Figure 1: Overview of the QoSiLAN key components.

CONTRIBUTION

In this section the main contributions of our research are presented and discussed. These are the statistical class-based bandwidth prediction (SCBP) algorithm and the QoSiLAN policing and admission modules. These two key solutions provide the core functionality to the QoSiLAN framework, since the bandwidth prediction is essential to support autonomous traffic management, which works independently of support from media applications. Additionally, the policing and admission control module processes all data from the other key technology modules to enable smart policing decisions. A complete overview is shown in Figure 1, where all modules are presented. Especially for self-organisation, the physical topology map of the LAN must be discovered, including a bottleneck bandwidth detection for the path, which is assisted by the iperf tool [10] (topology discovery). Also, the traffic must be monitored, analysed, identified, classified (Flow Identification and Classification), and predicted in an autonomous manner (Flow Bandwidth Prediction). For signalling, a new protocol is needed to enable QoS management communication between the hosts (QoS Signalling Protocol). For this purpose, a signalling solution built on top of the latest IETF recommendation is presented, including a critical examination on the overhead and scalability issues this approach causes. The policing and admission control enables the smart provisioning of resources, which employs cooperative traffic shaping (traffic shaping) on all hosts in the LAN to enforce bandwidth preservation (policing/admission control). In the following, these modules are presented in detail.

Topology Discovery

First, to manage the traffic on a per link basis, a complete map of the local network must be known. The map reveals the link layer interconnection between hosts, switches, and access points, which is needed for link based resource reservation. The QoSiLAN framework does not rely on network core element support. This means that only end-hosts are involved in the signalling and enforcement processes. Although the network is not involved in the QoS management, the network is actively monitored. To be able to control the traffic in the LAN, its physical topology must be known. This enables the QoSiLAN framework to manage resources link-based and to react on topology changes and congestion directly.

This is accomplished using the Link Layer Topology Discovery (LLTD) protocol. The LLTD protocol was presented firstly by Black et al. [11]. It is a layer 2 topology discovery protocol, which was developed within the Microsoft Rally program [12]. Later the LLTD protocol was introduced and distributed with Microsoft Windows since 2006. The protocol specification was published by the Microsoft Corporation [13]. It works on wired IEEE 802.3 and wireless IEEE 802.11 networks. It is based on probing packets sent by a central entity, called "mapper," to each LLTD supporting host, called "Responder," in the network. All end devices implementing the protocol appear in the network topology map the mapper builds. The protocol aims at investigating the address tables of Ethernet switches. Since one cannot read the Address Information Table (AIT) in most consumer switches, the mapper sends Emit packets to the hosts to make them send Probe packets to the switches using spoofed MAC addresses, according to the connections reasoning technique presented by Sun et al. [14]. Using this algorithm the mapper trains and probes each switch's address tables to find out if the hosts are attached to the same or different switches. According to the IEEE 802.3 specification a switch forwards packets with an unknown MAC address to all ports. Once it has received a packet with the MAC address as source one time it subsequently forwards incoming packets with this MAC as the destination address only to this single port. The other hosts in the network, which have also listened to the training packet also answer to the mapper if they also have received the packet or not. For this purpose, the LLTD protocol uses MAC address spoofing with addresses starting with 00-0D-3A. This is a dedicated MAC address range, reserved by Microsoft. In order to make use of the LLTD capabilities, we completely reimplemented the protocol and the mapper logic and integrated it into the QoSiLAN framework.

Flow Identification and Classification

To enable the QoSiLAN to work independently of applications, the traffic flows must be identified and classified in an autonomous manner. This is accomplished using our solution, the enhanced Statistical Protocol Identification (eSPID) algorithm [15]. We further developed the Statistical Protocol Identification (SPID) algorithm [16] to identify audio/video streams reliably. The SPID algorithms are based on the Kulback-Leibler divergence (KLD):using twelve different statistical measures of traffic behaviour, like bytes-per-direction, number-of-direction-changes, bytefrequency, and nine more. The eSPID algorithm needs to learn a protocol from 30 preclassified sample flows, as evaluated in our previous work [15]. The twelve statistical measures are applied to the sample flows and stored as probability distribution arrays in a database. This makes it robust against UDP/TCP port changes and up to a certain degree against encryption. The KLD in (1) is a logarithmic measure of the relation between the relative frequency of the observed (P) to the trained flows (Q), summed for each attribute measure. The ($P \parallel Q$) is matched to a database of learned $D(P \parallel Q)$ from other protocols. The protocol with the smallest divergence ($P \parallel Q$) is then identified. The distance represents the probability of matching.

$$D(P \parallel Q) = \mathrm{KL}(P, Q) = \sum_{x \in X} P(x) \log_2 \frac{P(x)}{Q(x)}, \qquad (1)$$

The eSPID algorithm allows for robust identification of flows after 20 packets, as shown in our previous work [15]. Therefore, it is a fast and reliable method for near real-time media identification. The outgoing traffic is identified and classified using the individual protocol name and the media type. These media types are, namely, audio, video, or unknown if no matching was found. New real-time protocols can be learned by the system in a semisupervised way. Needed are at least 30 sample flows, which are identified by the user. For these the KLD is calculated and the result is stored in the database. The identification probability of encrypted protocols is not substantially less. As the content based measures have no statistical information due to the entropy of the encrypted content, only the behaviour focused statistical measures apply. This does not need to essentially lower the recognition probability, especially not for different protocols, but for the content differentiation within a protocols.

Statistical Class-Based Bandwidth Prediction

Once a flow is identified and classified, the needed resources must be estimated in order to reserve them. This is enabled by a novel statistical class-based bandwidth prediction (SCBP) algorithm, which we developed for the special purposes of the QoSiLAN framework. As shown in Figure 1, it is applied after the eSPID process and the results are fed directly into the policing and admission control module.

The statistical class-based bandwidth prediction (SCBP) algorithm is our novel approach for Internet video traffic bandwidth prediction for single streams. It addresses the problem of different transmission characteristics of state-of-the-art streaming technology and the resulting low bandwidth forecasting accuracy. Nowadays, the traditional continuous streaming characteristic, for example, known from the Real-Time Transport Protocol (RTP), is highly underrepresented. Instead, HTTP based streaming technology like HTTP Dynamic Streaming (HDS) [17], HTTP Live Streaming (HLS), and the Real-Time Media Protocol (RTMP) is very common. Those streaming protocols support the feature of chunked data transfer. This allows the CDNs to significantly save their traffic costs, since only those parts of a video are transferred, which are actually consumed by the user. If a user stops a video the transfer also stops. If a user moves to a position at the end of a video, there is no need to transfer the parts before. So, the data is not transferred continuously according to the encoded bit rate, but in chunks, with a burst characteristic, often with several seconds of traffic silence in between the bursts. The goal for our SCBP algorithm is to predict the average bandwidth requirement of a flow, for the first minute of transfer, ten seconds after start. As shown in Figure 2, after 60 s the average of the last 60 s is chosen to update the reservation state. These values were chosen to fulfil system requirements for the QoSiLAN framework. So, after 60 s the reservation update is not using the SCBP values, but the measured average throughput of the flow from the last 60 s.

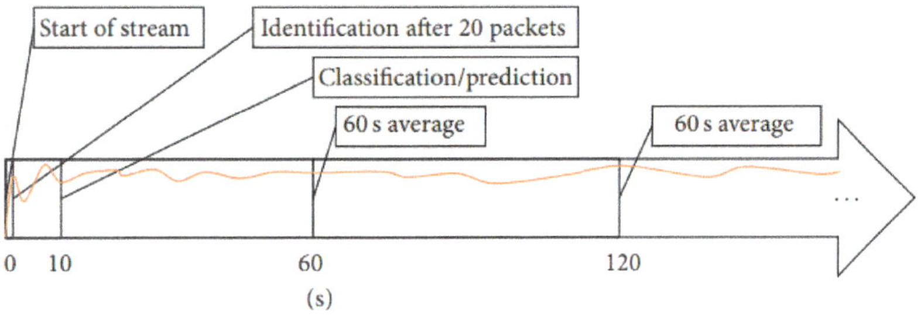

Figure 2: Bandwidth prediction procedure timeline.

Since the QoSiLAN framework needs to communicate with all hosts in the network to coordinate the resource reservations, it causes high signalling effort. Therefore, the reservation state live time was evaluated to be 60 s, to avoid too frequent state updates and therefore network congestion from signalling. That is why the SCBP algorithm is designed to predict the average bandwidth consumption for single multimedia streams for the first 60 s after 10 s recording time. According to our evaluations a minimum of 10 s recording time from the start of the flow was evaluated to be required to catch the flows characteristic and to enable proper predictions. As depicted in Figure 2, after 60 s of measurement, the reservation state is updated to the measured average bandwidth consumption $(\overline{B_{60}})$ of the last 60 s. Within this paper we present our simple but highly precise prediction algorithm and validate its applicability using evaluations, as presented in Section 5.1.

The SCBP algorithm classifies the traffic into six different traffic classes (A–F), according to their behaviour within the first ten seconds of transmission, as shown in Figure 3. To achieve the highest accuracy, the measurement must start at the very beginning of a connection. During the observation time I m throughput measurement samples χ_i are collected, where m is an even number. From this we get the set B, containing m bandwidth measurement samples. For better flow characterisation we divide the set of B into two subsets: $B_a \subset B := \{B_0, \ldots, B_{m/2}\}$ and $B_b \subset B := \{B_{m/2+1}, \ldots, B_m\}$, where we calculate the maximum (Ba,max and Bb,max) as well as the average (Ba and Bb) values. In addition also Bmax is determined as the maximum value in the set of B. The prediction is calculated at time I and forecasts the average bandwidth consumption for the whole first 60 s of transmission. The sampling interval is defined as $s = I/m$.

The evaluations are based on s = 10 s/10 samples = 1 s. The ratio R_c, defined in classifies the flows into the categories A–F, as shown in Table 1.

$$R_c := \frac{\overline{B}}{B_{max}}, \quad (2)$$

There, especially the ratio of bandwidth consumption within the first five and the next five seconds is taken into account. The classes represent dedicated constant values, which are applied to k_c in (3), the prediction algorithm. The SCBP algorithm predicts the bandwidth requirements for identified streams for the period of 60 seconds after 10 seconds of observation. These values come from the QoSiLAN framework requirements, which were defined to require a detection and prediction of QoS relevant flows within 10 seconds after they start. Additionally, to reduce the amount of signalling messages, QoS state updates should not be sent more frequently than each 60 seconds which requires for a prediction interval of 60 seconds. Table 1 shows samples for the characteristics in the first ten seconds for the different traffic classes. One can see that the criteria basically reflects the first burst length, which is typical for nowadays Internet streaming. With the first burst the first chunks of video frames are pushed to the client to fill the client video buffer for enabling a fast start of video playback. For that reason the first burst provides a first estimate on the expected average throughput rate. To enhance the estimate, the next bursts are analysed with the set of Bb. The class F addresses the special characteristic, when there are no samples in the set of Bb, but the stream has not finished yet. Figures 3(a)– 3(e) show samples for the first 10 s characteristic of the traffic classes. There, Figure 3(e) represents the classical continuous streaming case, whereas Figure 3(f) represents the case, with a burst at the beginning and no data within the last half of the observation interval of 10 s.

Table 1: Traffic classes by characteristics

Class name	Characteristic (R_c)
A	$0 \le \frac{\overline{B}}{B_{max}} \le 0.25$
B	$0.25 \le \frac{\overline{B}}{B_{max}} \le 0.5$
C	$0.5 \le \frac{\overline{B}}{B_{max}} \le 0.6$
D	$0.6 \le \frac{\overline{B}}{B_{max}} \le 0.8$
E	$0.8 \le \frac{\overline{B}}{B_{max}} \le 1$
F	$\frac{\overline{B}}{B_{max}} < 1 \wedge \overline{B_b} = 0$

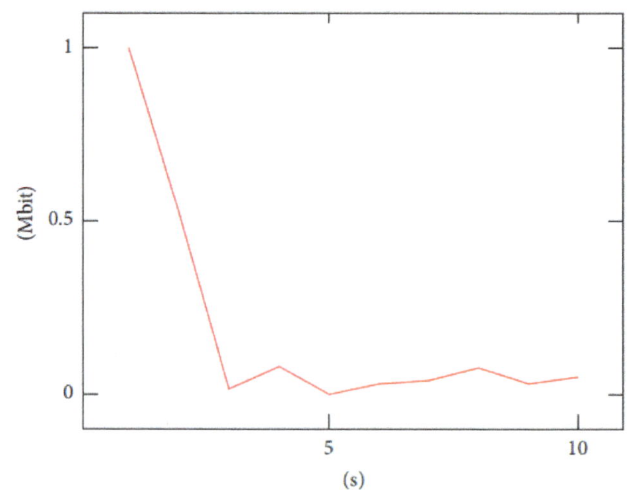

(a) Class A (R_c = 0.18)

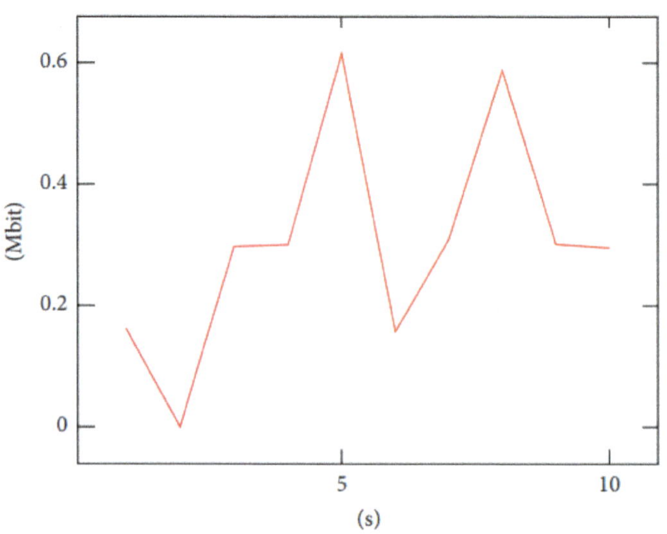

(b) Class B (R_c = 0.49)

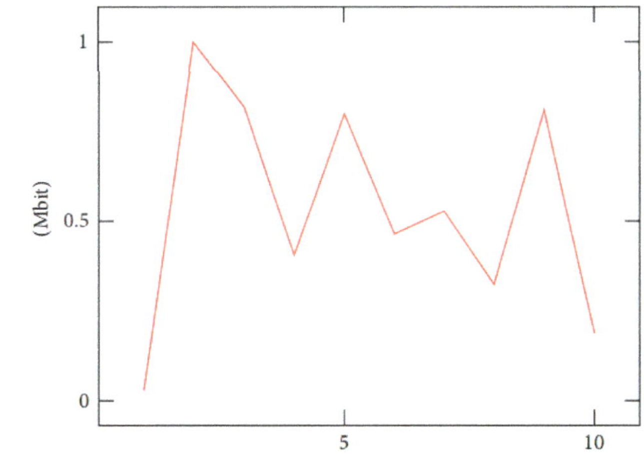

(c) Class C (R_c = 0.54)

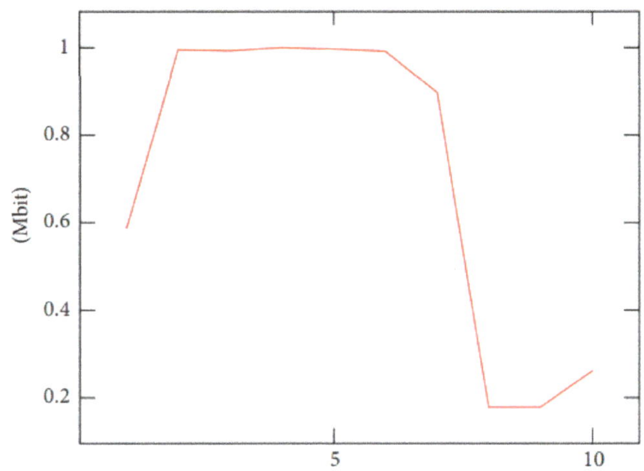

(d) Class D (R_c = 0.71)

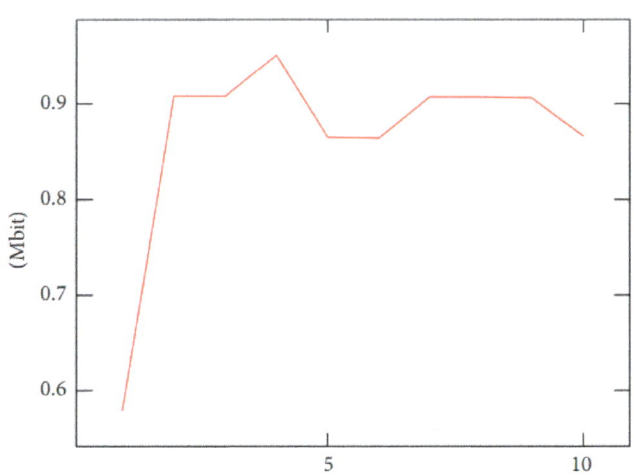

(e) Class E (R_c = 0.91)

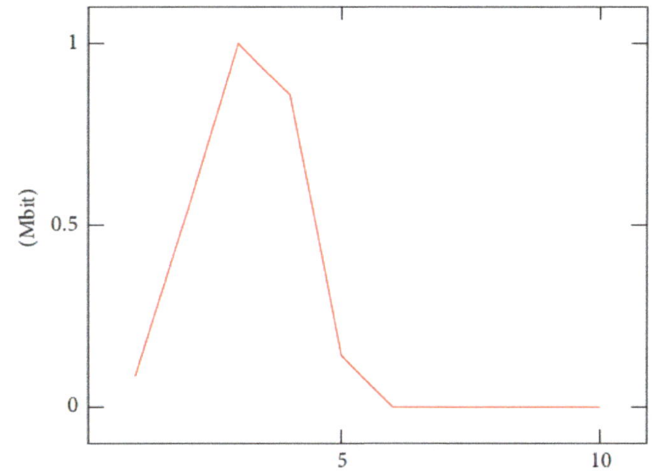

(f) Class F (R_c = 0.58)

Figure 3: Examples for the SCBP classes.

Through evaluations, we validated that the -values assigned to the classes A–F were applicable to the ranges as best defined in Table 1. Hence, the classes reflect the bandwidth characteristic, including the start-up behaviour of the flow in a simple way. For the class-range assignment evaluations, the measured error values were put into a density histogram to identify the ranges of similar deviations.

We designed the prediction formula, shown in

$$\overline{P_{10}} = \frac{\left((1/N_{10})\sum_{i=0}^{N_{10}} \chi_i\right)^2}{(1/N_5)\sum_{i=0}^{N_5} \chi_i} * k_c = \frac{\left(\overline{B}\right)^2}{\overline{B_a}} * k_c, \qquad (3)$$

for the balance of simplicity and accuracy. It takes into account the application in embedded systems with less computation power, which also saves battery life on mobile systems. The prediction formula in (3) implements the correction factor k_c, which reflects the class characteristics. The value for k_c was found using evaluations, as carried out in Section 5.3.

QoS Signalling Protocol

The QoSiLAN Signalling Layer Protocol (QSLP-LAN) provides the mechanism to exchange QoS information and signalling commands within the QoSiLAN hosts (QH) on top of the NSIS NSLP framework, adapted for the QoSiLAN QoS model. As as shown in Figure 1, the protocol is employed by the policing and admission control module to coordinate the QoS policies within the hosts in the network. The QSLP-LAN is designed according to the latest IETF Next-Steps-in-Signalling (NSIS) recommendations [18, 19], and named QoS Signalling Layer Protocol for QoSiLAN (QSLP-LAN). The core piece of the QoSiLAN approach is the policing and signalling procedures. Whereas present QoS protocols communicate end-to-end and QoS aware network elements where involved, in QoSiLAN it is different. One host, which preferred the originator of the traffic, informs a QoSiLAN Manager (QM) host, about the needed resources. A QM could be any host in the network. Using the network topology map, the QM generates sophisticated policy resource requests and sends them to all other hosts in the network to indirectly achieve resource reservation for the physical links along the data path.

In the following, we present the QSLP-LAN protocol messages and the signalling procedures. The protocol behaviour within the QoSiLAN framework is presented as examples within the evaluations in Section5.2.

QSLP-LAN Message Format

The QoS Signalling Layer Protocol for QoSiLAN is designed based on the NSIS message format, similar to the QoS NSLP header format described in [19], Section 5.1.

The QoSiLAN protocol uses, like other common QoS protocols, a soft state mechanism. This means, the hosts keep a reservation state as long as a time-out has not been reached. To keep states alive, a reservation refresh message (QoSiLAN_RESERVE), with the same parameters as the first one, must be sent before the time-out is reached.

QoSiLAN hosts (QH) inform the QM about their traffic situation and request for resources. The QM asks all QH for cooperation for currently active QoS states to establish the bandwidth reservations commonly.

The NSIS General Internet Signalling Transport (GIST) protocol [20] also brings along a host discovery feature, which is used to detect and identify the QoSiLAN enabled hosts in the network. The QoSiLAN Manager (QM) selection is performed by the smallest switch/hub-hop distance to the router, evaluated using the LLTD protocol. If the router itself is QoSiLAN enabled, it announces a distance of zero. If the router is not QoSiLAN enabled and two QH have the same distance, the QH with the longest uptime period is selected.

(i) Reservation (QoSiLAN_RESERVE). The reservation messages use the NSLP common header, as all GIST NSLP objects [20] do. The message contains a sequence number (RSN), a REFRESH_PERIOD, and a BOUND_SESSION_ID. The QSPEC object defines the QoS information parameters. It lists the requested resources using the TMOD-1 parameter, which contains the peak data rate for traffic shaping, and the Excess Treatment parameter, which defines the shaping policy, as defined in [21].

In addition, we introduced the new Reservation Path Parameter for IPv4, to communicate the five-tuple, which defines what flow the reservation is for, as shown in Figure 4. The first 32 bits are defined according to the QSPEC parameter header [21]. The source and destination IPv4 addresses as well as the source and destination ports and the transport protocol ID are included. For IPv6 a similar parameter header format with 64-bit IP address fields needs to be defined accordingly.

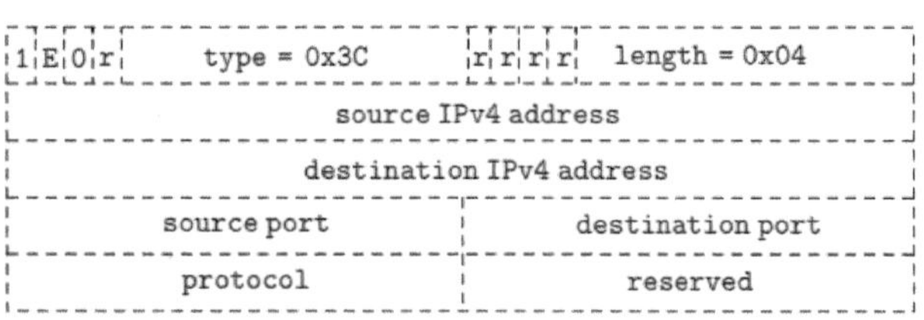

Figure 4: Reservation path parameter for IPv4.

Reservations are deleted either on soft state time-out or by sending a QoSiLAN_REQUEST message using the BOUND_SESSION_ID without a QSPEC object defined.

(ii) Response (QoSiLAN_RESPONSE). The response message is intended to report success or error codes to the requesting node. The success case is indicated using the error=0x00 value. If a reservation state is rejected, a negative acknowledgement is signalled through a error=0x47 value set in the INFO_SPEC header. The RSN object is taken from the corresponding QoSiLAN_REQUEST message to match the response to a request.

(iii) Notify (QoSiLAN_NOTIFY). The notify message is intended to report significant best effort traffic flow statistics to the QoSiLAN Manager (QM). This is needed to keep the QM informed about the current state of the network, especially when there is a lot of traffic occupying which is not classified for QoS. The message structure is similar to the corresponding QoSiLAN_REQUEST and QoSiLAN_RESPONSE messages as described before. The QoSiLAN_NOTIFY message also uses the Reservation Path Parameter for IPv4 within the QSPEV header to announce detected flows.

QSLP-LAN Signalling Procedure

In Figure 5(b) the signalling is shown to be exemplary and used to establish bandwidth reservation in a simple LAN scenario. In this LAN one QoSiLAN Manager (QM) host and three client QHs are connected using two different switches. All of them, except the switches, are QoSiLAN aware. The initiator (Host 1) sends a reservation request message (QoSiLAN_RESERVE) to the QM. The reservation request shall contain at least the physical addresses and the IP addresses of the two communicating parties and the requested resource, the predicted bandwidth to reserve. The QM analyses the location of the QHs and sends sophisticated reservation requests (QoSiLAN_RESERVE) for all other nodes (Host 1, Host 2, and Host 3) in the network, based upon the LAN topology and the LAN's traffic status knowledge, to encourage all QHs to obey the limitations for the affected physical links. In return, the nodes acknowledge the request to the QM (QoSiLAN_RESPONSE), and the QM reports (QoSiLAN_RESPONSE) the result/success to the initiator (Host 1) at the end. To cover the case where both the sending and receiving host do not support QoSiLAN, but the QM is a gateway and detects the flow, another example is given. As shown in Figure 5(a), on resource reservation initiation by a gateway, enabled as QM, no request/response communication to another initiation node is required in contrast to the host initiation case, depicted in Figure 5(b). In both cases the reservation requests/responses are sent to/from each QH in the network, initiated from the QM. To avoid unnecessary signalling effort, the hosts do not report their traffic statistics regularly, but only triggered by events. In case of significant best-effort traffic detection, a QH reports the monitored bandwidth of the stream to the QM using a QoSiLAN_RESPONSE message. Details on the policing and admission control algorithm are described in Section 2.5.3.

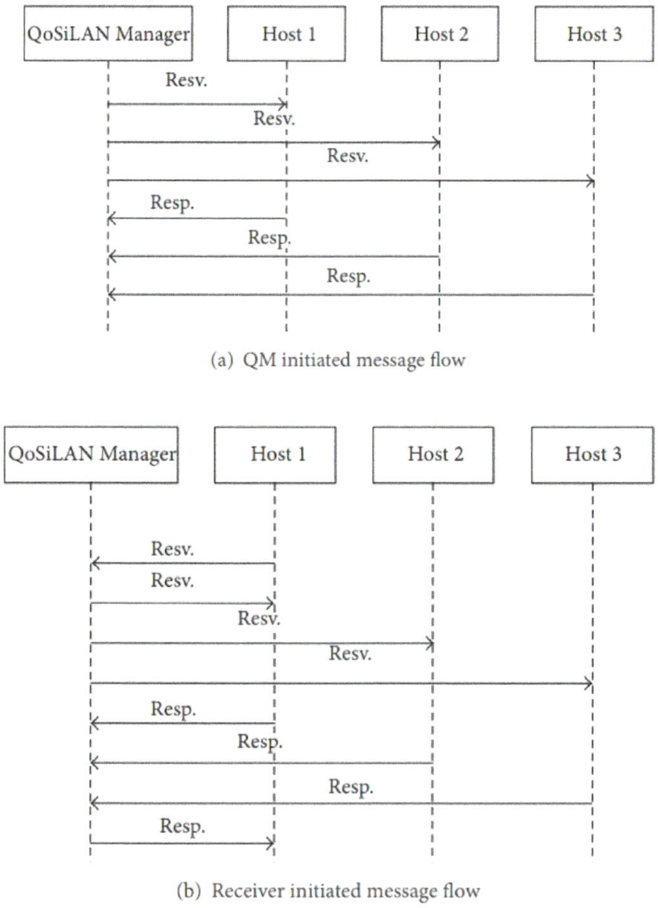

(a) QM initiated message flow

(b) Receiver initiated message flow

Figure 5: QM and receiver initiated message flow.

Policing/Admission Control

As shown in Figure 1, the policing and admission control algorithms are the key components to enable autonomous QoS management. Within this paper we propose appropriate policing and admission control schemes to enable the QoSiLAN framework. The resource management within a LAN requires detailed knowledge about the available resources on all links between the LAN entities. Only if the link layer topology and the capacities of its links are known, the QoSiLAN framework can autonomously manage the resources. In the following, we describe the management procedures to acquire the required information.

Resource Discovery

One host in the network, which preferred the gateway, fulfils the role of the QM. As such it maps the network topology and acts as resource coordinator. The mapping process is executed each time a new host is discovered in the network. The host discovery is based on broadcast and ARP packet monitoring. The map, generated by the LLTD Mapper module, described in Section 2.1, reflects the link layer topology between the hosts, switches, hubs, and access points in the LAN. Additionally to the topology itself, the bottleneck capacity of each link needs to be evaluated. This is done during network or link idle times. The mapper advises the hosts to measure the bottleneck bandwidth of their links by active probing. The QM gathers the results from the QHs and adds this information to the connection information table within the topology map.

Policing Procedure

Each QH in the network continuously monitors its outgoing traffic. To make autonomous QoS policing possible, the QM needs to gather and maintain all information about the LAN and its links, by using the LLTD topology mapper module. This includes the physical paths and measures their bottleneck bandwidth μ . As depicted in Figure 6, the eSPID module analyses on each QH the outgoing flows to identify data with QoS requirements, like video and audio transport. Once a host discovers, for example, a VoIP communication, it estimates the bandwidth requirements P_B for this particular flow using the SCBP algorithm. The QoSiLAN MBAC algorithm decides upon the admission of the reservation, taking into account the different measures. If the admission was granted, a QoSiLAN REQUEST message is sent to the QM to request the bandwidth reservation for the detected resources. A QoSiLAN REQUEST message contains a five-tuple: the sender and receiver IP and port addresses as well as the estimated bandwidth.

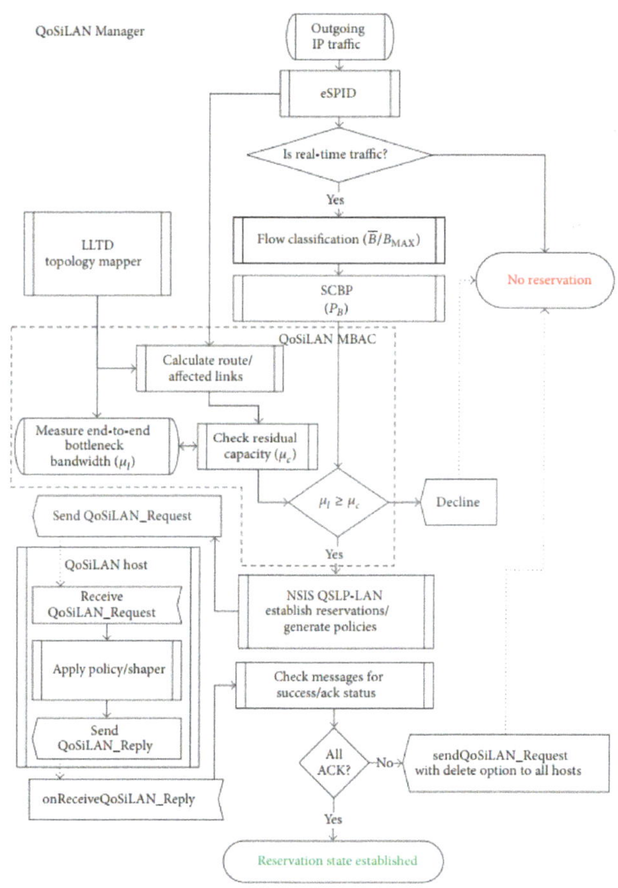

Figure 6: QoSiLAN policing information flow diagram.

The QM receives the QoSiLAN_REQUEST message and checks the map and the available resources for the flow's route within the LAN. If the requested resources are available, the QM sends individualQoSiLAN_REQUEST messages to each QH in the network. These messages contain a list of QSPEC parameters containing the flow's five-tuples and their bandwidth limits to be obeyed by the receiver. These messages are generated individually for each QH, since the affected links on a route to another QH in the LAN differs, depending on the location in the LAN's topology. Each QH checks the request for validity and if the requested resources are available locally. In any instance of an error or conflict, the QH sends a negative acknowledgement QoSiLAN_RESPONSE message back. If the request is accepted, the QH sends a positive acknowledgement QoSiLAN_RESPONSE message back to the QM.

Once all QHs in the network responded with a positive acknowledgement QoSiLAN_RESPONSE message, the QM confirms the resource request with a positive acknowledgement QoSiLAN_RESPONSE message to the requesting QH. From this moment, the flow is protected by traffic shaping rules on all QHs in the network, which apply to all flows, except the protected one. The reservation state is deleted either on soft state time-out or on end-of-stream discovery, like TCP FIN flag detection.

Admission Control

The proposed admission control algorithm works according to the principles of coordinated resource admission control. This shall prevent overbooking of resources. The QM provides the function of a final decision point. It carries out priority considerations in terms of network resource availability, based on client requests. It also takes care that resource reservation request does not block best effort signalling traffic and that individual links are not overbooked. According to comparative simulation results from Jamin et al. [22] a network utilisation rate of 77% is. achievable in a multihop scenario, with a utilisation target of 80% $=1-\mu_r$ and no packet loss due to congestion. For this, we defined a threshold of μ_r = 20% residual capacity, which shall not be blocked by reservations and is instead reserved for best-effort traffic. The following algorithm defines that a reservation will be denied by the QM: if the sum of current reservation states^] for one of the affected connections/links including the predicted bandwidth p_b and residual capacity μr for a flow α exceeds the link capacity μ_l.

$$\mu_l \geq \mu_c = p_b^{\alpha} + \mu_r + \sum_{i=1}^{N} \widehat{v}_i, \tag{4}$$

This algorithm enforces bandwidth allocation by collaborative shaping. By default, the QHs in the network shape their traffic to the residual bandwidth, to isolate the reservation's traffic from congestion. This works fine for a two-host network. The probability of multiple hosts using the full capacity of residual bandwidth and therefore exceeding it in sum grows with every host joining the network. Therefore, an additional control function is needed to manage the residual bandwidth and to share this resource for the best effort traffic among the hosts. A reactive approach, as proposed by Hock et al. [23] cannot be applied to this scheme, since the traffic characteristic is not predictable enough. As carried out in Section 2.3 the traffic characteristic is not continuous, but bursty with pause periods. Therefore, a QoS degradation by congestion is hard to detect by the receiver. Hence, our approach works as follows.

Since every QH in the network is monitoring its outgoing traffic continuously, it detects streams with significant best effort traffic rates. The rate is regarded as significant, if the output rate ro exceeds the residual capacity shared by the number of QHs $r_o \geq (1/n)_r$. If this is the case, the QH informs the QM about its current average best-effort traffic output rate and the destination of the stream. The QM collects this information from all QHs and maintains it per link in the network topology map. The QM takes care, that the sum of best-effort traffic from all QHs will not exceed μ_r for each single link in the LAN. If a reservation violation is detected by the QM, the affected QHs are advised to shape their traffic accordingly for traffic crossing the affected links.

RELATED WORK

In this section, related work for the new technology proposed in this paper is discussed. These are the QoS management in LANs, the statistical class-based bandwidth prediction for flows, and the policing and admission control in LANs.

Approaches for QoS in Local Area Networks

Beside the QoS approach presented in this work, other solutions for enabling QoS in LANs or home networks are described in the literature. The approaches vary from the access layer to the application layer. Since the QoSiLAN approach is an approach targeting cross access technology scenarios, other approaches working on layer 1 and layer 2 are not discussed.

An approach, most similar to the QoSiLAN framework, has been proposed by Louvel et al. [24–26], who propose a network resource management framework for multimedia applications distributed in heterogeneous home networks. In this solution to QoS for multimedia applications in LANs, also a central management entity, called the Global Resource Manager (GRM), is used as resource coordinator. On the local devices, the needed components are bundled in a Local Resource Manager (LRM). The LRM provides a resource estimation method, implemented using the Bienaymé-Chebyshev inequality algorithm [27] and a scheduling tool for traffic prioritisation, the Linux iproute2 tool's tc command [28]. The GRM measures the available bandwidth on the links using the iperf tool [10] and coordinates the resources. As main differentiation criteria, Louvel's proposal does not take into account the network topology and limits the approach to a one-hop star topology with heterogeneous network interfaces and different devices attached. Since the GRM as the central entity is able to manage all resources, a dedicated QoS protocol is not needed and obviously out of scope of the approach. This limits its practical applicability in home networks dramatically. In the defined topology it benefits from the nonintrusive and adaptable resource management approach, since the end-devices do not need to be modified essentially to achieve the desired QoS level.

A state-of-the-art approach for a common home network protocol comes from the Universal Plug and Play (UPnP) forum in forms of the UPnP-QoS Architecture [7] to enable QoS services in LANs, consisting of a single IP subnetwork. This architecture defines policing and admission control for prioritised, parametrised, and hybrid QoS control for individual links, as well as path property discovery for them. Three services are required to implement this functionality, as presented in Figure 7. The QosPolicyHolder Service gathers path information and provides appropriate policies for the traffic, described by a TrafficDescriptor structure. The QosManager Service, invoked by an application and implemented within a UPnP Control Point, requests the required resources from the QoSPolicyHolder Service. The QosDevice Service is responsible for establishing the QoS for a new traffic stream. To support end-to-end prioritised QoS, the QosDevice Service needs to be implemented on all network devices along the data path. For links not supporting the parametrised QoS on the path, prioritised QoS is selected hoping for DiffServ support by the network, resulting in an hybrid QoS operation. Network segments not supporting the UPnP-QoS architecture result in a QoS establishment failure for the whole end-to-end path. This is an aspect the proposed QoSiLAN framework overcomes, since it does not rely on network support and it can operate end-to-end, even if not all devices support the system. In addition, the UPnP-QoS framework requires not only implementation of its services on all devices, but also support by the applications causing the traffic. This problem was addressed by Laulajainen and Hirvonen [29], who propose a background service running on traffic causing devices, which performs fast application detection on basis of statistical analysis of the first four packet sizes of a stream, which provides a basic identification functionality. This measure is also a small part of the eSPID algorithm, described for the QoSiLAN framework in Section 2.2. Suraci et al. state that the UPnP-QoS architecture works well in the case of moderate traffic loads but may fail whenever the network becomes overloaded [30]. They demonstrate their admission control and drop solutions using test-bed evaluations. For the admission control algorithm they rely on the bandwidth information provided by the UPnP framework. If a network segment on the data path has no sufficient residual bandwidth, the admission is rejected; otherwise it is admitted. The drop strategy decision algorithm is realized using a binary tree to estimate lowest cost for packet dropping. They determine the cost by the importance/priority of the flow. The QoSiLAN framework also defines an admission control algorithm, which also supports not QoS aware network segments, in contrast to the presented solution. A dedicated drop strategy is implicitly given by the traffic shaping appliance the QoSiLAN requests from the operating system. Castrucci et al. go one step deeper in the scheduling of packets with their proposal for an application QoS management and session control in a heterogeneous home network using inter-MAC layer support [31]. They propose an architectural and procedural definition of the home context using the UPnP-QoS and SIP frameworks. Within this OMEGA called architecture they introduce a convergence layer between IP and MAC layer to manage all traffic using the information provided by the UPnP-QoS framework. This architecture requires implementation on all network devices and also uses a centralised coordinator within the network's gateway to manage the resources. Chen et al. [32] propose a DiffServ focused scheme for QoS management in heterogeneous home networks. it also adopts to the QoS-UPnP specification by adding monitoring and resource management functionality to the framework. They monitor real-time network traffic to adaptively control the bandwidth and manage to reduce jitter latency and packet loss significantly. The focus of this particular work is set on the last mile from the service provider to the home network, which is out of scope of the QoSiLAN framework. Since the QoSiLAN framework also may control the Internet gateway, it also manages these resources and controls the Internet line. Furthermore, Westberg et al. use the OSGi's resource management in DiffServ (RMD) [33] architecture to interface to the Per Hop Reservation (PHR) and Per Domain Reservation (PDR) protocols to manage the network traffic not on per flow basis, but on link basis. In this way they also cover wired and wireless QoS concerns into admission control using the proposed adaptive QoS mechanism, proved by evaluations in an heterogeneous test-bed. Lee et al. [34] propose an enhanced UPnP QoS architecture to support network-adaptive media streaming in home networks. They state that the initial UPnP QoS architecture does not provide methods for dynamic network monitoring. Thus, they propose to enhance it by adding a dynamic network monitoring and adaptation scheme. Although the UPnP QoS 2.0 specification introduced the GetRotameterInformation method to retrieve network status information of other important features, it still lacks the QoS-based adaptation method and the capability of guaranteeing streaming quality over time-varying networks. They propose to enhance the UPnP QoS Device with an dedicated Status Monitor component and the UPnP QoS Manager with an QoS Adapter. Their purpose is to acquire continuous network status information for a dynamic QoS management. They use this enhanced functionality to adapt the video streaming quality dynamically. This approach is different from the QoSiLAN framework, since it does not aim to prevent congestion, but only to react on network performance degradation, which leads to lower video quality and therefore probably lower QoE. Brewka et al. [35] propose an enhancement to UPnP QoS for automatic QoS provisioning, which is a missing feature to have a better comparability to the QoSiLAN framework. They describe the problem of autoclassification of the traffic from non-UPnP-QoS devices present in UPnPQoS enabled networks. A limitation of their proposal is the assumption that the home gateway and all network devices are UPnP QoS aware and support their enhancements. Only end-devices are allowed to be not UPnP QoS compliant. An advantage is the integration of the provider network using GMPLS transmission, which provides better QoS enforcement possibilities. Their simulation shows similar results as ours with the same setup time issues, which are inherited from the reactive traffic identification and classification approach.

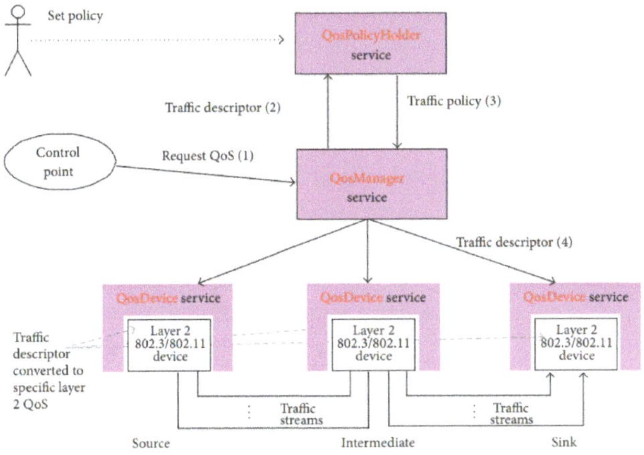

Figure 7: UPnP-QoS architecture averview [7, Figure].

Also the ITU-T proposes an architectural framework of a home network that supports multimedia services within the recommendation H.622 [6]. The ITU-T identifies two different roles that home networks fulfil and name them as primary and secondary domain. For the primary domain the home network is considered as an extension of the access network from the provider point of view. For the secondary domain, they consider the home network as an intra-LAN transmission medium for data distribution among home devices from the user point of view. As an extension of the access network, they state that providers expect it to behave similar to their access network with the same functional QoS services with security and management entities that can be found typically in provider networks. In the role of interconnecting home devices these features may not be needed. For QoS they also define two different QoS models: class-based QoS and session-based QoS. The session-based QoS is recommended to be realized as UPnP [36] and class-based QoS using [37, 38]. They emphasise the features of these models, like for class-based QoS the less complexity, scalability, and priority-based mechanism. For session-based mechanisms they criticise that some network devices may be unaware of signalling protocol, because network devices need a complicated mechanism and that additional session setup time is introduced by the resource reservation process. Interestingly, they also consider NSIS QoS NSLP [19] and UPnP QoS [7] as emerging new QoS technology which need further consideration. This is exactly what also the QoSiLAN framework does by further developing the ideas from NSIS and UPnP to enable autonomous session-based QoS for unmanaged networks. In that way the QoSiLAN framework complies with the H.622 recommendation for the primary as well as the secondary domain and fills the gaps of the identified drawbacks of existing and referenced solutions.

There are also QoS approaches for higher layer application, for example, the routing layer. Haikal et al. propose a distributed QoS adaptive routing engine architecture based on OSPFxQoS [39, 40]. This is an Open Shortest Path First (OSPF) link-state routing protocol extension, which works independently of the used QoS architecture. This kind of routing-level QoS architecture works well for large scale hierarchical, routed networks but does not provide a solution to unmanaged local networks using a single subnet, which is the target environment for to QoSiLAN framework.

The Data Distribution Service (DDS) for real-time systems [41] is a middleware architecture for device, service, and QoS management for data centric communication in highly dynamic distributed networks. It follows the publish-subscribe communication model and is able to provide QoS in any environment, where users, devices, and services are potentially mobile. Al-Roubaiey and Alkhiaty provide an architecture for a QoS aware DDS middleware in an ubiquitous environment [42]. Their proposed solution as well as the DDS specification does not provide technical solutions, but only high level descriptions of solution principles and are therefore not directly comparable to to QoSiLAN framework.

Bandwidth Prediction for Flows

In the past, the scientific community addressed the problem of traffic prediction mainly to continuous traffic flows, Internet backbone traffic or even more specific on video codec level. The algorithms, designed for encoding bandwidth prediction, use algorithms to exploit the nature of MPEG video to allocate the bandwidth on a scene basis [43]. The algorithms used for Internet backbone prediction address scenarios, where multiple streams run through one link and predictions aim on providing forecasts for the multiplex, the sum of streams [44]. In contrast, our solution addresses only single stream predictions, in a local network scenario. In publications addressing streaming media, mainly traditional streaming protocols were investigated. To the best of our knowledge there is no comparable scientific publication looking at the nature of real Internet traffic from modern cloud services and Content Delivery Networks (CDNs) on a per flow basis. Even in the area of traffic modelling no comparable work could be found. An often addressed problem is the traffic prediction on a large scale basis for Internet backbones [45], which aims on statistical predictions like number of streams, amount of bandwidth, and occurrence probability. Some general applicable algorithms, like the Recursive Last Square (RLS) in an application of traffic prediction [46] and machine learning algorithms like SVM [47], were investigated. It was found that those algorithms are on one hand designed to predict the traffic on a short term but do not perform very well in an inert framework like the QoSiLAN addresses, with forecasting intervals of 60 s. In addition, those algorithms cause high computation complexity, but the QoSiLAN framework's design requires for a lightweight approach with a minimum of computation costs, since it is designed to run on thin and also mobile systems with limited CPU and power sources. That is why we aim on a simple approach to predict the needed bandwidth as accurate as possible. These requirements are mostly hit by linear prediction algorithms. He et al. [48] distinguish between Formula Based (FB) and History Based (HB) algorithms. For the FB algorithms they propose linear prediction algorithms. Among others a Moving Average (MA) predictor was presented. We also employed and configured it for our application and referenced it as Mean Estimation (ME), for our evaluation of results in Section 5.3. The HB algorithms do not fit for our application, since they require a large set of throughput measurements from previous transfers in the same path, which behaved similar. In particular, the similar behaviour of protocols is an assumption we could not reproduce in our evaluations, where similar video streaming flows from different large CDNs behave very individually.

Policing and Admission Control in LANs

A framework for providing end-to-end QoS for individual flows was proposed by Yang et al. [49] with the goal of keeping the scalability of the DiffServ model. They propose the On-Demand QoS Path (ODP) framework, which supports per flow admission control and end-to-end bandwidth reservation. In contrast to our QoSiLAN framework, the ODP framework targets interdomain/Internet QoS by involving edge- and core-router. The ODP framework enables scalability by using class-based service differentiation in the network core. The ODP framework reduces the signalling effort by using a hierarchical bandwidth management scheme. From evaluations they conclude that the ODP Central Control and Router-Aided approaches provide end-to-end guarantees to individual flows with significantly less overhead than IntServ QoS like RSVP.

In terms of admission control, one can distinguish between parameter-based admission control (PBAC) and measurement-based admission control (MBAC) algorithms. Whereas the PBAC algorithms rely on a priori knowledge and accurate network traffic models to allot the resources, the MBAC algorithms rely on actual measurements and accurate estimation of QoS parameters. Brewer and Ayyagari [50] compare and analyse MPAC and PBAC in testbed evaluations. They conclude for bursty traffic patterns that the MBAC approach provides better network utilisation and a higher admission rate than the PBAC approach. Similar results from Mancuso and Neglia [51] prove true the superiority of MBAC algorithms about PBAC algorithms, in special for scenarios with bursty nature of self-similar flows. They discovered that MBAC algorithms make the system robust to statistical traffic properties. That is why we also decided to investigate more on MBAC algorithms and designed our approach according to this scheme. Moore [52] identified five characteristics for an appropriate MBAC algorithm. First a MBAC must provide a relationship between the traffic characteristic and the calibration control. Second, the estimator must incorporate the statistical nature of traffic. Third, the estimator and the MBAC must be matched to the task required. Fourth, the algorithms must be implementable with realistic resource requirements. Fifth, the policy performed by the MBAC influences the overall performance critically. Overall, he concludes that the correct maintenance of the current provision values is more important than the accuracy of short term traffic characterisation. Independently, we also designed our MBAC algorithm for QoSiLAN according to these principles and share the experiences. Jamin et al. [22] evaluated three MBAC and one PBAC algorithm in terms of performance for controlled load service. They configured the PBAC algorithm for capacity bounding. The three MBAC algorithms are based on equivalent bandwidth, acceptance region, and measured bandwidth. Although they do not aim on giving final conclusions on their simulation results, their evaluations reveal that a higher utilisation target than 80% causes packet loss in the network. In another survey Jamin and Shenker [53] observed that all known MBAC algorithms can be reduced to one formula, as shown in

$$\hat{v} < f(\cdot)\mu - g(\cdot), \tag{5}$$

and be tuned with parameters to give the same result curves. In (5) $\hat{v}$ is the measured load, μ is the link bandwidth, and $(\cdot)$ and $g(\cdot)$ are functions of the source's reserved rate and the number of admitted sources. Therefore, they conclude and propose to focus future research on the tuning parameters, instead of the algorithms itself. Another observation is the structural limitations ofMBAC algorithms. First, long lasting connections will statistically dominate the reservations over short lasting connections. Second, flows that traverse multihop paths have a higher risk of a rejected admission, if the switches perform the admission independently. For the QoSiLAN MBAC algorithm we considered the limitations and found solutions as described in the QoSiLAN policy algorithm Section 2.5.2.The application of MBAC algorithms in the context of QoS for Quality of Experience (QoE) was shown by Latre and De Turck [54]. The authors propose a ´ MBAC algorithm for provider based video rate controlling. They define policies of how providers can use MBAC algorithms and video rate control policing for the goal of revenue maximization or QoE. This is a passive approach to react on QoS degradation. Instead, the QoSiLAN framework aims on preventing congestion and interference traffic actively.

MATERIALS AND METHODS

This section discusses the approaches, environments, and scientific methods used to achieve the presented results and evaluations as well as the research methodology to develop the proposed research solutions. Firstly, it presents the evaluation test-bed most evaluations were based on. Afterwards, for each proposed QoSiLAN framework key module, the special evaluation or simulation setup is described.

Home Scenario Evaluation Testbed

The evaluation test-bed was selected to represent a typical home environment with six active hosts, as presented in Figure 8. Three of the hosts are connected using fixed line 100Base-T Ethernet links and three hosts are connected using WiFi IEEE 802.11g links. In special, the simplex/duplex nature of the different link types and the hybrid QoS behaviour are represented by this setup. Each one wireless and one wired host are serving as media server and therefore as data source. The others are configured as media clients to consume media and demand for resources interactively. The Host 4 was configured as QoSiLAN Manager (QM), to manage the resources, since the intra-LAN traffic is in focus for this scenario. For setups, where the Internet to LAN traffic is in focus, the router is configured as QM. The hosts are Netbook devices with Windows 8 operating system. The router is a Linksys WRT-54GL device [55] running with the Linux based DD-WRT operating system. All devices, including the router, are equipped with the portable QoSiLAN framework stack. The test-bed network is isolated from the laboratory's traffic using the router's NAT and firewall functionality. The Internet link is routed through the laboratory LAN, sharing a 100 Mbit Internet link, provided by the facilities of the University of Applied Sciences Mittelhessen, Germany, which is connected to the German Scientific Network (DFN) backbone [56]. The DFN Internet backbone X-WIN is a science network, connecting more than 60 universities, science institutes, and science related companies within Germany, Europe, and abroad using one of the most powerful fiber-based communication networks in the world.

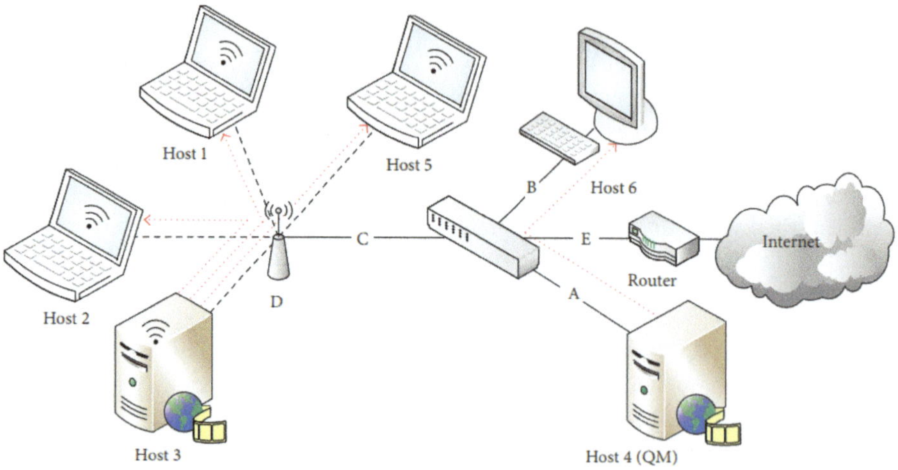

Figure 8: QoSiLAN evaluation scenario.

Link Layer Topology Discovery

The LLTD protocol was selected after intensive related work study [13, 14, 57] and comparison of existing topology discovery solutions [58–60]. It was found that the LLTD algorithm is the most appropriate state of the art approach of physical topology discovery in LANs. The protocol was implemented by Microsoft for their Windows operating system products since the release of Windows Vista, including a closed source LLTD Mapper service and LLTD Responder service for Microsoft Windows and an open source LLTD Responder for Linux based operating systems. The most important part, an API to the LLTD Mapper service or an open source implementation of it, is not available publicly. Although technical protocol descriptions exist and the algorithm was presented within a conference paper [57], a lot of implementation and algorithmic details of the LLTD mapping process are not published. So, to be able to use the technology within the QoSiLAN framework and for its evaluations the LLTD mapper had to be reverse engineered and reimplemented. This was a major task, since the mapping process is very complex and especially discovering deep segments and hosts is not trivial.

To reverse engineer the LLTD algorithm and to test the LLTD mapper during the implementation and reverse engineering phase, an Ethernet network simulator was developed, which simulates the behaviour of switches, hubs, and LLTD responder nodes. The network simulator, as shown in Figure 9 provides basic Ethernet functionality to emulate the Ethernet communication behaviour, addressing the switch's AIT building behaviour. In addition, the LLTD responder nodes also implement the LLTD responder behaviour for LLTD message sending and responding and the "sees" list. All addresses, tables, and lists are inspectable through the user interface. Additionally, the network simulator provides functionality to pause and continue the communication to provide rich debugging possibilities. It provides a live watch feature, to follow the Ethernet packet traversal through the LAN using animations. The LLTD mapper application, shown in Figure 10, is a separate component, which was developed to support both communication with the simulator through named pipes and portable Ethernet operation using the libpcap/winpcap API interfaces for Linux and Windows based systems [61, 62]. The LLTD mapper as well as the Ethernet Simulator was developed using the Microsoft .NET framework [63] and the Mono project framework [64] to support platform independence. For the other evaluation scenarios, which make use of the LLTD features and as final regression test, the LLTD mapper was tested and productively used within the evaluation test-bed, as presented in Figure 8. Further details on the work of the LLTD are not included in this paper, since we did not enhance this technology but only used it for the QoSiLAN framework and its test-beds.

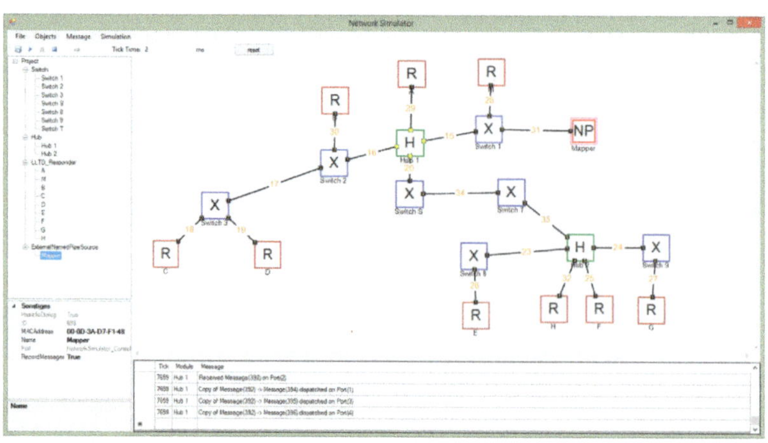

Figure 9: LLTD network simulator with the test topology loaded.

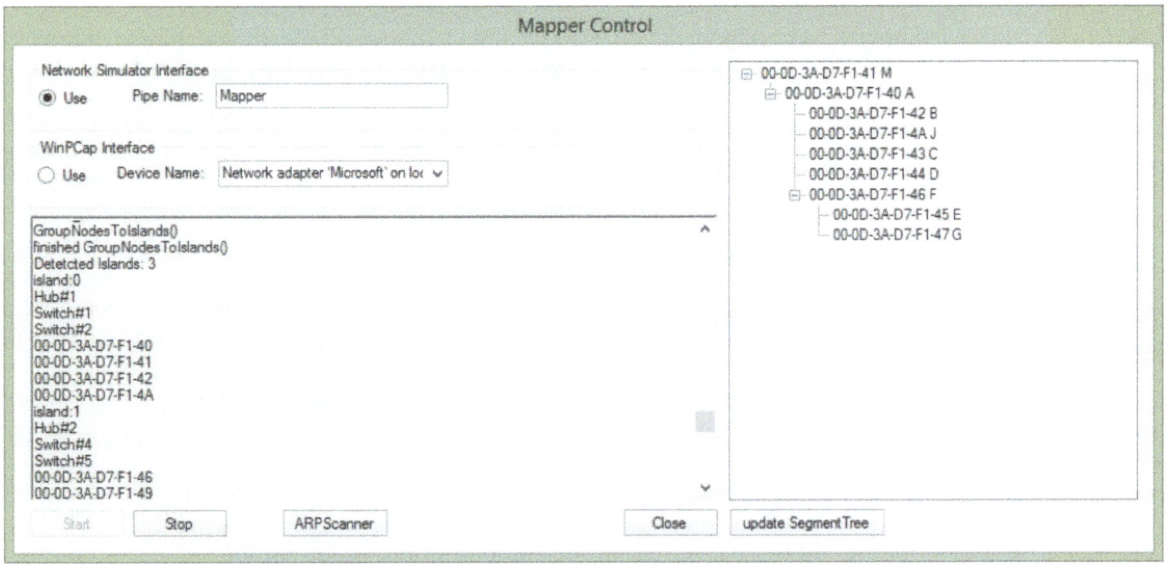

Figure 10: LLTD mapper application with the test topology's segment tree.

Enhanced Statistical Protocol Identification

Preceded by intensive related work study, the SPID algorithm was identified as best fitting for the QoSiLAN framework since it fulfils the requirements of the targeted environment. It is light weight of high precision and enables protocol identification and application payload identification at the same time, even for encrypted or compressed traffic. After related work study and first tests the SPID algorithm was selected as appropriate base. The published implementation was evaluated to be not well implemented in terms of performance and memory usage and needed to be reimplemented. In addition, laboratory test showed that the SPID performance was not as good as expected. Therefore, all measures and parameters were evaluated and optimised. In addition, the measures were reconfigured and additional once developed and tested, to find a better measure configuration for the QoSiLAN framework evaluation test-bed. The completely reengineered algorithm was called eSPID. The eSPID implementation is written in C++ using the libpcap/winpcap API interfaces [61, 62].

The eSPID evaluations to find the best measure and algorithm configuration were carried out using a set of 3135 flows from 17 different protocols. The set of evaluation flows was recorded from real web-browsing and application usage under various usage scenarios, to cover different protocol behaviours for the same protocol. During the development process and for the fine-tuning of the algorithm, the different measures were tested individually to verify their performance and usefulness for the whole set of measures.

Statistical Class-Based Bandwidth Prediction

The SCBP algorithm was developed from the motivation to have a simple and light-weight algorithm with low computing complexity. After literature research and investigation of real-world traffic from major video and audio streaming portals it was found that the state-of-the-art literature solutions do not handle the characteristics of nowadays Internet media streaming traffic explicitly. For that reason, the SCBP algorithm was designed from the practical observation that streams need a prior classification and case by case handling before predications should be applied. In particular, the first ten seconds of transmission were found as significant for the overall transfer behaviour. Dependent on the characteristic of the first ten second transfer behaviour, a systematic deviation from the expected results could be discovered. Therefore, intensive evaluations were carried out to optimise the classified results using individual correction factors for each class. In addition, different optimisation approaches were followed in parallel and compared to find the best optimisation set for the prediction results. All evaluations for the SCBP were performed with real Internet traffic from common WebTV, IPTV, Internet Radio, and on-demand platforms, located in Germany, United Kingdom, France, and the United States of America. The evaluation was carried out according to Figure 11 on Host 1. Host 1 is connected using 100BaseT Ethernet to an Internet gateway, which provides access to the University Of Applied Sciences Mittelhessen's (THM) Internet connection. The SCBP implementation is written in portable C++ using the libpcap/winpcap API interfaces [61, 62]. The streams were automatically identified using the eSPID algorithm [15] and classified according to the algorithm discussed in Section 2.2. Only streams with a minimum transfer time of 60 s were included in the evaluation, which resulted in a set sized of 463 samples. This allowed us to get the significant average bandwidth consumption value for the first 60 s $(\bar{B}_{60})$ for each flow. The $(\bar{B}_{60})$-value served as reference and was used to validate the prediction accuracy after ten seconds (A_{10}).

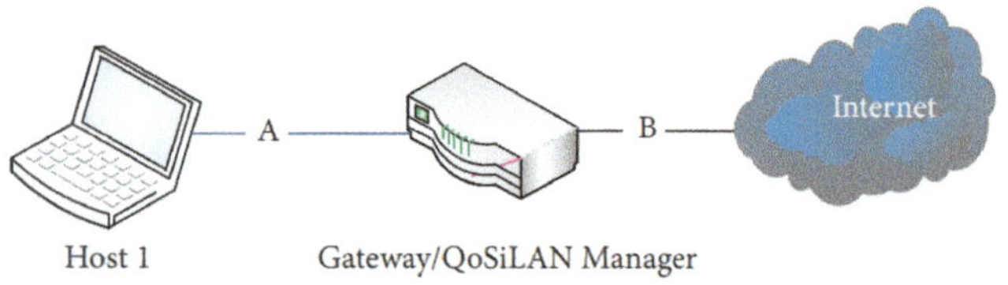

Figure 11: QoSiLAN evaluation scenario.

QoS Signalling Layer Protocol for Local Area Networks

The QSLP-LAN was designed after intensive literature research and state-of-the-art Internet protocol specification investigations. The latest IETF recommendations were followed very strictly to specify the new protocol accordingly for the novel QoSiLAN's QoS model. The evaluations also include a critical quantitative analytical view on the IETF's NSIS specification and the overhead it causes in a distributed scenario. The NSIS-based QSLP-LAN implementation is written in C++ using the ACE ACE-Wrapper communication framework for a light-weight, portable multithreading and socket communication support.

The QSLP-LAN was evaluated within the test-bed presented in Figure 8. The communication was tested on the Windows based hosts, as well as on the DD-WRT enabled router. The Wireshark- [65] and the Tcpdump-tools [66] were used to inspect and analyse the signalling data. The QSLP-LAN was also assessed indirectly within the evaluations for the policing and admission control function, presented in Section 2.5.3. Additionally, the analytical evaluation was performed using mathematical calculations and projections assisted by Microsoft's Excel [67] application.

Policing and Admission Control

The policing and admission control algorithm was designed according to the best-practices found in the literature and in existing systems. The literature research helped to identify the crucial parts and to select the appropriate approach. The concrete implementation of the algorithm was designed by employing the features of the different QoSiLAN framework's modules and to use them efficiently. The policing and admission control module is written in C++ employing APIs to all other module and additionally accessing the Microsoft Windows Traffic Control API [68] and the Linux netfilter-tc [68] tools for active traffic management and control. The intermodule communication is realised using local socket communication.

The policing and admission control evaluations show the integration of the whole QoSiLAN framework, its behaviour, and the interaction of the individual key components. Therefore, the evaluation uses the complete scenario, as shown in Figure 8. A complete resource reservation procedure was selected, which drives the network in an overloading situation with QoS degradation of the application streams with the QoS demands. The evaluation setup was also designed to assess the MBAC and policing algorithm in an demonstrative way.

RESULTS AND DISCUSSION

The evaluations were carried out in a real test-bed with Netbook hosts, connected using IEEE 802.11g and IEEE 802.3 100-BaseT Ethernet links, as shown in Figure 12. The presented scenario includes four wireless hosts, two fixed line hosts, an access point, a switch, and a router, which provides the Internet connection.

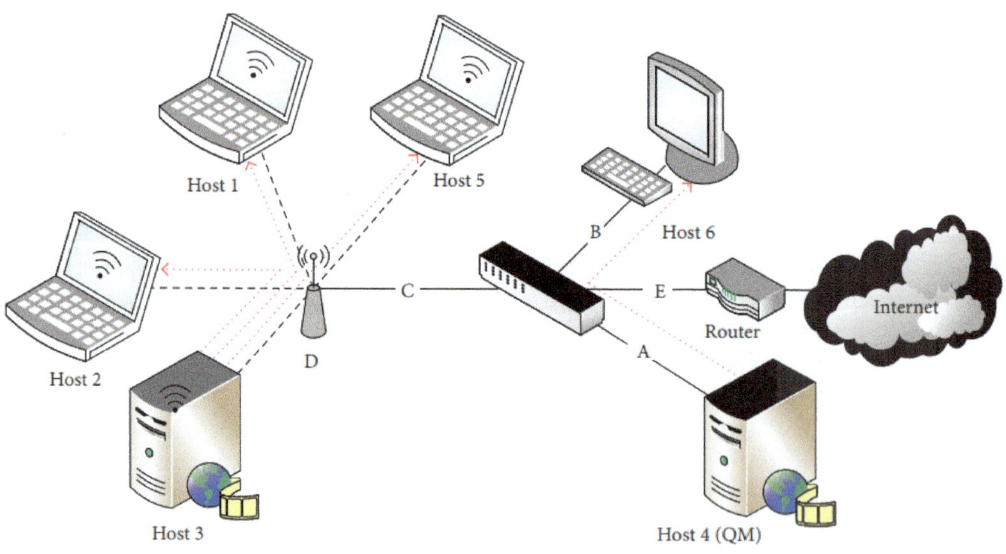

Figure 12: QoSiLAN evaluation scenario.

QoS Admission Control and Policing

To evaluate the concept of the QoSiLAN framework and the effectiveness of its admission and policing algorithms, the scenario shown in Figure 12 was configured to overload the network for proofing the system in a critical situation. In addition, the features of hybrid inter-access-medium QoS, per link bandwidth reservation, and simplex/duplex handling are shown within this example. To show the effectiveness of the QoS approach, Figure 13 depicts a direct comparison of a bandwidth conflict scenario with and without QoS enabled.

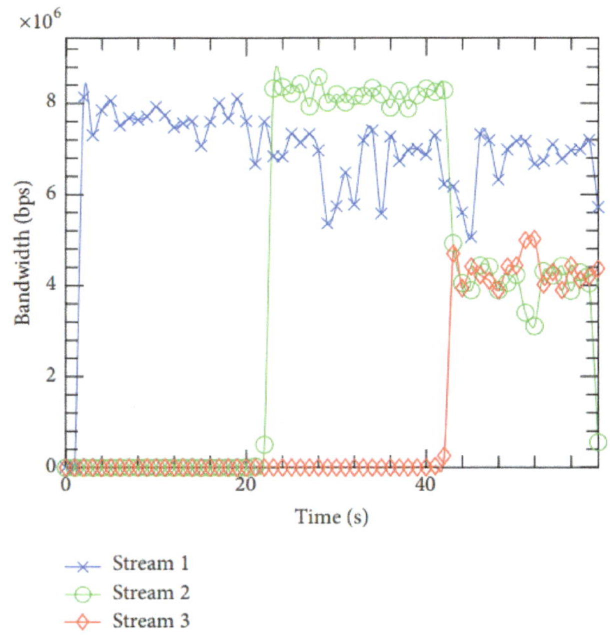

(a) Without QoS enabled

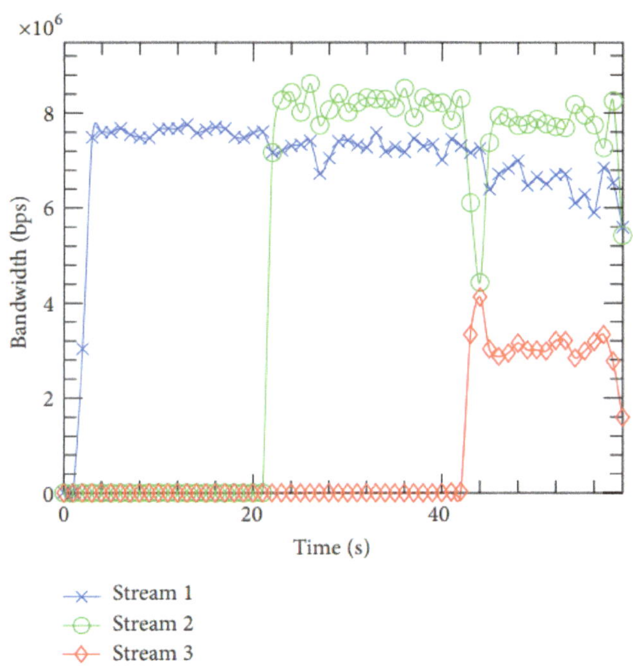

(b) With QoS enabled

Figure 13: Conflict evaluation with and without QoSiLAN QoS enabled.

QoSiLAN Framework Evaluation

The effectiveness of the QoSiLAN's QoS approach of reserving bandwidth within the LAN by cooperative traffic shaping is illustrated in Figure 13.

This comparative evaluation was executed within the test-bed shown in Figure 12. Host 1, Host 2, and Host 5 request TCP streams with 8 Mbps from Host 3. In Figure 13(a) the results are presented, where there is no QoS configured, whereas in Figure 13(b) the results were generated with QoSiLAN's QoS functionality enabled and requested for all of the streams. All stream have a bandwidth demand of 3 Mbps. Since they all are sharing the same access medium, which was assessed with a capacity of 20.6 Mbps before a bandwidth conflict occurs when all streams are running at the same time. In Figure 13(b), the conflict is resolved by QoSiLAN, which detects the overprovisioning and hence does not admit the reservation request for Stream 3. Therefore, it limits Stream 3 to 3 Mbps. First, Host 1 requests Stream 1 and can start without disturbance. After 20 s Host 2 requests Stream 2. Since the access medium capacity is not exceeded in both scenarios, no problem occurs. The main difference until that point in time is the visible effect of the traffic shaper, which harmonises the variance of the bandwidth consumption. After 40 s Host 5 requests Stream 3. Figure 13(a) shows that this harms the transmission of Stream 2, which shares the residual bandwidth with Stream 3, now. Also Stream 1 is affected and disturbed in transmission. Figure 13(b) shows the QoSiLAN approach's effect, where the start of Stream 3 does not harm the transmission of the other streams. Only in the beginning of Stream 3 there is a short disturbance of Stream 2 until the traffic shaper in Host 5 is applied after 20 packets of flow recognition and identification.

The whole QoSiLAN framework was also evaluated using the test-bed in Figure 12. There, Host 4 was setup as QoSiLAN Manager. Table 2 shows a tabular view on the actions performed within the evaluation.

Table 2: Evaluation action schedule

Time (sec)	Source host	Target host	Action
−10	4	4	LLTD mapping
−5	4	Any	Performance measurement
0	1	4	Request Stream 1
0	4	1	Start of Stream 1
2	4	Local	SPID identification [Stream 1: Video]
10	4	Local	SCBP prediction (Stream 1)
10	4	4	QoSiLAN_Req (Stream 1)
10	4	Any	QoSiLAN_Req (Stream 1)
19	2	3	Request Stream 2
19	3	2	Start of Stream 2
20	3	Local	SPID identification [Stream 2: None]
29	3	Local	SCBP prediction (Stream 2)
29	3	4	QoSiLAN_Status (Stream 2)
27	5	3	Request Stream 3
27	3	5	Start of Stream 3
28	3	Local	SPID identification [Stream 3: Video]
37	3	Local	SCBP prediction (Stream 3)
37	3	4	QoSiLAN_Req (Stream 3)
37	4	Any	QoSiLAN_Req (Stream 3)
37	any	Local	Apply new policy

Before the start of the evaluation, Host 4 already performed the LLTD mapping process and assessed the wireless link TCP throughput from the wireless Host 3 to the other wireless Host 1 with μ_l = 10.6 Mbps. This is a realistic throughput for IEEE 802.11g connections with both nodes connected to the same wireless access point, due to the simplex nature of the access medium. The tested throughput from the fixed Host 6 to the wireless Host 1 was measured to be 20.6 Mbps.

The maximum TCP throughput between the fixed Host 4 and Host 6 was tested with 87.7 Mbps. The tests were carried out under congestion free network conditions and a close physical link for the wireless hosts, using the iperf TCP and UDP bandwidth performance measurement tool [10]. In the beginning, the network is in idle state. For our evaluations, Host 1 starts requesting a video stream (Stream 1) from Host 4 with an average bandwidth of 8 Mbps, as shown in Figure 14. After 20 packets the eSPID module identified the stream type as video and after 10 s the average output bandwidth P_b^1 of Stream 1 was predicted with 8.0 Mbps. The admission control algorithm decided to admit the reservation, since it is in the rage of 80% link capacity 8.48 Mbps $= \mu_l \geq \mu_c =$ 8.0 Mbps of the wireless link D. The QM initiated the QoS signalling and advised all wireless hosts to shape their outgoing traffic to other wireless hosts to $\mu r =$ 2.12 Mbps residual bandwidth. Exactly 20 s after start, Host 2 also requests TCP data (Stream 2) from Host 3 with a data rate of 2 Mbps, which was predicted with $P_b^2 =$ 2.1 Mbps. This stream was not identified as audio/video stream and therefore no reservation was initiated. The predicted bandwidth of Stream 2 (P_b^2) is smaller than the residual bandwidth μr and thus causing no QoS problems. Although for this flow no reservation is requested, the QM is informed about the current bandwidth occupation.

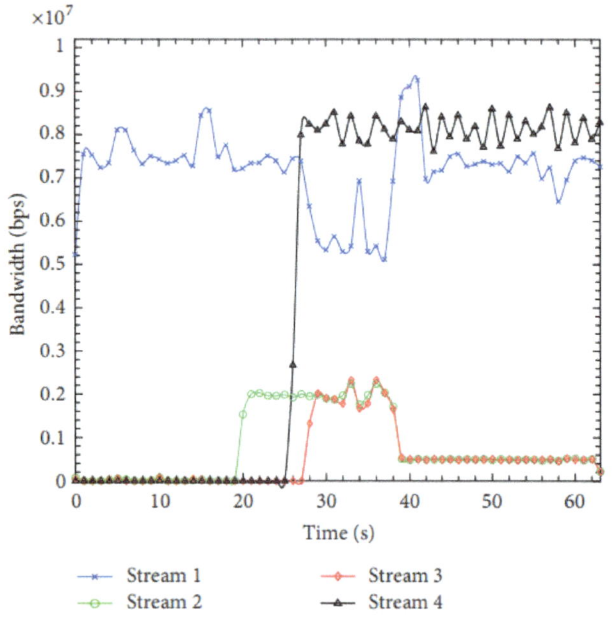

Figure 14: QoSiLAN evaluation.

Now, both streams are running in parallel without any disturbance or interference. When Host 5 also requests 2.1 Mbps TCP traffic (Stream 3) 27 s after start, the wireless link capacity is exceeded and Stream 1 is disturbed significantly, as shown in Figure 14. This situation represents an unmanaged state, where no QoS is applied. This situation lasts for 6 s. As soon as Host 3 detects the significant outgoing traffic, it informs the QM about its amount. The QM detects the conflict and advises all wireless hosts to shape their outgoing traffic to other wireless targets to 500 Kbps. This happens in second 33, where the new policies are applied. Now, the QoS protection for Stream 1 is adapted again and Stream 1 returns to its desired throughput level. For targets outside the wireless link D a shaping limit of 1 Mbit was communicated. As soon as this new policy is applied by the hosts, the throughput of Stream 1 recovers to its desired state, as depicted in Figure 14. In parallel, a video stream from Host 4 to Host 6 (Stream 4) with $P_b^5 =$ 8.3 Mbps is detected. Since no reservations are applied to the links A and B the reservation is admitted and does not affect the other reservations. This new reservation is also not communicated to the wireless hosts, since the bottleneck bandwidth for the path from the wireless hosts to Host 6 is lower than the residual bandwidth on link B. Host 6 has no limits to Host 4, due to the duplex nature of the Ethernet links and no reservations apply in that direction. In addition, there is no need to communicate the Ethernet reservation to the wireless nodes, since their outgoing traffic limit is lower than the one on the Ethernet links. Host 4 limits its outgoing traffic for other flows than Stream 4 to $P_b^3 - \mu_r^A =$ 8.3 Mbps − 70.16 Mbps = 61.86 Mbps according the policing rules. Table 3 shows the shaping policies as applied at the end of the evaluation, when all reservation states are active. As one can see, all host receive individual policies, according to their location in the network. In that way perlink reservation states are enforced.

Table 3: Traffic shaping policies

Source	Host 1	Host 2	Host 3	Host 4	Host 5	Host 6
Target			Limit			
Host 1	—	500 Kbps	500 Kbps	1 Mbps	500 Kbps	500 Kbps
Host 2	500 Kbps	—	500 Kbps	1 Mbps	500 Kbps	1 Mbps
Host 3	500 Kbps	500 Kbps	—	1 Mbps	500 Kbps	1 Mbps
Host 4	1 Mbps	1 Mbps	1 Mbps	—	1 Mbps	no limit
Host 5	500 Kbps	500 Kbps	500 Kbps	1 Mbps	—	500 Kbps
Host 6	1 Mbps	1 Mbps	1 Mbps	61.86 Mbps	1 Mbps	—

Conflict Management

Critical situations occur, if there are not enough resources available in the LAN. In this case the admission control function decides on three traffic priority levels:

(i) general Internet access (low priority);

(ii) AV-streaming/IPTV (higher priority);

(iii) VoIP/IP telephony (highest priority).

In the case of two conflicting reservation requests, the first come first served policy is applied. So, the last incoming conflicting request is declined, unless it belongs to a higher prioritised traffic class. If a higher prioritised request is recognised, the QH owning the lower one is informed with a tear down request for its reservation state, in forms of a QoSiLAN_RESERVE message with the tear flag set. Also all other QHs in the network are informed to delete the lower prioritised reservation state and to establish the higher one. This enables the QH to inform the user about the loss of QoS for the running service.

Limitations

Since the QoSiLAN approach relies on client support, most of the possible reasons limiting the framework's effectiveness are caused by lacking QoSiLAN support by hosts:

(i) One host, with lacking QoSiLAN support, can be managed by the corresponding host. In cases if the sender is not QoSiLAN aware, on behalf, the traffic-receiver may tell the QM about the needed resources. Both end-systems are not QoSiLAN aware, but the gateway discovered real-time traffic between them; the QM can initiate the reservation request on behalf of it, depending on matching policies. This is a probable scenario, if one node belongs to the LAN and is not QoSiLAN aware, and the correspondent host is located outside the LAN. In this case a QoSiLAN aware gateway may detect the need of resource reservation, since it is part of the path between the hosts.

(ii) Two hosts, with lacking QoSiLAN support, inside the LAN communicating with each other would cause uncontrolled and unknown traffic to the LAN. This may harm the communication of other hosts, since there is a way neither to prohibit the traffic nor to even get knowledge of it in a switched network. So, LAN internal communication between two hosts not supporting QoSiLAN has to be avoided by the administrators.

(iii) Data traffic, from or to hosts, which are not locatable by the LLTD protocol would cause QoSiLAN to limit the bandwidth, in case of reservations, network wide and not per link. Since the data path in the LAN's topology is not traceable by the QM, the reservation must be operative to all physical links in the whole LAN. This may reduce the overall performance of the network. In addition, the QM has to calculate the reserved capacities in the network and to take care that it reserves not more resources than available. It has to mind a minimal bandwidth capacity for all hosts in the network to enable best effort for at least signalling applications.

QoS Signalling Protocol

This section evaluates the quantity, scalability and performance of the protocol. A typical QoSiLAN_RESERVE message has a length of 124 bytes, including the UDP, IPv4, and GIST header. The GIST message header has a size of 12 bytes. The GIST NSLP data header has a length of 4 bytes. The GIST payload consists of a QoS message, which starts with a QoS NSLP header with a length of 4 bytes, followed by the QoS objects. All QoS objects start with a 2 byte common header. The minimum size is 4 bytes, additionally 32 bit fields are indicated by the length parameter at byte 2 of the QoS common object header. These are the RSN, EpochID, Refresh Period, Bound Session ID, and QSpec. The sizes of all headers are listed in Table 4. The QSpec contains QSpec objects with a Common QSpec header at the start. The QSpec objects start with a 4 byte parameter header, followed by the object's payload header. These are the TMOD-1, Excess Treatment, and the RPP-IPv4. The sum of headers gives a total message length of 116 bytes, as listed in Table 4.

Table 4: QoSiLAN request header sizes

Header name	Size [bytes]
GIST	12
GIST NSLP DATA	4
QoS NSLP	4
QoS RSN	4
QoS EpochID	8
QoS Refresh Period	4
QoS Bound Session ID	36
QSpec Common Object	4
QSpec Common QSpec	4
QSpec Object	4
QSpec TMOD-1	24
QSpec Excess Treatment	8
QSpec RPP-IPv4	20
Sum	136

The QoSiLAN_Response message has a size of 32 bytes, as listed in Table 5. The INFO_SPEC object consists of a 4 byte common header and the 4 byte ESI, which carries the IPv4 address of the message source. For each host in the network, the QM has to generate one message for each QH in the LAN, which leads to the network request message load (B_r), generated by the QM, as defined in

$$f(B_r) = (N_H - 1)^2 * s_{\text{req}} + (N_H - 1)^2 * s_{\text{rep}}. \tag{6}$$

There, N_H describes the number of host and s_{req} is the size of the request and s_{rep} the size of response messages, respectively. The messages from and to the QM itself are not routed to the network and therefore not relevant to the network load. Figure 15 shows the scalability problem of the proposed protocol. It shows the graphs of number of messages and the generated amount of data in one graph, scaled by the number of hosts in the network. As one can see, already 25 hosts in the network cause over 129,024 bytes of traffic occupied by 1,152 messages sent in the network for a single QoSiLAN reservation session establishment. The 1 MB mark is hit with 68 hosts causing 8,978 messages.The number of 213 hosts generates approximately 10 MB of traffic using 89,888 messages. Over 1 billion messages are needed for a LAN with 709 hosts, generating 112,283,136 bytes of data.

Table 5: QoSiLAN response header sizes

Header name	Size [bytes]
GIST	12
GIST NSLP DATA	4
QoS NSLP	4
QoS RSN	4
QoS INFO SPEC	8
Sum	32

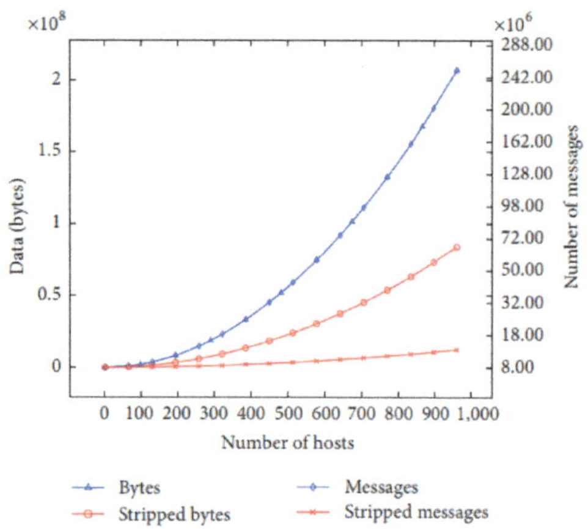

Figure 15: QoSiLAN signalling effort.

The QSLP-LAN was designed following the latest IETF recommendations for new signalling protocols. Since the QoSiLAN approach is designed only for small networks with not more than 25 hosts, the number of messages and data used for signalling is not regarded as relevant for the system. As expected, the signalling effort for a cooperative approach is very high. Anyway, the evaluation prooves that a redesign of the signalling procedure would be needed in case of higher scalability demands. An approach to reduce the number of message and the amount of data needed would be to pack the individual policy information affecting one host into one single message, using the maximum path MTU for the transfer. Also, a more minimalistic, proprietary message design with compression enabled would significantly save signalling resources. For example, a QoSiLAN_Request message could be stripped to 83 bytes instead of 136 bytes, when removing all structural NSIS information and keeping only the essential data, without data compression. This is reduction of approx. 39%. When using a MTU size of 1400 bytes, 16 messages would fit into one packet. As depicted in Figure 15, the amount of data needed to to establish a QoS state in a network with 709 nodes would be reduced from 112,283,136 bytes to 45,493,248 bytes, which is a reduction of 59%. The number of message would be reduced by 94% from 1,002,528 to 59,472. In a 25-node network the number of messages would reduce from 1152 to 39 and the number of amount of data needed would scale down from 105,984 bytes to 41,864 bytes.

Statistical Class-Based Bandwidth Prediction

The evaluation helped to calibrate the algorithm and to validate its accuracy. To improve the readability of this section, Abbreviations provides a compact overview about the most important abbreviations. All evaluations were performed with real Internet traffic from common WebTV, IPTV, Internet Radio, and on-demand platforms, located in Germany, UK, France, and the USA. The evaluation was carried out according to Figure 11 on Host 6.The streams were automatically identified using the eSPID algorithm [15] and classified according to the algorithm discussed in Section 2.2. All streams had a minimum transfer time of 60 s. This allowed us to get the significant average bandwidth consumption value for the first 60 s $(\overline{B}_{60})$. This value served as reference and was used to validate the prediction accuracy after ten seconds (A_{10}):

$$A_{10} = \frac{P_{10}}{\overline{B}_{60}}. \tag{7}$$

Other important measures are the Prediction Hit Rate (PHR), the Mean Prediction Accuracy Ratio (MPAR), and the OverEstimation Rate (OER):

(i) The Prediction Hit Rate specifies the number of predictions, which are in the range of 0.8 ⍰ A_{10} ⍰ 2, as percentage. This range was specified to filter unacceptable outliers for consumer media traffic prediction.

(ii) The Mean Prediction Accuracy Ratio specifies the mean prediction accuracy $\overline{A_{10}}$ over all samples. Since the prediction causes network blocking through QoSiLAN reservations, the Mean Prediction Accuracy Ratio reveals the average network blocking rate.

(iii) The Over-Estimation Rate specifies the number of prediction accuracy ratios with $A_{10} > 1$ in percentage. This is an important measure for QoS critical applications, since it reflects the QoS assurance probability a prediction algorithm configuration can achieve.

For the evaluations a set of 1442 monitored media streams was used. All these parameters were evaluated for the whole stream set Class Less (CL) and per class individually ClassBased (CB). The k-value in (3) was optimised for each of these three measures individually to find the best method for optimisation as defined in the following:

(i) The k-value for Prediction Hit Rate was evaluated for the maximum Prediction Hit Rate in (3), to receive the maximum number of results in the acceptable range.

(ii) For the MPHR, the k-value was evaluated to give in (3) a result in average of 1, which reflects the best mean network blocking/utilisation rate.

(iii) The QoS optimization's k-value was evaluated to result in (3) an average of 90% Over-Estimation Rate to ensure a minimum of 90% QoS assurance.

Finding the best optimisation configuration is challenging. First, the Mean Prediction Accuracy Ratio should be near to 1, to ensure the best network utilisation.This would be reflected by traditional error calculation like the Root Mean Square Error (RMSE). Second, at the same time as much A_{10} results should match the acceptable range. Third, since the QoS is important, as much as possible A_{10} results should be greater than 1. To find the best optimisation aspects, which meet all these requirements at the same time, the Euclidean distance (d) was employed, as shown in

$$\mathbf{d} = \sqrt{(1 - \text{MPAR})^2 + (1 - \text{PHR})^2 + (1 - \text{OER})^2}. \qquad (8)$$

It takes all three parameters into account and provides the minimum d-value, which reflects the best fitting algorithm configuration. In Figure 16(d) a smaller value of d indicates a better performance, taking into account the three measures MPAR, Prediction Hit Rate, and OER. Table 6 gives an overview about the results achieved for the different configurations. There, also the median $(\widetilde{\text{MPAR}})$ and the mean accuracy $(\overline{\text{MPAR}})$ values are listed, which enable a first assessment of the results. While the mean accuracy value emphasises the average network utilisation, the median accuracy value gives an indication about the distribution of values. Figures 16(a)–16(c) give an overview about the three different optimisation aspects, whereas Figure 16(d) shows the results after the Euclidean distance calculation, which reflects a combination of the previous ones. In Figure 16(a) the Over-Estimation Rate optimisation, with a target value of 1, indicates that the Mean Estimation (ME) and CLPHR aspects perform best. The CBQoS performs only on the third place together with CLQoS aspect. In Figure 16(b) the Mean Prediction Accuracy Ratio results with a target value of 1 that indicates the optimum for the CLMPAR and CBMPAR aspects, as expected, but the CBQoS aspect performs as next best. The Prediction Hit Rate aspect results in Figure 16(c) show the best performance for the CBPHR and the CBQoS results, which should be near to 1 to be the best. This is interesting and shows that the optimisation for Prediction Hit Rate without classes cannot provide an average ratio better than 0.77. The class-based approach gives a better density of results in the acceptable range. The Euclidean distance assessment in Figure 16(d) illustrates the advantage of the CBQoS approach, which does not perform best in all categories, but collectively over all optimisation aspects it shows the best performance.

Table 6: Overview of results

Optimization	k	$\widetilde{\text{MPAR}}$	d	$\overline{\text{MPAR}}$	PHR	PAR > 1	PAR < 1
CLME	1.0000	1.1561	1.3613	2.3241	68.93%	94.31%	5.69%
CBMPAR	Class based	0.8676	0.7218	1.0000	72.61%	33.22%	66.78%
CLMPAR	0.6335	1.2023	0.9824	1.0000	39.04%	22.95%	77.05%
CBPHR	Class based	1.1949	0.4790	1.4613	93.07%	89.11%	10.89%
CLPHR	1.0670	0.7324	0.7261	1.6842	76.63%	93.34%	6.66%
CBQoS	Class based	1.2335	0.4580	1.4408	92.51%	90.08%	9.92%
CLQoS	1.0189	1.1779	0.6597	1.6083	76.49%	90.01%	9.99%

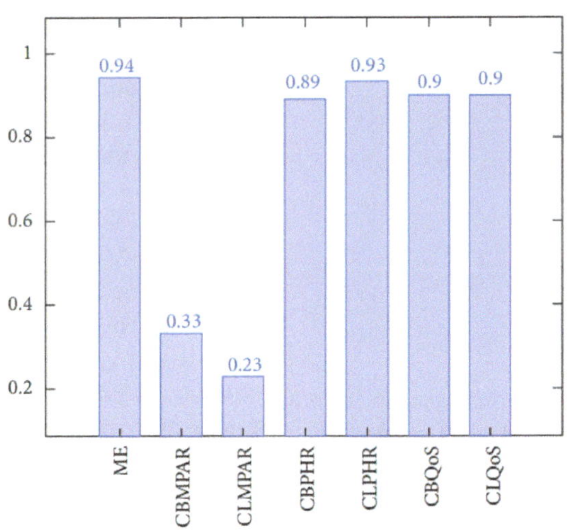

(a) OER

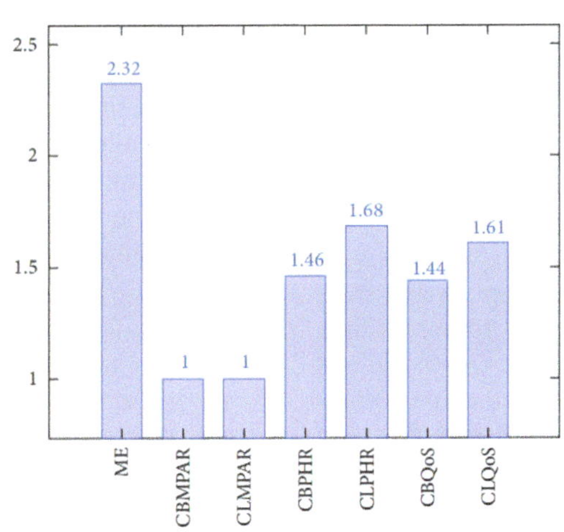

(b) MPAR

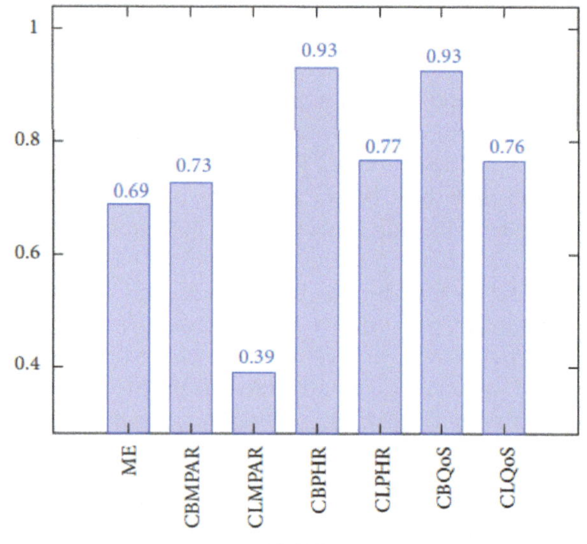

(c) PHR

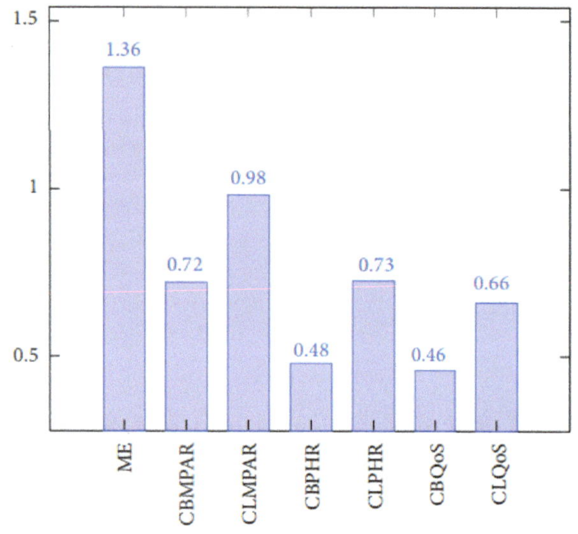

(d) Euclidean distance

Figure 16: Performance assessment of optimisation results.

The statistical class-based bandwidth prediction algorithm using the CBQoS optimisation configuration was proved to perform best for predicting bandwidth requirements for a relative long period of 60 s. On the first view the classless results look also very good and perform in some configurations similar to the class-based approach or even better. Finally the Euclidean distance comparison in Figure 16(d) reveals the advantage of the CBQoS optimisation approach, since it brings the deviation of results into account, combining the different measures. Also, we showed, as presented in Figure 16, that a 100% prediction accuracy with a minimum error is not desirable, as it causes a higher underestimation probability than, for example, an QoS optimisation case. Generally, it is more critical for the media streams, if their resources are underprovisioned, since they are not properly protected from congestion then. In contrast, blocking of more resources than needed is critical for the overall network performance and utilisation. In the application of QoS, a little overestimation of resources is also to be regarded as positive, since this allows the streams to prebuffer faster at the receiver, which results in more robustness against the variability of network performance and provides a better stream isolation against disturbing traffic and congestion.

CONCLUSION

In this paper we presented and evaluated the QoSiLAN framework in its whole for the first time. The interaction of the different key technology, which enable link based resource reservation by autonomous policing and admission control for QoS in LANs, was shown. The QoSiLAN admission control and policing algorithm was designed to take care not to block more resources in the network than needed, by allowing to react dynamically on reservation violations and network congestion in an appropriate manner autonomously. The QoSiLAN framework was presented to be an effective method to reserve bandwidth on individual links in LANs without the network's QoS assistance and therefore to provide self-organised QoS for unmanaged networks. The admission control and policing function in the QM utilizes the QH information from the topology mapping and the traffic-analysis and -reporting to take informed decisions for managing the LAN's resources efficiently. The new SCBP algorithm was presented along with detailed evaluations to optimise it for the best resource predication performance within the QoSiLAN framework. The evaluations show that QoS conflicts are detected reliably and a solution is enforced in an autonomous way. The novel QoSiLAN QoS model, designed to enforce cross-access-technology link-based bandwidth reservation by collaborative traffic shaping without network assistance using the dedicated QSLP-LAN protocol, was proved within the evaluations. The QoSiLAN framework is implementable in a lightweight manner. It does not rely on network support, but on host collaboration. In addition, not all hosts in the network need to support the framework essentially. For a proper operation, the support by at least one of the communication parties within the LAN is required, if the router is QoSiLAN aware. Traffic sources like Media-NAS devices and the Internet router may implement the framework preferably to allow for an optimised operation. This makes the QoSiLAN framework easy to implement and to be deployable in realistic scenarios. The autonomous configuration and operation features qualify the framework for nonexpert deployment and application.

REFERENCES

1. Cisco. Cisco data meter, 2013, http://www.ciscovni.com/data-meter/index.html.
2. Cisco, "Cisco Visual Networking Index: Forecast and Methodology, 2012–2017," white paper, 2013.
3. Qualcomm, "Qualcomm Introduces StreamBoost Technology to Optimize Performance and Capacity of Home Networks," 2013, https://www.qualcomm.com/news/releases/2013/01/04/qualcomm-introduces-streamboost-technology-optimize-performance-and.
4. R. Braden, L. Zhang, S. Berson, S. Herzog, and S. Jamin, "Resource ReSerVation Protocol (RSVP)—version 1 functional specification," Proposed Standard RFCs 2205, 2750, 3936, 4495, 5946, 6437, 6780, 1997, http://www.ietf.org/rfc/rfc2205.txt.
5. M. Cooperation, "Rsvp service," 2013, http://msdn.microsoft.com/en-us/library/windows/desktop/

aa374144(v=vs.85).aspx.

6. ITU, A Generic Home Network Architecture with Support for Multimedia Services (Recommendation ITU-T H.622), International Telecommunications Union, 2008.
7. U. Forum, "Upnp-qos architecture v3, for upnp version 1.0," 2014, http://upnp.org/specs/qos/UPnP-qos-Architecture-v3.pdf.
8. A. M. J. Manner and G. Karagiannis, Nslp for quality-ofservice signaling (qos nslp), internet draft (draft-ietf-nsisqos-nslp-16), work in progress, 2009, http://tools.ietf.org/html/draft-ietf-nsis-qos-nslp-16.
9. S. Akhshabi, A. C. Begen, and C. Dovrolis, "An experimental evaluation of rate-adaptation algorithms in adaptive streaming over HTTP," in Proceedings of the 2nd Annual ACM Multimedia Systems Conference (MMSys '11), pp. 157–168, February 2011.
10. iperf, "Tcp and udp bandwidth performance measurement tool," 2013, https://github.com/esnet/iperf.
11. R. Black, A. Donnelly, and C. Fournet, "Ethernet topology discovery without network assistance," inProceedings of the 12th IEEE International Conference on Network Protocols (ICNP '04), pp. 328–339, IEEE, Berlin, Germany, October 2004.
12. M. Corporation, "Lltd and qos for media experiences," 2013, http://msdn.microsoft.com/library/windows/hardware/gg463099/.
13. M. Corporation, "[MS-LLTD]: link layer topology discovery (LLTD) protocol specification," Open Specifications Documentation, 2009, http://msdn.microsoft.com/en-us/library/cc233983%28PROT.10%29.aspx.
14. Y. Sun, Z. Wu, and Z. Shi, "The physical topology discovery for switched ethernet based on connections reasoning technique," in Proceedings of the International Symposium on Communications and Information Technologies (ISCIT '05), pp. 44–47, IEEE, October 2005.
15. C. Köhnen, C. Überall, F. Adamsky, V. Rakočević, M. Rajarajan, and R. Jäger, "Enhancements to statistical protocol identification (SPID) for self-organised QoS in LANs," in Proceedings of the 19th International Conference on Computer Communications and Networks (ICCCN ‹10), pp. 1–6, IEEE, Zürich, Switzerland, August 2010.
16. E. Hjelmvik and W. John, "Statistical protocol identification with SPID: preliminary results," inProceedings of the Swedish National Computer Networking Workshop, 2009, http://spid.sourceforge.net/sncnw09-hjelmvik_john-CR.pdf.
17. A. S. Incorporated, "Http dynamic streaming (HDS)," 2013, http://www.adobe.com/de/products/hds-dynamic-streaming.html.
18. J. Manner, R. Bless, J. Loughney, and E. Davies, "Using and Extending the NSIS Protocol Family," RFC 5974 (Informational), 2010, http://www.ietf.org/rfc/rfc5978.txt.
19. J. Manner, G. Karagiannis, and A. McDonald, "NSIS Signaling Layer Protocol (NSLP) for quality-of-service signaling. (Experimental)," RFC 5974, 2010, http://www.ietf.org/rfc/rfc5974.txt.
20. H. Schulzrinne and R. Hancock, "GIST: general internet signalling transport," RFC 5971, 2010, http://www.ietf.org/rfc/rfc5971.txt.
21. G. Ash, A. Bader, C. Kappler, and D. Oran, "QSPEC Template for the Quality-of-Service NSIS Signaling Layer Protocol (NSLP)," RFC 5975 (Experimental), 2010, http://www.ietf.org/rfc/rfc5975.txt.
22. S. Jamin, S. J. Shenker, and P. B. Danzig, "Comparison of measurement-based admission control algorithms for controlled-load service," in Proceedings of the 16th Annual Joint Conference of the IEEE Computer and Communications Societies. Driving the Information Revolution (INFOCOM ‹97), vol. 3, pp. 973–980, IEEE, Kobe, Japan, April 1997.
23. D. Hock, N. Bayer, R. Pries et al., "QoS provisioning in WLAN mesh networks using dynamic bandwidth control," in Proceedings of the 14th European Wireless Conference (EW ‹08), pp. 1–7, IEEE, Prague, Czech Republic, June 2008.
24. M. Louvel, A. Plantec, and J.-P. Babau, "Resource management for multimedia applications, distributed in open and heterogeneous home networks," Journal of Systems Architecture—Embedded Systems Design, vol. 59, no. 3, pp. 121–134, 2013.
25. M. Louvel, P. Bonhomme, J.-P. Babau, and A. Plantec, "A network resource management framework for multimedia applications distributed in heterogeneous home networks," in Proceedings of the 25th IEEE International Conference on Advanced Information Networking and Applications (AINA ‹11), pp. 724–731, Singapore, March 2011.
26. M. Louvel, J. Pulou, A. Plantec, and J.-P. Babau, "Quantity of resource aggregation for heterogeneous resource reservation for multimedia applications," in Proceedings of the 15th IEEE International Conference on Emerging Technologies and Factory Automation (ETFA ‹10), pp. 1–4, IEEE, Bilbao, Spain, September 2010.
27. S. Ghahramani, Fundamentals of Probability: With Stochastic Processes, Pearson/Prentice Hall, 2005, http://books.google.ca/books?id=M1GUQgAACAAJ.
28. I. R. Tools, "tc—show/manipulate traffic control settings," 2014, http://www.linuxmanpages.com/man8/tc.8.php.
29. J.-P. Laulajainen and M. Hirvonen, "Automatic QoS control in UPnP home networks," in Proceedings of the IEEE Symposium on Computers and Communications (ISCC ‹09), pp. 455–460, IEEE, Sousse, Tunisia, July 2009.
30. V. Suraci, G. Oddi, N. Mattiacci, and A. Angelucci, "Admission control and drop strategies in a UPnP-QoS controlled home network," in Proceedings of the IEEE 21st International Symposium on Personal Indoor and Mobile Radio Communications (PIMRC ‹10), pp. 2811–2816, IEEE, Instanbul, Turkey, September 2010.

31. M. Castrucci, G. Oddi, G. Tamea, and V. Suraci, "Application QoS management and session control in a heterogeneous home network using Inter-MAC layer support," in Proceedings of the Future Network and Mobile Summit, pp. 1–9, Florence, Italy, June 2010.

32. J.-L. Chen, M.-C. Chen, and Y.-R. Chian, "QoS management in heterogeneous home networks," Computer Networks, vol. 51, no. 12, pp. 3368–3379, 2007.

33. L. Westberg, M. Jacobsson, M. de Kogel et al., "Resource management in diffserv on demand (roda) phr, internet draft (draft-westberg-rmd-od-phr-04), work in progress," 2003, http://tools.ietf.org/html/draft-westberg-rmd-od-phr-04.

34. H. Y. Lee, S. T. Moon, and J. W. Kim, "Enhanced UPnP QoS architecture for network-adaptive streaming service in home networks," IEEE Transactions on Consumer Electronics, vol. 53, no. 3, pp. 898–904, 2007.

35. L. Brewka, P. Sköldström, J. Nelis, H. Wessing, and C. Develder, "Automatic provisioning of end-to-end QoS into the home," IEEE Transactions on Consumer Electronics, vol. 57, no. 4, pp. 1670–1678, 2011.

36. ITU, Architecture of MediaHomeNet (Recommendation ITU-T J.190), International Telecommunications Union, Geneva, Switzerland, 2nd edition, 2007.

37. Home Gateway Initiative, "Home gateway technical requirements, release 1," Tech. Rep., Home Gateway Initiative, 2006.

38. The Architecture and Transport Working Group and DSL Home Technical Working Group, "Multiservice delivery framework for home networks," DSL Forum, Technical Report, 2004.

39. A. Y. Haikal, M. Badawy, and H. A. Ali, "Towards internet QoS provisioning based on generic distributed QoS adaptive routing engine," The Scientific World Journal, vol. 2014, Article ID 694847, 29 pages, 2014. ·

40. G. Apostolopoulos, S. Kama, D. Williams, R. Guerin, A. Orda, and T. Przygienda, "QoS Routing Mechanisms and OSPF Extensions," RFC 2676 (Experimental), 1999, http://www.ietf.org/rfc/rfc2676.txt.

41. Object Management Group, "Data distribution service for real-time systems," Object Management Group, 2007, http://www.omg.org/.

42. A. Al-Roubaiey and M. A. R. Alkhiaty, "Qos-aware middleware for ubiquitous environment: a review and proposed solution," Journal of Computational Engineering, vol. 2014, Article ID 725960, 7 pages, 2014.

43. G. Sivaradje and P. Dananjayan, "Dynamic resource allocation algorithm for next generation wireless multimedia. Services," in Proceedings of the 8th IEEE International Conference on Communication Systems (ICCS ‹02), vol. 2, pp. 752–754, IEEE, Singapore, November 2002.

44. K. Papagiannaki, N. Taft, Z.-L. Zhang, and C. Diot, "Long-term forecasting of Internet backbone traffic,"IEEE Transactions on Neural Networks, vol. 16, no. 5, pp. 1110–1124, 2005.

45. R. H. Filho and J. E. B. Maia, "Network traffic prediction using PCA and K-means," in Proceedings of the 12th IEEE/IFIP Network Operations and Management Symposium (NOMS ‹10), pp. 938–941, IEEE, Osaka, Japan, April 2010.

46. S. Chong, S.-Q. Li, and J. Ghosh, "Predictive dynamic bandwidth allocation for efficient transport of real-time VBR video over ATM," IEEE Journal on Selected Areas in Communications, vol. 13, no. 1, pp. 12–23, 1995.

47. H. Feng, Y. Shu, S. Wang, and M. Ma, "SVM-based models for predicting WLAN traffic," in Proceedings of the IEEE International Conference on Communications (ICC ‹06), pp. 597–602, Istanbul, Turkey, July 2006.

48. Q. He, C. Dovrolis, and M. Ammar, "On the predictability of large transfer TCP throughput," inProceedings of the Conference on Applications, Technologies, Architectures, and Protocols for Computer Communications (SIGCOMM ‹05), pp. 145–156, ACM, Philadelphia, Pa, USA, August 2005.

49. M. Yang, Y. Huang, J. Kim, M. Lee, T. Suda, and M. Daisuke, "An end-to-end QoS framework with on-demand bandwidth reconfiguration," in Proceedings of the 18th IEEE Annual Workshop on Computer Communications (CCW ‹03), pp. 66–74, IEEE, Dana Point, Calif, USA, October 2003. ·

50. O. T. Brewer and A. Ayyagari, "Comparison and analysis of measurement and parameter based admission control methods for Quality of Service (QoS) provisioning," in Proceedings of the IEEE Military Communications Conference (MILCOM ‹10), pp. 184–188, San Jose, Calif, USA, November 2010.

51. V. Mancuso and G. Neglia, "Performance improvements on self-similar traffic using measurement-based admission control," 2002, http://www-sop.inria.fr/members/Vincenzo.Mancuso/MNB02.pdf.

52. A. W. Moore, Measurement-based management of network resources [Ph.D. thesis], Corpus Christi College, University of Cambridge, Cambridge, UK, 2002, http://www.cl.cam.ac.uk/~awm22/publications/moore2002phd.pdf.

53. S. Jamin and S. Shenker, "Measurement-based admission control algorithms for controlled-load service: a structural examination," Tech. Rep. CSE-TR-333-97, University of Michigan, Ann Arbor, Mich, USA, 1997.

54. S. Latré and F. De Turck, "Joint in-network video rate adaptation and measurement-based admission control: algorithm design and evaluation," Journal of Network and Systems Management, vol. 21, no. 4, pp. 588–622, 2013.

55. T.F.E. Wikipedia, "Linksys wrt54g series," 2015, http://en.wikipedia.org/wiki/Linksys_WRT54G_series.

56. D.F.N.G.S. Network, "Das wissenschafftsnetz xwin," 2015, http://www.dfn.de/xwin.

57. R. Black, A. Donnelly, and C. Fournet, "Ethernet topology discovery without network assistance," inProceedings of the 12th IEEE International Conference on Network Protocols (ICNP ‹04), pp. 328–339, IEEE, Berlin, Germany, October 2004.

58. Y. Bejerano, Y. Breitbart, M. N. Garofalakis, and R. Rastogi, "Physical topology discovery for large multisubnet networks," in Proceedings of the 22nd Annual Joint Conference of the IEEE Computer and Communications (INFOCOM ‹03), vol. 1, pp. 342–352, IEEE, March-April 2003.
59. S. S. Ands, "Discovering internet topology," 1998, http://www.cs.cornell.edu/skeshav/papers/discovery.pdf.
60. M. Rose, "Management Information Base for network management of TCP/IP-based internets: MIB-II. RFC 1158 (Proposed Standard)," Obsoleted by RFC 1213, 1990, http://www.ietf.org/rfc/rfc1158.txt.
61. NRG, "Libpcap—the packet capture library," http://sourceforge.net/projects/libpcap/.
62. D.C. CACE Technologies, "Winpcap: The windows packet capture library," http://www.winpcap.org/.
63. Microsoft Corporation, "The microsoft net framework," 2002, http://www.microsoft.com/net.
64. Mono Project, "Cross platform, open source .net framework," 2004, http://www.mono-project.com/.
65. Wireshark Foundation, "Wireshark," 2015, https://www.wireshark.org/.
66. Tcpdump, "Tcpdump, a powerful command-line packet analyzer," 2015, http://www.tcpdump.org/.
67. Microsoft Corporation, "Excel application," 2015, https://products.office.com/en-us/Excel.
68. Microsoft Corporation, "Traffic control application programming interface (TC API)," 2015, https://msdn.microsoft.com/en-us/library/windows/desktop/aa374468%28v=vs.85%29.aspx.

CHAPTER 10

DEFINITION OF AN 802.11 INTERFACE MANAGEMENT PROCESS IN A PROPOSED SYSTEM FOR TRANSMISSION CAPACITY ENHANCEMENT IN WIRELESS MESH NETWORKS

Christian Köbel[1], Walter Baluja García[1], and Joachim Habermann[2]

[1]Departamento de Telecomunicaciones y Telemática, Instituto Superior Politécnico José Antonio Echeverría ISPJAE, Calle 114, No. 11901, e/Ciclovía y Rotonda, Marianao 19390, La Habana, Cuba

[2]Department for ICT, Electrical Engineering & Mechatronics, THM University of Applied Sciences, Wilhelm-Leuschner Straße 13, 61169 Friedberg, Germany

ABSTRACT

802.11-based wireless mesh networks (WMNs) as last mile solutions frequently become bottlenecks in the overall Internet communication structure. The lack of end-to-end capacity on routes also affects vertical traffic coming from or flowing towards external networks, such as the Internet. The presented approach aims to increase the overall network performance by exploiting channel diversity and to additionally favor vertical traffic. To achieve this, first we propose a general system that modifies an existing mesh node architecture, in order to prepare a more efficient resource management and to enhance the restricted transmission capacity in standard WMNs. The parallel use of nonoverlapping channels, based on a multiradio node, marks the starting point. The system treats aspects of channel assignment, traffic analysis, and fast layer 2 forwarding. Then, the impact of a novel Multihop Radio Resource Management process is discussed as a relevant component of this new system architecture. The process combines per-hop priority queuing and load balancing in a novel way. It was designed, developed, and evaluated in the presented paper, resulting in the fact that capacity in WMNs was significantly increased, Quality-of-Service parameters were improved, and more efficient use of multiple radios could be reached. The proposed process was validated using a simulation approach.

INTRODUCTION

Often, last mile networks become bottlenecks in the Internet delivery chain, since they have to fulfill increasing user demands, in terms of Quality-of-Service (QoS) guarantees. This work focuses on last mile wireless networks, which can be direct user-to-user networks, wireless backbones (e.g., a public, city-wide network), or both, in a hybrid form [1].

Wireless mesh network (WMN) technology is mostly used to create economic and flexible backbones. Planners of wireless consumer- and industry networks have seen the various advantages and diverse applications of WMNs and have begun to adapt the technology to market-ready solutions. Nevertheless, a broad acceptance is still missing, mainly due to the fact that WMNs are mostly based on single interface (IF) nodes [2]. An 802.11-based WMN naturally suffers from known risks of negative channel conditions on the Physical (PHY) layer in 802.11, like fading or distortion effects in a non-line-of-sight situation. Such effects ultimately turn the pure throughput of an 802.11 Wireless LAN (WLAN) IF into a highly conditional parameter.

Citation: Christian Köbel, Walter Baluja García, and Joachim Habermann, "Definition of an 802.11 Interface Management Process in a Proposed System for Transmission Capacity Enhancement in Wireless Mesh Networks," Journal of Computer Networks and Communications, vol. 2015, Article ID 898365, 13 pages, 2015. doi:10.1155/2015/898365

But there are other significant, more ad hoc-specific factors which may drastically restrict the transmission capacity of WLAN-based WMNs. 802.11g does not support full duplex communication [3], which causes a rapid performance- and capacity degradation on multihop routes [4, 5]. Although 802.11g is outdated in most high-performance setups, it may be still commonly used in mesh installations based on commodity hardware, for example, in rural scenarios [6–8]. Also, 802.11 Medium Access Control (MAC) is designed for shared channel access [9] and is partly based on random timers, making a consistent packet forwarding unreliable [10]. Route segments which are shared by multiple flows may be prone to congestion and unfair traffic treatment [11]. Finally, links of routes which are separated on layer 3 might still interfere within the same layer 2 collision domain [11].

In addition to the to various interference types, which should be always considered in an ad hoc network [12], traffic in WMN is often heterogeneous. Users with growing and wider external service demands create mostly vertical traffic in WMNs [13]. This leads to congestion [14] near those mesh nodes which serve as traffic gateways (GW) to outside networks, or the Internet. Vertical traffic is not protected on those routes and has the same priority as intramesh traffic. These basic limitations cause standard single-channel WMNs to have a limited transmission capacity.

To solve these issues, at first an improvement to a cross-layer mesh node architecture is proposed. It considers key functions and processes, in order to enhance the transmission capacity in WMNs. A multi-interface node offers a suitable basis for this intention, by exploiting its access to multiple orthogonal WLAN channels [15]. The novel cross-layer architecture combines and adapts methods of distributed Channel Assignment (CA) and traffic analysis and engineering, which have proven to be efficient as independent solutions. Then, a Multihop Radio Resource Management process becomes a relevant requirement within this modified architecture. This process aims to exploit capacity through packet scheduling (PS) modes and to support the protection of vertical traffic. Therefore, its development and a related proof-of-concept have priority in this work and represent the key contribution.

RELATED WORK

Several papers with the objective to exploit IF resources in a typical 802.11-based WMN have been identified in this section. To the best of our knowledge, none offers an integral or systemic answer for the described spectrum of problems so far. However, some ideas are considered as milestones by the authors towards future effective solutions.

An important definition is found in [3], which states that a carefully designed resource allocation strategy, which matches the node's availability of radios to the desired network behavior, is a crucial success factor. Mainly, this requires us to introduce a distributed or centralized CA scheme and subsequently a load balancing (LB) mechanism.

Before network parameters are optimized, basic 1-hop connectivity needs to be guaranteed. The CA approach in [16] focuses on this aspect. The centralized CA protocol of Robitzsch et al. [17] facilitates an autonomously controlled entrance of a node into WMN, considering Adjacent- and Intercarrier Interference (A/I-CI). Less interference may lead to a reduced energy consumption in node batteries [18], which benefits mobility-oriented setups. Most CA approaches do not distinguish between orthogonal and overlapping channels. Despite this fact, the CA approach in [19] explicitly foresees an optimization for partially overlapping channels.

Receiver-Based Channel Assignment (RCA) schemes [20, 21] are straight-forward, proactive, topology-considerate, and easy to implement. Negotiation-based Channel Assignment (NCA) schemes perform CA on-demand and allow interference free transmissions in most cases [20]. But their reactive nature makes them more suitable for MAC layer approaches, where the channel is negotiated framewise. Still, with simple RCA and NCA schemes, there is no consideration of 2-hop neighbors, the next-hop type, and the assignment of multiple radios per neighbor.

After CA, the next conceptual stage to exploit channel diversity often involves an unmanaged, non-LB related solution, based on additional radios. A common approach in a WMN backbone is to deploy edge nodes with two separate radios, in order to grant interference-free access to their local clients, at best using separate bands (2.4 GHz and 5 GHz, e.g., in [22]). A next stage denotes the use of two or more radios within the backbone itself, to minimize intraflow interference. Within Fraunhofer's Wireless Back-Haul (WiBACK) architecture [3], simply two 802.11 radios are deployed, with a gap of at least 60 MHz between two 20 MHz channels. This avoids a throughput decrease at each hop [23, 24]. In [25], full-duplex communication is achieved with a dual-radio scheme.

Managed scheduling depicts the next essential and logical step. If sufficient interface resources are available between two adjacent nodes, bundling is able to improve the resource utilization beyond CA measures [26]. Furthermore, channel bundling can be used to reduce signaling overhead [26]. Also, the allocation of channels to a single bundle group reduces computational cost, because when "all the channels in the same bundle are either available or busy simultaneously, a secondary user can sense each bundle of channels instead of each channel individually" [26].

Kim and Ko [27] describe a virtual interface (VI) which sits upon and controls multiple WLAN MACs. Within the VI, the IF with the best link quality is chosen for transmission, on a per-packet basis. Their approach segregates low performing interfaces in a bonded set of IFs. This may waste capacity in certain constellations. CA is not included whatsoever in the approach, which causes additional configuration efforts for the user. A neighbor table is maintained, to hold information on the interface availability and link states in the neighborhood. To signal a node's associate IF addresses, a modification of the Address Resolution Protocol (ARP) is used.

Hu confirms that establishing channel diversity (by having sole single channel links) is not enough; this diversity must be actively utilized, in order to improve capacity. In his work [28], a system model is described, which uses multiple radios for parallel transmission between nodes. Again, a VI with a virtual MAC address is used. In his simulator testbed, two kinds of Transmit- (TX-) oriented scheduling algorithms are tested. Although entirely different in their behavior, both consider hop-to-hop scheduling. Hu defends this decision with the varying nature of the wireless medium, making multihop/

flow coordinated scheduling too complex. The paper of Prabhavat et al. [29] is considered highly useful, as it provides a comprehensive review on the existing load distribution models. They claim that skewness between routes is a major issue in multipath LB. With hop-to-hop (single-path) load balancing (LB), skewness is of minor importance.

A key concept depicts the abstraction of resources for the sake of simplicity, compatibility, and modularity. Adding a cross-layer design has high benefits [30]. The CARMEN architecture [31] introduces an abstraction layer, which hides particularities of each access technology. An open virtual layer is also deployed in [32]. A bundling within the virtual layer is not applied. Like many other Multi-interface/Multichannel (MIMC) approaches, the group targets to optimize throughput and end-to-end delay as QoS parameters.

A virtual layer/interface is essential for MIMC WMNs which shall be compatible with different mesh protocols and metrics. A VI can be used to gather and reorganize different types of performance-critical cross-layer input. A well designed VI is further able to provide a usable platform to combine different measures, in order to improve capacity and support heterogeneous traffic.

TECHNICAL BACKGROUND

This section outlines a proposed cross-layer node scheme. This supporting node architecture is required, in order to host the core processes which are later described in Section 4.

In mesh backbones, limited multihop capacity and traffic unfairness have a negative influence on transmissions, particularly on those which flow to and from gateways. This work's focus lies on the enhancement of transmission capacity in mesh and on the optimization of these vertical flows. A node cannot determine the final route of a packet; therefore, the necessity to enhance the performance of every single next-hop link was identified. The proposed modified node architecture incorporates the combined use of various radios. A prior step was the adaption and assembly of standard schemes and components in a custom manner. The considered standard technologies include mesh routing, QoS and traffic engineering (TE), routing topology analysis, priority queuing, and load balancing. The latter two components are described in detail in the Multihop Radio Resource Management (MHRRM) process in Section 4.

General System Overview

The novel proposal for modifications in a standard mesh node architecture is shown in Figure 1 and contains basic components in the envisioned MIMC node, which are grouped in four blocks.

It has to be distinguished in Figure 1 between standard/legacy components, supporting components (treated in the current Section) and core MHRRM components. Characters in curly brackets refer to the relationships among different components, respectively, and the type of exchanged information.

The Mesh Routing Protocol in layer 3 sits above Channel Assignment (which is envisioned as an interchangeable protocol in the system) and the three remaining component blocks, which are nested in a middle-layer (2.5) solution. In the following, the details of each component block that completes the system are described.

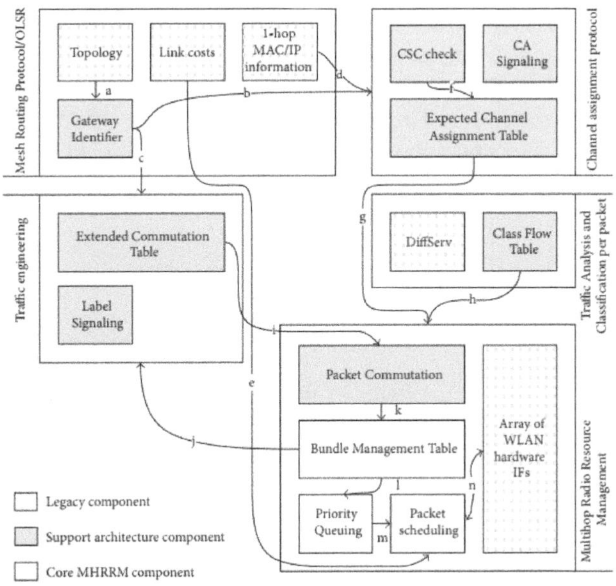

Figure 1: General system overview.

Mesh Routing Protocol

The internal host system/operation system provides local IP/MAC addresses and the routing table, as well as frame transmit- and channel switchaccess of each radio. It was intended to tightly integrate the Mesh Routing Protocol into the system architecture, mainly because it already provides performance-critical routing information through the protocol-specific routing metric. The authors recommend the deployment of optimized linkstate routing (OLSR) [33] protocol, but any proactive Mesh Routing Protocol which maintains proactive link states can be used. OLSR also provides connectivity and address information (MAC/IP of 1-hop neighbors) {d} of the 1-hop topology {a}. From the latter source, the identification of gateway nodes (Gateway Identifier) especially is relevant, since they inject, or receive vertical flows. With OLSR, the main IP address of the smallest index j of the totality of all local radios $\sum rj$ depicts the main IP and at the same time the node's identity in layer 3. The expected transmission time (ETT) metric [34] is recommended to be used with OLSR, since it introduces bandwidth-related link quality awareness. Proactive probing is performed with all radios by OLSR.

Traffic Analysis and Classification per Packet

Traffic Analysis and Classification (TAC) analyzes packets which enter or are created in the mesh network and thus pass the middle-layer module for the first time. A flow is identified via a five-tuple (Source (SRC)/Destination (DST) IP address and port, Transmission Control Protocol (TCP)/User Datagram Protocol (UDP)), and a class code c_k. c_k can be derived by a hash function which processes DiffServ Code Point (DSCP) encodings [35]. For the presented approach, five DSCP ranges have been summarized and mapped to five class codes; the network operator can determine further custom classes, alter the hashing, or process alternative input, such as the users' preference bandwidth [36]. The class code later determines the chosen priority queue per packet. Identified flows are stored in a Class Flow Table, provided by TAC to MHRRM {h}. The table is proposed in order to facilitate QoS-processing in the subsequent data plane components in MHRRM. Traffic classes can be freely defined, independent of the original DiffServ assignation. Even an arbitrary prioritization scheme contrary to the DiffServ priority order can be designed by the mesh network operator. The Class Flow Table then offers traffic engineering capabilities based on packet priorities, which may influence queuing and other QoS-control measures, such as bandwidth shaping or packet dropping.

Channel Assignment Protocol

CA is considered an external component in Figure 1, for the sake of having a modular architecture. CA is a necessary step to achieve a sensible utilization of resources. A set of requirements on the chosen CA protocolwas defined, as well as a static CA output. The expected minimum information in this output is gathered in theExpected CA Table in Table 1.

Table 1: Expected channel assignment table

Neighbor IP	Neighbor MAC	Channel
IP_1	MAC_1 of neighbor 1	$1 \cdots z$
IP_1	MAC_2 of neighbor 1	$1 \cdots z$
IP_1	MAC_n of neighbor 1	$1 \cdots z$
$\vdots$	$\vdots$	$\vdots$
IP_m	$MAC_{1 \cdots n}$ of neighbor m	$1 \cdots z$

Thus, Table 1 depicts a recommendation to the system to assign quantities of radios and channels to neighbors and may be further evaluated out of the CA component in Figure 1. Essential requirements on the CA protocolitself are as follows.

(i) Assure 1-hop connectivity (topology preservation).

(ii) Radios can operate on channels exclusively used with a single neighbor/next-hop or on channels shared with several neighbors.

(iii)If a gateway is present in the 1- or 2-hop neighborhood, this next-hop to the GW (or leading to it) is prioritized in the assignment phase; it receives more radios and better channels.

(iv) If no GW is present, channels/radios are equally distributed among neighbors.

(v) There is a possibility to configure a designated Control Channel (CC) [37].(vi)One can see CA Signaling between distributed CA Protocol instances in the 1-hop neighborhood to guarantee a synchronized channel switch/handshake between neighbors. CA Signaling shall avoid packet loss due to unsynchronized switches to channels without neighbor connectivity. A suitable framework for CA protocols (including signaling approaches) for the OMNeT++ simulation environment can be found in [38].

Within CA, a Channel Switching Cost (CSC) Check [39] as a prior step {f} and a predefined cost threshold should be considered to avoid the fact that channels are switched too often or that an unsuitable channel map is used, which limits connectivity or transmission capacity. In particular, those hops that are attached or close to gateways (identified via {b}) are frequently loaded in a WMN [14]. Deployed channels in these topology edges shall have a higher CSC, to avoid a temporary outage and to enable a more stable, inert channel map around GWs.

Traffic Engineering

Traffic engineering favors GW flows over horizontal traffic and paves the way for a faster processing of such in the Packet Commutation component. The TE component block foresees a Multiprotocol Label Switching- (MPLS-) inspired [40] TE Next-Hop Label (NHL) for selected packets. It can be either added in a separate custom header between the IP and MAC header or included in fields of the existing sublayer 3 headers. Only packets of vertical flows receive a NHL at the ingress mesh router. Gateways label all packets forwarded into the mesh cloud, whereas regular mesh routers label only vertical flows. The label is removed by the TE component block at the egress router/GW, or at the mesh DST node. The label allows a fast layer 2 forwarding of selected packets. In the ideal case, a packet is forwarded in intermediate nodes with complete transparency to the network layer. The sublayer 3 forwarding chain is depicted in Figure 2, including the required push, swap, and pop label operations.

In intermediate nodes, TE only performs the label swap operation and Packet Commutation, as shown in Figure2. Other packets (those of horizontal flows) receive a classic layer 3 forwarding (longest-prefix-match lookup in the routing table), which is potentially more time-consuming, depending on the actual routing table size [41]. To determine the affiliation to a GW flow in a non-GW node, the packet's DST IP must coincide with a mesh-external IP address. MPLS-like traffic steering via fixed Label Switched Paths (LSP) is not desired, as the concept of a predefined chain of routers is not conformable with the philosophy of ad hoc routing ("hop-to-hop" principle).

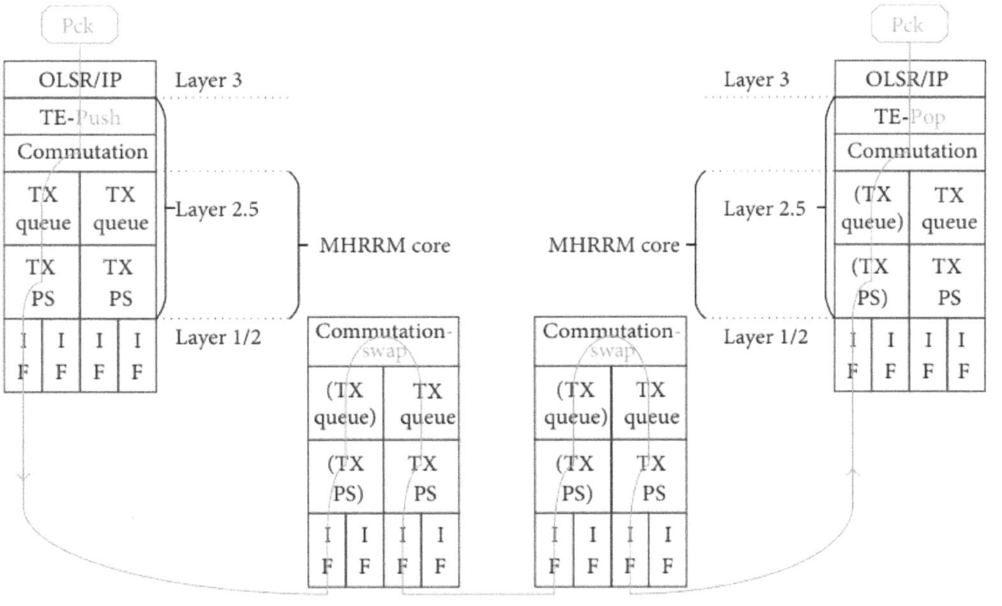

Figure 2: Label-based layer 2.5 Packet Commutation in WMNs.

With OLSR, GW nodes typically broadcast Host and Network Association (HNA) [33] messages, which allow us to determine the mesh-internal IP address of a gateway node. Information about which mesh nodes function as gateways is provided via {c}. This input is required to generate labels to all GWs in the topology. Labels are proactively generated by each node and maintained in the Extended Commutation Table, depicted in Table 2.

Table 2: Extended commutation table

In-label	In-bundle b_h	IP DST of s_o	Out-label	Out-bundle b_h
label	b_1	IP_0	label	b_1
⋮	⋮	⋮	⋮	⋮
label	b_m	IP_{l-1}	label	b_m

In Table 2, b is a bundle (of radios), h is its index, m is the current amount of registered 1-hop neighbors, and IP DST refers to an IP (v4) address of a mesh-internal GW flow endpoint (with an index o). l is the number of registered GW flow endpoints in the WMN. There is a unique bundle-index per 1-hop neighbor, which is provided to TE by MHRRM {j} in Figure 1. The out-label is unique within an out-bundle (resp., per next-hop). The next-hop specification for a DST is directly overtaken from the routing table, filled by the Mesh Routing Protocol. As with MPLS, Label Signaling is required, in order to guarantee a flawless swapping operation. A node can signal its out-labels either via a LDP-like [40] derivative or by including labels in proactive signaling messages generated by the Mesh Routing Protocol.

MULTIHOP RADIO RESOURCE MANAGEMENT

This section describes the technical core contribution of this work. Whether selective forwarding/Packet Commutation based on the Extended Commutation Table {i} is applied or not influences the swiftness of the next-hop selection per packet. The subsequent treatment within MHRRM {k} now further consists of enquiring {l} and scheduling {m} within a bundle. Both subprocesses represent the core operations of MHRRM and allow a mesh operator to fully exploit given radio resources and channels. This increases QoS-relevant performance parameters in the network, such as end-to-end throughput and delay. Figure 3 visualizes both subprocesses with the help of three representative packets, which enter a node (left side of the figure).

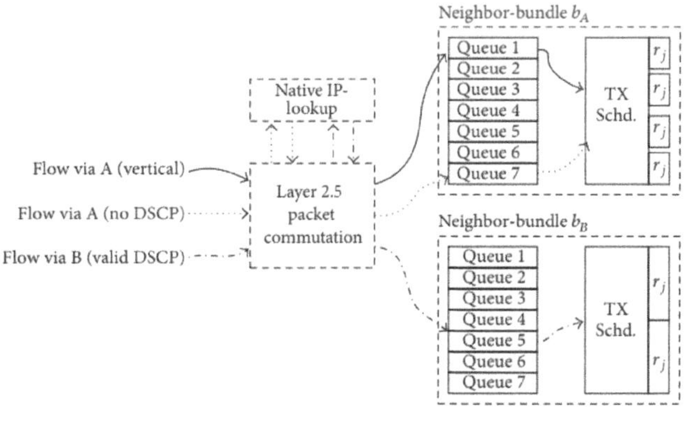

Figure 3: Packet treatment within MHRRM.

The first encapsulated packet belongs to a GW flow and is fast-forwarded. The second packet belongs to a horizontal flow. The third packet is also forwarded between two non-GW mesh nodes, but it additionally contains a valid class code/ DSCP value.

MHRRM also defines bundles and has direct control over aggregated capacities . The envisioned resource management scheme is depicted in Figure 4.

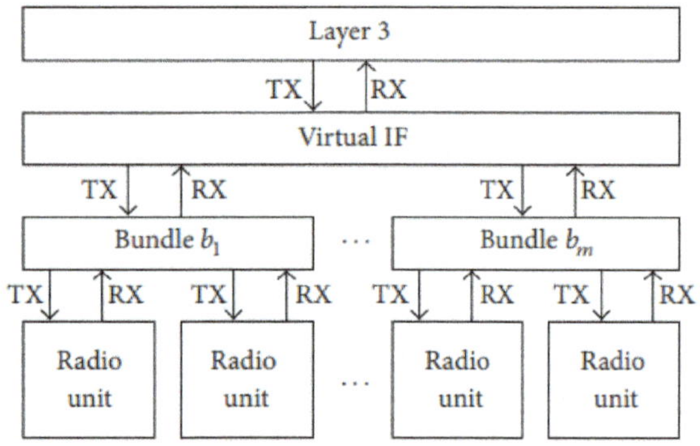

Figure 4: Virtual interface and bundle definition.

Different neighbors receive separate bundle indices $b1 \cdots m$. A radio unit refers to a physical WLAN radio. This single resource unit can be a radio which is tuned to an exclusive or to a shared channel. Thus, a physical radio can be assigned to multiple bundles at the same time. The same condition applies to a radio rj in Figure 3. A Bundle Management Table (BMT) to define bundles per neighbors is maintained within MHRRM. The table is primarily based on the Expected Channel Assignment Table {g} input (see Section 3.4). Additionally, the BMT stores statistical parameters for load balancing.

Priority Queuing

A corresponding queue $q_{1 \ldots 7}$ is chosen in the Priority Queuing component in Figure 1, based on Table 3. Class codes/DSCP ranges are mapped to queues in this table.

Table 3: Proposal for DiffServ- and topology-based traffic classes

Queue	Internal traffic class c_k	DiffServ equivalent [35]
q_1	Gateway traffic	None
q_2	c_1	EF
q_3	c_2	AF4
q_4	c_3	AF3
q_5	c_4	AF2
q_6	c_5	AF1
q_7	None/best effort	Default PHB

First, the internal traffic class code ck is determined on a per-packet basis, based on the Class Flow Table provided by TAC {h} (see Section 3.3). There is one queue set $q_{1 \ldots 7}$ per bundle/neighbor. Queues in Table 3 are listed in a descending order of priority. The priority of GW traffic (q_1) excels any other internal traffic class specifications. Queues $q_{2 \ldots 6}$ are reserved for horizontal flows which match a Class Flow Table entry. If multiple flows are directed towards the same nexthop, the queue set manipulates their packet sending order according to detected priorities. This manipulation becomes more effective with multiple hops and mainly favors vertical traffic (class c_1). Thus, GW and DiffServ packets experience a faster queue removal and have a higher chance for immediate forwarding when competing with flows of lower priorities. Queuing further enhances the subsequent multiradio packet scheduling: If Priority Queuing is combined with link-state sensitive packet scheduling, the best radios are offered to the most important packets/queues. A single set of queues is characterized by the following main parameters:

(i) fixed, tunable amount of queues;
(ii) tunable queue length (in packets);
(iii) tail drop principle [42] within each queue;
(iv) PFIFO principle [43] within each queue;
(v) dequeuing policy based on Weighted Fair Queuing (WFQ) [44, 45];
(vi) fixed, manually chosen weight w per queue.

Packet Scheduling

After a packet was dequeued, it is finally scheduled to be sent via one of the available radios in a bundle. A configurable set of load balancing modes is offered to a mesh operator. These modes are explained in the following. The mode parameter reflects two basic network response profiles: capacity- and stability-oriented networks. Both types tackle the pervasive issue of performance degradation due to single-radio hop-to-hop interference in mesh transmissions. Also, both profiles exploit channel diversity, but for different reasons. The first category uses channel resources in parallel, whereas the second may maintain extra resources as backup options. A mode is applied network-wide.

With the Weighted Fair Scheduling (WFS) mode, radios with the best quality shall bear the majority of packets. WFS calculates a TX probability per radio {n}, based on its estimated link cost{e}to determine the link's usage frequency. Thus, WFS integrates well with link-state routing. It supports the forwarding of vertical flows when combined with Priority Queuing. WFS also permits a fair treatment of interfaces with underperforming links, to prevent starvation of such. WFS mode is based on ETT, as it is the more accurate, QoS-related metric, which is commonly available with OLSR. Applied to system parameters, the sending probability is calculated with

$$g_j = \frac{v_j}{\sum_{i=1}^{n_{b_h}} v_i}, \tag{1}$$

where g is the TX probability of a radio r with the index j, V is the link state/metric value of a radio r, and n_{bh} is the number of radios in a bundle b_h.

The Round-Robin (RR) packet scheduling mode simply foresees that, for n radios in a bundle b, each radio r will transmit n^{-1} of incoming packets. The RR mode and the previously discussed WFS mode aim to exploit the capacity of multiple radios.

The third mode describes an extended version of the simple Round-Robin mode. From a given set of n radios in a bundle b, a fixed number of Fallback (FB) radios B, $0 \leq B < n$ are reserved. This mode focusses on network stability. Extra resources in form of WLAN IFs are used redundantly and on demand, while the exploitation of the available channel spectrum is still possible. This is suitable to create robust setups such as emergency networks, where performance is a secondary goal and reliable communication has a top priority [46]. Fallback radios are used in case one or more of the currently used radios might fail. When B=0, standard RR is applied. When $B = n-1$, single interface transmission is applied on this link, while $n-1$ radios remain inactive. B is specified by the user, so the operator has full control over the degree of WLAN hardware utilization. This is also relevant for fully mobile mesh nodes, where energy consumption is a limiting factor [18]. A fallback threshold rate $R=F_j/d_j$ per radio is maintained in the Bundle Management Table. R triggers the replacement of an active radio. As a starting point, F is the MAC frame loss rate between layers 1 and 2. Other advanced cross-layer information may be used related to the channel's quality [36].

MEASUREMENTS

Measurements were conducted within an OMNeT++ (OMNeT++ Network Simulation Library and Framework, https://omnetpp.org/) simulation environment. A general goal is to validate the bundle definition capabilities of the proposed architecture. Subsequently, the impact of the MHRRM process on transmissions in MIMC mesh networks shall be evaluated. Channel assignment is statically configured and c_k class codes are manually set for each packet generator.

Scenarios

Three scenarios have been selected to evaluate MHRRM functionalities. Nodes have multiple 802.11g radios, using typical PHY and MAC layer settings. They are aligned in a grid or in a chain formation and have a fixed distance of 140 m between each other. Based on the available parameterization in the INETMANET framework (INETMANET Framework for OMNEST/OMNeT++ 4.x (based on INET Framework), build "4116c0c371", https://github.com/inetmanet/inetmanet), a free-space radio environment was modelled. Circles in the following figures indicate the resulting minimum reception range; every packet received beyond this range is considered as noise. All 20 MHz 802.11a/b/g channels are considered orthogonal [38] in INETMANET. Also, contrary to the limitation of the standard, the used INETMANET build enables an arbitrary number of available orthogonal channels for 802.11g. Their index (0, 1, . . . , n) used in this work does not correspond to standardized 802.11g numeric channel numbers [9].

To show the impact of multiple radios on WMN capacity, the scenario in Figure 5 was designed.

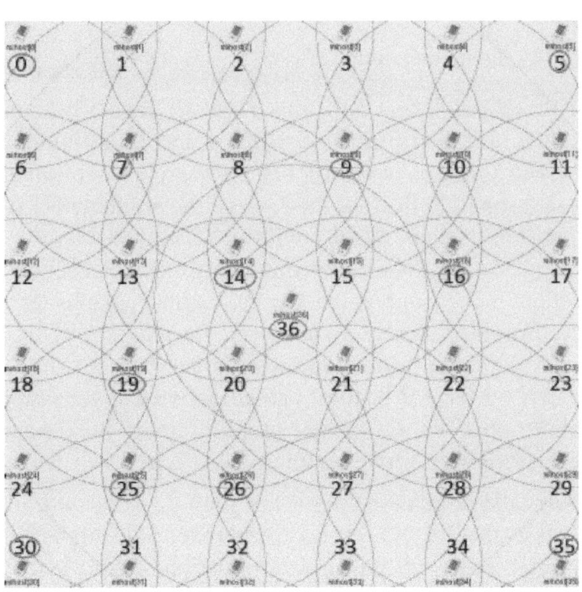

Figure 5: Grid setup with 1 GW.

The total simulation time is 55 s per run. Figure 5 depicts a mesh grid with 37 nodes, in which node number 36 functions as a GW. Here, all nodes bear the same amount of radios (1, 2, 4, or 6), which are tuned to the same common set of channels 0 to 5. OLSR is combined with the ETX [34] metric. RR mode is used network-wide. The 37 nodes have to cope with only a single, or up to 7 active GW flows. A representative set of flows has been defined for various hop distances. Multiple instances of a File Transfer Protocol (FTP) application initiate a download from the GW. One after another (in different simulations), the nodes 14, 9, 26, 0, 5, 35, and 30 become active (flow indices 1–7). The simulation shall confirm that the hop distance plays a major role in performance degradation and that the increasing amount of radios per node will raise the overall capacity.

In the scenario in Figure 6, the impact of different packet scheduling modes is tested.

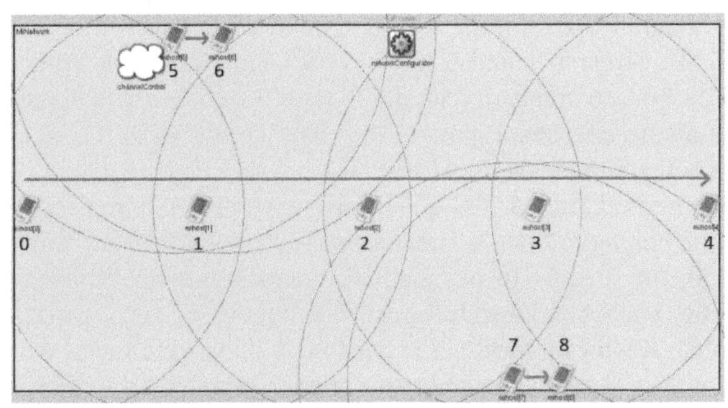

Figure 6: Chain setup with local interroute interference.

The shown chain between nodes 0 and 4 may as well represent a partial route towards a GW from the grid in Figure 5, but with a different traffic situation. A UDP-based stream from nodes 0 to 4 with a TX bandwidth of 5 Mbit/s (datagram sizes are set to 512 B/1.5 kB, start at 30 s; total simulation time: 100 s) is locally congested by two background streams from nodes 5 to 6 (start at 40 s) and from 7 to 8 (start at 60 s) (1 kB datagram size at 3 Mbit/s UDP TX for both streams). Nodes 5 to 8 have only one WLAN IF at their disposition. Congestion is caused on the single channels 0 (nodes 5 to 6) and 1 (nodes 7 to 8), while the nodes on the chain from 0 to 4 have 3 radios at their disposition, tuned to channels 0, 1, and 2. The two background flows interrupt the main flow from nodes 0 to 4 at different start times, to create a more heterogeneous traffic environment. The influence on network performance of all three scheduling modes included in the MHRRM process is evaluated. It is expected that the WFS mode will offer the best multihop performance, because link-state-based load balancing in MHRRM is supposed to avoid the congested channels 0 and 1. ETT is used.

The impact of different queue weighting schemes on parallel flows is tested with the last scenario shown in Figure 7. The total simulation time is 130 s.

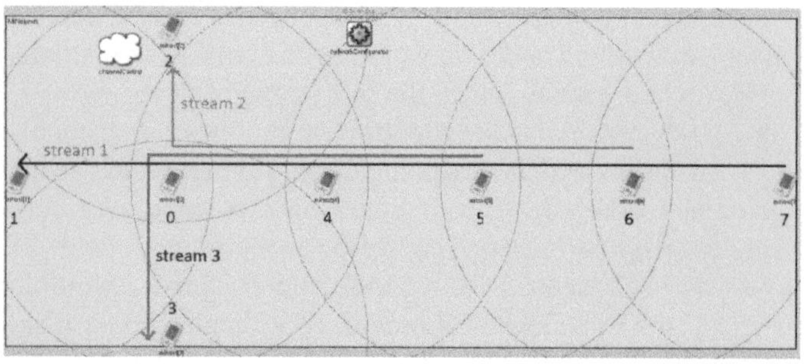

Figure 7: Setup with shared route fragments and intraroute interference.

Again a chain setup was chosen, which could be part of a larger WMN with multiple routes (see Figure 5). All nodes deploy one or two radios on channels 0 and 1 here; in the dual-radio case, the RR mode is used. UDP streams 1, 2, and 3 run from their prospective senders to destinations 1, 2, and 3. Datagram sizes for the three streams vary between 1 kB and 1.5 kB. Streams 1 and 3 have a TX bandwidth of 1 Mbit/s, while node 6 transmits stream 2 with 2 Mbit/s. It is forced that all streams share parts of the chain constellation between nodes 0 and nodes 4–6. At first, an uneven weight distribution scheme shall grant a 70% queue removal probability to packets which belong to flow 2. The remaining share of 30% is granted evenly to streams to destinations 1 and 3 and for broadcast traffic. The second weighting scheme includes an even removal probability for all traffic. The queue size in packets varies with parameter C. It is expected that stream 2, which may represent a GW flow, is favored in terms of endto-end delay, when the uneven weight scheme is used.

Results and Evaluation

Figures 8, 9, and 10 show the throughput results of flows 1, 2, and 3 in the grid setup from Figure 5.

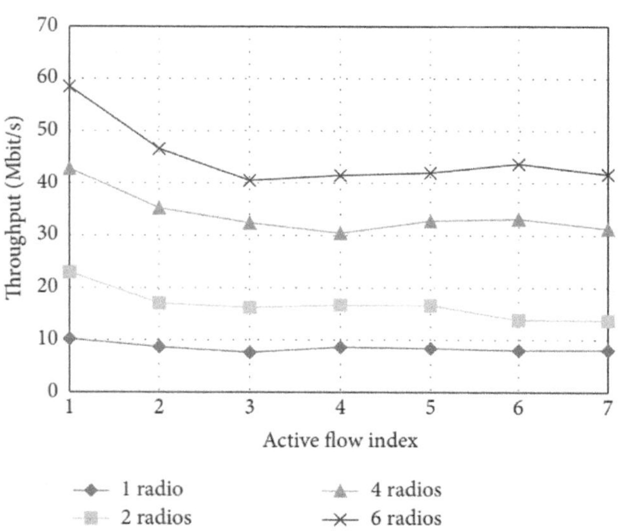

Figure 8: Throughput results of flow 1 using RR PS mode.

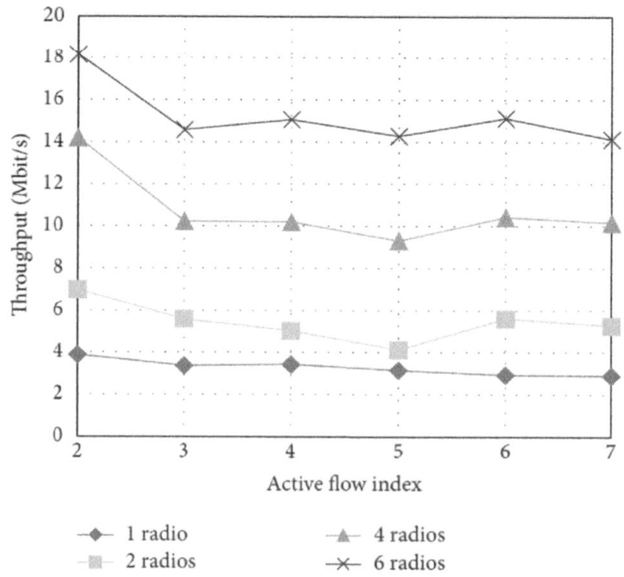

Figure 9: Throughput results of flow 2 using RR PS mode.

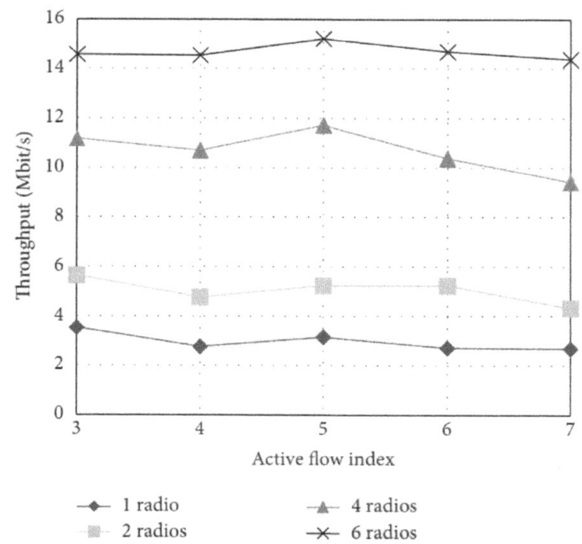

Figure 10: Throughput results of flow 3 using RR PS mode.

Throughput levels and thus network capacity levels of flows 1, 2, and 3 rise notably with an increasing number of radios. But the sole usage of RR PS cannot solve intraroute fairness issues for flows 4 to 7, because all channels in the network are loaded evenly with RR, not adaptively. Our data suggests that flows 4–7 underperform in terms of TCP throughput (The supplementary throughput graphs of flow 4–7 are provided on request.), despite the availability of extra radios. Still, if the hop count to GWs can be kept short (1-3 hops) in a WMN, RR becomes an attractive and yet simplistic scheme to improve throughput proportional to the amount of equipped radios, as proven with flows 1, 2, and 3.

Now, the remaining PS modes shall be evaluated. Figure 11 suggests that the WFS scheduling enables the highest mean throughput levels (for the entire simulation period) in the next scenario in Figure 6.

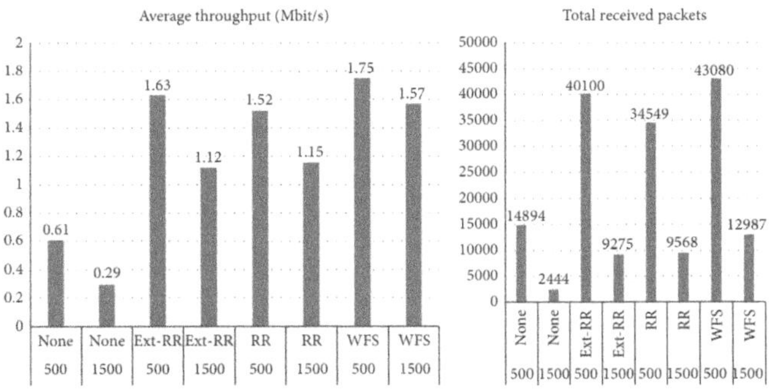

Figure 11: Throughput and packet RX results of the packet scheduling modes comparison.

This is due to the advantage that if ETT-based probing results drop on a single link in a bundle, adaptive PS with WFS assigns less load on it. WFS allows the multihop streams to exchange more packets in total, even if their route is selectively congested. Thus, the mode is recommended to facilitate the coexistence of different cross-flows suffering from interroute interference, what could be applied to vertical traffic. Also, weighted-fair-based scheduling is useful when a rerouting option is considered too cost expensive by OLSR. Available capacities on the reputed bad next-hop can still be optimized with WFS. The load shift within a bundle is not as radical as with the Extended RR mode, with which an absolute switch of an interface is forced.

Before the actual scheduling process, queues enable measures to improve performance of disadvantaged flows from the scenario depicted in Figure 7. The end-to-end delay is a crucial QoS parameter and can be selectively improved over other parallel flows, by applying per-hop queues. Figures 12 and 13 demonstrate these improvements.

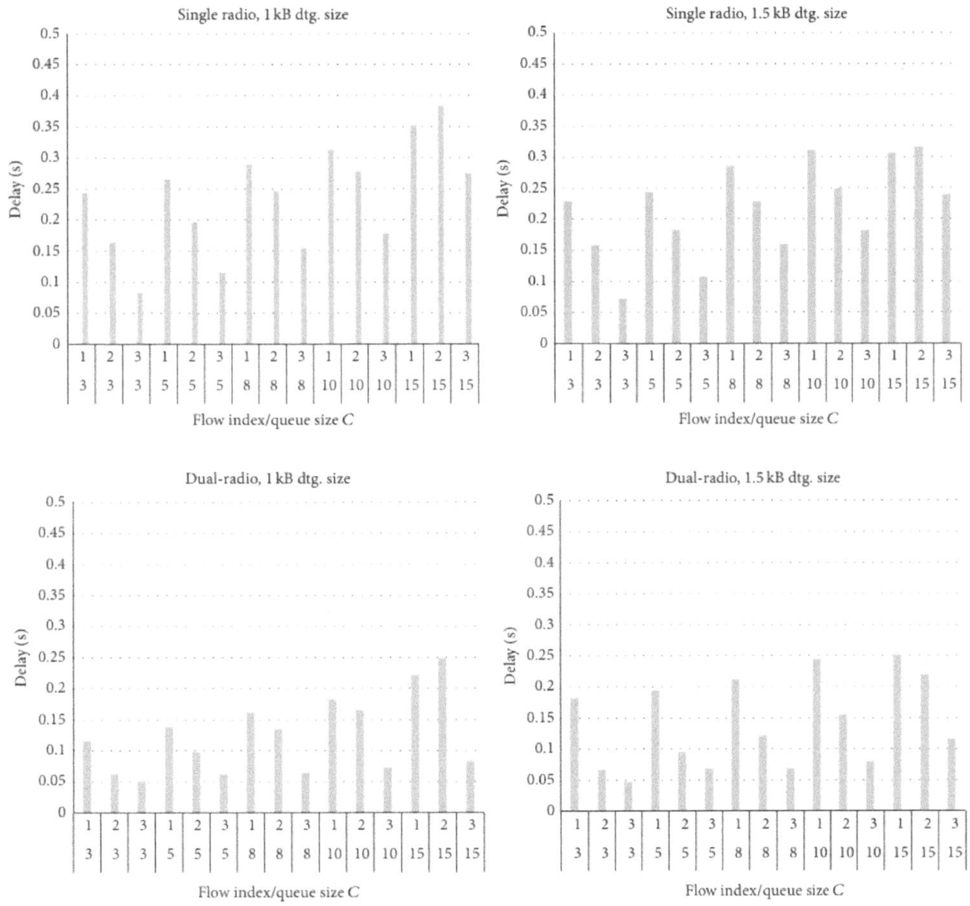

Figure 12: Delay results for the balanced queue scheme.

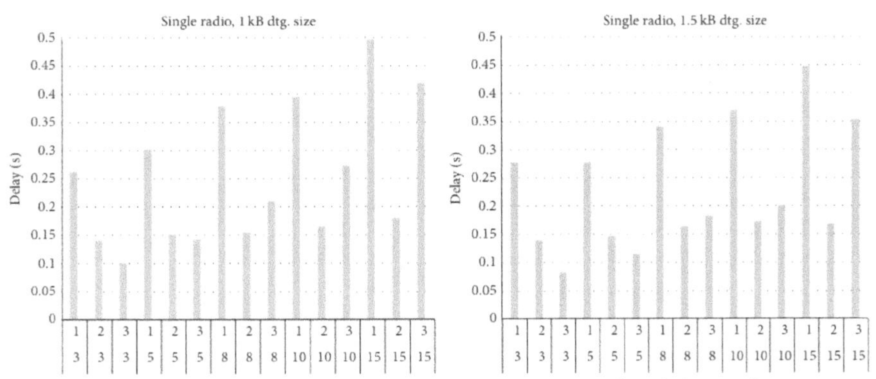

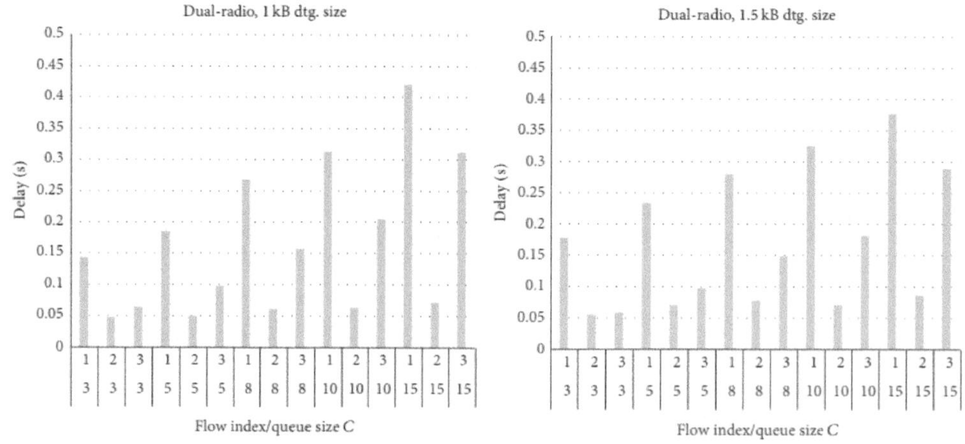

Figure 13: Delay results for the priority queue scheme.

In Figure 13, delay levels of flow 2 were reduced with a queue weighting scheme in its favor (70% removal probability). The effect visibly takes place when queue size C (in packets) is chosen between 3 and 8, depending on the available capacity on the route (dual-radio nodes allow a smaller C). The prioritization resolves unfairness due to intraroute interference and varying hop counts. Still, in this specific scenario there exists a trade-off between the artificial delay (introduced with a larger C) and the effectiveness of prioritization. Also, in some cases, flow 2 shows slightly longer delays than flow 1 with the balanced scheme (in Figure 12), which does not match the flows respective hop distances to their DSTs. This effect occurs due to heavy traffic congestion in this particular scenario. Measurements have shown that a queue length of 15 packets or more is not feasible here. The authors strongly suggest to adapt queue parameters (size C, weights) to the specific QoS demands of each mesh setup. Queuing is independent from bundling and has the potential to even favor streams on single-channel paths, given a customized prioritization scheme.

CONCLUSIONS

Standard, single-channel wireless mesh networks suffer from multihop and interference limitations and from the issue that vertical traffic cannot be properly protected. Several island solutions to exploit multiradio nodes, as well as QoS alternatives, can be applied. However, if applied isolated, each method may offer a discrete and independent benefit, but cannot ultimately solve the true issues of limited transmission capacity in WMNs.

A proposal, in general terms, for an improvement of the architecture of an 802.11-based mesh node is presented in this work for the first time. Standard node architecture is extended by combining different components, such as link-state routing information, Channel Assignment, and sublayer 3 traffic engineering in a novel way. The resulting system is built around a custom middle-layer module, which processes cross-layer information. Considering the idea to match a node's availability of radios with the desired network behavior as a milestone of the proposed system, the Multihop Radio Resource Management component, which is nested in the previously described cross-layer architecture, was prioritized in its design, development, and testing. Then, the complementary concepts of combining available radios in bundles, managing them through a virtual interface, using priority queue processing and DiffServ to further protect vertical flows against horizontal traffic, and implementing specific scheduling as load balancing modes within each bundle (drawing on information from proactive routing protocols), were deployed in a systemic form, respectively, applied from a systemic point of view. The Multihop Radio Resource Management enables a better use of nonoverlapping channels on multiple radios and is the key contribution of this work.

Selected scenarios have shown that due to the novel combination of these techniques, the capacity in the WMN was significantly increased and a more efficient use of multiple radios was reached. The link quality-sensitive WFS mode is tailored for proactive, link-state mesh routing, and conquers interference on congested channels. Tunable queue parameters provide a toolset to facilitate QoS policies, which lead to selective end-to-end delay improvements on multihop paths.

At the same time, the paper also offers an overview of current trends and the state-of-the art of those components, which can be sensibly combined in multiradio mesh node architectures. Furthermore, the work allows planners of practical mesh installations to select among various methods to enhance capacity and quickly evaluate their impact within the simulated scenarios.

Future work will focus on the complete development and evaluation of the integral system and other more specific tasks, such as testing the impact of channel switches during run-time and the impact of layer 2 labeling and commutation techniques, among others.

REFERENCES

1. I. F. Akyildiz, X. Wang, and W. Wang, "Wireless mesh networks: a survey," Computer Networks, vol. 47, no. 4, pp. 445–487, 2005.
2. D. Hock, N. Bayer, R. Pries et al., "QoS provisioning in WLAN mesh networks using dynamic bandwidth control," in Proceedings of the 14th European Wireless Conference (EW ‹08), pp. 1–7, June 2008.
3. M. Kretschmer, C. Niephaus, D. Henkel, and G. Ghinea, "QoS-aware wireless back-haul network for rural areas with support for broadcast services in practice," in

Proceedings of the IEEE 8th International Conference on Mobile Ad-hoc and Sensor Systems (MASS ‹11), pp. 758–764, October 2011.

4. K. N. Ramachandran, E. M. Belding, K. C. Almeroth, and M. M. Buddhikot, “Interference-aware channel assignment in multi-radio wireless mesh networks,” in Proceedings of the 25th IEEE International Conference on Computer Communications (INFOCOM ‹06), pp. 1–12, April 2006. ·

5. R. Draves, J. Padhye, and B. Zill, “Routing in multi-radio, multi-hop wireless mesh networks,” inProceedings of the 10th Annual International Conference on Mobile Computing and Networking, pp. 114–128, New York, NY, USA, October 2004.

6. D. Gokhale, S. Sen, K. Chebrolu, and B. Raman, “On the feasibility of the link abstraction in (rural) mesh networks,” in Proceedings of the 27th IEEE Communications Society Conference on Computer Communications (INFOCOM ‹08), IEEE, Phoenix, Ariz, USA, April 2008.

7. R. Bruno, M. Conti, and E. Gregori, “Mesh networks: commodity multihop ad hoc networks,” IEEE Communications Magazine, vol. 43, no. 3, pp. 123–131, 2005. ·

8. C. Köbel, W. B. García, and J. Habermann, “A survey on Wireless Mesh Network applications in rural areas and emerging countries,” in Proceedings of the 3rd IEEE Global Humanitarian Technology Conference (GHTC ‹13), pp. 389–394, October 2013.

9. IEEE Standard for Information technology—Telecommunications and information exchange between systems Local and metropolitan area networks—Specific requirements Part 11: Wireless LAN Medium Access Control (MAC) and Physical Layer (PHY) Specifications, IEEE Std 80211-2012 Revis. IEEE Std 80211-2007, pp. 1–2793, 2012.

10. Y. Cheng, H. Li, P.-J. Wan, and X. Wang, “Wireless mesh network capacity achievable over the CSMA/CA MAC,” IEEE Transactions on Vehicular Technology, vol. 61, no. 7, pp. 3151–3165, 2012. ·

11. J. Jun and M. L. Sichitiu, “The nominal capacity of wireless mesh networks,” IEEE Wireless Communications, vol. 10, no. 5, pp. 8–14, 2003.

12. L. Tan, X. Zhan, J. Li, and F. Zhao, “A novel tree-based broadcast algorithm for wireless ad hoc networks,”International Journal of Wireless and Mobile Computing, vol. 1, no. 2, pp. 156–162, 2006.

13. J. J. Gálvez, P. M. Ruiz, and A. F. G. Skarmeta, “A distributed algorithm for gateway load-balancing in wireless mesh networks,” in Proceedings of the 1st IFIP Wireless Days (WD ‹08), pp. 1–5, November 2008. ·

14. I. F. Akyildiz and X. Wang, “Introduction,” in Wireless Mesh Networks, chapter 1, pp. 1–16, John Wiley & Sons, New York, NY, USA, 2009.

15. N. Kaur and J. S. Saini, “Performance enhancement of 802.11 based wireless mesh network by using Multi-Radio Multi-Channel,” in Proceedings of the International Conference on Green Computing, Communication and Conservation of Energy (ICGCE ‹13), pp. 71–76, IEEE, Chennai, India, December 2013.

16. C. Teixeira De Oliveira, F. Theoleyre, and A. Duda, “Connectivity in multi-channel multi-interface wireless mesh networks,” in Proceedings of the 7th International Wireless Communications and Mobile Computing Conference (IWCMC ‹11), pp. 35–40, July 2011. ·

17. S. Robitzsch, S. Murphy, and P. Szczechowiak, “Architecture of a self configuration framework for 802.11-based multi-radio mesh networks,” in Proceedings of the 14th IEEE International Symposium on a World of Wireless, Mobile and Multimedia Networks (WoWMoM ‹13), pp. 1–8, Madrid, Spain, June 2013.

18. L. Tan, P. Yang, and S. Chan, “Error-aware and energy-efficient routing approach in MANETs,”International Journal of Communication Systems, vol. 22, no. 1, pp. 37–51, 2009.

19. D. Wang, P. Lv, Y. Chen, and M. Xu, “POCAM: partially overlapped channel assignment in multi-radio multi-channel wireless mesh network,” in Proceedings of the 11th International Symposium on Communications and Information Technologies (ISCIT ‹11), pp. 188–193, October 2011. ·

20. Y. Qu, C.-H. Lung, and A. Srinivasan, “Network layer negotiation-based channel assignment in multi-channel wireless networks,” in Proceedings of the 50th Annual IEEE Global Telecommunications Conference (GLOBECOM ‹07), pp. 759–763, November 2007. ·

21. H. A. Mogaibel and M. Othman, “Review of routing protocols and it›s metrics for wireless mesh networks,” in Proceedings of the International Association of Computer Science and Information Technology—Spring Conference (IACSIT-SC ‹09), pp. 62–70, April 2009.

22. V. Brik, S. Rayanchu, S. Saha, S. Sen, V. Shrivastava, and S. Baneriee, “A measurement study of a commercial-grade urban WiFi mesh,” in Proceedings of the 8th ACM SIGCOMM Conference on Internet Measurement, pp. 111–124, New York, NY, USA, October 2008.

23. S. Robitzsch, J. Fitzpatrick, S. Murphy, and L. Murphy, “Behind-the-scenes of IEEE 802.11a based multi-radio mesh networks: a measurement driven evaluation of inter-channel interference,” 2010.

24. V. Angelakis, S. Papadakis, V. A. Siris, and A. Traganitis, “Adjacent channel interference in 802.11a is harmful: testbed validation of a simple quantification model,” IEEE Communications Magazine, vol. 49, no. 3, pp. 160–166, 2011.

25. G. E. M. Zhioua and N. Tabbane, “A load and QoS aware scheduling algorithm for multi-channel multi-radio wireless mesh networks,” in Proceedings of the IEEE Wireless Communications and Networking Conference (WCNC ‹12), pp. 2043–2047, IEEE, Shanghai, China, April 2012.

26. H. T. Cheng, Radio resource management for wireless mesh networks supporting heterogeneous traffic [Ph.D. thesis], University of Waterloo, Waterloo, Canada, 2009.

27. S.-H. Kim and Y.-B. Ko, “Wireless bonding for maximizing throughput in multi-radio mesh networks,” in Proceedings of the 5th Annual IEEE

International Conference on Pervasive Computing and Communications Workshops (PerCom Workshops ‹07), pp. 570–574, March 2007.

28. Y. Hu, "Parallel-transmission: a new usage of multi-radio diversity in wireless mesh network,"International Journal of Communications, Network and System Sciences, vol. 2, no. 1, pp. 51–57, 2009.

29. S. Prabhavat, H. Nishiyama, N. Ansari, and N. Kato, "On load distribution over multipath networks,"IEEE Communications Surveys and Tutorials, vol. 14, no. 3, pp. 662–680, 2012.

30. P. Kyasanur, J. So, C. Chereddi, and N. F. Vaidya, "Multichannel mesh networks: challenges and protocols," IEEE Wireless Communications, vol. 13, no. 2, pp. 30–36, 2006.

31. A. Banchs, N. Bayer, D. Chieng et al., "CARMEN: delivering carrier grade services over wireless mesh networks," in Proceedings of the 19th IEEE International Symposium on Personal, Indoor and Mobile Radio Communications (PIMRC ‹08), Cannes, France, September 2008.

32. R. Tahar, A. Belghith, and R. Braham, "A generic mobile node architecture for multi-interface heterogenous wireless link layer," in Proceedings of the 3rd International Conference on the Network of the Future (NOF ‹12), pp. 1–5, November 2012.

33. OLSR Project, 2013, http://olsr.org/docs/README-Link-Quality.html.

34. P. M. Esposito, M. E. M. Campista, I. M. Moraes, L. H. M. K. Costa, O. C. M. B. Duarte, and M. G. Rubinstein, "Implementing the expected transmission time metric for OLSR wireless mesh networks," inProceedings of the 1st IFIP Wireless Days (WD ‹08), pp. 1–5, IEEE, Dubai, UAE, November 2008.

35. D. Grossman, "New Terminology and Clarifications for Diffserv," http://tools.ietf.org/html/rfc3260.

36. L. Tan, Z. Zhu, C. Yuan, and W. Zhang, "A novel approach for bandwidth allocation among soft QoS traffic in wireless networks," Transactions on Emerging Telecommunications Technologies, vol. 25, no. 5, pp. 479–484, 2014.

37. E. Z. Tragos, S. Zeadally, A. G. Fragkiadakis, and V. A. Siris, "Spectrum assignment in cognitive radio networks: a comprehensive survey," IEEE Communications Surveys and Tutorials, vol. 15, no. 3, pp. 1108–1135, 2013.

38. H. Kim, Q. Gu, M. Yu, W. Zang, and P. Liu, "A simulation framework for performance analysis of multi-interface and multi-channel wireless networks in INET/OMNET++," in Proceedings of the 2010 Spring Simulation Multiconference, pp. 101:1–101:8, Orlando, Fla, USA, 2010.

39. S. Avallone and G. D. Stasi, "An experimental study of the channel switching cost in multi-radio wireless mesh networks," IEEE Communications Magazine, vol. 51, no. 9, pp. 124–134, 2013. ·

40. R. Callon and E. C. Rosen, "Multiprotocol Label Switching Architecture," 2014, http://tools.ietf.org/html/rfc3031.

41. M. Bredel, Z. Bozakov, and Y. Jiang, "Analyzing router performance using network calculus with external measurements," in Proceedings of the IEEE 18th International Workshop on Quality of Service (IWQoS ‹10), pp. 1–9, June 2010.

42. A. Rao, A. Legout, Y.-S. Lim, D. Towsley, C. Barakat, and W. Dabbous, "Network characteristics of video streaming traffic," in Proceedings of the 7th ACM International Conference on Emerging Networking EXperiments and Technologies (CoNEXT ‹11), New York, NY, USA, December 2011. ·

43. V. Jacobson, B. Braden, S. Floyd et al., "Recommendations on Queue Management and Congestion Avoidance in the Internet," http://tools.ietf.org/html/rfc2309.

44. A. K. Parekh and R. G. Gallager, "A generalized processor sharing approach to flow control in integrated services networks: the multiple node case," IEEE/ACM Transactions on Networking, vol. 2, no. 2, pp. 137–150, 1994.

45. K. Wehrle, K. Nichols, and R. Bless, "A Lower Effort Per-Domain Behavior (PDB) for Differentiated Services," 2014, http://tools.ietf.org/html/rfc3662.

46. C. Lottermann, A. Klein, H. D. Schotten, and C. Mannweiler, "Enhancing service provisioning within heterogeneous wireless networks for emergency situations," in e-Infrastructure and e-Services for Developing Countries, R. Popescu-Zeletin, K. Jonas, I. A. Rai, R. Glitho, and A. Villafiorita, Eds., pp. 14–23, Springer, Berlin, Germany, 2012.

CHAPTER 11

SECURE MULTICAST ROUTING ALGORITHM FOR WIRELESS MESH NETWORKS

Rakesh Matam[1] and Somanath Tripathy[2]

[1]Indian Institute of Information Technology, Guwahati, Assam 781001, India

[2]Indian Institute of Technology Patna, Patna, Bihar 800013, India

ABSTRACT

Multicast is an indispensable communication technique in wireless mesh network (WMN). Many applications in WMN including multicast TV, audio and video conferencing, and multiplayer social gaming use multicast transmission. On the other hand, security in multicast transmissions is crucial, without which the network services are significantly disrupted. Existing secure routing protocols that address different active attacks are still vulnerable due to subtle nature of flaws in protocol design. Moreover, existing secure routing protocols assume that adversarial nodes cannot share an out-of-band communication channel which rules out the possibility of wormhole attack. In this paper, we propose SEMRAW (SEcure Multicast Routing Algorithm for Wireless mesh network) that is resistant against all known active threats including wormhole attack. SEMRAW employs digital signatures to prevent a malicious node from gaining illegitimate access to the message contents. Security of SEMRAW is evaluated using the simulation paradigm approach.

INTRODUCTION

Wireless mesh networks have emerged as a popular technology to provide wireless Internet access anywhere any time [1]. Recent popular applications of WMN include multicast TV, audio and video conferencing, and multiplayer social gaming. These multimedia streaming applications rely on multicast transmissions for transportation of content, as it is an efficient way of transmitting same data stream to several clients simultaneously [2]. Multicast data streams are characterized by their requirement of high bandwidth and low latency [3]. Therefore, majority of the existing works mainly focus on optimizing these requirements. At the same time, other requirements such as security are implicitly assumed. However, it has been already shown that failing to address security issues of a routing protocol for WMN can severely disrupt network services and significantly affect performance [4].

A multicast routing protocol is vulnerable to several active attacks. The nature of these attacks is similar in comparison to attacks launched against a unicast routing protocol. However, the impact of an attack in multicast environment is much higher compared to its unicast counterpart, as a single attacker can affect transmissions to multiple destinations at the same time. Therefore, addressing security attacks in multicast environment is considered to be more crucial. Very few works exist that specifically address the security aspects of a multicast routing protocol. The reason behind this can be attributed to the obvious similarity between unicast and

Citation: Rakesh Matam and Somanath Tripathy, "Secure Multicast Routing Algorithm for Wireless Mesh Networks,"Journal of Computer Networks and Communications, vol. 2016, Article ID 1563464, 11 pages, 2016. doi:10.1155/2016/1563464

multicast routing protocols and the attacks launched against them. This facilitates easy adaptation of unicast security solutions to multicast environment.

Security techniques employed by unicast routing protocols like secure on-demand distance vector protocol (SAODV) [5], authenticated routing in ad hoc networks (ARAN), and [6] security aware routing (SAR) [7] are based on AODV [8]. These security frameworks can be adapted by multicast routing protocols like MAODV [9] and on-demand multicast routing protocol (ODMRP) [10]. On the other hand, Ariadne [11] and secure routing protocol (SRP) [12] are based on dynamic source routing (DSR) [13] and therefore can be adapted by ad hoc multicast routing protocol (AMRIS) [14]. But vulnerabilities still exist mainly due to the subtle nature of flaws in these protocols [15]. Moreover, the adversary model employed by these secure routing protocols restricts colluding malicious nodes from sharing a hidden/out-of-band channel which rules out wormhole attack. So these drawbacks would be inherent to adapted secure multicast routing protocols. Alternative works like Byzantine-resilient multicast routing BMSR [16] and Secure-ODMRP [17] are multicast routing specific security protocols that rely on the transmission behavior of mesh routers to detect and avoid malicious nodes while establishing multicast routes. Therefore, there is a call for secure multicast routing schemes that can defend against all known active attacks.

In this paper, we present a secure multicast routing algorithm SEMRAW (SEcure Multicast Routing Algorithm for Wireless mesh network), the secure version of our previous work enhanced multicast routing algorithm for WMN EMRAW [18]. SEMRAW thus preserves the performance merits of EMRAW, by selecting paths that incur fewer number of transmissions and establishing a bandwidth minimal multicast tree. It scales well compared to other multicast algorithms, specifically in scenarios where multicast receivers are sparsely distributed. SEMRAW employs an integrated security approach to address different active security threats even relaxing the restrictions of active-n-m adversary model [19]. The security of the proposed protocol is formally evaluated using simulation paradigm approach [20, 21].

The rest of the paper is organized as follows. Section 2 presents related work. Section 3 presents the network and adversarial model and basic definitions of security used to evaluate the proposed protocol. Section 4presents the proposed algorithm secure EMRAW. The security proof of the proposed algorithm is presented in Section 5. Section 6 presents the simulation results of SEMRAW. In Section 7, we present a brief discussion on the robustness of SEMRAW and finally Section 8 provides the concluding remarks.

RELATED WORK

Even though the security frameworks of existing unicast secure routing protocols like SAODV [5], ARAN [6], SAR [7], Ariadne [11], and SRP [12] can be adapted by multicast routing protocols like M-AODV [9], ODMRP [10], and AMRIS [14], they are still vulnerable to some security threats. The formal analysis of these protocols has uncovered subtle flaws that are otherwise difficult to identify [15, 22–26]. Moreover, the security of these protocols is evaluated against an active-n-m adversary model that prohibits adversaries from sharing an out-of-band channel which rules out wormhole attacks [23].

Multicast specific secure routing protocols like BMSR [16] and SODMRP [17] focus on addressing Byzantine attacks like flood rushing, packet dropping, and wormhole attacks. These are essentially detection based schemes that rely on the transmission behavior of mesh routers to detect and avoid malicious nodes while establishing routes. BSMR is a Byzantine-resilient multicast protocol that detects Byzantine attacks (attacks launched by nodes that are legitimate part of the network) based on the packet dropping behavior of mesh routers. Specifically, nodes in BSMR determine the reliability of their direct links by comparing the observed data rate with the data rate advertised by the source node. If the observed data rate falls below the rate indicated by the source node by more than a threshold, the neighboring node sharing a direct link with the adversarial node updates its weight list and initiates a new route discovery process by including the weight lists of the links in the route requests. The major limitation of BSMR is its reliance on static detection threshold, which is independent of the channel quality and medium access collisions. Similarly, SODMRP is a secure high-throughput multicast protocol based on ODMRP and link layer metric, SPP (success probability product) [27]. SODMRP addresses packet dropping attacks by detecting the discrepancies between expected packet delivery ratio (ePDR) and perceived packet delivery ratio (pPDR). A node estimates the ePDR of a route from SPP of that route and a node determines the pPDR for a route by measuring the rate at which it receives data packets from its upstream node on that route. If ePDR-pPDR for a route becomes larger than a detection threshold, then nodes suspect that the route is under attack because the route failed to deliver data at a rate consistent with its claimed quality.

Besides these, other works like HASM [28], MeCA [29], and the secure multicast protocols proposed in [30–32] focus on key generation, key management, and secure group communication techniques to protect against outside attacks. Hierarchical agent based secure multicast (HASM) is one such agent based secure multicast algorithm for securing mobile multicast in WMNs. It aims at minimizing the overall network communication cost incurred by multicast packet delivery, security key management, group membership maintenance, and mobility management. HASM dynamically maintains a group of multicast agents running on mesh routers for integrated mobility and multicast service management and maintains a hierarchical multicast structure for efficient multicast packet delivery.

Mesh certification authority (MeCA), presented in [29], addresses the problem of authentication and key management without a trusted third party in wireless mesh networks. It relies on the self-configuring and self-organizing characteristics of WMN to distribute the functions of a certification authority over several mesh routers. Key functionalities like secret sharing and key distribution are based on threshold cryptography, which minimizes the possibility of secret disclosure even when some shareholders are compromised by adversaries. MeCA adopts the multicast tree building approach presented in [33] to reduce the operation overhead.

Similar to MeCA, the secure multicast framework proposed in [31] is decentralized and exploits the self-healing characteristics of wireless mesh network. It is based on the multihop proxy encryption scheme that is first employed in [34], to secure group communications. The source that initiates the communication generates the topology aware key encryption keys (KEK) after the initialization and the key path construction. The session key, used as the traffic encryption key (TEK), is distributed by a new multihop proxy encryption with the KEKs along the key path. Subprotocols like rekeying and self-healing are employed to handle new joins and router failures.

Reference [35] presents a certificateless architecture for multicast wireless mesh network. It uses certificateless proxy reencryption mechanism. It relies on a transformation technique that reduces cipher texts from $k{\cdot}n$ size to $k{+}n$, where k denotes the length of the best route from the source to the target multicast users and n denotes the number of valid receivers in the group.

A key point to note is that none of the existing schemes single handedly address all of the active security attacks on multicast routing protocols in WMN. The existing security frameworks for unicast routing protocols cannot be applied for multicast environment due to their vulnerabilities and limitations. Multicast routing specific protocols like BSMR [16] and SODMRP [17] employ different detection mechanisms to successfully address malicious packet dropping attacks. Other works like HASM [28] and MeCA [29] address issues like secure key distribution, key management, and secure group communication in multicast environment. In this paper, we present SEMRAW that employs integrated security framework to address all active attacks on multicast routing protocols in WMN.

SYSTEM MODEL

In this section, we present the network and adversarial model. We also briefly present the system model used to evaluate the security of the proposed protocol. The same system model has been employed in our earlier work [21] to prove security of another protocol. The definitions of system correctness and the security are similar to those defined in [21].

Network Model

We consider a typical wireless mesh network (WMN) architecture, where a set of MRs that are uniformly distributed, form the backbone of WMN. Few of these mesh routers (MRs) designated as gateways can be connected to the Internet. Mesh clients (MCs) are typical wireless clients connected to specific MRs with access point functionality. We model the backbone of the WMN as a undirected labelled graph (V, E), where V is the set of vertices and E is the set of edges. Each MR represents a node, and there is an edge between two vertices if and only if there is a communication link between the corresponding nodes. The communication links between nodes are assumed to be bidirectional. Each link is assigned a cost by a node connected to it with the help of a cost function $C_{\text{Link}}: E \rightarrow \mathrm{R}$, to represent the routing metric.

Security Model

Security Assumptions

We assume that all network nodes obtain a valid certificate signed by the certification authority (CA) that is later used for authentication. Nodes use authenticated identifiers for secure peer link establishment and construction of a multicast tree. SEMRAW relies on two-hop neighborhood information for establishing routes; therefore, during neighbor discovery, a node authenticates itself with all the nodes in its two-hop range by presenting a valid certificate and thereby validating its neighborhood. The set of node-identifiers are denoted by L and we label each vertex V of V in G with the identifiers used by the node corresponding to V. Each nonmalicious node in the network uses a single identifier that is unique in the network, whereas malicious nodes may use multiple identifiers of the compromised ones. The set of malicious nodes and their identifiers is represented by V^* and L^*, respectively. The assignment of identifiers to the nodes is represented by a labelling function $\Phi : V \rightarrow 2^L$, which returns the set of labels assigned to each vertex V in G. If V corresponds to a noncompromised node, then $\Phi(\mathrm{V})$ is a singleton and $\Phi(\mathrm{V}) \subsetneq \Phi(\mathrm{V}^*)$ holds for any other vertex V^*. Here, the configuration conf is represented as a 4-tuple $((V, E), V^*, \Phi, C\text{Link})$. It consists of a network graph, the set of compromised nodes, the labelling function, and cost function.

Adversarial Model

We consider a class IX attacker model as presented in [19]. A class IX adversary has all the capabilities of an active-n-m attacker and an additional capability that allows colluded malicious nodes to establish an out-of-band communication link between themselves to relay messages. In an active-n-m adversarial model n signifies the number of compromised MRs that hold keying material, and m is the total number of attacker nodes in the network. Usually, attacker nodes in the active-n-m attacker model have restricted capabilities that prevent them from sharing information through out-of-band channels, which rules out wormhole attacks. An attacker in a class IX attacker model can launch various kinds of active attacks involving modification, metric manipulation, and fabrication of routing messages. An adversary can also launch a wormhole attack by colluding with other malicious nodes. The major motivation of the attacker is to corrupt the routing protocol to launch various kinds of active denial of service (DoS) attacks, to disrupt network services.

System State

State of the system Q can be represented by the set of verified routing entries of routing tables of all noncompromised nodes. A routing entry in V's routing table can be represented as a five-tuple field $(v, l_{\text{tar}}, l^1_{\text{nxt}}, l^2_{\text{nxt}}, C)$ in Q with identifier l_{tar} as target and l^1_{nxt} as the one-hop and l^2_{nxt} as the two-hop identifier with routing metric C. Thus, the system state $Q \subset (V \setminus V^*)$ is a collection of such tuples. A system is said to be in a correct state if all the verified routing entries of noncompromised nodes are correct; that is, if V has a verified routing entry for target l_{tar} with one-hop l^1_{nxt} and two-hop l^2_{nxt} with cost C, then actually there exists a route that starts at node V and ends at node l_{tar} and the path through l^1_{nxt}, l^2_{nxt} is comprised of edges only belonging to E and with the metric value C.

Definition 1 (correct state). The state Q of a system is said to be correct if for every $(v, l_{\text{tar}}, l^1_{\text{nxt}}, l^2_{\text{nxt}}, C) \in Q$, there exists a sequence $\mathrm{V}_1, \mathrm{V}_2, \ldots, \mathrm{V}_p$ of vertices in V such that $(\mathrm{V}_i, \mathrm{V}_{i+1}) \in E$ (for all $1 \leq i$

(i) $v_1 = v$,

(ii) $l_{tar} \in \ell(v_p)$,

(iii) $l^1_{nxt} \in \ell(v_2)$,

(iv) $l^2_{nxt} \in \ell(v_3)$,

(v) $(l^1_{nxt}, l^2_{nxt}) \in E$,

(vi) $\sum C_{link} \leq C$.

Dynamic Representation of the System

Simulation Paradigm

SEMRAW is evaluated by simulation paradigm approach. The main idea of simulation-based approach is to construct two models, a real-world model and an ideal- world model to evaluate a protocol under investigation. A real-world model describes the operation of the protocol with all its details in a particular computational model whereas an ideal-world model describes the protocol in an abstract way mainly focusing on the services that the protocol should provide. Once constructed, the security of a real-world protocol is compared to that of an ideal-world implementation of the same task.

Both the models contain adversaries and their behavior is not constrained apart from the requirement that it has to run in polynomial time. The presence of an adversary in an ideal-world model essentially has no effect on the system due to the nature of its design. In other words, the ideal-world system is secure by its construction. The real-world model implements the actual protocol under consideration. Once both the models are implemented, the goal is to prove that for any real-world adversary there exists an ideal-world adversary that can achieve the same effects in the ideal-world model as those achieved by the real-world adversary in the real-world model. The security of a protocol interpreted from an adversary's generated view states that if the view generated by an adversary after executing a protocol in the real-world model can be solely generated from the information it legitimately possesses, then the protocol is termed to be secure. This implies that an adversary cannot gain extra information from the execution of a protocol, and everything that an adversary gathers can be generated by the adversary itself.

The real-world and ideal-world models are constructed as interacting Turing machines. The real-world model consists of honest and adversarial nodes represented by M_i and A_i, respectively. The nodes run the desired actual protocol in order to complete a specific task. Similarly, The ideal-world model too consists of honest and adversarial nodes, but the honest nodes interact with an ideal functionality F, running the ideal protocol ϕ.The functionality F is synonymous to the protocol to be evaluated, but it is provided with all the initial conditions that allows it to detect when the system goes into an incorrect state. An adversary in the ideal-world cannot gain any extra knowledge except for the information that F chooses to provide.

Definition 2 (statistical security). A routing protocol is said to be statistically secure if, for any configuration conf and any real-world adversary A, there exists an ideal-world adversary A' such that $\mathrm{Out}^{real}_{conf,A} \cong \mathrm{Out}^{ideal}_{conf,A'}$, where "$\cong$" means "statistically indistinguishable."

Intuitively, a routing protocol is said to statistically secure if the effect of a real-world adversary on a real-world model can be "almost perfectly" simulated by an ideal-world adversary in the ideal-world model. That is, no ideal-world adversary exists that can cause the ideal-world system to go into an incorrect state, and it follows that no real-world adversary can exist that can cause the real-world model to move into an incorrect state with nonnegligible probability because if such an adversary exists, then no ideal-world adversary can simulate it "almost perfectly."

SEMRAW: THE PROPOSED SECURE MULTICAST ROUTING ALGORITHM

The proposed secure multicast routing algorithm for WMN is based on our multicast routing protocol EMRAW [18]. SEMRAW employs an integrated security scheme to prevent all the active attacks on a multicast routing protocol in wireless mesh networks. SEMRAW requires every node to maintain secure neighborhood relations with all the nodes in its two-hop range. To prevent malicious nodes from manipulating the accumulated metric, the multicast routing messages are protected with the help of signatures. SEMRAW mainly prevents nodes from modifying the metric field appended by previous nodes in the network. Multicast tree formation in SEMRAW is accomplished by a broadcast tree establishment message from a source node that is replied back by the set of receivers.

SEMRAW uses signatures to provide authentication and message-integrity to the tree establishment process. Therefore, it uses the services of a trusted certificate server, whose public key is known to all valid nodes. Each node maintains a list of public keys of all the nodes in its one-hop and two-hop neighborhood. The public and private keys of a node A are represented by K^u_A and K^v_A, respectively. It also employs a wormhole detection mechanism presented in [36] to distinguish real links from links traversing a wormhole. The proposed SEMRAW operates in following 3 phases.

Request Phase

The request phase is initiated by the source S (source node in the sample network shown in Figure 1), whenever it needs to form a multicast group or establish/update routes with the members of multicast group. In either case, S needs to establish multicast routes with the set of group members (receivers). S initiates the request phase by flooding a Join Request (JRQ), advertising the multicast group. The contents of Join Request include Multicast Address (MA), Multicast Request ID (MID), Sequence Number (SN), Source Address (SA), Transmitter Address (TA), Hop Count (HC), Metric Value, and Time-to-Live (TTL). The Join Request identity (JRQ-ID) uniquely identifies a Join Request. On receiving a nonduplicate Join Request (JRQ), intermediate nodes rebroadcast it after creating a routing entry for the received Join Request. Meanwhile, multicast receivers that receive the Join Request respond to it with a Join Reply, initiating the Reply phase:

$$S \longrightarrow * : \{\text{JRQ}, 2\text{HA}, 3\text{HA}, 4\text{HA}\}\, K_S^v \,\{M_S, \text{HC}, S\_\text{SQ}\}\, K_S^v. \tag{1}$$

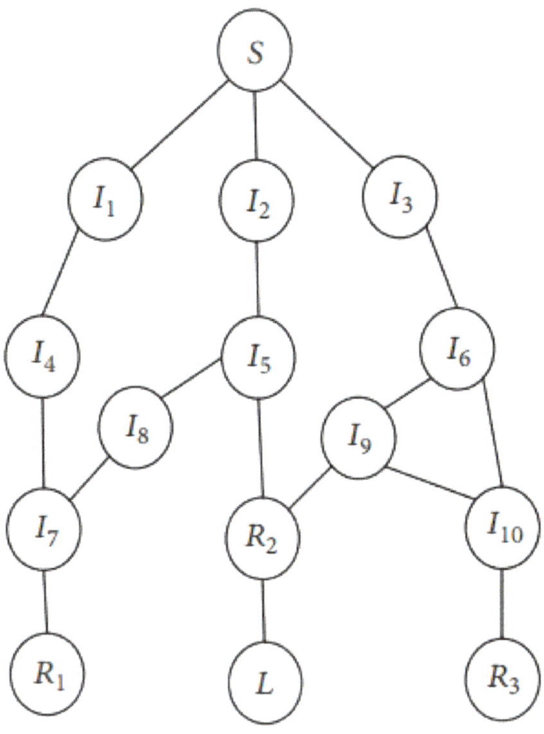

Figure 1: An example network connection.

JRQ represents the contents of the JRQ element. The 2HA represents the address of previous hop from which the current transmitting node received the JRQ. It is not applicable to the source node transmitting the JRQ. 3HA and 4HA represent the 3rd and 4th hop address that the JRQ has traversed. 3HA and 4HA enable SEMRAW to distinguish real links from out-of-band links. SEMRAW allows nodes to monitor the two-hop subpath on a received Join Request and identify a JRQ that traverses an out-of-band link like a wormhole. A JRQ that traverses an out-of-band link would not satisfy the necessary wormhole-free path criterion [36], which can be detected at the neighbors of a wormhole node and is quarantined. A path is said to be free from wormhole links if and only if for each subpath of length 2R there exists an alternate subpath of maximum length 4R, where R is the transmission range of a node. The proof of concept is presented in [36]. SEMRAW thrives on the fact that the probability of finding alternate paths between nodes separated by a distance d ($R < d < 2R$) (in a network where nodes are uniformly distributed) is high. The JRQ element is further extended to include an authenticated metric field that contains the metric, hop count, and source sequence number (S SQ).

Nodes I_1, I_2, I_3 that receive the JRQ from S verify its authenticity by validating the signatures. Once verified, a node creates a multicast routing entry towards the source. All routing entries in SEMRAW are by default considered to be in transient state. They are elevated to stable state only after a JRQ is verified to be wormhole-free.

An intermediate node $I1$ begins the wormhole verification process by checking for an existing transient routing entry corresponding to the MID and sequence number received in JRQ. Multiple transient routing entries may exist for the same MID that are received through a unique two-hop node. Node $I1$ then compares the two-hop address present in JRQ with the two-hop addresses of a set of existing routing entries represented by $\{\text{JRQ}O\}$. If it matches with any of the existing routing entries JRQO, it is updated with JRQ provided that it offers better metric. In case of no matching address, node I further compares the three-hop and fourhop addresses present in JRQ with the two-hop addresses of routing entries represented by JRQO or vice versa (provided the 2HA of JRQ does not match with TA address of JRQO or vice versa). If any one of the two addresses match (two-hop address in JRQ with three/four-hop addresses of JRQO or vice versa), an optimal of the two JRQs (JRQO or JRQ) is selected and state of the routing entry is set to stable. If none of the comparisons match, a new transient routing entry is created for the corresponding JRQ-ID. This matching of addresses is carried out to select an optimal wormhole-free path.

Before rebroadcasting the JRQ, nodes $_{I1,}$ I_2, and I_3 set the 2HA field with address of S, respectively. Nodes I_1, I_2, and I_3 also compute the cumulative metrics M_{I_1}, M_{I_2}, and M_{I_3} (from $I_1 \to S$, $I_2 \to S$, and $I_3 \to S$), respectively. The metric field along with the source sequence number (S SQ) is independently signed and appended to the JRQ. The source sequence number in the appended metric field ensures the freshness of the JRQ. The metric originally appended by S is kept intact:

$$I_1 \longrightarrow * : \{\text{JRQ}, S, 3\text{HA}, 4\text{HA}\}\, K_{I_1}^v \,\{M_S, \text{HC}, S\_\text{SQ}\}\, K_S^v \,\{M_{I_1}, \text{HC}, S\_\text{SQ}\}\, K_{I_1}^v. \tag{2}$$

Similarly, I_2 and I_3 broadcast the received JRQ after acting on it accordingly. I_4 (also I_5 and I_6) that receives the JRQ from I_1 (also I_5 from I_2 and I_6 from I_3) verifies the authenticity of the JRQ and the authenticated metric field appended by S and I_1. On verifying the authenticity, I_4 acts accordingly on the JRQ by computing the cumulative metric, incrementing the hop count and updating the 2HA and 3HA fields. The authenticated metric field appended by S is discarded to include the current cumulative metric M_{I_4}, signed and appended by I_4. This process is repeated by each intermediate node until the JRQ reaches the set of receivers. The JRQ broadcasted by I_4 is given by

$$I_1 \longrightarrow * : \{\text{JRQ}, S, I_1, 4\text{HA}\}\, K_{I_4}^v \,\{M_{I_1}, \text{HC}, S\_\text{SQ}\}\, K_{I_1}^v \,\{M_{I_4}, \text{HC}, S\_\text{SQ}\}\, K_{I_4}^v. \tag{3}$$

Reply Phase

The reply phase can be considered as request phase concurrently initiated by the set of receivers to optimize the multicast tree. Reply phase begins when a receiver(s) responds to a Join Request by broadcasting a Join Reply(JRP). If a receiver receives multiple copies of the same Join Request from different neighbors, a route selection decision is made in favour of the node that offers better metric. A Join Reply is broadcasted by a receiver after a corresponding stable route entry has been created.

The JRP requires additional address fields to store the addresses of multicast receiver and the selected next-hop node towards the source. Two important fields, hop count (HC) and effective hop count (EHC), are introduced in Join Reply packet. The effective hop count (EHC) allows a node to compute effective distance from a receiver. The hop count is set to the value received in Join Request and EHC is set to 0 by a multicast receiver broadcasting the Join Reply. The EHC field of JRP is added to the authenticated metric field to prevent from malicious manipulation. The JRP broadcasted by R_1 is given by

$$R_1 \longrightarrow * : \{\text{JRP}, 2\text{HA}, 3\text{HA}, 4\text{HA}\} K^v_{R_1} \{M_{R_1}, \text{HC}, \text{EHC}, D\_\text{SQ}\} K^v_{R_1}. \quad (4)$$

Processing of Join Replies by intermediate nodes varies depending on the type of node that receives the Join Reply. The proposed algorithm categorizes intermediate nodes into one of the two types: free nodes and potential forwarders. Nodes that are not part of the forwarding process for the current multicast tree are called free nodes, whereas a potential forwarder is a node that has been selected as forwarder by a receiver and awaits final confirmation from the source. In other words, a potential forwarder is a node that has recently received a Join Replywith next-hop address matching its own address. On receiving a nonduplicate Join Reply, a node I initially checks for the address present in nexthop (NH) address field. If it matches with its own address, a corresponding routing entry is created and thereafter I becomes a potential forwarder for that particular multicast group. The Join Reply is broadcasted after appropriately setting the next-hop address, hop count, and effective hop count. A Join Reply is considered original (not-duplicate) by a node only if it has not processed a similar Join Reply for a particular receiver

A free node that receives a broadcasted Join Reply, compares the hop count and effective hop count values after decrementing and incrementing them, respectively. A Join Reply is broadcasted further only if HC ≥ EHC; else it is suppressed. Similarly, a potential forwarder receiving a broadcasted Join Reply increments the hop count, leaving the effective hop count unaltered. It propagates the received Join Reply through the established route towards the source. This allows a source node S to realize the existence of an alternate path that minimizes overall transmission count.

Similar to request phase, each intermediate node verifies the authenticity of signed JRP messages and metric fields. It appends a new authenticated metric field by discarding the old field appended by the two-hop node. Each node also verifies for the presence of out-of-band links by using the real-link detection mechanism discussed in the request phase.

Route Commit Phase

The route commit phase is carried out by the source S after receiving Join Replies from the set of receivers. The source selects a route based on the received Join Replies that minimizes overall transmission count in the network. The route is committed by the source by explicitly sending a commit message (RCOM). The contents of route commit message include Multicast Address (MA), Sequence Number (SN), Source Address (SA), Transmitter Address (TA), and Selected Next-Hop address. SNH is the address of selected next-hop that allows a node to realize the path to be followed to a receiver. The route commit message transmitted by source S in the example network is given by

$$S \longrightarrow I_2 : \{\text{RCOM}\} K^v_S. \quad (5)$$

Each intermediate propagates the received route commit message through the selected next-hop node towards the receiver(s), after appropriately signing it. Intermediate nodes that act as forwarders for multiple receivers (like I_5 in the current example), propagate an individually signed route commit message through the respective selected forwarder.

SECURITY PROOF

Theorem 3. The proposed SEMRAW is statistically secure if the signature scheme is secure against chosen message attacks.

Proof. In order to prove the security of SEMRAW, let us construct an appropriate ideal-world adversary A' as discussed in Section 3 for any real-world adversary A. Next, initialize both the systems with the same configuration conf and the same random input r. The proposed algorithm is said to be secure if the output $(\text{Out}^{\text{ideal}}_{\text{conf},A'})$ of the ideal-world model for idealworld adversary A' is statistically indistinguishable from the output of a real-world model (Outreal conf,) for any adversary A. In this case, $\text{sys}^{\text{real}}_{\text{conf},A}$ and $\text{sys}^{\text{ideal}}_{\text{conf},A'}$ are identical implying that, in each step, the state of the corresponding machines and the content of the corresponding tapes are the same. On the other hand, if an incorrect state is encountered, the output configurations of both the models do not match as the idealworld model outputs a special symbol ($).

A system moves into an incorrect state when a routing entry of a noncompromised node V is incorrect. Node V sets a routing entry $(l_{\text{tar}}, l^1_{\text{nxt}}, l^2_{\text{nxt}}, C)$ for a target l_{tar} only if it has received a signed JRQ message which has been traversed through l^2_{nxt} and l^1_{nxt} with metric equal to C and the edge $(l^2_{\text{nxt}}, l^1_{\text{nxt}}) \in E$.

Now, the node V shares one-hop and two-hop neighborhood relations with l^1_{nxt} and l^2_{nxt}. The routing entry can be made incorrect forcing one of the following cases to occur.

- Case 1. There is no route from V to a node that uses the label l_{tar}, but attacker forces l_{tar} to accept the corresponding message.
- Case 2.There are routes from V to a node that uses the label l_{tar}, going through the one-hop and two-hop neighbors l^1_{nxt} and l^2_{nxt} of V. But the link between $(l^1_{\text{nxt}}, l^2_{\text{nxt}}) \notin E$. That is, the link is not present in the set of valid edges.
- Case 3. There are routes from V to a node that uses the label l_{tar}, but the sequence number received in the message through (l^1_{nxt} and $l^2_{\text{nxt}}$of V) is higher than the original source sequence number.
- Case 4. There are routes from V to a node that uses the label l_{tar} going through l^1_{nxt} and $l^2_{\text{nxt}}$of V. But attacker changes the metric values with cost lower/higher than the actual cost C.

To succeed in Case 1, an attacker needs to generate a fabricated JRQ/JRP message that contains the JRQ element and the signed metric fields of the PrvHopNode (through which the JRQ has traversed) and own signed metric field.

In Case 2, to force a genuine node V into accepting an outof-band link as a routing entry, it must have also received a Join Request through an alternate path connecting the twohop node l^2_{nxt} within a maximum of 4-hops, provided l^2_{nxt} of newly arrived JRQ does not match with transmitter address of existing Join Request or vice versa. But it has been already proven that finding such an alternate path is negligible in [36]. Therefore, the only way to accept such an incorrect routing entry is by fabricating an alternate Join Request traversing a nonexisting alternate subpath.

In Case 3, for a genuine node V to accept an incorrect routing entry with higher sequence number, the attacker must modify the contents of a JRQ/JRP message such that it has traversed through l^2_{nxt} and l^1_{nxt}. To perform this, the signature mechanism needs to be forged. Alternatively, if the attacker uses the label (l^*) of other malicious nodes, node V does not accept such a message since a message traversing l^* and l^1_{nxt} fails in Case 2.

In Case 4, an attacker needs to modify the metric field appended by a PrvHopNode in JRQ/JRP message to force the genuine node V in accepting a route whose metric value is lower/higher than the actual cost C. Let C' be the minimum of the costs of routes in R. If the signatures of l^2_{nxt} and l^1_{nxt} have not been forged, the JRQ must have taken one of the routes in R. However, since the metric C is independently signed, the value signed by l^2_{nxt} cannot be acted upon by l^1_{nxt} without forging the signature of l^2_{nxt}. Therefore, for C' to be selected over C, either C' has to be forged or C' is in fact the best of all the available metric values, which is not the case as C has been selected over C'.

Thus the ideal-world model enters into an incorrect state, only if the signature mechanism is forgeable. Fortunately, the probability of forging a cryptographic signature mechanism is computationally infeasible. So the output configuration of both the real-world and the ideal-world models are identical, that is, $\text{Out}^{\text{ideal}}_{\text{conf},A'} = \text{Out}^{\text{real}}_{\text{conf},A}$.

SIMULATION RESULTS

In this section, we present the simulation results of SEMRAW. The results are compared with SODMRP [17], a popular secure multicast routing protocol based on on-demand multicast routing protocol (ODMRP). SODMRP is a detection (and reaction) based security protocol that identifies attacker nodes based on their forwarding behavior in the network. Even though such a protocol would not be the first choice to compare with a prevention based mechanism like SEMRAW, to the best of our knowledge we could not find another alternate multicast protocol that employs a prevention based approach. At first, the performance of both the protocols is compared for packet delivery ratio (PDR) in presence of malicious nodes, and later for the additional overhead incurred to provide security.

The experiments were carried out on OMNeT++ 4.2.1, a discrete event network simulator [37]. The network set-up consists of varying number of MRs (50–100) for different experiments, forming the mesh backbone. The transmission range of a MR is set to 100 m. MRs implement the 802.11s MAC protocol with a channel data rate of 54 Mbps. Source (or root of the tree) and multicast receivers are selected at random for each experiment. The simulation is repeated for randomly generated seed values, and the average results are plotted in the graphs.

Figure 2 shows the performance comparison of SEMRAW and SODMRP in presence of varying number of malicious nodes, in terms of percentage of packet delivered. The network set-up consists of 100 MRs distributed over an area of 1000 m^2. Randomly selected source nodes transmit CBR (constant bit rate) data traffic over UDP to a set of randomly selected multicast receivers. Packet size was set to 1024 bytes. The simulations were run for 500 seconds. Over time, different multicast sources become active to send 1 MB of data traffic (≈100 data packets) to different receivers. Malicious nodes are strategically selected in such a way that they could affect more number of data flows in the network. Malicious nodes actively try to disrupt network services by launching attacks like metric manipulation attack, route corruption attack, and replay and wormhole attack. The principle goal of these malicious nodes is to degrade network performance and disrupt network services by dropping data packets.

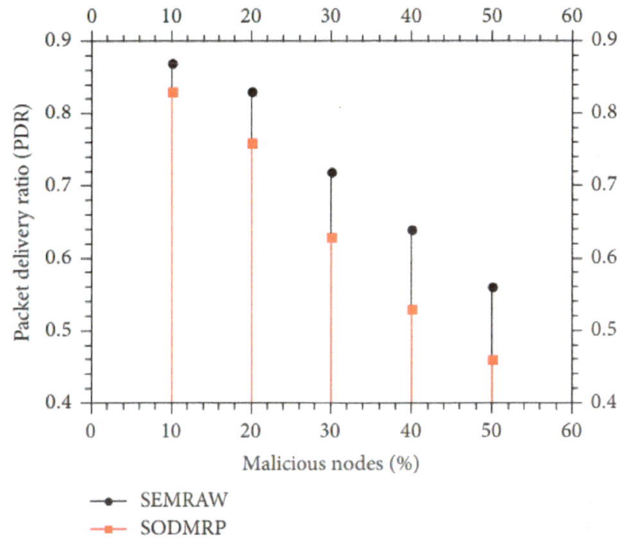

Figure 2: Performance comparison in terms of PDR.

SODMRP, similar to SEMRAW, relies on Join Query and Join Reply phase, where the multicast receivers broadcast their join tables to establish multicast routes to the source. SODMRP employs a reactive based approach to detect an attack. Each node that is part of the multicast forwarding group continuously monitors the discrepancy between effective PDR (ePDR) and perceived PDR (pPDR) and the route is considered to be under attack if ePDR − pPDR > δ. (δ is the predefined detection threshold) A downstream monitoring node on detecting malicious behavior accuses the upstream suspected node by flooding an accusation message that contains its identity and the identity of the accused node, as well as the duration of the accusation. For the duration of accusation the accused node would not be considered in route selection process. Figure 2 shows that SEMRAW performs better compared to SODMRP. Since SODMRP employs a reactive based approach it suffers from initial packet losses till the malicious behavior of an attacker node is detected.

Our later experiments were carried out to compute the overhead incurred by SEMRAW and SODMRP due to their respective security enhancements. First, we study the route creation overhead (in terms of additional bytes per packet) incurred for varying number of malicious attacker nodes. The network set-up comprised of 100 MRs spread over 1000 m^2. Figure 3 shows the overhead of SEMRAW in comparison to SODMRP. SEMRAW incurs constant overhead (in terms of additional bytes) as it requires three additional addresses to identify a wormhole link. Overhead of SEMRAW remains constant, irrespective of the number of malicious nodes as it employs a preventive based approach and the security scheme does not change with increase in the number of attackers. Therefore, when the network is free of attackers, SODMRP incurs less overhead compared to SEMRAW. However, with the increase in number of attackers SODMRP requires broadcasting accusation messages (contains identities of the accuser and suspected node, and the duration of accusation) across the network that requires additional bytes. With increase in number of attackers, higher number of accusation messages need to be transmitted and therefore incur more overhead than SEMRAW.

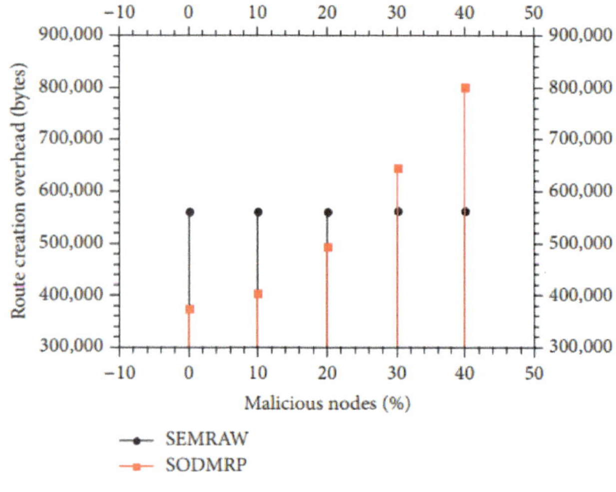

Figure 3: Route creation overhead for varying number of malicious nodes.

Finally, we compare the computation overhead in terms of signatures for SEMRAW and SODMRP for varying number of malicious nodes in a network of 50 MRs and a fixed average length of the route of 5. Figure 4 shows that with increasing number of attacker nodes the number of signatures required to protect messages in SODMRP is much higher compared to SEMRAW. It should be noted that, by increasing the number of malicious nodes in the network, we equally increase the number of source nodes that request for data transmission. SEMRAW requires two signatures per packet irrespective of the number of attacker nodes in the network. Therefore, the linear increase in total number of signatures in SEMRAW is due to increase in number of simultaneous multicast route formation processes. But on the other hand number of signatures in SODMRP increases with the increase in number of attacker nodes as more number of accusation messages are generated. Each node that generates an accusation message needs to sign it, so that the receiving node can appropriately verify it for authenticity. Thus, more attackers simply mean more number of accusation messages which result in more signatures.

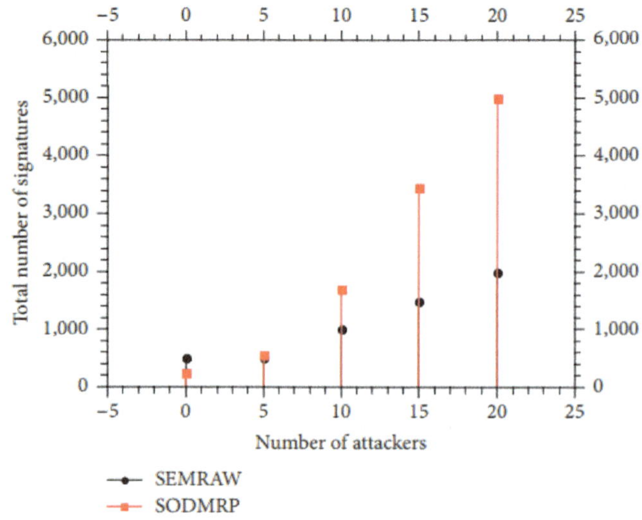

Figure 4: Signature overhead for varying number of attacker nodes.

DISCUSSION

SEMRAW is the secure version of our multicast routing algorithm EMRAW [18]. The proposed algorithm preserves the performance merits of EMRAW as such, by selecting paths that incur fewer number of transmissions and establishing a bandwidth minimal multicast tree.

To address the security requirements, SEMRAW employs an integrated security framework to defend against all known active threats in multicast routing environment. It uses digital signatures to prevent attacks that involve malicious manipulations while it employs a wormhole detection mechanism to distinguish real links from wormhole links. The authenticated metric field protects mutable content in the JRQ and JRP message, thereby allowing the source and receivers to construct a secure multicast tree. SEMRAW allows an intermediate node to verify the content of routing messages in two steps. First, a node verifies the authenticity of the authenticated metric field appended by 2-hop node. This represents the cumulative content along the traversed path, acting as a check point. Secondly, it verifies the authenticity of the authenticated metric field appended by the previous hop. These two steps restrict intermediate nodes from acting on contents appended by previous hops, thus completely securing the multicast tree formation. In other words, each node acts as a checkpoint that allows downstream nodes to verify the authenticity of multicast routing messages. Since each node verifies the validity of the path traversed by a routing message, it is infeasible for an attacker to launch an attack without being detected by a processing node.

The wormhole detection mechanism employed by SEMRAW works concurrently in conjunction with the tree selection mechanism. It facilitates nodes to monitor their two-hop subpaths and selects only such routes that are verified to be wormhole-free. It relies on the observations made in [36] to distinguish out-of-band links from real links. It relies on the fact that, in a uniformly distributed network, alternate routes within a maximum of 4-hops exist between node separated by a distance of 2R, where *R* is the transmission range of a node.

However, SEMRAW is not without any limitations as any other algorithm. It requires the minimum length of wormhole link to be greater than 2R to successfully distinguish real links from wormholes. Since wormhole links of length less than 2R have negligible impact on the tree construction process, we safely ignore this limitation.

SEMRAW incurs additional computation and message overhead over EMRAW. This additional overhead results from the signatures employed during the secure tree construction process and due to the presence of additional addresses to detect wormhole attack. All the intermediate nodes that participate in route discovery, sign tree selection elements: Join Request, join reply, and route commit messages. At any instance, the Join Request (or join reply) element contains the signatures of the one-hop and two-hop nodes. Each intermediate node verifies the signatures of its immediate neighbor and its two-hop node, which adds to the computation overhead. Also, each intermediate node processes the addresses of previous hops for detecting wormhole links, adding to overhead in computations. Similarly, the presence of previous and current hop signatures slightly increases the message overhead. The presence of separate metric field increases the size of a message by a byte. However, the majority of the additional message overhead is due to the addresses of previous 4 hops for detecting wormhole links. Any intermediate node that receives a Join Request (or join reply) signs the path-selection element and the metric field separately and updates the addresses, before propagating it further into the network. Even though SEMRAW incurs additional overhead, the security provided by SEMRAW in an open operating environment of WMN overweighs this additional overhead.

Table 1 presents a security comparison of various existing unicast and multicast protocols. It can be observed that none of the existing protocols are secure against all known active attacks in wireless mesh network. Multicast routing protocols like BMSR [16] and SODMRP [17] can defend against Byzantine attacks, but they are essentially detection schemes that suffer from initial packet losses.

Table 1: Security comparison of different protocols

Protocol	Metric manipulation attack	Route corruption attack	Routing loop attack	Wormhole attack
SAODV [5]	Resistant	Not resistant	Resistant	Not resistant
ARAN [6]	Resistant	Not resistant	Not resistant	Not resistant
Ariadne [11]	Resistant	Not resistant	Resistant	Not resistant
SRP [12]	Not resistant	Not resistant	Resistant	Not resistant
SODMRP [17]	Resistant	Not resistant	Resistant	Not resistant
EMRAW [18]	Not resistant	Not resistant	Not resistant	Not resistant
SEMRAW	Resistant	Resistant	Resistant	Resistant

CONCLUSION

Securing multicast communications is essential to meet the performance requirements of wireless mesh network. In this paper, we proposed a secure multicast routing algorithm SEMRAW, to defend against all known active threats including wormhole attack. The security of the proposed protocol is analysed using simulation paradigm approach, which confirms its resistance against different active threats in a multicast routing environment. Later, the performance of SEMRAW is compared with a detection based protocol SODMRP in terms of packet delivery ratio and additional overhead incurred to provide security.

REFERENCES

1. I. F. Akyildiz, X. Wang, and W. Wang, "Wireless mesh networks: a survey," Computer Networks, vol. 47, no. 4, pp. 445–487, 2005.
2. P. A. K. Acharya and E. M. Belding, "MARS: link-layer rate selection for multicast transmissions in wireless mesh networks," Ad Hoc Networks, vol. 9, no. 1, pp. 48–60, 2011.
3. N. Nandiraju, D. Nandiraju, L. Santhanam, B. He, J. Wang, and D. P. Agrawal, "Wireless mesh networks: current challenges and future directions of web-in-the-sky," IEEE Wireless Communications, vol. 14, no. 4, pp. 79–89, 2007.
4. S. Paul, Multicast on the Internet and Its Applications, Kluwer Academic, New York, NY, USA, 1998.
5. M. Zapata and N. Asokan, "Securing ad hoc routing protocols," in Proceedings of the ACM Workshop on Wireless Security (WiSE ‹02), pp. 1–10, Atlanta , Ga, USA, September 2002.
6. K. Sanzgiri, B. Dahill, B. N. Levine, C. Shields, and E. M. Belding-Royer, "A secure routing protocol for ad hoc networks," in Proceedings of the 10th IEEE International Conference on Network Protocols (ICNP ‹02), pp. 78–87, IEEE, Paris, France, November 2002.
7. R. Kravets, S. Yi, and P. Naldurg, "A security-aware routing protocol for wireless ad hoc networks," inProceedings of the ACM Symposium on Mobile Ad-Hoc Networking and Computing, Long Beach, Calif, USA, October 2001.
8. C. E. Perkins and E. M. Royer, "Ad-hoc on-demand distance vector routing," in Proceedings of the 2nd IEEE Workshop on Mobile Computing Systems and Applications (WMCSA ‹99), pp. 90–100, New Orleans, La, USA, February 1999.
9. E. M. Royer and C. E. Perkins, "Multicast operation of the ad-hoc on-demand distance vector routing protocol," in Proceedings of the 5th Annual ACM/IEEE International Conference on Mobile Computing and Networking, pp. 207–218, August 1999.
10. S.-J. Lee, W. Su, and M. Gerla, "On-demand multicast routing protocol in multihop wireless mobile networks," Mobile Networks and Applications, vol. 7, no. 6, pp. 441–453, 2002.

11. Y.-C. Hu, A. Perrig, and D. B. Johnson, "Ariadne: a secure on-demand routing protocol for ad hoc networks," in Proceedings of The 8th Annual International Conference on Mobile Computing and Networking (Mobicom ‹02), pp. 12–23, September 2002.

12. P. Papadimitratos and Z. J. Haas, "Secure routing for mobile ad-hoc networks," in Proceedings of the SCS Communication Networks and Distributed Systems Modelling and Simulation Conference (CNDS ‹02), San Antonio, Tex, USA, January 2002.

13. D. Johnson and D. Maltz, "The Dynamic Source Routing Protocol (DSR) for mobile ad hoc networks for IPv4," Tech. Rep., 2007, http://tools.ietf.org/html/RFC4728.

14. C. W. Wu and Y. C. Tay, "AMRIS: a multicast protocol for ad hoc wireless networks," in Proceedings of the IEEE Conference on Military Communications, pp. 25–29, Atlantic City, NJ, USA, 1999.

15. G. Acs, L. Buttyan, and I. Vajda, "Provably secure on-demand source routing in mobile ad hoc networks,"IEEE Transactions on Mobile Computing, vol. 5, no. 11, pp. 1533–1546, 2006.

16. R. Curtmola and C. Nita-Rotaru, "BSMR: byzantine-resilient secure multicast routing in multihop wireless networks," IEEE Transactions on Mobile Computing, vol. 8, no. 4, pp. 445–459, 2009.

17. J. Dong, R. Curtmola, and C. N. Rotaru, "Secure high-throughput multicast routing in wireless mesh networks," IEEE Transactions on Mobile Computing, vol. 10, no. 5, pp. 653–668, 2011. ·

18. R. Matam and S. Tripathy, "Improved heuristics for multicast routing in wireless mesh networks,"Wireless Networks, vol. 19, no. 8, pp. 1829–1837, 2013.

19. T. R. Andel and A. Yasinsac, "Adaptive threat modeling for secure Ad Hoc routing protocols," Electronic Notes in Theoretical Computer Science, vol. 197, no. 2, pp. 3–14, 2008.

20. T. R. Andel and A. Yasinsac, "Surveying security analysis techniques in MANET routing protocols," IEEE Communications Surveys and Tutorials, vol. 9, no. 4, pp. 70–84, 2007.

21. R. Matam and S. Tripathy, "Provably secure routing protocol for wireless mesh networks," International Journal of Network Security, vol. 16, no. 3, pp. 168–178, 2014.

22. M. Burmester and B. D. Medeiros, "Towards provable security for route discovery protocols in mobile ad hoc networks," IACR Cryptology ePrint Archive, 2007.

23. G. Ács, L. Buttyán, and I. Vajda, "Provable security of on-demand distance vector routing in wireless ad hoc networks," in Security and Privacy in Ad-Hoc and Sensor Networks, R. Molva, G. Tsudik, and D. Westhoff, Eds., vol. 3813 of Lecture Notes in Computer Science, pp. 113–127, 2005. ·

24. L. Mao and J. Ma, "Towards provably secure on-demand distance vector routing in MANET," inProceedings of the International Conference on Computational Intelligence and Security (CIS ‹08), pp. 417–420, Suzhou, China, December 2008.

25. Q. Niu, "Formal analysis of secure routing protocol for ad hoc networks," in Proceedings of the International Conference on Wireless Communications and Signal Processing (WCSP ‹09), Nanjing, China, November 2009.

26. L. Buttyán and T. V. Thong, "Formal verification of secure ad-hoc network routing protocols using deductive model-checking," in Proceedings of the 3rd Joint IFIP Wireless and Mobile Networking Conference (WMNC ‹10), pp. 1–6, Budapest, Hungary, October 2010.

27. S. Roy, D. Koutsonikolas, S. Das, and C. Hu, "High-throughput multicast routing metrics in wireless mesh networks," in Proceedings of the 26th IEEE International Conference on Distributed Computing Systems (ICDCS ‹06), p. 48, IEEE, July 2006.

28. Y. Li and I.-R. Chen, "Hierarchical agent-based secure multicast for wireless mesh networks," inProceedings of the IEEE International Conference on Communications (ICC ‹11), pp. 1–6, Kyoto, Japan, June 2011.

29. J. Kim and S. Bahk, "Design of certification authority using secret redistribution and multicast routing in wireless mesh networks," Computer Networks, vol. 53, no. 1, pp. 98–109, 2009.

30. A. Perrig, R. Canetti, D. Song, and J. D. Tygar, "Efficient and secure source authentication for multicast," in Proceedings of the Network and Distributed System Security Symposium (NDSS ‹01), San Diego, Calif, USA, February 2001.

31. Y. Han, X. Gui, X. Wu, and X. Yang, "Proxy encryption based secure multicast in wireless mesh networks," Journal of Network and Computer Applications, vol. 34, no. 2, pp. 469–477, 2011.

32. S. Zhao, A. Aggarwal, S. Liu, and H. Wu, "A secure routing protocol in proactive security approach for mobile ad-hoc networks," in Proceedings of the IEEE Wireless Communications and Networking Conference (WCNC ‹08), pp. 2627–2632, IEEE, April 2008.

33. P. M. Ruiz and A. F. Gomez-Skarmeta, "Heuristic algorithms for minimum bandwith consumption multicast routing in wireless mesh networks," in Ad-Hoc, Mobile, and Wireless Networks, V. R. Syrotiuk and E. Chávez, Eds., vol. 3738 of Lecture Notes in Computer Science, pp. 258–270, 2005. ·

34. R. Mukherjee and J. W. Atwood, "Scalable solutions for secure group communications," Computer Networks, vol. 51, no. 12, pp. 3525–3548, 2007.

35. H. Wang, Z. Cao, and L. Wei, "A scalable certificateless architecture for multicast wireless mesh network using proxy re-encryption," Security and Communication Networks, vol. 7, no. 1, pp. 14–32, 2014.

36. R. Matam and S. Tripathy, "WRSR: wormhole resistant secure routing for wireless mesh networks,"Eurasip Journal of Wireless Communications and Networking, vol. 2013, article 180, 2013.

37. The OMNeT++ Network Simulator, http://www.omnetpp.org.

CHAPTER 12

A TWO-LEVEL MARKOV MODEL FOR PACKET LOSS IN UDP/IP-BASED REAL-TIME VIDEO APPLICATIONS TARGETING RESIDENTIAL USERS

Martin Ellis [a], Dimitrios P. Pezaros [a], Theodore Kypraios [b], and Colin Perkins [a]

[a]School of Computing Science, University of Glasgow, Glasgow G12 8QQ, UK

[b]School of Mathematical Sciences, University of Nottingham, Nottingham NG7 2RD, UK

ABSTRACT

The packet loss characteristics of Internet paths that include residential broadband links are not well understood, and there are no good models for their behaviour. This complicates the design of real-time video applications targeting home users, since it is difficult to choose appropriate error correction and concealment algorithms without a good model for the types of loss observed. Using measurements of residential broadband networks in the UK and Finland, we show that existing models for packet loss, such as the Gilbert model and simple hidden Markov models, do not effectively model the loss patterns seen in this environment. We present a new two-level Markov model for packet loss that can more accurately describe the characteristics of these links, and quantify the effectiveness of this model. We demonstrate that our new packet loss model allows for improved application design, by using it to model the performance of forward error correction on such links.

INTRODUCTION

Studies show that video comprises more than 50% of global consumer Internet traffic, and it is predicted that this will rise to 80–90% by 2017 [1]. This video traffic can be split into two categories: on-demand streaming of near real-time content, primarily movies and catch-up TV (e.g., NetFlix, BBC iPlayer), and real-time traffic in the form of live TV broadcasts and video conferencing. Much has been written about near real-time applications. These typically make use of dynamic adaptive streaming over HTTP (DASH) [2] and accept TCP congestion control and in-order reliable delivery, with the multi-second play-out delays this entails, in return for being able to build on the web infrastructure of content delivery networks. By way of contrast, real-time applications require shorter play-out buffers, typically on the order of tens of milliseconds, and so eschew the DASH model and instead build custom UDP/IP transport protocols and infrastructure. By accepting this complexity, real-time applications can gain visibility into the timing and reliability of the packet delivery process, allowing them to optimise the transport to reduce latency.

In order to design effective low-latency real-time transport protocols, new forward error correction (FEC) schemes, or improved packet loss concealment algorithms, we need to create an accurate model of the packet delivery process. Such a model will allow analytic and simulation studies to evaluate the performance of new applications and services in advance of full-scale deployments, testing the effectiveness of the

Citation: Martin Ellis, Dimitrios P. Pezaros, Theodore Kypraios, Colin Perkins, A two-level Markov model for packet loss in UDP/IP-based real-time video applications targeting residential users, Computer Networks, Volume 70, 9 September 2014, Pages 384-399, ISSN 1389-1286, http://dx.doi.org/10.1016/j.comnet.2014.05.013.

design. Previous studies have used Markov models, such as the classical Gilbert model [3], to evaluate video streaming applications [4] and forward error correction [5]. These models are popular due to their relative simplicity, and because they are easy to implement and understand. Using measurements of packet loss between academic sites, more complex Markov models [6] and [7] and hidden Markov models [8] and [9] have also been proposed to describe Internet packet loss. However, the accuracy of these models for characterising packet loss on residential broadband networks remains poorly understood. There is some evidence that packet loss characteristics of residential networks are different to those on academic networks [10], so it is important to study the accuracy of the models in this context.

In this paper, we use measurements of packet loss from real-time video on residential broadband links [10] to show that well-known Markov models of network packet loss do not effectively capture the characteristics of such links. We introduce a new two-level model that uses both packet loss and delay information to better understand the state of the network, using delay data to give insight into whether packet loss is due to congestion or link noise. Finally, we show that this new model captures packet loss processes seen on residential ADSL and cable links more accurately than the previous models. This paper is an extended version of [11] that refines and expands our analysis, and makes two new contributions: (1) we present a new technique for classifying congestion for use in the two-level model and (2) we apply the two-level model to simulation of FEC performance, to evaluate its improved accuracy over existing models in a realistic scenario.

We structure the remainder of this paper as follows. We begin, in Section 2, by describing the experimental dataset used in our work. Section 3 then outlines existing approaches to modelling packet loss patterns in the Internet, and Section 4 explores the limitations of these existing approaches, based on an evaluation using our dataset. In Section 5, we introduce a new type of packet loss model, then show how this improves accuracy when modelling residential links in Section 6. Section 7 compares the different packet loss models using simulation of FEC performance, and Section 8 outlines how the two-level model can be applied to other scenarios. We discuss related work in Section 9, and conclude in Section 10.

MEASUREMENT OF PACKET LOSS ON RESIDENTIAL LINKS

We use a dataset we have previously collected, which is described in [10], to evaluate the performance of the existing packet loss models against traces of packet loss on residential links. This dataset contains end-to-end measurements of one-way Real-time Transport Protocol (RTP) [12] traffic sent over UDP/IP at a range of bit-rates (1–8.5 Mbps) from a well-connected server to measurement hosts located in residential premises. The server was located at the University of Glasgow, while the residential measurement hosts were located in the UK and Finland. A range of experimental factors were considered: the traces were collected at different bit-rates, at different times of day, and from residences connected to the Internet via several different Internet Service Providers (ISPs) using a mix of ADSL and cable modem links. The measurements were taken in 2009 and 2010.

A sequence number and transmission timestamp was attached to each packet, i , allowing us to obtain an observation sequence of packet losses, Z_i (Z_i=0 for received packets, Z_i=1 for lost packets) and arrival timestamps, T_i, for those packets that were received. We use the timestamps to estimate the queueing delay (*DQ*) experienced by each received packet, correcting for clock skew as in [13], to understand the correlation between the queueing conditions experienced by the stream and the loss behaviour. These packet loss and delay observations are then used as input to the packet loss models.

The dataset contains ~3800 RTP packet traces varying between one and ten minutes in duration, with sending data rates ranging from 1–8.5 Mb/s depending on the edge link capacity. This gives between 6000 and approximately 600,000 packets per trace. Within the traces, there are a range of different loss and delay characteristics, showing cases where the network is overloaded and causing packet loss due to congestion, cases of time-of-day variation in packet loss behaviour, as well as many traces where no packet loss at all was encountered. More information on the dataset, including how to download the raw traces, can be found in [10].

Few consistent patterns can be identified in the packet loss characteristics of the traces. Different links exhibited quite different behaviours. For example, some ADSL links showed signs of time-of-day variation in packet loss, with significant spikes during the evening (perhaps associated with more load on the network), while other ADSL links showed no such behaviour. Similarly, in some cases, the same links showed different behaviours across the two years when the measurements were taken (possibly due to network upgrades by the ISP during this period). For this reason, the analysis presented here uses each trace individually, as a separate observation of the behaviour of the network, and does not aggregate across traces. For further details on the high-level characteristics of the traces, as well as in-depth analysis of the packet loss and delay measurements, see [14].

EXISTING APPROACHES TO MODELLING LOSS PATTERNS

Numerous attempts have been made to model the packet loss patterns seen on the network. These can be roughly categorised into end-to-end packet loss models and link-layer specific packet loss models. We are interested in end-to-end packet loss models, since it is end-to-end performance that is observed by applications. We do not further consider link-layer specific models for two reasons: (1) their effects are subsumed into the end-to-end model of the packet loss patterns and (2) most of the work on link-layer specific models has considered wireless links, since those have the most complex loss patterns. We are not aware of widely available link-layer specific models for ADSL and cable modem links that could be incorporated into an end-to-end model, and even if such were available, they would only address part of the end-to-end path. We rather consider end-to-end packet loss models trained based on the measurement data outlined in Section 2.

Commonly used end-to-end models of packet loss are based on either simple multi-state Markov models, or on more complex hidden Markov models. Perhaps the most straightforward of the simple Markov models is the two-state Markov chain, proposed by Gilbert [3], also referred to as the

Simple Gilbert Model (SGM) [15]. In the SGM, the state of the model directly represents Z_i, as shown in Fig. 1 (i.e., the BAD state always produces packet losses, while the GOOD state never does). Transitions between the states are per-packet, and independent of the previous states. The parameters of the model are p, the probability of losing a packet, given the previous one was received; and q, the probability of receiving a packet, given that the previous one was lost. These parameters can be expressed as a matrix, as in Eq. (1):

$$\textbf{SGM} = \begin{bmatrix} (1-p) & p \\ q & (1-q) \end{bmatrix} \quad (1)$$

These parameters are estimated by counting the number of transitions between states, as discussed in [16].

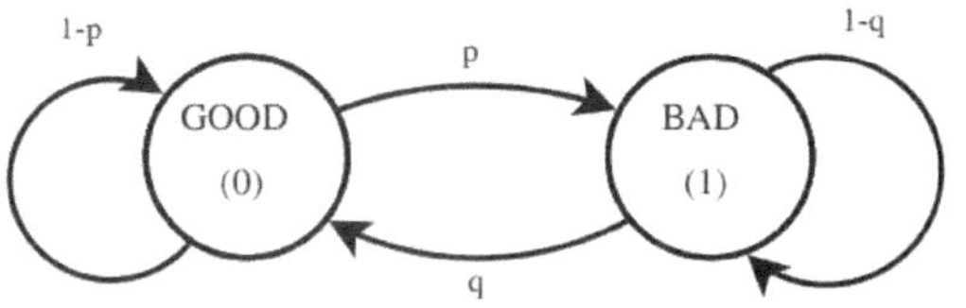

Figure 1: Simple Gilbert Model (SGM).

The SGM has been heavily used for evaluating application performance, especially after early work on academic networks found it to be suitable for describing the loss processes seen in these networks [6]. For example, recent evaluations of network video streaming systems [4] and video quality estimation tools [17] have used SGM models to generate their loss processes. Analytical evaluations of forward error correction (FEC) performance have also used the SGM as the basis for their work (e.g., [18] and [5]).

One of the drawbacks of the SGM is that there are only two states and the model is memoryless so it does not capture bursty behaviour in packet loss. To address this, a new model was proposed [7] and [16] where the number of states to represent losses is extended from one (as in the SGM) to m, as illustrated in Fig. 2. We refer to this as the Extended Gilbert Model (EGM). This extended model allows us to describe loss bursts of up to m packets, with each state representing a loss burst of a particular length. That is, state j (where $j<m$) represents a loss burst of j packets, while state m represents a loss burst of *at least* m packets. Received packets are represented by state 0, and the run-lengths of received packets are not specifically captured by the model. Considering all of the measured packet traces in our dataset [10], the 99*th* percentile loss burst length is four packets as shown in Fig. 3. Accordingly, we consider extended Gilbert models with m=4in this paper. The parameters of an EGM with m=4 can be expressed as the matrix shown in Eq. (2):

$$\textbf{EGM} = \begin{bmatrix} p_{00} & p_{01} & 0 & 0 & 0 \\ p_{10} & 0 & p_{12} & 0 & 0 \\ p_{20} & 0 & 0 & p_{23} & 0 \\ p_{30} & 0 & 0 & 0 & p_{34} \\ p_{40} & 0 & 0 & 0 & p_{44} \end{bmatrix} \quad (2)$$

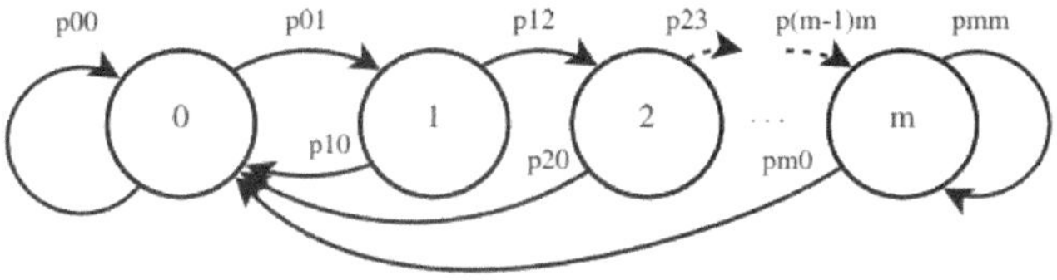

Figure 2: Extended Gilbert Model (EGM).

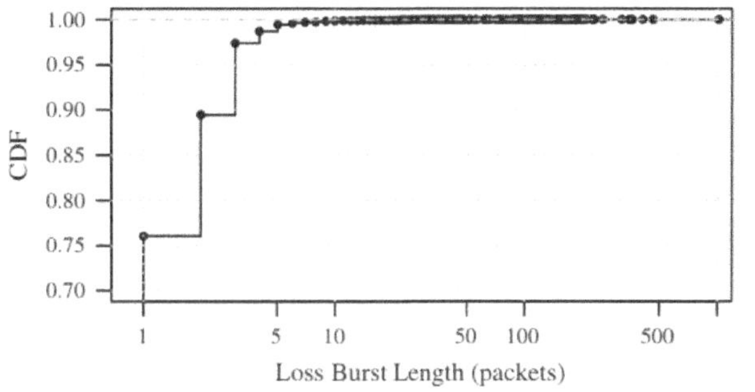

Figure 3: Cumulative distribution of observed loss burst lengths.

Finally, an extension to the Gilbert model was proposed by Elliott [19], where *both* states produce errors with different probabilities, as shown in Fig. 4. The motivation behind this approach is that one of the states (GOOD) produces losses with a low probability, corresponding to isolated loss events, whereas the other state (BAD) produces losses with a higher probability, corresponding to packet loss bursts. One way to implement this model is as a two-state Hidden Markov Model (HMM), where only the observations of packet loss can be seen, while the actual state (GOOD or BAD) is hidden. The parameters of the HMM can be expressed as matrices HMM A, which defines transition probabilities between the hidden states, and HMM B, which defines the probability of packet loss in each hidden state, as in Eqs. (3) and (4):

$$\textbf{HMM A} = \begin{bmatrix} (1-p) & p \\ q & (1-q) \end{bmatrix} \quad (3)$$

$$\textbf{HMM B} = [(1-k) \quad (1-h)] \quad (4)$$

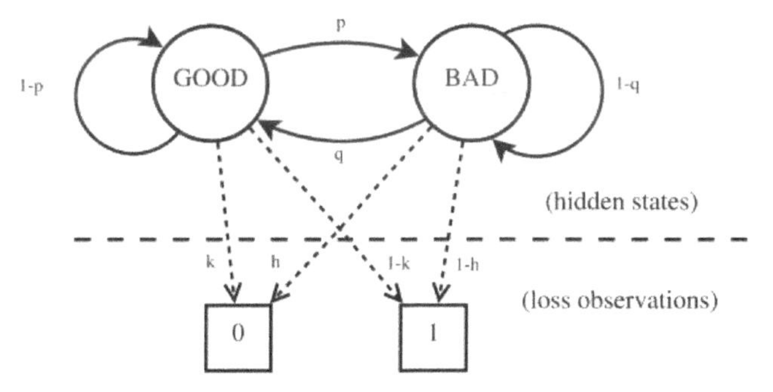

Figure 4: Two-state Hidden Markov Model (2HMM).

In HMMs, the transition probabilities between hidden states and the loss probabilities for each hidden state are estimated from the observed data. This process is more complex than for the SGM and EGM, and involves the use of expectation–maximisation algorithms as described in [20]. An HMM can be extended to contain more than two states. This will improve its accuracy, although in practice the complexity of the estimation process limits the number of states, since the estimation time increases quadratically with the number of states in the HMM. In this work, we will focus on two- and three-state HMMs, since these are computationally feasible to calculate, and since the states can be associated with a physical interpretation with different states representing different causes of network congestion (we discuss the physical interpretation of the states in Section 5.1).

HMMs were first employed for modelling packet loss in [8], where HMMs of varying numbers of states were applied to active measurement traces, finding that in the majority of cases, two- and three-state HMMs were sufficient. The HMMs were used to estimate the transitions between hidden states for these traces, and showed that greater resolution can be obtained using HMMs than the simpler SGM and EGM. Further work has used HMMs to model the behaviour of both packet loss and delay in Internet measurement traces between academic sites [21] and [9], and to predict network conditions and apply these to dynamic adaptation of FEC parameters [22].

LIMITATIONS OF EXISTING PACKET LOSS MODELS

In this section we evaluate the performance of the SGM, EGM, and two- and three-state HMM (2HMM and 3HMM) packet loss models outlined in Section 3 against the measured loss traces described in Section 2. The model parameters for each of the models studied in this paper, as trained on each of the packet loss traces described in [10], can be found at http://martin-ellis.net/research/loss-modelling.

Trace classification and example loss patterns

An initial manual examination of the packet loss traces showed that they can be divided into three groups: those with zero or very low packet loss, those with non-bursty loss, and those with bursty loss. Separating out traces with very low levels of loss allows further analysis to be more significant, focusing on bursty or non-bursty loss patterns that are not meaningful when there are only occasional packet losses. For those traces visually identified to be very low loss, over 90% had 15 or fewer lost packets, so the threshold for a trace to be considered very low loss was set to 15 packets lost. A total of 2890 traces are categorised as very low loss. Of these 1679 are loss free, while the remaining 1211 have between 1 and 15 lost packets.

Among the traces with higher loss, the distinction between bursty and non-bursty loss was made by visual examination of the trace sequences. This finds 486 non-bursty traces and 433 traces with bursty packet loss. Representative samples of non-bursty and bursty packet loss behaviour are shown in Fig. 5 and Fig. 7 respectively. The bars indicate whether packets were lost (black) or received (grey). The top panel of each figure ("raw data") shows the measured loss sequence, while the lower four panels show sample synthetic loss sequences generated using the SGM, EGM, 2HMM, and 3HMM packet loss models with parameters estimated from the trace, as will be described in Section 4.2. The SGM, EGM, 2HMM, and 3HMM parameters estimated from the non-bursty and bursty traces are shown in Figs. 6 and 8, respectively. Fig. 9 and Fig. 10 show packet loss burstiness metrics to illustrate the differences between the bursty and non-bursty trace data. These figures show that the traces classified here as bursty indeed have a higher fraction of packet loss bursts than the non-bursty traces, using the metrics for bursty packet loss introduced in [23] (using G_{min}=16 as recommended) and [24] respectively.

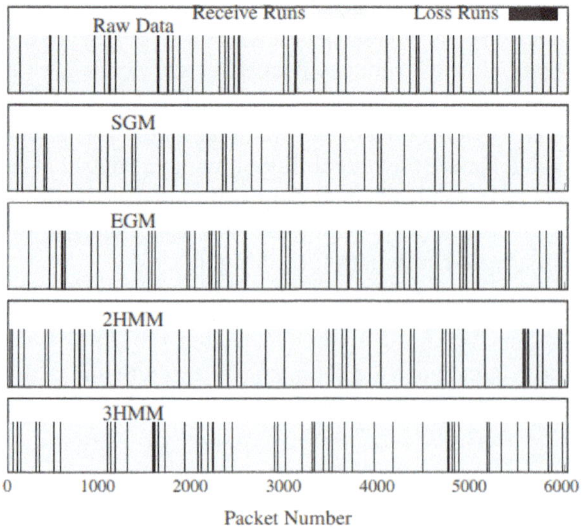

Figure 5: Example non-bursty trace: original/synthetic loss sequences.

$$\textbf{SGM} = \begin{bmatrix} 0.9904 & 0.0096 \\ 0.9661 & 0.0339 \end{bmatrix}$$

$$\textbf{EGM} = \begin{bmatrix} 0.9904 & 0.0096 & 0 & 0 & 0 \\ 0.9649 & 0 & 0.0351 & 0 & 0 \\ 1 & 0 & 0 & 0 & 0 \\ 1 & 0 & 0 & 0 & 0 \\ 1 & 0 & 0 & 0 & 0 \end{bmatrix}$$

$$\textbf{2HMM A} = \begin{bmatrix} 0.677 & 0.323 \\ 0.109 & 0.891 \end{bmatrix}$$

$$\textbf{2HMM B} = \begin{bmatrix} 0.0327 & 0.0021 \end{bmatrix}$$

$$\textbf{3HMM A} = \begin{bmatrix} 0.5455 & 0.1807 & 0.2738 \\ 0.0661 & 0.7275 & 0.2065 \\ 0.0476 & 0.0984 & 0.8540 \end{bmatrix}$$

$$\textbf{3HMM B} = \begin{bmatrix} 0.0652 & 0.0067 & 0.0017 \end{bmatrix}$$

Figure 6: Example non-bursty trace: model parameters.

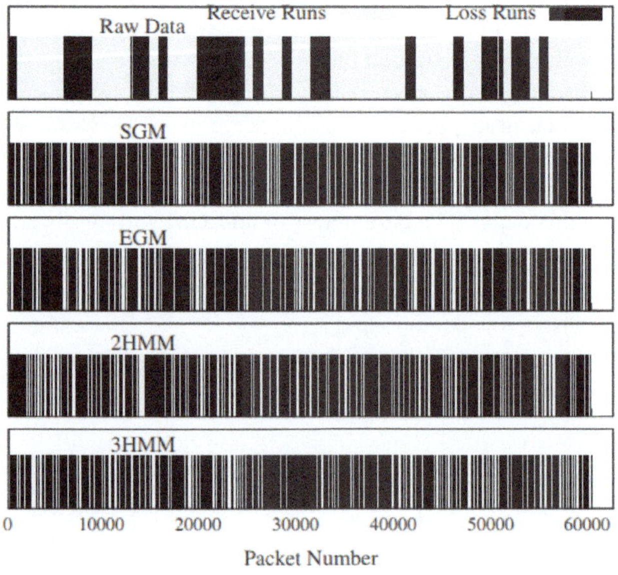

Figure 7: Example bursty trace: original/synthetic loss sequences.

$$\mathbf{SGM} = \begin{bmatrix} 0.9883 & 0.0117 \\ 0.9106 & 0.0894 \end{bmatrix}$$

$$\mathbf{EGM} = \begin{bmatrix} 0.9883 & 0.0117 & 0 & 0 & 0 \\ 0.9062 & 0 & 0.0938 & 0 & 0 \\ 0.9538 & 0 & 0 & 0.0462 & 0 \\ 1 & 0 & 0 & 0 & 0 \\ 1 & 0 & 0 & 0 & 0 \end{bmatrix}$$

$$\mathbf{2HMM\ A} = \begin{bmatrix} 0.703 & 0.297 \\ 0.080 & 0.920 \end{bmatrix}$$

$$\mathbf{2HMM\ B} = \begin{bmatrix} 0.0596 & 0.0000 \end{bmatrix}$$

$$\mathbf{3HMM\ A} = \begin{bmatrix} 0.6652 & 0.1400 & 0.1948 \\ 0.0562 & 0.7283 & 0.2155 \\ 0.0343 & 0.0946 & 0.8711 \end{bmatrix}$$

$$\mathbf{3HMM\ B} = \begin{bmatrix} 0.1128 & 0.0011 & 0.0001 \end{bmatrix}$$

Figure 8: Example bursty trace: SGM, EGM, and HMM parameters.

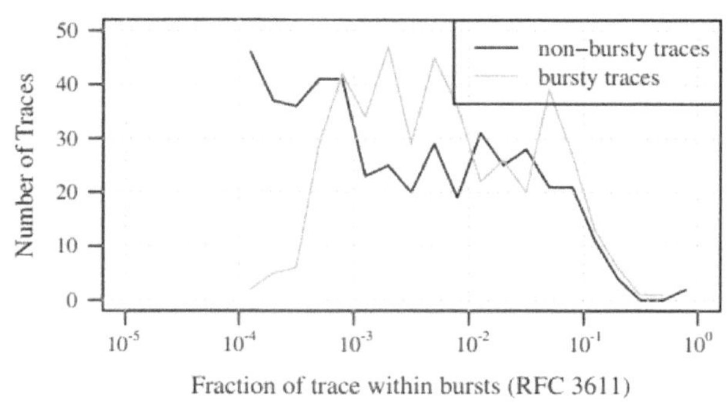

Figure 9: Distribution of trace burstiness, using metric from [23].

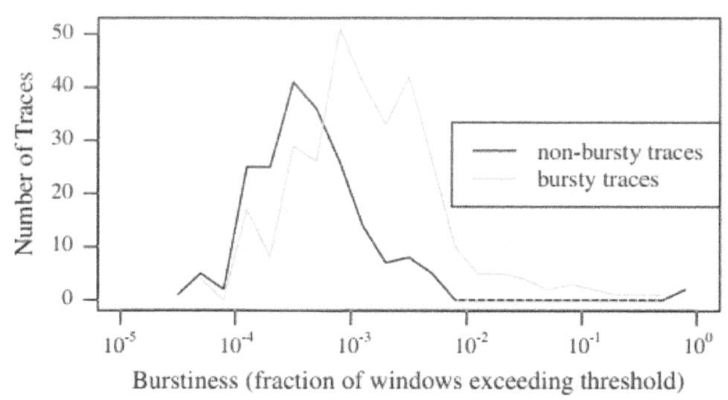

Figure 10: Distribution of trace burstiness, using metric from [24].

Returning to Fig. 5, we see that the synthetic packet loss sequences generated by the SGM, EGM, 2HMM, and 3HMM are comparable to the non-bursty packet loss in the measured trace. This indicates that these models are suitable for this type of loss behaviour, matching results from previous work [6], [16] and [8]. Fig. 7 shows a sequence with bursty periods of loss in the raw data, with long runs of received packets between them. In this case, however, it is apparent that the SGM, EGM, 2HMM, and 3HMM generate synthetic packet loss sequences that differ significantly from the measured trace.

There is no clear link between the burstiness of traces and experimental variables such as time of day. As discussed in [10], some of the measured links showed evidence of time-of-day variation in loss behaviour, although others do not. Moreover, since there are variations in behaviour within some of the traces, we choose to perform further analysis at a per-trace level.

Evaluation using Parametric Bootstrap

Fig. 5 and Fig. 7 give a clear visual representation of the goodness-of-fit of the models to the original data, but do not provide a quantitative measure of accuracy. To quantify model accuracy, we need a procedure to test how well the original data is captured by the model. That is, we need a numeric measure of the goodness-of-fit for the models.

To do this, we adapt a commonly used statistical technique known as *bootstrapping*. This proceeds as follows. We first estimate model parameters from each trace, using the process described in [16] for the SGM and EGM, and the *R* package *hmm.discnp* [25] for the 2HMM and 3HMM. Then, we use these parameters to generate a large number of synthetic sequences from each model (in our case, we use 1000 sequences, a typical choice). We then calculate a set of statistics, *S*, relating to each generated sequence, as described in Section 4.3. For each of these statistics S_k, the values obtained from calculating the S_k on each of the synthetic sequences are used to produce a distribution, S_k^{synth}, which is compared to S_k^{raw} (the value of S_k obtained from the raw data). This is a similar approach to [26], which tested the "curvature" of distributions when testing for long-tailed behaviour in Internet traffic. Since this technique generates new sequences using the parameterised models, we refer to it as *parametric bootstrap*, in contrast to traditional bootstrap techniques which involve resampling from within the existing data[27].

To assess the model's goodness-of-fit, we test the null hypothesis that the observed value of S_k^{raw} is a typical draw from the distribution S_k^{synth}. If the null hypothesis is not rejected, this suggests that the model offers a good fit to the data, since the realisations of the fitted model are similar to the observed data (always in terms of the summary statistic S_k). We test this hypothesis by calculating a central 95% confidence interval and checking if S_k^{raw} falls into that interval. This is equivalent to a hypothesis test at significance level 5% where the probability of rejecting the null hypothesis given that the null hypothesis is true is 5%[28]. Although setting 5% is a typical choice for statistical hypothesis testing, a larger significance level which leads to a narrower interval does not alter our results considerably. Goodness of fit results are presented in Section 4.4.

Choice of statistics for parametric bootstrap

The parametric bootstrap aims to measure the accuracy by which the models describe the observed packet loss processes, and must therefore be based on packet loss metrics. We calculate two metrics of packet loss: the mean packet loss fraction and the run-length distributions of lost and received packets (loss run-lengths are defined as the number of packets lost in a row, while receive run-lengths are defined as the number of packets received in a row; analysing both these metrics together is necessary, since they give insight into packet loss correlation). The former measures the total level of packet loss experienced in each trace, while the latter describes the loss patterns in the traces. These metrics form the base from which we calculate the statistics needed for parametric bootstrap.

The set of statistics, S , calculated from our raw and synthetic sequences and used for parametric bootstrap is therefore: the mean packet loss rate over the whole trace; the 5th, 25th, 50th, 75th, and 95th percentiles of the receive run-length distribution; the mean, median, and maximum loss run-lengths; and the number of receive runs in each order of magnitude (i.e., number of runs of order $10^0, 10^1, 10^2, 10^3, 10^4, 10^5$ packets).

These statistics include the loss and receive run-length distributions to assess whether the loss patterns of the raw data are matched by the models. They cover a large range of the receive run-length distribution, along with the key points of the loss run-length distribution (which is less variable). Since the receive run-lengths can range from very short (i.e., single packets) to tens of thousands of packets within a single trace, it is important that the models can capture this range. To test this, we count the number of receive run-lengths in each order of magnitude. Statistics related to the run-length distributions have been chosen, since in previous work we found the run-lengths to be a key factor in explaining the effect of packet loss on real-time applications [24].

We use these empirical metrics to describe the run-length behaviour in the traces, rather than attempting to fit probability distributions to the loss and receive run-length observations, because they can be more fairly compared between different sequences. Indeed, it is not clear which distribution is appropriate, or even whether it is possible to describe the empirical run-length distributions with any single well-known probability distribution. For example, when the loss run-lengths of two different sequences are characterised by different distributions (e.g., one showing Poisson-distributed loss run-lengths, and the other showing geometrically distributed loss run-lengths), it is unclear how they should be compared. This is especially true since loss run-lengths might be characterised by a mixture of such distributions. Another reason against fitting the run-lengths to a distribution is that the degree of fit would also have to be taken into consideration, alongside the estimated distribution parameters. For the purposes of parametric bootstrap, we feel that using empirical metrics which can be simply calculated and compared between sequences is most appropriate.

Results of parametric bootstrap

Goodness-of-fit results from applying the parametric bootstrap technique with 1000 synthetic sequences per model to the SGM, EGM, 2HMM, and 3HMM models are shown in Fig. 11a for the 486 non-bursty traces, and Fig. 11b for the 433 bursty traces in the dataset. These figures show, for each statistic S_k (y -axis), the number of traces where the model had good fit to the packet traces, in terms of S_k. Visually, for each statistic, bars that extend further right mean that the corresponding model offers a good fit to that statistic in more traces. We see that:

- All models capture the mean loss rate, offering a good fit for both the bursty and non-bursty traces.
- In terms of the receive run-lengths, the SGM, EGM, 2HMM, and 3HMM all perform poorly, i.e., offer a good fit to a relatively small number of traces, for the bursty traces, and only a little better for the non-bursty traces (recall from the example in Fig. 7 that bursty loss was not well captured by these models). Interestingly, there are differences between the models for different types of trace. The SGM and EGM appear to capture the receive run-lengths better in the non-bursty traces, while the 2HMM and 3HMM are slightly better for short receive run-lengths in the bursty traces. Since the 2HMM and 3HMM aim to capture the changes in loss states, they perform slightly better in bursty traces. This extra complexity does not help when the loss pattern is not bursty.
- The patterns in the loss run-length results are similar for both non-bursty and bursty traces (with better performance on non-bursty traces, as expected). The SGM and EGM perform particularly well, capturing mean and median of the loss run-lengths for most traces. The 2HMM and 3HMM capture the mean loss run-length less well, although they do capture the median (since most loss bursts consist of a single packet, the median loss run-length is likely to be 1; even in bursty periods, individual loss runs are short, but fall close together). Although loss run-length statistics are well-captured, this does not mean the trace is accurately modelled (since receive run-length statistics are not well-captured by the models), and can lead to loss patterns that are quite different to the raw data, as seen in Fig. 7.

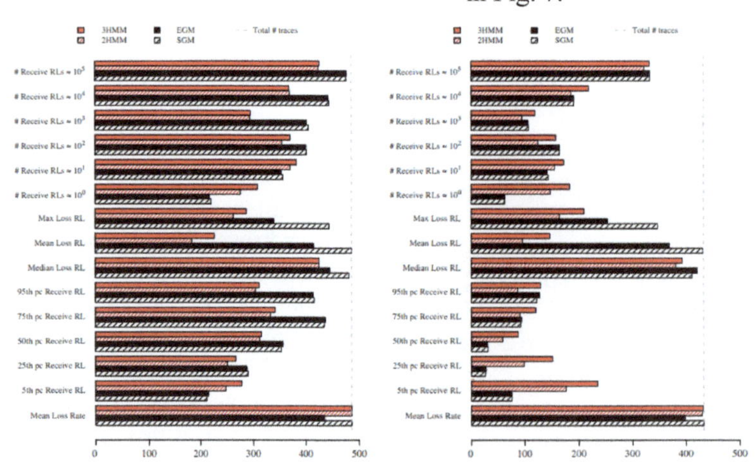

(a) non-bursty traces (out of 486 traces)

(b) bursty traces (out of 433 traces)

Figure 11: Parametric bootstrap results (loss models).

To summarise, the parametric bootstrap results show that although the SGM, EGM, 2HMM, and 3HMM perform adequately on certain types of traces and in terms of some metrics, they do not accurately capture the loss patterns of the most bursty traces (as illustrated by the example in Fig. 7). Although bursty packet loss does not occur in all traces, over 10% of traces were classified as bursty. The implications of this loss behaviour for the performance of streaming video are too important to be ignored, since bursty packet loss severely degrades the performance of the FEC schemes needed to ensure acceptable video quality at residential receivers [24].

To understand the real-world performance of such schemes, and more generally, to understand end-to-end video quality, it is important to ensure that the packet loss simulation used in testing is accurate. The results shown in this section have illustrated that the existing packet loss models studied here are inaccurate in the presence of bursty packet loss (such as that seen on residential ADSL and Cable networks). Therefore, an alternative modelling approach that is more capable of modelling bursty packet loss is needed to better understand FEC performance and the overall video quality experienced by residential Internet users.

A NEW TWO-LEVEL MODEL FOR PACKET LOSS

Section 4 showed that the existing models cannot accurately model the bursty packet loss behaviour seen in some of our traces. To improve the models, we begin with the observation that periods of bursty loss are often associated with network congestion in environments using drop-tail queues, and that the location of those queues within the network will influence the degree of statistical multiplexing of flows, and hence the impact of loss bursts on individual flows. Both the nature and location of the loss event is important.

We hence propose a new *two-level* model that explicitly considers the congestion state of the network, and the location of congestion within the network, to more accurately model bursty loss. This model is similar to the layered model outlined in [29], which divides traces into separate sub-traces based on loss rate. However, our model differs in the following ways. First, we explicitly consider the bursty nature of packet loss, rather than just the overall loss rate. Second, we incorporate additional delay information captured in the measurement data [10] to give insight into the causes of loss. Finally, the outer states of our model were chosen specifically to model the location of congestion within the network, rather than being purely data-driven. Our new model uses the combination of packet loss and delay information to obtain a more accurate picture of the network conditions. Understanding the relationship between delay and loss is important because packet delay gives insight into the likely location of congestion within the network, potentially allowing us to distinguish losses due to congestion and queue overflow in the core network, from losses caused by other factors (e.g., electrical noise on the last mile link).

In our two-level model, the outer states represent the network state (i.e., congested or uncongested) and the location of the congestion, while the inner states capture the packet loss process. Although it is possible that several of these conditions might occur at the same time (e.g., both edge and core congestion), we focus on the *dominant* loss mode, allowing us to represent the current network conditions as one of the outer states of the model. For example, given that a single flow makes up a relatively higher fraction of the traffic at the network edge than it would in the core, congestion at the edge is likely to have a more dominant effect than congestion elsewhere.

In this two-level approach, the trace being used to train the model is split up into fixed duration windows, and the outer state for each window is explicitly chosen by applying a simple classification algorithm to the loss and delay data (described in Section 5.1). The window duration was one second, chosen to balance the need to capture the dynamics of the system while including enough data points within a single window to train the inner model; investigating the effects of different window durations is for future work. Self-transitions between the outer states are possible, allowing the model to capture the situation where conditions stay the same for an extended period of time. The transitions between outer states are modelled as a Markov chain, and the transition probabilities are estimated by counting the number of transitions between windows of each outer state. The parameters of this outer model, therefore, can be represented as a transition probability matrix, A_{outer}:

$$\mathbf{A_{outer}} = \begin{bmatrix} p_{uu} & p_{ue} & p_{uc} \\ p_{eu} & p_{ee} & p_{ec} \\ p_{cu} & p_{ce} & p_{cc} \end{bmatrix} \tag{5}$$

More formally, the probability of moving from outer state α to outer state β is calculated using the number of transitions from α to β,$n_{\alpha\beta}$, and the total number of transitions fromα, n_α, as in Eq. (6) (following [30]):

$$\mathbf{A_{outer}}[\alpha, \beta] = \frac{n_{\alpha\beta}}{n_\alpha} \tag{6}$$

The observation sequence Z_i from all windows classified as being in a particular outer state is used to calculate the parameters of the inner packet loss model for that outer state, as discussed in Section 5.2.

Classification schemes to identify outer states

Fig. 12 illustrates an example of the two-level model, with three outer states (corresponding to different conditions on the underlying network), and inner models to capture packet loss within each outer state. The outer states for the model correspond to the different sources of packet loss along the end-to-end path that our measurement data traversed:

- *access link noise*, where issues with the physical layer cause IP-layer packet loss;
- *edge congestion*, where queue overflows at the ISP edge (i.e., DSLAM or CMTS) cause packet loss; and
- *core congestion*, where queue overflows occur at routers within the core IP networks.

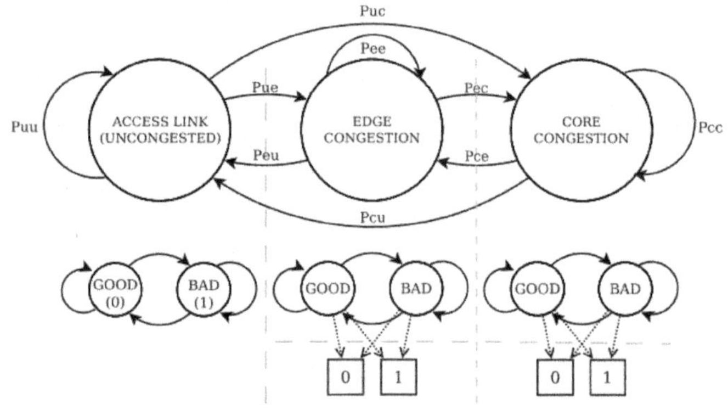

Figure 12: Two-level model, SGM/2HMM/2HMM configuration.

In terms of the physical effects seen in the data, access link noise will cause low levels of uncongested loss regardless of the levels of delay. Edge congestion will cause higher levels of loss, which will be associated with higher delay since the building queues at edge routers will noticeably increase queueing delay *DQ* due to the low levels of statistical multiplexing expected on edge links. Core congestion will also cause higher loss, but without the noticeable effect in *DQ* since higher statistical multiplexing at core routers means that the effects of queueing on *DQ* will be less obvious at the receiver. These intuitive insights into the effects of congestion on packet loss and delay form the basis of the classification schemes presented here.

We consider two classification schemes for the outer states. One is based on fixed thresholds for loss and delay (the *ld* classifier), while the other looks for increasing trends in queueing delay before loss (the *ldbl* classifier).

Both classifiers consider fixed one-second windows of trace data, and in each window examine the number of losses (N), number of loss bursts (M), and median *DQ* ($\widetilde{DQ}$). Other schemes for classification are possible, and due to the two-level nature of the model, could be used in place of the classifiers we consider.

The *ld* classifier is described in Algorithm 1. It uses thresholds for N and M to identify periods of high loss, which indicate congestion, and another threshold for $\widetilde{DQ}$ to distinguish between core and edge congestion.

The loss thresholds (N>2 or M>2indicating congestion) are chosen based on the assumption, backed up by analysis of our dataset, that non-congestive loss is unlikely to create more than two separate loss events with a one second window, and that a loss burst of longer than two packets is likely to be due to congestion.

The $\widetilde{DQ}$ threshold (5 ms) is also based on examination of the trace data; traces with non-bursty loss typically exhibit *DQ*<5 ms. These thresholds are based on the dataset in [10], and while we expect them to be valid for residential ADSL and Cable links of the type we have measured, some calibration may be needed before they can be applied to other sorts of network.

```
if (state = "uncongested") then
  if (N > 2) or (M > 2) then        #"high loss"
    if (DQ~ > 5 ms) then        #"elevated DQ"
      state ← "edge congestion"
    else
      state ← "core congestion"
    end if
  end if
else
  if (N ⩽ 2) and (M ⩽ 2) and (DQ~ ⩽ 5 ms) then
    state ← "uncongested"
  end if
end if
```

Algorithm 1: Loss/Delay (ld) classifier

The *ldbl* classifier is described in Algorithm 2. It is a generalisation of the *ld* classifier, that no longer uses a fixed $\widetilde{DQ}$ threshold to distinguish between edge and core congestion. Instead, when congestion is identified (as before, when N>2 or M>2), *ldbl* looks at the median *DQ* from packets immediately before the loss event ($\widetilde{DQ}_{BL}$), and compares this against $\widetilde{DQ}$. If $\widetilde{DQ}_{BL}$ is more than twice $\widetilde{DQ}$ (i.e., delays preceding losses are elevated above the average), then the window is classified as edge congestion; otherwise, the window is classified as core congestion. In the core congestion state, *DQ* does not give insight into congestion, so if N and M fall below their thresholds, the state returns to uncongested. However, in the edge congestion state, *DQ* is important; so, an extra check is needed to test for the slow fall in delay observed when the congested queue empties (i.e., at an ISP-edge router). Once the losses from congestion have stopped and $\widetilde{DQ}$ has fallen within 10% of the $\widetilde{DQ}$ in the last uncongested state ($\widetilde{DQ}_{UC}$), the state switches back to uncongested. To do this, in Algorithm 2, we test $\widetilde{DQ} \leqslant k\widetilde{DQ}_{UC}$, where k=1.1. This tolerance of 10% is chosen to prevent the model remaining in a congested state for longer than necessary, simply because the delay has not fallen to precisely the pre-congestion level. A final addition to the *ldbl* classifier is to test for cases when *DQ* increases *before*any losses are observed (e.g., to detect the increase in queue lengths at the edge router). If a sudden increase in *DQ* is detected within a window (defined as 25% of the difference between maximum and minimum *DQ* for the whole trace), the window is classified as showing edge congestion. This threshold was chosen based on examples of such sudden increases in the dataset.

```
if (state = "uncongested") then
  if (N > 2) or (M > 2) then        #"high loss"
    if (DQ~_BL > 2DQ~) then        #"elevated DQ"
      state ← "edge congestion"
    else
      state ← "core congestion"
    end if
    DQ~_UC ← DQ~
  end if
else if (state = "edge congestion") then
  if (N ⩽ 2) and (M ⩽ 2) and (DQ~ ⩽ kDQ~_UC) then
    state ← "uncongested"
  end if
else if (state = "core congestion") then
  if (N ⩽ 2) and (M ⩽ 2) then
    state ← "uncongested"
  end if
end if
```

Algorithm 2: Loss/Delay Before Loss (ldbl) classifier

The thresholds chosen for the classifiers are appropriate for this dataset. Applying these classification algorithms to other network scenarios may require a different choice of thresholds. When choosing these thresholds, it is important to select values that can be used to distinguish between different network states. For example, understanding typical rates of uncongested packet loss are necessary when choosing thresholds for N and M. Further work might develop ways to self-configure the threshold values, by looking at the patterns in the loss and delay time-series. The requirement of such techniques is that they must be able to identify between the different outer states of the model.

Parameter choice for inner states

The outer states of the model correspond to different network conditions (core congestion, edge congestion, and access link noise), modelled as a three-state Markov chain. Within each outer state, an inner packet loss model is used to model the observed loss processes.

The inner model can be either a SGM or a 2HMM, as described in Section 3. The two configurations used for the inner models are SGM/SGM/SGM, where packet loss is modelled by an SGM in each outer state, and SGM/2HMM/2HMM, where the outer states potentially subject to congestion are modelled by a 2HMM. Since Section 4 showed that non-bursty loss is well-modelled by the SGM, it is suitable for uncongested loss due to access link noise. The SGM/2HMM/2HMM configuration tests whether using HMM s*within* the pre-classified states also improves performance. Configurations using the EGM or 3HMM are also possible, but based on the results in Section 4 we believe they would offer little benefit, while being significantly more complex.

PERFORMANCE OF THE TWO-LEVEL MODEL

In Fig. 13, we present sample results using the two-level model on the example bursty packet loss trace shown in Fig. 7. The top panel shows the measured trace data, while the lower four panels show synthetic traces generated using different configurations of the two-level model: we use each of the *ld* and *ldbl* classifiers for the outer states with both the SGM/SGM/SGM and SGM/2HMM/2HMM inner models.

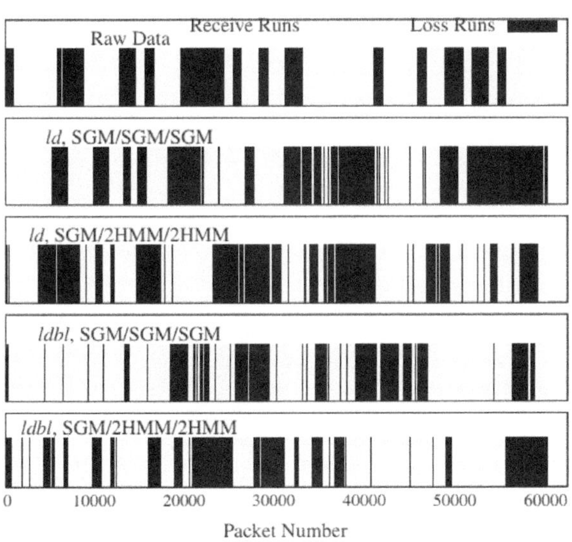

Figure 13: Example bursty trace (two-level loss/delay models).

As the lower panels in Fig. 13 show, the sequences generated by the new models match the bursty nature of the measured data more closely than those from the previous models shown in Fig. 7. We observe that the models show periods of bursty loss, separated by long runs of successfully received packets. This differs from the previous models, which generated losses throughout the trace. It is clear that the receive run-length distributions in bursty traces are more accurately captured by the two-level model than by the simple models.

The model parameters for this example trace are shown in Fig. 14 and Fig. 15 for the two-level models using the SGM/SGM/SGM inner model, and Fig. 16 and Fig. 17 for the two-level models using the SGM/2HMM/2HMM inner model. Observe that in this particular trace, the model switches between the uncongested and core congestion states; neither algorithm has classified any window as showing edge congestion, since the median queueing delay does not exceed the threshold of either classifier. It is also worth noting that for this trace, both classifiers agree on the classification of the outer states, and yield the same transition probability matrix for the outer states. However, this is not the case for all traces, which is why different classification algorithms have different overall performance.

$$\text{Outer States } \mathbf{TPM} = \begin{bmatrix} 0.9263 & 0 & 0.0632 \\ 0 & 0 & 0 \\ 0.1182 & 0 & 0.8818 \end{bmatrix}$$

$$\text{Uncongested } \mathbf{SGM} = \begin{bmatrix} 0.999526 & 0.000474 \\ 1 & 0 \end{bmatrix}$$

$$\text{Edge congestion } \mathbf{SGM} = \begin{bmatrix} 1 & 0 \\ 0 & 1 \end{bmatrix}$$

$$\text{Core congestion } \mathbf{SGM} = \begin{bmatrix} 0.9682 & 0.0318 \\ 0.9071 & 0.0929 \end{bmatrix}$$

Figure 14: Example bursty trace: *ld*, SGM/SGM/SGM.

$$\text{Outer States } \mathbf{TPM} = \begin{bmatrix} 0.9263 & 0 & 0.0632 \\ 0 & 0 & 0 \\ 0.1182 & 0 & 0.8818 \end{bmatrix}$$

$$\text{Uncongested } \mathbf{SGM} = \begin{bmatrix} 0.999526 & 0.000474 \\ 1 & 0 \end{bmatrix}$$

$$\text{Edge congestion } \mathbf{SGM} = \begin{bmatrix} 1 & 0 \\ 0 & 1 \end{bmatrix}$$

$$\text{Core congestion } \mathbf{SGM} = \begin{bmatrix} 0.9682 & 0.0318 \\ 0.9071 & 0.0929 \end{bmatrix}$$

Figure 15: Example bursty trace: *ldbl*, SGM/SGM/SGM.

$$\text{Outer States } \mathbf{TPM} = \begin{bmatrix} 0.9263 & 0 & 0.0632 \\ 0 & 0 & 0 \\ 0.1182 & 0 & 0.8818 \end{bmatrix}$$

$$\text{Uncongested } \mathbf{SGM} = \begin{bmatrix} 0.999526 & 0.000474 \\ 1 & 0 \end{bmatrix}$$

$$\text{Edge congestion } \mathbf{2HMM\ A} = \begin{bmatrix} NA & NA \\ NA & NA \end{bmatrix}$$

$$\text{Edge congestion } \mathbf{2HMM\ B} = \begin{bmatrix} NA & NA \end{bmatrix}$$

$$\text{Core congestion } \mathbf{2HMM\ A} = \begin{bmatrix} 0.674 & 0.326 \\ 0.112 & 0.888 \end{bmatrix}$$

$$\text{Core congestion } \mathbf{2HMM\ B} = \begin{bmatrix} 0.1057 & 0.0092 \end{bmatrix}$$

Figure 16: Example bursty trace: *ld*, SGM/2HMM/2HMM.

$$\text{Outer States } \mathbf{TPM} = \begin{bmatrix} 0.9263 & 0 & 0.0632 \\ 0 & 0 & 0 \\ 0.1182 & 0 & 0.8818 \end{bmatrix}$$

$$\text{Uncongested } \mathbf{SGM} = \begin{bmatrix} 0.999526 & 0.000474 \\ 1 & 0 \end{bmatrix}$$

$$\text{Edge congestion } \mathbf{2HMM\ A} = \begin{bmatrix} NA & NA \\ NA & NA \end{bmatrix}$$

$$\text{Edge congestion } \mathbf{2HMM\ B} = \begin{bmatrix} NA & NA \end{bmatrix}$$

$$\text{Core congestion } \mathbf{2HMM\ A} = \begin{bmatrix} 0.674 & 0.326 \\ 0.112 & 0.888 \end{bmatrix}$$

$$\text{Core congestion } \mathbf{2HMM\ B} = \begin{bmatrix} 0.1057 & 0.0092 \end{bmatrix}$$

Figure 17: Example bursty trace: *ldbl*, SGM/2HMM/2HMM.

The performance of the different configurations of the two-level model is shown in Fig. 18a and b, which show the results of applying parametric bootstrap with 1000 synthetic sequences to the 486 non-bursty and 433 bursty traces identified earlier. These demonstrate the improved modelling accuracy shown in Fig. 13 over all the traces. As before, the performance of the models on the non-bursty traces is better than for the bursty traces. However, the two-level models also show improved performance in terms of all the metrics, for both non-bursty and bursty traces, with more traces offering a good fit for these models than the previous models. For comparison, examine the number of traces where the model offers a good fit for the existing loss models in Fig. 11 with those inFig. 18.

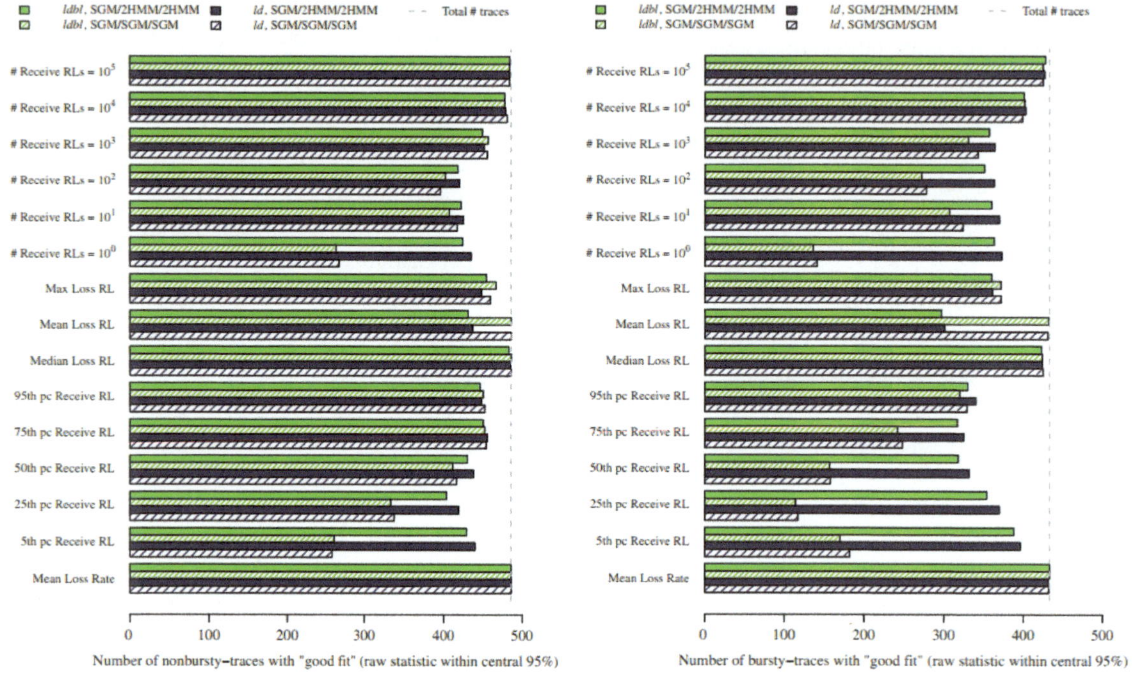

(a) non-bursty traces (out of 486 traces)

(b) bursty traces (out of 433 traces)

Figure 18: Parametric bootstrap results (two-level loss/delay models).

Both the *ld* and *ldbl* classifiers appear to have similar performance. However, the choice of inner model configurations has a large impact on the performance of the two-level model. The SGM/SGM/SGM configuration improves slightly on the single-level SGM, EGM, and HMMs using only loss data, although the percentiles of the receive run-length distribution are still not well-modelled in the majority of traces. However, the two-level models using the SGM/2HMM/2HMM configuration show much improved performance over the previous models, with the majority of traces being well-modelled in terms of every statistic of interest (and many showing over 75% of traces as well-modelled). This is because they more accurately capture the different states in packet loss, and use the most appropriate model for each (i.e., SGM for uncongested, and 2HMM for congested periods).

To quantify the improvement obtained from the new models, we use a metric showing the performance of each model M relative to the SGM. The metric of model improvement is calculated for each S_k as in Eq. (7):

$$\mathcal{I}_{S_k}(\mathcal{M}) = \frac{\#traces\ with\ good\ fit\ for\ S_k(\mathcal{M})}{\#traces\ with\ good\ fit\ for\ S_k(SGM)} \quad (7)$$

Model improvement averaged over all S_k, denoted by $\overline{\mathcal{I}}(\mathcal{M})$, is calculated as in Eq. (8), and shown in Fig. 19:

$$\overline{\mathcal{I}}(\mathcal{M}) = \frac{\sum_{i=1}^{n} \mathcal{I}_{S_k}(\mathcal{M})}{n} \quad (8)$$

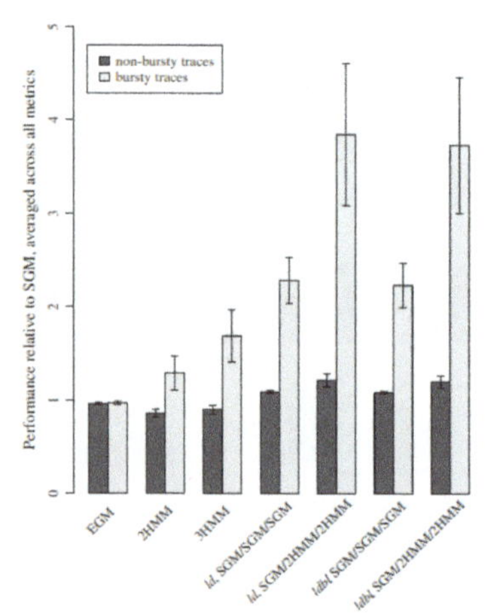

Figure 19: Performance improvement of new models, relative to SGM.

The results shown in Fig. 19 demonstrate the difference between non-bursty and bursty traces, showing that while only a slight improvement is obtained by using the two-level model for the non-bursty traces, the improvement is much larger for bursty traces. The two-level models (SGM/SGM/SGM configuration) produce a good fit in roughly twice as many bursty traces as the SGM (on average). With the SGM/2HMM/2HMM configuration, almost four times as many bursty traces are well-modelled compared to the SGM.

These results show that the two-level delay/loss models (using the SGM/2HMM/2HMM configuration) are more accurate than the previous single-level SGM, EGM, or HMMs. For the traces previously identified as non-bursty, the two-level models with the SGM/2HMM/2HMM configuration are suitable in almost all cases. In terms of the bursty traces, most of which were poorly modelled by the previous models, the two-level models again show a clear improvement, as illustrated in the example of Fig. 13. Looking at the percentiles of the receive run-length distribution (which the previous models failed to model accurately), the importance of the choice of inner model configuration is made clear. Two-level models with the SGM/SGM/SGM configuration perform better than the single-level SGM and EGM models for all the receive run-length percentiles, but not as well as the HMMs for the 5th and 25th percentiles. However, by using the SGM/2HMM/2HMM configuration, the performance is better than the single-level SGM, EGM, and HMMs, for all the statistics. In terms of the computational complexity and estimation time, we note that since the two-level model treats the different outer state separately, parameter estimation is often faster than when using the HMMs. This is due to the simpler SGM estimation procedure used for the uncongested portions of the trace; the more time consuming HMM estimation process is only applied to the portions of the trace classified as showing congestion.

APPLICATION TO MODELLING FEC EFFECTIVENESS

Forward error correction (FEC) can be used to maintain video quality in IPTV applications[31]. These typically use FEC at the application level, adding redundant packets to the media stream that can be used to repair packet loss. The effectiveness of FEC is highly dependent on the packet loss characteristics of the network. Therefore, it is important to tune the FEC parameters to suit the network conditions to maximise the FEC recovery rate while minimising the bandwidth overhead. With ongoing commercial deployment of multicast IPTV service to residential Internet users, it is becoming important to understand how to tune FEC parameters to suit such services. In particular, it is important to understand how the loss patterns of ADSL and cable access links differ from more widely studied backbone network links, and how this impacts media quality and user experience.

Section 6 showed that the two-level model is more accurate in modelling packet loss statistics than previous models. In this section, the two-level model is applied to model the performance of FEC, and the accuracy of this model for FEC performance is compared to the single-level SGM and uniform random loss, using input packet loss sequences generated by these models. This is important since FEC performance can be evaluated using packet loss models, rather than requiring full measurement traces (provided that the models induce similar FEC performance to the raw data). Since the SGM is already widely used for this purpose (e.g., [18], [32], [33], [5] and [4]), this section demonstrates that the two-level model is more suitable when simulating the packet loss patterns of residential broadband networks.

Comparing models to raw data

To compare performance of the models when evaluating FEC effectiveness, we follow the same experimental procedure as described in [24], where simulations of the OpenFEC library were conducted using the packet loss traces described in Section 4. Here, we compare the performance of the best performing FEC scheme in OpenFEC, Low-Density Parity Check (LDPC) codes [34], using two different parameter settings. As in [24] we evaluate FEC recovery using the performance evaluation tool of OpenFEC, eperftool. Our aim is to compare the improved accuracy of the two-level model, when predicting FEC performance, compared to previous approaches (e.g., using uniform random packet loss, or generating loss sequences using the SGM).

To demonstrate the improved accuracy of the two-level models using FEC as an example application, the FEC performance results obtained from these synthetic sequences are compared to the results obtained from the original raw data. For each trace, this gives FEC performance measured from:

- the original raw trace data, showing measured packet loss;
- a synthetic trace subject to uniform random loss, with a loss probability matching the average loss probability seen in the raw trace data;
- a synthetic sequence calculated using the SGM with model parameters derived from the raw trace data; and
- a synthetic sequence calculated using the *ld*, SGM/2HMM/2HMM model with parameters derived from the raw trace data.

The FEC performance from each of the models is compared to the performance calculated on the raw data, to assess the accuracy of the models, in terms of simulating FEC repair performance.

Improved accuracy of two-level models

Fig. 20 compares the performance of FEC obtained from the loss traces (as discussed earlier) against FEC performance results using synthetic data from (1) uniform random packet loss; (2) packet loss generated by the SGM model; and (3) packet loss generated by the *ld*, SGM/2HMM/2HMM model. The metric for performance is *FEC effectiveness*(i.e., number of source packets repaired divided by number of source packets lost). This is used instead of residual loss rate, as it better illustrates performance differences between the models.

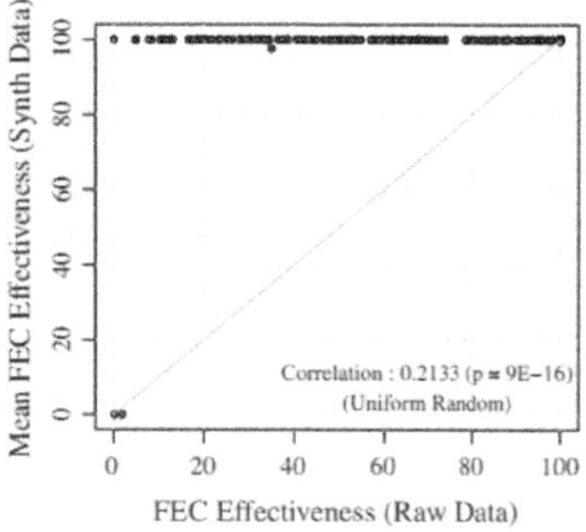

(a) Uniform Random

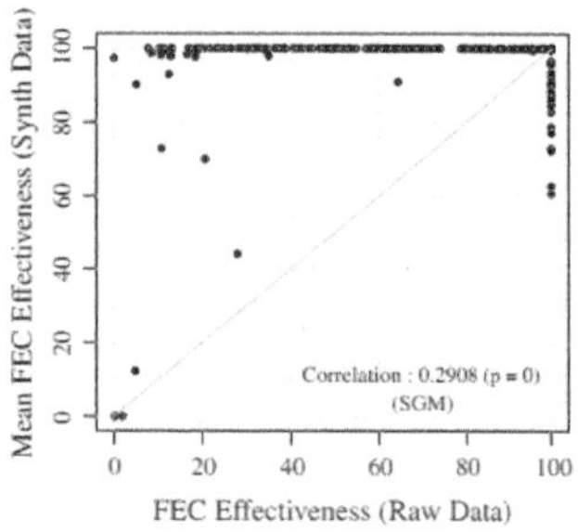

(b) SGM

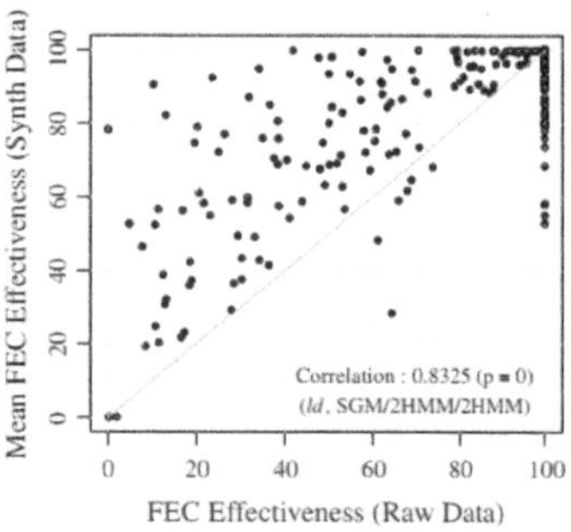

(c) *ld*, SGM/2HMM/2HMM

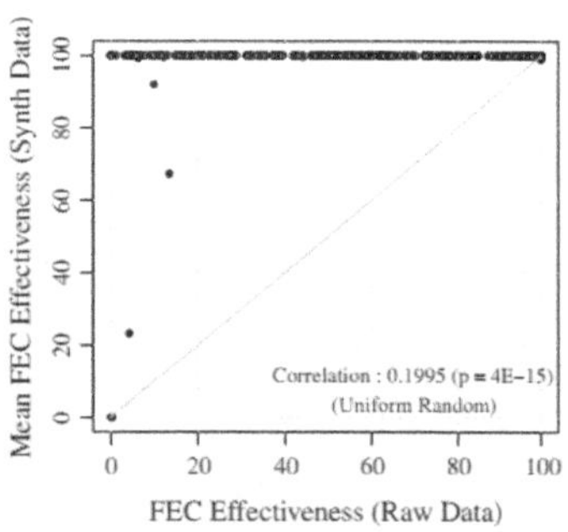

(d) Uniform Random

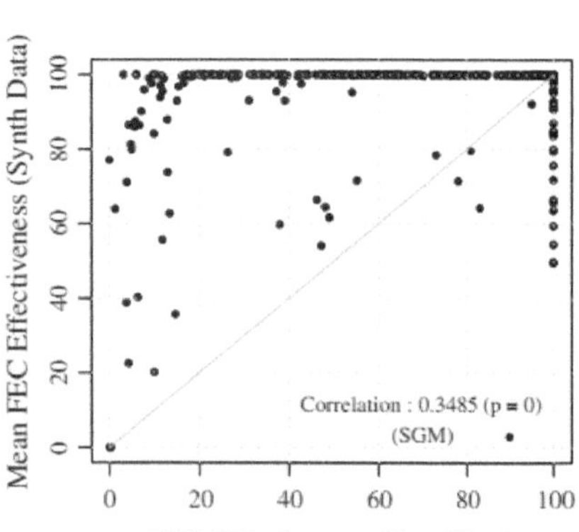

(e) SGM

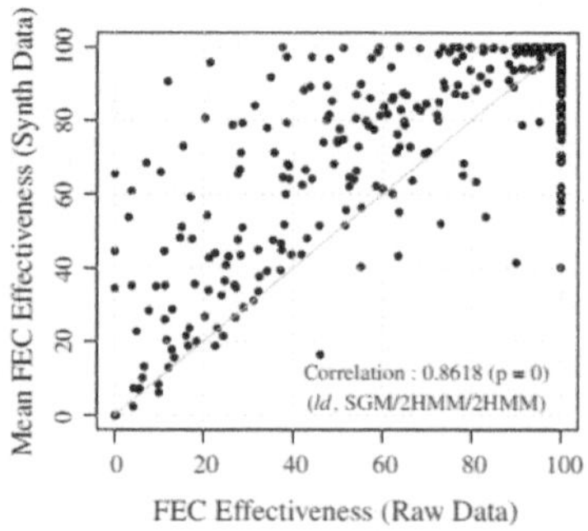

(f) *ld*, SGM/2HMM/2HMM

Figure 20: FEC performance on raw and synthetic data (top row: LDPC (k=67,r=33); bottom row: LDPC(k=80,r=20)).

From each raw data trace, ten synthetic sequences were generated (within eperftool for uniform random loss model, using the approach described in Section 4 for the single-level SGM, and the approach described in Section 5 for the two-level *ld*, SGM/2HMM/2HMM model). Each point on the scatter plots in Fig. 20 represents a measurement trace, and shows the FEC effectiveness obtained from the raw data (x-axis), and the mean of the FEC effectiveness obtained from the 10 synthetic sequences. This demonstrates the typical FEC performance that would be obtained from simulation using these models. If the models perfectly matched the raw data, the points would fall on a 45° diagonal line. Deviations from this line show the extent to which the FEC performance obtained from the models is different to that obtained from the raw data.

The left column of Fig. 20 shows the results from uniform random loss, the middle column shows results from the SGM model, and the column on the right shows results from the *ld* , SGM/2HMM/2HMM model. The top row shows results from the LDPC (k=67,r=33)scheme, and the bottom row shows results from LDPC (k=80,r=20).

From Fig. 20a and d, it is clear that the FEC performance obtained by simulating uniform random loss is quite different from that in the real data. This is as we have discussed in[24], but is visible in the line present across the top of Fig. 20a and d, corresponding to the case where the synthetic sequence resulted in 100% FEC recovery, while the original raw data sequence was not fully recovered. Fig. 20b and e show that the performance of the SGM is only slightly better than using uniform random loss. The lines of points representing 100% recovery is also present for the SGM. In contrast, the *ld*, SGM/2HMM/2HMM model, as shown in Fig. 20c and f, tends to generate synthetic sequences that show FEC performance closer to the measured data, with the points clustering nearer to the 45° diagonal.

The vertical line around x=100 on the plots for the SGM and *ld*, SGM/2HMM/2HMM models indicates cases where 100% recovery was achieved in the original trace, while the synthetic trace resulted in lower recovery. In these cases, the model appears to be somewhat pessimistic about the FEC performance. However, looking at the correlation between raw FEC effectiveness, and mean synthetic FEC effectiveness (displayed on each plot), it is clear that the two-level model is more accurate, with correlation of over 0.8. This is a strong improvement over the correlation of ~0.2 (for uniform random loss) and ~0.3 (for the SGM).

Compared to the uniform random loss model, and the widely used single-level SGM model), it is clear that the two-level model we propose gives more accurate, but not perfect, FEC performance results. This suggests that our two-level model is more suitable for simulation of FEC performance on video streaming over residential broadband networks.

APPLICATION TO OTHER NETWORK SCENARIOS

To apply the two-level model presented in this paper to different network scenarios, with characteristics that differ significantly from the residential broadband links we studied, it is necessary to understand the conditions of the network to be modelled. There are two elements to this: analysing the system architecture to consider the possible sources of packet loss and the reasons for this loss (i.e., the outer states of the model), and collecting measurement traces of the network. Analysis of the traces (using packet loss and delay measurements, as discussed in Section 5, or other relevant metrics) can then be used to assist in developing a classification algorithm to identify the network state.

To apply the two-level model as presented in Section 5, with the same outer states, it would be sufficient to study the measurement traces for the new type of network, and develop a suitable classifier to determine the congestion state of the network from the measurements. This might be as simple as choosing appropriate thresholds to use with the algorithms presented in Section 5.1. Following this, the next step would be to estimate the model parameters from the trace data, and apply the same model evaluation procedure described in Section 4.4. Scripts to generate synthetic traces using all of the packet loss models studied in this paper are available at http://martin-ellis.net/research/loss-modelling. These synthetic traces can then be used to evaluate the two-level model (in the configuration described in Section 5, or a different one), once appropriately tuned, to simulate network behaviour for performance evaluation of applications.

The two-level model described in this paper can be directly used to evaluate the behaviour of other applications on residential broadband networks. The parameter files and scripts needed to generate synthetic trace data for such networks have also been made available at http://martin-ellis.net/research/loss-modelling. Application of these parameters will allow simulation of typical loss characteristics of ADSL and cable networks of the type we measured, and will hence allow application performance on such networks to be evaluated.

It may be more difficult to directly simulate loss behaviour of other environments, such as WiFi or mobile networks, since the model parameters we calculate for residential broadband links will not match those environments. Nonetheless, the two-level model approach outlined here could be reused. Through analysis of the possible network conditions and empirical measurement, the two-level model framework presented in this paper could be used in future work to simulate both the longer-term changes in network behaviour through the outer states of the model, and the short-term, correlated packet loss behaviour using the inner models. In this case, different classification algorithms might be used, and could even consider using not just packet loss and delay data, but also available bandwidth, capacity, or jitter estimates. An interesting avenue for future work would be the application of online classification algorithms to learn the network conditions associated with different environments, and use these to improve the simulation of more diverse scenarios.

RELATED WORK

Related models have been proposed to model frame errors in wireless networks. These include a four-state Markov chain model, which includes separate states for long and short loss and receive run-lengths [35]. The thresholds for long and short are defined in terms of the physical-layer characteristics of the wireless channel, making this approach hard to directly apply to Internet losses. The Markov-based trace analysis (MTA) [36]technique uses a data-preconditioning approach, similar to our pre-classification of network state, aiming to classify frame error traces from GSM networks into lossy or loss-free sub-traces, then concatenating and modelling these separately.

In [37], the MTA approach and other Markov models were evaluated against a new alternative, the extended on/off model (modelling loss and receive runs with lengths derived from mixtures of geometric distributions). The results of [37] show that the extended on/off model improves modelling accuracy, although only a single trace was used throughout the evaluations making it unclear that the results hold in general. In another comparison study [38], the performance of the SGM, the four-state Markov-chain model, and the MTA technique are compared using error measurements from DVB-H networks. This latter study concluded that the good performance and relative simplicity of the four-state model makes it well-suited for simulation of DVB-H errors. However, since their approach relied on manually estimating model parameters, it is difficult to scale up for large-scale use.

Hidden *Semi-Markov* Models (HSMMs), were applied to validate estimates of Internet packet loss from PlanetLab measurements [39]. HSMMs extend HMMs, considering the packet loss process as an alternating on/off process (i.e., loss and receive runs), but allowing the run-lengths to be drawn from non-exponential distributions (unlike HMMs, where run-lengths are drawn from an exponential distribution). This approach is more general than the HMMs we consider, although the parameter estimation is more complex. However, future work could use an HSMM model within our two-level model, possibly further improving performance.

CONCLUSIONS AND FUTURE WORK

In this paper, we evaluated the accuracy of commonly used packet loss models using traces measured from residential access networks, and found that they are insufficient to capture the bursty loss conditions present on such networks. We introduced a new two-level model that more accurately captures these loss conditions. The results of Section 6show that our new model performs better than the previous widely-used models (SGM, EGM, 2HMM, and 3HMM) across all types of traces. Our two-level model uses a three-state outer Markov chain to model network state, with inner loss models to capture packet loss processes. Combining the simplicity of the SGM for non-congestive loss, and the extra power of HMMs for capturing bursty, congestive loss, the SGM/2HMM/2HMM inner model configuration has been shown to accurately model measured packet loss on a range of residential ADSL and cable links.

Accurate simulation of packet loss relies on understanding the end-to-end path the traffic is likely to take (e.g., across the Internet, over the ISP backbone, through an access router and finally across an ADSL or cable modem link). By measuring the end-to-end performance on a representative link, and using this to train the two-level packet loss model we have proposed, realistic simulation results can be obtained. This is demonstrated in Section 7, which compared the performance of FEC simulations to real data, showed that the two-level model we propose provides better accuracy than previous models.

Although this study has focused on the use of the two-level model in residential broadband networks, it is possible to apply it to other network types, as discussed in Section 8. An important element of this would be to understand the different sources of loss in the network to be modelled, and capture these in the outer states of the two-level model. For example, an 802.11 wireless link can be expected to have very different behaviour than an ADSL link, so the single outer state representing edge congestion in our model might need to be replaced with multiple states to model different link behaviours. This type of extension can be done within the framework of the two-level model we have defined.

An interesting area for future work would be to add on-line classification algorithms, to deduce the outer states dynamically according to observed data (and similarly to choose the correct combination of models for the inner states). Such an approach would require a significant new effort, including collection of a large quantity of additional trace data from multiple types of networks, development of new classification algorithms, and thorough validation of the technique. However, it would also represent a significant advance in improving the accuracy of network models.

Our results show that future work on simulating FEC performance on networks with bursty packet loss, such as the residential broadband we have measured, would benefit from using the two-level model rather than the single-level SGM. Another potential use for the new models is in adaptive FEC, where the receiver uses the classification and modelling mechanisms presented in Section 5 as input to a control loop which determines which FEC parameters should be used (e.g., similar to [40]). For example, the ratio of video data to FEC could be adjusted, so that a higher video bit-rate can be offered while network conditions are good, while more error resilience is available when conditions degrade. The issues involved in the design and optimisation of such a system are an interesting direction for future work.

ACKNOWLEDGEMENTS

This work was supported in part by a gift from The Cisco University Research Program Fund, a corporate advised fund of Silicon Valley Community Foundation, and by the UK Engineering and Physical Sciences Research Council (Grant Nos. EP/P50418X/1 and EP/L005255/1). Thanks to Maurizio Filippone for advice on the use of parametric bootstrap.

REFERENCES

1. Cisco, Visual Networking Index: Forecast and Methodology, 2012– 2017, White Paper, 2013.
2. T. Stockhammer, Dynamic adaptive streaming over HTTP – standards and design principles, in: Proceedings ACM MMSys, ACM, San Jose, CA, USA, 2011.
3. E. Gilbert, Capacity of a burst-noise channel, Bell Syst. Tech. J. 39 (1960).
4. P.U. Tournoux et al., On-the-fly erasure coding for real-time video applications, IEEE Trans. Multimedia 13 (2011).
5. S.-R. Kang, D. Loguinov, Modeling best-effort and FEC streaming of scalable video in lossy network channels, IEEE/ACM Trans. Netw. 15 (2007).
6. M. Yajnik, et al., Measurement and modelling of the temporal dependence in packet loss, in: Proc. IEEE Infocom, 1999.
7. H. Sanneck, G. Carle, A framework model for packet loss metrics based on loss runlengths, in: Proc. SPIE/ ACM MMCN, 2000.
8. K. Salamatian, S. Vaton, Hidden Markov modeling for network communication channels, in: Proc. ACM SIGMETRICS, 2001.
9. P. Salvo Rossi et al., Joint end-to-end loss-delay hidden Markov model for periodic UDP traffic over the internet, IEEE Trans. Signal Proc. 54 (2006).
10. M. Ellis, et al., End-to-end and network-internal measurements of real-time traffic to residential users, in: Proc. ACM MMSys, 2011.
11. M. Ellis, et al., Modelling packet loss in RTP-based streaming video for residential users, in: Proc. IEEE LCN, 2012.
12. H. Schulzrinne, et al., RTP: A Transport Protocol for Real-Time Applications, IETF, 2003 (RFC 3550).
13. S. B. Moon, et al., Estimation and removal of clock skew from network delay measurements, in: Proc. IEEE Infocom, 1999.
14. M. Ellis, Understanding the Performance of Internet Video over Residential Networks, Ph.D. thesis, University of Glasgow, 2012.
15. O. Hohlfeld, Statistical Error Model to Impair an H.264 Decoder, Master's thesis, Technische Universität Darmstadt, 2008.
16. W. Jiang, H. Schulzrinne, Modeling of packet loss and delay and their effect on real-time multimedia service quality, in: Proc. NOSSDAV, 2000.
17. S. Tao et al., Real-time monitoring of video quality in IP networks, IEEE/ACM Trans. Netw. 16 (2008).
18. P. Frossard, FEC performance in multimedia streaming, IEEE Commun. Lett. 5 (2001).
19. E.O. Elliott, Estimates of error rates for codes on burst-noise channels, Bell Syst. Tech. J. 42 (1963).
20. L.R. Rabiner, A tutorial on hidden Markov models and selected applications in speech recognition, Proc. IEEE 77 (1989).

21. W. Wei et al., Continuous-time hidden Markov models for network performance evaluation, Perform. Eval. 49 (2002).
22. F. Silveira, E. de Souza e Silva, Predicting packet loss statistics with hidden Markov models, Perform. Eval. Rev. 35 (2007).
23. T. Friedman, R. Caceres, A. Clark, RTP Control Protocol Extended Reports (RTCP XR), IETF, 2003 (RFC 3611).
24. M. Ellis, et al., Performance analysis of AL-FEC for RTP-based streaming video traffic to residential users, in: Proc. Intl. Packet Video Workshop, 2012.
25. R. Turner, L. Liu, hmm.discnp: hidden Markov models with discrete non-parametric observation distributions, 2012 (R package v. 0.1-8).
26. A.B. Downey, Evidence for long-tailed distributions in the internet, in: Proc. ACM IMW, 2001.
27. M.R. Chernick, Bootstrap Methods: A Practitioner's Guide, John Wiley & Sons, 1999.
28. J.S. Bendat, A.G. Piersol, Random Data: Analysis and Measurement Procedures, third ed., John Wiley & Sons, 2000.
29. S. Tao, R. Guérin, On-line estimation of internet path performance: an application perspective, in: Proc. IEEE Infocom, 2004.
30. W. Zucchini, I.L. MacDonald, Hidden Markov Models for Time Series: An Introduction Using R, Chapman & Hall, CRC, 2009.
31. M. Luby, T. Stockhammer, M. Watson, Application layer FEC in IPTV services, IEEE Commun. Mag. 46 (2008) 94–101.
32. P. Frossard, O. Verscheure, Joint source/FEC rate selection for quality-optimal MPEG-2 video delivery, IEEE Trans. Image Process. 10 (2001).
33. C. Neumann, et al., Impacts of packet scheduling and packet loss distribution on FEC performances: observations and recommendations, in: Proc. ACM CoNEXT, 2005.
34. V. Roca, et al., Low Density Parity Check (LDPC) Staircase and Triangle Forward Error Correction (FEC) Schemes, IETF, 2008 (RFC 5170).
35. Y. Yu, S. L. Miller, A four-state Markov frame error model for the wireless physical layer, in: Proc. IEEE WCNC, 2007.
36. A. Konrad et al., A Markov-based channel model algorithm for wireless networks, Wirel. Netw. 9 (2003).
37. P. Ji et al., Modeling frame-level errors in GSM wireless channels, Perform. Eval. 55 (2004).
38. J. Poikonen, J. Paavola, Error models for the transport stream packet channel in the DVB-H link layer, in: Proc. IEEE ICC, 2006.
39. H. X. Nguyen, M. Roughan, Rigorous statistical analysis of internet loss measurements, in: Proc. ACM SIGMETRICS, 2010.
40. F. Silveira Filho, et al., Adaptive forward error correction for interactive streaming over the internet, in: Proc. IEEE Globecom, 2006.

CHAPTER 13 EFFICIENT CLUSTERING ROUTING ALGORITHM BASED ON OPPORTUNISTIC ROUTING

Fan Wang[1], Yan Yang[2], Kunpeng Wang[1], Xiaopeng Hu[1], and Ning Zhang[1]

[1] School of Computer Science and Technology, Dalian University of Technology, Dalian, China

[2] School of Computer and Information Technology, Liaoning Normal University, Dalian, China

ABSTRACT

Based on the analysis of the existing classic clustering routing algorithm HEED, this paper proposes an efficient dynamic clustering routing algorithm ED-HEED. In the cluster selection process, in order to optimize the network topology and select more proper nodes as the cluster head, the proposed clustering algorithm considers the shortest path prediction of the node to the destination sink and the congestion situation. In the data transmission procedure, the high-efficiency CEDOR opportunistic routing algorithm is applied into the ED-HEED as the data transmission mode between cluster headers. A novel adaptive dynamic clustering mechanism is also considered into the algorithm, as well as the data redundancy and security control. Our Simulation demonstrates that the ED-HEED algorithm can reduce the energy consumption, prolong the network life and keep the security and availability of the network compared with the HEED algorithm.

INTRODUCTION

With the rapid development of mobile communication, embedded computing and sensing technology, wireless sensor network is considered as a more convenient and economical solution in many scopes [1]. Network topology control is one of the core techniques in wireless sensor network and has always been a research hotspot. Every routing protocol is designed on basis of a specific network topology. Therefore, it's important to organize a better network topology for wireless sensor network [2].

Citation: Wang, F., Yang, Y., Wang, K.P., Hu, X.P. and Zhang, N. (2016) Efficient Clustering Routing Algorithm Based on Opportunistic Routing. Int. J. Communications, Network and System Sciences, 9, 198-208. http://dx.doi.org/10.4236/ijcns.2016.95019

Clustering routing technique have lots of advantages and is becoming the major content in the research of wireless sensor network [3]. It can easily control the network topology. Clustering can also conserve the communication cost and make it convenient for intra-cluster data aggregation. In a clustering algorithm, the network is grouped into a set of clusters. Each cluster has a leader, often referred to as the cluster-head (CH), and many member nodes. However, in a special situation, there is only one single node (CH) in a cluster. Nodes in one cluster only communicate with their respective cluster head. They are in charge of collecting data, transmitting data, and receiving the command from the cluster head. Accordingly, the cluster head is responsible for: 1) Analysis and aggregation of received data. 2) Transmission of the processing result to the sink. In the work [3], researchers prove that clustering algorithm can solve the energy consumption problem better and extend the network lifetime effectively.

LEACH (Low-Energy Adaptive Clustering Hierarchy) [4] is the earliest clustering algorithms in wireless sensor network. Clusters in the network are formed periodically. Cluster head are randomly selected in order to distribute the energy load among the sensors and prolong the network lifetime. In the later research, a number of efficient algorithms are presented based on the idea of LEACH, such as TEEN (Threshold Sensitive Energy Efficient Sensor Network Protocol) [5], DCHS (Deterministic Cluster-head Selection) [6], HEED (Hybrid Energy-efficient Distributed Clustering) [7], etc.

An energy-efficient routing protocol using message success rate in wireless sensor networks is proposed in [8]. Its main idea is to reduce the communication overhead and guarantee the data communication reliability. The algorithm is based on node connectivity and message success rate. However, the complexity of the protocol is higher. In [9], the authors present an energy-efficient and flexible approach using hierarchical agglomerative clustering in wireless sensor networks (DHAC). The protocol only considers one-hop node information to compute the resemblance matrix. The similar nodes are divided into one small cluster. Then, some small clusters are merging into one cluster based on the predefined cluster size threshold. Cluster heads are selected in these clusters. The problem is that the network traffic load is not considered. There still exists unnecessary energy consumption during communication.

In these above algorithms, the network topology is reasonable and cluster heads are well distributed. However, the network performance can still be improved. In this paper, we propose an efficiency dynamic clustering routing algorithm (ED-HEED). We improve HEED protocol including cluster head selection, inter-cluster routing method, re-clustering mechanism, data redundancy and network security control. Compared with HEED protocol, our algorithm reduces the energy consumption, prolongs the network life and keeps the security and validity of the network. This paper is organized as follows. Section 1 is the introduction. In Section 2, we present the existing problem of HEED and our improvement. Section 3 describes the details of the clustering algorithm (ED-HEED). Section 4 discusses the simulation results and evaluates the algorithm performance. We give the conclusion in section 5.

PROBLEM ANALYSIS

HEED Routing Protocol

HEED (Hybrid Energy-efficient Distributed Clustering) [7] protocol is proposed by Younis O and Fahmy S in 2004. During the cluster head selection, the algorithm considers the residual energy as the primary parameter and the intra-cluster communication cost as the secondary parameter. The node with more residual energy has a larger probability to be selected as a cluster head temporally. Then the average minimum reachability power (AMRP) between the candidate and all its neighbors is calculated to measure the communication cost. Thus, the cluster heads are selected more properly and the energy within a cluster is more balanced. The HEED protocol has the following features: a distributed method to select the cluster heads; the cluster head selection phase is within limited iterations; the cluster heads distribution is balanced. The HEED protocol performs faster during the clustering. At the same time, the network topology is reasonable and cluster heads are well distributed.

Problems are still existed in HEED protocol. When a node locates in an area within the range of several different clusters, it will choose a cluster head with the minimal average power. In a practical application, this method may ignore some factors such as the distance between a node and its cluster head, the distance between cluster heads and the sink node and so on. Large amounts of nodes join a cluster within which its cluster head has a long distance from the sink node. So the communication cost of the cluster head is too high. Besides, network traffic also plays an important role in the algorithm.

Improvement of HEED

To overcome the above shortcomings, we improve the HEED protocol by proposing an efficiency dynamic clustering routing algorithm (ED-HEED). During the cluster head selection, we comprehensively consider the residual energy, shortest distance from the node to the sink node and the network traffic congestion. So the clus-ter heads are selected more properly. Then, we uses an opportunistic routing protocol for inter-cluster data transmission. We also present a novel adaptive dynamic re-clustering algorithm, the network security control and data redundancy control mechanism.

ED-HEED Clustering Routing Algorithm

ED-HEED is an efficient dynamic clustering routing algorithm. It is designed with the following ideas. 1) In cluster formation, we consider not only the node residual energy, but also the shortest distance prediction and node traffic congestion. 2) During data transmission phase, cluster member nodes communicate with the cluster head directly, but multi-hop cluster head to cluster head connectivity uses an opportunistic routing protocol (CEDOR [10]).

In order to avoid the fast energy consumption of the cluster heads, we adopt an adaptive dynamic re-clustering mechanism to our ED-HEED. The network will re-clustering when the Sink real-timely detects the energy of some cluster head has dropped below the predefined threshold or the node is invalidate. The strategy will indeed improve the network performance. According to the idea that nodes broadcast HELLO frames to probe network link in traditional dynamic routing protocol (AODV), we use the similar way to detect the working state of each node. In our algorithm, each node periodically broadcasts HELLO frames to all its neighbors to find their working state. Then, we can ensure the security and validity of the network. At the same time, cluster head need broadcast three thresholds to all member nodes for further reducing the redundant data and energy consumption of the member nodes. Actually, we use the simple HELLO frame mentioned above to carry the thresholds value, which will minimize the control message.

Cluster Formation Algorithm

In order to reduce energy consumption more efficiently and guarantee the network security and validity, we consider the shortest distance from node to the base station (the sink node) and traffic congestion as another two parameters during cluster head selection. The probability of becoming a cluster head is modified as follows.

$$CH_{prob} = C_{prob} \times \left(\alpha \times \frac{E_{Residual}}{E_{Max}} + \beta \times DP_i + \gamma \times C_i \right) \qquad \alpha + \beta + \gamma = 1 \tag{1}$$

where α, β and γ are the weights of the current residual energy, shortest distance and node congestion. They can set to different value according to specific situation. In this paper, we don't discuss it much and just make them satisfied the equation $\alpha=\beta=\gamma = 1/3$. $E_{Residual}$ is the estimated current residual energy of the node and E_{Max} is a reference maximum energy. DPi is the prediction of the shortest distance from the node to the sink node.

ED-HEED algorithm uses the multiple priority queue model described in [10] when computed the node congestion. However, we only consider the high priority queue while computing the traffic congestion of the node. The congestion factor, C_i is described as follows.

$$C_i = \sum_{i=1}^{N_H} LH_i \Big/ Buf_H \tag{2}$$

where N_H is the number of packet in the current high priority queue. LH_i is packet length (bit) of the high priority queue. Buf_H is the buffer size (bit) of the high priority queue.

Inter-Cluster Routing Protocol

In the work [10], the algorithm CEDOR (Congestion Control Based on Multi-priority Data for Opportunistic Routing) was proposed. It comprehensively considers the shortest distance from the node to the Sink, the current residual energy and traffic congestion of the node. So we apply CEDOR as the inter-cluster routing protocol. The network security, effectiveness and the data transmission efficiency are all improved.

When we apply CEDOR routing algorithm, there's some work we need to do. Firstly, we define the neigh-bours set of each node, S_{nbr}. Secondly, we compute the delivery utility (DU_i) of each cluster head to find candidate forward node set. Then cluster head broadcasts data to each node in the candidate forward node set. Finally, data is transmitted to the Sink through multi-hop. So after cluster formation phase, each cluster head knows its cluster head neighbour node set and its own depth. During data transmission, the node current congestion is obtained by computing the priority of forwarding data. The pseudo code of cluster head routing algorithm is shown in Figure 1.

Re-Clustering Mechanism

In classical clustering routing algorithms (e.g. LEACH, HEED), clustering occurs after a fixed period. The period is predefined before running the algorithm. However, selecting an appropriate period will directly affect the performance of clustering routing algorithm [11]. The cluster head will die for fast energy consumption if the period is too long. And if the period is too short, frequent clustering will affect the efficiency of data transmission.

To overcome the shortcomings, a novel adaptive dynamic re-clustering mechanism is proposed. Cluster head records its current residual energy (E_{Record}) before stable data transmission. Cluster heads are real-timely monitoring its current energy and compares it with αE_{Record} (we assume that $\alpha = 0.5$). If the current residual energy is less than that, cluster head will send an emergency high priority packet to the Sink which means sending a request for re-clustering. On the other hand, the network also starts re-clustering if some cluster node is found invalidate or dead (see Chapter 3.4). The pseudo code of the re-clustering mechanism algorithm is shown in Figure 2.

Algorithm 5: Cluster Header Routing Algorithm.

```
begin
    Initial the cluster neighbor node set → s_nbr_CH
    if ( s_nbr_CH == Ø)
        Select the Sink as the next hop
    else
        Compute the delivery utility of each cluster header in s_nbr_CH
            DU_i = W_1 × C_i + W_2 × (E_init − E_left)/E_init + W_3 × D_i/D_max
        Compute the expected value of the delivery utility
            DU‾ = (Σ_{j=1}^{N} DU_ij) / N
        for (each V_i ∈ s_nbr_CH)
            if (DU_i < DU‾)
                set priority of V_i according to the DU_i
                CN_CH_i = CN_CH_i ∪ V_i
            endif
        endfor
        // Broadcast packets to the node in CN_CH_i
        Sendbroadcast(packet, CN_CH_i)
        for (each V_i ∈ s_nbr_CH)
            if (V_i's priority is the highest)
                // Broadcast the ACK to the other nodes in CN_CH_i
                Sendbroadcast(ACK, CN_CH_i)
                break
            else
                // Wait the ACK from the nodes whose priority is higher than V_i
                Wait (CN_CH_i)
                if (The node does not receive any packet in a period)
                    // Broadcast the ACK to the other nodes in CN_CH_i
                    Sendbroadcast(ACK, CN_CH_i)
                    break
                endif
            endif
        endfor
    endif
end
```

Figure 1: The cluster header selection pseudo-code

Algorithm 6: The Re-clustering Mechanism Algorithm.

```
begin
    // Record current residual energy locally for every cluster header nodes
    E_Record = E_Left
    for (each V_i ∈ S_CH)
        if ( V_i == Sink)
            // Receive message,and judge whether it is equal to cluster
            GetMessage (msg)
            if (msg == cluster)
                // Sink broadcast synchronization cluster signal to the network
                Sendbroadcast (cluster)
            endif
        else
            if (E_Left ≤ E_Record/2)
                //Request for re-clustering
                SendMessage(cluster, high-priority, Sink)
            endif
        endif
    endfor
end
```

Figure 2: The re-clustering mechanism pseudo-code.

Network Security and Redundancy Control

In wireless sensor network application, nodes may suddenly fail or die for some reason. We need to know their working state real-timely, so we can take measures to make sure the network is validate and secure. Depending on the idea that nodes broadcast HELLO frames to probe network link in traditional dynamic routing protocol (AODV), we use the similar way to resolve the problem. Each node of the network maintains a neighbour connection list and a timer. The neighbour connection list describes the node connectivity with all its neighbours. We assume each node exchanges information with all its neighbours directly. We define a simple HELLO frame and let TTL = 1. Each node broadcasts it to all its neighbour after a fixed period, HELLO_INTERVAL. If a node does receive the HELLO frame from its neighbour, the connectivity between them is certainly normal and the connectivity information will be recorded in its neighbour connection list. The list will update during the running of the network. At last, each node knows the connectivity situation with all its neighbours.

However, if the node doesn't receive any data or the HELLO frame from one of its neighbours after a limited time, ALLOWED_HELLO_LOSS*HELLO_INTERVAL, it's possible that the neighbour node is failed. Then it will immediately send an emergency high priority packet to the sink. Receiving the packet, the sink will take measures to handle it.

After the cluster formation phase, the sink will generate three thresholds (T_{hard1} , $T_{hard\,2}$, T_{soft}) depending on the effective range of the current received sensor data. Then the thresholds will be broadcasted to every node of the network. Where T_{hard1} is the lower bound of the effective range. $_{\text{Thard 2}}$ is the upper bound of the effective range. T_{soft} is the maximum variation range of the sensor data. In general, the threshold information is carried in the above HELLO frame. So extra communication cost is reduced effectively.

During the stable data transmission phase, the first data collected by each node is transmitted to the cluster head respectively and recorded locally as msg_record. After that, each node will compare the current data with the thresholds as follows: the node will send raw data under the condition that the data message is beyond the scope of T_{hard1} to $T_{hard\,2}$ or the difference between the data and the msg_record is bigger than T_{soft} . Otherwise, the node will simply transmits a control packet to cluster head instead of the sensor data. Thus, not only the network function well but also the total number of transmission and reception data and the energy consumption of cluster member node is reduced effectively. However, there's still a serious problem existed which is that if the cluster head didn't receive the data from some member node, it's hard to tell the member node is failed or doesn't need to send data temporarily. To solve this problem, the network security mechanism presented above is applied to failure detection in our ED-HEED algorithm. So the network is running safely and reliably. Figure 3 describes the data redundancy control algorithm.

SIMULATION AND PERFORMANCE EVALUATION

Simulation Setup

The ED-HEED algorithm proposed in this paper is experimented in a simulation platform based on the NS-2 software. We set up our simulation parameters as shown in Table 1. 150 nodes are randomly deployed in a rectangle region of 25 m × 25 m. There is only one base station which is located in the center of the network. The result of the deployment is shown in Figure 4. The little red circle is the normal node and the blue one represents the sink in the figure.

Algorithm 7: Data Redundancy Control Algorithm.

```
begin
    // Record data locally
    msg_record = message
    // Collect data for the first time
    if (fisrt)
        SendMessage (message,CH)
    else
        // Data is beyond the scope of the effective threshold
        if (message < T_Hard1 || message > T_Hard2 )
            SendMessage (message,CH)
        // Data fluctuation is too big than T_Soft
        elseif (abs(message − msg_record > T_Soft))
            SendMessage (message,CH)
        else
            sleep()
        endif
    endif
end
```

Figure 3: Data redundancy control pseudo-code.

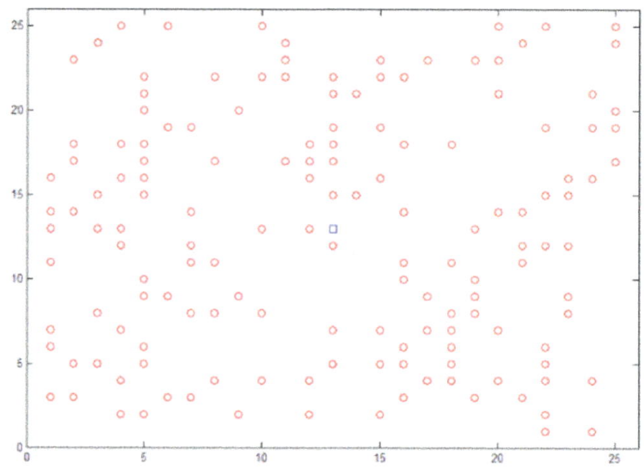

Figure 4: The random deployment of all nodes in the network.

Table 1: Parameter of the experiment

Parameter	Value
Network Size	(0, 0) - (25, 25)
Number of Nodes	150
Coordinates of the Sink	(12, 12)
Initial Energy	50 J
Energy Consumption for Processing One Bit [12]	0.01 J/bit
Amplifier Parameter of Free Space Model [12]	0.01 J/bit/m^2
Amplifier Parameter of Multipath Model [12]	0.0013 J/bit/m^2
Size of Control Packet	64 bit
Size of Data Packet	500 bit

We provide comparison experiments between our ED-HEED clustering algorithm and the HEED algorithm in some aspects of the network performance.

The Comparison of Network Lifetime

Network lifetime has always been one of the most important criterions to evaluate the network performance. The experiment is aiming at the comparison of network lifetime using different algorithms in terms of the number of alive nodes. Our experiments collected the statistical information of the network after a fixed period instead of each round. The energy of each node was monitored continuously. When its initial energy was lost, a node would stop working.

Figure 5 depicts that the number of alive nodes changes over time. From the figure, we can see some nodes had lost all of its energy when time reached 200 s in HEED algorithm. But the phenomenon began at 350 s by our method. ED-HEED algorithm we proposed improves HEED in terms of the cluster formation, inter-cluster transmission, data redundancy control and so on. Therefore, the nodes survive one time longer. The network lifetime is extended effectively.

The Comparison of Energy Balance

We ran HEED and ED-HEED algorithm under the same experimental condition. Once some node died, the residual energy of each node was computed. According to the statistic of the data, we got the distribution of nodes' residual energy which is shown in Figure 6. Where X-axis means the different distributed range of the residual energy and Y-axis is the number of nodes.

The experiment results can measure the energy balance problem. From Figure 6, we can see that half of the nodes in the network have less than 30% of the maximum energy when HEED was adopted. Whereas, there're more than 75% of the nodes in the network in ED-HEED. So our algorithm can achieve energy balance more effectively

The Comparison of Re-Clustering Time Interval and Data Transmission Rate

In this research, we assume that the fixed period between each round is 50 s in HEED. Each re-clustering round schedule is shown in Table 2 as follows.

In ED-HEED, the cluster head won't be reselected until the energy of some cluster head has dropped down for a half. From Table 2, we can draw a conclusion that all nodes were full of energy at the beginning so that the re-clustering time interval was longer. Then the stable data transmission would certainly last for a relative longer time. With time went on, the re-clustering time interval was getting shorter. Thus, the energy consumption is reduced.

Through the above analysis, we know ED-HEED can extend network lifetime effectively and improve the reliability and security. Now we compare the data transmission rate between ED-HEED and HEED. We count the number of packet successfully received within a fixed time to represent the network transmission efficiency. The result is shown in Figure 7.

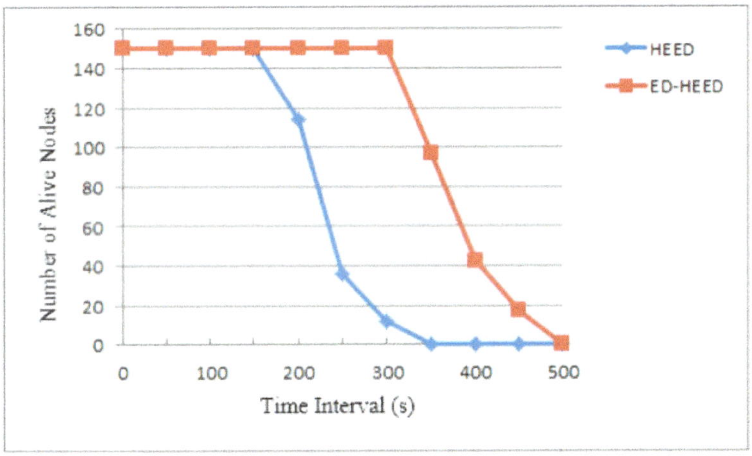

Figure 5: Number of alive nodes diagram.

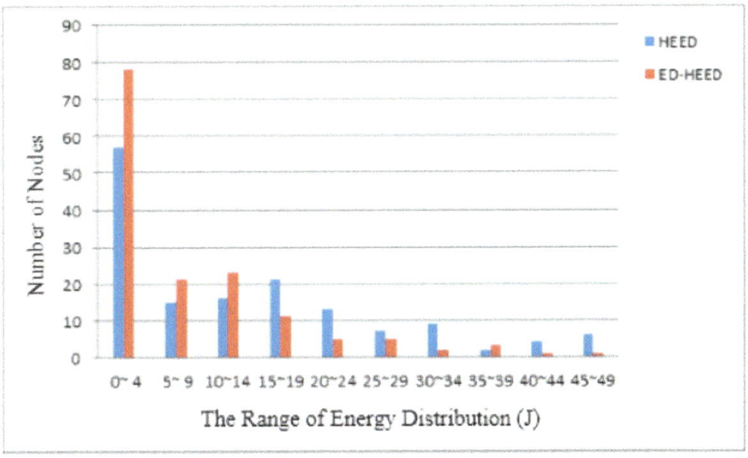

Figure 6: The comparison of residual energy distribution.

Table 2: Each re-clustering round schedule table

Round	1	2	3	4	5	6
HEED	50 s	100 s	150 s	200 s	250 s	300 s
ED-HEED	154 s	268 s	334 s	391 s	428 s	456 s

The Comparison of Transmission Latency

We carry on this experiment to evaluate that ED-HEED algorithm can effectively reduce network transmission latency. So that emergency high priority packets can be sent to the sink as soon as possible. To make the comparison convenient, we randomly selected a cluster head. Let the node send a high priority packet to the sink. Then, we traced the packet and recorded the latency when it arrived at the sink. The result is described in Figure 8.

Figure 8 shows us that ED-HEED has a lower transmission latency than HEED. Therefore, ED-HEED clustering routing algorithm can process the high priority packets perfectly in time. The network security and reliability are guaranteed.

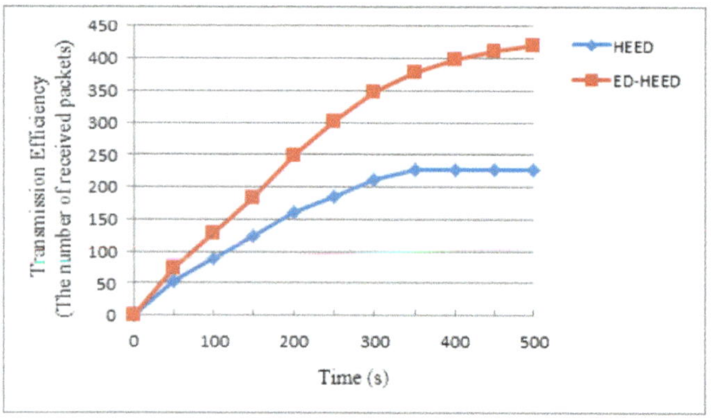

Figure 7: The comparison of transmission efficiency.

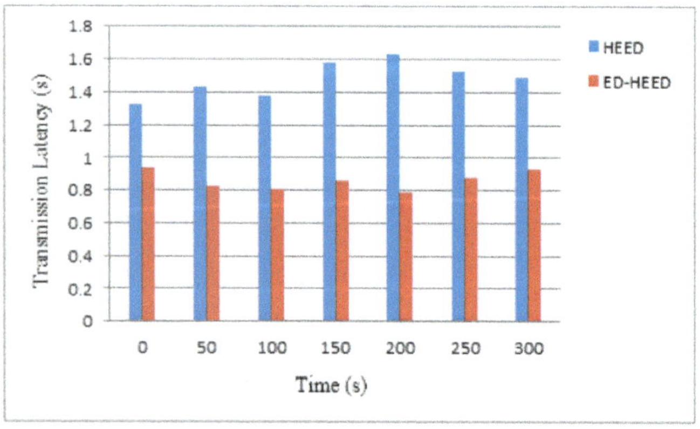

Figure 8: Transmission latency diagram.

The Comparison of Data Redundancy Control

As is known to all, sensor data collected by a single node are always correlated temporally. We gathered the data transmitted by one node every 10 s to evaluate the validity of data redundancy control mechanism. Figure 9 is the analysis diagram of data redundancy control.

From the figure, we can see that there's no difference between ED-HEED and HEED when the node sent data to its cluster head the first time. However, after that, the data gathered by the node hardly changed and stayed stable. So there's no need to send the redundant data to its cluster head. In ED-HEED, only a simple control packet was transmitted to inform the cluster head that the node was operating well. Thus, the data volume is apparently reduced.

CONCLUSION

In this paper, we propose an efficiency dynamic clustering routing algorithm ED-HEED based on comparison and analysis of the existing classic clustering routing algorithm HEED. We improve the algorithm as follows: 1) for the purpose of optimizing the network topology and selecting more appropriate cluster head, we take the prediction of shortest path from the node to the Sink and node congestion into consideration during cluster formation phase. 2) In data transmission phase, the high-efficiency CEDOR opportunistic routing algorithm is applied to ED-HEED as the data transmission mode between cluster headers. 3) We also present a novel adaptive dynamic re-clustering algorithm, the network security control and data redundancy control mechanism. The simulation results demonstrate that ED-HEED is more effective in reducing network energy consumption and extending network lifetime. The transmission latency of high priority packets is also lower and the network is more secure and reliable.

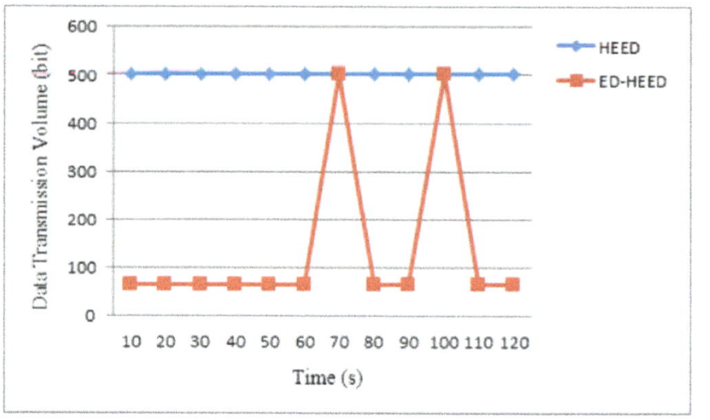

Figure 9: The analysis of data redundancy control.

ACKNOWLEDGEMENTS

This research was supported by "National Natural Science Foundation of China" (No.61272523), "the National Key Project of Science and Technology of China" (No.2011ZX05039-003-4) and "the Fundamental Research Funds for the Central Universities".

REFERENCES

1. Ren, F.Y., Huang, H.N. and Lin, C. (2003) Wireless Sensor Networks. Journal of Software, 14, 1282-1291.
2. Zhao, T., Guo, T.D. and Yang, W.G. (2009) Energy Balancing Routing Model and Its Algorithm in Wireless Sensor Networks. Journal of Software, 20, 3023-3033. http://dx.doi.org/10.3724/SP.J.1001.2009.03384
3. Pantazis, N.A., Nikolidakis, S.A. and Vergados, D.D. (2013) Energy-Efficient Routing Protocols in Wireless Sensor Networks: A Survey. IEEE Communications Surveys & Tutorials, 15, 551-591. http://dx.doi.

org/10.1109/SURV.2012.062612.00084

4. Heinzelman, W.R., Chandrankasan, A. and Balakrishnan, H. (2000) Energy-Efficient Communication Protocol for Wireless Microsensor Networks. Proceedings of the 33rd Annual Hawaii International Conference on System Sciences, Hawaii, 4-7 January 2000, Vol. 2, 10. http://dx.doi.org/10.1109/hicss.2000.926982
5. Manjeshwar, A. and Agrawal, D.P. (2001) TEEN: A Routing Protocol for Enhanced Efficiency in Wireless Sensor Networks. IPDPS, 1, 189. http://dx.doi.org/10.1109/ipdps.2001.925197
6. Handy, M.J., Haase, M. and Timmermann, D. (2002) Low Energy Adaptive Clustering Hierarchy with Deterministic Cluster-Head Selection. 2002 IEEE 4th International Workshop on Mobile and Wireless Communications Network, 368-372. http://dx.doi.org/10.1109/mwcn.2002.1045790
7. Younis, O. and Fahmy, S. (2004) HEED: A Hybrid, Energy-Efficient, Distributed Clustering Approach for Ad Hoc Sensor Networks. IEEE Transactions on Mobile Computing, 3, 366-379. http://dx.doi.org/10.1109/TMC.2004.41
8. Yoon, M., Kim, Y.K. and Chang. J.W. (2013) An Energy-Efficient Routing Protocol Using Message Success Rate in Wireless Sensor Networks. Journal of Convergence, 4, 15-22.
9. Lung, C.H. and Zhou, C. (2010) Using Hierarchical Agglomerative Clustering in Wireless Sensor Networks: An Energy-Efficient and Flexible Approach. Ad Hoc Networks, 8, 328-344. http://dx.doi.org/10.1016/j.adhoc.2009.09.004
10. Ding, N., Tan, G.-z., You, D. and Zhang, W. (2013) Opportunistic Routing Algorithm Based on Topological TimeVarying and Residual-Energy Balance in Wireless Sensor Network. Journal of Electronics & Information Technology, 35, 715-720.
11. Heinzelman, W.B., Chandrakasan, A.P. and Balakrishnan, H. (2002) An Application-Specific Protocol Architecture for Wireless Microsensor Networks. IEEE Transactions on Wireless Communications, 1, 660-670. http://dx.doi.org/10.1109/TWC.2002.804190
12. Rappaport, T.S. (2006) Wireless Communications: Principles and Practice. Prentice Hall PTR.

CHAPTER 14

A COMPARATIVE SIMULATION STUDY OF IP, MPLS, MPLS-TE FOR LATENCY AND PACKET LOSS REDUCTION OVER A WAN

Adewale Adeyinka A[1], Adagunodo Emmanuel R[2], John Samuel N[1], and Ndujiuba Charles[1]

[1]Covenant University, Canaanland, Ota, Nigeria

[2]Obafemi Awolowo University, Ile-Ife, Nigeria

ABSTRACT

The need for improved network performance towards providing reliable services in the face of growing demand on enterprise network and internet service across all sectors of the economy has become very paramount. Latency and packet loss as quality of service (QoS) metrics are issues of concern since different multimedia applications, voice and data packets have to be delivered to end systems over long distances. This study investigated the technology behind the delivery of the packets by comparing the performance of each of IP, MPLS and MPLS-TE on the same congested WAN design. The results showed that MPLS-TE had the least latency and barely any packet loss.

INTRODUCTION

An increase in the number of users and deployment of new applications, memory intensive applications and devices contending for network resources have necessitated the need for improvement in the overall architecture of internet and enterprise networks. Hence, an ever evolving model, technologies and devices to match are needed [1]. The network designer is faced with the challenge of optimizing network performance at lowest cost for maximum operation. IP Networks are used for data exchange on the internet, but in spite of its good functionality; it is no longer enough to provide the needed quality of service for delay sensitive applications. IP packet forwarding analyzes the destination IP address contained in the network layer header of each packet as the packet travels from its source to its final destination. Multiprotocol label switching (MPLS) uses labels which are advertised between routers so that they can build a label-to-label mapping. These labels are attached to the IP packets, enabling the routers to forward the traffic by looking at the label and not the destination IP address that is packets are forwarded by label switching instead of by IP switching resulting in greater speed of delivery of packets [3, 5]. Some of the problems associated with a poorly designed network include congestion, poor mapping of mapping of traffic streams to network resources, poor redundancy and backup links resulting in poor service quality (IP telephony, IP video and wireless communications) in terms of the latency, jilter and loss of packets [2]. Traffic Engineering (TE) can be used to resolve some of these design flaws and improve overall network performance of the Core/Backbone, enterprise topology, branch / WAN, data center, and Internet edge [4]. This research examined the effects of MPLS and traffic engineering (MPLS-TE) on latency and packet loss in a congested WAN (enterprise network) by simulation

Citation: Adewale Adeyinka A, Adagunodo Emmanuel R, John Samuel N, Ndujiuba Charles, A Comparative Simulation Study of IP, MPLS, MPLS-TE for Latency and Packet Loss Reduction over a WAN, doi:10.5923/j.ijnc.20160601.01

study using GNS3. The rest of this paper is divided into four sections. The literature review comes after this section followed by network design in section 3. The section 4 is the implementation followed by a conclusion of the paper.

LITERATURE REVIEW

Routing in IP networks is governed by the need to get the traffic across the network as quickly as possible. That is why IP routing is based on the least-cost routing principle. Every IP routing protocol has a cost associated with the links in the networks. In MPLS, devices that support IP forwarding, the IP routing tables are used to build IP forwarding tables, also called forwarding information base (FIB) [6, 7]. After the IP routing tables have been built, MPLS labels are assigned to individual entries in the IP routing table (individual IP prefixes) and propagated to adjacent MPLS devices through a Label Distribution Protocol (LDP). Every label assigned by an MPLS device is entered as an input label in its label forwarding information base (LFIB), which is the forwarding table used for label switching [9].

Most label assignments, both local as well as those made by adjacent devices, are entered into a table called the label information base (LIB). The label that the IP next-hop assigns for a particular IP prefix is entered as an output label in the local LFIB to enable pure label forwarding. In devices that support IP forwarding, such a label is also entered into the FIB to support IP-to-label forwarding. After the IP routing tables, IP forwarding tables, and label forwarding tables have been built, the MPLS devices can start to forward IP traffic. All MPLS devices must support label forwarding; whenever they receive a labeled packet, they perform a label lookup in the LFIB, replace the input label with the output label, and forward the labeled packet to the next-hop LSR. Some MPLS devices (ingress LSRs) can receive IP datagrams, perform a lookup in the FIB, insert an MPLS label stack in front of the IP datagram based on information stored in the FIB, and forward the labeled packet to the next-hop LSR. The PE router within the MPLS VPN architecture is an example of such a device. Other MPLS devices (egress LSR) can receive labeled packets, perform an LFIB lookup, and (based on the absence of an output label in the LFIB) remove the label from the ingress labeled datagram and forward the IP datagram to the next-hop IP router [11]. MPLS Traffic Engineering (MPLS-TE) is a growing implementation in today's service provider (SP) networks. MPLS adoption in SP networks has increased greatly due to its inherent TE capabilities. The SPs use the MPLS-TE to ensure reliability and fast movement of data over the network, as it essential for SPs to recognize networks which need to be managed, secured and made reliable for the resources of the network for customers [2, 11].

MPLS-TE allows for a TE scheme where the head end router of a label switched path (LSP) can calculate the most efficient route through the network toward the tail end router of the LSP [4, 6, 10]. TE consists of three main steps which are measure, model and control. The operator measures the physical layout of the network which is necessary for tasks like capacity planning and network visualization followed by estimation of possible settings of the links, knowing how much an IGP setting affects the traffic flow. IGP protocol is a routing protocol which is used with the group of IP networks under the control of one entity which gives a common routing policy for the internet [6, 11]. The Cisco IOS IP Service Level Agreements (SLAs) Internet Control Message Protocol (ICMP) echo operation is used to monitor end-to-end response time between a Cisco router and devices using IP. Also, ICMP echo is useful for troubleshooting network connectivity issues. IP SLAs is a portfolio of technology embedded in most devices that run Cisco IOS software, which allows Cisco customers to analyze IP service levels for IP applications and services, to increase productivity, to lower operational costs, and to reduce the frequency of network outages [12].

The law of large numbers (LLN), which states that as an experiment is repeated, the observed frequency of a specific outcome approaches the theoretical frequency of that outcome over an entire population is the statistical concept employed by Traffic Engineering. The LLN when put in telecommunication terms simply means that the overall behavior of a large network can be predicted with reasonable certainty even if the behavior of any single packet cannot be predicted.

If the level of network traffic nears, reaches or exceeds the design maximum, the network is said to be congested. In a telephone network, traffic is measured in call seconds (CCS) or erlangs. One CCS is equal to 100 seconds of telephone time. One erlang is equal to one hour or 36 CCS of telephone time. If a subscriber attempts to send a message or place a call in a congested network, one of three things may occur which includes: rejection, return or loss of a message, the user may receive a busy signal, a message can be placed in a queue and is eventually delivered according to set parameters. The network is said to be in a high-loss condition when message queues become unacceptably lengthy or the frequency of busy signals becomes unacceptably high, one of the major objectives of traffic engineering is to reduce high-loss situations. Under normal circumstances the number of rejected messages or failed call attempts should be as close to zero as possible. Balancing the quality of service against the cost of operation and maintenance of the network are other goals of TE [13].

When multiple TE tunnels have the same cost, traffic can be load-balanced across them. Traffic can also be load-balanced between the native IP path and TE tunnels if the cost of the routing is the same. A times, the load balancing can be unequal cost load balancing hence, the load balancing of traffic is weighted proportionally to the bandwidth requirement of the TE tunnels that is If you have one tunnel with 60 MB and one with 40 MB of reserved bandwidth, the load-balancing ratio is 3:2, or the first tunnel should get one and a half times more traffic than the second tunnel. However, the load-balancing ratio is an approximation, because Cisco Express Forwarding (CEF) has only 16 hash buckets [14]. When an LSR performs the load balancing over one or more IP paths and one or more TE tunnels, it is always equal cost load balancing. This means that every path gets the same amount of traffic. Multiple TE tunnels can be handy when the amount of bandwidth to be reserved between a pair of routers is more than the bandwidth capacity of the links. You can then just create multiple TE tunnels with each a piece of the required bandwidth.

IP routing is a rather general name for an assemblage of protocols that accomplish routing by implementing specific routing algorithm. Routing is the transfer of a packet from a device on one network to a device on a different network. IP routing protocols allow routers to build up forwarding tables that correspond with final destinations and next hop addresses. Some of the routing protocols are: IGRP (Interior Gateway Routing Protocol) which operates within an autonomous system (AS) that is a system under single administration. OSPF (Open Shortest Path First) a link state protocol that uses speed as its metric. RIP (routing Information Protocol) is a distance vector protocol [12, 14].

NETWORK DESIGN/IMPLEMENTATION

It is envisaged that when the core network is congested (flooded) with packets or occurrence of a link failure, there is tendency of high latency in the core network and communication between the layers may become practically impossible over the network. This scenario was created in this design and was used as the basis of comparison of the IPv4 and the label switching techniques and its traffic engineering techniques.

Meanwhile, practice in network designs has shown that a network should be built in a hierarchical and modular way. This is to ensure scalability, redundancy and limitation of the size of failure domains if they occur. The network was designed following the Cisco recommended hierarchical model as in figure1. It utilized a layer 3 routed core to which the other architectural building blocks were connected. Basic layer 3 connectivity were established in the core and between distribution switches before virtualization. MPLS was enabled on all interfaces connected to providers' routers and on all interfaces interconnecting the distribution layer switches and globally in the router configuration. MPLS labels were exchanged for all routes in the routers IPv4 routing table each having its own label protocol. This can be seen from the MPLS forwarding table of any provider edge (PE) router.

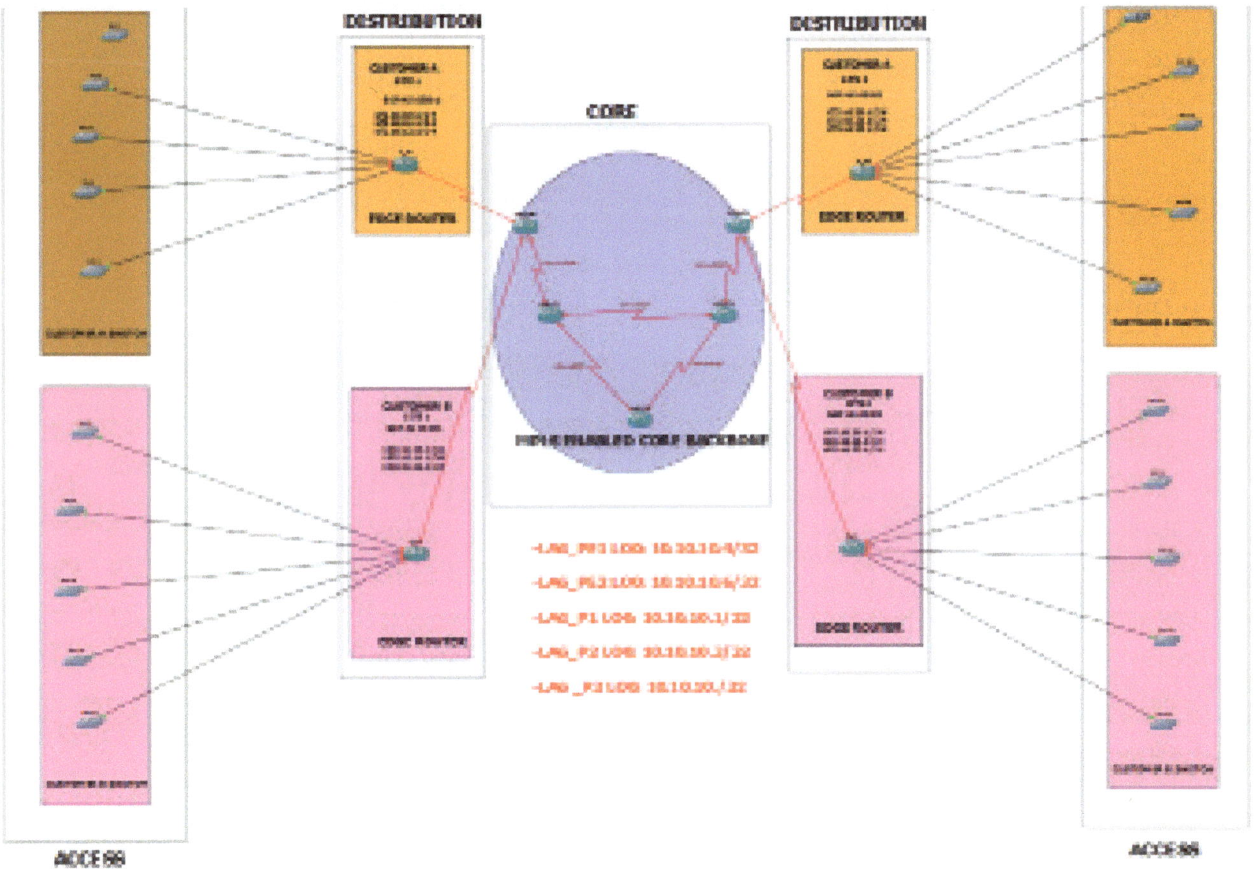

Figure 1: Hierarchical Block diagram.

MPLS forwarding-table build-up is shown in figure 2. Among others, it showed the incoming and outgoing label tags for the packets through each of the router interfaces. For MPLS VPNs to work appropriately, the control plane and data plane have to be successfully built. BGP (Border gateway protocol) was used for the buildup of the control plane. The control plane holds all routes advertised in and into the routing domain. It is chosen because due to its possession of extended communities, larger-than-32bit routes can be sent over the network. In other words, it is capable of carrying overlapping IP addresses unlike other routing protocols.

```
Router#sh mpls forwarding table
Local   Outgoing    Prefix           Bytes tag   Outgoing    Next Hop
tag     tag or VC   or Tunnel Id     switched    interface
16      16          10.10.10.5/32    0           Se1/3       point2point
17      17          10.10.10.3/32    0           Se1/3       point2point
18      20          10.10.10.2/32    0           Se1/3       point2point
19      Pop tag     10.10.10.1/32    0           Se1/3       point2point
20      21          10.1.1.20/30     0           Se1/3       point2point
21      Pop tag     10.1.1.16/30     0           Se1/3       point2point
22      18          10.1.1.8/30      0           Se1/3       point2point
23      Pop tag     10.1.1.4/30      0           Se1/3       point2point
24      Pop tag     10.1.1.0/30      0           Se1/3       point2point
25      22          10.10.10.6/32    0           Se1/3       point2point
Router#
Router#
```

Figure 2: Buildup of MPLS Forwarding table

The core was kept BGP free. In fact, the purpose of the provider P routers is to label switch routes and provide a high speed connection between PE routers. Now that the control plane has been built, the data plane for each virtual network (VRF) was created and then populated. This is done by the creation of VRF instances on the PE/distribution routers and then the mapping of the respective VLANS in each distribution block to the appropriate VRF.

```
Router#sh ip bgp sum
BGP router identifier 172.16.1.2, local AS number 65001
BGP table version is 1,main routing table version 1

Neighbor        V        AS  MsgRcvd MsgSent    TblVer  InQ  OutQ Up/Down  State/PfxRcd
172.16.1.1      4        1        11      11         1    0     0 00:07:43        0
Router#
Router#
```

```
!
router bgp 65001
no synchronization
bgp log-neighbor-changes
neighbor 172..16.10.0 mask 255.255.255.0
neighbor 172..16.11.0 mask 255.255.255.0
neighbor 172..16.12.0 mask 255.255.255.0
redistribute connected route-map bgp_redist
neighbor 172..16.1.1 remote-as 1
no auto-summary
!
ip http server
ip forward-protocol
!
!
!
!
ip access-list standard redist
permit 172.16.11.0 0.0.0.255
permit 172.16.11.0 0.0.0.255
!
route-map bgp_redist permit 10
match ip address redist
!
```

Figure 3: Configuration of BGP customer edge (CE) -PE on Route Reflectors for Control Plane Buildup

Traffic engineering (TE) was enabled globally and on interfaces that were possible candidates for TE paths. Resource reservation protocol (RSVP) as an extension of the resources reservation protocol for traffic engineering was used to reserve resources and indicate nature (bandwidth, jitter, maximum burst) of the packet streams received across the IP network. In MPLS-TE, the command used to establish a tunnel on the network or through routers is MPLS TRAFFIC-ENG TUNNELS which was entered globally and on the interface level. In the IP rsvp band X Y, X states the size of the possible pool and Y states the size of a single traffic flow. The tunnel destination is LAG_PE2 and it has a Loopback interface IP of 10.10.10.6. The 'tunnel mpls traffic-eng priority X Y', X is the set-up priority which was used when signaling an LSP to determine which existing LSP can be pre-emptied, Y is hold priority which was used to determine whether the LSP should be pre-emptied by other LSPs with lower priority. The 'tunnel mpls traffic-eng bandwidth' specified the LSP's bandwidth. Path-option configured the tunnel to use a named IP explicit path or a path dynamically calculated from the traffic engineering topology database as shown in figure 4 and 5, tunnel1 and tunnel 2 respectively. A dynamic path is used if an explicit path is currently unavailable. The 'tunnel mpls traffic-eng AutoRoute announce' command, configured the tunnel interface to be announced into the IGP routing table.

```
LAG_PE1(config)#ip explicit-path name
LAG_PE1(config)#ip explicit-path name LSP1
LAG_PE1(cfg-ip-expl-path)#
LAG_PE1(cfg-ip-expl-path)#next
LAG_PE1(cfg-ip-expl-path)#next-address 10.1.1.13
Explicit Path name LSP1:
    1: next-address 10.1.1.13
LAG_PE1(cfg-ip-expl-path)#next-address 10.1.1.6
Explicit Path name LSP1:
     1: next-address 10.1.1.13
     2: next-address 10.1.1.6
LAG_PE1(cfg-ip-expl-path)#next-address 10.10.10.6
Explicit Path name LSP1:
     1: next-address 10.1.1.13
     2: next-address 10.1.1.6
     3: next-address 10.10.10.6
```

Figure 4: Tunnel 1 (LSP1), Explicit Path Addresses Configuration

In this configurations (that is figure 4 and 5), the IGP is OSPF and all the above configurations were carried out on all LSRs that are possible candidate for TE path-options. Cisco IOS IP Service Level Agreements (SLAs) ICMP echo operation was used to monitor end-to-end response time and troubleshoot network connectivity issues between a router and devices using IP.

```
LAG_PE1(config-if)#int tun 2
LAG_PE1(config-if)#ip unnumbered lo0
LAG_PE1(config-if)#tunnel mode mpls tunnel traffic-eng
LAG_PE1(config-if)#
LAG_PE1(config-if)#tunnel destination 10.10.10.6
LAG_PE1(config-if)#
LAG_PE1(config-if)#
LAG_PE1(config-if)#tunnel mpls traffic-eng priority 3 3
LAG_PE1(config-if)#
LAG_PE1(config-if)#tunnel mpls traffic-eng bandwidth 100
LAG_PE1(config-if)#tunnel mpls traffic-eng path-option 2 explicit LSP2
LAG_PE1(config-if)#
LAG_PE1(config-if)#tunnel mpls traffic-eng autoroute announce
LAG_PE1(config-if)#exit
LAG_PE1(config)#ip explicit-path name LSP2
LAG_PE1(cfg-ip-expl-path)#next
LAG_PE1(cfg-ip-expl-path)#next-address 10.1.1.13
Explicit Path name LSP1:
    1: next-address 10.1.1.13
LAG_PE1(cfg-ip-expl-path)#next-address 10.1.1.2
Explicit Path name LSP1:
     1: next-address 10.1.1.13
     2: next-address 10.1.1.2
LAG_PE1(cfg-ip-expl-path)#next-address 10.10.10.9
Explicit Path name LSP1:
     1: next-address 10.1.1.13
     2: next-address 10.1.1.6
     3: next-address 10.1.1.9
LAG_PE1(cfg-ip-expl-path)#next-address 10.10.10.6
Explicit Path name LSP2:
     1: next-address 10.1.1.13
     2: next-address 10.1.1.6
     3: next-address 10.1.1.9
     4: next-address 10.10.10.6
```

Figure 5: Tunnel 2 (LSP2), Explicit Path Addresses Configuration

RESULTS

Each router was connected using a four port serial link into the slot one 1 space provided. Open Shortest Path First (OSPF) as an open standard routing protocol being implemented by a lot of network vendors was used as routing protocol for this design and the network simulator employed was GNS3. Wireshark was used to monitor packet loss. To increase scalability, the Resource Reservation Protocol (RSVP) was used to automate the procedure. The packets forwarded according to MPLS-TE had a stack of two labels (imposed by the ingress router). The top-most label identifies a specific LSP to use to reach another router at the other end of the tunnel. The second label indicates what the router at the far end of the LSP should do with the packet. By selecting the appropriate LSP, traffic can be directed explicitly. Some of the configurations and tunnels setup are shown below in Figures 6 to 8.

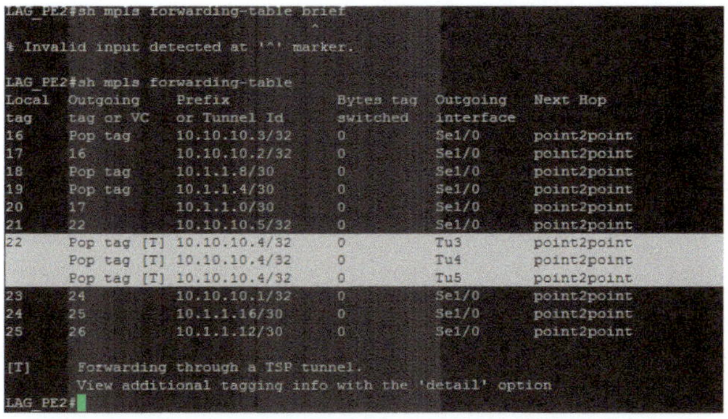

Figure 6: Successful Build-up of Tunnels Across Router Interfaces

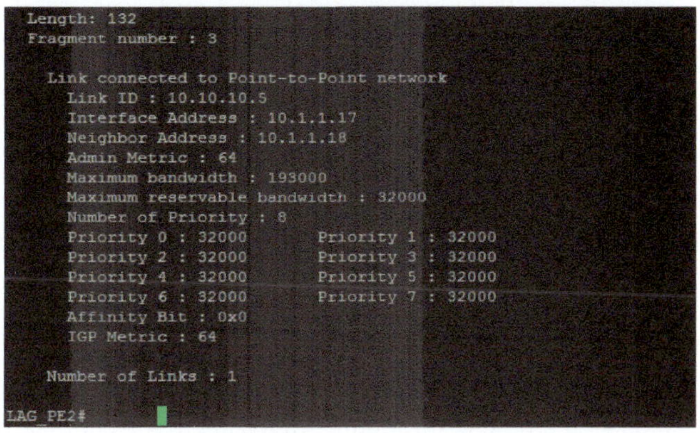

Figure 7: OSPF OPAQUE LSA

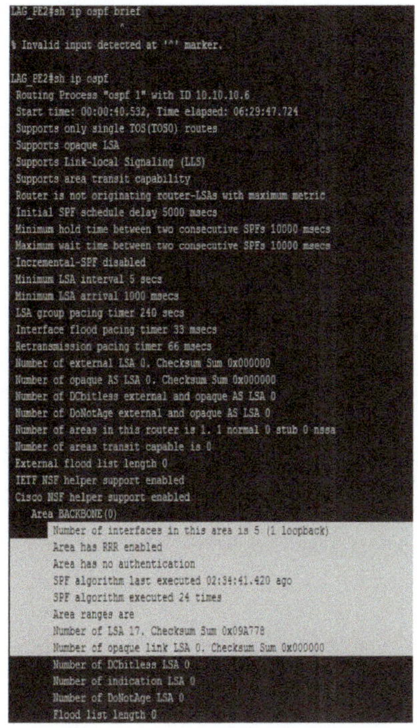

Figure 8: Verifying MPLS-TE for OSPF

This shows the extension of all the operation occurring in the network involving MPLS and MPLS-TE.

The IP, MPLS and MPLS-TE networks were of the same topology and were subjected to the same ping tests. The network in turn was congested with increasing number of packet in the core network and ping tests were carried out to measure the latency (RTT). The results of the ping tests are presented in Table1 below. It should be noted that once an MPLS network is disabled, it operates as an IPv4 network.

Table 1: Values of RTT and Packet loss for each Network Protocol

	Packets in the Core Network	IP Network	MPLS Network	MPLS-TE Network
RTT in ms	18000	1785	1934	1148
	15000	1778	1894	1015
	10000	1405	1562	681
	5000	777	880	574
	100	204	260	214
Packet Loss	18000	260	290	000
	15000	170	280	000
	10000	030	060	000
	5000	000	000	000
	100	000	000	000

The graphical views of the results are illustrated graphically in Figure12 and Figure13.

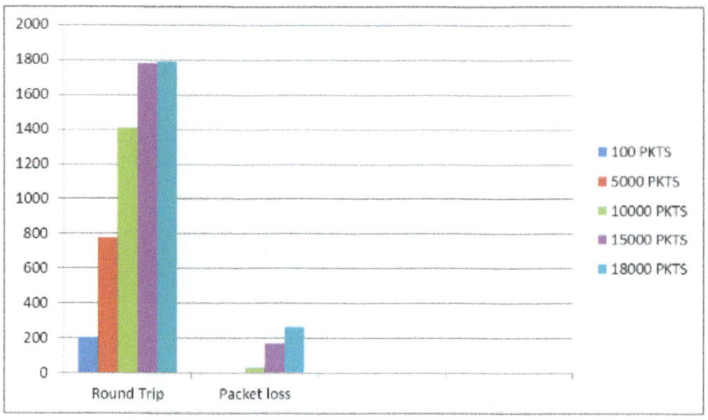

Figure 9: Latency and Packet Loss of IP Network

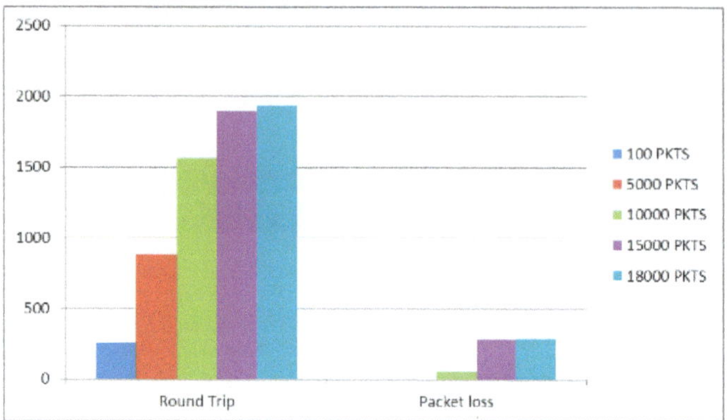

Figure 10: Latency and Packet loss of MPLS

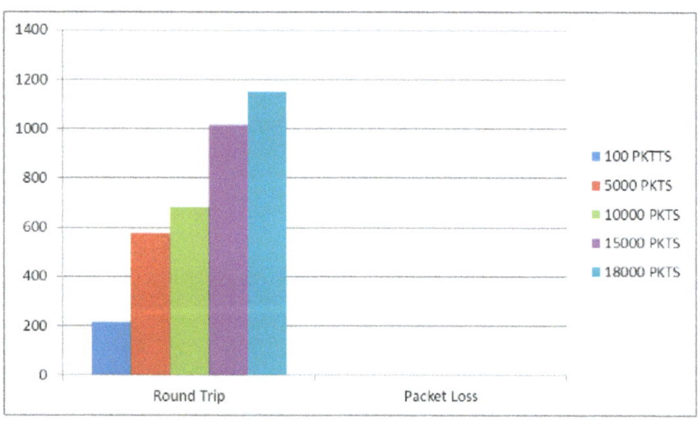

Figure 11: Latency for MPLS-TE Network

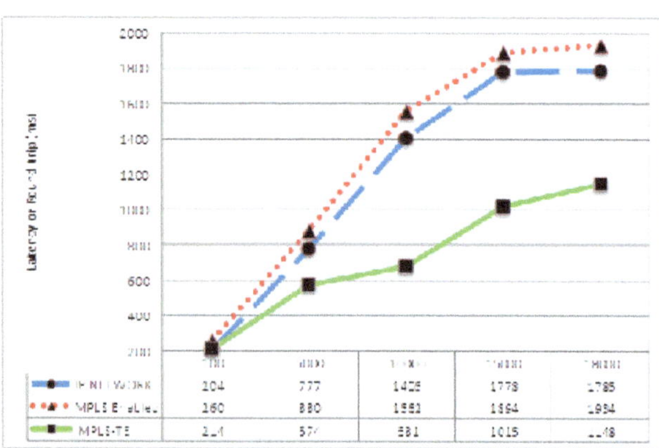

Figure 12: Comparison of Latencies of IP/MPLS/MPLS TE over a WAN

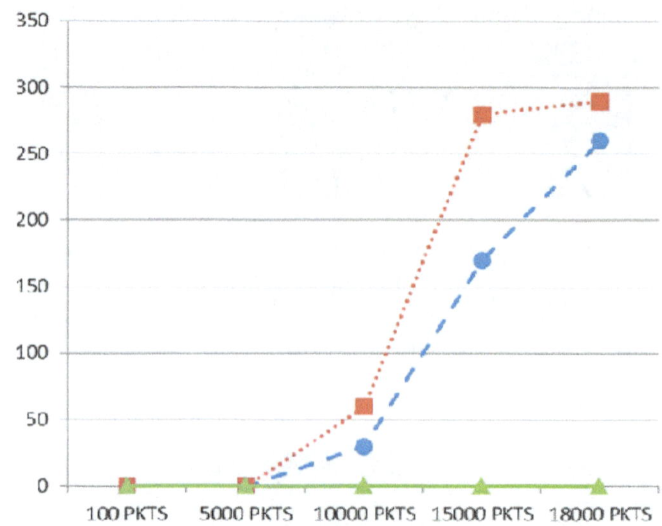

Figure 13: Comparison of Packet Loss over a WAN

In the line graph in the Figure12 below, for an IP network there is an increase in the round trip time for it to send packets, also in the MPLS network there is slight reduction RTT from that of the IP network while the reduction is substantial for MPLS-TE.

The line graph of Figure13 showed that, for an IP network there is an increase in the number of packet loss when sending packets and also the same for an MPLS Network but no packet loss was noticed for the for MPLS-TE when sending packets.

CONCLUSIONS

The MPLS-TE solution has been used as a network virtualization or path isolation tool in service provider core networks to improve the redundancy of the MPLS and MPLS VPN. However, with slight modification to its logic, it can be applied to the campus enterprise network and when this is done, it provides ability to create as many networks as possible, redundancy, load balancing, backup route and link protection. The need for network planning and traffic engineering in a core network has driven multiprotocol label switching traffic engineering (MPLS-TE) towards becoming a standard within service provider core networks. The explosive growth of the Internet presents serious challenge to service providers and equipment sellers in terms of traffic escalation. There is also the demand to create differentiated IP services and other challenges include the cost of mapping IP over layer 2 networks, as well as difficulties in identifying better network utilization and fault handling. However, this research has shown by simulation experiments comparison between IP, MPLS and the MPLS-TE network. The results showed a drastic reduction in latency and no packet loss as the network becomes more congested for the MPLS-TE network implying that traffic engineering combined with label switching will be a good option to decongest a core network or service provider network.

REFERENCES

1. F. Baker Requirements for IP Version 4 Routers, RFC1812, June 1995.
2. Network Virtualization - Path Isolation Design Guide, Cisco Validated Design, 2009.

3. D. O. Awduche, "MPLS and Traffic Engineering in IP Networks," University of Minnesota, IEEE communication magazine, December 1999.
4. D. Awduche, A. Chiu, A. Elwalid, I. Widjaja, X. Xiao "Overview and Principles of Internet Traffic Engineering", RFC 3272, May 2002.
5. B. Fortz, J. Rexford, M. Thorup, "Traffic Engineering with Traditional IP Routing Protocols" IEEE Communications Magazine, October 2002.
6. K. G. Coffman, A. M. Odlyzko, "Internet growth: Is there a Moore's Law for data traffic?" AT&T Labs – Research Revised version, June 4, 2001.
7. D. D. Clark, W. Fang, "Explicit Allocation of Best-Effort Packet Delivery Service", IEEE/ACM Transactions on Networking (TON) Volume 6 Issue 4, 1998, pp. 362-373.
8. V. P. Kumar, T. V. Lakshman, D. Stiliadis, "Beyond Best Effort: Router Architectures for the Differentiated Services ofTomorrow's Internet", IEEE Communications Magazine, May, 1998.
9. Guichard and Pepelnjak, MPLS and VPN Architectures, Volume I, Cisco Press, 2001.
10. Callon, Rosen and Visawanathan, RFC 3031, Multiprotocol Label Switching Architecture, January 2001.
11. Guichard and Pepelnjak, MPLS and VPN Architectures, Volume II, Cisco Press, 2001.
12. Cisco documents: IP slas-analyzing IP service levels using the ICMP ECHO operation.www.cisco.com/en/US/docs/ios/12_4/ip_sla/configuration/guide/hsoverv.html. Retrieved, May 2014.
13. Villy B. Iversen, "Teletraffic Engineering and Network Planning", Technical University of Denmark, DK-2800 Kgs-Lyngby, Revised May 20, 2010. Retrieved June10, 2015 from http://oldwww.com.dtu.dk/education/34340.
14. Todd Lammle, CCNA: Cisco Certified Network Associate Study Guide, 6th Edition, Wiley Publishing, 2007.

CHAPTER 15

ANALYZING THE EVOLUTION AND THE FUTURE OF THE INTERNET TOPOLOGY FOCUSING ON FLOW HIERARCHY

Yu Nakata, Shin'ichi Arakawa, and Masayuki Murata

Graduate School of Information, Science and Technology, Osaka University, 1-5, Yamadaoka, Suita, Osaka 565-0871, Japan

ABSTRACT

In the Internet, Autonomous Systems (ASes) exchange traffic through interconnected links. As traffic demand increases, more traffic becomes concentrated on such links. The traffic concentrations depend heavily on the global structure of the Internet topology. Therefore, a topological evolution considering the global structure is necessary to continually accommodate future traffic amount. In this paper, we first develop a method to identify the hierarchical nature of traffic aggregation on the Internet topology and use this method to discuss the long-term changes in traffic flow. Our basic approach is to extract the "flow hierarchy," which is a hierarchical structure associated with traffic aggregation. Our results show that the current connection policy will lead to a severe traffic concentration in the future. We then examine a new evolution process that attempts to reduce this traffic concentration. Our proposed evolution process increases the number of links in the deeper level in the hierarchy, thus relaxing the traffic concentration. We apply our evolution process to the Internet topology in 2000 and evolve this scenario over 13 years. The results show that our evolution process could reduce the traffic concentration by more than half compared with that without our evolution process.

INTRODUCTION

The Internet is the largest network system in the world and is becoming ever larger. The amount of traffic on the Internet has been increasing owing to the increase in the number of network users, network services, and communication devices, such as PCs, smartphones, and tablet devices. An AS is a network that is managed by an organization under a single administrative control. The Internet consists of many ASes and the connections among ASes. According to Border Gateway Protocol (BGP) data in [1, 2], the number of ASes has doubled over the last decade; as of November 15, 2013, there were at least 45,980 ASes and 105,540 interconnected links. The number of ASes is estimated to continue increasing in response to the increase in mobile traffic, which doubles each year, and traffic from new and emerging applications using, for example, sensor devices with a communication function [3, 4].

As the traffic amount increases, more traffic will concentrate on existing links. To relax the traffic concentration, each AS tries to form new links with ASes that have not yet been connected. An AS usually has its own policy for selecting which ASes to connect with from among the many candidates. For example, an AS attempts to connect with another AS such that the cost, revenue, and performance after connecting are optimized. That is, new links are constructed based on the local

Citation: Yu Nakata, Shin'ichi Arakawa, and Masayuki Murata, "Analyzing the Evolution and the Future of the Internet Topology Focusing on Flow Hierarchy," Journal of Computer Networks and Communications, vol. 2015, Article ID 736870, 18 pages, 2015. doi:10.1155/2015/736870

decision of two ASes. They do not consider the global structure of the Internet topology. However, because the degree of traffic concentration on links depends heavily on the global structure of the topology [5], local decision-making is inadequate to fundamentally avoid the future traffic concentration associated with the increase in traffic. An evolution that considers the global structure of the Internet topology is necessary to continually accommodate future traffic amount.

The evolution of the Internet topology has been studied intensively in recent years [6–8]. Dhamdhere and Dovrolis [6] investigated the long-term change in the number of peering/transit links. The authors also discussed the factors behind the emergence of the current topological structure and gave graph generation models for the Internet topology. Shavitt and Weinsberg [8] used the clustering coefficient [9] and betweenness centrality [10] to characterize this evolution, while Gregoria et al. [7] extracted well-connected subgraphs from the Internet topology and discussed how these subgraphs were connected to the rest of the Internet topology. These studies longitudinally analyzed the change in the Internet topology from a graph metrics perspective. However, a more important metric to avoid future traffic concentration is related to the change in the structure of the Internet topology associated with spatial dynamics of the traffic flow. An analysis of the change in the structure associated with traffic flow can help to reveal where the traffic concentration occurs and how to deal with it.

We therefore develop a method to identify the hierarchical nature of traffic aggregation in the Internet topology and use this method to discuss the long-term changes in traffic flow. Our basic approach is to extract the "flow hierarchy," which is a hierarchical structure associated with traffic aggregation, from the Internet topology. Many works have shown that the Internet has a hierarchical structure [11–13]. Within this hierarchical structure, an AS aggregates traffic from lower-level ASes and relays the traffic to higher-level ASes. Such traffic aggregation leads to a hierarchy of traffic aggregation, which in turn leads to the traffic concentration on links. Recently, the structure of the Internet topology is becoming "flat" [14], and the trend of traffic flow also is changing from centralized to more distributed. Nevertheless, the flow hierarchy has not disappeared because the flat structure is formed by adding links to existing hierarchical structure. To extract the flow hierarchy, we focus on structures called "modules" as the unit of traffic aggregation and retrieve the hierarchy of modules that appear in the Internet topology. A module consists of a set of ASes that are densely connected with each other, and each module is sparsely connected with other modules [15]. The outgoing traffic from one module is first aggregated inside that module, and then the traffic is transferred to the other module through the sparsely connected links. A module may be divided into two or more submodules; that is, there is a containment relationship between the module and submodules. By repeating the division of modules and revealing their containment relationships, we can extract the flow hierarchy of the Internet topology. We then investigate the long-term changes in the flow hierarchy of the Internet topology. Our results show that the increase in traffic amount at the top-level module is larger than that at middle-level or low-level module and particularly has slightly accelerated since 2011. This suggests that the current connection policy will lead to a severe traffic concentration in the future Internet topology. Therefore, we urgently need an evolution process that considers the global structure of the Internet topology to slow down the increase in traffic concentration. In this paper, we examine a new evolution process that attempts to increase the number of links between lower-level modules to relax the traffic concentration in higher-level modules. We apply our evolution process to the Internet topology in 2000 and evolve this scenario for 13 years. We then evaluate the traffic concentration at various levels of containment following the evolution. The results show that our evolution process can suppress the traffic concentration by more than half compared with that without our evolution process.

This paper is organized as follows. Section 2 gives an overview of some related work in the analysis of the Internet topology. Section 3 describes the hierarchy concept based on the containment relationship of modules and presents the method of extracting the flow hierarchy from the Internet topology. Section 4 discusses the long-term change in the flow hierarchy of the Internet topology. We first investigate the internal structure in a module and then illustrate the structure between top-level modules in the flow hierarchy, because a large amount of traffic traverses the links between top-level modules. Finally, we investigate the long-term change in the structure of each level in the flow hierarchy. Section 5 studies the links on which a lot of traffic is aggregated. In Section 6, we examine a new evolution process that attempts to increase the number of links between lower-level modules. We apply the evolution process to the Internet topology in 2000 and confirm that it suppresses the traffic concentration across links between top-level modules. Section 7 shows that the appearance of Hyper Giants does not enable the continued accommodation of an increase in traffic amount. Section 8 concludes this paper.

RELATED WORK

Understanding and analyzing the structure of the Internet topology is important, because the properties of the Internet are used for network design. The network performance, such as the amount of traffic that can be accommodated across the Internet, is dependent on the structure of the Internet topology, because this strongly affects the traffic flow. Therefore, when a network operator of an AS adds new links and network equipment, a design based on the properties of the topology is needed to improve the network performance. Determining the structure of the Internet topology is also vital to evaluate the performance of new applications and protocols on a topology reflecting the structure and properties of the Internet. For example, a topology reflecting properties of the Internet is required to evaluate the scalability of BGP [16].

For the past dozen years, various structural properties of the Internet topology have been widely investigated. References [17, 18] visualized the Internet topology to determine its structural properties. However, it is difficult to characterize structural properties from pictures of the Internet topology generated by these studies, because the Internet topology is large and complex. Some studies have investigated structural properties using various graph metrics. In [19], Faloutsos et al. revealed that the degree distribution of the Internet topology exhibits power-law attributes, and Pastor-Satorras et al. [12] showed that the distribution of betweenness centrality also follows a power law. However, these studies analyzed the structural properties at a point in time. Network design requires the prediction of the future structure of the Internet topology. To predict the future structure, the trend in changes to the Internet topology has to be clarified. In [6], Dhamdhere and Dovrolis quantified the ability of an AS to attract customer ASes that pay a transit fee for traversing traffic and found that Internet Service Providers (ISPs) connecting to a lot of customer ASes had acquired more customer ASes. These studies analyzed the evolution of the Internet topology using some graph metrics. Each graph metric shows a characteristic of the Internet topology; however, these are not directly related to network performance. For instance, even if two networks have the same degree of distribution, the amount of network equipment needed to accommodate traffic demand will differ depending on the structure of the networks. For example, [5] found that the degree of traffic concentration on links is heavily dependent on the global structure of the topology. Actually, the Internet topology suffers from traffic congestion more than a random network [20]. It is important to understand the global structure related to the spatial dynamics of traffic flow to develop a new evolution process that avoids the current and future traffic concentration suffered by the Internet topology.

In [8], Shavitt and Weinsberg analyzed changes in topological structure, such as betweenness centrality and link density, by focusing on large content providers, also referred to as Hyper Giants [14, 21]. From this analysis, it was found that the structure of the Internet topology has changed from a hierarchical to a flat structure. This is because large content providers construct links with a lot of small ISPs. Because they have influenced the Internet topology, considerable attention is currently focused on these Hyper Giants. However, Hyper Giants do not contribute to the moderation of traffic concentration over certain parts of the links, because the traffic flow between two ASes does not traverse the Hyper Giants; that is, the traffic is not aggregated at the links controlled by the Hyper Giants. Thus, the Hyper Giants are not relevant to an evolution process to reduce traffic concentration at these links. In this study, we focus on the structure of traditional links, such as those between ISPs.

THE FLOW HIERARCHY

Concept of the Flow Hierarchy

We use the flow hierarchy to reveal where and how traffic is aggregated. The structure of the flow hierarchy is the hierarchical structure based on containment relationship of modules. We note that the flow hierarchy is not a hierarchy of "tier" based on the ISP's business scale but the structure indicating a gradual traffic aggregation in the Internet topology. Such a containment relationship has appeared in the history of the Internet evolution, and then the traffic is aggregated in accordance with the flow hierarchy. This makes the flow hierarchy be useful for analyzing degree of traffic aggregation. In the late 1960s, some academic organizations deployed network equipment and connected with all other organizations. This is the origin of the Internet, and the organizations became to be called ASes later. To participate in the early Internet, new ASes needed to connect with all other ASes. However, as the scale of the Internet became larger, it was increasingly difficult to sustain the full mesh network. Because the construction and maintenance costs of long or high-capacity links are high, new ASes tend to connect with only a few "senior" ASes that have long or high-capacity links. As a result, sets of ASes centered on senior ASes, that is, modules, were generated. However, as the number of ASes connecting to senior ASes increases, the amount of traffic aggregated at senior ASes and global links increases, and the risk of suffering traffic congestion increases. To reduce the traffic load at senior ASes, some ASes have locally aggregated traffic. Because a hierarchical structure has appeared in the Internet under this process of traffic aggregation, the flow hierarchy reflects the hierarchical nature of traffic aggregation. Therefore, we use the flow hierarchy to reveal where and how traffic is aggregated.

Extraction of the Flow Hierarchy

We now extract and investigate the flow hierarchy in the Internet topology. First, we obtain the topology data of ASes and links in the Internet topology (Section 3.2.1). We then extract the hierarchical structure based on containment relationship of modules from the Internet topology (Section 3.2.2). We finally give the traffic demand to the hierarchical structure because the flow hierarchy is derived by adding the traffic amount on each link to the hierarchical structure (Section 3.2.3).

Obtaining Topology Data

We obtain the topology data of ASes and links in the Internet topology. We extract the topology data from the BGP routing tables that have been recorded in the gateway routers of large ISPs and have been gathered. Various organizations, such as UCLA [22] and CAIDA [17], create the Internet topology data and these topology data include more links [23, 24]. However, these topology data are not suitable for a longitudinal topological analysis because the number of monitors that observe BGP tables and traceroute results that are used to create topology data has greatly increased. That is, we cannot distinguish between actual evolution of the topology which is contributed by the real change of the topology and changes caused by the increase of monitors. Instead of the data provided by UCLA and CAIDA, we use the BGP tables gathered by a part of servers of RouteViews Project and RIPE NCC. The part of servers has been gathering the BGP tables from almost the same ISPs after starting up their projects. Although the number of links observed is fewer than the topology data of UCLA and CAIDA, the BGP tables from RouteViews Project and RIPE NCC are suitable for a longitudinal topological analysis because they are consistently comparable over time. BGP tables contain AS paths, which are the routes between two ASes. The AS path is described as a list of ASes that the traffic traverses. From the AS paths in the BGP tables, we obtain the ASes and links in the Internet topology. We use BGP routing tables stored in http://archive.routeviews.org/oix-route-views/, which is a RouteViews Project server, and rrc00.ripe.net, which is a RIPE NCC server. The reason why we use these servers is that they are the oldest ones that are still working. Table 1 shows the number of ASes and links that we can extract. Unfortunately, [6, 25] reported that this method cannot capture over 40% of the peering links on which traffic is exchanged without a transit fee. Since a huge amount of traffic traverses peering links through IX, missing of peering links decreases the accuracy of estimated amount of traffic traversing each link. However, the use of BGP routing tables is not a problem for this study because the purpose of this study is to reveal the impact of the global structure of the Internet on the traffic concentration rather than to show the actual traffic amount.

Table 1: Number of ASes, links, and AS paths in the Internet topology

	June 15, 2000	June 15, 2004	June 15, 2008	November 15, 2013
# of ASes	8,162	18,015	29,320	45,980
# of links	17,533	40,205	64,305	105,540
# of AS paths	299,434	1,108,704	1,901,745	3,136,820

Extracting the Hierarchy of Modules Based on Containment Relationship

The structure of the flow hierarchy is the hierarchical structure based on containment relationship of modules. We extract the hierarchical structure from the Internet topology. The hierarchical structure based on containment relationship of modules is extracted by repeating the division of modules into submodules. Several methods for division of modules have been proposed such as the Infomap method [26], the OSLOM method [27], and the Louvain method [28]. Since our main concern is the traffic aggregation, we select the Louvain method for our analysis. The Infomap method uses the probability flow of random walks on a network as a proxy for information flows in the real system and divides the network into modules by compressing a description of the probability flow [26, 29]. However, since the traffic flow of the Internet is not random walk, we cannot capture links where the traffic is aggregated from the Infomap method. The OSLOM method uses a measure indicating how obvious module structure is in the network against a random null model graph. Therefore, the OSLOM method can detect the obvious module structure against the random null model graph. However, the traffic concentration is expected to be observed in also the random null model graph and the OSLOM method cannot capture the traffic concentration. Unlike the Infomap and the OSLOM methods, the Louvain method derives modules so that the number of intermodule links relative to that of the intramodule links is minimized. The traffic originated inside a module is first conveyed and aggregated by the intramodule links and then transferred by the intramodule links. The Louvain method incrementally merges modules into a module, so we can gradually capture links where the traffic is aggregated by using the Louvain method.

In the Louvain method, the topology is divided in such a way as to maximize the modularity. The modularity is a measure of the strength of interconnection among modules when a particular division P of a topology is given and is defined by

$$M(P) = \frac{1}{2m}\sum_{ij}\left[A_{ij} - \frac{k_i k_j}{2m}\right]\delta_{S_i S_j}. \quad (1)$$

Descriptions of the variables in (1) are shown in Table 2. Here, we regard the maximum of (P) for all divisions as the modularity of the topology. The modularity of a topology ranges from 0 to 1. The modularity is high in case that links between ASes in the same module are densely connected and links between ASes in different modules are sparsely connected. The modularity of a complete graph and a star graph is 0, because these graphs do not consist of sets of nodes densely connected to each other.

Table 2: Definition of notation for modularity (1).

Notation	Definition
m	Number of links
i, j	Node
A_{ij}	Element of adjacency matrix
k_i	Degree of node i
S_i	Module that contains node i
$\delta_{S_i S_j}$	Kronecker delta. If S_i and S_j are the same, $\delta_{S_i S_j}$ is 1, otherwise 0

After dividing the Internet topology into modules as described above, we divide each module into smaller submodules. Furthermore, we divide these submodules into even smaller submodules. By repeating this dividing process, the hierarchical structure based on the containment relationship is extracted. If the modularity of a module is 0, it cannot be divided into submodules because the module does not consist of sets of densely connected nodes. All modules are repeatedly divided until their modularity is 0. We define the "containment level" (CL) as the level of the hierarchical structure. As shown in Figure 1, CL1 modules are modules that are extracted in the first division of the Internet topology. Submodules of CL1 modules are CL2 modules, and submodules of CL_n modules are CL_{n+1} modules, where n is a nonnegative integer.

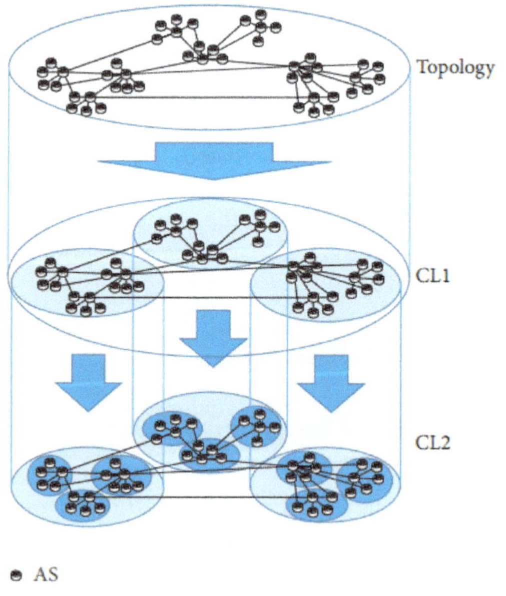

Figure 1: Extraction of hierarchical structure based on the containment relationship of modules.

Assigning Traffic Demand

We assign traffic demand to the hierarchical structure of the containment relationship of modules. Since the actual traffic amount on most paths is closed information, we give the traffic demand based on the gravity model [30]. The gravity model is a simple method for estimating the traffic demand [30, 31] and is used in some studies [32, 33]. The traffic demand of AS i is proportional to the degree of AS i since the business scale of AS i is related to its degree [5, 34]. Note that, as discussed in [35], the gravity model does not capture self-similarity and long-range dependence of traffic. However, we use the gravity model for assigning traffic demand since our study focuses on the increase in the degree of traffic concentration rather than short-term traffic fluctuation. The gravity model is represented by the following expression:

$$e_{ij} = \gamma \cdot x_i \cdot x_j, \quad (2)$$

where e_{ij} is traffic amount on the path between AS i and AS j. x_i and x_j are the traffic demand of AS i and AS j, respectively, and γ is a scaling factor and is set to 1 hereafter. Note that this setting may not reflect actual traffic amount. However, our focus here is to reveal the traffic concentration on some links rather than actual traffic amount on each link.

Note that Hyper Giants send huge amounts of traffic compared with the other ASes. In particular, Google and Akamai are defined as Hyper Giants by some studies [5, 14]. We check names of organizations managing ASes in CIDR report [36], and we regard ASes whose names contain "Google," "Akamai" as Hyper Giants. Then, γ is set to 1 if both of AS i and AS j are not Hyper Giants; otherwise γ is set to 895. These values are determined based on a Cisco report [37, 38] that quantifies the traffic amount on the Internet. Cisco reported the traffic over the whole of the Internet to be 369 exabytes in 2011 and that between users and data centers to be 116 exabytes. The number of ASes registered by the Internet Registry is 60538, and the number of famous content providers is about 30. Therefore, the average amount of traffic at each AS is 4.18 petabytes (= (369 − 116)/(60538 − 30) exabytes), and the average amount of traffic sent by a large content provider is 3.74 exabytes (= 116/30 exabytes). Thus, we set γ to 895 (= 3.74 · 1000/4.18) for the Hyper Giants. The value of γ may not reflect actual traffic amount. However, our focus here is to reveal the traffic concentration on some links rather than actual traffic amount on each link. Note that Microsoft is also called as Hyper Giants in some studies [5, 14]; however, we regard only Google and Akamai as Hyper Giants because the degree of Microsoft (AS number is 8075) has greatly changed.

When we derive the amount of traffic that traverses each link from the amount of traffic between AS pairs, the path between two ASes is required. Unfortunately, most paths between AS pairs are undocumented. Thus, we assume that the path between two ASes is a minimum hop path, although this is not always the case for actual BGP routings [39]. This assumption is sufficient to observe the change in traffic aggregation, because [8] reported that the number of minimum hop paths that traverse an AS is similar to the actual amount of traffic that traverses that AS. Thus, we consider minimum hop paths to be useful for analyzing the changes in traffic aggregation.

LONG-TERM CHANGE OF THE FLOW HIERARCHY

The traffic concentration at links between modules is dependent on the structure within modules and the structure between modules. An investigation of the change in the flow hierarchy is important for discussing the future evolution of the Internet topology. Therefore, in this section, we first analyze the internal structure of modules. Through this analysis, we investigate ASes that have a lot of links between modules to confirm where traffic is aggregated in the module. We then analyze the between-module structure. In particular, we investigate the structure between CL1 modules, which are top-level modules in the flow hierarchy, because it is thought that large amounts of traffic are aggregated in the links between CL1 modules. Finally, we investigate the long-term change in the structure of each level in the flow hierarchy to reveal the trend of traffic aggregation at links between modules at each level.

Internal Structure of Modules

In this section, we reveal the internal structure of modules using various graph metrics. Here, we do not divide CL5 modules even when some CL5 modules can be divided to CL6 modules. The reason is that the number of CL6 modules and the size of CL6 modules are too small to see the change of internal structure of the CL5 module. Figure 2 shows the longitudinal change in the graph metrics of modules. From the analyses in Figure2, we confirm that the internal structure of modules gives a star-like graph. Figure 2(a) shows the mean ratio of ASes that have degree one or two. For the modules in most CLs, the ratio of these ASes is over 80%. Figure 2(b)shows the mean of the maximum degree in the modules. Whereas over 80% of ASes in a module have only one or two links, the degree of hub ASes in CL1 modules is over 100, and that in CL2 modules is over 30. Furthermore, the degree of hub ASes in these CLs has been increasing. Although the degree of hub ASes in CL4 and CL5 is less than 10, they connect to most of the ASes in the module. Thus, it is found that the degree of most ASes in a module is small, but the degree of some ASes is large. To reveal where the links are constructed in a module, we now investigate the assortativity of modules. Assortativity is an index indicating that a node in a network connects with ASes that have a similar degree [40]. If all links are constructed between nodes that have the same degree, the assortativity of the network is 1. On the contrary, the assortativity is 0 when there is no correlation between the degrees of two nodes that are connected with each other. When the nodes with small degrees are likely to be connected to the nodes with large degrees, the assortativity is close to −1. As shown in Figure 2(c), the assortativity of modules in all CLs is small, which means that ASes that have a small degree connect to hub ASes. Figure 2(d) shows the clustering coefficient of modules in each CL to investigate the connection between neighbor ASes. The clustering coefficient of an AS is an index indicating the ratio of connected pairs to all neighbor nodes' pairs of an AS and ranges from 0 to 1. As shown in Figure 2(d), the clustering coefficient of each module is small. This means that neighbor ASes of a given AS do not connect with each other. The result suggests that hub ASes link to a lot of ASes that have a small degree, and ASes with a small degree are not connected to each other. Finally, Figure 2(e) shows the mean diameter of modules. As the CL increases, the module diameter approaches 2. To summarize the points in Figure 2, it is obvious that the internal structure of each module is a star-like graph.

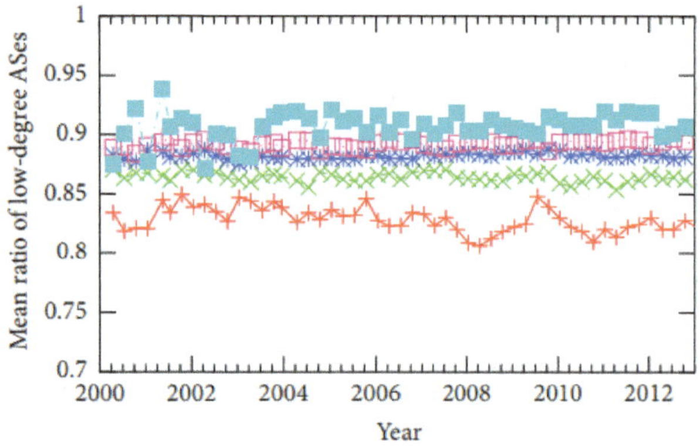

(a) Mean ratio of the number of one- or two-degree ASes to the number of all ASes in a module

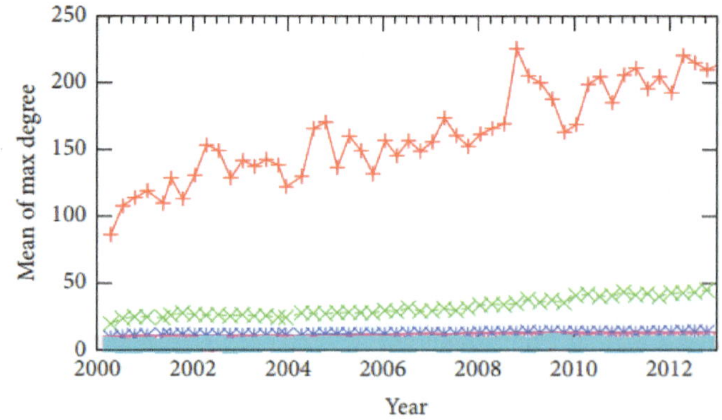

(b) Mean of max degree

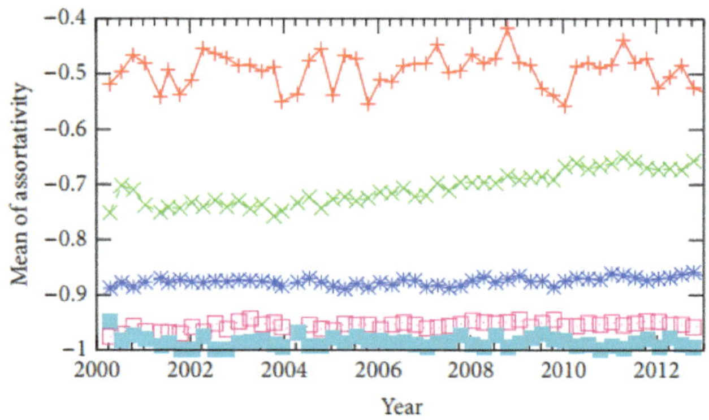

(c) Mean of assortativity

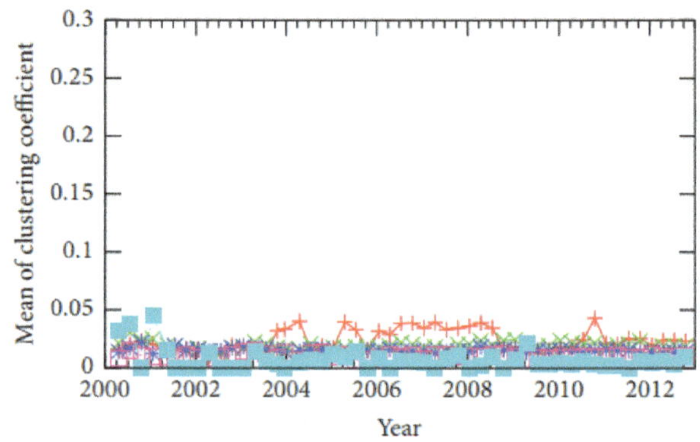

(d) Mean of clustering coefficient

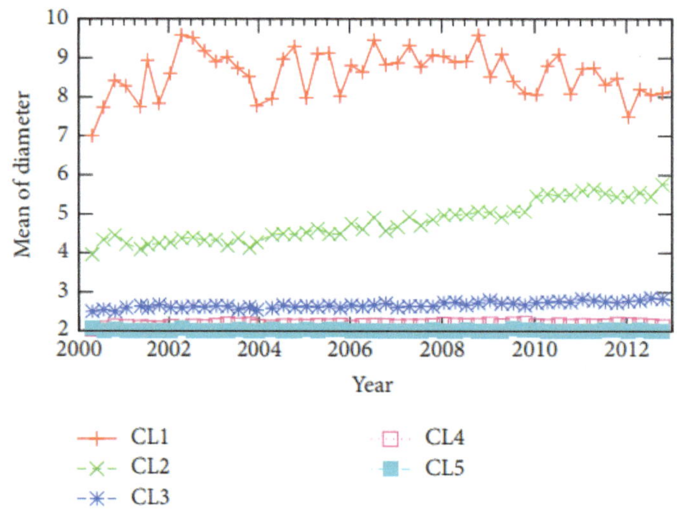

(e) Mean of diameter

Figure 2: Mean value of graph metrics of modules in each CL.

ASes with a Number of Links between Modules

The large amount of traffic that is generated within a module is aggregated at links between modules. We reveal the relationship between the degree of ASes and the number of links between modules. We first investigate whether a hub AS or an AS that has a small degree has more links between modules. Here, we define hub ASes as those having a degree that is more than half of the maximum in the module. Table 3 shows the average ratio of links between modules to all links of an AS in the Internet topology on 15 July 2013. This shows that hub ASes have a higher ratio than low-degree ASes. This means that low-degree ASes tend to connect to only the hub ASes belonging to the same module. The hub ASes link to both ASes in the same module and ASes in other modules. Therefore, the traffic between modules is aggregated at the hub ASes and then transferred to ASes in other modules.

Table 3: Ratio of intermodule links of hub ASes and ratio of intermodule links of low-degree ASes.

	Hub ASes	Low-degree ASes
CL1	0.244	0.137
CL2	0.396	0.269
CL3	0.476	0.293
CL4	0.463	0.267
CL5	0.406	0.093

Next, we examine which types of ASes have many links between modules. In the Internet, there are various types of ASes. ISPs are classified into four types, Tier-1 to Tier-3 and sub-Tier-1. We define sub-Tier-1 as ISPs for which there is no consensus as to whether they should be categorized as Tier-1 or Tier-2. The other ASes are classified as Hyper Giants or Academic. In this study, ASes are ranked based on two types of links: transit links and peering links. A transit link is one in which traffic is exchanged with a transit fee. A peering link is one where traffic is exchanged without a transit fee. Unfortunately, information about the type of link is generally unknown. The method of [17] can infer the link type with an accuracy rate of 99.1%, and so we use this approach. We classify ASes based on the following steps. First, we extract "peering links" and ASes that have peering links. We regard a connected component consisting of peering links as one tier, because two ASes connected with a peering link generally process the same amount of traffic. Next, we check the commercial name of the AS in each connected component and determine the tier of each connected component from six types. Finally, we regard the tier of the connected component that contains the AS to be the type of AS. There is a hierarchy in the Internet based on link types [11–13]. Note that a hierarchy based on AS types is different from the flow hierarchy. The hierarchy based on link types shows the difference in the amount of traffic exchanged by two connected ASes. The flow hierarchy describes the amount of traffic aggregated at ASes or links based on the global structure of the topology.

Table 4 shows the average number of links between modules for each AS type. e_x is the average number of links between modules of an AS in CL_x. Table 4 shows that e_x decreases as x increases. This means that Tier-1 ASes have more links between modules than other ASes, because most Tier-1 ISPs have a global network spanning multiple continents and connected with many ISPs all over the world.

Table 4: Average number of links between modules.

	e_1	e_2	e_3	e_4	e_5	e_6
Tier-1	989.54	158	624.31	0.54	22.77	0
Sub-Tier-1	191.03	75.23	160.82	2.31	14.31	0
Tier-2	52.76	29.39	52.63	0.93	7.74	0.03
Tier-3	16	11.33	33.08	0.58	2.42	0.17

According to our findings, the flow hierarchy can be illustrated as in Figure 3. In Figure 3, the number of ASes, number of links between ASes in different tiers, and number of links between ASes in the same tier are 1/5 of those in the actual Internet topology in 2012. In Figure 3, ISPs are arranged from top to bottom in descending order of amount of traversing traffic, and the triangles represent modules. As shown in Figure 3, there is a hierarchy in the Internet based on AS type. Note that this hierarchy is different from the flow hierarchy. The major difference is that the hierarchy based on AS type is not reflected by the structure of the topology. Each module contains ASes in different tiers, and ASes in higher tiers have more links between modules. A module in the flow hierarchy is a part of a vertically divided Internet topology. From the structure in Figure 3, we can see that Tier-1 ISPs exchange traffic traversing from/to other modules. The traffic concentrates at Tier-1 ISPs, because they aggregate the traffic that is generated in the modules.

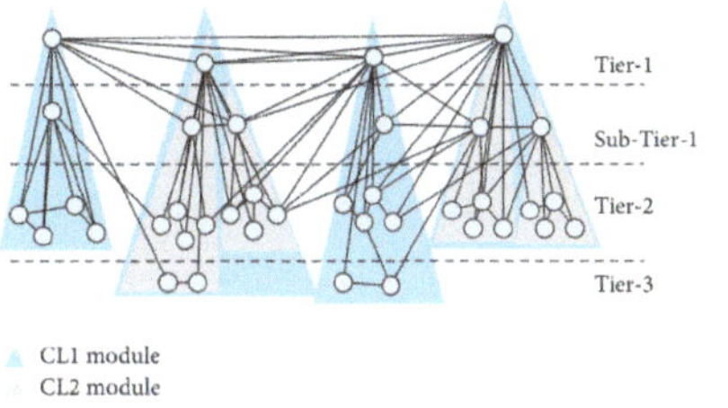

Figure 3: Outline drawing of the flow hierarchy in the Internet topology.

Long-Term Change in Structure of Top-Level Modules in the Flow Hierarchy

A hub AS connects links to a lot of ASes in other modules. Thus, a hub AS aggregates traffic generated in the module and relays the traffic to the other modules. Therefore, it is considered that an immense amount of traffic generated in CL1 modules is aggregated at the links between top-level (CL1) modules. In the future, when traffic concentrates at links between CL1 modules, an evolution process is needed that avoids traffic concentration, allowing the Internet topology to accommodate this increase in traffic amount. Thus, the change of traffic concentration at links between CL1 modules must be clarified. For this purpose, we analyze the long-term change in the structure between CL1 modules, because the degree of traffic concentration at the links depends on the connections between CL1 modules.

We first investigate the long-term change in modularity of the Internet topology to investigate the structure between CL1 modules. Since the value of modularity itself is not suitable measure to investigate the modular structure [41–43], we compare the modularity between the ER random model, hierarchical scale-free graph, and the Internet topology. Figure 4 shows the long-term change in modularity of these graphs. For the hierarchical scale-free graph, a module having a scale-free degree distribution is first generated, and this is incrementally added to the graph until the numbers of nodes and links exceed those of the Internet topology. We create the hierarchical scale-free graph that has the same number of nodes and links as the Internet topology. In Figure 4, we use (19) in [41] for calculating the modularity of the ER random model. Equation (19) is an equation to analytically calculate the maximum modularity of the ER random model without the module detection, and the modularity derived by (19) in [41] is close to the modularity derived by the simulated annealing method [41]. There is another approach to calculate the maximum modularity [43]. However, the modularity derived by the equation in [41] is slightly closer to the modularity derived by the simulated annealing method in case that the average degree is fewer than 10 (see Figure 12 in [43]). Since the average degree of the Internet topology is also fewer than 10, we use the equation in [41].

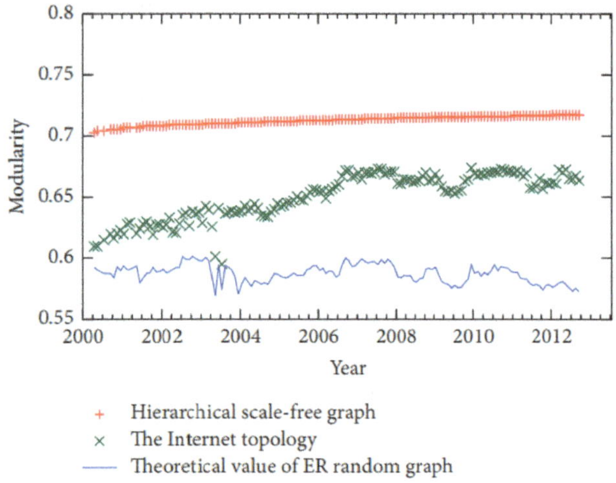

Figure 4: Long-term change in modularity.

As shown in Figure 4, the hierarchical scale-free graph has the largest modularity, and the ER random graph has the smallest. In the hierarchical scale-free graph, a large amount of traffic tends to be aggregated at the links between modules, because the large modularity indicates a low density of links between modules. In Figure 4, the modularity of the hierarchical scale-free graph and the ER random graph remains constant. On the other hand, the trend in modularity of the Internet topology changed sometime around 2007. This suggests that the overall structure started to change at this time. The dashed line in Figure 4 denotes 1 January 2007. Until this point, the modularity of the Internet topology had been increasing. This suggests that new links had tended to be locally constructed between two ASes in a module. It is thought that when new ASes are created in the Internet topology, they connect to ASes having links between higher-level modules. Since 2007, the modularity of the Internet topology has remained constant. However, the number of links between modules has increased since 2007.

To clarify the factors affecting the change in the modularity trend around 2007, we investigate the long-term change of variables in the definition of modularity (1). The modularity depends on the ratio of links between nodes in a module to all links and the node degree in each module. The key terms in (1) are α is the ratio of links between two nodes in a module to all links, and β is the probability of drawing a link between nodes that are in the same module when the link is randomly deployed on the topology.The higher the degree of node i and node j, the higher the value of β. α and β are normalized by the number of links in the Internet topology. Figure 5 shows the long-term change in these terms. Figure 5(b)shows that β has decreased continuously since 2000. As there is no change in this trend around 2007, β is not considered to be a factor in the change in modularity. On the other hand, Figure 5(a) shows that the trend of α changed around 2007. α was increasing until 2007, with minor fluctuations, and decreases after 2007. Thus, we assert that the change in the trend of α affected the modularity of the Internet topology. Even though the scale of the Internet topology has increased since 2007, the ratio of links between nodes in a module has decreased; that is, the number of links between top-level modules has increased. We believe that the factors behind the increase in links between top-level modules are the reduction in the price of constructing links and the increase in IXes (Internet eXchanges), which are relaying points for traffic between two connected ASes. These factors lead to an increase in intermodule links between ASes that do not have a lot of links between top-level modules. As a result, the modularity of the Internet topology has decreased.

$$\alpha = \frac{1}{m}\sum_{ij} A_{ij}\delta_{S_i S_j},$$

$$\beta = \frac{1}{m}\sum_{ij} \frac{k_i k_j}{2m}\delta_{S_i S_j}. \quad (3)$$

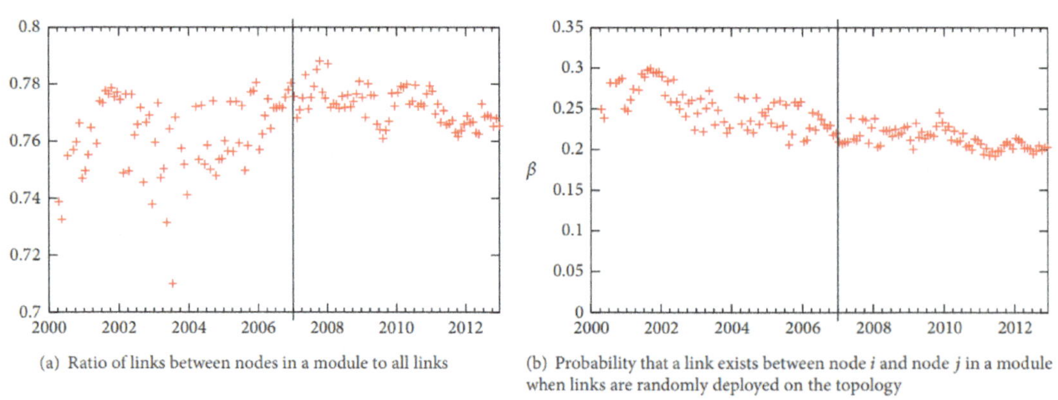

Figure 5: Long-term change of variables in the definition of modularity.

Long-Term Change of Each Level in the Flow Hierarchy

More links between modules are needed to avoid an increase in traffic concentration at links between top-level modules. New links between modules should be constructed between two ASes that locally aggregate traffic. This is because a part of the traffic that traverses the existing links between top-level modules will traverse links between two ASes that locally aggregate traffic. We investigate the traffic aggregation at links between modules in each CL to reveal where the ASes that locally aggregate traffic are located. The degree of traffic aggregation at the links between modules in each level of the flow hierarchy depends on the structure between the modules in each level. Therefore, in this section, we investigate the long-term change in the structure of each level in the flow hierarchy.

There are two ways in which the flow hierarchy can evolve: by expanding in depth and by expanding in width. There are two further subcategories for the expansion of the width. One is to increase the number of modules in each CL, and the other is to increase the number of ASes in each module. Figure 6 illustrates these expansions of the flow hierarchy. White nodes indicate ASes that exist before the growth, and red nodes indicate those added after the expansion. In the left-hand growth pattern in Figure 6, the number of modules in each CL increases as the topology grows. In this case, the links between modules also increase in number. By increasing the links between modules, the concentration of traffic at existing links is relaxed. In the center growth pattern in Figure 6, a star-like graph in each module becomes larger because additional ASes connect to the hub ASes in each module. As a result, the amount of traffic aggregated at hub ASes and on links between modules increases. In the right-hand growth pattern in Figure 6, submodules are generated in each module. The generation of submodules increases the maximum number of CLs, which corresponds to the depth of the flow hierarchy. If the depth of the flow hierarchy in the Internet topology grows, the amount of traffic aggregated on the links between top-level modules will decrease. This is because the paths between ASes belonging to the same module do not traverse the links between modules in the upper CL.

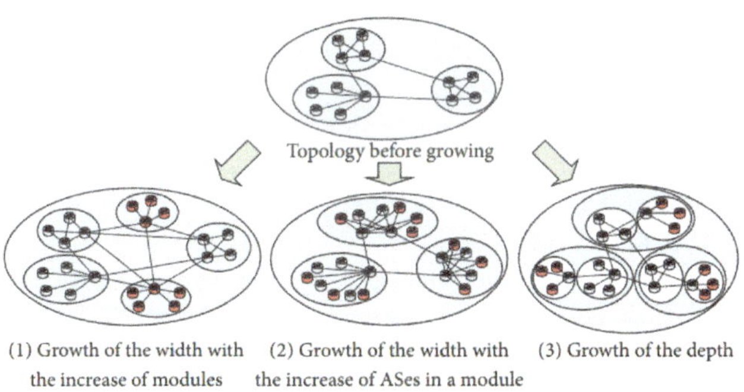

Figure 6: Evolution of the flow hierarchy with the increase of modules, the number of ASes in a module, or width.

We first investigate whether the depth of the flow hierarchy has been expanding or not. The depth of the flow hierarchy is defined by the containment level where a module at the level cannot be divided into submodules. Hereafter, we call modules that do not have submodules terminal modules. Figure 7 shows the number of terminal modules at each CL. The value of y-axis is normalized by the total number of terminal modules. We observe that most of terminal modules are located at CL3 and CL4, and the depth of these modules has increased from 2000 to 2012. However, the increase in terminal modules in CL4 is only 10%. Moreover, the average depth of terminal modules is slightly increased, from 3.42 to 3.71. The depth of the deepest terminal module remains steady at six from 2003 to 2013. Therefore, we conclude that the depth of the flow hierarchy has not changed greatly.

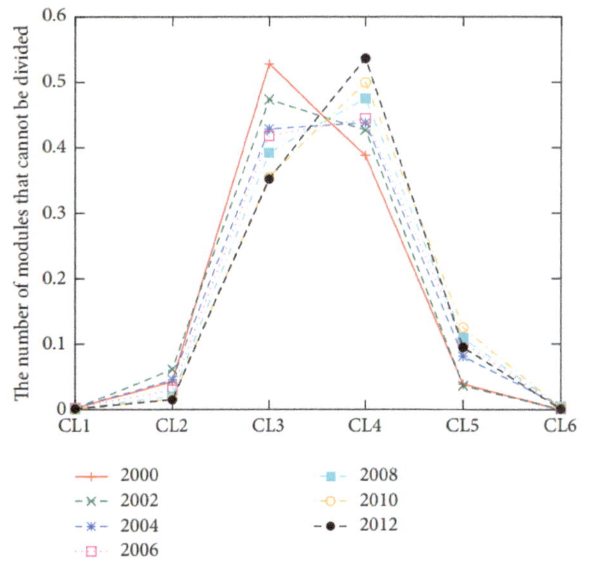

Figure 7: Containment level where a module at the level cannot be divided anymore.

We next investigate whether the growth in the flow hierarchy has followed the left-hand pattern or the center pattern in Figure 6. Table 5 shows the number of modules in each CL. The number of modules in CL3 and CL4 is greater than that in other CLs. Furthermore, the number of modules at CL3 and above has increased more rapidly than the number at CL1 and CL2. This means that the structure in CL3 and above has grown in similar fashion to the left-hand pattern in Figure 6. Table 6 shows the average number of ASes in a module. From 2000 to 2012, the average number of ASes in CL1 modules increased by a factor of 4.07, and that in each CL2 module increased 2.96 times. The number of ASes in modules in these CLs increased at a faster rate than in the other CLs. This suggests that the structure in CL1 and CL2 has expanded by increasing the number of ASes within a module. That is, the structure of these CLs has expanded according to the center pattern in Figure 6. The expansion in width with the increase of ASes in a module leads to an increase in the amount of traffic aggregated at links between modules. Therefore, more traffic has been concentrated at links between CL1 modules and links between CL2 modules. Note that it is known that the Louvain method suffers from a resolution limit. The resolution limit is the characteristic scale of the smallest size of a module that the method can detect. We checked the effect of the resolution limit by comparing divisions by the Infomap method, which is known to mitigate the resolution limit better than the Louvain method [44]. We found that the division by the Louvain method is affected by the resolution limit: the number of small-size (<10 ASes) modules is about ten times fewer than that by the Infomap method. However, we also found that the impact of the resolution limit on analyzing the evolution of flow hierarchy is marginal (see Appendix A for detail). The main reason is that the evolution of the flow hierarchy depends on the relation between the large-size module at the CL and the large-size module at lower-level CL. That is, the evolution of flow hierarchy indicates how the large-size module at a CL can be divided into submodules at lower-level CL. Our result shows that the resolution limit of the Louvain method is enough to capture the large-size module and is enough to understand the way of traffic aggregation in the flow hierarchy. Another reason is that although the Infomap method can detect some "periphery nodes" (which in turn form a small-size module), such small-size modules are detected at each CL. Thus, the relation between the large-size module at the CL and the large-size module at lower-level CL is not suffered from the resolution limit.

Table 5: Number of modules in each CL

Year	CL1	CL2	CL3	CL4	CL5	CL6
2000	26	255	812	529	71	0
2002	37	384	1215	881	131	6
2004	43	462	1526	1173	208	6
2006	40	479	1883	1562	299	4
2008	40	508	2437	2088	389	6
2010	42	490	2795	2641	438	2
2012	51	578	3153	3181	638	12

Table 6: Mean number of ASes contained in one module

Year	CL1	CL2	CL3	CL4	CL5	CL6
2000	224.97	24.78	8.41	4.01	3.22	2
2002	424.32	35.73	9.81	4.32	3.35	2.75
2004	414.07	37.84	10.41	4.67	3.59	3.5
2006	528.33	43.54	11.25	5.43	3.59	2
2008	695.98	57.18	12.20	6.20	3.71	2
2010	841.98	69.16	12.26	5.71	3.81	2.17
2012	915.93	73.31	12.93	6.36	3.74	2.89

LONG-TERM CHANGE IN TRAFFIC AGGREGATION

Section 4 showed that the structure within a module can be represented as a star-like graph. It was also revealed that the structure in higher CLs has expanded by increasing the number of ASes within a module, whereas the structure in lower CLs has expanded with an increase in the number of modules. In this section, we use this structural analysis to investigate where the traffic will become concentrated. In particular, we focus on the traffic amount over intermodule links where large amounts of traffic are exchanged.

Relationship between Intermodule Links and Traffic Aggregation

The traffic concentration on links between modules is dependent on the structure of the Internet topology. In particular, the number of submodules influences the amount of traffic aggregated on the links between modules. This is because traffic aggregated inside each submodule is aggregated at an AS in a higher-level module, and the traffic aggregated at this AS is relayed via links between modules. We therefore investigate the number of submodules contained in a module. Figure 8 shows the average number of submodules contained in a module in each CL. The average number of submodules contained in a CL1 module increased until 2007, after which it can be seen to have slightly decreased. In levels below CL2, the average number of submodules has remained almost constant. In CL2, the average number of submodules has increased. The reason for this increase is that the number of CL3 modules has increased more than the number of CL2 modules, as shown in Section 4.4. Thus, more traffic has become concentrated on the links between CL2 modules.

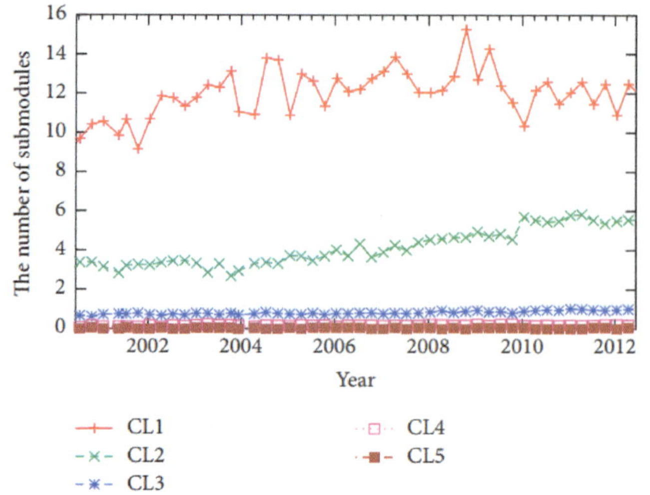

Figure 8: Average number of submodules contained in a module in each CL.

Amount of Traffic Traversing Links between Modules

We now investigate the traffic concentration on links between modules. Figure 9 shows the increase in the average amount of traffic traversing links between modules in each CL. In obtaining the figure, we use (2) as a traffic demand between ASes and then calculate traffic amount of links. The average amount of traffic on links between CL1 modules has increased more than in other CLs. If this trend continues, more traffic will become concentrated on links between CL1 modules. The amount of traffic traversing links between CL2 modules also increased compared to the other CLs. In particular, the amount of traffic traversing links between CL2 modules in Figure 9 has slightly accelerated since 2011. The reason for the shift in 2011 may relate to the change of structure in CL2 modules. In Figures 2(c) and 2(e), we can see that the increase in the assortativity and diameter of CL2 modules stopped around 2011. This implies that ASes having few links have tended to connect to an AS with the highest degree in a CL2 module after 2011. This trend leads to the increase in traffic aggregated on links between CL2 modules, and the acceleration in the amount of traffic on links between CL2 modules prevents the Internet from accommodating the overall increase in traffic. To determine how sensitive to γ our result is, we also examine by changing the value of γ from 238 at year 2004 to 3804 at year 2012 in Figure 15. From Figure 15, a similar tendency of traffic concentration is observed. By the traffic concentration, the operating and investment costs of routers increase. For example, the increase in processing cost leads to heatings problem and the power cost to cool routers, which is the primary contributor to an energy footprint, exponentially increases [45]. Moreover, an expansion of network equipment is needed according to the increase in the traffic volume. However, the transit fee that an AS receives from the other ASes does not increase more largely than the increase of traffic traversing the AS [5]. The traffic concentration will prevent

ASes from continual maintenance and expansion of network equipment. Therefore, a new evolution process is needed to slow down the traffic concentration on links between CL1 modules and links between CL2 modules.

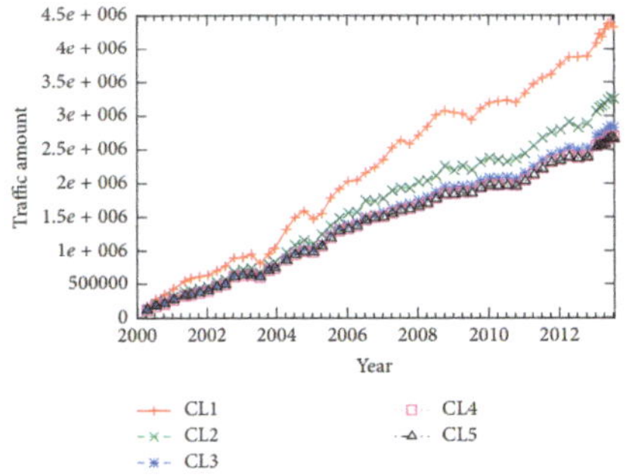

Figure 9: Average traffic amount on intermodule links in each CL.

EVOLUTION TO ACCOMMODATE THE INCREASE IN TRAFFIC AMOUNT

Our analysis of the flow hierarchy shows that traffic is concentrated on links between CL1 modules and links between CL2 modules. Therefore, an evolution process that considers the global structure of the Internet topology is needed to slow down this increase in concentration. In this section, we examine a new evolution process that attempts to increase the number of links between lower-level modules to reduce the traffic concentration among higher-level modules. We explain our evolution process in Section 6.1 and then evaluate its performance in Section 6.2.

Evolution Process to Slow Down Traffic Concentration

The results presented in Section 5 show that traffic has become increasingly concentrated on links between CL1 modules and links between CL2 modules. This is mainly because the number of ASes within CL1 and CL2 modules has increased, leading to an increase in the traffic generated in these modules. To continually accommodate the increase in traffic amount, the Internet topology requires a new evolution process to reduce this concentration at the links. Because the degree of traffic concentration on the links depends heavily on the global structure of the topology, our focus here is a global structure that can accommodate more traffic without increasing the concentration. For this purpose, we apply our evolution process in a centralized manner, rather than in the autonomous manner currently employed by ASes.

The basic approach of our evolution process is to construct more links between modules at lower CLs. With the links between lower CL modules, the traffic concentration in the current Internet can be relaxed, as some of the traffic will no longer have to traverse links between higher-level modules. On the one hand, our evolution process is necessary to avoid traffic concentration among higher-level modules associated with the increase in traffic amount. On the other hand, our evolution process relies to some extent on the current topological characteristic that attempts to aggregate many paths into one link. In fact, the Internet topology has evolved such that a hub AS attracts more intramodule links (see discussion of Figure 2(b)). The hub AS aggregates and exchanges traffic from/to other modules. In the proposed evolution process, we must avoid traffic concentration among higher-level modules while retaining the characteristic of traffic aggregation used in the past. We therefore introduce a parameter w to represent the threshold of the number of links between hub ASes in different modules. As we increase w, the number of links between modules increases, which will lead to a relaxation in traffic concentration at higher-level modules. By changing the value of w, we are able to examine how the number of links between modules slows down the traffic concentration in links between higher-level modules. Formally, w is defined as follows. Let $E_V(\mathrm{CL}x)$ be the set of links between a hub AS and another AS in a CLx module, and let $E_h(\mathrm{CL}x)$ be the set of links between CLx modules. We define the ratio (CLx) of links in $E_h(\mathrm{CL}x)$ to both $E_V(\mathrm{CL}x)$ and $E_h(\mathrm{CL}x)$ at CLx as

$$R(\mathrm{CL}x) = \frac{|E_h(\mathrm{CL}x)|}{|E_v(\mathrm{CL}x)| + |E_h(\mathrm{CL}x)|}. \quad (4)$$

Then, our evolution process increases the links in $E_h(\mathrm{CL}x)$ until $R(\mathrm{CL}x)$ exceeds the threshold w. Figure 10 illustrates how (CLx) is calculated. A red node denotes a hub AS, which we call the gateway AS hereafter, in a module. A link between two red nodes is a link in $E_h(\mathrm{CL}x)$, which is shown as a blue line. A link between a red node and a white node is a link in $E_V(\mathrm{CL}x)$, which is shown as a red line. By increasing w, links in $E_h(\mathrm{CL}x)$ are constructed between blue nodes. We then evolve a topology T using the following evolution process.

Step 1. Add new ASes to T.

Step 2. Add only one link for each new AS in T such that the new AS connects links to T.

Step 3. Calculate the flow hierarchy of T.

Step 4. Repeat the following steps from CL6 to CL1.

Step 4.1. Add a link between modules at the same CL.

Step 4.2. Calculate (CLx).

Step 4.3. If (CLx) $< w$ and the connection among CLx modules is not a full mesh, return to Step 4.1.

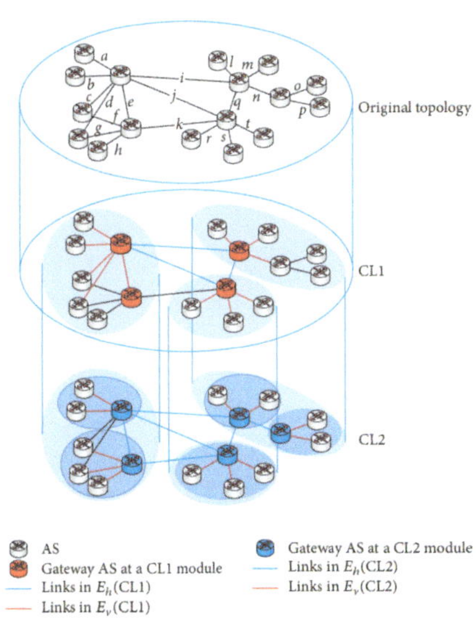

Figure 10: Illustrative example for $E_V(\mathrm{CL}x)$ and $E_h(\mathrm{CL}x)$; $E_h(\mathrm{CL1})$ is $\{a, b, c, d, e, l, m, n, r, s, t\}$ and $E_V(\mathrm{CL1})$ is $\{i, j, q\}$. $E_h(\mathrm{CL2})$ is $\{a, b, f, g, h, l, m, o, p, r, s, t\}$ and $E_V(\mathrm{CL2})$ is $\{e, i, j, k, n, q\}$. Thus, (CL1) is 3/14 and R(CL2) is 6/18.

In Step 4.1, the link is constructed between gateway ASes, because a certain degree of traffic aggregation should be retained to preserve its characteristics.

Note that the current Internet does not have a mechanism which lets an AS know the location and the CL of the other gateway ASes. However, each AS can estimate whether an AS is a gateway from the AS paths in BGP tables. When most AS paths traverse a specific AS, the AS is considered as a gateway AS. Since the amount of traffic on links between modules in the same CL differs according to CL, as shown in Figure 9, the traffic amount on links connecting to gateway ASes also varies with the CL. By investigating the number of AS paths that traverse the gateway AS, the CL of the gateway AS can be estimated.

Effect of the Evolution Process

Backtracking the Internet Topology

We examine the effect of our evolution process in terms of slowing down the traffic concentration. For this purpose, we apply our evolution process to the Internet topology in the year 2000 and evolve the topology until 2013. Then, we compare the degree of traffic concentration in the evolved topology with that of the actual Internet topology in 2013.

To apply our evolution process, we first check the ASes and links added from year y to year $y + 1$ from (y) and $G(y + 1)$. Here, (y) represents the actual Internet topology at year y. We then evolve the topology such that the ASes are the same as those in the Internet topology in the next year. Links between ASes are constructed by the proposed evolution process described in Section 6.1. The evolution process is repeatedly applied 13 times; that is, the topology (y) is evolved to $T(y + 13)$. Note that when some ASes vanish at ($y + 1$), we remove them and their links from $T(y + 1)$ just after Step 1. If the topology ($y + 1$) becomes unconnected by this removal process, we select the largest connected component for further evolution. Selecting the largest connected component leads to a decrease in the number of ASes and links. However, we can confirm that the number of ASes in unselected connected components is less than 1% of all ASes, so the impact of this decrease is negligible.

At Step 3, we recalculate the flow hierarchy after adding links in Step 2 such that the flow hierarchy reflects the change of traffic aggregation altered by the link addition. At Step 4.1, we randomly select a pair of gateway ASes to construct a link on E_h(CLx). Instead, we could calculate the optimal pair that minimizes the amount of traffic traversing links between higher-level modules. However, such a calculation is difficult in practice, because it requires complete information about the Internet topology and AS paths. Therefore, we randomly select a pair of gateway ASes and estimate the change in the amount of traffic traversing links. In this paper, we evolve the Internet 10 times with different random seeds and present the average change in the amount of traffic traversing links. After Step 4.1, when the number of links in ($y + 1$) is the same as the number of links in $G(y +1)$, we stop applying our evolution process. After Step 4.3, we ensure that the number of links in ($y +1$) is equal to that of $G(y +1)$ for the purpose of comparison. We randomly select links from a set that is not included in ($y + 1$) but is included in $G(y + 1)$ and add the selected links to $T(y + 1)$. Finally, y is set to $y + 1$, and our evolution process is again applied until y becomes 2013.

Evaluation Results of the Proposed Evolution Process

To investigate how the number of links in E_h(CLx) should be increased in the Internet topology, we evaluate the amount of traffic at links between higher-level modules in the topology evolved by our evolution policy. Figure 11 shows the average and the range of traffic amount on CL1 and CL2 intermodules links of 10 evolutions with different random seeds.The figures show results for $w = 0.2$, 0.4, and 0.6. Note that the evolved topology has more links in E_h(CLx) as we increase w. Figure 11 shows that the evolution policy slows down the increase in traffic at links between higher-level modules. When w is 0.2, this slowdown is small, because the size of E_h(CLx) is small. In contrast, when the threshold w is set to 0.4 or 0.6, the slowdown effect is high. This is because traffic no longer needs to traverse links between higherlevel modules. More importantly, the increase in traffic on links between CL2 modules has accelerated since 2011 in the original evolution, but this trend is not observed in Figure 11(b). We observe that the traffic concentration given by our evolution policy with $w = 0.6$ is not significantly different from that when $w = 0.4$. This suggests that when the size of E_h(CLx) is above some threshold, the slowdown effect is not enhanced. We consider the traffic aggregated at links between higher-level modules to be adequately reduced when w is set to 0.4.

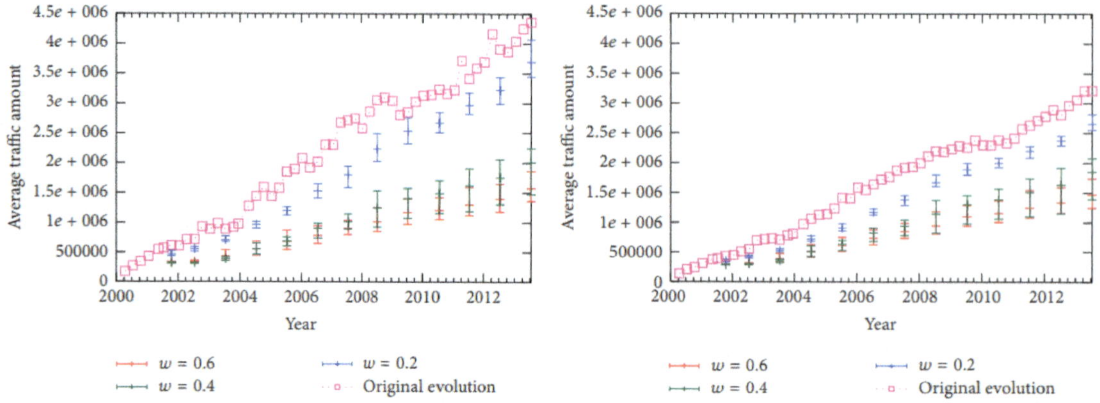

(a) Average traffic amount at CL1 intermodule links

(b) Average traffic amount at CL2 intermodule links

Figure 11: Average traffic amount at CL1 and CL2 intermodule links in the topology grown by applying the proposed evolution process.

We finally investigate the influence of our evolution policy on the characteristics of the Internet. Figure 12 shows the average path length and the clustering coefficient of the Internet topology in January 2015 and the graphs evolved by our evolution policy. Average path length of topologies evolved by our evolution policy is larger than the Internet topology. However, when parameter w of our evolution policy is 0.4, the difference is marginal. Clustering coefficient of topology evolved by our evolution policy is lower than that of the Internet topology. However, since clustering coefficient of the Internet topology is also quite small, the difference of absolute value of clustering coefficient is small. These mean that the influence of our evolution policy on the characteristics of the Internet topology is marginal.

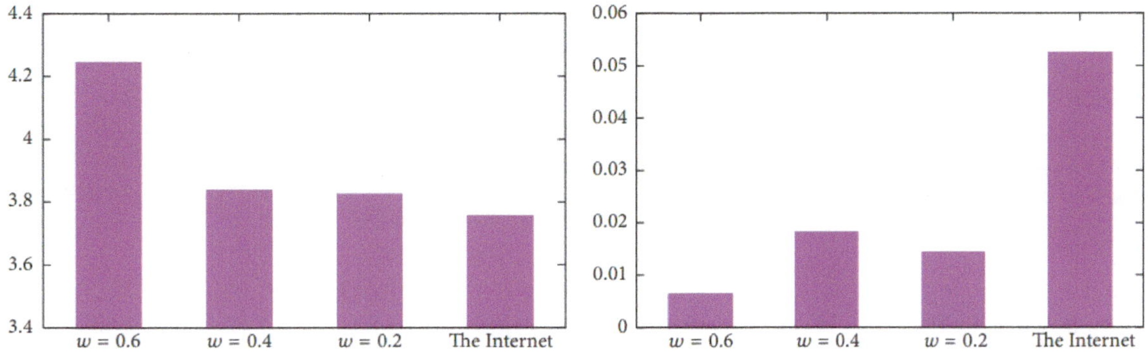

(a) Average path length

(b) Clustering coefficient

Figure 12: The influence on graph metrics by the evolution policy.

These results mean that a suitable structure is derived when the threshold w is 0.4. Although our evolution policy with $w = 0.4$ slows down the traffic concentration, the volume of traffic on links between higher-level modules increases slightly. Therefore, there is a possibility that the traffic concentration will become a problem in the distant future. To further reduce the traffic concentration on these links, each AS exchanges information about which AS is a gateway in the modules at each CL. Thus, some feedback mechanism is required to achieve a suitable global structure and global performance. Under such a feedback mechanism, more suitable pairs of gateway ASes can be selected to construct links in $E_h(\mathrm{CL}x)$. This evolution process may be difficult to realize in the current mechanism of link construction of ASes because this evolution process does not include the economic incentive for ASes. Our focus is not to develop a rigid evolution policy but investigate how the principles of evolution policy lead to the difference of the evolution of the global structure and whether it is possible to relax the future traffic concentration or not. Results show that our proposed evolution process can relax the traffic concentration on links between top-level modules by a half of the traffic concentration in the original evolution as shown in Figure 11. In practice, some economic incentives for promoting ASes to construct links based on the evolution process are necessary to optimize the performance of the global Internet, which is left for our future work.

ARE HYPER GIANTS NECESSARY FOR THE EVOLUTION OF THE INTERNET?

Recently, the appearance of Hyper Giants, such as Google and Akamai, has impacted the traffic flow and evolution of the Internet topology. They generate huge amounts of traffic and send this across the Internet. Reference [14] found that the traffic amount sent by Hyper Giants is about 30% of the whole amount across the Internet, and the traffic amount generated and sent by Hyper Giants is expected to increase [5]. The appearance of Hyper Giants has influenced the structure of the Internet topology [5, 6, 8, 14, 46]. Hyper Giants construct peering links to ASes that use services provided by Hyper Giants, so that traffic sent by Hyper Giants does not traverse large ISPs. The primary reason that Hyper Giants construct a lot of peering links is to reduce the transit cost of traffic traversing large ISPs.

The increased number of peering links partly helps the Internet topology to achieve a suitable structure to continually accommodate an increase in traffic amount. This is because peering links are connected between modules, which are links in $E_h(\mathrm{CL}x)$. However, the appearance of Hyper Giants alone will not allow the Internet topology to evolve sufficiently to accommodate the increase in traffic amount, because only traffic between a Hyper Giant and an ISP can be exchanged over the peering links. To accommodate the increase in traffic amount, some of the traffic aggregated at links suffering from overconcentration must traverse the other links. The peering links of Hyper Giants do not exchange traffic, but links between ISPs can. Therefore, it is important to consider not only the peering links of Hyper Giants, but also the connection among ISPs.

CONCLUSION

An evolution process that considers the global structure of the Internet topology is needed to accommodate future traffic amount. An analysis of the structure in the topology reveals where the traffic is concentrated, which enables us to develop an evolution policy to relax the overconcentration. Many works have shown that the Internet has a hierarchical structure [11–13]. Within this hierarchical structure, an AS aggregates traffic from lower-level ASes and relays the traffic to higher-level ASes. To identify the hierarchical nature of traffic aggregation, we investigated the long-term change in the structure of the Internet topology by analyzing the flow hierarchy. By examining the internal structure of a module, we found that each hub AS in a module is a gateway that aggregates and exchanges traffic from/to other modules. Furthermore, when the traffic demand is given by the gravity model, we showed that the amount of traffic traversing links between top-level modules and link between second-level modules has been rapidly increasing.

We considered a new evolution policy to avoid traffic concentration and then examined how this policy could slow down the traffic concentration compared with the actual evolution of the Internet topology.The basic approach behind our evolution policy is to construct more links between gateway ASes in different modules at the same level of the flow hierarchy, particularly at lower levels. While the topology retains the characteristic of traffic aggregation, a new policy is needed to avoid traffic concentration. To retain this characteristic, links between a gateway AS and other ASes in the same module should be preserved. We therefore introduced a threshold that determines the ratio of links between gateway ASes in different modules to the links between a gateway AS and other ASes. By varying this threshold, we examined how many links between gateway ASes are needed to slow down the traffic concentration. In evaluating the effect of our evolution policy, we found that the traffic concentration at links between higher-level modules decreased noticeably when the threshold was 0.4 or 0.6. We thus considered the traffic aggregated at links between higher-level modules to be adequately reduced when $w = 0.4$.

In future work, we will develop an evolution policy that considers the merits of each AS. Because the evolution of the Internet topology is not centrally controlled but an ensemble of individual link construction by each AS, the evolution policy should be applied to each AS. Indeed, [5, 47] investigated the evolution of the Internet topology from the viewpoint of game theoretic behavior by each AS. Future evolution policies must consider both the merit to individual ASes and the merit for the global structure of the Internet.

APPENDIX

The Impact of Resolution Limit on Analysis of the Evolution of the Flow Hierarchy

In Section 4, we analyzed the evolution of the Internet topology by investigating the evolution of the flow hierarchy. In the investigation, we used the Louvain method to exploit the flow hierarchy from the Internet topology. However, it is known that the Louvain method suffers from a resolution limit. The resolution limit is the characteristic scale of the smallest size of a module that the method can detect. To determine the effect of resolution limit on the analysis of the evolution of the flow hierarchy as shown in Table 5 and Figure 6, we analyze the evolution of each CL with the Infomap method [26], which does not much suffer from the resolution limit [44].

Analysis of the Size of Module by Infomap Method

We first investigated the size of module derived by the Louvain method and the Infomap method. Figure 13 shows the size of CL1 modules derived by the Louvain method on 15 November 2013. x axis indicates the size of a module and y axis indicates the number of modules. The width of a bar is 2 in both of Figures 13(a) and 13(b). The number of modules containing fewer than 10 ASes is only about 10 and there are a few large modules containing more than 5000 ASes. Figure 14 shows the size of CL1 modules derived by the Infomap method on 15 November 2013. x axis and y axis show the size of CL1 modules derived by the Infomap method and the number of modules, respectively. By the Infomap method, much more amount of small-size modules appears compared to the Louvain method. This means that there is the effect of resolution limit on our analysis of the modular structure.

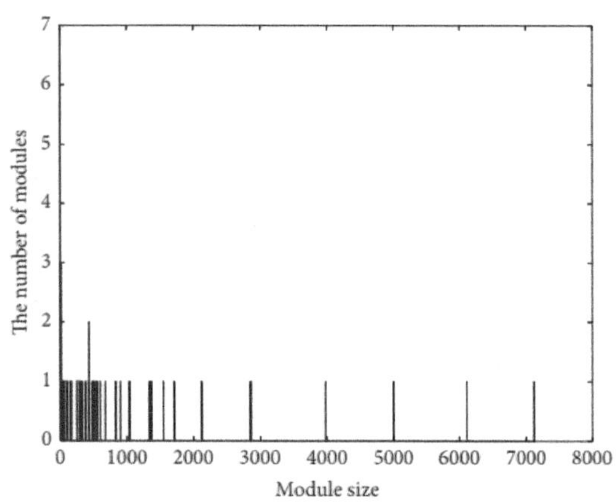

(a) All modules

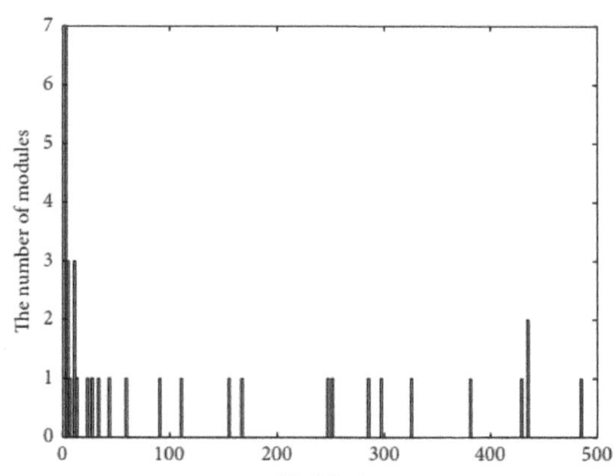

(b) Modules that contain smaller than 500 nodes

Figure 13: The size of CL1 modules that are divided by the Louvain method.

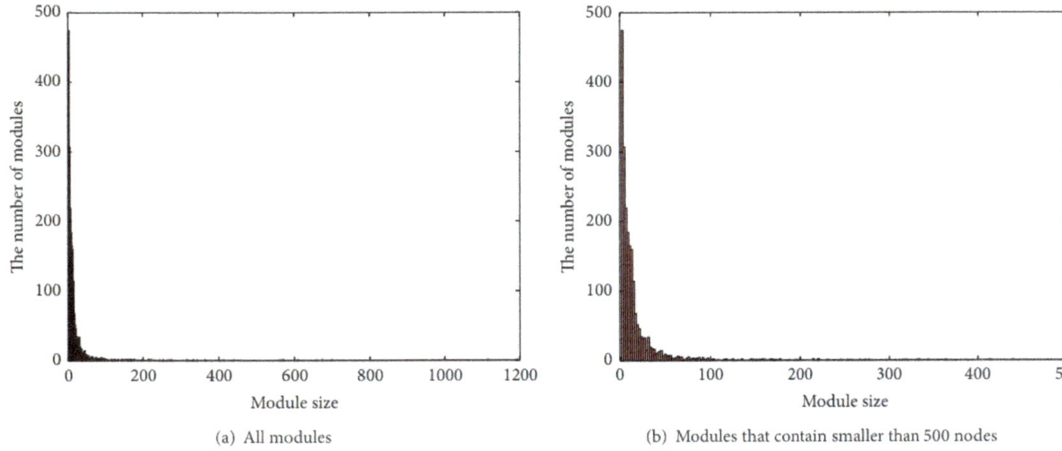

Figure 14: The size of CL1 modules that are divided by the Infomap method.

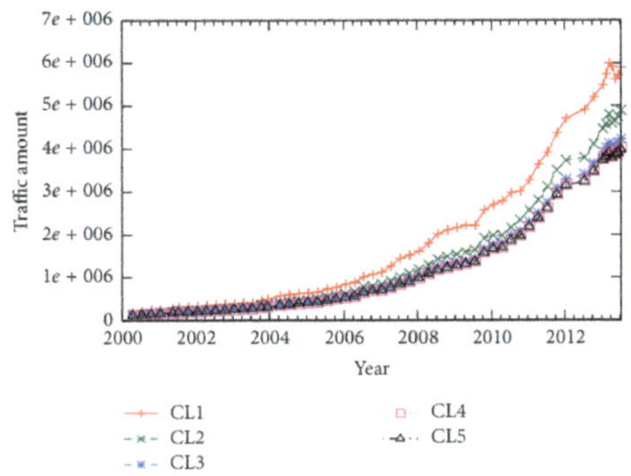

Figure 15: The average traffic amount on intermodule links in each CL as the increase of γ.

Analysis of the Evolution of the Flow Hierarchy by Infomap Method

We next clarify whether our analysis of Table 5 and Figure 6 in our first submitted paper is affected by the resolution limit. Table 7 shows the number of modules in each CL derived by the Infomap method. The depth of the deepest module is always 3 from 2000 to 2012; that is, the depth has not changed. This result is the same as the result with the Louvain method. The number of modules in middle or bottom level such as CL2 and CL3 has more greatly increased than CL1 modules which is top level. This result also agrees with the result with the Louvain method.

Table 7: The number of modules in each CL derived by the Infomap method

Year	CL1	CL2	CL3
2000	445	573	4
2002	752	950	19
2004	887	1313	53
2006	1127	1625	25
2008	1379	2221	42
2010	1757	2604	49
2012	1991	3177	64

Table 8 shows the average number of ASes in a module derived by the Infomap method. The increase of ASes in a CL1 module is slight. The reason is that there are a much more number of small-size CL1 modules as shown in Figure 14. Nevertheless, the number of ASes in CL1 modules has increased compared to CL2 and CL3. This suggests that the number of ASes in large-size CL1 modules has greatly increased. From Tables 7 and 8, we consider that the structure in top level has expanded with the center pattern in Figure 6 since the structure in top level has expanded by increasing the number of ASes within a module. The structure in low level has expanded with the left pattern in Figure 6 since modules have increased more than top level. This result agrees with the result of analysis with the Louvain method.

Table 8: The average number of ASes in a module derived by the Infomap method

Year	CL1	CL2	CL3
2000	18.34	10.33	4
2002	18.1	9.16	5.95
2004	20.31	10.56	7.66
2006	20.34	10.87	4.52
2008	21.26	10.74	4.83
2010	20.26	10.91	17.67
2012	21.1	10.67	6.03

REFERENCES

1. University of Oregon, "Route Views project," 2013, http://www.routeviews.org/.

2. RIPE NCC, "RIS Raw Data," 2013, http://www.ripe.net/data-tools/stats/ris/ris-raw-data.

3. L. Atzori, A. Iera, and G. Morabito, "The internet of things: a survey," Computer Networks, vol. 54, no. 15, pp. 2787–2805, 2010.

4. D. Miorandi, S. Sicari, F. De Pellegrini, and I. Chlamtac, "Internet of things: vision, applications and research challenges," Ad Hoc Networks, vol. 10, no. 7, pp. 1497–1516, 2012.

5. A. Dhamdhere and C. Dovrolis, "The Internet is flat: modeling the transition from a transit hierarchy to a peering mesh,," in Proceedings of the ACM 6th International Conference (Co-NEXT ‹10), pp. 1–12, December 2010.

6. A. Dhamdhere and C. Dovrolis, "Twelve years in the evolution of the internet ecosystem," IEEE/ACM Transactions on Networking, vol. 19, no. 5, pp. 1420–1433, 2011.

7. E. Gregoria, L. Lenzinib, and C. Orsini, "k-dense communities in the Internet AS-level topology,"Computer Networks, vol. 57, pp. 1–10, 2013.

8. Y. Shavitt and U. Weinsberg, "Topological trends of Internet content providers," in Proceedings of the 4th Annual Workshop on Simplifying Complex Networks for Practitioners (SIMPLEX ‹12), pp. 13–18, ACM, Lyon, France, April 2012.

9. D. J. Watts and S. H. Strogatz, "Collective dynamics of 'small-world' networks," Nature, vol. 393, no. 6684, pp. 440–442, 1998.

10. L. C. Freeman, "A set of measures of centrality based on betweenness," Sociometry, vol. 40, no. 1, pp. 35–41, 1977.

11. Z. G. Daniel, D. R. Figueiredo, S. Jaiswal, and L. Gao, "On the hierarchical structure of the logical Internet graph," in Proceedings of the Scalibility and Traffic Control in IP Networks, vol. 4526, pp. 208–222, 2001.

12. R. Pastor-Satorras, A. Vázquez, and A. Vespignani, "Topology, hierarchy, and correlations in Internet graphs," Complex Networks, vol. 650, pp. 425–440, 2004.

13. H. Tangmunarunkit, R. Govindan, S. Jamin, S. Shenker, and W. Willinger, "Network topologies, power laws, and hierarchy," Computer Communication Review, vol. 32, p. 76, 2002.

14. C. Labovitz, S. Iekel-Johnson, D. McPherson, J. Oberheide, and F. Jahanian, "Internet inter-domain traffic," in Proceedings of the 7th International Conference on Autonomic Computing (SIGCOMM ‹10), pp. 75–86, September 2010.

15. M. E. J. Newman, "Modularity and community structure in networks," Proceedings of the National Academy of Sciences of the United States of America, vol. 103, no. 23, pp. 8577–8582, 2006.

16. A. Elmokashfi, A. Kvalbein, and C. Dovrolis, "On the scalability of BGP: the roles of topology growth and update rate-limiting," in Proceedings of the 4th ACM International Conference on Emerging Networking Experiments and Technologies (CoNEXT ‹08), pp. 1250–1261, ACM, Madrid, Spain, December 20098.

17. CAIDA, "The cooperative association for Internet data analysis," 2013, http://www.caida.org/home/.

18. S. C. Au, C. Leckie, A. Parhar, and G. Wong, "Efficient visualization of large routing topologies,"International Journal of Network Management, vol. 14, no. 2, pp. 105–118, 2004.

19. M. Faloutsos, P. Faloutsos, and C. Faioutsos, "On power-law relationships of the internet topology," inProceedings of the Conference on Applications, Technologies, Architectures, and Protocols for Computer Communication (SIGCOMM ‹99), pp. 251–262, September 1999.

20. V. Rosato, L. Issacharoff, S. Meloni, D. Caligiore, and F. Tiriticco, "Is the topology of the internet network really fit to sustain its function?" Physica A, vol. 387, no. 7, pp. 1689–1704, 2008.

21. I. Poese, B. Frank, B. Ager, G. Smaragdakis, S. Uhlig, and A. Feldmann, "Improving content delivery with PaDIS," IEEE Internet Computing, vol. 16, no. 3, pp. 46–52, 2012.

22. Y. Zhang, "Internet as-level topology archive," http://irl.cs.ucla.edu/topology/.

23. B. Zhang, R. Liu, D. Massey, and L. Zhang, "Collecting the Internet AS-level topology," ACM SIGCOMM Computer Communication Review, vol. 35, pp. 53–61, 2005.

24. B. Huffaker, M. Fomenkov, and K. Claffy, "Internet topology data comparison," CAIDA Technical Report, 2012.

25. R. Cohen, "The Internet dark matter: on the missing links in the AS connectivity map," in Proceedings of the IEEE Conference on Computer Communications (INFOCOM ‹06), pp. 1–12, April 2006.

26. M. Rosvall and C. T. Bergstrom, "Maps of information flow reveal community structure in complex networks," Proceedings of the National Academy of Sciences, vol. 105, pp. 1118–1123, 2008.

27. A. Lancichinetti, F. Radicchi, J. J. Ramasco, and S. Fortunato, "Finding statistically significant communities in networks," PLoS ONE, vol. 6, no. 4, Article ID e18961, 2011.

28. V. D. Blondel, J. L. Guillaume, R. Lambiotte, and E. Lefebvre, "Fast unfolding of communities in large networks," Journal of Statistical Mechanics: Theory and Experiment, vol. 2008, no. 10, Article ID P10008, 2008.

29. M. Rosvall and C. T. Bergstrom, "Maps of random walks on complex networks reveal community structure," Proceedings of the National Academy of Sciences of the United States of America, vol. 105, no. 4, pp. 1118–1123, 2008.

30. M. Roughan, A. Greenberg, C. Kalmanek, M. Rumsewicz, J. Yates, and Y. Zhang, "Experience in measuring backbone traffic variability: models, metrics, measurements and meaning," in Proceedings of the 2nd ACM SIGCOMM Internet Measurement Workshop (IMW ‹02), pp. 91–92, November 2002.

31. Y. Zhang, M. Roughan, N. Duffield, and A. Greenberg, "Fast accurate computation of large-scale IP traffic matrices from link loads," in Proceedings of the ACM SIGMETRICS International Conference on Measurement and Modeling of Computer Systems (SIGMETRICS ‹03), pp. 206–217, June 2003.
32. H. Chang, S. Jamin, and W. Willinger, "To peer or not to peer: modeling the evolution of the Internet›s AS-level topology," in Proceedings of the 25th IEEE International Conference on Computer Communications (INFOCOM ‹06), pp. 1–12, April 2006.
33. H. Chang, S. Jamin, Z. M. Mao, and W. Willinger, "An empirical approach to modeling inter-AS traffic matrices," in Proceedings of the 5th ACM SIGCOMM Conference on Internet Measurement (IMC ‹05), vol. 5, pp. 139–152, August 2005.
34. Q. Chen, H. Chang, R. Govindan, S. Jamin, S. J. Shenker, and W. Willinger, "The origin of power laws in Internet topologies revisited," in Proceedings of the IEEE INFOCOM, pp. 608–617, June 2002.
35. D. Jiang and G. Hu, "GARCH model-based large-scale IP traffic matrix estimation," IEEE Communications Letters, vol. 13, no. 1, pp. 52–54, 2009.
36. G. Huston, "CIDR-report," 2013, http://www.cidr-report.org/as2.0/.
37. Cisco, "Cisco global cloud index: forecast and methodology, 2011–2016," 2012, http://www.itworldcanada.com/assets/cisco-global-cloud-index-forecast-and-methodology-2011-2016.
38. Cisco, "Cisco global cloud index forecasts cloud traffic to grow sixfold by 2016," 2012, http://newsroom.cisco.com/release/1091855.
39. L. Gao, "On inferring autonomous system relationships in the Internet," IEEE/ACM Transactions on Networking, vol. 9, no. 6, pp. 733–745, 2001.
40. M. E. Newman, "Mixing patterns in networks," Physical Review E: Statistical, Nonlinear, and Soft Matter Physics, vol. 67, no. 2, 2003.
41. R. Guimerà, M. Sales-Pardo, and L. A. N. Amaral, "Modularity from fluctuations in random graphs and complex networks," Physical Review E: Statistical, Nonlinear, and Soft Matter Physics, vol. 70, no. 2, Article ID 025101, 2004.
42. S. Fortunato, "Community detection in graphs," Physics Reports, vol. 486, no. 3–5, pp. 75–174, 2010. ·
43. J. Reichardt and S. Bornholdt, "Statistical mechanics of community detection," Physical Review E, vol. 74, no. 1, Article ID 016110, 2006.
44. A. Lancichinetti and S. Fortunato, "Community detection algorithms: a comparative analysis," Physical Review E: Statistical, Nonlinear, and Soft Matter Physics, vol. 80, no. 5, Article ID 056117, 2009.
45. X. Ma and K. Harfoush, "Traffic concentration for a green Internet," in Proceedings of the 9th International Conference on High Capacity Optical Networks and Enabling Technologies (HONET ‹12), vol. 9, pp. 142–146, December 2012.
46. B. Krogfoss, M. Weldon, and L. Sofman, "Internet architecture evolution and the complex economies of content peering," Bell Labs Technical Journal, vol. 17, no. 1, pp. 163–184, 2012.
47. A. Lodhi, A. Dhamdhere, and C. Dovrolis, "Peering strategy adoption by transit providers in the internet: a game theoretic approach," ACM SIGMETRICS Performance Evaluation Review, vol. 40, no. 2, pp. 38–41, 2012.

CHAPTER 16

TOWARDS INTERNET OF THINGS: SURVEY AND FUTURE VISION

Omar Said[1] and Mehedi Masud[2]

[1]IT/ College of Computers and Information Technology Taif University Taif, Saudi Arabia.

[2]CS/ College of Computers and Information Technology Taif University Taif, Saudi Arabia.

ABSTRACT

Internet of things is a promising research due to its importance in many commerce, industry, and education applications. Recently, new applications and research challenges in numerous areas of Internet of things are fired. In this paper, we discuss the history of Internet of things, different proposed architectures of Internet of things, research challenges and open problems related to the Internet of things. We also introduce the concept of Internet of things database and discuss about the future vision of Internet of things. These are the manuscript preparation guidelines used as a standard template for all journal submissions. Author must follow these instructions while preparing/modifying these guidelines.

INTRODUCTION

Recently, the concept of the Internet as a set of connected computer devices is changed to a set of connected surrounding things of human's living space, such as home appliances, machines, transportation, business storage, and goods etc. The number of things in the living space is larger than the number of world population. Research is going on how to make these things to communicate with each other like computer devices communicate through Internet. The communication among these things is referred as Internet of Things (IoT). Till now, there is no specific definition or standard architecture of IoT. Some researchers define the IoT as a new model that contains all of wireless communication technologies such as wireless sensor networks, mobile networks, and actuators. Each element of IoT is called a thing and should have a unique address. Things communicate using the Radio-Frequency Identification (RFID) technology and work in harmony to reach a common goal. In addition, the IoT should contain a strategy to determine its users and their privileges and restrictions. The US National Intelligence council has stated that by 2025 the IoT will connect everything in our life [1]. For this target new architectures are proposed and more research challenges are opened. Authors in [1] highlight some research challenges. Despite new architectures are proposed in the recent years, however, the future vision of IoT is still unclear. Considering the research challenges and future vision of IoT, in this paper we present a detail survey. At the end of the paper, we also present our recommendations.

The rest of the paper proceeds as follows. Section 2 demonstrates the history of IoT. Section 3 introduces the currently proposed IoT architectures. Section 4 introduces the IoT research challenges and open problems. Section 5 presents

Citation: Omar, and Mehedi Masud. "Towards internet of things: Survey and future vision." International Journal of Computer Networks 5, no. 1 (2013): 1-17.

the IoT database. Section 6 discusses future vision of IoT. Section 7, demonstrates the comparison between our survey and other surveys. Finally, the paper concludes in Section 8.

THE IOT HISTORY

IoT Definition

Internet has become more prevalent in our lives in a shorter time period than any other technology in the history. It revolutionized the communicate way of people. Currently, the Internet involves the process of connecting machines, equipment, software, and things in our surroundings. This connection will be through the use of the unique Internet protocol address that permits things for communicating to each other without human intervention. This new scenario is called IoT [2]. The term IOT is formalized by MIT Auto-ID center at [3]. Till now there is no accepted or standard definition for IoT.

The IoT Applications

There can be many applications of IoT. The famous IoT application is in marketing. We know that a market contains many goods and electrical machines. By using IoT, an item can automatically contact its provider and inform its situation in case of stock decreasing [4]. The cooperation between the traffic lights and the sensors for environment pollution is another example that uses the IoT technology [1]. This cooperation using IoT may provide a life with new advantages such as the normal distribution of cars in the roads and the adaptive time for each sign to be on or off [5]. There is also a range of IoT applications in France. For example, the use of glass containers equipped with ultrasonic sensors that send information about its level of filling [1]. When the level reaches to three-quarters of the container, the collection, loading and unloading processes are started automatically. In the United States, there are many applications exist such as garbage cans that are provided with sensors. When the garbage reaches a certain weight or level, warning is sent to the municipality in order to send the garbage cars, which leads to reduce the taxes on homeowners and reduce the cost and the time of communication process [1]. Also, IoT and RFID technology are used to recycle information about automotives factories in china [6]. In addition, there are some projects, which are still under progress, e.g., e-learning, healthcare, smart environment (home, office, plant), and industrial fields [1, 7, 8].

Regarding the IoT and Internet applications, it is clear that the IoT applications and the Internet applications are similar. Based on the ontology, both applications have a common character. There are some close relations such as Hypertext and text, XML and electronic tag, and Standardization and free restrictions. The ascendancy of IoT comes from product information and Internet. The IoT is tangible restriction to the product information. The product information must be written on an electronic tag, with fixed format and standardized and general words. Internet of Things can be considered as a special application of Semantic Web. It tries to appreciate the mentally processing and sharing the product information based on the Semantic Web platform [9, 10].

THE IOT ARCHITECTURES

Recently, there are two IoT architectures are suggested (i) 3–layer architecture and (ii) 5-layer architecture, and other special purpose architectures, respectively [11, 12, 13, 14]. In the following, we present these architectures.

The 3-Layer architecture

Beginning of the IoT, the accepted architecture was the 3-layer architecture. It consists of three layers which are called perception, network, and application. The purpose of perception layer is to identify each thing in the IoT system. This is done by gathering information about each object. This layer contains RFID tags, sensors, cameras, etc. The second layer is the network layer. The network layer is the core of the IoT. It transmits the information gathered by the perception layer. It contains the software and hardware instrumentations of internet network in addition to the management and information centers. The third layer is the application layer. The application layer's target is to converge between the IoT social needs and industrial technology (i.e. it can be considered as the middle tier between the industry technologies and how it can be controlled to cover the human needs) [11], see Fig. 1.

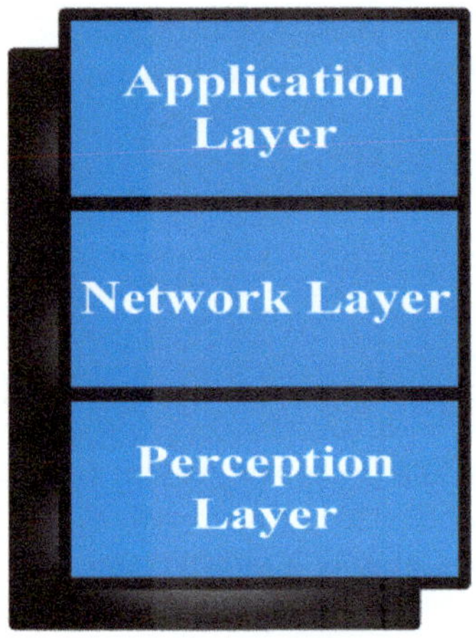

Figure 1: The IoT 3-Layer Architecture [11].

The 5-Layer Architecture

The 3-layer architecture became not sufficient due to the expected IoT development. Therefore, 5-layer architecture is proposed. The first layer is called business. The purpose of this layer is to define the IOT applications charge and management. Also, it is responsible about the user's privacy and all research related to IOT applications. The second layer is called application. The target of this layer is determining the types of applications, which will be used in the IoT. Also, it develops the IOT applications to be more intelligence, authenticated, and safe. The third layer is called processing. Its responsibility is to handle the information gathered by perception layer. The handling process contains two main topics; storing and analyzing. The target of this layer is extremely hard due to the huge gathered information about system things. So, it uses some techniques such as database software, cloud computing, ubiquitous computing, and intelligent processing in information processing and storing. The fourth layer is called transport. It seems like the network layer in the 3-layer architecture. It transmits and receives the information from the perception layer to the processing layer and via versa. It contains many technologies such as infrared, Wi-Fi, and Bluetooth. Also, the target of this layer is to address each thing in the system using IPV6. The fifth layer is called perception. The target of this layer is to define the physical meaning of each thing in the IoT system such as locations and temperatures. It also gathers the information about each object in the system and transforms this data to signals. In addition, it contains the technologies that are used in the IoT such as the RFID and the GPRS [11]. Fig. 2 presents the 5-Layer architecture.

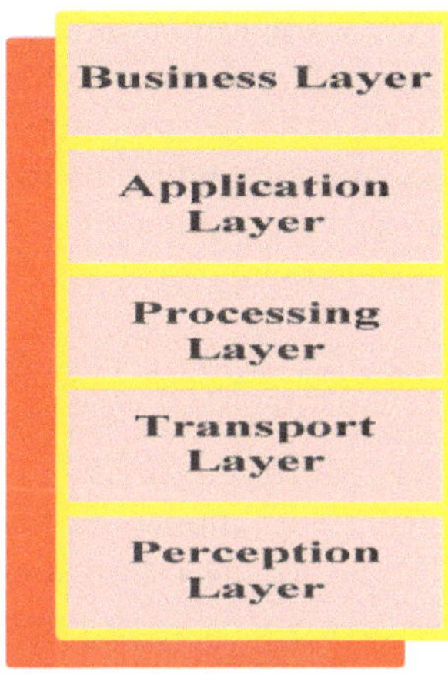

Figure 2: The IoT 5-Layer Architecture [11].

Special Purpose Architectures

There are some special purpose IoT architectures. The first architecture [15] is related to mediaaware traffic security architecture. This architecture is based on the given traffic classification to enable various multimedia services being available anywhere and anytime. The second architecture [16] is new clock synchronization architecture of network for IoT. This clock synchronization architecture of IoT is the key technology to resolve the problems, which are released due to manage the IoT nodes effectively and to ensure high clock synchronization precision. It includes three levels: adaptation level, organization level and region level. The adaptation level architecture is to resolve the problem about the adaptability of IoT; the organization level architecture is to organize and manage of the clock synchronization system; the region level architecture is to ensure clock synchronization accuracy and security. The third architecture [17] is for trusted security systems. This architecture is based on cholars' researches and combined with the security requirements and characteristics of IoT. This architecture also includes trusted safety management system, security gateway, unified service platforms of IoT, security infrastructure, and unified information exchange platform. The fourth architecture [18] is mankind neural system. This architecture introduces two aspects: Unit IoT and Ubiquitous IoT. The Unite IoT focus on special targets (provides solutions for special applications), and its infrastructure is a man-like nervous system. The Ubiquitous IoT focus on the collection of multiple unites of IoTs with ubiquitous views (assemble the special organization to be manageable by one powerful application). Also, there are some special purpose architectures [19, 20, 21] which cannot be considered a standard architecture.

IOT CHALLENGES AND OPEN PROBLEMS

There are numerous challenges in the IoT which are still under research. The IoT challenges and open problems are raised due to two main reasons. These reasons for mass gathering information for each thing in the IoT system and the communication among system hardware, see Fig. 3.

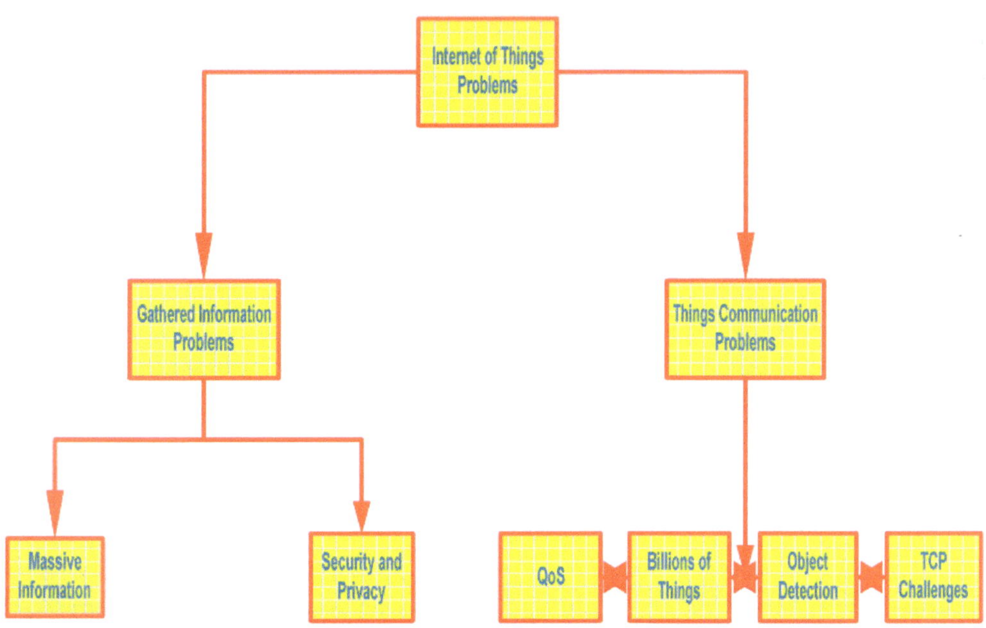

Figure 3: IoT Challenges and Problems.

Information Gathering Problems

These problems can be divided to two main classes. The first one is related to the massive information that is gathered by RFID about huge number of things which are found at IoT system. The second is the security and the privacy of information due to wireless transmission media.

Massive gathered information: The IoT systems should have millions if not billions of objects. Each object should radiate information to express about itself. This information should be gathered. The quantity of gathered information is massive due to the huge number of IoT objects. So, there are several problems which are raised due to a lot of gathered information. These problems are transmission, storing, and processing. Transmission problem means that it is required to transmit all of things data in real time and this is not a guaranteed issue [22, 23]. This is because of the bandwidth issue, which is required to transmit this information, may be not available. It is well known that the information travels in a trip starting from the things and ends to its control web application. This trip may contain more bandwidth bottlenecks which mean that a required bandwidth is mostly not available. The problem of data storing is raised due to the quantity of media required to store and backup this information. The processing operation means that the things information should be handled by IoT web applications to determine the control actions for each thing. This handling process should be done in a real time mode [24, 25].

Security and privacy: It's well known that the data is transmitted between IoT objects inside a wireless medium. So, the security and privacy issues are very important and should be discussed. Regarding the security problem, there are numerous causes to make the IoT information in danger. These causes are physical attack, wireless information attack, and low self-defense. The physical attack means that the hacker may tamper with the IoT devices due to presence of these devices alone most of the time. Hence, anyone can hack it physically. The wireless information attack means that the hacker can acquire the information from the medium before it is received by the destination and there are more researches in this topic [26, 27, 28, 29]. The low self defense means that most of IoT devices didn't have an ability to accept security package(s) for partially saving [30, 31, 32]. The privacy is an important issue in civilized countries. It means that the information provider is only able to infer by observing the use of the system related to each system client (at least, inference should be very hard to conduct). The data collection, handling, and mining are accomplished in the IoT systems in completely different form that we know. This is because there are more situations that may occur in the IoT system such as home resources control system. So, to guarantee the privacy of things personal information, we should make sure of three main items; (1) who collects the personal data, (2) how these data are collected, and (3) the time of collection process. Furthermore, the personal data that are collected should be used by authorized the person, stored in an authorized server, and accessed by authorized clients [33, 34, 35]. The security and privacy needs three main requirements: resilience to attack, data authentication, and client privacy. Also, some questions related to human rights and constitutional framework are raised such as if new international laws are needed, if legislation is envisaged [1, 36].

Things Communication Problems

The problem related to the communication between IoT things components, is divided into two classes. The first is addressing of things problem and the second is RFID problems in reading, writing, and transmission of objects information. In the following, we discuss the things communication problems.

Billions of IoT things: When we think in communication process among a large number of things, we observe a big problem due to many issues. Sample of these issues are: what is the hardware, which is required for communicating this massive number of things? What is the ideal addressing technique (protocol) for each thing in the resulted system? If the answer is IPV6, another question will be raised; if IPV6 is suitable for the IoT future? The compatibility between a huge number of required hardware, which consist the IoT systems, can be considered as a communication factor or not? and others. There are many attempts that have emerged to answer these issues [37, 38, 39, 40, 41, 42, 43], but most of these researches are theoretical and lack in practice. Furthermore, they did not specify the IoT future vision and parameters. The problem of the tools, which are proposed so far to build an integrated IoT system, is incomplete and lacking in standard. Another trial for accessing the information instead of using hardware communications (RFID) is presented in [44]. This trail uses the computer vision and image processing techniques to access the thing information and suffers from delay due to the time consumption in object image handling process (see subsection entitled real time object detection).

IoT and TCP challenge: The IoT infrastructure is similar to the Internet backbone. So, the data transmission will use TCP or UDP protocols as a transmission protocol. The UDP is not reliable protocol and this is opposite of our target. Hence, TCP should be selected to act as a transport layer for IoT systems. The TCP has more challenges related to the IoT systems such as connection setup, congestion control, and data buffering. The connection setup may not be considered in most cases in the IoT systems due to the need to transmit small amount of data between objects. In addition, the communication resources in IoT are mostly sensors, RFID tags, and PDAs which cannot handle the data required for connection setup. The congestion control is a challenge in the wireless medium which is the same medium of IoT systems. Also, in case of small transmitted information between IoT objects, the congestion control data is not required. The data buffering in TCP is required at the source for retransmission process and destination for ordering process. The data buffering processes are costly for the battery-less devices such as RFID tags. So, the conclusion is UDP is not suitable and TCP has more challenges and in most IoT cases is not required. Many researchers studied the characteristics and actions of transmitted information inside IoT objects such as WSN and RFID systems [22, 23, 24].

Real time objects detection: When we concentrate in IoT system, we find two ambiguous queries; how we can define each thing and how we can acquire its information. It is natural if we answer by using the RFID, the EPC, or the UID technologies. But, these technologies have several problems such as radiation, privacy, violation, and inconvenience of information updating. In addition, it is not easy to define all of these technologies with the entire world things shortly. There are many researches tried to solve these problems such as [45], [46]. Authors in [44] introduce another idea which changes the concept of using above technologies for things definition. Instead of using the RFID, the EPC, or the UID, we can use the computer vision and image processing techniques such that each object can extract other objects by vision. Also, this idea faces another challenge, namely the real time handling. The real time handling means that the relation between the IoT system objects, which contains three main steps; seeing, analysis, and information extraction should be accomplished in real time mode.

IoT QoS: There are many researches in the internet QoS such as [47, 48]. But these scenarios are not suitable for the IoT systems. This is because the QoS researches considered a localized area in the IoT such as Wireless Sensor Network (WSN) and not for other areas such as the RFID. The research of QoS may be applied on the IoT systems but this can be considered as a short term solution. In addition, the QoS results are executed on the M2M communication. But, in case of IoT, there are different paradigms due to the mixture of IoT objects each one has a different characteristics and behavior [1, 2].

Core Challenge

The most important factor in the IoT is to build a standard and universal architecture. So, now we try to construct this architecture based on our daily live. The attempt, which is introduced in [18], is much closed idea to our trial. This attempt is limited. The limitation of this architecture comes from the consideration that the entire IoT systems have the same features and layers. This is not true in most cases. In IoT infrastructure, there are many systems with different targets, applications, and features. Hence, we should expand the architecture, which is introduced in [18], to be the most common one that will communicate these different systems (work in this architecture in progress).

IOT DATABASE

Internet of Things system produces mass information. The format of RFID contains three parts EPC which represents the unique identifier read by an RFID reader; location is the place where the reader is found, and time of reading process. It is well known that RFID raw needs approximately 18 bytes. If we took a supermarket as an example, there are about 700,000 RFID tags. If the supermarket has readers that scan the items every second, about 12.6 GB RFID data will be produced per second, and the data will reach 544TB per day. So, it is necessary to find effective methods for storing, filtering and modifying RFID raw data. The Internet of Things gathered information can be classified into numerous types: RFID data stream, address/unique identifiers, descriptive data, positional data, environment data and sensor network data etc. [49]. It is a great challenge to manage the Internet of Things information. Many trials have appeared to suggest models for dealing with this type of intensive database. Reference [50] provides a new model called ROAM and used for variance detection in moving objects. Reference [51] developed a novel partition-and-detect model for faraway trajectory detection of moving object. Reference [52] also put forward a new method called TraClass using trajectory-based clustering and hierarchical region-based. Reference [53] introduced a new model in trajectory clustering of moving object which is called a partition-and-group. Reference [54] proposed a general model to supervise learning under the conditions of power, computational, and memory limitations. The special characteristics of IoT such as mass data, distributed data, time-related data, and heterogeneous environment bring several problems to centralized data mining architecture [55]. The last trial [56] suggested four different models. The first model, called multi-layer data mining model for IoT, which consists of four layers each one accomplishes some functions. These layers are data management layer, event processing layer, data mining service layer, and data collection layer, and each layer has many functions. The second model is called distributed data mining model for IoT. In this model, there is a core for entire data mining system which is called the global control node. It determines the data mining algorithm and the data sets for mining, and then search about the sub-nodes containing these data sets. Hence, these sub-nodes receive the raw data from various smart things. These information is filtered, abstracted, and compressed, and then is saved in the local data warehouse. The third model is called grid based data mining model for IoT. IoT objects should intelligent, context-awareness, and long-range operable. Therefore smart IoT objects are considered as a kind of resources for grid computing. Thus, using the data mining services of grid to implement the data mining operations for IoT is the core of this model idea. The fourth model is called data mining model for IoT from multi-technology integration perspective. In this model, the context-awareness provides the IoT system with data individually or from smart objects. IPV6 protocol is used in objects addressing. There are different ubiquitous ways are used for accessing the future Internet such as, sensor devices, RFID, WiMAX, etc. Credibility and controllability of data transmission are adapted by a trusted control plane. So, data mining tools and algorithms are carried out, and different service-oriented applications such as intelligent transportation, intelligent logistics accepts the gained knowledge.

Suggested IoT Database Architecture

We propose a multilayer data mining model for the proposed system based on [56]. The model consists of six layers: IoT layer, data collection layer, data warehousing layer, event processing layer, data mining service layer, and application layer. Table 1 describes each layer's functions while Fig. 4 presents a general view of the data model. Table 1demonstrates Functions of the Data Model Layers.

Table 1: Functions of the Data Model Layers

Layer Name	Layer Function
IoT layer	This layer contains all the system objects such as sensors, PDA, desktops, cameras, actuators, etc. In this layer each object is identified using RFID and IPv6.
Data collection layer	This layer collects the objects' data. Each type of data needs different collection strategies such as misreading, repeated reading, fault tolerance, data filtering and communications, etc. This is a challenging task and should be solved appropriately.
Data warehousing layer	The collected data is stored in a data warehouse after three processes: object identification, data abstraction and compression. For example, the style of an RFID stream is "Electronic Product Code (EPC), location, time", where EPC marks smart object's ID. After data cleaning, we can obtain a Stay table that contains records of the format "EPC, location, time_in, time_out". We can, then, use a data warehouse like RFID-CUBOID to save and manage the data, including tables such as Info table, Stay table and Map table. Based on RFID-CUBOID, users can access online RFID data conveniently. Also, it may contain some XML modules that can be adopted to describe data in IoT. The connection between IoT smart objects are mostly achieved via the data warehousing layer in the IoT.
Event processing layer	Event processing layer is used to analyze events in IoT effectively. The data should be aggregated, organized and analyzed according to events. Hence, we can issue an event-based query or conduct an event-analysis in this layer. To that end, we should filter out primitive events so only complex events that concern user(s) are kept.
Data mining service layer	The data mining layer relies on both the data warehousing layer and the event processing layer. Object-based or event-based data mining services, such as association analysis, patterns mining data classification, data forecasting, data clustering, or outlier detection are available for applications. The architecture of this layer is service-oriented.
Application layer	The application layer contains three sub-layers: the local manager sub-layer, general manager sub-layer, and inelegant applications sub-layer. The fist sub-layer is used to implement some data mining algorithms for complex events that cannot be done in the data mining layer. The second sub-layer is used to aggregate, adapt, and filter the results that come from the local managers. The results are transformed to instructions and then into actions to be executed by the application sub-layer.
Multi-Agent system	Layers 2 to 6 are controlled by the multi-agent system.

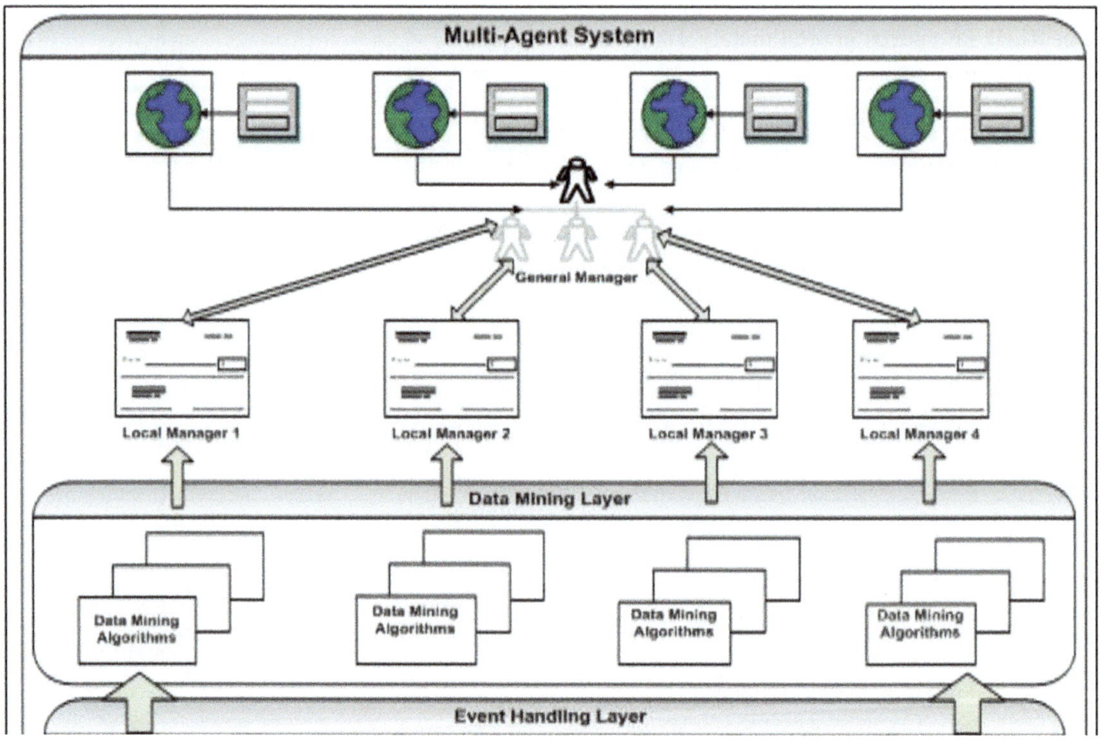

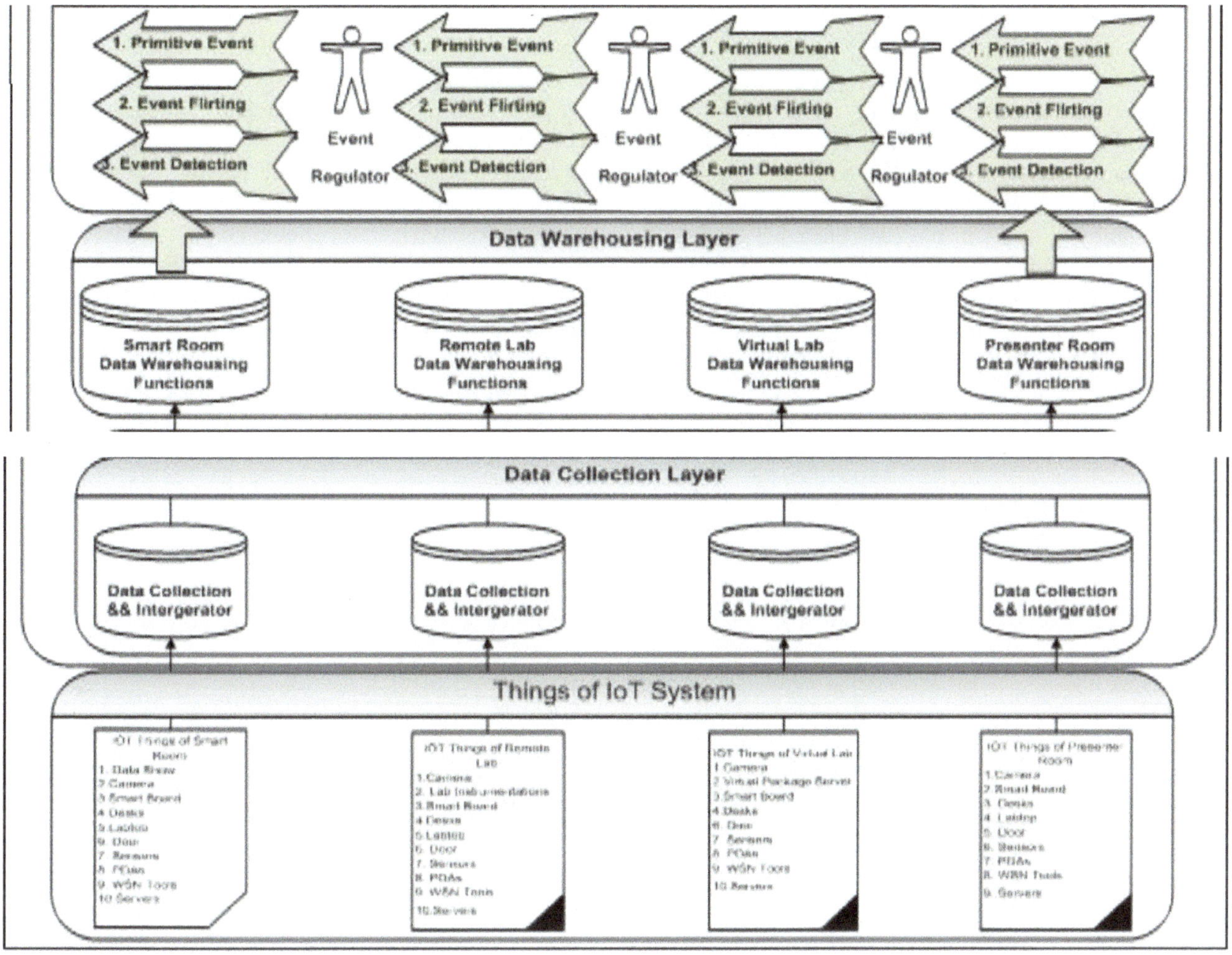

Figure 4: General View of the Data Model.

IOT DISCUSSION AND FUTURE VISION

In this section we discuss some issues regarding the IoT. Before we demonstrate our vision in IoT we first give an example: Consider a scenario where a person lives in a smart city. When the person wakes up from sleep, there is a set of events occurs between his waking up until he returns to his home (i.e. work hours events). First, he goes to the bathroom. The bathroom door is automatically opened. Then the faucet water is opened for adaptive interval time. As this person comes in the front of the apartment door, it is opened. While the person moves to the elevator, its door will be opened and the elevator is adapted to stop at the person desired level. These smart actions from the things that will be used by this person will continue until he reaches his work. If he wants to know information about something within the trip, he can easily access it by other things which are closed to the target one. This scenario is accomplished by communicating the system things (bathroom door, faucet water, apartment door, elevator, etc.) to be one network using IoT technology (smart application). This network makes the objects behavior like a human.

From above example, it's clear that our future vision of IoT is to make everything like an autonomous robot. This is a truth, which should be reached, but nowadays, this is not easy to accomplish. Science, there are more things which are passive. In addition, to transform each thing in our live, even it is active, from human control to full smartness is extremely expensive [57, 58]. Without complexity, the full smartness of a thing can be defined as the ability to make this thing behavior like a human behavior using software and hardware. Let us take a thing such as smart board and imagine that we would like to transform it into full smartness. The smart board can be considered as an active thing. This smart board should sense a human (student or professor) desires in addition to its around hardware tools such as data show and cameras. To accomplish these two simple characteristics, we need camera, image processing technique, processor, actuator, and intelligent program to adapt the smart board motion. All of these components are needed for transforming the active thing from static situation (i.e., with human controlled) to smartness.

From our point of view, in the near future we will find that most of these things in our range of living will be smart. In this case, we will find ourselves facing an amazing programming challenge to achieve the ultimate goal of IoT, see Fig. 5.

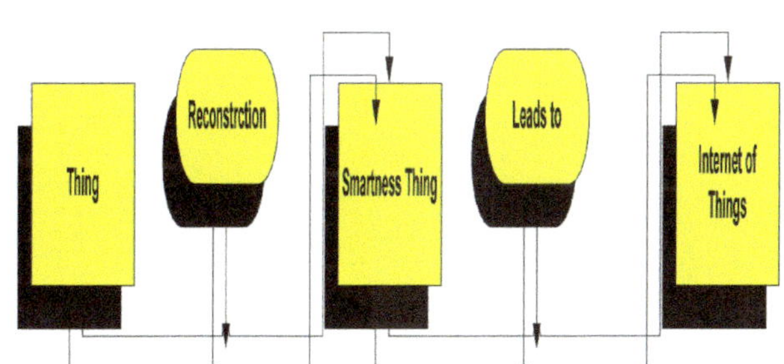

Figure 5: Live Cycle of Thing To Be in The IoT System.

If everything is transformed to smartness another problem will be raised that is called standardization. The standardization in the IoT system means the capability of replacing or changing hardware with something else; permitting mutual substitution without loss of function or suitability. The standardization itself may be a good solution for most of IoT problems if it is accomplished for most of the world things. It is well known that there are many systems in the IoT. Each IoT system is constructed using some hardware and software programs. The hardware in each system may be adapted in some way which cannot be used by other systems. For example, the marketing is a famous application in the IoT. The refrigerator is one of essential components in the market. The IoT refrigerator is adapted to call the service provider automatically in case of near to finish. If we use this refrigerator to be in a hospital, there are two different parameters. The first parameter is to whom the alarm message will be sent from the hospital refrigerator (i.e., there are more persons should be alarmed with the refrigerator situation) and the second one is the content sensitivity (the refrigerator should contain cadavers). Also, the IoT software may differ from one application to others. So, our recommendation is to strive for setting a standard specs for IoT hardware and software to be ready to work when transferred from one place to another. This thing will lead us to reduce the complexity of IoT and solves more problems such as compatibility, cost, and communication complexity, see Fig. 6.

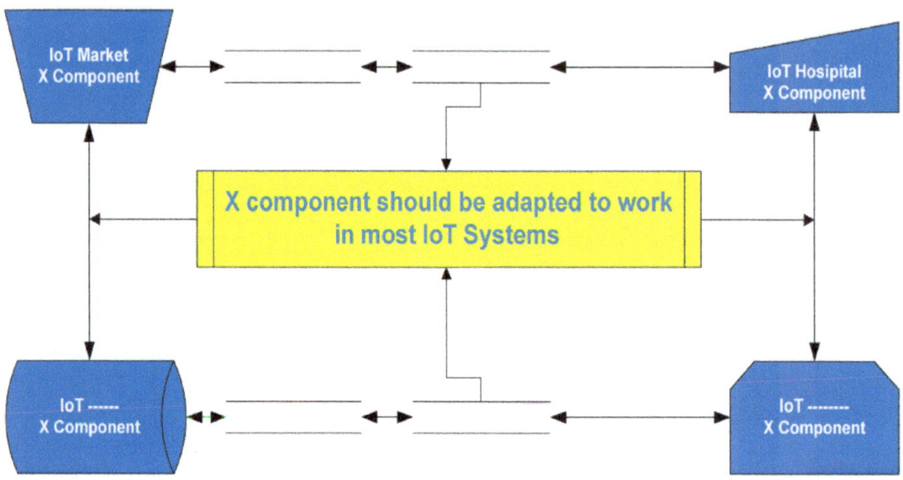

Figure 6: Standardization of Things In The IoT Systems.

Regarding the mass gathered information, I think we should determine the information, which is strictly useful for IoT and should be gathered. This determination will decrease the size of gathered information, hence the time that should be taken in gathering, transmission, processing, and filtering processes will be decreased. The standardization may participate to reach this target. If the hardware and the software characteristics for IoT systems are settled, only the information, which will be useful systems, is determined and accessed. The determination process may be accomplished using some techniques such as back propagation or feedback. When we install many IoT applications, the data of each system component, which is used in control mechanism, should be filtered and minimized. The filtering process will continue till the fully useful data is exactly determined. When the data of each component will be preciously known, the data can be stored on one server and accessed for the same components found all over the world. At this moment the number of gigabytes required for storing the IoT system information and the time required for process are minimized, see Fig. 7.

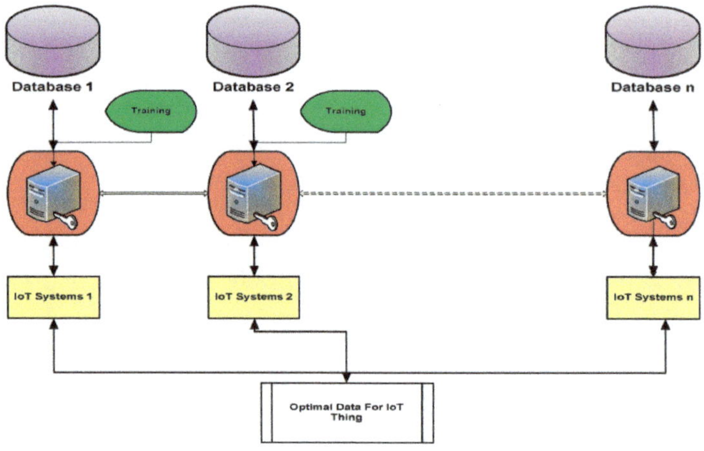

Figure 7: Accurate Information About Each IoT Thing.

Also, it's notable that the main problems are raised from the s character which is found in the things word. So, if we change our vision of IoT as a number of terrible things in a single network to little number of networks connected by one network, the problems may calm down. The division of the IoT system into IoT subsystems provides the researchers with more concentration in building an optimal infrastructure of IoT systems, see Fig. 8. For example, we consider the healthcare, the transportation and the marketing are three standalone IoT applications. In fact, we should change our vision and consider these applications as one application and is divided into three sub applications. This will lead us to delete the things duplication. The things duplication may be raised from the shared things in each IoT application. These shared things such as shelves, tickets, camera, desks, etc. it is sufficient to store the minimal control data about the thing one time instead of more times. In addition, we should construct a relation between the IoT subsystems. These relations help us in solving many of IoT challenges like things addressing.

The acronyms M2M stands for machine to machine communication. This abbreviation means that each machine can connect and construct a dialog with other machines. This expression is not new but it strongly appears with the IoT technology. Our vision in this issue is transforming the M2M communication to Data-to-Data (D2D) communication. Really, the IoT technology relies on the communication between the system machines and makes them in cooperation without human intervention, but this cooperation depends on the information, which is exchanged between devices, and the management information, which is used by the control web applications. Hence, the communication and control infrastructures are accomplished basically by the data. This concept fires the acronyms D2D instead of M2M., see Fig. 8.

The addressing problem is raised due to the massive number of things in IoT system. As stated above that the IPV4 and IPV6 may be used in addressing. The IPV4's main problem is addressing limitation. The problems in IPV6 are the security, routing, and mobility. There are more trials are found to solve the compatibility between the IPV6 backbone to be adapted with the IoT infrastructure specially in addressing of RFID tags. Recently, mixing of RFID tags into

IPv6 networks has been researched and techniques to add RFID identifiers and IPv6 addresses have been demonstrated in [59]. For example, the 64 bits are used to address the gateway between the internet and RFID system, and the other 64 bits are used to as an identifier of the IPv6 address to report the RFID tag identifier [60]. This trial cannot be used in case of 96 bits RFID identifier as found at EPCglobal. This problem is solved by deploying an agent to maps the RFID identifier into 64 bits to be used as an ID of IPV6 address. This mapping should be kept by this agent [61]. Another trial is introduced in [RFID URL]. This trial illustrates that IPV6 packet contains the body and the header of RFID message. There is another important issue regarding IPV6 and IoT addressing that is called mobility. We still in need to a technique describe the mobility issue in the IoT systems with guarantee of scalability and reliability with IoT heterogeneous environment. Also, How to obtain the IoT system addresses is an important issue should be adapted. In the IoT, the Object Name Service (ONS) should be able to combine the RFID tag identifier with the explanation of its object, and vice versa. The reversion process requires special techniques such as Object Code Mapping Service (OCMS) [62, 63].

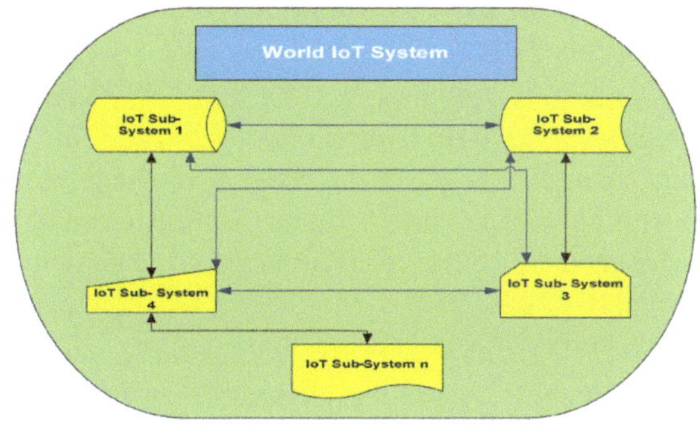

Figure 8: The IoT Should Be One System Contains Number of Related Sub-Systems.

OUR SURVEY VS. OTHER SURVEYS

The difference between our survey and other surveys [1], [23] is demonstrated below in Table 2. There are many parameters which are discussed in our survey and neglected in others such as IoT database and IoT core challenges. Also, there are some parameters which are extremely discussed in our survey and briefly discussed in others like IoT architectures.

Table 2: The Comparison Between IoT Surveys

Criteria	Our Survey	First Survey [1]	Second Survey [23]
IoT Application	Briefly Discussed	Extremely Described	Extremely Described
IoT Architecture	Extremely Discussed	Not Found	Not Found
IoT Database	Discussed	Not Found	Not Found
IoT Challenges	Discussed	Described	Extremely Described
IoT Future Vision	Extremely Discussed	Not Found	Briefly Discussed
IoT Open Issues	Described	Described	Not Found

CONCLUSION

In this paper, an IoT survey is presented. IoT history, which contains the IoT definition and the applications, are demonstrated. Also, the IoT architectures, which are called 3-layer and 5-layer, with recent special purpose ones are showed. The IoT challenges such as the mass gathered information, security, privacy, and some networking challenges are introduced. In addition, the IoT database requirements, trials, and models are demonstrated. Finally, our IoT future vision is discussed.

REFERENCES

1. Luigi A., Antonio I., Giacomo M. 2010.The Internet of Things: A survey. Science Direct journal of Computer Networks, Volume 54, Pages: 2787–2805.

2. Yinghui H., Guanyu L., 2010. Descriptive Models for Internet of Things. IEEE International Conference on Intelligent Control and Information Processing, Dalian, China, Pages: 483- 486.

3. Mealling M, 2003 Auto-ID Object Name Service (ONS) v1.0, Auto-ID Center Working Draft.

4. Bo Y., Guangwen H., 2008. Application of RFID and Internet of Things in Monitoring and Anticounterfeiting for Products. International Seminar on Business and

Information, Wuhan, Hubei, China, Pages: 392- 395.

5. Zouganeli E., Einar Svinnset I., 2009. Connected Objects and the Internet of Things - a Paradigm Shift. International Conference on Photonics in Switching, Pisa, Italy, Pages: 1-4.

6. Tongzhu Z., Xueping W., Jiangwei C., Xianghai L., Pengfei C., 2010 .Automotive recycling information management based on the internet of things and RFID technology. IEEE International Conference on Advanced Management Science (ICAMS), Changchun, China, page(s): 620 – 622.

7. Muriel D., Juan F., 2010. Expanding the learning environment: combining physicality and virtuality The Internet of Things for eLearning. IEEE International Conference on Advanced Learning Technologies (ICALT), Sousse, Tunisia, Pages: 730- 731.

8. Gustavo G, Mario O., Carlos K., 2008. Early infrastructure of an Internet of Things in Spaces for Learning. Eighth IEEE International Conference on Advanced Learning Technologies, Cantabria, Spain, Pages: 381-383.

9. Yinghui H., Guanyu L., 2010. A Semantic Analysis for Internet of Things. IEEE International Conference on Intelligent Computation Technology and Automation, Shenzhen, China, Pages: 336- 339.

10. Yuxi Liu, Guohui Zhou, Key Technologies and Applications of Internet of Things, IEEE Fifth International Conference on Intelligent Computation Technology and Automation, Hunan China, pp: 197-200, 2012.

11. Miao W., Ting L., Fei L., ling S., Hui D., 2010. Research on the architecture of Internet of things. IEEE International Conference on Advanced Computer Theory and Engineering (ICACTE), Sichuan province, China, Pages: 484-487.

12. Jinxin Z., Mangui L., 2010. A New Architecture for Converged Internet of Things. International Conference on Internet Technology and Applications, Beijing, China, Pages: 1 - 4.

13. Zhang J, Liang M., 2010. A New Architecture for Converged Internet of Things. IEEE International Conference on Internet Technology and Applications, Wuhan, China, Pages: 1- 4.

14. Inge G., 2008. Architecture for the Internet of Things (IoT): API and interconnect. 2nd International Conference on Sensor Technologies and Applications, Cap Esterel, France, Pages: 802-807.

15. Liang Z., Han-Chieh Chao, Multimedia Traffic Security Architecture for the Internet of Things, IEEE Networks, 2011. VOL.25, NO. 3, Pages: 35-40.

16. Junwei Lv, 11, Xiaohu Yuan and Haiyan Li, 2011. A New Clock Synchronization Architecture of Network for Internet of Things, International Conference on Information Science and Technology March 26-28, 2011 Nanjing, .Jiangsu, China, Pages: 685-688.

17. Xiong Li, Zhou Xuan,Liu Wen, 2011. Research on the Architecture of Trusted Security System Based on the Internet of Things, Fourth International Conference on Intelligent Computation Technology and Automation, Shenzhen, China, Pages: 1172-1175.

18. Huansheng N., Ziou Wang, 2011. Future Internet of Things Architecture: Like Mankind Neural System or Social Organization Framework?, IEEE COMMUNICATIONS LETTERS, VOL. 15, NO. 4, Pages: 461

19. Castellani, et. al., 2010. Architecture and Protocols for the Internet of Things: A Case Study, IEEE Pervasive Computing and Communication Workshops (PERCOM Workshop), Mannheim, Germany, Pages: 678-683

20. Castro, M. et. al., 2011. Oxygen Cylinders Management Architecture Based on Internet of Things, International Conference on computational science and its applications (ICCSA), Murica, Spain, Pages: 271-274.

21. Neil Bergmann, Peter J. Robinson, Server-Based Internet of Things Architecture, The 9th Annual IEEE Consumer Communications and Networking Conference, Brisbane, Australia, pp: 360 – 361, China, 2012.

22. Botterman M., 2009. for the European Commission Information Society and Media Directorate General, Networked Enterprise & RFID Unit – D4, Internet of Things: An Early Reality of the Future Internet, Report of the Internet of Things Workshop, Prague, Czech Republic.

23. INFSO D.4 Networked Enterprise, RFID INFSO G.2 Micro & Nanosystems, in: Co-operation with the Working Group RFID of the ETP EPOSS, 2008. Internet of Things in 2020, Roadmap for the Future, Version 1.1.

24. Vilamovska A, Hattziandreu, E., et al., 2009. RFID Application in Healthcare – Scoping and Identifying Areas for RFID Deployment in Healthcare Delivery, RAND Europe.

25. Lakshman T., Madhow U, 1997. The performance of TCP/IP for networks with high bandwidth-delay products and random loss. IEEE/ACM Transactions on Networking 5 (3) Pages: 336–350.

26. Jules A., 2006. RFID security and privacy: a research survey. IEEE Journal on Selected Areas in Communications, 24 (2), Pages: 381–394.

27. Lu T.,Neng W., 2010. Future Internet: The Internet of Things. IEEE International Conference on Advanced Computer Theory and Engineering (ICACTE), China, Pages: 376-380.

28. Odrigo R., Cristina A., 2011. Key management systems for sensor networks in the context of the Internet of Things. Elsevier, Computers and Electrical Engineering, Article in Press.

29. Sachin Babar, Parikshit Mahalle, Antonietta Stango, Neeli Prasad and Ramjee Prasad, 2010, Proposed Security Model and Threat Taxonomy for the Internet of Things (IoT). Springer

30. Nilssen A., 2009. Security and privacy standardization in internet of things, in: eMatch. 09 – Future Internet Workshop, Oslo, Norway.

31. Eschenauer L., Gligor V., 2002. A key-management scheme for distributed sensor networks. The Ninth ACM Conference on Computer and Communications Security, Washington, DC, USA.

32. Chenghua Yan, Kun Feng, Zhiming Zhang, Impact

of Internet of things on security grade evaluation, International Conference on Computer Science and Electronics Engineering, PP: 289 – 292, China, 2012.

33. Chan H., Perrig A., 2003. Security and privacy in sensor networks, IEEE Computer 36 (10) Pages: 103–105.

34. Weber R., 2010. Internet of Things – New security and privacy challenges. Elsevier Computer Law and Security Review, Volume 26, Pages 23-30.

35. Jie Liu, Xu Hu, Zhiqiang Wei, Dongning Jia, Chao Song, Location privacy protect model based on positioning middleware among the internet of things, International Conference on Computer Science and Electronics Engineering, pp: 288 – 291, China, 2012

36. Hui Suoa,, Jiafu Wan, Caifeng Zoua, Jianqi Liua, Security in the Internet of Things: A Review, IEEE International Conference on Computer Science and Electronics Engineering, pp: 648- 651, Zhejiang, China, 2012

37. Dunkels A., Vasseur J., 2008. IP for Smart Objects, Internet Protocol for Smart Objects (IPSO) Alliance, White Paper #1. http://www.ipso-alliance.org.

38. Hui J., Culler D., Chakrabarti S., 2009. 6LoWPAN: Incorporating IEEE 802.15.4 Into the IP Architecture – Internet Protocol for Smart Objects (IPSO) Alliance, White Paper #3, January 2009, http:// www.ipso-alliance.org.

39. Kushalnagar N, Montenegro G., Schumacher C., 2007. IPv6 Over Low Power Wireless Personal Area Networks (6LoWPANs): Overview, Assumptions, Problem Statement, and Goals, IETF RFC 4919.

40. Y.-W. Ma, C.-F. Lai, Y.-M. Huang, J.-L. Chen, 2009. Mobile RFID with IPv6 for phone services, in: Proceedings of IEEE ISCE, Kyoto, Japan.

41. S.-D. Lee, M.-K. Shin, H.-J. Kim, 2007. EPC vs. IPv6 mapping mechanism, in: Proceedings of Ninth International Conference on Advanced Communication Technology, Phoenix Park, South Korea.

42. Minkeun Ha, Seong Hoon Kim, Hyungseok Kim, Kiwoong Kwon, Nam Giang, and Daeyoung Kim, SNAIL Gateway: Dual-mode Wireless Access Points for WiFi and IP-based Wireless Sensor Networks in the Internet of Things, The 9th Annual IEEE Consumer Communications and Networking Conference - Smart Spaces and Personal Area Networks, , Page(s): 169 – 173, Daejeon, Korea, 2012

43. Shancang Li, Da Xu, and Xinheng Wang, 2012, Compressed Sensing Signal and Data Acquisition in Wireless Sensor Networks and Internet of Things, IEEE Transactions on Industrial Informatics, Issue: 99.

44. Zhanjie W., Guoyuan M., Keqiu L., 2010. Research on the Real-time of the Perception between Objects in Internet of Things based on Image. The Fifth IEEE Annual ChinaGrid Conference, China, Pages: 92-97.

45. Runian L, 2009. Study on the Internet of Things Based on RFID Technique," Journal of CAEIT, 6(4):pp.594-597.

46. Hao W, 2009. RFID, EPC and Things of Internet. Radio Frequency Identification Technologies and Applications: Pages:17-20.

47. Chen D., Varshney P., 2004. QoS support in wireless sensor networks: a survey, in: International Conference on Wireless Networks 2004, Las Vegas, NE, USA.

48. Harald S., Patrick G., Peter F., Sylvie W., 2010 .Vision and Challenges for Realising the Internet of Things. Cluster of erponean research projects on the Internet of Things.

49. Cooper J, 2009. A. Challenges for Database Management in the Internet of Things. IETE Tech Rev, 26:320-9.

50. Xiaolei Li, Jiawei H., Sangkyum K., 2007. Hector G., ROAM: Rule- and Motif-Based Anomaly Detection in Massive Moving Object Data Sets. SDM.

51. J.-G. L., Han J., and X. Li. 2008. Trajectory outlier detection: A partition-and-detect framework," Proc. 24th Int'l Conf. on Data Engineering, pages140-149, Cancun, Mexico.

52. Jae-Gil L., Jiawei H., Xiaolei L., Hector G.: 2008. TraClass: trajectory classification using hierarchical region-based and trajectory-based clustering. PVLDB 1(1): 1081-1094.

53. Jae-Gil Lee, Jiawei Han, Kyu-Young Whang. 2007. Trajectory clustering: a partition-andgroup framework. SIGMOD 593-604.

54. Joydeep G, 2007. Probabilistic Framework for Mining Distributed Sensory Data under Data Sharing Constraints. First International Workshop on Knowledge Discovery from Sensor Data.

55. James A., Cooper J., Jeffery K., Saake G. 2009. Research Directions in Database Architectures for the Internet of Things. A Communication of the First International Workshop on Database Architectures for the internet of things, Pages: 225-233.

56. Shen Bin, Liu Yuan, Wang Xiaoyi, 2010. Research on Data Mining Models for the Internet of Things. International Conference on Image Analysis and Signal Processing (IASP), Pages: 127 – 132, Zhejiang, China.

57. Kiritsis D., 2010. Closed-loop PLM for intelligent products in the era of the Internet of Things. Elsevier, In press.

58. Gerd K., Fahim K., Daniel F., Vasughi S., 2010. Smart Objects as Building Blocks for the Internet of Things. IEEE Internet Computing, vol. 14, no. 1 pages: 44-51.

59. Ma Y., Lai C., Y., M. Huang M, J., Chen L., 2009. Mobile RFID with IPv6 for phone services. IEEE ISCE, Kyoto, Japan.

60. S.-D. Lee, M.-K. Shin, H.-J. Kim, 2007. EPC vs. IPv6 mapping mechanism. Ninth International Conference on Advanced Communication Technology, Phoenix Park, South Korea.

61. D.G. Y, D.H. Lee, C.H. Seo, S.G. Choi, 2008. RFID networking mechanism using address management agent, in: Proceedings of NCM, Gyeongju, South Korea.

62. <http://ipv6.com/articles/applications/Using-RFID-and-IPv6.htm>.

63. Vasseur J., Dunkels A., 2010. Chapter 4 - IPv6 for Smart Object Networks and the Internet of Things, Elsevier Interconnecting Smart Objects with IP, Pages: Pages 39-49.

INDEX